The Church Of God In[...] Presiding Bishop

Bishop Charles E. Blake, Sr.

Fighting for Salvation and Righteousness In A Violent And Immoral World

"Fight the good fight of faith, lay hold on eternal life..."
- 1 Timothy 6:12 (KJV)

Order materials today from the Power for Living Series:

Church Of God In Christ Publishing House
2500 Lamar Avenue, Memphis, Tennessee 38114
P.O. Box 140636, Memphis, Tennessee 38114
Toll Free: 1-877-746-8578 | Fax: (901) 743-1555
Website: www.cogicpublishinghouse.net
Email: sales@cogicpublishinghouse.net

CHURCH OF GOD IN CHRIST, INC.
ANNUAL SUNDAY SCHOOL LESSON COMMENTARY 2016–2017
INTERNATIONAL SUNDAY SCHOOL LESSONS

Mark A. Ellis

Chairman, Publishing Board

Copyright © 2016 by Urban Ministries, Inc.

Bible art: Aaron and Alan Hicks

Copyright © 2016 by Urban Ministries, Inc.

Item No.: 1-2011. ISBN-13: 978-1-60997-170-0. ISBN-10: 1-60997-170-1,
PFL Large Print Item No.: 1-2612. ISBN-13: 978-1-60997-174-8. ISBN-10: 1-60997-176-0
Publishers: COGIC Publishing House, Memphis, TN 38114
To place an order, call 877-746-8578 or visit our website at www.cogicpublishinghouse.net

TABLE OF CONTENTS

Fall Quarter 2016

THE SOVEREIGNTY OF GOD

LESSONS
Unit 1 • The Sovereignty of God
SEPTEMBER

Unit 2 • The Sovereignty of Jesus
OCTOBER

Unit 3 • Alpha and Omega
NOVEMBER

Winter Quarter 2016–2017

CREATION: A DIVINE CYCLE

LESSONS
Unit 1 • The Savior is Born
DECEMBER

Unit 2 • All Creation Praises God
JANUARY

Unit 3 • The Church is Born
FEBRUARY

Spring Quarter 2017

Summer Quarter 2017

FROM THE PRESIDING BISHOP'S DESK

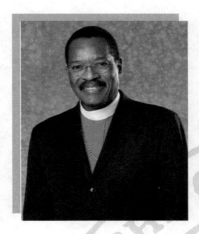

Blessings in the Name of the Lord Jesus Christ,

What an honor and privilege it is to see the Church Of God In Christ moving forward in deliverance, ministry, and community involvement. Hundreds of ministries across the world are stepping up the fight against the devil and his kingdom. The Gospel of Christ is being preached harder than ever before; reports of people being reclaimed, saved, and baptized in the Holy Ghost are off the scale. Yet with all of these things happening, the most stable ground in allowing all of this to come to fruition is Sunday School.

Yes, it is in Sunday School that we as children learn about God, and an appreciation for God grows within our hearts. Sunday School is the bedrock of every Christian organization, and the reason is that we are constantly learning and digging deep into the Word of God to try to understand God. The one thing we first learn about in Sunday School is the creation of our universe and the earth upon which we live. We also learn in Sunday School that God created all vegetation upon the Earth. **"So God said, 'Let the earth sprout [tender] vegetation, plants yielding seed, and fruit trees bearing fruit according to (limited to, consistent with) their kind, whose seed is in them upon the earth'; and it was so"** (Genesis 1:11, AMP).

Sunday School is the fruit that allows us to grow stronger and stronger within the Lord; it is also a seed that will continue to produce tree after tree after tree. Each tree that grows within us grounds us in the knowledge of God. For instance, when we learn about the Creation in Sunday School as children, it is a seed that is planted within us; as we learn more and more about God, we learn more about the Sovereignty of God. In Sunday School, we learn about the Resurrection of Jesus Christ, and as the seed that was planted grows, we begin to understand that God established a divine cycle for our personal salvation, and that we must live a sanctified life in Him.

Just like water and food is vital to the human body, Sunday School is vital to the Christian's soul. **"Thy word have I hid in mine heart, that I might not sin against thee. Blessed art thou, O LORD: teach me thy statutes. With my lips have I declared all the judgments of thy mouth. I have rejoiced in the way of thy testimonies, as much as in all riches. I will meditate in thy precepts, and have respect unto thy ways. I will delight myself in thy statutes: I will not forget thy word"** (Psalm 119:11–16, KJV).

It is God's Word that keeps us unified in Him. It is His Word that gives us life more abundantly. It is His Word that allows us to declare that I am the head and not the tail. I am above and not beneath. The Word of God is planted within us because of Sunday School. As I close this letter, I want to say, thank you, thank you, thank you. To all the grandparents who take their grandchildren to Sunday School. To all the aunts and uncles who strive to promote the importance of Christian education. To all the parents who know that Sunday School is like a farmer who plants the seed in a child's mind to be better than his or her circumstances. **"Train up a child in the way he should go [teaching him to seek God's wisdom and will for his abilities and talents], Even when he is old he will not depart from it" (Proverbs 22:6, AMP).**

Yours for Service,

Bishop Charles Edward Blake Sr.
Presiding Bishop of the Church Of God In Christ, Inc.
Seventh in Succession

FROM THE DESK OF CHAIRMAN MARK ELLIS

Greetings to all of God's People,

I want to encourage each and every one of you today by saying that no matter what you are going through, nothing can separate us from the love of Jesus Christ. **"For I am persuaded, that neither death, nor life, nor angels, nor principalities, nor powers, nor things present, nor things to come, nor height, nor depth, nor any other creature, shall be able to separate us from the love of God, which is in Christ Jesus our Lord"** (Romans 8:38–39, KJV).

It is in knowing this that we, the children of God, are blessed. In fact we are more than just blessed; we are endowed with power from on high, and it is God's power and love that take us through the storm. In Sunday School, as children we learned of the terrible storms that happened in the Bible; we learned of Noah and the Great Flood, Jonah and the Whale, the storm when Jesus was asleep in the boat, and the storm in which Paul was shipwrecked. Yet it was through these lessons that we learned that no matter what life tosses in our direction, God is still with us, guiding us and constantly molding us in His image.

This is what makes Sunday School so important, that we are taught as children and adults the building blocks to a better relationship with God. See, the important thing about Sunday School is that it doesn't matter whether you've been attending one day or fifty years, we all learn something new about our great God. We learn powerful Scriptures that help us hold during hard times like Psalm 37:25: **"I have been young, and now am old; yet have I not seen the righteous forsaken nor his seed begging bread."**

Remember when we as children sometimes did not feel like being dragged to another service, yet again we heard another Scripture no doubt taught in Sunday School, from Joshua 24:15: **"But as for me and my house, we will serve the LORD."** All of these Scriptures, stories, and life lessons that our parents taught us did not all come from just experiencing life, but from Sunday School. Just like our parents learned and studied the Bible in Sunday School, we too should be doing the very same thing.

Our National Sunday School Department, which is being headed up by Bishop Alton Galton, is on the march forward in Sunday School. They have a wonderful working relationship with Mother Sandra Smith Jones and the Publishing Board because we all collaborate together to bring you the best tools to equip God's people. Now for those of you who might not know, the Publishing House has a new Bible game that has come out. This game operates on the PC (personal computer) and can be a wonderful addition to any Sunday School class, as it will show you, the parent and the teacher, all that your students have learned from our material. It also will show with the adult level how much you have learned yourself in Sunday School.

In my final words, I want to encourage each and every student, teacher, and pastor to purchase a copy of the Bible game on our website; but more importantly, reach out and bring someone to Sunday School, and watch them grow in the knowledge, love, and happiness of God.

Yours for Service,

Superintendent Mark A. Ellis
Chairman of the Publishing Board
Church Of God In Christ, Inc.

FROM THE CHAIRMAN OF MARKETING

Greetings in the matchless Name of Jesus Christ,

I count it a privilege and an honor to still be able to present to you our new 2016–2017 Annual Commentary for the year. The reason I am privileged is because Bishop Blake, our Presiding Bishop, continues to push for the best for the people of God and ensures that we provide the best; and I am honored because of the wonderful comments that we have received about the commentary down through the years. I am so on fire for God and His people that I make sure that you are given the best, because I feel that nothing substandard should be handed out to the people of God.

Just like Haggai was determined to build a house to God, I am determined that our Annual Commentary is the best for God's people. I know this letter is a bit more on the personal side, but that's because everything that I do for God, I take personally. I remember my grandmother walking me to Sunday School and other church functions when I was a little girl. I remember going to Sunday School with my brother, sister, and cousins, and my mother.

Sunday School is so important because it helps us understand: why and how we must live holy; why and how we must live a separated life; why and how we must pray to Jesus and God our Father. On Sunday morning, the sermon is to uplift and present to you the chance of changing your life. Once that change has been made, it is the duty of Sunday School to impart the Word of God in you and bring forth those hidden gifts and talents that God birthed in you. It is in Sunday School where we learn how to speak in front of an audience, how to study God's Word, and where we learn that we need to fall in love with Jesus Christ. **"He that hath my commandments, and keepeth them, he it is that loveth me: and he that loveth me shall be loved of my Father, and I will love him, and will manifest myself to him"** (John 14:21, KJV).

How many of you learned in Sunday School the Bible verses you know now? Do you remember the fun times you had in Sunday School? I bet you can remember your favorite Sunday School teacher—just like many other Sunday School memories. Let's create them for other children. It is important for not only adults but also children to learn and grow. The Bible says if you train up a child in the way he should go, when he gets old, he shall not depart from it. It is our responsibility as people of God to ensure that everyone has that same right, that same chance that we had to enjoy and love Sunday School.

Sunday School is another form of marketing for God! It is an established foundation that places the Word of God and His teachings in the forefront. Our partnership with UMI (Urban Ministries, Inc.) is making that marketing strategy for God much more efficient. As you will notice, we have made a change to the Annual Commentary, as we are replacing the tainted New International Version (NIV) with the Amplified Version (AMP). We want to bring you the best, because you deserve the best, because we are the best. We are the best because we have Christ in our lives, and we belong to God.

So as you're reading and studying through this commentary, remember to pick up a child or a loved one and share the experience of Sunday School with them because remember ... A Child Saved is a Soul Saved, Plus a Life.

Many thanks to the Saints of God, the Church Of God In Christ Publishing Board, and the Publishing House for their continued dedication to the Word and work of the Lord. Thanks to all the departments and churches across the country for their loyal support of the Church Of God In Christ's literature. As always, let me personally thank each of you for your continued support and encouragement by purchasing the curriculum. Remember, without you, this dream wouldn't have become a reality, and a church without its people is just an empty shell.

Yours for Service,

Evangelist Sandra Smith Jones
Trustee Board Member
Vice President of Publishing Board
Chairman of Marketing for Publishing House
Church Of God In Christ, Inc.

FROM THE SENIOR ADVISOR TO THE PUBLISHING HOUSE

Dear Sunday School Scholar,

Another year and another opportunity for the publishing ministry of our fine institution to release our annual Sunday School Commentary. I am overjoyed with the work of the committee that put this curriculum together. The Word of God has ever greater presence in our lives because the need is so compelling. The Church Of God In Christ Publishing House issues the *Power For Living* curriculum to help make students better able to live in a dynamic world. This literature is timely and significant for training, educating, and fostering a biblically literate future generation. This goal is germane among the objectives the Publishing Board desires to achieve.

I was on my farm last summer and noticed my neighbor's land next to mine. This gentleman dedicated acres of land and planted rows of trees. These trees are now roughly 20 years old. They are strong, straight, and well-managed. This man will be dead and in his grave when the trees will be harvested. I know that his goal was to leave a treasure for the future generations of his family. Our goal should be as tangible. How many times have you heard some misguided soul say, "Let them make it on their own. Nobody left me nothing and why should I leave them something?" In our world of material wealth, those who can leave treasure for their children encourage future blessings. In this church, we Saints of God should be like-minded. Each family is responsible to plant and leave a legacy of spiritual knowledge to the coming generation. Certainly, the money would help, but a well-disciplined spiritual life is more necessary!

Take your children to Sunday School weekly and provide them with a gift of the Word. Remember, as Paul expressed to the Corinthian Church, "Which things also we speak, not in the words which man's wisdom teacheth, but which the Holy Ghost teacheth; comparing spiritual things with spiritual" (1 Corinthians 2:13). The staff at the Church Of God In Christ Publishing House want the next generation to be prepared for the life ahead. Plant trees of righteousness and assure the possibility of spiritual legacy for the coming generation.

Remember in Sunday School the endeavor and unabridged intent is impacting students' lives. Each lesson will provide a systematic and well-grounded approach for educating young and old alike. May this yearly commentary provide you with the material to get the job done. Therefore, put it in the car and take it to work. Read at the doctor's office or resting in your favorite chair. Challenge those on the jobs, at the house, or over the fence to read and discuss next week's lesson with you. Be prepared as never before to teach the lesson and enrich someone's life.

Bishop David Allen Hall Sr.
Church Of God In Christ, Inc.

FROM THE INTERNATIONAL
SUNDAY SCHOOL PRESIDENT

Greetings, Sunday School Family!

What a privilege it is to greet you again on behalf of the greatest school in the world, *SUNDAY SCHOOL!*

From its inception in England during the 1780s by Robert Raikes, Sunday School has made a tremendous impact in the lives of those who attend! It was established to teach working and orphaned children who otherwise roamed the streets on Sundays through a focus on reading, writing, and Bible study.

The streets of our world today are filled with violence and immorality. Hopeless lives seek peace from every source but the right one: Jesus Christ. There's a war going on… physically and spiritually! And if we, the Body of Christ, endeavor to win, we must *know what we believe, why we believe it,* and *how we're going to defeat the enemy,* which can be found in the study of God's Word, through the ministry of Sunday School.

The Church Of God In Christ's theme for 2016 from our Presiding Bishop, *"Fighting for Salvation and Righteousness in a Violent and Immoral World,"* so appropriately describes our plight in the earth. As Matthew states in his Gospel: *"And from the days of John the Baptist until now the kingdom of heaven suffereth violence, and the violent take it by force"* (11:12).

Our force shall not be taken with knives, guns, or other such weapons. *"For though we walk in the flesh, we do not war after the flesh: (For the weapons of our warfare are not carnal, but mighty through God to the pulling down of strong holds)"* (2 Corinthians 10:3–4).

Sunday School superintendents, teachers, workers, and students, let's put on the whole armor of God, as counseled in Ephesians 6:10–18, so that we may be able to withstand in these evil days! Let us ask God—amid our study, prayer, and instruction—to guide us in helping *every student* sharpen the ability to use the Sword of the Spirit, which is the Word of God!

Your Servant,

Bishop Alton E. Gatlin
President, International Sunday School Department
Prelate, First Ecclesiastical Jurisdiction Trinidad/Tobago
Church Of God In Christ, Inc.

FROM THE COGIC-UMI SUNDAY SCHOOL LIAISON

Dear Sunday School Scholar,

Inasmuch as you are an owner of the commentary published by your denomination, you are a scholar and a loyal member of the Church Of God In Christ. I think you would appreciate the work of Evangelist Sandra Jones, the Marketing Chair of the publishing house, who contributes toward ensuring that our product is one of the best Sunday School commentaries in the nation.

She sometimes spends hours, with the support of the COGIC Liaison, encouraging one of the top African American publishing companies to make sure our book is second to none. I am sure your learning experience will be enriched with this book and that it will equip you to teach and preach the Word with a deeper appreciation for the Scripture.

The September quarter will show how peace in the world should be our highest aim. The quarter will also emphasize God's universal love for all people, the importance of interceding for others, and the power of faith.

The December quarter will focus on God's divine plan of salvation. Luke's Gospel, several psalms, and the epistle to the Galatians are used to explore God's ongoing actions in blessing and reconciling the whole creation.

In March, the lessons are about how God's love for us is evident in Scripture from the creation of the first humans through His constant interactions with individuals and groups of people through historical circumstances and developments. A survey of select Old and New Testament Scriptures reveals dynamic and encouraging aspects of God's constant love for humankind.

The theme for the June quarter reminds us that God continues to speak to us through His written Word. God calls ordinary people from diverse backgrounds to make a difference. From the days of the judges to the prophets to the early church leaders, God called and the faithful answered. We encourage all instructors to integrate the theme of the Presiding Bishop as much as possible in their class discussion.

Fighting for Salvation and Righteousness in a Violent and Immoral World — 1 Timothy 6:12

Bishop J. L. Whitehead Jr., B.A., M.Div.
Church Of God In Christ, Inc. Liaison

Review Team:
Pastor Charles Hawthorne, Ph.D., Elder Herman W. Hullum, B.A., M.A., D.Min., Evangelist Iretha Sanford, Th.D. (candidate), Pastor Ronald Alexander, M.A.; Eld. Scott Bradley, B.A.

COGIC PUBLISHING BOARD
2016-2017

Mark Ellis
Chairman of the Board

Uleses Henderson
1st Vice Chairman
(Incumbent)

Sandra S. Jones
Vice Chairman
(Incumbent)

Dr. Joe Chase Jr.
Secretary
(Incumbent)

Bishop E. Charles Connor
(Incumbent)

Bishop David Hall Sr.

Bishop Welton Lawrence
(Incumbent)

Bishop O.L. Meadows
(Incumbent)

Stephen Savage
COGIC Photographer
(Incumbent)

Reggie Witherspoon
(Incumbent)

Superintendent Tony Campbell

Dr. Sabrina Ellis

Supervisor Gracie Davis Harris

Administrative Assistant Dr. Philip Jackson

The team who works diligently every day to bring the best in scriptural discipleship publications to you and your Church.

Vickie Burse
Chief Operations Officer

Veronica Johnson
Executive Admin Assistant

LaTrina Smith
Accounting Manager

Margaret Hinton
Accounting Lead

Dorothy Driver
Accounting Clerk

Delores Johnson
Receptionist

Barachias Irons
Manuscript Supervisor

Darius Willis
Special Projects Coordinator

Anissa Everett
Design Artist

Erica Wilkins
Proofreader

Myers Jimerson
Proofreader

Phyllis Dearing
Proofreader

James Ross
Picker, Packer, Shipper

Samantha Martin
Operations Supervisor

Willie Simms
Picker, Packer, Shipper

John Davis
Auditor

Cebron Lee
Picker

Joseph Davis IV
Picker

LaQuanta Reed
Auditor

Tiffany Douglas
Auditor

Sherri Elrod
Auditor

Gloria Lee
CSR

Judy Booth
CSR

Damonic David
CSR

Tephanie Calvin
CSR

Edward Broen
CSR

LaTonya Rogers
CSR

LaTonya Richardson
CSR

The Publishing House Team Customer Service Department
They process credit card payments for phone orders
Handle all email and mail-in orders with an up-to-date tracking system

Warehouse/Shipping Department
Utilize state-of-the-art inventory control and order picking technology

Production/Pre-press Department
One six-pocket Muller Martini Saddle Stitcher

Manuscript Department
Responsible for all reading, proofing, editing, and editorial enhancing of all literature

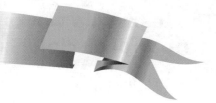

In the first decade of the 20th century, God caused His Kingdom to come and His will to be done in earth as it is in heaven at the legendary Azusa Street Revival and with the Grand Ole' Church Of God In Christ. At Azusa, He confounded the wisdom of the wise, and caused the very last to be first, pouring out His Holy Spirit, first of all, on the sons and daughters of slaves in His initiation of a worldwide revival, while the Church Of God In Christ became a primary ongoing vehicle for this mighty move of God. Yet the Holy Spirit began laying the foundations long before, as He raised those sanctified pioneers from poverty and oppression to spiritual power and influence. Among them was a man of great humility, love, ability, and charisma, Overseer David Johnson Young.

D. J. Young was born a slave in Chester, South Carolina, in about 1861. His father carried him to freedom before the close of the Civil War. During his childhood, he showed exceptional academic progress while attending local schools in South Carolina, and later at Morehouse College in Atlanta, Georgia. Upon matriculation, Young set out to improve the living conditions of his fellow freedmen, becoming an educator in public schools and involving himself in political affairs.

Unsatisfied with these admirable but inadequate means of fulfillment, Young surrendered to Christ and was converted in 1881. Soon after, he realized that the Gospel was of far greater importance than education or political advancement, and he was licensed to preach in the African Methodist Episcopal Zion Church. Young's early ministry met with great success as he became widely known for his prolific preaching, scholarly abilities, and compassion for souls. Throughout Young's life, much of his drive derived from his love for people. Many would say of him, "to know him was to love him." During these years he pastored churches and evangelized throughout the South and the Midwest, as far north as Indianapolis.

In 1895, D. J. Young married Priscilla Louise Jones, a master musician and highly endowed woman of God, with whom he fathered seven children. Despite his many successes, he was increasingly dissatisfied, until he finally answered the call to the "higher life," and accepted the grace of entire sanctification. Then, filled with divine love and equipped with the message of uncompromising holiness, Young joined the growing ranks of holiness preachers in the South, where he forged a lasting friendship with Charles Harrison Mason, and became a preacher in the early Church Of God In Christ. Although he settled in Arkansas, he largely spread the message of holiness through evangelistic crusades. During these early years, Young was distinguished as an ecstatic worshiper and intellectual, a powerful preacher and an effective evangelist.

In 1907, Young was one of the sanctified trio sent by holiness leader C. P. Jones to investigate the Azusa Street Revival in Los Angeles, California. At old Azusa, Mason, Young, and a brother named J. E. Jeter received the Baptism of the Holy Ghost. This profound spiritual awakening further empowered Young for ministry while enhancing his understanding and commitment to heart purity, divine love, Christian unity, and racial reconciliation.

However, the much celebrated Baptism of the Holy Ghost was not well received by many of their brethren in the South, and when the right hand of fellowship was withdrawn, Young stood with Mason as one of the original members of the Pentecostal Assembly of the reorganized Church Of God In Christ. When that primordial group of Saints gathered to discuss who should lead the church, Young advocated for prayer. After a period of prayer, Young spoke in tongues and gave the interpretation that God had given them C. H. Mason for their leader. Young was immediately given a leading role and became one of Mason's ablest assistants. He was appointed the first editor of the *The Whole Truth*, an important instrument for the spread of the biblical truths on which the church was founded. Young also served as an early Overseer in Arkansas and later Texas, where he planted a number of new churches.

In 1910, while still a resident of Pine Bluff, Arkansas, God graced D. J. Young with an invention that catapulted his ministry: the "Musical Attachment for Automobiles." This ingenious device enabled him to play harmonious chords and amplify the sound for long distances during revivals, drawing the attention of passersby in parks and other public areas. Although he obtained patents in the U. S., Canada, and Europe, the evangelist-inventor became a victim of patent theft. Nevertheless, it served as a valuable adjunct to Young's evangelistic crusades as he carried the Gospel around the country. Its later widespread use by ice-cream trucks serves as a ringing reminder of how God endows His people with "witty inventions," Proverbs 8:12, for the furtherance of the Gospel.

During this difficult period in American history, none other than the Holy Ghost enabled Bishop Mason and his followers to persevere amid great persecution, with much opposition against both Blacks as well as the Holiness-Pentecostal Movement. A letter from the mayor of Houston, dated 1914, requesting the citizens' support of Overseer Young's efforts to raise money for the state convocation is evidence of the invaluable ministry of those early Saints.

In 1916, D. J. Young made his last earthly transition, to the heart of the country, in Kansas City, Kansas. He immediately gathered area Pentecostals to form the first Church Of God In Christ in the state. After his appointment as overseer, Young resisted much persecution and successfully established more than 25 churches across the Great Plains over the next 10 years.

That same year, D. J. Young was led by God to implement a formal education system in the church. While many believed that the only book needed by the Saints was the Bible, Young, always a staunch advocate for higher learning, pleaded for books and gained the approval of Bishop Mason to introduce Sunday School literature, the first official educational instrument of the church. Ultimately, the literature would prove to be a fundamental training tool for countless preachers, evangelists, missionaries, and Saints throughout the country and overseas.

After Young's transition to glory, in 1927, Bishop Mason, recognizing the tremendous effect of the literature on the growth of the church, commissioned Young's widow to continue the work, allowing the D. J. Young Publishing Company to continue providing quality printed materials for the Sanctified Church for more than half a century. With the proceeds of the business, Mother Young regularly made reports to the international church that met or exceeded expectations.

In 1948, a building was erected to expand the business. The land and printing equipment was purchased by Mother Priscilla Young, who used her own personal savings for the business venture. Printed materials included tracts, souvenir journals for national meetings, and the denomination's first hymnals, in addition to the quarterly Sunday School periodicals, which they sent to foreign missions at no charge. Despite Black oppression, limited resources, both World Wars, and the Great Depression, the company flourished.

Madame Young lived just long enough to finalize the plans and see the newly constructed building, but their children, duly trained, stepped in and took the business to a new level of productivity and impact. Under the leadership of Pastor Harold C. Young, Elder Melvin Young, Mother Rosette Young-Lockett, Ceolya Young-Richardson, the company's services were extended to meet the needs of the greater Kansas City community and beyond. With their motto, "Printing to fit your needs," the publishing house began printing various materials, such as programs for churches of other reformations, obituaries, business cards, advertisements for area businesses, and "Get out the vote" fliers for the NAACP.

In addition to providing full-time employment for several employees, a number of Saints worked and received wages alongside the Youngs' children and grandchildren. Notably, three Church Of God In Christ jurisdictional supervisors helped to "get the books out" during their youth: the late Mother Margaret Loretta Richardson (Missouri Western First), Mother Mary K. Sims (Kansas East 2005-2012), and Supervisor Betty Joe Morrison (Kansas East). At times the business would print and distribute materials, but receive little or no compensation, yet the D. J. Young Publishing Company trudged forward. The Saints knew that this was much more than an economic enterprise—it was a ministry ordained by God and a labor of love, for D. J. Young and all those who followed in this pious publishing tradition.

In the words of Bishop Lemuel F. Thuston, Prelate of the Kansas East Ecclesiastical Jurisdiction and Vice Chairman of the General Assembly of the Church Of God In Christ, "Overseer D. J. Young is one of the most unsung heroes of Kansas, COGIC, and Post Reconstruction America." Without question, D. J. Young's unequivocal contributions advanced the church's mission of spreading the Gospel of Jesus Christ through holiness crusades, Holy Spirit empowered preaching, widespread church planting, and Holiness-Pentecostal publications, leaving future generations an enduring heritage of holiness.

Ladrian P. Brown, M. D.
International Chairlady
Charles Harrison Mason Historical Society
Church Of God In Christ, Inc.

Ladrian P. Brown, M.D. is a native of Kansas City, Kansas, where she first experienced the power and presence of God at Young Memorial Church Of God In Christ. The historic church was founded by her great-great grandfather, Overseer D. J. Young, one of the leading pioneers of the denomination.

Ladrian obtained a Bachelor of Science degree in Chemistry and Biology at the University of Saint Mary, Leavenworth, Kansas, and went on to pursue a career in medicine, obtaining a Doctor of Medicine from the University of Kansas School of Medicine in 2002. During her years in medical school, she became the loving and devoted mother of two beautiful daughters, Eliana and Ariel. However, at the age of 22, Ladrian fully surrendered and committed her all to Jesus Christ, which led to an unimaginable shift in her life-course and career trajectory.

After completing one year of post-graduate training at the University of Missouri Kansas City, she utilized her training in the pharmaceutical-biotech industry supporting basic science research and Phase I-IV clinical trials. While advancing her career, Sister Brown was graced with a passion to help restore the heritage of holiness embodied in the Holiness-Pentecostal Movement and embedded in the foundation of the Church Of God In Christ. With this vision, she established the D. J. Young Heritage Foundation in 2008, with its aim to preserve the powerful collective testimony of our sainted forefathers through ministry, ecumenical conferences, and historical preservation. Through her efforts to preserve the original D. J. Young Publishing Company property, some of the original equipment was rescued from local government proceedings and shipped to Church Of God In Christ headquarters, Memphis, TN. Ladrian also led the foundation's work with the Pentecostal and Charismatic Research Archive (PCRA), through the University of Southern California, funded by the John Templeton Foundation. Through this initiative, numerous unique historical materials from the formative years of the church were published online and are currently accessible through the USC Digital Library.

In June 2011, Dr. Brown was appointed International Chairlady of the Charles Harrison Mason Historical Society of the Church Of God In Christ, Inc., by Supt. Mack C. Mason, President. During the past decade, Dr. Brown has served as guest speaker at numerous conferences and churches, where she enjoys sharing the Gospel of Jesus Christ in light of God's "wonderful works to the children of men" in the Holiness-Pentecostal tradition. Sister Brown serves faithfully as a member of Boone Tabernacle Church of God in Christ, in Kansas City, Missouri, where Bishop Lemuel F. Thuston is pastor.

This year, 2016, marks the centennial of the establishment of the Sunday School literature of the Church Of God In Christ and the planting of its first church in the state of Kansas by Overseer David Johnson Young. The D. J. Young Centennial Celebration Committee, led by Superintendent Samuel Mason Young Sr. (Pastor of Young Memorial Church Of God In Christ, 2401 N. 9th Street, Kansas City, KS, 66101), extends an invitation to the Saints to critically reflect on our heritage of holiness and to celebrate with us as we glorify God for the enormous contributions of D. J. Young and other early pioneers under the leadership of our Chief Apostle and Senior Founder Bishop C. H. Mason. With the generous *supply of the Spirit of Jesus Christ*, let's continue to build upon the wonderful foundation laid by the founders of this Grand Ole' Church Of God In Christ!

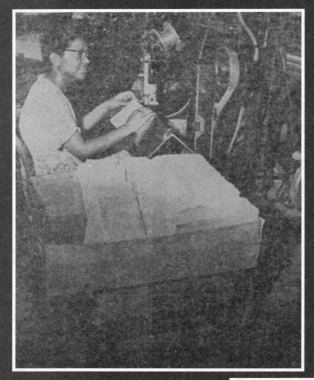

Scenes from the interior of the D. J. Young Publishing Company. Publishers of "Sunday School and other Literature" for the Church Of God In Christ, U.S.A. "Where the books are edited, printed and mailed." Kansas City 1, Kansas. "Yours for a Better Sunday School."

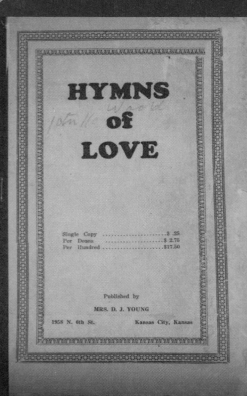

HYMNS
of
LOVE

Single Copy ....$ .25
Per Dozen ....$ 2.75
Per Hundred $17.50

Published by
MRS. D. J. YOUNG

1958 N. 6th St.   Kansas City, Kansas

W. I. C.

Washington, D.C.   May 1-6, 1962

Name...

State...

JESUS ANSWERS HARD QUESTIONS

Lesson Material—Matthew 22: 15-22

Memory Verse—"Do that which is right and good
in the sight of the Lord."—Deuteronomy 6: 18a.

SUNDAY SCHOOL PEP SONGS

Published by the
D. J. YOUNG PUBLISHING COMPANY
Publishers of
Sunday School and Other Literature
for the Church of God in Christ, International
642-44 Chelsea Trafficway, Kansas City, Kansas
Price—50 cents

COPYRIGHTED 1958, D. J. YOUNG PUBLISHING COMPANY

Minister's License or Commendation

This is to certify that Brother ....
is a member of Our Lord Jesus Christ with the Church of God in
Christ at.............................. Being led, as we
believe, through the Spirit to regard him as called to the Gospel
Ministry, and profitable for the same, we hereby so certify, com-
mending him to the brotherhood in Christ everywhere. Praying
God's choicest blessings upon his labors, and faithfulness unto the
very end, we subscribe ourselves in Jesus' name.
This ....day of ....192......

.... P. C.
.... Deacon
.... Clerk

49th National
CONVOCATION
CHURCH OF GOD IN CHRIST
MASON TEMPLE
930 Mason Street
MEMPHIS, TENN.
BISHOP C. H. MASON, Presiding
LILLIAN BROOKS COFFEY, Supervisor of Women
NOVEMBER 25th TO DECEMBER 15th
1956

The New Administration Building

Souvenir Program
FIFTEENTH ANNUAL
YOUTH CONGRESS
of
KANSAS
of the
CHURCHES OF GOD IN CHRIST

1217 East Murdock Street   Wichita, Kansas
AUGUST 31 — SEPTEMBER 6, 1954
ELDER L. V. STITT, State President

WOMEN'S
INTERNATIONAL
CONVENTION
CHURCH OF GOD IN CHRIST

DETROIT, MICHIGAN
MAY 7 to 12, 1957

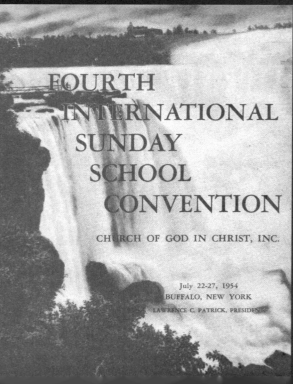

FOURTH
INTERNATIONAL
SUNDAY
SCHOOL
CONVENTION

CHURCH OF GOD IN CHRIST, INC.

July 22-27, 1954
BUFFALO, NEW YORK
LAWRENCE C. PATRICK, PRESIDENT

INTERNATIONAL
SUNDAY SCHOOL DEPARTMENT

Greetings Sunday School Scholars!

Our 2016 Church Of God In Christ theme speaks to the violent and immoral world we live in, challenging us to fight for salvation and righteousness! This fight begins with knowing God and His Word! The ministry of Sunday School is the vehicle that provides opportunities for the study and application of God's Word.

We are again overjoyed to have the awesome privilege of partnering with the Publishing Board of the Church Of God In Christ.

Continuing the success of the 2015–16 Annual Commentary, quarterly commentaries are provided at the beginning of each quarter's lessons. This invaluable tool provides additional scriptural insight and motivates Sunday School teachers and students to dig even deeper in preparation for their weekly lesson.

The following Sunday School scholars and leaders have provided invaluable insight for us this year.

- **FALL QUARTER:** Dr. Jeannette H. Donald – Louisiana East First Jurisdiction

- **WINTER QUARTER:** Evangelist Yvonne Atkins – Texas Northeast Second Jurisdiction

- **SPRING QUARTER:** Superintendent Larry L. Polk – Texas Northeast First Jurisdiction

- **SUMMER QUARTER:** Dr. William C. McCoy – Wisconsin First Jurisdiction

We encourage you to browse through your commentary before using it. At the beginning of each quarter's lessons, you will find phenomenal *Teaching Tips* written by another group of talented Sunday School teachers and leaders. Please share these Teaching Tips with your local Sunday School staff to use them as a training tool in your staff meetings.

We release blessings and growth upon every local Sunday School!

For the Kingdom,

Vice President Althea Sims
SSD Associate Editor
Church Of God In Christ, Inc.

Vice President Althea Sims serves as a member of Bishop Alton E. Gatlin's Cabinet for the leadership of the International Sunday School Department (ISSD), where she is responsible for the department's Branding, PR & Marketing, Social Media, and Department Publications, and serves as Liaison for the Publishing Board and ISSD Associate Editor for the COGIC Annual Sunday School Commentary.

In November 2015, at the Holy Convocation in St. Louis, Sims was recognized and honored as one of the 150 Influential Women of the Church Of God In Christ by "The Whole Truth" publication.

She was appointed to the office of 3rd Vice President of the ISSD in January 2013 by Presiding Bishop Charles E. Blake and Bishop Alton E. Gatlin. At AIM 2012, Sims was the first recipient of the prestigious Patrick Williams Macklin Award as Director of the Year for Leadership Ministry.

Previously, Sims has served the ISSD as Director of Education for Leadership Ministry in the International Sunday School University; Covenant Partners Director; Department Trainer; and an ISSD Women's Conference speaker

Sims also serves as the Jurisdictional Sunday School Superintendent of the First Ecclesiastical Jurisdiction of Southern California, under the leadership of Bishop Joe L. Ealy and Assistant General Supervisor/Jurisdictional Supervisor, Mother Barbara McCoo Lewis. She provides leadership for the growth, development, and training of the 220 local Sunday School ministries within its six regions and twenty-two districts.

VP Sims is the wife of Superintendent Emeritus Reginald D. Sims, founding pastor of The Dwelling Place Church Of God In Christ in Inglewood, CA, where Elder Ryan David Sims is the senior pastor and she serves as co-pastor. They are the proud parents of 5 and loving grandparents of 11.

QUARTERLY COMMENTARY
"THE SOVEREIGNTY OF GOD"

by Dr. Jeannette H. Donald

TEACHER'S TIPS
"WHAT QUALIFIES A TEACHER TO TEACH?"
by Dr. Jeannette H. Donald

#TSSGTEACHINGTIP –
"FACILITATORS AND TEACHERS MAKING A DIFFERENCE"
by Evangelist Waynell Henson

THE SOVEREIGNTY OF GOD

BY DR. JEANNETTE H. DONALD

If you look up the definition of the word *"sovereign"* in the dictionary, you would find words like *"possessing supreme or ultimate power," "greatest," "ruler,"* and *"authority."* The way I like to explain God's sovereignty best is simply by saying, "God's supremacy" (*the state of having more power, authority, or status than anyone else*). The greatest act of God's sovereignty was creation:

> *"God that made the world and all things therein, seeing that he is Lord of heaven and earth, dwelleth not in temples made with hands; Neither is worshipped with men's hands, as though he needed any thing, seeing he giveth to all life, and breath, and all things; And hath made of one blood all nations of men for to dwell on all the face of the earth, and hath determined the times before appointed, and the bounds of their habitation"* (Acts 17:24–26, KJV).

Have you ever thought clearly about how the physical heavens up above literally rule over the earth? The seasons change, as does the climate that warms us or cools us, ruins us or blesses us. The heavens are the creation of God, but they also illustrate His sovereign, majestic control over our lives. One of our problems today is that we have lost the biblical perspective of the majestic greatness of our God, and we are truly out of focus. God created humanity with a volition, a free will. It does not matter what decisions a person makes—the Sovereignty of God will not be affected.

UNIT 1 – THE SOVEREIGNTY OF GOD

As we study this unit, imagine Isaiah, this strong and courageous man of God, proclaiming God's Word. Listen to his message with your mind and heart, and how it relates to your own life, his message to return, repent, and be renewed. We must trust in God's redemptive powers through the Messiah, Jesus Christ, and rejoice. Isaiah the prophet's name means *"the salvation of the Lord"* or *"the Lord is salvation."* He is the author of the book of Isaiah, and is called the Prince of Prophets, who shines above all other writers and prophets of the Scripture. Isaiah was educated, distinguished, and privileged, but remained deep in his spiritual beliefs. He was committed to obedience in ministry as a prophet of God for 55 to 60 years. Isaiah was a man in touch with God. He heard God's message, and he brought the nation back to Him before it was too late. Isaiah loved his nation, using the phrase *"my people"* at least twenty-six times in his book. He pleaded with Judah to return to God and warned kings when their foreign policy was contrary to His will. Isaiah was skilled in communicating God's truth to the people, and he hated sin and sham religion.

Isaiah prophesied during the days of Uzziah, Jotham, Ahaz, and Hezekiah, kings of Judah. *"The vision of Isaiah the son of Amoz, which he saw concerning Judah and Jerusalem in the days of Uzziah, Jotham, Ahaz, and Hezekiah, kings of Judah"* (Isaiah 1:1).

The first 39 chapters of Isaiah carry the message of judgment for sin to Judah, Israel, and surrounding pagan nations. Judah had a form of godliness, but their hearts were corrupt. Isaiah's warnings told of God's compassion, love, and justice. Isaiah indicated their balance and their significance when he wrote, *"And in mercy shall the throne be established: and he shall sit upon it in truth in the tabernacle of David, judging, and seeking judgment, and hasting righteousness"* (Isaiah 16:5). This verse is the essence of what the book of Isaiah is about. The book of Isaiah reveals a prophetic message from God, who cares for His people to be their judge and would provide for them a Savior. This Savior will come from *"the house of David,"* who would eventually bear the entire judgment for their rebellion and disobedience. *"And there shall come forth a rod out of the stem of Jesse, and a Branch shall grow out of his roots: And the spirit of the LORD shall rest upon him, the spirit of wisdom and understanding, the spirit of counsel and might, the spirit of knowledge and of the fear of the LORD"* (Isaiah 11:1–2).

The second half, chapters 40–66, delivers a message of forgiveness, comfort, and hope. This message of hope unfolds God's promise for the future, *"the coming of the Messiah."* Isaiah speaks of the Messiah as both a suffering servant and a sovereign Lord. As you study this quarter, imagine a strong and courageous man of God, proclaiming His Word and His message in regards to life— *return*, *repent*, and *renewal*. Isaiah saw God forgiving His people, delivering them from captivity, and taking them back to Jerusalem to rebuild the Temple and restoring the nation. He prophesies of the coming of the Lord Jesus Christ as the Messiah, Savior, and King. The Messiah will certainly bring salvation to the world. The world needs to know that God loves us enough to WARN us about real danger!

God asked Isaiah to remind His people that love and justice are at the heart of all His promises. Our loving God sets two ways before His people: t*he way of truth, life, and light; and the way of deception, death, and darkness.* God's message carried by His prophets is always the same: "Repent, turn to God, and be saved."

Isaiah describes a *"Peaceable Kingdom"* in the coming of a messianic kingdom, not only for humans, but all of God's creatures, to live together in peace and harmony. God will send the Messiah to save His people. His kingdom will be set up as the faithful Prince of Peace. The Messiah will come as sovereign Lord, who will take away sins.

"But God commendeth his love toward us, in that, while we were yet sinners, Christ died for us" (Romans 5:8, KJV).

UNIT 2 – THE SOVEREIGNTY OF JESUS

In this quarter, the book of Hebrews will open your mind to the fact that Christ is supreme over more than just roles and systems. *"The Son is the radiance of God's glory and the exact representation of His being, sustaining all things by his powerful word"* (Hebrews 1:3a, NIV). The main theme of the book of Hebrews is explaining the work of Jesus' ministry in the context of the Old Testament. Jesus was the fulfillment of the Old Testament. He does not represent a new way of doing things, but rather, He is the fulfillment of the old way of doing things and therefore greater than those ways, because He fulfills the promises and prophecies of the Old Testament. The Jews believed in the Old Testament, but they rejected Jesus as the long-awaited Messiah. Christ is superior to the angels, Moses, and high priests. The New Testament helps us as believers to avoid drifting away from our faith in Christ, because He died for the sins of all.

In the Old Testament, the mediator between God and His people was the high priest. His job was to regularly offer animal sacrifices to intercede before God for the people's sins. Jesus Christ is now our High Priest. He came to earth as a human being, therefore He understands our weaknesses. He has paid the penalty for our sins by His own sacrificial death. Moses, a great biblical hero, led the Israelites from Egyptian bondage to the Promised Land; but Jesus is more than a human servant, He is God Himself (Hebrews 1:3).

The best way we can probably explain God's sovereignty is simply to say, "*God is in control.*" Nothing that happens on this earth is outside of God's influence and authority. God has no limitations. Here are a few claims the Bible makes about God:

- "The LORD hath prepared his throne in the heavens; and his kingdom ruleth over all" (Psalm 103:19, KJV).

- "O the depth of the riches both of the wisdom and knowledge of God! how unsearchable are his judgments, and his ways past finding out!" (Romans 11:33, KJV).

- "And he said unto me, It is done. I am Alpha and Omega, the beginning and the end. I will give unto him that is athirst of the fountain of the water of life freely" (Revelation 21:6, KJV).

UNIT 3 – ALPHA AND OMEGA

John wrote the book of Revelation, a book of prophecy about the future and present. The book offers eternity for those who have suffered for their faith. Jesus gave John the message in a vision, allowing him to see and record future events to be an encouragement to all believers. No matter what oppositions we encounter in this life, God's people will be victorious!

One of the meanings of Jesus being the "*Alpha and Omega*" is that He was at the beginning of all things and will be at the end. He has always existed and always will exist. The phrase "*Alpha and Omega*" identifies Him as the God of the Old Testament. Isaiah ascribes Jesus in the Scriptures, "I the LORD, the first, and with the last; I am he" (Isaiah 41:4); "I am the first, and I am the last; and beside me there is no God" (Isaiah 44:6); "Hearken unto me, O Jacob and Israel, my called; I am He; I am the first, I also am the last" (Isaiah 48:12).

At the end of every road is God. God can meet all as "*light and life*" or as "*fire and torment.*" To the thirsty, He will give water without price from the fountain of the water of life. Let everyone who hears Him say "Come!" "*And the Spirit and the bride say, Come. And let him that heareth say, Come. And let him that is athirst come. And whosoever will, let him take the water of life freely*" (Revelation 22:17). Absolutely nothing that happens in this universe is outside of God's influence and authority. He is King of kings and Lord of lords; God is sovereign and He loves us! Nothing will ever come into our lives that He does not either decree or allow! No matter what trials or tribulations you face in this life, we can take comfort in the fact that God is sovereign.

"The Lord is not slack concerning his promise, as some men count slackness; but is longsuffering to us-ward, not willing that any should perish, but that all should come to repentance" (2 Peter 3:9).

Dr. Jeannette Head Donald is the First Lady of the Gospel Temple Church Of God In Christ, Pine Grove, LA, she is married to Elder Peter Donald, mother of three children, and grandmother to three grandchildren. She is a graduate from Walker High School, Walker, LA; Graduate of Southeastern Louisiana University, Hammond, LA, in Office & Business Administration, Certified & Licensed Belief Therapist (*Therapon Institute of New Orleans, Louisiana*), IFFC Bible Institute of Baton Rouge, LA (*Diploma in Theology*), and Life Christian University (*Bachelor's Degree in Christian Counseling and Bachelor Degree, Master's Degree & Doctoral Degree in Theology*), Zachary, LA. She is a woman of integrity and character called to do a work in the harvest for God; her motto is "Each One Reaching One." Dr. Jeannette serves as Assoc. Professor of Life Christian University (Zachary, LA). She is Director of Leadership Ministry in the International Sunday School Department. She was the owner of J'Nettes Bridal Gallery (Baton Rouge, LA). She serves at her local church as the chairperson of the Women's Department, Intercessor & Prayer Warriors, and a Sunday School Teacher. She serves in the Louisiana Eastern First Jurisdiction as Asst. Dean of the W. K. Gordon Institute and the Jurisdictional Sunday School Field Representative under Bishop Alphonso Denson Sr., Prelate, and Mother Dorothy Richardson, Supervisor of Women.

WHAT QUALIFIES A TEACHER TO TEACH?

BY DR. JEANNETTE H. DONALD

A Sunday School teacher requires spiritual maturity and should be endorsed by the pastor. The most important lesson to learn in Sunday School is **PRAYER**. Prayer should be the first and foremost act that a teacher should do before class begins and the last act at the end of the class. As teachers, you must always acknowledge that you can only know the things of God by His Spirit, so you should ask Him to lead you to help the students understand what is being taught, what the context is, and what the outcome should be. The Apostle Paul says,

"Now I beseech you, brethren, by the name of our Lord Jesus Christ, that ye all speak the same thing, and that there be no divisions among you; but that ye be perfectly joined together in the same mind and in the same judgment. For it hath been declared unto me of you, my brethren, by them which are of the house of Chloe, that there are contentions among you. Now this I say, that every one of you saith, I am of Paul; and I of Apollos; and I of Cephas; and I of Christ. Is Christ divided? was Paul crucified for you? or were ye baptized in the name of Paul? I thank God that I baptized none of you, but Crispus and Gaius" (1 Corinthians 1:10–14, KJV).

A person steeped in worldly ways does not accept the things of the Spirit of God, and is not able to understand them because these spiritual things do not comport to worldly thinking. Jesus said, *"But the Comforter, which is the Holy Ghost, whom the Father will send in my name, he shall teach you all things, and bring all things to your remembrance, whatsoever I have said unto you"* (John 14:26) and that the *"anointing which ye have received of him abideth in you, and ye need not that any man teach you: but as the same anointing teacheth you of all things, and is truth, and is no lie, and even as it hath taught you, ye shall abide in him"* (1 John 2:27).

If an individual is spiritually mature, he or she would have learned to draw near to God, to study the Scripture, and meditate on the Word. The Scripture says, *"Gather the people together, men and women, and children, and thy stranger that is within thy gates, that they may hear, and that they may learn, and fear the Lord your God, and observe to do all the words of this law"* (Deuteronomy 31:12).

RESPONSIBILITY OF A SUNDAY SCHOOL TEACHER

- *"And whoso shall receive one such little child in my name receiveth me. But whoso shall offend one of these little ones which believe in me, it were better for him that a millstone were hanged about his neck, and that he were drowned in the depth of the sea"* (Matthew 18:5–6).

MOTIVATION OF A SUNDAY SCHOOL TEACHER

- *"Hereby perceive we the love of God, because he laid down his life for us: and we ought to lay down our lives for the brethren. But whoso hath this world's good, and seeth his brother have need, and shutteth up his bowels of compassion from him, how dwelleth the love of God in him?"* (1 John 3:16–17).

QUALIFICATIONS OF A GOOD TEACHER:

I.   HAVE A RELATIONSHIP WITH GOD

1. "For God so loved the world" (John 3:16).

2. "Sanctify them through thy truth: thy word is truth" (John 17:17).

3. "That if thou shalt confess with thy mouth the Lord Jesus, and shalt believe in thine heart that God hath raised him from the dead, thou shalt be saved. For with the heart man believeth unto righteousness; and with the mouth confession is made unto salvation" (Romans 10:9–10).

II.   STUDENT OF THE WORD

1. "Study to shew thyself approved unto God" (2 Timothy 2:15).

2. "This book of the law shall not depart out of thy mouth" (Joshua 1:8–9).

3. "Meditate upon these things, give thyself wholly to them" (1 Timothy 4:15).

III.   PRAYER

1. "My voice shalt thou hear in the morning" (Psalm 5:3).

2. "Seek ye the LORD while he may be found" (Isaiah 55:6).

3. "...my God will meet all your needs according to the riches of his glory in Christ Jesus." (Philippians 4:19).

4. "Pray without ceasing" (1 Thessalonians 5:17).

IV.   BE PREPARED

1. Use reference materials (other Bible versions, dictionaries, and commentaries)

2. Teach with love and compassion

3. Spend time alone with God

4. Be a good communicator

The greatest teacher of children was Jesus Christ. His method included parables. Develop a workable plan for your church. What works for one church might not work in another. You must assess your church and come up with a plan which ensures you will have capable, trained instructors for your Sunday School.

Dr. Jeannette Head Donald is the First Lady of the Gospel Temple Church Of God In Christ, Pine Grove, LA, she is married to Elder Peter Donald, mother of three children, and grandmother to three grandchildren. She is a graduate from Walker High School, Walker, LA; Graduate of Southeastern Louisiana University, Hammond, LA, in Office & Business Administration, Certified & Licensed Belief Therapist (*Therapon Institute of New Orleans, Louisiana*), IFFC Bible Institute of Baton Rouge, LA (*Diploma in Theology*), and Life Christian University (*Bachelor's Degree in Christian Counseling and Bachelor Degree, Master's Degree & Doctoral Degree in Theology*), Zachary, LA. She is a woman of integrity and character called to do a work in the harvest for God; her motto is "Each One Reaching One." Dr. Jeannette serves as Assoc. Professor of Life Christian University (Zachary, LA). She is Director of Leadership Ministry in the International Sunday School Department. She was the owner of J'Nettes Bridal Gallery (Baton Rouge, LA). She serves at her local church as the chairperson of the Women's Department, Intercessor & Prayer Warriors, and a Sunday School Teacher. She serves in the Louisiana Eastern First Jurisdiction as Asst. Dean of the W. K. Gordon Institute and the Jurisdictional Sunday School Field Representative under Bishop Alphonso Denson Sr., Prelate, and Mother Dorothy Richardson, Supervisor of Women.

#TSSGTEACHINGTIP – FACILITATORS AND TEACHERS MAKING A DIFFERENCE

BY EVANGELIST WAYNELL HENSON

I love sharing my life story and my love of Sunday School. I am really a Sunday School girl. I was even born on a Sunday during Sunday School! How funny is that? I was also reared in a "family church." It's not a big place, but there is a tremendous love for God and love for His people! We didn't have fancy classrooms. Our Sunday School was held in the sanctuary divided into 3 classes—adult, young children, and older children. Yet in the most simple of models, Sunday School was genuinely a time I enjoyed and to which I looked forward. My grandmother, the late Chairlady Mayla Henson, was my teacher. The late Mother Inetta Franklin was our superintendent. And at the end of each lesson, my pastor (who happens to be my awesome grandfather), Dr. Supt. A. H. Henson, facilitated a discussion and wrap up review. I thought class was fun and I had a special job: Sunday School secretary. And I felt empowered as a child to participate in the wrap-up questions presented by the pastor. I reflect on those times and realize those years were incredible seeds. But I also reflect on what helped to create success in the simplest of Sunday School models.

Each week every student, both current and potential, faces the same decisions. To go to class or not to go to class? That is the question. Should I set my alarm? Should I get that extra hour of sleep? Will my teacher be prepared? Will other people be there? Succeeding isn't at all about our budgets or building. So this raises the question, how can we win? I believe the true answer was given by retail giant Wal-Mart, who many years ago said, "It's our people who make the difference." The same is true with Sunday School. As a #MinistryLeaderCoach, I will always tell you the truth. Students don't get out of bed for class due to a deficit of preached Word or simply because it's on the schedule. They typically decide based on their evaluation of "what's in it for me?" Adult learners thrive where community is created in both relationship and learning. The relationship and the environment that you, the teacher/facilitator, create will cause your class to grow. So what types of teachers are making a difference and winning?

1. GENUINELY PASSIONATE

Teaching/facilitating IS WORK! Great teachers are in a constant state of reading, learning, and looking for new ways to share. It should be enjoyable! You will only be great if you are passionate about both people and the study of the Word! Don't expect your students to enjoy if you don't enjoy what you're presenting. You will make it hard for yourself and see it reflected in attendance and consistency. Passion pushes you to make the learning time engaging and fun. And be fair to yourself and your leader. Burnout is real! So if you're in place with no passion, consider having an honest discussion about perhaps having a little break. Better to return full steam than to serve without joy and fulfillment!

2. BE A DIFFERENCE AND A DIFFERENCE MAKER

Being a teacher/facilitator comes with an awesome responsibility. "To whom much is given, much is required" (Luke 12:48). Keep this in mind and never underestimate the weight of that responsibility. Gen-X'ers, Gen-Y'ers and particularly millennials don't expect you to be perfect, but they expect that if you teach it, you live it. Be a positive influence in the lives of students.

3. CREATE A SAFE ENVIRONMENT

It's really great to create an environment of "self-feeders." Class is very different when students have prepared for the lesson and come ready to discuss. That said, you must create a safe environment where no question is a silly question. With the building of community also comes the safety of asking questions without fear of discussion outside of the class setting. Create an environment where discussions (even points of difference) are discussed with respect.

4. BE POSITIVE AND GIVE YOUR ALL

Bring positive energy to class every week! We often don't know what someone has faced in a week or even that morning before coming to class. Your positivity could be the thing that changes the course of their day! Some days, no one knows just what it took for you to walk in the door. But students who sacrifice to be with you deserve every effort to rise above frustration. We have a duty to create a positive learning experience. Smile and give encouraging feedback! Don't forget—your positive energy is contagious! When you open your class, you owe 100%!

5. GET PERSONAL

Relationships are NOT created nor do they grow simply because of one hour of weekly class time. They grow when you make the effort to get to know your students and find meaningful ways to connect with them. Get to know your students and their interests. It will create other ways for you to engage and build relationships. Don't be shy about sharing your interests with them.

6. BE OPEN

Adult learners value the opportunity to share their perspective. This will mean that as students study, they too will have insights and thoughts on the lesson. As prepared as we might be, it is important to know that we do not have ALL of the answers. We too can be open and find learning moments with students.

7. FIND INSPIRATION

Being creative doesn't mean creating everything. As you study, seek out resources to find your own inspiration. Find a teacher who inspires you! What do you like or appreciate about their style/method? Keep in mind options such as books, blogs, Pinterest, YouTube, Facebook, and Twitter. There's a world of information around you!

 **Evangelist Waynell Henson** is a member of Dominion Word Ministries Church Of God In Christ, Elder Michael McWilliams, Pastor. She has a heartbeat for connecting in relevant and meaningful ways to inspire people to abundant living through the truth of God's Word. A gifted administrator and #MinistryLeaderCoach, she serves as the Executive Secretary of the International Sunday School Department (COGIC) and Co-Chairman of Auxiliaries in Ministry for the Kansas East Jurisdiction COGIC, Bishop L.F. Thuston, Prelate. With a heightened awareness of connecting with Gen-X'ers, G-Y'ers, and millennials, she impacts a social media "community" of more than 1,000 lovers of Sunday School. She shares the weekly lesson, growth strategies, and resources through platforms as YouTube, Facebook, Instagram, Pinterest, Twitter, and SnapChat. Have YOU joined "The Community"?

#HappyTeaching

Find more great ideas (#TeachingTipTuesday) on www.ThatSundaySchoolGirl.com.

QUARTERLY QUIZ

The questions on this page may be used in several ways: as a pretest at the beginning of the quarter; as a review at the end of the quarter; or as a review after each lesson. The questions are based on the Scripture text of each lesson (King James Version).

LESSON 1

1. Create a list of the powerful animals that will live in peace (**Isaiah 11:6–8**). Evaluate the "powerful" or antagonistic barriers that need to be changed or eradicated in your life to help you, your family, and the global community live in peace.

_____

_____

2. Critique the difference between how we judge others and how God judges us (**vv. 3–5**)?

_____

_____

LESSON 2

1. Judge the benefits of those who are invited to God's feast in **Isaiah 25:6–7**.

_____

_____

2. Explain how the "hand of the LORD" in **v. 10** is evidenced in the Christian community.

_____

_____

LESSON 3

1. Isaiah's uses the image of soaring on an eagle to give hope to those who are discouraged. Infer how one can soar on eagles' wings in practical terms (**Isaiah 40:31**).

_____

_____

2. According to Isaiah, people thought that they could hide from God (**v. 27**). Do you agree that this is true in the church today and for you personally? Explain.

_____

_____

LESSON 4

1. Describe the type of clothing in **Isaiah 61:10** that God will give to His people and the relationship between the clothing and God's people.

_____

_____

2. Create an analogy in nature that describes how you see the relationship between God, righteousness, and praise (**v. 11**).

_____

_____

LESSON 5

1. God spoke to His people through the prophets (**Hebrews 1:1**). How does God speak to believers today, and what is the most effective way that you listen to Him?

_____

_____

QUARTERLY QUIZ

2. The writer of Hebrews describes the superiority of Jesus. Who is Jesus to you, and would you describe Him as the authority in your life?

_____

_____

LESSON 6

1. Jesus taught that not doing God's Word is like building a house on sand; it cannot resist the winds and forces of life (**Matthew 7:26–27**). Reflect on the choices that you make and why you make them. What causes you to build your foundation on things that will crumble and not support you?

_____

_____

2. Jesus spoke with great authority, and the people were amazed (**v. 29**). What evidence can you share that demonstrates the power of Jesus' transforming Word in you?

_____

_____

LESSON 7

1. How should believers approach our High Priest, Jesus (**Hebrews 4:16**)? What is your response to an unbeliever who asks you to explain your response?

_____

_____

2. God's love for creation is experienced through Jesus' sacrifice on the Cross and Resurrection. Do you agree that believers accept God's love? Defend your response and give an example.

_____

_____

LESSON 8

1. What is the importance of Abraham's approach to Melchisedec and our approach to Jesus as our High Priest?

_____

_____

2. Jesus is the High Priest who lives forever and is greater than all of creation. Compare and contrast ways that Jesus is superior to the former things that gave you joy over Him.

_____

_____

LESSON 9

1. The writer of Hebrews presents that endurance is necessary to handle hardships (**Hebrew 12:7**). Create a short song or poem that expresses how to strengthen your trust in God during difficult times.

_____

_____

QUARTERLY QUIZ

2. No one likes to be punished, but the author of Hebrews reminds the reader that after God's punishment, believers can enjoy the "peaceable fruit and righteousness" (**v. 11**). Identify reasons how that this applies to your life and to your testimony to others about Christ.

_____

_____

LESSON 10

1. What results could occur if God's people believed that God is the Alpha, Omega, Beginning, and the End (**Revelation 21:6**)?

_____

_____

2. Compose a list of who should be fearful of the lake of fire and brimstone and the second death (**v. 8**). What approaches does the church use to effectively minister to people who live this way?

_____

_____

LESSON 11

1. Based on **Revelation 21:13–14**, think of three questions that might come to mind about the gates and the foundation for believers and unbelievers.

_____

_____

2. What is the relationship between Jesus, the Lamb, as the light (**v. 23**) in heaven and Jesus is the light of world (**John 8:12**)?

_____

_____

LESSON 12

1. How do you respond to the fact that John's vision includes the marking on the foreheads with God's name for those who are now living with Him forever (**Revelation 22:4**)?

_____

_____

2. John writes that Jesus will soon return (**v. 7**). Why does John emphasize Jesus' return?

_____

_____

LESSON 13

1. Identify two significant points that John shares about the new heaven and new earth.

_____

_____

2. After reading this lesson, how will you share with your family members who are unbelievers about accepting Jesus into their lives and tell them about His return?

_____

_____

_____

Answers to Quarterly Quiz can be found on page 460

THE PEACEFUL KINGDOM

BIBLE BASIS: ISAIAH 11:1–9

BIBLE TRUTH: The sovereignty of God will bring peace and an end to painful problems, persistent evil, and other troubles.

MEMORY VERSE: "They shall not hurt nor destroy in all my holy mountain: for the earth shall be full of the knowledge of the LORD, as the waters cover the sea" (Isaiah 11:9).

LESSON AIM: By the end of the lesson we will: DISTINGUISH the key descriptors of God's peaceful Kingdom; ANTICIPATE the day when Christian communities will be known for their godly life of peace; and EVALUATE an area of church or community life that does not meet God's intention for peace and develop a strategy to address it.

TEACHER PREPARATION

MATERIALS NEEDED: Quarterly Commentary/Teacher Manual, Adult Quarterly, Adult resources—charts, worksheets, and other teaching tools, paper, pens, pencils, Bibles (several different versions)

OTHER MATERIALS NEEDED / TEACHER'S NOTES:

_____

_____

LESSON OVERVIEW

LIFE NEED FOR TODAY'S LESSON
Our world is filled with hatred, troubles, divisions, and chaos.

BIBLE APPLICATION
Christians discover various ways to help live in God's peace within the world.

BIBLE LEARNING
Isaiah's prophecy reveals that the sovereign God will bring about a world of peace.

STUDENTS' RESPONSES
Believers can share what things may keep them from meeting the needs of those in their communities.

LESSON SCRIPTURE

ISAIAH 11:1–9, KJV

1 And there shall come forth a rod out of the stem of Jesse, and a Branch shall grow out of his roots:

2 And the spirit of the LORD shall rest upon him, the spirit of wisdom and understanding,

ISAIAH 11:1–9, AMP

1 Then a Shoot (the Messiah) will spring from the stock of Jesse [David's father], and a Branch from his roots will bear fruit.

2 And the Spirit of the LORD will rest on Him—the Spirit of wisdom and

the spirit of counsel and might, the spirit of knowledge and of the fear of the LORD;

3 And shall make him of quick understanding in the fear of the LORD: and he shall not judge after the sight of his eyes, neither reprove after the hearing of his ears:

4 But with righteousness shall he judge the poor, and reprove with equity for the meek of the earth: and he shall smite the earth: with the rod of his mouth, and with the breath of his lips shall he slay the wicked.

5 And righteousness shall be the girdle of his loins, and faithfulness the girdle of his reins.

6 The wolf also shall dwell with the lamb, and the leopard shall lie down with the kid; and the calf and the young lion and the fatling together; and a little child shall lead them.

7 And the cow and the bear shall feed; their young ones shall lie down together: and the lion shall eat straw like the ox.

8 And the suckling child shall play on the hole of the asp, and the weaned child shall put his hand on the cockatrice' den.

9 They shall not hurt nor destroy in all my holy mountain: for the earth shall be full of the knowledge of the LORD, as the waters cover the sea.

understanding, the Spirit of counsel and strength, the Spirit of knowledge and of the [reverential and obedient] fear of the LORD—

3 And He will delight in the fear of the LORD, and He will not judge by what His eyes see, nor make decisions by what His ears hear;

4 But with righteousness and justice He will judge the poor, and decide with fairness for the downtrodden of the earth; and He shall strike the earth with the rod of His mouth, and with the breath of His lips He shall slay the wicked.

5 And righteousness will be the belt around His loins, And faithfulness the belt around His waist.

6 And the wolf will dwell with the lamb, And the leopard will lie down with the young goat, and the calf and the young lion and the fatted steer together; and a little child will lead them.

7 And the cow and the bear will graze [together], their young will lie down together, and the lion shall eat straw like the ox.

8 And the nursing child will [safely] play over the hole of the cobra, and the weaned child will put his hand on the viper's den [and not be hurt].

9 They will not hurt or destroy in all My holy mountain, for the earth will be full of the knowledge of the LORD as the waters cover the sea.

LIGHT ON THE WORD

Jesse. Jesse was the grandson of Ruth and Boaz. He was a shepherd and raised his sons in that occupation. Jesse was the father to eight sons. The youngest of these sons was David, who eventually became King of Israel. Not much is said about Jesse after David takes him and his wife to live in Moab (**1 Samuel 22:3–4**), because David became a fugitive hunted by Saul.

The Branch. The Branch is a term that symbolized the Davidic Messiah. The term can be found in the prophets (**Jeremiah 23:5, Zechariah 3:8**), but its origins may have stemmed from other uses of the word "branch" in reference to rulers. In **Daniel 11:7,** the word is used to reference political strife that will occur between a ruler and her offspring. Elsewhere, Isaiah speaks of God's people collectively being a branch planted by God that will grow (**60:21**).

TEACHING THE BIBLE LESSON

LIFE NEED FOR TODAY'S LESSON

AIM: Students are reminded that our world is filled with hatred, troubles, divisions, and chaos.

INTRODUCTION

Freedom from Oppression

As in much of Isaiah's prophecies, the present and future can be intermingled. In **chapter 10**, Isaiah speaks of the Assyrian oppression and captivity. This speaks to the situation of Israel at the time of Assyrian world dominance. The Assyrians were used by God to discipline the Children of Israel. Isaiah then speaks of this dominance fading away and the Assyrian yoke destroyed.

At the same time, intermingled with verses of liberation from Assyrian oppression, Isaiah speaks of a time when the remnant of Israel and Judah will return, the time of the consummated kingdom of God. Isaiah fully describes this period of time in **chapter 11**—a time of peace and prosperity, security and safety. This is not because of any inherent goodness in the time itself, but the glory and greatness of the King who will reign: Jesus Christ.

BIBLE LEARNING

AIM: Students will learn Isaiah's prophecy reveals that the sovereign God will bring about a world of peace.

I. THE MESSIAH GIVES REAL HOPE (Isaiah 11:1–5)

These Scriptures in Isaiah speak about hope. This kind of hope cannot be in man. God promised David that he would have someone from his family to reign over his throne forever (**1 Chronicles 22:10**). **Verse 1** says in part, "there shall come forth a rod out of the stem of Jesse." David came from Jesse's lineage. During Isaiah's time, Judah experienced fluctuation in their kings, despite all of them being from the lineage of Jesse and David. Whether the ruler at the time of the prophecy here was generally godly like Hezekiah or corrupt like Manasseh, all were human and made mistakes. But the ruler and judge Isaiah here refers to is not an ordinary man—He is the Messiah.

He is the one who would give hope to God's people to trust, believe, and hope in Him again. This new King will be different from all the other kings. He will be the Savior of the world, the King who will sit on the throne forever. He is equipped to handle the monumental task of giving hope and bringing peace.

Isaiah 11:1–5

1 And there shall come forth a rod out of the stem of Jesse, and a Branch shall grow out of his roots:

Jesse was King David's father, placing him in the lineage of Jesus (**1 Samuel 17:12; Matthew 1:6**). Referring to the Messiah as a Branch (Heb. *netser*, **NEH-tser**) from the felled Davidic tree is not unique to this verse (see **Isaiah 4:2; Jeremiah 23:5, 33:15; Zechariah 3:8; 6:12**), but note that in each instance the word is capitalized. These other verses use a different Hebrew word for branch than **Isaiah 11:1**, but the idea is the same. Cutting off dead branches allows the branches to grow back healthier than before.

2 And the spirit of the LORD shall rest upon him, the spirit of wisdom and understanding,

the spirit of counsel and might, the spirit of knowledge and of the fear of the LORD; 3 And shall make him of quick understanding in the fear of the LORD: and he shall not judge after the sight of his eyes, neither reprove after the hearing of his ears:

The spirit of the Lord is more than just our understanding of an existence outside bodily form. In Hebrew it means one's very breath (*ruakh*, **ROO-akh**). Isaiah promises that the Messiah will be filled with God's breath, and as a result, with God's wisdom, understanding, counsel, might, knowledge and reverence. These are all characteristics of a righteous ruler, characteristics not always exhibited by human rulers, even those who seek God's guidance and the good of the people in all things. The word "rest" (Heb. *nuakh*, **NU-akh**) is deeper than the idea of a bird landing, resting, and then flying away, but has a much more settled and profound sense. Whenever the Holy Spirit rested on an Old Testament figure, it was in the sense of an anointing and filling, and always for a purpose (cf. **Numbers 11:25; 2 Kings 2:15**). Essentially, the Messianic King is completely equipped by God with everything He will need to rule righteously and effectively over Israel and the whole earth (cf. **Isaiah 9:6–7, 11:10–12**).

Most scholars recognize that whenever a term or phrase is repeated in Scripture, the emphasis is significant. In this case, the aspect of the fear of the Lord could be seen to be integral to the sum of the qualities of the Messiah King, especially when combined with the rest of the passage. This Messiah would not use His own understanding or personal judgment, but the standard of God's righteousness when weighing matters of grave importance—such as the fate of oppressors or the worthiness of the oppressed for salvation. In the end, even the strongest and wisest are subject to God, who directs the minds of kings even when they are unaware of it (**Proverbs 21:1**). Jesus made it clear throughout His ministry that He

was there not to do His will, but His Father's (**John 6:38**).

4 But with righteousness shall he judge the poor, and reprove with equity for the meek of the earth: and he shall smite the earth: with the rod of his mouth, and with the breath of his lips shall he slay the wicked. 5 And righteousness shall be the girdle of his loins, and faithfulness the girdle of his reins.

The poor have experienced far too much corruption and injustice, and waited far too long, so they very much need a righteous judge. For these afflicted souls, just judgment is synonymous with salvation. Fulfilling His righteous role, the Messiah King judges as the embodied, all-powerful Word of God (**Revelation 19:11–13**). Scholars concur that the girdle, belt, or sash was a critical item in Middle Eastern clothing, holding the rest of the garments together—and also earning a New Testament mention in Paul's description of the well-armed believer girding his waist with truth (**Ephesians 6:14**).

II. THE MESSIAH GIVES REAL PEACE (Isaiah 11:6–9)

Isaiah's readers and hearers know that the prophet is referring to the Messiah here, because He is so different from earthly rulers. They were all temporary, but He is everlasting; He will reign forever. His Kingdom should be totally different than any other kingdom, especially our present earthly kingdom. **Verse 6** says the wolf and the lamb will dwell together, even though the lamb is food for the wolf.

The Scripture continues: "The leopard shall lie down with the kid; and the calf and the young lion and the fatling together; and a little child shall lead them." This is so different from our present world. A child could not lead a lion and fatling; the lion would devour them both. Yet Isaiah speaks of a time when the Messiah will bring peace to all of creation. He alone can bring peace for every aspect of our lives. All things that cause destruction—fire, tsunamis, frigid temperatures—will no longer exist. In this Kingdom, everyone will get along, even predators and prey.

Isaiah 11:6–9

6 The wolf also shall dwell with the lamb, and the leopard shall lie down with the kid; and the calf and the young lion and the fatling together; and a little child shall lead them. 7 And the cow and the bear shall feed; their young ones shall lie down together: and the lion shall eat straw like the ox. 8 And the sucking child shall play on the hole of the asp, and the weaned child shall put his hand on the cockatrice' den.

This idyllic, utopian scene has been the subject of countless paintings, songs, and literature; indeed, the peaceful co-existence of natural enemies and human babies, a world restored to an Eden-like state in the Messiah's reign, has sparked the imagination and dreams of humanity ever since the prophet penned the words. An asp (Heb. *pethen*, **PEH-then**) means a snake or venomous serpent, which is synonymous with cockatrice (Heb. *tsepha'*, **TSEH-fah**), perhaps a cobra, adder, or viper (cf. **Isaiah 59:5**, "viper's brood"). The serpent has a unique role in human history dating from the garden temptation (**Genesis 3**) and has been symbolic of evil ever since. Clearly, if children and infants can play with poisonous snakes, the curse or enmity (**Genesis 3:15**) pronounced on Adam and Eve has been removed—and more than that, Kingdom peace reigns over all.

9 They shall not hurt nor destroy in all my holy mountain: for the earth shall be full of the knowledge of the LORD, as the waters cover the sea.

These verses are similar to **Isaiah 65:25** and **Habakkuk 2:14**. The reference to the holy mountain, or Mt. Zion, is a recurring theme throughout Isaiah, which also will be explored in next week's lesson (**25:6, 10**; cf. **10:32**). Nature is restored, peace envelops the world.

SEARCH THE SCRIPTURES

QUESTION 1

Isaiah speaks of Jesus when he says, "There shall come forth a rod out of the stem of Jesse, and a Branch shall grow out of his roots" (**Isaiah 11:1**). Draw a genealogical chart that outlines Jesse's family tree all the way to Jesus (**Matthew 1:1–17**).

Jesse; David and Bathsheba; Solomon and Naamah; Rehoboam; Abijam; Asa; Jehosaphat; Jehoram; Uzziah; Jotham; Ahaz; Hezekiah; Manasseh; Amon; Josiah; Jeconiah; Shealtiel; Zerubbabel; Abiud; Eliakim; Azor; Zadok; Achim; Eliud; Eleazar; Matthan; Jacob; Joseph and Mary; Jesus.

QUESTION 2

How do we reconcile Christians being soldiers or police officers with Isaiah's words that "they shall not hurt or destroy in all my holy mountain" (**v. 9**)?

Total peace happens because Christ will reign over everything and everyone.

LIGHT ON THE WORD

Future Hope

Isaiah wanted God's people to know that the Messiah came fully equipped with the wisdom/understanding, counsel/might, knowledge, and the fear of the Lord. He came to introduce the Kingdom of God. His role is to implement God's righteousness on earth, not self-glorification. The words and images of this passage originated during Israel's captivity and exile, and therefore spoke to a future hope radically different from present circumstances.

BIBLE APPLICATION

AIM: Students will agree to live with God's peace in the world.

Peaceful is not a word that describes our current times. Nations are in uproar and wars are fought on many fronts. Unrest persists even in our national government and politics. Our young people are being slain in the streets. One day the Lord will bring peace to this world. For now, we must access the peace that He offers those who trust in Christ, and strive to work for peace in our neighborhoods and in our nation.

STUDENTS' RESPONSES

AIM: Students will agree to share God's peace in their communities.

As you consider God's peace, are there areas in your family life, neighborhood, or church that call for God's peaceful intervention? What Scriptures come to mind to guide your thought life and influence your actions?

Psalm 23; Galatians 5:22; Ephesians 6:10-15; Philippians 4: 6, 7 are some examples.

PRAYER

Father, in these troubled times, the concept of peace seems difficult to grasp. We invite the Holy Spirit to guard our hearts and minds according to **Philippians 4:6, 7**. In the Name of Jesus we pray. Amen.

HOW TO SAY IT

Cockatrice.   **KA**-ka-treese.

Reprove.   ree-**PROOV**.

DIG A LITTLE DEEPER

This section provides an additional research article to further your study of the lesson:

Isaiah 11 is a message of hope. It paints a vivid picture of the manifestation of God's plan for peace, a plan not limited to cultural notions of justice and diversity but one that includes much more. In his article "If You Only Knew What Would Bring Peace," Terry McGonigal provides a rich understanding of the outworking of peace or shalom. With Jesus as the model, McGonigal challenges the reader to look beyond culturally ingrained ideas and embrace the radical ideal that challenged its biblical hearers.

http://studentlife.biola.edu/page_attachments/0000/1395/ShalomTheology-TerryMcGonigal.pdf

PREPARE FOR NEXT SUNDAY

Read **Isaiah 25:6–10a** and "The Mountain of God."

DAILY HOME BIBLE READINGS

MONDAY
God's Offer to Solomon
(1 Kings 3:3–9)

TUESDAY
God is Pleased with Solomon's Requests
(1 Kings 3:10–15)

WEDNESDAY
Live Together in Harmony
(1 Peter 3:8–13)

THURSDAY
Build a Peaceful Lifestyle
(2 Peter 1:3–11)

FRIDAY
Support the Interests of Others
(Philippians 2:1–11)

SATURDAY
Build a Just and Righteous Community
(Psalm 72:1–7)

SUNDAY
The Peaceful Kingdom
(Isaiah 11:1–9)

THE MOUNTAIN OF GOD

BIBLE BASIS: ISAIAH 25:6–10a

BIBLE TRUTH: The Lord will create a feast for the faithful and end death forever.

MEMORY VERSE: "He will swallow up death in victory; and the Lord GOD will wipe away tears from off all faces; and the rebuke of his people shall he take away from off all the earth: for the LORD hath spoken" (Isaiah 25:8).

LESSON AIM: By the end of the lesson we will: DECIDE that God acts in the best interest of all peoples and nations; APPRECIATE that God removes barriers that cause people to feel separated from Him and one another; and REJOICE that God gives hope to all oppressed peoples.

TEACHER PREPARATION

MATERIALS NEEDED: Quarterly Commentary/Teacher Manual, Adult Quarterly, Adult resources—charts, worksheets, and other teaching tools, paper, pens, pencils, Bibles (several different versions)

OTHER MATERIALS NEEDED / TEACHER'S NOTES:

_____

_____

LESSON OVERVIEW

LIFE NEED FOR TODAY'S LESSON
Oppressed people always seek relief from their injustices.

BIBLE APPLICATION
Isaiah's prophecy reveals that the sovereign God will give deliverance from oppression.

BIBLE LEARNING
God is a God for all people and whose promises and plans are true.

STUDENTS' RESPONSES
Christians agree that God breaks down barriers that separate us from the Lord and from one another.

LESSON SCRIPTURE

ISAIAH 25:6–10a, KJV

6 And in this mountain shall the LORD of hosts make unto all people a feast of fat things, a feast of wines on the lees, of fat things full of marrow, of wines on the lees well refined.

7 And he will destroy in this mountain the face of the covering cast over all people, and the

ISAIAH 25:6–10a, AMP

6 On this mountain [Zion] the LORD of hosts will prepare a lavish banquet for all peoples [to welcome His reign on earth], a banquet of aged wines—choice pieces [flavored] with marrow, of refined, aged wines.

7 And on this mountain He will destroy the

vail that is spread over all nations.

8 He will swallow up death in victory; and the Lord GOD will wipe away tears from off all faces; and the rebuke of his people shall he take away from off all the earth: for the LORD hath spoken it.

9 And it shall be said in that day, Lo, this is our God; we have waited for him, and he will save us: this is the LORD; we have waited for him, we will be glad and rejoice in his salvation.

10a For in this mountain shall the hand of the LORD rest.

covering that is [cast] over all peoples, and the veil [of death] that is woven and spread over all the nations.

8 He will swallow up death [and abolish it] for all time. And the Lord GOD will wipe away tears from all faces, and He will take away the disgrace of His people from all the earth; for the LORD has spoken.

9 It will be said in that day, "Indeed, this is our God for whom we have waited that He would save us. This is the LORD for whom we have waited; let us shout for joy and rejoice in His salvation."

10a For the hand of the LORD will rest on this mountain [Zion].

LIGHT ON THE WORD

God's Restoration Plan. In **chapter 24**, Isaiah prophesies cosmic judgment and God's reign over all the earth. The very earth is pictured as reeling to and fro like a drunkard. Isaiah speaks of it being dissolved clean. Although this may sound discouraging, God will not leave the earth desolate. He will bring restoration through His coming reign, which is then described in full, rich detail in **chapter 25**. The joy of God's people and the blessings that will accompany His reign will be the result of His abolishing sin and death.

TEACHING THE BIBLE LESSON

LIFE NEED FOR TODAY'S LESSON

AIM: Students witness how oppressed people always seek relief from their injustice.

INTRODUCTION

The New Jerusalem

Isaiah **chapter 25** paints the picture of God's judgment on the nations and establishment of His Kingdom. These chapters are especially focused on the end of the world; they speak of what will happen in the last days and what has already begun to happen, as the Kingdom of God has been inaugurated with the coming of Christ.

BIBLE LEARNING

AIM: Students will agree that God is a God for all people and His promises and plans are true.

I. GOD HOSTS A PARTY
(Isaiah 25:6–7)

Verses 1–5 comprise a hymn, including a confession of faith (**v. 1**), praising God for delivering His people from oppression (**Isaiah 24**). Only God can break oppression and end bondages imposed by the evil one. **Isaiah 25:6** talks about God throwing a feast that will end oppression. This feast will be for all people, and will be full of wine and the richest foods. This feast would have stirred the imagination of the Hebrew mind at the time. The imagery is one of plenteous food and joy.

Next Isaiah alludes to the Lord destroying a shroud or covering that is over all people. This shroud, which connects all people, no matter what ethnicity or culture, is death. The feast is for all people because this shroud will one day be destroyed.

Isaiah 25:6–7

6 And in this mountain shall the LORD of hosts make unto all people a feast of fat things, a feast of wines on the lees, of fat things full of marrow, of wines on the lees well refined. 7 And he will destroy in this mountain the face of the covering cast over all people, and the vail that is spread over all nations.

"In this mountain" refers again to Mt. Zion, which Isaiah establishes early on (**2:1–5**; cf. **24:23**), and "unto all people" refers to the gathering of Israel and all other nations (cf. **Zechariah 14:16**) for the momentous occasion of a great feast. Indeed, it bears an undeniable resemblance to the "great supper," the wedding feast of the Lamb described in **Luke 14:15–24**. Just like in the parable, the guest list is open to all, although not all will attend—even among the first invitees. As can be imagined, this is the ultimate feast, and God spares no good thing, even for former enemies. In this sense, it is perhaps intentionally reminiscent of the prodigal son, whose father threw a lavish feast to welcome home his lost son, which speaks directly to the father's character. There is an interesting reiteration with dual usage of "a feast of fat things" (Heb. *shemen*, **SHEH-men**) and dual usage of "a feast of wines on the lees" (Heb. *shemer*, **SHEH-mer**), which might be similar to someone today extravagantly describing a "no expense spared, fully appointed,

everything under the sun, fit for a king" feast. Lees is the name of the residual yeast that settles to the bottom of beverages during the fermentation process. This can include anything from wine to vinegar. Lees were also designed to preserve or keep.

II. DEATH WILL BE DESTROYED (v. 8)

Isaiah 25:8 talks about God removing the shadow of death. With this cloud of gloom removed from over His people, they can see the bigger picture: God is Sovereign and in control, and He can do whatever He chooses. We as believers look forward to the celebration that marks the end of all oppression. We wait for death to be done away with, for the New Heaven, the New Earth, and the New Jerusalem.

The strength and fear of death will be destroyed so that it no longer exists. Oppression will be completely severed. Our God says to all people who put their trust in Him that He will wipe away all tears. Not only will He swallow death and wipe away all tears, but the sting of insults and mockery will be removed against His land and people. The reputation of His people would be restored.

Isaiah 25:8

8 He will swallow up death in victory; and the Lord GOD will wipe away tears from off all faces; and the rebuke of his people shall he take away from off all the earth: for the LORD hath spoken it.

Paul quotes from this verse in **1 Corinthians 15:54**: "So when this corruptible shall have put on incorruption, and this mortal shall have put on immortality, then shall be brought to pass the saying that is written, death is swallowed up in victory," rendered "forever" in NLT. The Hebrew word (*netsakh*, **NET-sakh**) can mean glory or success as well as eternity. Isaiah takes advantage of the dual meaning in order to make his point. It will be an eternal victory when God destroys death. The process of its demise is called the end times, with the end of death being just one of the climaxes prior to the inauguration of God's Kingdom. Directly related to other aspects of the curse, all suffering, pain, and crying will end as well, along with all oppression and its associated disgrace, reproach, and shame (see **Zephaniah 3:18; Joel 2:19**). As with much of the Old Testament, the Scripture emphasizes the unique plight of Israel's persecutions, repeated in waves of anti-Semitism through history, which continue to the present day. In the KJV, Isaiah promises God will take away his people's rebuke. The NIV renders this word "disgrace" (Heb. *kherpah*, **kher-PAH**), which is more accurate for contemporary English because what Isaiah is promising is that the disgrace that God's people have faced through centuries of oppression will be done away with. Oppressors removed God's people from their home and devastated God's land, and now He uses Israel as the gathering place for righting the wrongs other nations have committed against her, focused on general humanity as well as specifically Israel. Because of this view, ancient church father Ambrose called Isaiah not only a prophet but "the first apostle and evangelist" (Ibid., 192). God is committed to Israel but cares for all people of all nations; within this concern, however, is their need to respond to Him and turn toward Him, no longer rejecting Him. God's concern for the world is universal, but the world's response certainly hasn't been nor ever will be as universal; thus the distinction even in this grandest of promises of "his people" from all others. Many similar verses, such as **Revelation 21:4** ("And God shall wipe away all tears from their eyes; and there shall be no more death, neither sorrow, nor crying, neither shall there be any more pain"), have been quoted at many funerals, as they speak to the core of the abiding faith and future hope of believers through the centuries.

III. GOD'S HAND OF PROTECTION (vv. 9–10a)

God's people will proclaim "He is our God!" Here, they are basically saying, "We trusted in Him and He saved us. This is the Lord, in whom we have trusted. The people of God have come back and declared that Yahweh is our God because He has delivered them to freedom." This declaration points to our salvation in Jesus Christ. The believer can exclaim the same thing: He is our God. Next Isaiah speaks of God's hand of protection and blessings which will rest upon His people. It will be evident and clear that all believers are God's people. This is the hope and expectation of those who trust in Him. They will be vindicated in the age to come.

Isaiah 25:9–10a

9 And it shall be said in that day, Lo, this is our God; we have waited for him, and he will save us: this is the LORD; we have waited for him, we will be glad and rejoice in his salvation. 10a For in this mountain shall the hand of the LORD rest.

Once again, continuing the psalm of praise he used to start the chapter, Isaiah again breaks into song. Indeed, such celebration is found throughout the prophet's writings (among numerous examples, see the closely associated **24:14–16**; cf. **12:1–6**, et al.). Those who hope in God will not be let down; He has heard every prayer ever uttered, He will save us, and then we will rejoice greatly as all our suffering finally, mercifully, and permanently ends. This is God's final answer to every evil known to man from the Fall, the fulfillment of every promise in every prophecy. "The hand of God" is a phrase found throughout both testaments, from recognizing God's hand at work in both trials (e.g., **Job 19:21**) and victories (e.g., **Exodus 32:11**), to Jesus Himself being exalted to the place of God's right hand (**Acts 2:33**), to a context for discipleship ("humble yourself under the mighty hand of God," **1 Peter 5:6**). God's hand is a symbol of power, used for judgment, destruction, and creation. In this oracle of salvation, Isaiah promises that after the power of God's judgment will come the power of God's rest.

SEARCH THE SCRIPTURES

QUESTION 1

What did Isaiah mean when he said, "He will swallow up death in victory; and the Lord GOD will wipe away tears from off all faces; and the rebuke of his people shall he take away from off all the earth: for the LORD hath spoken it" (**Isaiah 25:8**)?

No more death and shame.

QUESTION 2

How can we discern if God's hand of blessing is on our lives (**v. 10**)?

Answers will vary.

QUESTION 3

Injustice and oppression are all around us. Is it better to accept it and wait until Jesus returns or to get involved in an opportunity to fight injustice and oppression?

It is better to get involved in an opportunity to fight injustice and oppression. We are God's agents in the earth. (Answers will vary.)

LIGHT ON THE WORD

Joyous Celebration

In biblical times, weddings, harvest periods, and peace treaties were among the many occasions for feasting. These occasions symbolize everything that will take place in the future: Christ's marriage to His bride the church will be consummated, the harvest of His people will be gathered, and the peace between Him and His people will be celebrated.

We are reminded through Isaiah's words of encouragement to those who accept salvation that no matter how great or painful the loss, all will be made right through God in the end. All loved ones will be reunited and all tears of sorrow will give way to eternal gladness and rejoicing (cf. **Psalm 126:5; Isaiah 35:10**). God's sovereignty will make right the wrongs caused by the unfathomable suffering that has been ever present on the earth.

BIBLE APPLICATION

AIM: Students discover that Isaiah's prophecy reveals that the sovereign God will give deliverance from oppression.

Fifteen years after the attacks on New York City's World Trade Towers on September 11, 2001, the world seems to be an even more dangerous place, with terrorists seemingly coming out of the woodwork and multiplying like cockroaches. The news is regularly filled with new attacks, both in America and other nations; sometimes, the attacks target Christians in the most incomprehensibly inhumane ways. When and how will it all come to an end? Believers through the centuries have placed their hope in God, especially in times of great darkness and oppression.

Oppression is an awful experience for anyone. We must ask ourselves if we can be set free. God expects us to cry out to Him for deliverance. We cannot save ourselves; our salvation is tied up in Jesus Christ. What will you decide?

STUDENTS' RESPONSES

AIM: Students will agree that God breaks down barriers that separate us from Him and from one another.

If you turn on the evening news or surf the Internet, you can find out what people put their trust in. Many hope and trust in the government. Some put their trust in the economy, others in their health. All of these things will ultimately fail. Today's lesson tells people to put their hope in the Lord and His Kingdom, where all of their aspirations will come true. The violence, oppression, and death that plague us will one day be destroyed.

PRAYER

God of justice, righteousness, and joy, we praise and bless You. Your sovereignty and glory reveal the majestic and mighty ways that You deliver and bring justice to the oppressed and condemn the unjust. Use us, we pray. In the Name of Jesus we pray. Amen.

HOW TO SAY IT

Lees.   **LEES.**

Vail.   **VAY**-il.

DIG A LITTLE DEEPER

This section provides an additional research article to further your study of the lesson:

The vastness of God and the delicacies of His creation are overwhelming to the mere spectator. As we reflect on God's creation, there's a sense of awe. In this article, "The Large and Small Things in God's Creation," the student is guided on a path of reflection and introspection. With links to images, it provides a visual reminder of God's supreme love for His creation.

http://studentsoul.intervarsity.org/large-small

PREPARE FOR NEXT SUNDAY

Read **Isaiah 40:21–31** and "Foundations of the Earth."

DAILY HOME BIBLE READINGS

MONDAY
Praise for Deliverance From Oppression
(Isaiah 25:1–5)

TUESDAY
Healing Can't Wait
(Luke 14:1–6)

WEDNESDAY
Wait to Be Seated
(Luke 14:7–11)

THURSDAY
Invite the Needy to Your Table
(Luke 14:12–14)

FRIDAY
Dinner Will Be Served
(Luke 14:15–20)

SATURDAY
Christ Died for Our Sins
(1 Corinthians 15:1–11)

SUNDAY
The Mountain of God
(Isaiah 25:6–10)

COMMENTS / NOTES:

_____
_____
_____
_____
_____
_____
_____
_____
_____
_____
_____
_____

FOUNDATIONS OF THE EARTH

BIBLE BASIS: ISAIAH 40:21–31

BIBLE TRUTH: Isaiah declares that God is the absolute power in whom we should depend.

MEMORY VERSE: "Hast thou not known? hast thou not heard, that the everlasting God, the LORD, the Creator of the ends of the earth, fainteth not, neither is weary? there is no searching of his understanding" (Isaiah 40:28).

LESSON AIM: By the end of this lesson we will: DISTINGUISH God's power to control and effect change with human inability to do the same; REFLECT on the poetic imagery the writer uses to witness to God's sovereign power and personal presence with the people; and EMBRACE God's sovereignty and ability to address people's situations and needs.

TEACHER PREPARATION

MATERIALS NEEDED: Quarterly Commentary/Teacher Manual, Adult Quarterly, Adult resources—charts, worksheets, and other teaching tools, paper, pens, pencils, Bibles (several different versions)

OTHER MATERIALS NEEDED / TEACHER'S NOTES:

_____

_____

LESSON OVERVIEW

LIFE NEED FOR TODAY'S LESSON
We often place loyalty in people or systems to sustain and guide our lives.

BIBLE APPLICATION
Believers know that God can change the circumstances in the lives of God's people.

BIBLE LEARNING
Christians have the blessed assurance that God is in control and not humanity.

STUDENTS' RESPONSES
Believers agree that God can do the impossible in their lives.

LESSON SCRIPTURE

ISAIAH 40:21–31, KJV

21 Have ye not known? have ye not heard? hath it not been told you from the beginning? have ye not understood from the foundations of the earth?

22 It is he that sitteth upon the circle of the earth, and the inhabitants thereof are as grasshoppers; that stretcheth out the

ISAIAH 40:21–31, AMP

21 Do you [who worship idols] not know? Have you not heard? Has it not been told to you from the beginning? Have you not understood from the foundations of the earth [the omnipotence of God and the stupidity of bowing to idols]?

22 It is He who sits above the circle of the earth, and its inhabitants are like

heavens as a curtain, and spreadeth them out as a tent to dwell in:

23 That bringeth the princes to nothing; he maketh the judges of the earth as vanity.

24 Yea, they shall not be planted; yea, they shall not be sown: yea, their stock shall not take root in the earth: and he shall also blow upon them, and they shall wither, and the whirlwind shall take them away as stubble.

25 To whom then will ye liken me, or shall I be equal? saith the Holy One.

26 Lift up your eyes on high, and behold who hath created these things, that bringeth out their host by number: he calleth them all by names by the greatness of his might, for that he is strong in power; not one faileth.

27 Why sayest thou, O Jacob, and speakest, O Israel, My way is hid from the LORD, and my judgment is passed over from my God?

28 Hast thou not known? hast thou not heard, that the everlasting God, the LORD, the Creator of the ends of the earth, fainteth not, neither is weary? there is no searching of his understanding.

29 He giveth power to the faint; and to them that have no might he increaseth strength.

30 Even the youths shall faint and be weary, and the young men shall utterly fall:

31 But they that wait upon the LORD shall renew their strength; they shall mount up with wings as eagles; they shall run, and not be weary; and they shall walk, and not faint.

grasshoppers; [It is He] who stretches out the heavens like a veil and spreads them out like a tent to dwell in.

23 It is He who reduces dignitaries to nothing, who makes the judges (rulers) of the earth meaningless (useless).

24 Scarcely have they been planted, scarcely have they been sown, scarcely has their stock taken root in the earth, but He merely blows on them, and they wither, and a strong wind carries them away like stubble.

25 "To whom then will you compare Me that I would be his equal?" says the Holy One.

26 Lift up your eyes on high and see who has created these heavenly bodies, the One who brings out their host by number, He calls them all by name; because of the greatness of His might and the strength of His power, not one is missing.

27 Why, O Jacob, do you say, and declare, O Israel, "My way is hidden from the LORD, and the justice due me escapes the notice of my God"?

28 Do you not know? Have you not heard? The Everlasting God, the LORD, the Creator of the ends of the earth does not become tired or grow weary; there is no searching of His understanding.

29 He gives strength to the weary, and to him who has no might He increases power.

30 Even youths grow weary and tired, and vigorous young men stumble badly,

31 But those who wait for the LORD [who expect, look for, and hope in Him] will gain new strength and renew their power; they will lift up their wings [and rise up close to God] like eagles [rising toward the sun]; they will run and not become weary, they will walk and not grow tired.

LIGHT ON THE WORD

Judgment and Joy. Isaiah 40 is a significant turning point in the book of Isaiah. Up until now, the prophetic oracles have largely been about impending judgment on Judah and the other nations of the world. Judah worshiped idols and committed oppression; as a result, they will be judged with other nations. This judgment will result in exile, and the people of God will be scattered to the ends of the earth. The talk of judgment is interspersed with talk of the joy and peace of God's coming Kingdom.

TEACHING THE BIBLE LESSON

LIFE NEED FOR TODAY'S LESSON

AIM: Students agree that they should not place loyalty in people or systems to sustain and guide our lives.

INTRODUCTION

Isaiah's Vision of God

Isaiah has just written to the Israelites about the absurdity of worshiping idols. People are worshiping something they made out of the materials that our Creator-God made. We may think that we would not do something so crazy as worshiping idols, but anytime we elevate material things above the spiritual, we are guilty of this very sin. Isaiah had an amazing vision of God (**Isaiah 6:1–4**), and now he is sharing with the Hebrew people a little bit of how big God is. This should be nothing new to His people. From their beginning as a nation, God has been revealing Himself to them. Even before then, God was making Himself known to those with eyes to see and hearts to receive.

BIBLE LEARNING

AIM: Students will decide that they have the blessed assurance that God is in control.

I. GOD'S POWER OVER CREATION (Isaiah 40:21–22)

21 Have ye not known? have ye not heard? hath it not been told you from the beginning? have ye not understood from the foundations of the earth? 22 It is he that sitteth upon the circle of the earth, and the inhabitants thereof are as grasshoppers; that stretcheth out the heavens as a curtain, and spreadeth them out as a tent to dwell in:

Isaiah begins by asking his audience if they really understand who God is. The greatness of God, the Creator, should be evident to anyone whether they are familiar with the Bible or not. Paul echoes this thought in **Romans 1:20**: "For the invisible things of him from the creation of the world are clearly seen, being understood by the things that are made, even his eternal power and Godhead; so that they are without excuse." **Genesis 1–2** gives us a creation theology that informs our understanding of God's nature. He is not a part of His creation, but distinct from it. There is God, and everything else is not God, including us, His created beings. Any belief that calls us gods is wrong.

The phrase "circle of the earth" fits into the ancient Near Eastern world view on the structure of the universe. In ancient cosmology, the sky was a round dome over the earth, partly because stars and other celestial bodies were thought to move from horizon to horizon in a half circle. The earth in turn sat on primordial waters, and underneath lay a netherworld or underworld. In the ancient world, the earth was seen as a circle rather than a sphere, more than likely due to the disk-shaped curvature of the horizon. Isaiah is both declaring that God dwells on the horizon—just in sight—and playing on the sound of the words for horizon (Heb. *khug*, **KHOOG**) and grasshopper (Heb. *khagab*, **KHAH-gahv**), which begin with similar sounds that represent the expanse of God's creation from the vast horizon to the multitude of small insects.

Isaiah compares our significance to grasshoppers. These insects were so prolific and familiar to the Israelites that the Old Testament contains about a dozen different words for them. This passage emphasizes the smallness of the grasshopper. Isaiah pictures the heavens above the earth as a great vault. If we go outside in an open field on a starry night, we can look up at the stars above as well as the horizon all around, which appears as a great circle. Imagine God sitting up in the star-filled sky and looking down upon the earth at us. We appear as small to God as a tiny grasshopper would appear to us. Just as we can stomp on a grasshopper and end it, so God has the destiny of every human life in His hands. This thought should cause us to tremble in awe before our almighty God! How do you respond to the awesome creations of God?

II. GOD'S POWER OVER HUMAN AUTHORITY (Isaiah 40:23–27)

Isaiah is prophesying the period of Babylonian captivity, which imposed new human authority over God's people, who relish their unique identity in the known world of their time. Isaiah reminds the people that while they are at times subject to human authority, they should not worship or put trust in human authority. Even as God has allowed a change in designation, He still retains control of their destiny, and must continue to be worshiped and praised for deliverance.

23 That bringeth the princes to nothing; he maketh the judges of the earth as vanity. 24 Yea, they shall not be planted; yea, they shall not be sown: yea, their stock shall not take root in the earth: and he shall also blow upon them, and they shall wither, and the whirlwind shall take them away as stubble.

The Hebrew word for "vanity" is *tohu* (**TOE-hoo**). Among the synonyms for this word are a desolation, a desert, a worthless thing, confusion, an empty place without form, nothingness, a waste, or wilderness. Great civilizations have come and gone, such as the great African empires, the Aztec and Incan empires, and the Roman empire. All people are capable of great civilizations, but these are very fragile. The study of history helps us to see the bigger picture, but all of this is known to God. He sees the beginning and end of all the kingdoms and empires of the world. He is the God of both history and creation.

The Israelites were looking at the mighty Babylonian empire and trembling. But we worship the God of the long view. God dwells in eternal time; He can simultaneously see seconds, years, and even millions of years—past, present, and future. Individual rulers may be in charge almost their entire lifetimes and empires may last hundreds of years, but this is just a little blip in God's eternal plans. Earlier in this chapter (**40:7–8**), we read that people are just like grass—transitory. None of us will last forever. Even kingdoms of great cultures have come and gone. So we should not idolize or fear a mighty ruler, the head of the corporation we work for, or even our middle-level manager. Just like chaff/stubble, the loose shells that were separated from grain, so will those who are not righteous or just. They are also like the husks that were then blown away with the wind and the edible grain would remain. These became a metaphor for the wicked who would be judged by God: They would be driven away by the wrath of His judgment, and only the righteous would remain.

25 To whom then will ye liken me, or shall I be equal? saith the Holy One. 26 Lift up your eyes on high, and behold who hath created these things, that bringeth out their host by number: he calleth them all by names by the greatness of his might, for that he is strong in power; not one faileth. 27 Why sayest thou, O Jacob, and speakest, O Israel, My

way is hid from the Lord, and my judgment is passed over from my God?

The Hebrew word for equal is *shavah* (**shah-VAH**), a word that invites comparison as to whether something is of equal value or quality. The answer is that no one, no god, nothing can compare to God, the Holy One; nothing is equal to Him.

Just as many people do today, the Babylonians consulted their horoscopes to see what was in their future. Isaiah points out that the stars are all under God's command. Why consult the stars, when we know the God who created and controls them? He has a name for each star. Just the Milky Way alone contains 100 billion stars. To count them all would take about 3,000 years, to say nothing of the task of naming them. This causes us to remember that God knows each one of us by name and even knows how many hairs there are on our heads (**Matthew 10:30**).

We may think that no one sees the things we do in secret or knows the things we think about, but God does. Not only does He know everything about us, but He is the one who judges us. Judgment (Heb. *mishpat*, **mish-POT**) means a judicial verdict (whether favorable or unfavorable). So this is a paradox. God loves us far more than we could imagine, but He is completely holy and cannot let sin into His presence. This is why each of us needs the Cross. On the Cross our sins were judged, and through the resurrection, we are assured that God has accepted the sacrifice of Jesus for our sins.

III. GOD'S POWER OVER OUR AUTHORITY (Isaiah 40:28–31)

28 Hast thou not known? hast thou not heard, that the everlasting God, the Lord, the Creator of the ends of the earth, fainteth not, neither is weary? there is no searching of his understanding. 29 He giveth power to the faint; and to them that have no might he increaseth strength. 30 Even the youths shall faint and be weary, and the young men shall utterly fall: 31 But they that wait upon the Lord shall renew their strength; they shall mount up with wings as eagles; they shall run, and not be weary; and they shall walk, and not faint.

This often quoted Scripture is at once poetic, provocative, and powerful. The hypothetical "have you not known, have you not heard" are rhetorical questions that seek to comfort the believer who expresses doubt or exasperation at God's timing and motivations. The very heartfelt encouragements within these verses acknowledge both God's power and His concern over our lives. He is not distant, if He created and dwells in the ends of the earth. He knows when we are faint and re-energizes us. He increases the physical, mental, and moral strength of those helpless to fend off opponents. Essentially, the foundation that we enjoy in God is not based on our place in society, our obedience to government, or even our diligence toward His works. He alone is our foundation, meaning He provides and protects us completely on His own!

To wait on God (**v. 31**) must then mean that we actively and excitedly seek and see God's involvement at all times. If there is no searching of His understanding, this means there is no limit to what He can do to remedy our situations. Paul expresses this idea in **Philippians 4:19**: "My God shall supply all your need, according to his riches in glory by Christ Jesus." Waiting on God means that we surrender to His authority personally. Our individual yielding to God allows us to intimately benefit from the strength and supply that He provides.

The primary difference between God's sovereignty and human authority is motivation. In most cases, the powers of humankind could very easily end poverty, war, and brutality. Even the advances in science technology and medicine could sharply reduce disease and suffering for millions, if not billions of people. Sadly, however, human authority erects barriers to access and thus, progress, because of our greed and quest for power while neglecting the needs of others. God's model, by contrast, is to renew strength. Waiting on God is not waiting in a bureaucratic line, but rather waiting with hope and expectation for the miraculous to happen among the mundane. As the prophet Isaiah issues this song of expectation, he elicits worship out of worry and converts panic into praise. The end result is not just deliverance for personal gain, but deliverance of all who witness the victory that comes after the wait.

SEARCH THE SCRIPTURES

QUESTION 1
When looking at humanity in comparison to the Lord, what is one humble action you can choose to acknowledge God's greatness (**Isaiah 40:22**)?

Gratitude, praise, and thanksgiving. Answers will vary.

QUESTION 2
If God reduces "princes to nothing" and makes "judges of the earth as vanity," what attitude should we as believers have when engaging in politics (**v. 23**)?

Answers will vary.

QUESTION 3
Isaiah speaks of God renewing our strength. In what way does God renew your strength when you are tired and discouraged?

Answers will vary.

LIGHT ON THE WORD

God Sees Everything All the Time
"Everlasting" (Heb. *'olam*, **oh-LOM**) means existing beyond time, before time began, and without any end. As humans, we understand history in terms of a timeline, but the everlasting God sees everything at all times. This is why we can trust our futures to Him. He knows the things that have happened and brought us to this point. He also sees what lies beyond today, and controls all the ages; certainly He has our futures in His hands.

BIBLE APPLICATION

AIM: Students will accept that God can change the circumstances in the lives of God's people.

Today's political seasons seem to last longer than the actual term of office. Often politicians wage campaigns built on the promise of change and reform, yet once in office, they continue to support archaic systems that continue to leave the least powerful people impoverished and hungry. In America, citizens enjoy not only a vote, but also the right to pray and worship freely. Despite political parties' claims of morality and righteousness, it is the citizens who have the ultimate ability to invoke God's presence and obey His will even while serving under an unjust or ungodly administration.

STUDENTS' RESPONSES

AIM: Students will agree that God can do the impossible in their lives.

Isaiah 40 speaks peace in the midst of turmoil. While our lives may not be rife with grave injustice on a daily basis, it is still good to know that hope in God and trust in His foundation will guarantee eventual good. "They that wait upon the Lord" cannot simply be a platitude or a comforting saying. Waiting is an action word, meaning that faith is put to work, resulting in a closer relationship with God and a deeper respect for our place within His creation.

PRAYER

O God, You renew our strength when we are weary. Lord, You care for us when we are tired and need care to give us hope and love. Your mercy is everlasting and we are grateful. In the Name of Jesus we pray. Amen.

HOW TO SAY IT

Orthoptera.   Or-**THOP**-ter-a.

Liken.   **LIE**-kin.

DIG A LITTLE DEEPER

This section provides an additional research article to further your study of the lesson:

Isaiah 40:28 asks the reader questions regarding the Eternal Creator who is not bound by physical restraints of fatigue nor plagued by limitations of knowledge. Neither is God limited in His ability to preserve His Word throughout the generations. New discoveries of ancient copies of the Bible are exciting! The Dead Sea Scrolls are perhaps one of the greatest finds and a confirmation of the power of God to preserve the integrity of His Word. In this article in *Biola University Magazine* is a discussion about the discovery of the Great Isaiah Scroll, one of the Dead Sea Scrolls, and the impact it has on those who are able to review its contents.

http://magazine.biola.edu/article/11-winter/dead-sea-living-word/

PREPARE FOR NEXT SUNDAY

Read **Isaiah 61:1–4, 8–11** and "Everlasting Covenant."

DAILY HOME BIBLE READINGS

MONDAY
See God's Saving Power
(Luke 3:2–6)

TUESDAY
Power to Overcome Illness
(Isaiah 38:9–20)

WEDNESDAY
God's Word Stands Forever
(Isaiah 40:1–8)

THURSDAY
God Leads Like a Shepherd
(Isaiah 40:9–11)

FRIDAY
God's Wisdom is Unmatched
(Isaiah 40:12–14)

SATURDAY
God Unlike the Nations and Idols
(Isaiah 40:15–20)

SUNDAY
Foundations of the Earth
(Isaiah 40:21–31)

COMMENTS / NOTES:

_____
_____
_____
_____
_____
_____
_____
_____
_____
_____
_____
_____
_____
_____
_____
_____

EVERLASTING COVENANT

BIBLE BASIS: ISAIAH 61:1–4, 8–11

BIBLE TRUTH: God promises an everlasting covenant.

MEMORY VERSE: "For I the LORD love judgment, I hate robbery for burnt offering; and I will direct their work in truth, and I will make an everlasting covenant with them" (Isaiah 61:8).

LESSON AIM: By the end of the lesson, we will: DECIDE that God has high ethical standards and enters into secure and enduring covenants with people; APPRECIATE what it means to live justly and faithfully according to God's covenant expectations; and PREPARE a statement in response to God's covenant that reflects life today.

TEACHER PREPARATION

MATERIALS NEEDED: Quarterly Commentary/Teacher Manual, Adult Quarterly, Adult resources—charts, worksheets, and other teaching tools, paper, pens, pencils, Bibles (several different versions)

OTHER MATERIALS NEEDED / TEACHER'S NOTES:

_____

_____

LESSON OVERVIEW

LIFE NEED FOR TODAY'S LESSON
People make agreements they intend to keep but too often break, causing stress and dismay.

BIBLE APPLICATION
God makes an everlasting covenant that God will never break.

BIBLE LEARNING
God loves justice, hates robbery and wrongdoing, and rewards those who are faithful with a covenant relationship.

STUDENTS' RESPONSES
Christians can choose to live justly and faithfully in God's covenant.

LESSON SCRIPTURE

ISAIAH 61:1–4, 8–11, KJV

1 The Spirit of the Lord GOD is upon me; because the LORD hath anointed me to preach good tidings unto the meek; he hath sent me to bind up the brokenhearted, to proclaim liberty to the captives, and the opening of the prison to them that are bound;

ISAIAH 61:1–4, 8–11, AMP

1 The Spirit of the Lord GOD is upon me, because the LORD has anointed and commissioned me to bring good news to the humble and afflicted; He has sent me to bind up [the wounds of] the brokenhearted, to proclaim release [from confinement and

2 To proclaim the acceptable year of the LORD, and the day of vengeance of our God; to comfort all that mourn;

3 To appoint unto them that mourn in Zion, to give unto them beauty for ashes, the oil of joy for mourning, the garment of praise for the spirit of heaviness; that they might be called trees of righteousness, the planting of the LORD, that he might be glorified.

4 And they shall build the old wastes, they shall raise up the former desolations, and they shall repair the waste cities, the desolations of many generations.

8 For I the LORD love judgment, I hate robbery for burnt offering; and I will direct their work in truth, and I will make an everlasting covenant with them.

9 And their seed shall be known among the Gentiles, and their offspring among the people: all that see them shall acknowledge them, that they are the seed which the LORD hath blessed.

10 I will greatly rejoice in the LORD, my soul shall be joyful in my God; for he hath clothed me with the garments of salvation, he hath covered me with the robe of righteousness, as a bridegroom decketh himself with ornaments, and as a bride adorneth herself with her jewels.

11 For as the earth bringeth forth her bud, and as the garden causeth the things that are sown in it to spring forth; so the Lord GOD will cause righteousness and praise to spring forth before all the nations.

condemnation] to the [physical and spiritual] captives and freedom to prisoners,

2 To proclaim the favorable year of the LORD, and the day of vengeance and retribution of our God, to comfort all who mourn,

3 To grant to those who mourn in Zion the following: to give them a turban instead of dust [on their heads, a sign of mourning], the oil of joy instead of mourning, The garment [expressive] of praise instead of a disheartened spirit. So they will be called the trees of righteousness [strong and magnificent, distinguished for integrity, justice, and right standing with God], the planting of the LORD, that He may be glorified.

4 Then they will rebuild the ancient ruins, they will raise up and restore the former desolations; and they will renew the ruined cities, the desolations (deserted settlements) of many generations.

8 For I, the LORD, love justice; I hate robbery with a burnt offering. And I will faithfully reward them, and make an everlasting covenant with them.

9 Then their offspring will be known among the nations, and their descendants among the peoples. All who see them [in their prosperity] will recognize and acknowledge them that they are the people whom the LORD has blessed.

10 I will rejoice greatly in the LORD, my soul will exult in my God; for He has clothed me with garments of salvation, He has covered me with a robe of righteousness, as a bridegroom puts on a turban, and as a bride adorns herself with her jewels.

11 For as the earth brings forth its sprouts, and as a garden causes what is sown in it to spring up, so the Lord GOD will [most certainly] cause righteousness and justice and praise to spring up before all the nations [through the power of His word].

LIGHT ON THE WORD

Oil. In ancient times, oil was commonly derived from olives (and sometimes myrrh). Oil was utilized for various purposes, including anointing people in office such as priests and kings. More commonly, it was used as a cosmetic to moisturize the body. It could also be used for medicinal purposes to soothe wounds, and as a fuel for lamps.

TEACHING THE BIBLE LESSON

LIFE NEED FOR TODAY'S LESSON

AIM: Students will agree that people make agreements they intend to keep but too often break, causing stress and dismay.

INTRODUCTION

God's Proclamation

Chapter 61 can be viewed as a stage play. First comes the Anointed One's soliloquy, or speech to the audience (**vv. 1–4**). In **verses 8 and 9** we hear from God Himself, who addresses the Israelites in the audience. He proclaims that the blessings mentioned in the previous verses are a gift from Him. Finally, in the last two verses, the audience responds in thanksgiving for all that God has done.

BIBLE LEARNING

AIM: Students will validate that God loves justice, hates robbery and wrongdoing, and rewards those who are faithful with a covenant relationship.

I. ETERNAL PROMISE (Isaiah 61:1–2)

Isaiah's proclamation of good tidings reflects the essence of God's interaction with humankind. The "good tidings" he mentions here are reflected much later by Jesus as He invokes this entire passage (**Luke 4:18**). Surely any word from God should be considered good news, although the prophets had the difficult task of issuing both pleasant and fearful messages from above. Contrary to the normal practices of those in political or social power, here God directs the prophet to share a message of hope to those who lack influence.

1 The Spirit of the Lord GOD is upon me; because the Lord hath anointed me to preach good tidings unto the meek; he hath sent me to bind up the brokenhearted, to proclaim liberty to the captives, and the opening of the prison to them that are bound; 2 To proclaim the acceptable year of the LORD, and the day of vengeance of our God; to comfort all that mourn.

The speaker in these verses is the Anointed One. Anointing in the Old Testament usually announced a new kingly dynasty, prophet, or high priest. In this case, the anointing with oil is closely associated with the Holy Spirit, so the speaker is filled with God's presence. The Hebrew for anointed is *mashach* (**maw-SHAKH**), where our word "Messiah" comes from; when Jesus read these words, He said that they were fulfilled in Him (**Luke 4:17–21**). Some have called the words in **Luke 4:18–19** the ordination speech of our Savior and Messiah. When we look at what Jesus read and applied to Himself, we can have a greater understanding of this prophecy from Isaiah.

Next we see that our Messiah has come to "proclaim liberty to the captives, and the opening of the prison to them that are bound." God has always desired to set free slaves and all who are imprisoned. In fact, the Jews were given a special year to set captives free—the Year of Jubilee, which was scheduled for every 50 years (**Leviticus 25**). Unfortunately, there is no record of this year ever being observed. God designed His Law to create a society with no permanent underclass, and observing this would have helped lessen the effect of class distinctions.

Jesus completed His quotation of these verses just before "and the day of vengeance of our God." Many biblical scholars believe that this indicates that the final day of judgment is in the future. We must remember that where abuse exists, judgment must eventually come to provide justice. For those of us who have been victims of injustice, these words of judgment come as a comfort. God will repay those who have hurt us (**Romans 12:19**).

SEARCH THE SCRIPTURES

QUESTION 1

Who is the source of empowerment for preaching good tidings (**Isaiah 61:1**)?

The Holy Spirit empowers us.

II. ETERNAL SALVATION (vv. 3–4)

3 To appoint unto them that mourn in Zion, to give unto them beauty for ashes, the oil of joy for mourning, the garment of praise for the spirit of heaviness; that they might be called trees of righteousness, the planting of the LORD, that he might be glorified. 4 And they shall build the old wastes, they shall raise up the former desolations, and they shall repair the waste cities, the desolations of many generations.

As surely as God is sovereign, and therefore singular in His authority to judge, He is also the author of love, and He is generous with favor to those He chooses to bless. The symbols of salvation are consistent with God's desire to bless, even if at times He has to warn or punish. The crown of beauty symbolizes the reign in which the redeemed will share, once they have passed their sinful states. As weeping is exchanged for rejoicing, it becomes clear that God's promises and His salvation will not be revoked. Human interaction is inconsistent compared to God's stability. Even before entering God's heavenly presence, we are afforded the opportunity to experience the benefits of His great joy via our salvation. If humans had the power to withhold salvation for a ransom or force certain behavior, most likely we would. Yet God uses the great oaks as a mighty and sturdy example of what it means to be rooted in His favor, and the permanence of the gift of salvation. **Psalm 1:1–3** heralds the person who delights in God's law, and he or she will be like a tree planted by a river. Security in God's law includes security in His promises, especially those that will save and preserve His people for eternity.

The imagery of rebuilding ancient ruins is a compelling vision of restoration after the Babylonian captivity. It also is a hint at the finite nature of humankind. While we build grand tributes to ourselves in the form of large buildings and great cities, any of them could come to ruin at any time for a number of reasons, and all of them will decay over time. Our bodies in a similar way can become great specimens of physical prowess, but age will eventually render us helpless, if death does not snatch us away first. Ultimately we must accept that God's salvation allows our souls to have a more permanent security than our physical bodies can provide. Through God's salvation, we are granted restoration beyond a simple renovation, given without restriction.

SEARCH THE SCRIPTURES

QUESTION 2

Are we sure we know what the Lord loves and what He hates (**v. 8**)? Create a list of what the Lord loves and what He hates. Here are a few examples to get you started: **Psalm 33:5, Deuteronomy 7:9, Proverbs 6:17–19, Malachi 2:16.**

The Lord loves righteousness, justice, keeping His covenant; He hates divorce, those who cover violence with their garments, "a proud look [the attitude that makes one overestimate oneself and discount others], a lying tongue, and hands that shed innocent blood, a

heart that creates wicked plans, feet that run swiftly to evil, a false witness who breathes out lies [even half-truths], and one who spreads discord (rumors) among brothers" (Proverbs 6:17–19, AMP).

LIGHT ON THE WORD

Rebuilding from the Ashes

This prophecy points toward Judah's return from exile and its ultimate fulfillment as the kingdom being consummated at the end of the age. They will face a time when their beautiful Temple and city will be burned to the ground, leaving only ashes and broken stones, but Isaiah prophecies a wonderful time of rebuilding. Many of our inner cities look almost the same, but we have the same God who can empower us to bring new life to our communities.

III. ETERNAL COVENANT (vv. 8–11)

Judgment, justice, righteousness, rightness—these not only describe what God loves, but embody who He is! If our God loves judgment, then He conversely must hate injustice and dishonesty, particularly when they victimize His people. As Isaiah elaborated in **verse 2** (and would later reiterate), and as Paul recalled in his letter to the Romans, God's vengeance is not a threat; it is indeed among His promises (**Isaiah 63:4; Romans 12:19**). God issued warnings and advisories through the prophets for the people's benefit. He also exacted acts of vengeance for correction. The entire Babylonian captivity is proof of God's long-suffering when it comes to sin.

8 For I the LORD love judgment, I hate robbery for burnt offering; and I will direct their work in truth, and I will make an everlasting covenant with them. 9 And their seed shall be known among the Gentiles, and their offspring among the people: all that see them shall acknowledge them, that they are the seed which the LORD hath blessed.

The word "judgment" (Heb. *mishpat*, **mish-POT**) can also be translated as justice. The word can also mean a decision free from favoritism and bias. As such, the decision conforms to established rules and laws, and it is fair and right toward those it affects. Justice is one of the themes of the book of Isaiah; the prophet uses this word 42 times in the book.

We can see from this first phrase how closely our Lord identifies Himself with justice. We see that God is not pleased with what His people are doing. The solution is an everlasting covenant that can come only through His grace, not anything that the people deserved.

In **verse 9**, we realize that God's commitment to the Israelite/Jewish people did not end with the exile. God is still planning to bless them, and all people will acknowledge them as His people.

10 I will greatly rejoice in the LORD, my soul shall be joyful in my God; for he hath clothed me with the garments of salvation, he hath covered me with the robe of righteousness, as a bridegroom decketh himself with ornaments, and as a bride adorneth herself with her jewels. 11 For as the earth bringeth forth her bud, and as the garden causeth the things that are sown in it to spring forth; so the Lord GOD will cause righteousness and praise to spring forth before all the nations.

Now we switch from God speaking, to the people responding in thankful praise. Garments of salvation and a robe of righteousness are the cause of their rejoicing. People of God proudly display these as a "bridegroom decketh himself with ornaments" and a "bride adorneth herself with her jewels." The word "decketh" (Heb. *kahan*, **ka-HAN**) means to dress ornately, as in priestly garments. This is underscored by the word for ornaments, which actually means a headdress or turban, which is what the high priest wore as part of his ceremonial garments. The next image is of a bride who "adorneth herself with her jewels." The word for "adorneth" is *adah* (Heb. **ah-DAH**) and carries the sense of making more attractive by adding ornament or color. From this imagery, we see God's people as proudly rejoicing and displaying the joy that comes from being made righteous before Him. Next Isaiah switches to a garden metaphor. Perhaps the nations had concluded that Yahweh was irrelevant, but the Jewish people are going to continue to be God's object lesson in His grace. The springtime garden is our example. Most of the plants seem to be dead all winter long, but in the spring, all the springtime bulbs wake up with the warming temperatures and show their beauty. This is how our God views righteousness and justice and how He wants us to prepare for this same growth in our lives.

SEARCH THE SCRIPTURES

QUESTION 3
How can we express the principles of God's everlasting covenant with those who are not yet Christians? Write a statement to share.

God's love is expressed in our lives and words.

LIGHT ON THE WORD

While the wages of sin is death (**Romans 6:23**), and the Law is filled with lists of crimes and their appropriate punishments, God is no common murderer. He does not kill for sport or pleasure, but He allows us to be our own best examples of why not to disobey His word. Even though sin is forgiven, disobedience has consequences which may sometimes be devastating.

BIBLE APPLICATION

AIM: Students will validate that God's everlasting covenant will never break.

Today's world and culture is rife with evidence that we need stronger covenant relationships.

Parents lament when their children land in jail or fail to complete their education, but often embrace a philosophy that "you're on your own" after a certain age. Similarly, interpersonal relationships can struggle with intimacy because of distrust and previous hurt. An "every person for him/herself" mentality is not about survival, but fear. Instead of fearing what others can take from us or do to us, we are instructed to fear God. That fear is not cowering to prevent abuse or harm, but instead it's a great respect and love for a sovereign God who acts out of love and keeps His covenant to bless us despite our shortcomings.

STUDENTS' RESPONSES

AIM: Students will accept that Christians can choose to live justly and faithfully in God's covenant.

We can apply the words of **Isaiah 61:1–2** to our own communities as we carry out the mission of our Lord. The Hebrew word for "meek" (Heb. *'anav*, **ah-NAHV**) can also be translated as poor, the meaning Jesus relates when He quotes these verses. There in Luke, also, many translations use the word "gospel" instead of "good tidings," because the words have the same meaning, although "gospel" also connotes salvation. If preaching to the poor is Jesus' mission, it should be ours as well. What better task for us than preaching the Gospel to the poor, whether economically or spiritually? Our actions should reflect advocating for changes, justice, and mercy for the poor and the oppressed. Jesus continues that He also came to heal the brokenhearted, another task for us as His followers.

PRAYER

Dear Lord, we praise You and we bless You for loving justice and expecting us to be just with one another and ourselves. Grant us the strength and the courage to live and love justly with all of your creation. In the Name of Jesus we pray. Amen.

HOW TO SAY IT

Soliloquy So-**LIH**-lo-quee.

DIG A LITTLE DEEPER

This section provides an additional research article to further your study of the lesson:

The Institute of Creation Research provides this article that is a brief discourse regarding the controversial issue of dual authorship in Isaiah. This introductory discussion provides insight into biblical interpretation and textual authenticity.

http://www.icr.org/article/4188/299/

PREPARE FOR NEXT SUNDAY

Read **Hebrews 1:1–9** and "The Imprint of God."

DAILY HOME BIBLE READINGS

MONDAY
A Light to the Nations
(Isaiah 42:5–9)

TUESDAY
Anointed for Ministry
(Luke 4:16–21)

WEDNESDAY
No Ministry in Our Backyard
(Luke 4:22–30)

THURSDAY
The Exiles Will Return
(Isaiah 60:1–5)

FRIDAY
The Glory of the Nation Restored
(Isaiah 60:19–22)

SATURDAY
With Everlasting Love and Compassion
(Isaiah 54:4–8)

SUNDAY
Everlasting Covenant
(Isaiah 61:1–4, 8-11)

COMMENTS / NOTES:

_____
_____
_____
_____
_____
_____
_____
_____
_____
_____
_____
_____
_____
_____
_____
_____
_____
_____
_____
_____
_____
_____
_____
_____
_____
_____

THE IMPRINT OF GOD

BIBLE BASIS: HEBREWS 1:1–9

BIBLE TRUTH: Christ is the reflection of God's glory, and addresses life's questions with a powerful and sustaining Word.

MEMORY VERSE: "Who [Jesus] being the brightness of his glory, and the express image of his person, and upholding all things by the word of his power" (Hebrews 1:3a).

LESSON AIM: By the end of the lesson, we will: JUDGE that Jesus expresses fully God's very being in the world; APPRECIATE that Jesus during His earthly life experienced the full range of human experience; and CREATE ways to seek Jesus' continued guidance in our lives.

TEACHER PREPARATION

MATERIALS NEEDED: Quarterly Commentary/Teacher Manual, Adult Quarterly, Adult resources—charts, worksheets, and other teaching tools, paper, pens, pencils, Bibles (several different versions)

OTHER MATERIALS NEEDED / TEACHER'S NOTES:

_____

_____

LESSON OVERVIEW

LIFE NEED FOR TODAY'S LESSON
People seek guidance for their lives but do not know to whom to turn for direction.

BIBLE APPLICATION
Christians should trust Jesus to give directions in all aspects of our lives.

BIBLE LEARNING
Jesus' human presence was God's presence in the world.

STUDENTS' RESPONSES
Believers accept that Jesus is the light for all of the world.

LESSON SCRIPTURE

HEBREWS 1:1–9, KJV

1 God, who at sundry times and in divers manners spake in time past unto the fathers by the prophets,

2 Hath in these last days spoken unto us by his Son, whom he hath appointed heir of all things, by whom also he made the worlds;

3 Who being the brightness of his glory,

HEBREWS 1:1–9, AMP

1 God, having spoken to the fathers long ago in [the voices and writings of] the prophets in many separate revelations [each of which set forth a portion of the truth], and in many ways,

2 has in these last days spoken [with finality] to us in [the person of One who is by

and the express image of his person, and upholding all things by the word of his power, when he had by himself purged our sins, sat down on the right hand of the Majesty on high:

4 Being made so much better than the angels, as he hath by inheritance obtained a more excellent name than they.

5 For unto which of the angels said he at any time, Thou art my Son, this day have I begotten thee? And again, I will be to him a Father, and he shall be to me a Son?

6 And again, when he bringeth in the first begotten into the world, he saith, And let all the angels of God worship him.

7 And of the angels he saith, Who maketh his angels spirits, and his ministers a flame of fire.

8 But unto the Son he saith, Thy throne, O God, is for ever and ever: a sceptre of righteousness is the sceptre of thy kingdom.

9 Thou hast loved righteousness, and hated iniquity; therefore God, even thy God, hath anointed thee with the oil of gladness above thy fellows.

His character and nature] His Son [namely Jesus], whom He appointed heir and lawful owner of all things, through whom also He created the universe [that is, the universe as a space-time-matter continuum].

3 The Son is the radiance and only expression of the glory of [our awesome] God [reflecting God's Shekinah glory, the Light-being, the brilliant light of the divine], and the exact representation and perfect imprint of His [Father's] essence, and upholding and maintaining and propelling all things [the entire physical and spiritual universe] by His powerful word [carrying the universe along to its predetermined goal]. When He [Himself and no other] had [by offering Himself on the cross as a sacrifice for sin] accomplished purification from sins and established our freedom from guilt, He sat down [revealing His completed work] at the right hand of the Majesty on high [revealing His Divine authority],

4 having become as much superior to angels, since He has inherited a more excellent and glorious name than they [that is, Son—the name above all names].

5 For to which of the angels did the Father ever say, "YOU ARE MY SON, TODAY I HAVE BEGOTTEN (fathered) YOU [established You as a Son, with kingly dignity]"? And again [did He ever say to the angels], "I SHALL BE A FATHER TO HIM AND HE SHALL BE A SON TO ME"?

6 And when He again brings the firstborn [highest-ranking Son] into the world, He says, "AND ALL THE ANGELS OF GOD ARE TO WORSHIP HIM."

7 And concerning the angels He says, "WHO MAKES HIS ANGELS WINDS, AND HIS MINISTERING SERVANTS FLAMES OF FIRE [to do His bidding]."

8 But about the Son [the Father says to Him], "YOUR THRONE, O GOD, IS FOREVER AND EVER, AND THE SCEPTER OF [absolute] RIGHTEOUSNESS IS THE SCEPTER OF HIS KINGDOM.

9 "YOU HAVE LOVED RIGHTEOUSNESS [integrity, virtue, uprightness in purpose] AND HAVE HATED LAWLESSNESS [injustice, sin]. THEREFORE GOD, YOUR GOD, HAS ANOINTED YOU WITH THE OIL OF GLADNESS ABOVE YOUR COMPANIONS."

LIGHT ON THE WORD

Hebrews Author Unknown. Aside from 1 John, Hebrews is the only letter in the New Testament without a greeting. Written in the style of an essay or sermon, the epistle contains references to the Old Testament. The language and quotations of the Old Testament suggests the intended audience may have been Jews who had converted to Christianity. However, several aspects of the epistle are unclear. Initially, the author is not identified. Although traditionally ascribed to the Apostle Paul, the book's language and vocabulary differ from his other known authored letters, and the biblical book itself does not claim to be written by Paul. The author may have known or been heavily associated with those who knew Paul. Secondly, the date of the epistle is also unclear. Since the author's believed goal was to showcase how Christianity replaced Judaism, with the destruction of the Temple, one possibility is that the latter was written after 70 AD. However, there are no clear references to the Temple's destruction, so it may have been written as early as 65–70 AD. A reference to Italy (**13:24**) is the only hint of where it could have been written.

TEACHING THE BIBLE LESSON

LIFE NEED FOR TODAY'S LESSON

AIM: Students will agree that people seek guidance for their lives but often do not know to whom to turn for direction.

INTRODUCTION

Jesus is the Reason

The author of Hebrews sought to persuade his audience that Jesus is superior to all that was valued in Jewish traditions. Consequently, this is why language familiarity and cultural awareness were important areas for the author; the letter sought to dissuade and inform converted Jews who were tempted to revert to Judaism because of their lack of understanding about Jesus. The theme of Jesus as absolute and complete adequacy fuels this passage. Through the lens of the Old Testament, Christ is revealed as the most excellent of all previous prophets, such as Moses, Samuel, and Elijah.

The person Jesus is superior to angels. An angel is superior to animals and human beings through power and intelligence. Angels possess superhuman power but do not have power equal with God. Created by God, they were present to exult in the Creation of the world (**Job 38:4–7**).

Angels can be either holy or fallen. Satan is the primary example of a fallen angel. Holy angels can be visible to humans, and their rare appearances invoke amazement (e.g., **Luke 2:9**). They are not known to assist evil spirits; on the contrary, they have been known to aid humans with personal and spiritual direction.

BIBLE LEARNING

AIM: Students will agree that Jesus' human presence was God's presence in the world.

I. THE EMINENCE OF JESUS (Hebrews 1:1–4)

The unknown author of Hebrews showcases seven facts to show Jesus' superior greatness. (1) He was deemed the heir of creation. (2) Jesus is the creator of all things made. (3) His radiance revealed God's glory. (4) He is the exact character of God. (5) Jesus is the personified Word of God. (6) He is the priest who provided sacrifice for our sins. (7) He sits on the throne at God's right hand.

1 God, who at sundry times and in divers manners spake in time past unto the fathers by the prophets, 2 Hath in these last days spoken unto us by his Son, whom he hath appointed heir of all things, by whom also he made the worlds;

The first four verses of Hebrews are only a single sentence in the Greek text. Unlike modern translations that have three or four sentences, the King James Version of the Bible retains the sense of the original Greek text in one rich, complete sentence.

The phrase, "in these last days," refers to both the present and end times. There is a clear sense that God has reached the climax of His self-revelation. He has saved the best for last. The writer intends to show that this last revelation of God is superior to what He has done in the past. The fact that God has already "spoken unto us by his Son" suggests that at the time of the writing of this epistle, the revelation had been completed.

Even though most English translations say "his Son" or "the Son," the Greek has no definite article. The writer assumes that the readers know he is talking about Christ. The use of the phrase "appointed heir of all things, by whom also he made the worlds" indicates that Christ embodies a dual motif of sonship and priesthood. When speaking of Jesus as God's heir, **Psalm 2:7–8** says, "Thou art my Son; this day have I begotten thee. Ask of me, and I shall give thee the heathen for thine inheritance, and the uttermost parts of the earth for thy possession." Everything God has belongs to Jesus. The Bible also reveals that Jesus is co-Creator with God (John 1:3; **Colossians 1:16–17**).

The word translated as "worlds" or "universe" (**Hebrews 1:2**, NIV) is *aionas* (**eye-OWE-nas**) in Greek, which literally means "ages" or "times." The preferred interpretation is "ages," which suggests that Jesus not only created the world, but He also controls the events of history.

3 Who being the brightness of his glory, and the express image of his person, and upholding all things by the word of his power, when he had by himself purged our sins, sat down on the right hand of the Majesty on high.

In **verse 3**, we get a complete Christology. The first part of the verse talks about the Son's relationship with God, the second part deals with Christ's work, and the third part refers to His exaltation—the pre-existence, incarnation, and exaltation of Christ. The phrase "brightness of his glory" means that Jesus is the reflection or the radiance of the glory of God. The Bible tells us that God is inapproachable, but Jesus makes it possible to know Him truly and intimately.

What a blessing! The "express image of his person" literally means "the imprint or seal of God's nature," and the word *hypostasis* (Gk. **hoo-POH-sta-sis**), translated as "person," means "the reality or actuality of His being." Thus, Jesus fully represents God (cf. **Colossians 2:9**). The exaltation of Christ is an allusion to **Psalm 110**; "the Majesty" is a euphemism for God.

4 Being made so much better than the angels, as he hath by inheritance obtained a more excellent name than they.

The phrase "better than" or "superior to" is used 13 times in the Christology presented in the Hebrews. **Verse 4** introduces the major subjects—Christ and the angels—of the discussion to follow. To counter the worship of angels, the writer shows the real position of the angels in relation to Christ.

SEARCH THE SCRIPTURES

QUESTION 1
Why is Jesus' superiority to prophets and angels important (**Hebrews 1:3–4**)?

He is the "exact representation and perfect imprint" of God's essence (Hebrews 1:3, AMP). Jesus' position above the angels counters the idea of worshiping angels.

LIGHT ON THE WORD

In this epistle, the writer begins with God, the initiator of revelation; therefore, the focus is on Him, not on people. The first and second verses compare God's methods of communication in the past and the present. The phrase "at sundry times and in divers manners" refers to the fact that God chose the times and methods to communicate. The Old Testament records the clouds, dreams, visions, and other methods that God used to communicate with His people. God also used the prophets to reveal what He was saying. The reference to "prophets" here is not limited to the traditional prophets but it includes men of God such as Moses, David, and Solomon.

II. THE DIVINITY OF JESUS (vv. 5–9)

To further reinforce Jesus' divinity, the author utilizes several quotes from the Old Testament. God addresses Jesus as "my Son" (**2 Samuel 7:14; Psalm 2:7**). Additionally, the writer states He is the "begotten" or firstborn Son to the world and that even angels must worship Him because He created them (**Psalm 97:7, 104:4**). Finally, He is on the throne where He rules with all righteousness (**Psalm 45:6–7**). Through these illustrations, the author hoped to show and persuade Jews that Jesus was the foretold Messiah and God's Son.

5 For unto which of the angels said he at any time, Thou art my Son, this day have I begotten thee? And again, I will be to him a Father, and he shall be to me a Son?

Hebrews 1:5–14 continues the explanation of who Jesus Christ is, and **2:1–4** challenges the reader to respond appropriately. The author follows this pattern throughout the epistle. Beginning with **verse 5**, we find frequent references to or quotations from the Old Testament (30 or more), especially the Psalms. **Verse 5** is a combination of two Old Testament verses: **Psalm 2:7** and **2 Samuel 7:14**. The truth from **Psalm 2:7** ("Thou art my Son; this day have I begotten thee") concerning Jesus' relationship to God was very significant for the early church's understanding of Christ. This truth was announced from Heaven at Jesus' baptism (**Mark 1:10–11**) and preached by Paul (**Acts 13:33–34**). The author of Hebrews also adapts a declaration the Lord made about David, whose kingship Jesus completes, from **2 Samuel 7:14**, as a way of reminding the audience of God's relationship to Christ.

6 And again, when he bringeth in the first begotten into the world, he saith, And let all the angels of God worship him.

The term "first begotten" is translated from the Greek word *prototokos* (**proe-TOE-toe-kos**). It does not mean the first to be created, but it indicates privilege, authority, inheritance, and responsibility that comes with being the first-born in a family. Christ has the highest authority. The phrase "all the angels of God worship him" emphasizes His exalted state as God because only God can be worshiped. This is not an exaltation of His human nature, but it's a recognition of His divinity.

7 And of the angels he saith, Who maketh his angels spirits, and his ministers a flame of fire.

Verse 7 contains an Old Testament quotation from **Psalm 104:4**. The meaning of this verse is clear when it is read in conjunction with **verses 8 and 9**. This verse is not saying that angels are Christ's messengers, though this is true. Instead, it teaches that while Christ is eternal, angels are temporal and transient.

8 But unto the Son he saith, Thy throne, O God, is for ever and ever: a sceptre of righteousness is the scepter of thy kingdom. 9 Thou hast loved righteousness, and hated iniquity; therefore God, even thy God, hath anointed thee with the oil of gladness above thy fellows.

These verses are a direct quotation of **Psalm 45:6–7**. **Psalm 45** is a royal marriage psalm calling a princess of Tyre (**vv. 12–14**) to heed the king's call and "forget also thy people and thine father's house" (**v. 10**) in order to enter the king's palace, where there is great joy. This king loves righteousness and hates sin. This psalm has many Messianic applications. **Hebrews 1:8–9** refer to the Son as God and say that His throne is exalted forever. Christ is superior to the angels—"anointed with the oil of gladness above thy fellows."

SEARCH THE SCRIPTURES

QUESTION 2
What is the meaning of "first begotten" (**v. 6**)?

The privilege and responsibility of being the firstborn; Christ has the highest authority.

LIGHT ON THE WORD

Jesus Is Higher Than the Angels

The author continues by further explaining Jesus' eminence through His humanness and divinity. This was done to assist readers into appreciating that Jesus fulfilled the prophecy of the Old Testament. In doing so, the author wanted the people to gain a larger respect for Jesus as divine over their ideals of angels. Angels were important in Judaism because they aided in important pronouncements (**Genesis 16:9; Exodus 3:2**) and helped at Mount Sinai with the Mosaic Law (**Deuteronomy 33:2**). This could have been an area of contention for many Jews, to believe that a man was higher in rank than angels.

BIBLE APPLICATION

AIM: Students will decide that Christians should trust Jesus to give directions in all aspects of our lives.

Frequently, believers tend to focus on Jesus' divinity, but He is also human and faced challenges similar to what we face today. Through His example, we can believe that also we can overcome. "I have told you all this so that you may have peace in me. Here on earth you will have many trials and sorrows. But take heart, because I have overcome the world" (**John 16:33**, NLT).

STUDENTS' RESPONSES

AIM: Students will agree that Jesus is the light for all of the world.

In a society where long suffering often overshadows hope, many Christians fail to see Jesus' greatness. For that reason, people have continually sought other means for personal fulfillment. Inspirational and empowerment teachings seem to be society's recipe for personal greatness. An understanding of who Jesus is to us trumps them all. The knowledge of Jesus' identity and the greatness of His ever-present power in our lives allow us to know that God truly cares about His children.

PRAYER

Thank You, Lord Jesus. You are worthy of all praise and worship. Jesus, You are higher than the angels and all glory and honor are Yours. We need You in our lives to lead us, guide us, and care for us. In the Name of Jesus we pray. Amen.

HOW TO SAY IT

Divers.   **DY**-vers.

Sceptre.   **SEP**-ter.

DIG A LITTLE DEEPER

This section provides an additional research article to further your study of the lesson:

Billy Graham offers a practical outline to seeking God's guidance. His formula is both biblically grounded and time tested. What a blessing to study from one who has, by his lifestyle and testimony, demonstrated such rich insight into God's Word.

http://billygraham.org/decision-magazine/february-2003/how-to-seek-gods-guidance/

PREPARE FOR NEXT SUNDAY

Read **Hebrews 3:1–6; Matthew 7:24–29** and "Builder of the House."

DAILY HOME BIBLE READINGS

MONDAY
Becoming Children of God
(John 1:1–14)

TUESDAY
Receiving Grace Upon Grace
(John 1:15–18)

WEDNESDAY
From Death to Life
(John 5:24–27)

THURSDAY
Jesus, Superior to the Angels
(Hebrews 1:10–14)

FRIDAY
Jesus Reconciles All Things
(Colossians 1:15–20)

SATURDAY
Jesus, Author of All Spiritual Blessings
(Ephesians 1:3–8a)

SUNDAY
The Imprint of God
(Hebrews 1:1–9)

COMMENTS / NOTES:

_____
_____
_____
_____
_____
_____
_____
_____
_____
_____
_____
_____

BUILDER OF THE HOUSE

BIBLE BASIS: HEBREWS 3:1–6; MATTHEW 7:24–29

BIBLE TRUTH: Jesus is the one who is faithful while accomplishing God's plan.

MEMORY VERSE: "For this man [Jesus] was counted worthy of more glory than Moses, inasmuch as he who hath builded the house hath more honour than the house" (Hebrews 3:3).

LESSON AIM: By the end of the lesson, we will: VALIDATE that Jesus, with divine authority, carried out God's intentions; AFFIRM that Jesus is the model for a life of dedication and service to the will of God; and DEDICATE our lives to Jesus with a commitment to engage in Christ-centered speech and actions.

TEACHER PREPARATION

MATERIALS NEEDED: Quarterly Commentary/Teacher Manual, Adult Quarterly, Adult resources—charts, worksheets, and other teaching tools, paper, pens, pencils, Bibles (several different versions)

OTHER MATERIALS NEEDED / TEACHER'S NOTES:

_____

_____

LESSON OVERVIEW

LIFE NEED FOR TODAY'S LESSON
People often give credit for accomplishments to those who carry out the work rather than to the one who created the plan.

BIBLE LEARNING
Jesus is more worthy of more glory than all the prophets, including Moses.

BIBLE APPLICATION
Believers affirm Jesus' greatness and His divine authority to transforms lives.

STUDENTS' RESPONSES
Christians can trust Jesus, who is wise and faithful.

LESSON SCRIPTURE

HEBREWS 3:1–6; MATTHEW 7:24–29, KJV

1 Wherefore, holy brethren, partakers of the heavenly calling, consider the Apostle and High Priest of our profession, Christ Jesus;

2 Who was faithful to him that appointed

HEBREWS 3:1–6; MATTHEW 7:24–29, AMP

1 Therefore, holy brothers and sisters, who share in the heavenly calling, [thoughtfully and attentively] consider the Apostle and High Priest whom we confessed [as ours when we accepted Him as Savior], namely, Jesus;

him, as also Moses was faithful in all his house.

3 For this man was counted worthy of more glory than Moses, inasmuch as he who hath builded the house hath more honour than the house.

4 For every house is builded by some man; but he that built all things is God.

5 And Moses verily was faithful in all his house, as a servant, for a testimony of those things which were to be spoken after;

6 But Christ as a son over his own house; whose house are we, if we hold fast the confidence and the rejoicing of the hope firm unto the end.

Matthew 7:24 Therefore whosoever heareth these sayings of mine, and doeth them, I will liken him unto a wise man, which built his house upon a rock:

25 And the rain descended, and the floods came, and the winds blew, and beat upon that house; and it fell not: for it was founded upon a rock.

26 And every one that heareth these sayings of mine, and doeth them not, shall be likened unto a foolish man, which built his house upon the sand:

27 And the rain descended, and the floods came, and the winds blew, and beat upon that house; and it fell: and great was the fall of it.

28 And it came to pass, when Jesus had ended these sayings, the people were astonished at his doctrine:

29 For he taught them as one having authority, and not as the scribes.

2 He was faithful to Him who appointed Him [Apostle and High Priest], as Moses also was faithful in all God's house.

3 Yet Jesus has been considered worthy of much greater glory and honor than Moses, just as the builder of a house has more honor than the house.

4 For every house is built by someone, but the builder of all things is God.

5 Now Moses was faithful in [the administration of] all God's house, [but only] as a ministering servant, [his ministry serving] as a testimony of the things which were to be spoken afterward [the revelation to come in Christ];

6 but Christ is faithful as a Son over His [Father's] house. And we are His house if we hold fast our confidence and sense of triumph in our hope [in Christ].

Matthew 7:24 "So everyone who hears these words of Mine and acts on them, will be like a wise man [a far-sighted, practical, and sensible man] who built his house on the rock.

25 And the rain fell, and the floods and torrents came, and the winds blew and slammed against that house; yet it did not fall, because it had been founded on the rock.

26 And everyone who hears these words of Mine and does not do them, will be like a foolish (stupid) man who built his house on the sand.

27 And the rain fell, and the floods and torrents came, and the winds blew and slammed against that house; and it fell—and great and complete was its fall."

28 When Jesus had finished [speaking] these words [on the mountain], the crowds were astonished and overwhelmed at His teaching;

29 for He was teaching them as one who had authority [to teach entirely of His own volition], and not as their scribes [who relied on others to confirm their authority].

LIGHT ON THE WORD

Jesus' Humanity and Son of God. There is some question about the author of the book of Hebrews; while it is commonly attributed to the Apostle Paul, the lack of concrete evidence leaves the authorship uncertain. The author of Hebrews focuses his attention on Jesus' humanity, emphasizing His being both the Son of God and the Son of Man. Moreover, the author wanted to use this as a platform to assist the Jews warning them about the risk of drifting away from the Gospel.

TEACHING THE BIBLE LESSON

LIFE NEED FOR TODAY'S LESSON

AIM: Students will agree that people often give credit for accomplishments to those who carry out the work rather than to those who created the plan.

INTRODUCTION

Jesus' Authority

The book of Hebrews shows how it was necessary for Jesus to take on the form of humanity and die. First, His presence and suffering displayed His identification with human suffering. Secondly, Jesus' death signified the ultimate defeat of Satan and the power of death. For that reason, believers should never fear death. Finally, His death permits Jesus to be the merciful and faithful High Priest on behalf of God. As an intermediary, Jesus has the authority to go to the Father on behalf of believers.

BIBLE LEARNING

AIM: Students will agree that Jesus is more worthy of glory than all the prophets, including Moses.

I. THE GREATNESS OF JESUS (Hebrews 3:1–6)

In **Hebrews 3:1–6**, the author of Hebrews therefore carefully and skillfully sets up the comparison between Moses and Jesus not by disparaging Moses, but by endorsing the verdict of **Numbers 12:7** that Moses was "faithful in all (God's) house." This emphasizes similarity rather than contrast in that Jesus, like Moses, was "faithful" (**v. 2**), but the mention of the "house" prompts the further argument (**vv. 3–6**) that, while in that house Moses was merely a "servant" (**Numbers 12:7**). Jesus as the Son "has greater honor" (**Hebrews 3:3**, NIV) in His Father's house.

1 Wherefore, holy brethren, partakers of the heavenly calling, consider the Apostle and High Priest of our profession, Christ Jesus; 2 Who was faithful to him that appointed him, as also Moses was faithful in all his house.

In **verse 1**, the author for the first time addresses his readers directly as "brethren," or "brothers and sisters," an important term previously used in **2:11–12, 17**. To this designation he adds the word "holy" (Gk. *hagios*, **HA-gee-os**; sometimes translated "saints"), a term which here, as in **6:10** and **13:24** and often in the New Testament, distinguishes the people of God who are "made holy" by Christ (**2:11**) from mere earthly relationship. The author of Hebrews knows the community shares in the life of Christ together in the same manner that Christ has shared in their lives. Moreover, the author stresses that their calling is from Heaven, implying that both the source and goal of their call is God Himself. Christians today are reminded that our calling is a heavenly calling. We are not simply members of a civic club, social organization, or academic and business community. The divine nature of our calling demands and challenges us to be serious about our response. The author then invites the community to "consider" or—as the Greek word *katanoeo* (**ka-ta-no-EH-oh**) implies here—"fix your mind intently on" Jesus, thereby alerting them that he is now about to explain another aspect of Jesus' special significance and superiority. He proceeds to introduce Him in a unique manner—with a double title, "Apostle and High Priest." Interestingly, this is the only place Jesus is described as "Apostle" in the New Testament. This title denotes a representative sent by God, more often given to the men whom Jesus sent with His Gospel message. Since the word means "one who is sent," it is easy to see how this applies to Jesus, as He was sent by the Father. The term "High Priest" attributes to Jesus a role allocated not to Moses but to his brother Aaron. The author of Hebrews will go into Christ's role as High Priest as well as His superiority over other high priests later in the letter (**Hebrews 4:14–16, 7:23–28**). "Apostle" and "High Priest" are thus two different aspects of the special authority Christians confess or acknowledge.

3 For this man was counted worthy of more glory than Moses, inasmuch as he who hath builded the house hath more honour than the house 4 For every house is builded by some man; but he that built all things is God.

Moses' status as "servant" will be discussed more directly in **v. 5**, but first Jesus' superiority is demonstrated by an argument that focuses not on Moses, but instead on the "house" in which his faithful service was performed. The Greek word translated "house" (*oikos*, **OY-kos**) is open to different meanings (God's heavenly household, the people of Israel, the Davidic dynasty, Jewish and Christian communities). However, in **Numbers 12:7**, the "house" was probably understood as the people of Israel, conceived as God's "household" or estate within which Moses acted as chief steward. If Moses was the servant in the "house," the house takes priority over the one who serves in it, whereas the householder, God, takes priority over the house He has founded.

5 And Moses verily was faithful in all his house, as a servant, for a testimony of those things which were to be spoken after, 6 But Christ as a son over his own house; whose house are we, if we hold fast the confidence and the rejoicing of the hope firm unto the end.

The author picks up from the quotation in v. 2 and draws the obvious conclusion that because **Numbers 12:7** describes Moses as the "servant" in God's house, he is not on the same level as the Son, who, by His family status, has authority over the house. Both servant and son have tasks to perform faithfully for the householder. But while the former will always be looking after someone else's property, the latter will one day own it. Moses' ministry, no less than that of the prophets, was not complete in itself but looked forward to a coming time of fulfillment. He was looking after the house the Son would later inherit. What was the future for Moses was now a present reality. That "house" is now identified as "we"—the author, his readers, and all the people of faith whom they represent—the household over which the Son holds authority. But our status as that "household" is not automatic. It depends on our keeping a firm hold on our "confidence" and "hope"; note the similar conditional clause in **3:14** and the negative counterpart in **10:26**. This will be sounded repeatedly throughout the letter and leads the author directly into a lengthy warning on the danger of failing to keep that hope. He fears that for his readers, the Christian "confidence and hope," which should be their greatest boast, is in danger of becoming a matter of uncertainty and shame. The exhortation in Ephesians matches the warning of the author of Hebrews and is very much appropriate today—"to live a life worthy of the calling to which you have been called" (**Ephesians 4:1**, AMP).

SEARCH THE SCRIPTURES

QUESTION 1

Remaining confident in our hope in Christ is the evidence that we are a part of Christ's house (**Hebrews 3:6**). Create a plan that will assist you in keeping your hope centered on Christ.

Prayer, Bible study, church. Answers will vary.

LIGHT ON THE WORD

Faithfulness is the overarching theme in this section, with the word "faithful" used for Moses (**3:2, 5**) and Christ (**3:2, 6**) and implied in the treatment of the readers (**3:6**). **Verse 2** recalls **Numbers 12:1–8**, where God rebukes Aaron and Miriam for their failure to respect Moses, and it describes him as "my servant Moses ... faithful in all mine house" (**v. 7**). Here the author of Hebrews starts to show that Jesus exceeds even Moses in authority, since the Son is more than a "servant." But first he discusses Moses' attribute of faithfulness or trustworthiness and points out that Jesus also deserves that accolade as the "faithful high priest" (**2:17**) who has undertaken the task His Father assigned and fulfilled it despite all opposition (**12:2**).

II. THE TEACHINGS OF JESUS (Matthew 7:24–29)

These verses contain a serious spiritual warning. The wise person hears the words of Jesus and puts them into practice (**7:24**). The result of such obedience is stability and security—the house does not fall in the midst of the storms and trials of life. The foolish person hears the words of Jesus and does not put them into practice (**7:26**). The result of such disobedience is destruction, as **verse 27** so picturesquely portrays. The first meaning of Jesus' parable here refers to His Sermon on the Mount. Obedience to the sermon will bring security; disobedience will result in destruction.

Matthew 7:24 Therefore whosoever heareth these sayings of mine, and doeth them, I will liken him unto a wise man, which built his house upon a rock: 25 And the rain descended, and the floods came, and the winds blew, and beat upon that house; and it fell not: for it was founded upon a rock. 26 And every one that heareth these sayings of mine, and doeth them not, shall be likened unto a foolish man, which built his house upon the sand: 27 And the rain descended, and the floods came, and the winds blew, and beat upon that house; and it fell: and great was the fall of it.

Verses 24–27 present the parable of the wise and foolish builders. Told in a parable-style format, the passage encourages the audience to be not only hearers of the Word, but also doers. The imagery suggests that people who build their lives according to God's Word are on a stable foundation, like a rock. When they press through difficulty, their lives will not crumble. However, a hearer of the same Word who does not act on what he hears, is as foolish as someone building on unstable sand. According to Jesus, the juxtaposition of wise and foolish is a choice for each believer. The life devoted to God obeys His Words. Although both will be subject to judgment, the wise will avoid punishment, while the foolish will be held accountable. The concluding thought surrounding this account was the fact that the people were astonished at Jesus' teaching prowess. His teachings were not like the scribes, which were handed down through tradition and Jewish teachers. Jesus taught with and in His own authority. He had the power to interpret the Law without the assistance of rabbis and His interpretation was fact, not conjecture.

28 And it came to pass, when Jesus had ended these sayings, the people were astonished at his doctrine: 29 For he taught them as one having authority, and not as the scribes.

The final section of the Sermon on the Mount (**Matthew 7:13–29**) consists of a series of warnings. **Matthew 7:13–14** contrasts two ways of approaching life. **Verses 15–23** warn against false prophets. Jesus then presents the parable of the wise and foolish builders in **verses 24–27**. The common theme in these passages is the importance of obedience. Heeding Christ's words and following His example is not optional for entry into the kingdom. Jesus impresses on the hearers the difference between real and merely nominal Christian obedience.

Following the conclusion of Jesus' teachings in the Sermon on the Mount, Matthew provides his own concluding comments in **verses 28–29**. The words when Jesus had ended these sayings (**7:28**) mark the end of the first block of teaching material in Matthew: the Sermon on the Mount. These words will reappear at the end of each teaching section in Matthew's Gospel (**19:1, 26:1**). The author notes that the people were amazed at His teaching because Jesus taught as one who had authority, not as their teachers of the Law (**7:29**).

SEARCH THE SCRIPTURES

QUESTION 2
Why is not only hearing but understanding God so important (**Matthew 7:24**)?

It creates a strong foundation for our lives, allowing us to weather the storms of the world.

QUESTION 3
In the Scripture, we are informed that although people hear the same message, they can respond differently. Why do you think this is important to remember? Does that mean the person who did the opposite does not love God?

Answers will vary.

LIGHT ON THE WORD
A Life of Obedience
The parable Jesus shares invites us to a life of obedience. Words are not a substitute for obedience. Preaching, casting out demons, and performing miracles can be divinely inspired, but they give no assurance of salvation. We should hear God's words and do them (see **James 1:22–25**). We must not stop with only hearing (or studying) His words; our hearing must result in doing. This is what it means to build on the rock foundation. What is your house built on?

BIBLE APPLICATION

AIM: Students will appreciate Jesus' greatness and divine authority to transform lives.

People can hear the same information and still respond differently. This happens with siblings in the same house, as well as co-workers in the same business and people in the same church. Some people automatically put what they hear into practice while others resist change and drag their feet. For some, the information just goes in one ear and out the other, with no benefit. The difference is true belief.

STUDENTS' RESPONSES

AIM: Students will agree that Christians trust Jesus, who is wise and faithful.

Christ's ultimate sacrifice on the cross demonstrates the love of God to us. As we read the Bible and spend time in prayer, praise, and devotions, the Holy Spirit guides us into all truth. We are confident that God's will is being accomplished in our lives.

PRAYER

Lord Jesus, thank You for interceding on our behalf and guiding us as we follow Your words. Let our actions show our dedication and love for You. May we encourage others to know and love You. In the Name of Jesus we pray. Amen.

HOW TO SAY IT

Accolade.   **AH**-koe-laid.

Picturesquely.   pik-chuh-**RESK**-lee.

DIG A LITTLE DEEPER

This section provides an additional research article to further your study of the lesson:

What is God's will for our lives? We don't have to wonder, because God's will is His Word. As we read, study, and apply biblical principles to our lives, God's will is expressed through our day-to-day experiences. For a daily devotional plan that echoes the heart of God, visit the Daily Direction Reading Plan by Dr. Melvin Banks.

https://www.bible.com/reading-plans/457-precepts-for-living-daily-direction/day/1

PREPARE FOR NEXT SUNDAY

Read **Hebrews 4:14–5:10** and "Our Great High Priest."

DAILY HOME BIBLE READINGS

MONDAY
Angels in God's Plan
(Hebrews 2:5–8b)

TUESDAY
Keep Your Commitment to Christ
(Hebrews 3:7–15)

WEDNESDAY
Hold Fast to Our Confession
(Hebrews 10:19–25)

THURSDAY
Jesus Christ, the Only Foundation
(1 Corinthians 3:10–12)

FRIDAY
Requesting Then Receiving Help
(Matthew 7:7–11)

SATURDAY
Obedient Actions Required of All Members
(Matthew 7:19–23)

SUNDAY
Builder of the House
(Hebrews 3:1–6; Matthew 7:24–29)

COMMENTS / NOTES:

_____

_____

_____

_____

_____

_____

_____

_____

_____

_____

_____

_____

_____

_____

_____

_____

OUR GREAT HIGH PRIEST

BIBLE BASIS: HEBREWS 4:14–5:10

BIBLE TRUTH: God appointed Jesus, the High Priest, as an intercessor on behalf of His people.

MEMORY VERSE: "Seeing then that we have a great high priest, that is passed into the heavens, Jesus the Son of God, let us hold fast our profession" (Hebrews 4:14).

LESSON AIM: By the end of the lesson, we will: AGREE that God appointed Jesus as High Priest for the people; APPRECIATE that Jesus, in His humanity, fully understands and identifies with the daily life of all peoples; and ASPIRE to become the kind of leaders who suffer, serve, and obey God's intentions in the spirit of Jesus.

TEACHER PREPARATION

MATERIALS NEEDED: Quarterly Commentary/Teacher Manual, Adult Quarterly, Adult resources—charts, worksheets, and other teaching tools, paper, pens, pencils, Bibles (several different versions)

OTHER MATERIALS NEEDED / TEACHER'S NOTES:

_____

_____

LESSON OVERVIEW

LIFE NEED FOR TODAY'S LESSON
People often have someone who makes special efforts on their behalf.

BIBLE LEARNING
Jesus is our redeemer, seated at the right hand of God with all power and majesty.

BIBLE APPLICATION
Christians accept that Jesus, our High Priest, is the author of eternal salvation for all who obey Him.

STUDENTS' RESPONSES
Followers of Christ know that advocating for the needs of others is obedience to Jesus in action.

LESSON SCRIPTURE

HEBREWS 4:14–5:10, KJV

14 Seeing then that we have a great high priest, that is passed into the heavens, Jesus the Son of God, let us hold fast our profession.

15 For we have not an high priest which cannot be touched with the feeling of our

HEBREWS 4:14–5:10, AMP

14 Inasmuch then as we [believers] have a great High Priest who has [already ascended and] passed through the heavens, Jesus the Son of God, let us hold fast our confession [of faith and cling tenaciously to our absolute trust in Him as Savior].

infirmities; but was in all points tempted like as we are, yet without sin.

16 Let us therefore come boldly unto the throne of grace, that we may obtain mercy, and find grace to help in time of need.

5:1 For every high priest taken from among men is ordained for men in things pertaining to God, that he may offer both gifts and sacrifices for sins:

2 Who can have compassion on the ignorant, and on them that are out of the way; for that he himself also is compassed with infirmity.

3 And by reason hereof he ought, as for the people, so also for himself, to offer for sins.

4 And no man taketh this honour unto himself, but he that is called of God, as was Aaron.

5 So also Christ glorified not himself to be made an high priest; but he that said unto him, Thou art my Son, to day have I begotten thee.

6 As he saith also in another place, Thou art a priest for ever after the order of Melchisedec.

7 Who in the days of his flesh, when he had offered up prayers and supplications with strong crying and tears unto him that was able to save him from death, and was heard in that he feared;

8 Though he were a Son, yet learned he obedience by the things which he suffered;

9 And being made perfect, he became the author of eternal salvation unto all them that obey him;

10 Called of God an high priest after the order of Melchisedec.

15 For we do not have a High Priest who is unable to sympathize and understand our weaknesses and temptations, but One who has been tempted [knowing exactly how it feels to be human] in every respect as we are, yet without [committing any] sin.

16 Therefore let us [with privilege] approach the throne of grace [that is, the throne of God's gracious favor] with confidence and without fear, so that we may receive mercy [for our failures] and find [His amazing] grace to help in time of need [an appropriate blessing, coming just at the right moment].

5:1 For every high priest chosen from among men is appointed [to act] on behalf of men in things relating to God, so that he may offer both gifts and sacrifices for sins.

2 He is able to deal gently with the spiritually ignorant and misguided, since he is also subject to human weakness;

3 and because of this [human weakness] he is required to offer sacrifices for sins, for himself as well as for the people.

4 And besides, one does not appropriate for himself the honor [of being high priest], but he who is called by God, just as Aaron was.

5 So too Christ did not glorify Himself so as to be made a high priest, but He [was exalted and appointed by the One] who said to Him, "YOU ARE MY SON, TODAY I HAVE BEGOTTEN (fathered) YOU [declared Your authority and rule over the nations]";

6 just as He also says in another place, "YOU ARE A PRIEST [appointed] FOREVER ACCORDING TO THE ORDER OF MELCHIZEDEK."

7 In the days of His earthly life, Jesus offered up both [specific] petitions and [urgent] supplications [for that which He needed] with

fervent crying and tears to the One who was [always] able to save Him from death, and He was heard because of His reverent submission toward God [His sinlessness and His unfailing determination to do the Father's will].

8 Although He was a Son [who had never been disobedient to the Father], He learned [active, special] obedience through what He suffered.

9 And having been made perfect [uniquely equipped and prepared as Savior and retaining His integrity amid opposition], He became the source of eternal salvation [an eternal inheritance] to all those who obey Him,

10 being designated by God as High Priest according to the order of Melchizedek.

LIGHT ON THE WORD

Melchisedec. Melchisedec is first referenced in Genesis as the king of Salem and "priest of the most high God" (**Genesis 14:17–20**). Even though there is no biblical record of Melchisedec's ancestry, he is a real person. Since he lived in Canaan, an area occupied by descendants of Ham, it is quite possible his ancestry is Hamitic, from which Africans descended. His encounter with Abram (who would later be renamed Abraham) was after the defeat of Chedorlaomer and his allies, including the king of Sodom. Abraham's victory was not a single-handed success, but was given by the hand of the Lord, who moved on his behalf. King Melchisedec, whose name means "My king is righteousness," brought out bread and wine to celebrate Abram and spoke a blessing over him. In response to God's goodness and honor, Abram gave King Melchisedec, the priest of the Most High God, one-tenth of the spoils of his victory. This is the first biblical instance of tithing.

TEACHING THE BIBLE LESSON

LIFE NEED FOR TODAY'S LESSON

AIM: Students will agree that people often have someone who makes special efforts on their behalf.

INTRODUCTION

Hold onto Your Faith

The book of Hebrews, one of the general epistles, was tailored and penned to reach a primarily Jewish Christian audience and is rich with examples that compare and contrast the Torah and the New Covenant. Its purpose is to exhort a second-generation church that had experienced persecution not to lose their faith. They were in danger of reverting to practices that neglected their faith in the power of Christ's life and death, so Hebrews often reminds the community of Christ's preeminent position of authority alongside God.

BIBLE LEARNING

AIM: Students will agree that Jesus is our Elder brother and High Priest, seated at the right hand of God with all power and majesty.

I. JESUS THE GREAT HIGH PRIEST (Hebrews 4:14–16)

Jesus in His role as our High Priest ends the need to petition anyone else for the forgiveness of sins. The writer reiterates to his audience that Jesus as the Son of God is the profession of the faith, and that because of Him, we are able to approach God's throne. Through this passage, Christians are invited to stand strong in this belief in the face of those who disagree. Throughout the opening of Hebrews, the writer makes the point that Jesus is the express image of God, just as in the world a child is the very reflection of his or her father in DNA, behavior, and character (**Hebrews 1:3**). Because of what Jesus accomplished through His death and resurrection, He is seated at the right hand of the Father with all power and majesty.

14 Seeing then that we have a great high priest, that is passed into the heavens, Jesus the Son of God, let us hold fast our profession. 15 For we have not an high priest which cannot be touched with the feeling of our infirmities; but was in all points tempted like as we are, yet without sin. 16 Let us therefore come boldly unto the throne of grace, that we may obtain mercy, and find grace to help in time of need.

The author turns our attention to Jesus as the great High Priest. The adjective "great" (Gk. *megas*, **MEH-gahs**) places Him in a different category from any other high priest; He is the High Priest of all high priests. The phrase "passed into the heavens" is similar to what the high priest did on the Day of Atonement (**Leviticus 16:2–3, 17–18**). He "passed through" the curtain of the Temple and entered the Holy of Holies, where the Ark of the Covenant was placed. The Holy of Holies was where God resided. Jesus' passing into the heavens suggests that He has gone into the very presence of God. This passage has two admonitions: to hold firmly to our faith and approach the throne of grace. Both are possible only through Jesus Christ, our great High Priest. Jesus was "touched with the feeling of our infirmities." This does not mean that He experienced every circumstance that we have experienced, but that He experienced and felt the same emotions and pain we feel in our own moments of weakness and suffering. As a human, Jesus experienced what we are going through, so we know that when we approach God in prayer, we will receive empathy and understanding. When we pray, we can also approach God with great hope and expectation because we know we will find forgiveness, mercy, and help to overcome our problems. The mention of the "throne of grace" alludes to the area of the Ark of the Covenant that was called the mercy seat, where the high priest sprinkled the blood of the sacrifice to make atonement with God for the people. The author is saying that unlike those other high priests who went into the Holy of Holies trembling, we can come boldly to God because of the work of Jesus, our great High Priest.

SEARCH THE SCRIPTURES

QUESTION 1

In what way was Christ "in all points tempted like as we are, yet without sin" (4:15)?

Jesus was human, experiencing emotions and pain as we did.

QUESTION 2

What are the unique and very significant ways that we need Jesus as our High Priest?

Because Jesus experienced what we go through, we receive empathy and understanding when we approach God. Although the other high priests went into the Holy of Holies trembling, Jesus' work means we can approach God boldly.

LIGHT ON THE WORD

A major theme of the book of Hebrews is showing Jesus as the Christ, the Son of God, in His position in the lives of believers as Savior, Priest, and King through His deity and humanity. It should also be noted that this audience of believers was the second generation of the church, who were enduring persecution for their faith. Hebrews sought to provide sound doctrine for them to follow, to further root them in the faith by teaching Christ's superiority over angels and prophets, including Moses, and His position as the great High Priest.

Hebrews 5:1–3

5:1 For every high priest taken from among men is ordained for men in things pertaining to God, that he may offer both gifts and sacrifices for sins:

This section does not discuss all the features of this office, but it highlights those that correspond with what the author wants to say about Jesus as High Priest (**vv. 1–4**). A high priest must be one of the people in order to fulfill his role effectively. He is taken from among the people to mediate between them and God. These points are essential in understanding Jesus' priesthood. One of the high priest's functions is to "offer both gifts and sacrifices" or make atonement for sin. The high priest must be holy in all that he is and does, when representing a person or people before God. The high priest's life was governed by a particular set of rules regulating his behavior, even down to his apparel when offering sacrifices for the people. The high priest was a representative for the people in "things pertaining to God." Jesus is also holy, pure, and able to represent the people before God, not because of what He wears or by adhering to certain ritual regulations, but because He is holy in His very nature.

2 Who can have compassion on the ignorant, and on them that are out of the way; for that he himself also is compassed with infirmity.

Another function of the priest is to empathize with the people. Even though this is not one of Aaron's specific requirements, it is implied to be his responsibility. The word translated "compassion" is *metriopatheo* (Gk. **meh-treeoh-pah-THEH-oh**), used only here in the New Testament and meaning to act in moderation or control one's emotion. A high priest is expected to have compassion toward those who are ignorant and "on them that are out of the way" ("going astray," NIV; see also **Leviticus 4**; **Numbers 15:22–29**). The high priest should be compassionate toward those who have ignorantly sinned against the Lord. He should neither dismiss sin lightly nor severely condemn the sinner, but he should act in moderation. Jesus is able to have compassion because He was a human, and although He was without sin, He could identify with human weakness.

3 And by reason hereof he ought, as for the people, so also for himself, to offer for sins.

The high priest in the Old Testament also had to offer sacrifices for himself (**Leviticus 16:11**) because, like the people, he had sinned. His task, therefore, was not to condemn sinners, but to stand in solidarity with them. In doing so, he could offer a sacrifice for them. By recognizing his own weakness, he could be deeply compassionate toward and patient with those who were not walking in the truth.

Hebrews 5:4–5

4 And no man taketh this honour unto himself, but he that is called of God, as was Aaron.

A high priest must be "called" (Gk. *kaloumenos*, **kah-LOO-men-ose**) or selected by God. One cannot just decide to enter into this high office and mediate between God and people. Since sinful humanity has violated God's righteous law, we cannot select the mediator. Only God can decide whom He wants as mediator. Aaron and his sons were appointed as priests by God Himself (**Exodus 28:1**).

5 So also Christ glorified not himself to be made an high priest; but he that said unto him, Thou art my Son, to day have I begotten thee.

Although Christ is compared to the high priest and they are both called by God, Christ is superior. In **verse 4**, the word "called" indicates that the calling to the office of the high priest is an honor that God gives to whom He chooses. However, a stronger word, *doxazo* (**doke-SAHD-zo**), which means "to glorify, praise, or honor," is used to describe Jesus' becoming High Priest. Christ is glorified or exalted to this office. In **verse 5**, God's call is expressed in the words of **Psalm 2:7** (which was also quoted in **Hebrews 1:5**).

II. JESUS IS OUR HIGH PRIEST FOREVER (vv. 6–10)

Verse 6 is a quotation of **Psalm 110** (which was also quoted in **Hebrews 1:13**). Unlike Aaron, Melchisedec was both king and priest. No king in Israel functioned as both king and priest. As priest and king, Melchisedec had no predecessor nor successor. Similarly, Christ is our High Priest forever. His perfect work of atonement is perpetual; He cannot be succeeded. Jesus Christ is the Son of God, our High Priest and King.

7 Who in the days of his flesh, when he had offered up prayers and supplications with strong crying and tears unto him that was able to save him from death, and was heard in that he feared.

Verse 7 emphasizes the humanity of Jesus, which was previously mentioned in **Hebrews 2:9–18**. The phrase "in the days of his flesh" refers to His earthly ministry. The phrase "offered up prayers and supplications" is a reference to Jesus' "High Priestly" prayer in the Garden of Gethsemane (**Matthew 26:36–46; Mark 14:32–42; Luke 22:40–46**). The Gospel accounts clearly describe the fervency and intensity of this prayer. This shows that Jesus can completely empathize with our human condition of weakness. Jesus prayed for deliverance from death, and was heard. God's answer was not that He would escape death, but that He could be resurrected.

The writer closes this phase of his argument by introducing the order of Melchisedec and makes the link that Jesus is the High Priest forever. He draws this conclusion because in Old Testament Scripture, Melchisedec has no recorded father, his priesthood predates Aaron's, he is also a king, and he has no recorded end. **Psalm 110:3–5** is a prophetic foreshadow of Christ saying: "The LORD has taken an oath and will not break his vow: You are a priest forever in the order of Melchizedek" (**v. 4**, NLT).

8 Though he were a Son, yet learned he obedience by the things which he suffered.

Through His suffering, Jesus learned obedience. This does not mean that He was at any time disobedient, but He learned how to submit in obedience, laying down His will and rights. The writer engages in wordplay between the verb forms for "learned" (Gk. *emathen*, **EH-mah-thehn**) and "suffered" (Gk. *epathen*, **EH-pah-thehn**). In doing so, the writer suggests the falsity of the common understanding that obedience always results in peace and disobedience in suffering. Jesus' life and His death on the Cross prove that obedience can lead to suffering.

9 And being made perfect, he became the author of eternal salvation unto all them that obey him.

The phrase "being made perfect" (a single word in Greek; Gk. *teleiotheis*, **teh-lay-oh-THASE**) is not a reference to moral perfection, but the satisfactory completion of Christ's role as High Priest. The same word is used in the Greek translation of the Old Testament to refer to consecration and ordination (**Leviticus 8:33**; **Numbers 3:3**). Upon completion of this responsibility, Jesus became the "author" or source of eternal salvation for all who obey Him, just as He learned to obey God. The Greek word for "author" (*aitios*, **EYE-tee-ose**) could also be translated as "cause." The term "eternal salvation" is to be equated with eternal life, which Christ offers to those who believe in Him. Therefore, the reference to eternal salvation here is a description of Christ's work. His work of procuring salvation as our High Priest is eternally powerful—a perpetual priesthood.

10 Called of God an high priest after the order of Melchisedec.

Verse 10 ends this discussion of Jesus as our High Priest the way it began: with God's calling. It also introduces the new thought "after the order of Melchisedec," which points to His role as both Priest and King. He is a High Priest, but a different kind of high priest. As the pre-incarnate Son of God, He is one with royal authority.

SEARCH THE SCRIPTURES

QUESTION 3

What does it mean for us today that Jesus while in the flesh "offered up prayers and supplications," and though He was a Son He learned "obedience by the things which he suffered" (**Hebrews 5:7–8**)?

Jesus can empathize with our human weakness, and His death demonstrates how obedience can lead to suffering.

QUESTION 4

How does knowing Jesus as our High Priest add value to your relationship with Him?

Answers will vary.

LIGHT ON THE WORD

The High Priest, Set Apart

Under the Mosaic Law, God set apart the high priest to represent Himself to the people and the people to Him. God specifically established the priesthood to hail from the lineage of Aaron; he wore special clothing while functioning as priest. While before the people, he wore a uniform of great grandeur, and each piece represented a facet of his office on behalf of the people. However, when he went before the Lord in the Holy of Holies, he was stripped of that grandeur to represent the people. The high priest entered the Holy of Holies once a year to make atonement of sins for himself and the people. The point the writer makes is that God the Father established His Son as the high priest when He called Him out in His humanity to represent the people by bearing our sins and glorifying His name (**v. 5, John 12:28**).

BIBLE APPLICATION

AIM: Students will evaluate the role of Jesus as our High Priest who is the author of eternal salvation for all who obey Him.

We have a great High Priest who sympathizes with our weakness. He invites us to come boldly to the throne of grace that we may obtain mercy and find grace to help in the time of need (**Hebrews 4:16**). Do you have a prayer request that seems too big to ask? Why not pray a bold prayer today?

STUDENTS' RESPONSES

AIM: Students will validate that followers of Christ know that advocating for the needs of others is obedience to Jesus in action.

It is wonderful to know that in Heaven, we have the best representation that money cannot buy, purchased with the blood of Christ. **Hebrews 7:25** says "He always lives to intercede and intervene on their behalf [with God]" (AMP). Praise God that Jesus intercedes for us!

Reflect and share how you can advocate for those whose voices and needs are overlooked or underrepresented in your family, job, and in church.

PRAYER

We lift You up, our High Priest, Jesus. You have all authority from God. We are Your vessels to break open the good news of who You are and in whom we can trust. Create in us clean hearts so that we may serve You, Jesus, and tell others of the saving love that You have for all. In Your name we pray. Amen.

HOW TO SAY IT

Melchisedec.   mel-**KI**-si-dek.

Infirmity.   in-**FER**-mi-tee.

DIG A LITTLE DEEPER

This section provides an additional research article to further your study of the lesson:

Dr. Claude Mariottini discusses Jesus' role as High Priest. In this article, he validates the lineage of Jesus, which makes Him a legitimate claimant to the Priesthood. This paper provides insight into the role of priests according to Old Testament tradition. *Note: the spelling of Melchisedec (Melchizedek) varies according to the Bible translation but references the same person.*

http://claudemariottini.com/2007/04/09/jesus-a-high-priest-after-the-order-of-melchizedek/

PREPARE FOR NEXT SUNDAY

Read **Hebrews 7:1–3, 19b–28** and "The High Priest Forever."

DAILY HOME BIBLE READINGS

MONDAY
Gifts for the Work of Ministry
(Ephesians 4:7–13)

TUESDAY
Grateful for God's Mercy
(1 Timothy 1:12–17)

WEDNESDAY
Maintain Faith and a Good Conscience
(1 Timothy 1:18–10)

THURSDAY
Guard Your Faith with Powerful Love
(2 Timothy 1:3–14)

FRIDAY
A Good Soldier of Jesus Christ
(2 Timothy 2:1–7)

SATURDAY
Jesus Carries Forward the Father's Will
(Matthew 26:36–39)

SUNDAY
Our Great High Priest
(Hebrews 4:14–5:10)

THE HIGH PRIEST FOREVER

BIBLE BASIS: HEBREWS 7:1–3, 19b–28

BIBLE TRUTH: Jesus' priesthood will last forever because He lives forever.

MEMORY VERSE: "But this man, because he continueth ever, hath an unchangeable priesthood" (Hebrews 7:24).

LESSON AIM: By the end of the lesson, we will: CONSIDER the relationship between Melchisedec, "priest of the Most High God," with Jesus, the "Priest forever"; APPRECIATE that people have someone who intercedes for them to God; and RESPOND to the realization that Jesus will always be our ultimate spiritual leader.

TEACHER PREPARATION

MATERIALS NEEDED: Quarterly Commentary/Teacher Manual, Adult Quarterly, Adult resources—charts, worksheets, and other teaching tools, paper, pens, pencils, Bibles (several different versions)

OTHER MATERIALS NEEDED / TEACHER'S NOTES:

_____

_____

LESSON OVERVIEW

LIFE NEED FOR TODAY'S LESSON
Practices, traditions, and institutions are expected to continue into the future.

BIBLE APPLICATION
Jesus is our ultimate spiritual leader and superior over all.

BIBLE LEARNING
Jesus gave the practices, traditions, and institutions established by God their ultimate meaning and role for all generations.

STUDENTS' RESPONSES
Believers should develop qualities and characteristics that are Christ-like.

LESSON SCRIPTURE

HEBREWS 7:1–3, 19b–28, KJV

1 For this Melchisedec, king of Salem, priest of the most high God, who met Abraham returning from the slaughter of the kings, and blessed him;

2 To whom also Abraham gave a tenth part of all; first being by interpretation King of righteousness, and after that also King of Salem, which is, King of peace;

HEBREWS 7:1–3, 19b–28, AMP

1 For this Melchizedek, king of Salem, priest of the Most High God, met Abraham as he returned from the slaughter of the kings and blessed him,

2 and Abraham gave him a tenth of all [the spoil]. He is, first of all, by the translation of his name, king of righteousness, and then he is also king of Salem, which means king of peace.

3 Without father, without mother, without descent, having neither beginning of days, nor end of life; but made like unto the Son of God; abideth a priest continually.

19b but the bringing in of a better hope did; by the which we draw nigh unto God.

20 And inasmuch as not without an oath he was made priest:

21 (For those priests were made without an oath; but this with an oath by him that said unto him, The Lord sware and will not repent, Thou art a priest for ever after the order of Melchisedec:)

22 By so much was Jesus made a surety of a better testament.

23 And they truly were many priests, because they were not suffered to continue by reason of death:

24 But this man, because he continueth ever, hath an unchangeable priesthood.

25 Wherefore he is able also to save them to the uttermost that come unto God by him, seeing he ever liveth to make intercession for them.

26 For such an high priest became us, who is holy, harmless, undefiled, separate from sinners, and made higher than the heavens;

27 Who needeth not daily, as those high priests, to offer up sacrifice, first for his own sins, and then for the people's: for this he did once, when he offered up himself.

28 For the law maketh men high priests which have infirmity; but the word of the oath, which was since the law, maketh the Son, who is consecrated for evermore.

3 Without [any record of] father or mother, nor ancestral line, without [any record of] beginning of days (birth) nor ending of life (death), but having been made like the Son of God, he remains a priest without interruption and without successor.

19b a better hope is introduced through which we now continually draw near to God.

20 And indeed it was not without the taking of an oath [that Christ was made priest]

21 (for those Levites who formerly became priests [received their office] without [its being confirmed by the taking of] an oath, but this One [was designated] with an oath through the One who said to Him, "THE LORD HAS SWORN AND WILL NOT CHANGE HIS MIND OR REGRET IT, 'YOU (CHRIST) ARE A PRIEST FOREVER'").

22 And so [because of the oath's greater strength and force] Jesus has become the certain guarantee of a better covenant [a more excellent and more advantageous agreement; one that will never be replaced or annulled].

23 The [former successive line of] priests, on the one hand, existed in greater numbers because they were each prevented by death from continuing [perpetually in office];

24 but, on the other hand, Jesus holds His priesthood permanently and without change, because He lives on forever.

25 Therefore He is able also to save forever (completely, perfectly, for eternity) those who come to God through Him, since He always lives to intercede and intervene on their behalf [with God].

26 It was fitting for us to have such a High Priest [perfectly adapted to our needs], holy, blameless, unstained [by sin], separated from sinners and exalted higher than the heavens;

27 who has no day by day need, like those high priests, to offer sacrifices, first of all for his own [personal] sins and then for those of the people, because He [met all the requirements and] did this once for all when He offered up Himself [as a willing sacrifice].

28 For the Law appoints men as high priests who are weak [frail, sinful, dying men], but the word of the oath [of God], which came after [the institution of] the Law, permanently appoints [as priest] a Son who has been made perfect forever.

LIGHT ON THE WORD

King-Priest. In chapter 7, the writer introduces this king who was also a priest: Melchisedec. As if anticipating their questions, he recounts how this king-priest met Abraham, blessed him, and received tithes from him. He also explains that the name Melchisedec means "king of righteousness" and "king of peace" and tells readers that his genealogy and dates of birth and death are not known. This description exalted Melchisedec above Abraham and portrayed the king-priest as a type of Christ, representing Jesus' eternal existence and unending priesthood.

TEACHING THE BIBLE LESSON

LIFE NEED FOR TODAY'S LESSON

AIM: Students will agree that some practices, traditions, and institutions are expected to continue into the future.

INTRODUCTION

The Imperfect and Perfect Priesthood
Synonymous with Aaronic priesthood and derived from the Law of Moses, this system restricted priestly duties to the tribe of Levi.

Levitical priests were appointed by inheritance. They offered up animal sacrifices to the Lord daily for their own sins and for the people. This system was imperfect and impermanent because it relied on the existence of a tabernacle or temple and the ability of humans to carry out the tasks.

The Levitical system disqualified Jesus from becoming a priest since He was not from the tribe of Levi, so a change in the order of the priesthood required a change in the priestly laws/instructions as well. However, Jesus' priesthood was of a higher order, not an earthly and imperfect one like the Levitical priesthood.

BIBLE LEARNING

AIM: Students affirm that Jesus gave the practices, traditions, and institutions established by God their ultimate meaning and role for all generations.

I. AN UNENDING LIFE
(Hebrews 7:1–3)

Melchisedec is introduced as a king and priest of God Most High in **Genesis 14:17–24**, AMP. This king and priest blessed Abraham and received tithes from him. His name and title allude to a connection to Christ.

7:1 For this Melchisedec, king of Salem, priest of the most high God, who met Abraham returning from the slaughter of the kings, and blessed him; 2 To whom also Abraham gave a tenth part of all; first being by interpretation King of righteousness, and after that also King of Salem, which is, King of peace; 3 Without father, without mother, without descent, having neither beginning of days, nor end of life; but made like unto the Son of God; abideth a priest continually.

The writer of Hebrews highlights the character of Melchisedec in order to explain the kind of high priest we have in Christ. Melchisedec blessed Abraham after he came back from the battle of the five kings (**Genesis 14:17–20**). He also received a tithe from him. Melchisedec's two titles are unusual, as he is both a priest and a king in the same way that Christ is our High Priest and also the King of Kings and Lord of Lords. Melchisedec's name means "king of righteousness," and asking of Salem, his title means "king of peace." These titles can both be applied to Christ.

The writer points out the most distinguishing feature of Melchisedec—he has no record of ancestry or death. In this way, he is said to live forever, and through this distinction, Melchisedec is most like Christ. His eternal priesthood causes Melchisedec to resemble (Gk. *aphomoio*, **ah-fo-moy-OH-oh**) or be made analogous to the Son of God.

SEARCH THE SCRIPTURES

QUESTION 1
What is the significance of Melchisedec being "Without father, without mother, without descent, having neither beginning of days, nor end of life" (**Hebrews 7:3**)?

Because there is no record of his ancestry or death, he is most like Christ, causing him to resemble the Son of God.

LIGHT ON THE WORD
The Prince of Peace
The Scriptures do not mention Melchisedec's ancestry or priestly pedigree. His name means "King of Righteousness." Salem, the name of his city, signified "peace." Thus, as king of peace, he typified Christ, the Prince of Peace, the One whose saving work reconciles God and humankind.

II. AN UNBREAKABLE OATH (vv. 19b–22)

This new priesthood was marked by many changes. One such change was God's endorsement of the priest. God swore in Jesus with a solemn oath, "Thou art a priest for ever after the order of Melchisedec" (**v. 21**). Never had God done that in the Levitical priesthood. Jesus' priesthood, pledged in Psalm 110, was superior because it was divinely affirmed with an oath.

19b but the bringing in of a better hope did; by the which we draw nigh unto God.

The writer of Hebrews notes that with the coming of Jesus, the Levitical priesthood was set aside because it was weak and unprofitable (**Hebrews 7:18**). "A better hope" was introduced, "by the which we draw nigh unto God" (**v. 19**). The law could only remove our sins and bring us in relationship with God temporarily. Instead of being made right with God on an annual basis through sacrifices, now we can continually draw near to God through Jesus' intercession. Jesus did not sacrifice an animal, but He sacrificed Himself for our sins. Therefore, no other sacrifice is needed—ever. We now have (and will forever have) Jesus, who intercedes with the Father for us.

20 And inasmuch as not without an oath he was made priest.

This is the writer's way of saying Jesus' priesthood is of a higher order than Levitical succession. Jesus' priesthood was established by God with an oath, meaning God has sworn and will not change His mind. Just as God kept His covenant with Abraham, He will keep His promise regarding Jesus' priesthood. Jesus' priesthood is permanent, unlike the temporary Levitical priesthood.

21 (For those priests were made without an oath; but this with an oath by him that said unto him, The Lord sware and will not repent, Thou art a priest for ever after the order of Melchisedec:)

The Levitical priesthood established under Aaron (**Exodus 28:1**) was conditional. It was instituted without an oath and therefore lacked permanence. Christ's priesthood was confirmed by an oath, and He is therefore "a priest for ever." The fact that Jesus' priesthood is confirmed by divine oath leaves no room for qualification because of any human weakness, sin, or failure. The writer of Hebrews aims to show that Christ's priesthood is superior to the Levitical priesthood. To strengthen the argument, the writer references **Psalm 110:4**, which is understood to be God's comment to Christ. Hebrews is the only New Testament book that makes a direct reference to Melchisedec. This name appears in two passages in the Old Testament (**Genesis 14:18–20; Psalm 110:4**). In **Genesis 14:18–20**, he is referred to as "the king of Salem" and "the priest of the most high God." The Bible is intentional in giving a limited amount of information regarding Melchisedec. However, some earlier Christian writers and scholars are aware of his existence in biblical history. The lack of clarity for some regarding his role does not diminish the truth of the superiority of permanence of Christ's priesthood.

22 By so much was Jesus made a surety of a better testament.

Here the writer of Hebrews surprisingly moves his line of reasoning from the priesthood to a testament or covenant. The Greek word *diatheke* (**dee-ah-THAY-kay**, testament or covenant) is used in conjunction with the Greek word *egguos* (**EN-gue-oss**, surety; the guarantee that a promise will be fulfilled). These two words are meant to make perfectly clear the incontestability of God's oath whereby Jesus was made "a priest for ever." God made the promise, and Jesus is the guarantee that the promise will be fulfilled.

LIGHT ON THE WORD
God's Oath

It is understood that a will or testament is final and absolute and therefore cannot be amended except by the testator, the person. God firmly established the terms of Christ's priesthood once and for all time. Jesus' life and God's oath makes unnecessary a succession of priests after Christ.

III. AN UNCHANGEABLE PRIESTHOOD (vv. 23–28)

According to **verse 25**, this Mediator of the new covenant "ever liveth to make intercession for them." This signified another change in the priesthood—Christ's priesthood was permanent and unchangeable. Whereas priests of the law died, leaving a vacancy in the priesthood until they were replaced, Jesus Christ as High Priest meant there will never be a vacancy in the priesthood. At all times, in all things, He will be available to negotiate our spiritual concerns in Heaven, by interceding with the Father on our behalf.

23 And they truly were many priests, because they were not suffered to continue by reason of death:

The writer of Hebrews continues to contrast Jesus with the Levitical priests. Historians tell us that from the time of Aaron to the destruction of the Temple in AD 70, between 80 and 85 high priests served. If a priest was careless in his preparation to enter the Holy of Holies, he fell dead immediately and would be pulled out by a rope that was tied to his ankle. Even if meticulous in his preparation, a priest was a mere mortal who would die eventually. For these reasons, numerous replacements were necessary.

24 But this man, because he continueth ever, hath an unchangeable priesthood.

Unlike the Levitical priests, Jesus' priesthood "continueth ever." He has "an unchangeable priesthood." The Greek word for unchangeable, *aparabatos* (**ahp-ar-AH-bah-toss**, something that cannot be transgressed or transferred to another), conveys the idea that Jesus' priesthood lives with Him through eternity. Since Jesus Himself "continueth ever," His priesthood can be "unchangeable." Jesus' priesthood cannot be transferred to another. It extends into eternity. Thus, He will be able to intercede for us and for all people in every generation yet unborn.

25 Wherefore he is able also to save them to the uttermost that come unto God by him, seeing he ever liveth to make intercession for them.

The basic and most significant content of this verse is contained in the Greek verb *sozo* (**SOHD-zoh**, to save, deliver, make whole, or to preserve from danger, loss, and destruction). More specifically, in the context of Hebrews, it is salvation in its broadest and fullest meaning. It implies complete deliverance, no matter what our need, including deliverance from the punishment resulting from sin. In Jesus, we have a Savior able to bring complete salvation to all who "come unto God by him." Jesus lives to make intercession for us. Because He lives forever, His priestly concern for us never ends.

Whatever our need, at any time or in any place, Jesus Christ stands ready to petition God the Father on our behalf. He is able and always available to speak for us, and go before God and plead our case.

26 For such an high priest became us, who is holy, harmless, undefiled, separate from sinners, and made higher than the heavens.

All priests who served in the Temple where God's presence dwelt were obliged to be holy, harmless, undefiled, and separate from sinners. In essence, they should be free of any impurity—any actions or circumstances that would render them unclean according to the Mosaic Law. Any defilement rendered the priest incapable of interceding for the people. The writer of Hebrews wants his readers to know that Jesus fulfills all of these requirements. He is holy, harmless, and undefiled, and although He is a friend of sinners, He has been "made higher than the heavens." While Jesus is apart from sinners, He nonetheless intercedes for sinners in ways that show His capacity to identify with even the outcasts of society. In fact, **Hebrews 4:15** reminds us, "For we have not an high priest which cannot be touched with the feeling of our infirmities; but was in all points tempted like as we are, yet without sin." Christ's undefiled character attests to His capacity to go before God on our behalf.

27 Who needeth not daily, as those high priests, to offer up sacrifice, first for his own sins, and then for the people's: for this he did once, when he offered up himself.

This verse presents meticulous students of the Scriptures with a problem. A careful reading of the relevant text will show that while sacrifices were offered daily, the high priest was not required to offer the daily sacrifices personally (**Numbers 28:3**). Those sacrifices requiring the high priest's attention were offered yearly, not daily (cf. **Hebrews 9:7, 25, 10:1**). However, the writer wishes to make the point that Jesus has no need to offer sacrifices daily or yearly for His own sins, because He was sinless (**4:15**). His perfect sacrifice was sufficient for all time. The writer's use of the phrase translated "for this he did once" is a critically important affirmation. It speaks not only of the eternal completeness and efficacy of Christ's sacrifice of Himself but it also nullifies every other sacrificial system because Jesus' sacrifice was complete and any other sacrifice is unnecessary. Christ's sacrifice of Himself was final, complete, and eternally adequate for our salvation.

28 For the law maketh men high priests which have infirmity; but the word of the oath, which was since the law, maketh the Son, who is consecrated for evermore.

Here the writer again compares the Levitical priests and Jesus. Under Levitical law, which was imperfect, priests were ordinary men appointed by ordinary men. Therefore priests, even the high priest, are limited, just as all men are limited and weak. They are subject to death.

Standing in clear contrast to the Law is "the word of the oath," which came much later than the Law. One could ask: If the Law was perfect, making provision for the appointment of perfect priests, what need would there be for "the word of the oath"? The mere fact that "the word of the oath" came after the Law points to the inadequacies of the Aaronic priesthood. This verse is really a summary of the preceding verses. It reiterates the thought that Jesus, the Son, is superior to all the priests appointed under the law. The continuous replacement of imperfect priests is contrasted with the permanent placement of the perfect Jesus "who is consecrated," or perfected (Gk. *teleioo*, **te-layoh-OH**). This word means to make

perfect or full and specifically in this sense to be perfect in character and qualifications. This is the high priest who always lives to make intercession for us.

SEARCH THE SCRIPTURES

QUESTION 2
What makes Jesus the kind of High Priest we need (**v. 26**)? Create a list of the qualities of Jesus and the qualifications of the high priest from **Leviticus 21**. Note the similarities and differences.

Jesus is the High Priest we need because He was human and understands our human weakness, allowing us to boldly approach God. The high priest must not leave his hair uncombed, tear his clothing, or go near a dead body; he must also marry a virgin.

QUESTION 3
Since Christ is always interceding for us, does this give us a license to sin? Why or why not?

No; answers will vary.

QUESTION 4
In **verse 26**, the high priests were to have what characteristics? Should these same characteristics apply to all leaders and believers today?

Holy, harmless, undefiled, and separate from sinners.

LIGHT ON THE WORD
Without Blemish
Unlike the Levitical priests, Jesus has no need to offer a sacrifice for Himself. By virtue of His undefiled character, He was qualified to offer Himself as the atoning sacrifice for our sins. He was the "lamb without blemish and without spot" (from **1 Peter 1:19**).

BIBLE APPLICATION

AIM: Students will agree that Jesus is our ultimate spiritual leader and superior over all.

Only Jesus is equipped to appear before a holy God. We can only go to God because Jesus is our High Priest. Without His ministry on our behalf, our prayers cannot be heard. It is one thing to pray, but it's another thing for God to hear our prayers and move on our behalf. This is what it means to have Jesus, God the Son, as our High Priest.

STUDENTS' RESPONSES

AIM: Students value the holiness of God and aspire to live holy.

High priests who entered the Holy of Holies encountered the very presence of God. That's why there was a veil separating sinful man from a holy God. Because of Christ in our lives, we, too, can live holy (**1 Peter 1:16**). In what ways are you demonstrating the holiness of God?

PRAYER

Dear Jesus, thank You for being the One that we need to plead our case before the Lord. You are blameless and Holy. Jesus, You are without sin, and we are sinners. Yet, You gave Your life for us, and You were resurrected. We adore You Jesus and praise You now and through eternity. In Your Name we pray. Amen.

HOW TO SAY IT

Melchisedec.   mel-**KIH**-zi-dek.

Consecrated.   **KHAN**-se-kra-tid.

DIG A LITTLE DEEPER

This section provides an additional research article to further your study of the lesson:

Melchizedek as a type of Christ for the Hebrew audience was an important connection for their comprehension of Jesus' role. And it's important for us to understand today. *Why You Need Know About Melchizedek* is an article that is both informative and concise.

https://bible.org/seriespage/lesson-20-why-you-need-know-about-melchizedek-hebrews-71-10

PREPARE FOR NEXT SUNDAY

Read **Hebrews 12:1–13** and "Pioneer and Perfecter of Our Faith."

DAILY HOME BIBLE READINGS

MONDAY
Victory of God's Priest King
(Psalm 110)

TUESDAY
Service by and Support of Priests
(Numbers 18:21–24)

WEDNESDAY
Believers' Inheritance in Christ
(Ephesians 1:11–16)

THURSDAY
Power of God Invested in Christ
(Ephesians 1:17–23)

FRIDAY
Jesus, Permanent Priest Forever
(Hebrews 1:1–3, 23–25)

SATURDAY
Power of an Indestructible Life
(Hebrews 7:15–17)

SUNDAY
The High Priest Forever
(Hebrews 7:1–3, 19b–28)

PIONEER AND PERFECTER OF OUR FAITH

BIBLE BASIS: HEBREWS 12:1–13

BIBLE TRUTH: God disciplines and punishes those He loves.

MEMORY VERSE: "Let us run with patience the race that is set before us, looking unto Jesus the author and finisher of our faith" (from Hebrews 12:1–2).

LESSON AIM: By the end of the lesson, we will: EVALUATE the importance of discipline in the family, in the congregation, and in other human settings; APPRECIATE the help provided by others who have experienced discipline; and SHARE personal struggles that resulted in a victorious and growing faith.

TEACHER PREPARATION

MATERIALS NEEDED: Quarterly Commentary/Teacher Manual, Adult Quarterly, Adult resources—charts, worksheets, and other teaching tools, paper, pens, pencils, Bibles (several different versions)

OTHER MATERIALS NEEDED / TEACHER'S NOTES:

_____

_____

LESSON OVERVIEW

LIFE NEED FOR TODAY'S LESSON
In life, there are many trials, and struggles.

BIBLE LEARNING
Faith sustains us in difficult times.

BIBLE APPLICATION
Jesus provides us the support needed to endure our troubles.

STUDENTS' RESPONSES
Believers appreciate that God's discipline makes us stronger and increases our faith.

LESSON SCRIPTURE

HEBREWS 12:1–13, KJV

1 Wherefore seeing we also are compassed about with so great a cloud of witnesses, let us lay aside every weight, and the sin which doth so easily beset us, and let us run with patience the race that is set before us,

2 Looking unto Jesus the author and finisher of our faith; who for the joy that was set before him endured the cross, despising the

HEBREWS 12:1–13, AMP

1 Therefore, since we are surrounded by so great a cloud of witnesses [who by faith have testified to the truth of God's absolute faithfulness], stripping off every unnecessary weight and the sin which so easily and cleverly entangles us, let us run with endurance and active persistence the race that is set before us,

shame, and is set down at the right hand of the throne of God.

3 For consider him that endured such contradiction of sinners against himself, lest ye be wearied and faint in your minds.

4 Ye have not yet resisted unto blood, striving against sin.

5 And ye have forgotten the exhortation which speaketh unto you as unto children, My son, despise not thou the chastening of the Lord, nor faint when thou art rebuked of him:

6 For whom the Lord loveth he chasteneth, and scourgeth every son whom he receiveth.

7 If ye endure chastening, God dealeth with you as with sons; for what son is he whom the father chasteneth not?

8 But if ye be without chastisement, whereof all are partakers, then are ye bastards, and not sons.

9 Furthermore we have had fathers of our flesh which corrected us, and we gave them reverence: shall we not much rather be in subjection unto the Father of spirits, and live?

10 For they verily for a few days chastened us after their own pleasure; but he for our profit, that we might be partakers of his holiness.

11 Now no chastening for the present seemeth to be joyous, but grievous: nevertheless afterward it yieldeth the peaceable fruit of righteousness unto them which are exercised thereby.

12 Wherefore lift up the hands which hang down, and the feeble knees;

2 [looking away from all that will distract us and] focusing our eyes on Jesus, who is the Author and Perfecter of faith [the first incentive for our belief and the One who brings our faith to maturity], who for the joy [of accomplishing the goal] set before Him endured the cross, disregarding the shame, and sat down at the right hand of the throne of God [revealing His deity, His authority, and the completion of His work].

3 Just consider and meditate on Him who endured from sinners such bitter hostility against Himself [consider it all in comparison with your trials], so that you will not grow weary and lose heart.

4 You have not yet struggled to the point of shedding blood in your striving against sin;

5 and you have forgotten the divine word of encouragement which is addressed to you as sons, "MY SON, DO NOT MAKE LIGHT OF THE DISCIPLINE OF THE LORD, And DO NOT LOSE HEART and GIVE UP WHEN YOU ARE CORRECTED BY HIM;

6 FOR THE LORD DISCIPLINES and CORRECTS THOSE WHOM HE LOVES, And HE PUNISHES EVERY SON WHOM HE RECEIVES AND WELCOMES [TO HIS HEART]."

7 You must submit to [correction for the purpose of] discipline; God is dealing with you as with sons; for what son is there whom his father does not discipline?

8 Now if you are exempt from correction and without discipline, in which all [of God's children] share, then you are illegitimate children and not sons [at all].

9 Moreover, we have had earthly fathers who disciplined us, and we submitted and respected them [for training us]; shall we not much more willingly submit to the Father of spirits, and live [by learning from His discipline]?

13 And make straight paths for your feet, lest that which is lame be turned out of the way; but let it rather be healed.

10 For our earthly fathers disciplined us for only a short time as seemed best to them; but He disciplines us for our good, so that we may share His holiness.

11 For the time being no discipline brings joy, but seems sad and painful; yet to those who have been trained by it, afterwards it yields the peaceful fruit of righteousness [right standing with God and a lifestyle and attitude that seeks conformity to God's will and purpose].

12 So then, strengthen hands that are weak and knees that tremble.

13 Cut through and make smooth, straight paths for your feet [that are safe and go in the right direction], so that the leg which is lame may not be put out of joint, but rather may be healed.

LIGHT ON THE WORD

Multitude of Witnesses. In **chapter 11**, the writer of Hebrews provides a brief history of people who demonstrated great faith in God, beginning in Genesis with Abel, and continuing with "others ... tortured [to death], refusing to accept release [offered on the condition of denying their faith], so that they would be resurrected to a better life" (**Hebrews 11:35**, AMP). These people of the faith make up this large multitude of witnesses, people who believed God, and testify to His faithfulness and power. The Greek term used for "witnesses" is *martus*, where we derive "martyr," and can be translated as "a spectator, witness, or testifier."

TEACHING THE BIBLE LESSON

LIFE NEED FOR TODAY'S LESSON

AIM: Students will agree that life has many trials and struggles.

INTRODUCTION

Hebrews

Abram (Abraham) is the first person to be called a "Hebrew," and his descendants through Isaac would go on to be known as "Hebrews" (also called Israelites and Jews). The origin of the term is debated. Some scholars believe it is derived from the name Eber, one of Abram's ancestors (**Genesis 11:14–17**). Still others hold that it comes from the term *ha ibhri* from the Hebrew word *abar*, which means "to cross over." This phrase is used in Genesis to describe Abram "crossing over" the river Euphrates. It is believed that the book of Hebrews was written to a largely Jewish audience who had converted to Christianity some time prior to the writing of the epistle.

BIBLE LEARNING

AIM: Students will agree that faith sustains us in difficult times.

I. BE FAITHFUL (Hebrews 12:1–4)

The "great ... cloud of witnesses" refers to the people mentioned in **chapter 11**. Here, the writer is saying that those who have gone before are examples to others of living the life of faith. God has confirmed their faithfulness, and they can be seen as examples of those who endured. Therefore, in light of our inspiring audience, we must rid ourselves of "every weight" and "run with patience."

1 Wherefore seeing we also are compassed about with so great a cloud of witnesses, let us lay aside every weight, and the sin which doth so easily beset us, and let us run with patience the race that is set before us,

The writer of Hebrews uses an illustration of a race, a common athletic event during Greco-Roman times. There are runners and witnesses. These "witnesses" are examples, though they were not "made perfect" (**11:40**). They trusted God and lived for Him to the end. Their testimonies encourage others to do the same. The writer exhorts his audience (runners) to "strip off" (i.e., take off excess clothing or weights while running) anything that hinders living faithfully, particularly sin (**12:1**).

2 Looking unto Jesus the author and finisher of our faith; who for the joy that was set before him endured the cross, despising the shame, and is set down at the right hand of the throne of God. 3 For consider him that endured such contradiction of sinners against himself, lest ye be wearied and faint in your minds.

Instead of being sidetracked and encumbered, believers should run with endurance by focusing on Christ, the One who founded the Christian faith (**v. 2**) and created a path forward for those to come. He not only started it but He is the ultimate example—the One who demonstrates how perfect faith looks, and equips us.

To run the race, a person must stay focused on Jesus, as implied here by the use of the Greek word *aphorao* (**ah-foe-RAH-oh**), translated as "looking." *Aphorao* means "to focus attention, to see something clearly"—namely Jesus. We do so because Jesus is the "author" (Gk. *archegos*, **ar-khay-GOSS**), meaning chief leader. This term was used for heroes and founders of philosophical schools, as well as those who paved the way for others and were exalted for their efforts. So Jesus is the "pioneer" and the "finisher" (Gk. *teleiotes*, **teh-lay-oh-TACE**), which means "completer" of faith. In other words, His life and death make faith complete. The word "endured" comes from *hupomeno* (Gk. **hoo-poe-MEN-oh**), meaning "to remain or tarry." Jesus chose to remain on the Cross and bear the shame of crucifixion to save humanity. He focused on the future and finished the work of our redemption, bringing many to glory (**Hebrews 2:10**).

When the temptation arises to be overwhelmed in the face of trials, the writer encourages believers not to "become weary and give up" (**v. 3**), as one would be toward the end of a race. Instead, believers should be motivated by remembering how Christ endured a humiliating and excruciatingly painful death to overcome sin and restore our relationship with God.

4 Ye have not yet resisted unto blood, striving against sin.

Here, the readers are reminded that although they may have suffered great persecution (**Hebrews 10:32–34**), none of them have shed blood and died like Jesus did. None had yet become martyrs because of their confession of Jesus as their Messiah or Savior.

SEARCH THE SCRIPTURES

QUESTION 1

How can we determine the weights in our lives and the sin that so easily besets us (**Hebrews 12:1**)?

Look away from distractions and focus on Jesus, who brings our faith to maturity.

LIGHT OF THE WORD

Jesus' Supremacy

The writer sets forth to establish the supremacy of Christ—speaking of His incarnation, death, priesthood, and His elevation above the angels, Moses, Joshua, and high priests. He then focuses on faith, providing its definition as "the substance of things hoped for, the evidence of things not seen" (**Hebrews 11:1**), and goes on to list those from Jewish history who are in the "Great Hall of Faith." In so doing, he reminds readers of the necessity of faith in Christ, how "without faith it is impossible to please God" (**11:6**, NIV), and how faith supersedes rituals and sacrifices.

II. BE DISCIPLINED (vv. 5–11)

5 And ye have forgotten the exhortation that speaketh unto you as unto children, My son, despise not thou the chastening of the Lord, nor faint when thou art rebuked of him: 6 For whom the Lord loveth he chasteneth, and scourgeth every son he receiveth.

In **verses 5 and 6**, the author quotes **Proverbs 3:11–12**. In these verses, the reader is reminded of the parent-child relationship. Undisciplined children are unloved children. In this instance, the use of the Greek word *paideia* (**pie-DAY-ah**) means "nurturing" or "giving instruction." The writer is saying that one should not make light of God's instruction but welcome it as a means of spiritual growth.

7 If ye endure chastening, God dealeth with you as with sons; for what son is he whom the father chasteneth not? 8 But if ye be without chastisement, whereof all are partakers, then are ye bastards, and not sons.

Christians should view trials as a form of divine discipline. Just as a parent would discipline a child, God deals with the sinner. No wise father or mother would allow his or her children to continue bad behavior without correcting it. Therefore, receiving discipline can be viewed as a sign of God's fatherly love.

9 Furthermore we have had fathers of our flesh which corrected us, and we gave them reverence: shall we not much rather be in subjection unto the Father of spirits, and live?

Here, God is called "the Father of spirits" (an expression in the New Testament which occurs only here)—in contrast to the human "fathers of our flesh." The writer makes a comparison between an earthly father and the heavenly Father—the argument being, if earthly parents discipline us and we respect them for it in the long run, then we should respect our Heavenly Father who gives us His Holy Spirit even more. God has power over every soul because it belongs to Him.

10 For they verily for a few days chastened us after their own pleasure; but he for our profit, that we might be partakers of his holiness.

Verse 10 points out the difference between human discipline and Heaven's discipline. Our earthly parents discipline us "for a few days," whereas God's discipline gives us an eternal benefit. Human discipline is often inconsistent and usually provides a temporary benefit. However, the long-range goal in God's discipline is that we might be "partakers" of His holiness. Nothing pleases God more than children who grow to emulate Him.

11 Now no chastening for the present seemeth to be joyous, but grievous:

nevertheless afterward it yieldeth the peaceable fruit of righteousness unto them which are exercised thereby.

Present discipline seems painful because it is! The purpose of our pain is to produce Christlike behavior. Sometimes we have to endure painful discipline. The Greek word for "exercised" is *gumnazo* (**goom-NAHD-zoh**), and as used here, it implies exercise of the mind in order to endure persecution. The word is usually used for going to the gym to work out, much as we would today. This physical training was a key part of the *paideia* (**PIE-ee-dee-uh**) or education a young person was expected to undergo. Here, the author states it is also a key part of the discipline that God has His children undergo, exercising the mind in order to endure persecution, so that they can later enjoy the "fruit of righteousness."

SEARCH THE SCRIPTURES

QUESTION 2
How do we develop an appropriate response to experiencing discipline from God (**vv. 4–7**)?

Remember that our relationship with God is one of parent and child, and view trials as fatherly correction.

QUESTION 3
Very rarely is discipline viewed in the context of faith and growth. However, **Hebrews 12:10** says that God's discipline is "for our profit." Create a timeline of your own experiences of God's discipline. Share with the class how they affected your faith, character, and growth. What lessons can others learn from your example?

Answers will vary.

LIGHT ON THE WORD
Spiritual Discipline
Many people talk about needing to "exercise discipline" or "be disciplined." However, few people understand or appreciate the process.

Discipline involves training, educating, and correcting, and it is accomplished in various ways. It requires effort, love, time, consistency, sacrifice, pain, and a degree of difficulty, but it is necessary in order to experience growth.

III. BE STRONG (vv. 12–13)

12 Wherefore lift up the hands which hang down, and the feeble knees; 13 And make straight paths for your feet, lest that which is lame be turned out of the way; but let it rather be healed.

These two verses encourage the Hebrew Christians to become strong, and by becoming stronger, they will be able to help even the weakest among them. In the race of faith, they are called to lift up their weak hands and knees. This is likely an allusion to **Isaiah 35:3**, a prophecy to Israel regarding the inaugurated Kingdom of God. Through this, the writer implies that now Jesus' followers have experienced the inbreaking of the coming Kingdom. This inbreaking, which is signified by the baptism of the Holy Spirit, is the basis for the believer's strengthened faith in the present as well as in the future.

The wording of **verse 13** might have **Proverbs 4:26** in mind. This verse is an exhortation to not stray away from the godly path. The writer of Hebrews says that by following the correct path, those who are already lame may become healed. They will avoid further suffering and spiritual disability.

SEARCH THE SCRIPTURES

QUESTION 4
What does the writer of Hebrews mean by saying "lift up the hands which hang down, and the feeble knees" (**vv. 12–13**)?

Be strong, and keep up your strength to help the weak in need.

LIGHT ON THE WORD

Authorship Questions

The book of Hebrews has a few unknowns. Origen, a Christian interpreter from the second-third centuries, engages in a debate regarding whether or not Paul wrote Hebrews. He determines that the style is different but that Paul's theology certainly influenced Hebrews strongly enough to include it in the tradition of Paul, even if only God can be sure whether or not Paul wrote the document.

BIBLE APPLICATION

AIM: Students will decide that Jesus provides us the support needed to endure our troubles.

This lesson causes us to re-examine our view of suffering and discipline. Joseph's tumultuous journey ended with his being second-in-command in Egypt. The faith of Daniel's friends grew as they experienced God's deliverance in the furnace, and Daniel's faith grew as he was delivered from the lion's den. Suffering is painful. But good can come from it. How are you challenged to change your view of suffering? What trials do you have now? Is there anything that needs to change in how you approach discipline in your life? Your children? Pray that God will give you the ability to see what He is doing and faith to endure.

STUDENTS' RESPONSES

AIM: Students will appreciate God's discipline that makes them stronger and increases their faith.

Very rarely is discipline viewed in the context of faith and growth. However, the writer has them intertwined. **James 1:2–4** says, "Dear brothers and sisters, when troubles of any kind come your way, consider it an opportunity for great joy. For you know that when your faith is tested, your endurance has a chance to grow.

So let it grow, for when your endurance is fully developed, you will be perfect and complete, needing nothing" (NLT). What hardships have you experienced that you now see were God's discipline? How did they affect your faith? Your character? Your growth? What lessons can others learn from your example?

PRAYER

Dear Heavenly Father, we are privileged to be Your children. Thank You for loving us to discipline and care for us to become stronger in our faith. We want to walk by faith in all that we do and say. Your faithfulness gives us grace and mercy each and every day. In the Name of Jesus we pray. Amen.

HOW TO SAY IT

Exhortation.   eks-**ZOR**-tay-shun.

Chaseneth.   **CHAY**-sen-ith.

DIG A LITTLE DEEPER

This section provides an additional research study of the lesson:

Perhaps one of mankind's greatest desires is the elimination of pain. In a search to reconcile his wife's disability with his own faith, the author embodies the struggles of many Christians. This candid discussion engages the reader with the hard truths of life.

http://www.dts.edu/read/christianity-disability-thinking-theologically-about-brokenness/

PREPARE FOR NEXT SUNDAY

Read **Revelation 21:1–8** and "Everything's Brand New."

DAILY HOME BIBLE READINGS

MONDAY
I Know Their Suffering
(Exodus 3:7–10)

TUESDAY
Cry for Help Answered
(Psalm 22:1–5)

WEDNESDAY
By His Bruises We Are Healed
(Isaiah 53:1–6)

THURSDAY
Run the Race to Win
(1 Corinthians 9:24–27)

FRIDAY
Endure Discipline, Share in God's Holiness
(Hebrews 10:35–39)

SATURDAY
You Are Blessed for Enduring Suffering
(James 1:12–16)

SUNDAY
Pioneer and Perfecter of Our Faith
(Hebrews 12:1–13)

COMMENTS / NOTES:

EVERYTHING'S BRAND NEW

BIBLE BASIS: REVELATION 21:1–8

BIBLE TRUTH: God will create a new Heaven and earth where life's challenges and stresses will be banished forever.

MEMORY VERSE: "And God shall wipe away all tears from their eyes; and there shall be no more death, neither sorrow, nor crying, neither shall there be any more pain: for the former things are passed away" (Revelation 21:4).

LESSON AIM: By the end of the lesson, we will: EVALUATE the "apocalypse" genre that characterizes the book of Revelation to discern how to understand its message; CONTEMPLATE the coming of "a new heaven and a new earth" for the hope that this vision brings; and EMBRACE the peace of God that begins in this life with Jesus.

TEACHER PREPARATION

MATERIALS NEEDED: Quarterly Commentary/Teacher Manual, Adult Quarterly, Adult resources—charts, worksheets, and other teaching tools, paper, pens, pencils, Bibles (several different versions)

OTHER MATERIALS NEEDED / TEACHER'S NOTES:

_____

_____

LESSON OVERVIEW

LIFE NEED FOR TODAY'S LESSON
People look for a place and time where life stresses will not exist.

BIBLE APPLICATION
Believers see the vision of hope that God gives for our future life.

BIBLE LEARNING
The book of Revelation gives us God's redemptive plan for Heaven and earth.

STUDENTS' RESPONSES
Christians can experience the peace of God wiping away the tears from their eyes and peace in their lives.

LESSON SCRIPTURE

REVELATION 21:1–8, KJV

1 And I saw a new heaven and a new earth: for the first heaven and the first earth were passed away ; and there was no more sea.

2 And I John saw the holy city, new

REVELATION 21:1–8, AMP

1 Then I saw a new heaven and a new earth; for the first heaven and the first earth had passed away (vanished), and there is no longer any sea.

Jerusalem, coming down from God out of heaven, prepared as a bride adorned for her husband.

3 And I heard a great voice out of heaven saying, Behold, the tabernacle of God is with men, and he will dwell with them, and they shall be his people, and God himself shall be with them, and be their God.

4 And God shall wipe away all tears from their eyes; and there shall be no more death, neither sorrow, nor crying, neither shall there be any more pain: for the former things are passed away.

5 And he that sat upon the throne said, Behold, I make all things new. And he said unto me, Write: for these words are true and faithful.

6 And he said unto me, It is done. I am Alpha and Omega, the beginning and the end. I will give unto him that is athirst of the fountain of the water of life freely.

7 He that overcometh shall inherit all things; and I will be his God, and he shall be my son.

8 But the fearful, and unbelieving, and the abominable, and murderers, and whoremongers, and sorcerers, and idolaters, and all liars, shall have their part in the lake which burneth with fire and brimstone: which is the second death.

2 And I saw the holy city, new Jerusalem, coming down out of heaven from God, arrayed like a bride adorned for her husband;

3 and then I heard a loud voice from the throne, saying, "See! The tabernacle of God is among men, and He will live among them, and they will be His people, and God Himself will be with them [as their God,]

4 and He will wipe away every tear from their eyes; and there will no longer be death; there will no longer be sorrow and anguish, or crying, or pain; for the former order of things has passed away."

5 And He who sits on the throne said, "Behold, I am making all things new." Also He said, "Write, for these words are faithful and true [they are accurate, incorruptible, and trustworthy]."

6 And He said to me, "It is done. I am the Alpha and the Omega, the Beginning and the End. To the one who thirsts I will give [water] from the fountain of the water of life without cost.

7 He who overcomes [the world by adhering faithfully to Christ Jesus as Lord and Savior] will inherit these things, and I will be his God and he will be My son.

8 But as for the cowards and unbelieving and abominable [who are devoid of character and personal integrity and practice or tolerate immorality], and murderers, and sorcerers [with intoxicating drugs], and idolaters and occultists [who practice and teach false religions], and all the liars [who knowingly deceive and twist truth], their part will be in the lake that blazes with fire and brimstone, which is the second death."

LIGHT ON THE WORD

Jerusalem. Jerusalem is recorded as being founded by Canaanites (see **Ezekiel 16:3**) and either named after one of their gods (Shalim) or adapted from the Hebrew word "shalom," which means peace. It is purportedly one of the oldest continuously inhabited cities in the world, highly sought after—and fought over. Jerusalem has been besieged, attacked, and captured dozens of times, divided by Jews and Arabs (1948–1967), destroyed twice—and rebuilt. The city was captured by King David and became known as the "city of David" (**2 Samuel 5:7**). It is the place where Solomon's Temple (and subsequent temples) was built, and the place where events leading up to the Crucifixion, the Day of Pentecost, and much of the history of Acts occurred. It is claimed as the rightful possession of both Israeli and Palestinian nationals. Jerusalem is known as the "holy city" for three major world religions: Christianity, Judaism, and Islam.

TEACHING THE BIBLE LESSON

LIFE NEED FOR TODAY'S LESSON

AIM: Students will agree that people look for a place and time where life stresses will not exist.

INTRODUCTION

Last But Not Least

Although Revelation is the last book of the Bible, it is not necessarily chronologically the last book to be written. John's original visions may have occurred shortly before the destruction of the Temple (AD 70), but some aspects of the book suggest that the apocalypse as we know it could also represent visions that occurred after the destruction of the Temple. Similar to portions of Ezekiel and Daniel, the book is apocalyptic literature filled with symbolism, poetry, and prophecy, specifically about the end times. Because of the symbolic language, it can be difficult to understand, and there are many interpretations of how or when particular events will occur (or whether they have occurred already). However, John makes it clear that this is a revelation of Christ, affirming God's sovereignty. This revelation serves as a warning to some, and it provides hope in the second coming of Christ and final victory over sin, Satan, and death for those who believe in Christ. With vivid imagery, he shares about events that will occur, signs of end times, the awesome glory of God, and the beauty of a new Heaven and new earth. **Revelation 21** is one of the last two chapters of the book, and it grants a glimpse of eternity.

BIBLE LEARNING

AIM: Students will agree that the book of Revelation gives us God's redemptive plan for Heaven and earth.

I. ALL NEW (Revelation 21:1–2)

John begins this chapter by sharing his vision of a new Heaven and earth, a fulfillment of **Isaiah 65:17–18**. This could be a restored and wholly cleansed version of God's creation, or it could be an unused, fresh Heaven and earth that replaces the one that was marred by sin and its effects—death, sorrow, and chaos. In the ancient Near East, the sea was a symbol of chaos (the Canaanites said Yam controlled the seas). John notes that the sea no longer exists, thus implying the establishment of complete order in the new creation.

1 And I saw a new heaven and a new earth: for the first heaven and the first earth were passed away; and there was no more sea.

John received a divine revelation from God concerning what He had purposed for the final stage of His created order, the final result of His creating activities. The adjectives "new" and "first" seem to describe a previous and latter cosmos standing in opposition to each other. The previous had "passed away" (Gk. *aperchomai*, **ap-AIR-kho-my**), which means to depart from a location. The sense is that the old Heaven and earth have vanished and disappeared. The latter had come to take its place, and God intends that it stay forever without ever reversing into a negative direction again (**Isaiah 65:17**). John also recognized that there was no more sea. The ancient mind feared the sea as a place of terror and chaos, and it was to be avoided. Evil beasts lurked in the sea, such as Leviathan, who represented the enemies of God. The fact that the sea was gone points toward a new creation that is orderly and absent of conflict and evil.

2 And I John saw the holy city, new Jerusalem, coming down from God out of heaven, prepared as a bride adorned for her husband.

The Apostle John saw the New Jerusalem, God's Holy City, descending from His presence, from Heaven. The city is God's place for renewing and refreshing His people after both their turbulence and success. It has no tears, sorrow, or pain; it is a place where we never die and wickedness is totally shut out. God Himself specially prepared it for His people. John uses a metaphor of a good and promising marriage to describe the power and reality of what the new order brings to God's people. The city is personified as a bride adorned for a husband. The word "adorned" (Gk. *kosmeo*, **KAHS-meh-oh**) is appropriate and fitting for the city; it is also connected with the word for "world" in Greek, from which English gets the word cosmos (Gk. *kosmos*, **KOS-mos**; decoration; order; universe). The careful preparation and arrangement of a bride embodies the gift that God is giving to His people. This is no ordinary city; the new home for God's people is excellent beyond all our human imaginations or dreams. It has been already prepared for us and is waiting for us.

It is the new and permanent place that Christ went ahead to prepare for us (**John 14:2–3**).

II. GOD DWELLS (Revelation 21:3–5)

Now that a new, holy, and perfect Heaven, earth, and Jerusalem have been created, God is free to live among His people. The tabernacle was known as the place where God's glory resided temporarily (**Exodus 25:8**). When the cloud or pillar of fire (God's presence) moved, it indicated when the Israelites should pack up their tents and the Tabernacle, and move along with Him. In Revelation, God from His throne says He will set up His tent and live with the people. Human kings do not reside among the people, but God, reminiscent of the incarnation of Christ who "became flesh, and made his dwelling among us" (**John 1:14**, NIV), chooses to do so.

3 And I heard a great voice out of heaven saying, Behold, the tabernacle of God is with men, and he will dwell with them, and they shall be his people, and God himself shall be with them, and be their God.

God's everlasting presence will be with His people in our new home. God has declared that He will never leave us nor forsake us (**Hebrews 13:5**). This is a reiteration of the covenant promise God gave to His people, which now at the consummation of the age is being fulfilled (**Leviticus 26:11–12**). In fact, the Tabernacle was a symbol of God's dwelling among His people (**Exodus 25:8–9**). However, in our new home, the content and context of God's abiding presence is totally different. The word "tabernacle" (Gk. *skene*, **ske-NAY**) used in this text does not literally mean the physical Temple or sanctuary described in the Old Testament (**Exodus 29:44; 1 Kings 6:12–13**). Rather, it figuratively referred to a dwelling place of God. It includes the idea of God's Kingdom, glory, and power tangibly filling up this "renewed" world that He created for His people. The consequences and impact of a fallen human nature and society will be no more. God's presence in the new world becomes the light that dispels all forces of evil and destruction. The Almighty God will be our provider and protector from all kinds of evil. The concept of "Emmanuel" (God with us) will become an everlasting reality in this new world.

4 And God shall wipe away all tears from their eyes; and there shall be no more death, neither sorrow, nor crying, neither shall there be any more pain: for the former things are passed away. 5 And he that sat upon the throne said, Behold, I make all things new. And he said unto me, Write: for these words are true and faithful.

The fall in Eden brought with it death, sickness, and poverty. The Bible teaches about three types of death: spiritual death is the result of the broken relationship between God and humankind (**Ephesians 2:1** ff.); physical death occurs when our spirit is separated from the body (**James 2:26**); and eternal death occurs when sinners depart forever into condemnation by spending eternity in the lake of fire (**Revelation 20:14–15, 21:8**). But in our new home, the Scriptures reveal that all of these kinds of death "shall be no more."

Sickness is often the evidence of disease. Humankind is broken spiritually, psychologically, and physically. Poverty has stricken society on many levels, expressed spiritually as a lack of the knowledge of God; physically as poor health and malfunctioning of the body; materially as a lack of resources and money; and socially as political vulnerability and social oppression. Poverty has produced misery and mourning in families and society. However, God has promised us that there shall no more be pain in the new world (**Revelation 20:4**).

When we go to our new home, "there shall be no more death, neither sorrow, nor crying." The "former things are passed away" because the fallen world system will be transformed into a new created order where God's entire creation is launched into an era of shalom. This is sealed by God's promising declaration: "Behold, I make all things new."

III. ALL DONE (Revelation 21:6–8)

"It is done!" While the events recorded by John have not yet occurred, this is a promise of completion from the all-powerful, all-knowing One—the Creator who is the beginning (Alpha, the first letter of the Greek alphabet) and the end (Omega, the final letter of the alphabet).

6 And he said unto me, It is done. I am Alpha and Omega, the beginning and the end. I will give unto him that is athirst of the fountain of the water of life freely.

The descent of the New Jerusalem from Heaven and its attendant blessings is now considered accomplished as God tells John, "It is done." God further says, "I am Alpha and Omega, the beginning and the end." This claim was previously made by the risen Christ in **Revelation 1:8**. Again John hears the same voice that the great prophets had heard: "I am the first, and I am the last; besides me there is no God" (from **Isaiah 44:6**). This figure of speech, called a merism, states the opposite poles of something in order to emphasize the totality of all that lies between. Alpha is the first letter of the Greek alphabet, and omega is the last. God is the beginning and the end. The word for "beginning" is *arche* (**ar-KHAY**). It does not simply mean first in point of time, but it means the source of all things. The word for "end" is *telos* (**TEH-loce**). It does not simply mean the end as a point of time, but it means the end as the completed goal. John is saying that all life begins in God and ends in God. Paul expresses the same thing in **Romans 11:36** and **Ephesians 4:6**.

To the announcement is added the promise of the "living water" or "the water of life," which may refer both to spiritual life now and eternal life in the new Heaven and new earth. In the same manner as in the Gospel of John, this is an invitation to the spiritually thirsty to come and drink of the "water of life," but here and in **22:17** John adds "freely" (Gk. *dorean*, **do-reh-AN**). This word comes from the noun *doron* (**doh-rahn**), which means gift. The water of life is a gift that can be taken freely. This may also reflect Isaiah 55:1, which adds to the invitation "come to the waters" and the further promise, "And you who have no money, come, buy, and eat" (NASB).

7 He that overcometh shall inherit all things; and I will be his God, and he shall be my son.

The section concludes with a challenge to the readers to recognize the difference between those who are faithful and those who are not; that is, to decide whether to be an overcomer (**v. 7**) or a "coward" (**v. 8**, NLT). The opening, "he that overcometh," is drawn from the conclusion of each of the seven letters in **Revelation 2–3**, where it is followed by the promises given to all those who were victorious over the world with its temptations and suffering. The exalted Christ promises that the overcomers, who remain faithful in the face of opposition, will eat from the tree of life (**2:7**), escape the second death (**2:11**), receive a new name (**2:17**), receive authority over the nations (**2:26**), remain in the book of life (**3:5**), be eternally united with God in the heavenly city (**3:12**), and share the rule of Christ (**3:21**). The overcomers shall inherit these blessings of the eternal state. The language of overcoming or triumph in the messages to the seven churches seems to be echoed closely in the scene here. To these blessings of eternity is added the gift of life-giving water from a sovereign God (**v. 6**). The last part of the verse sums up both the Abrahamic and Davidic covenants. In Genesis, God established a covenant with Abraham "to be your God and the God of your descendants after you" (from **Genesis 17:7,**

NIV), and to David, He made a promise concerning Solomon: "I will be his father, and he will be my son" (from **2 Samuel 7:14**, NIV). The covenant is fulfilled to all who are Abraham's heir by faith (**Galatians 3:29**). God declares that the overcomer will be His child, and He will be their God. This expresses the intimate relationship between the Saints and God. Hearers will experience the fulfillment of the promise for the end times that the overcomer will become a "son" of God. What a staggering promise and joyous hope!

8 But the fearful, and unbelieving, and the abominable, and murderers, and whoremongers, and sorcerers, and idolaters, and all liars, shall have their part in the lake which burneth with fire and brimstone: which is the second death.

In contrast to the overcomers in **verse 7** are all those who cowered in the face of persecution and joined the company of sinners. Here we see the character of those who follow sin instead of the Lamb, and wish to exclude themselves from the presence of God in the New Jerusalem. The fact that the list begins with the fearful and ends with "all liars" suggests that the list is not a general statement about cowardice and falsehood, but instead it defines those who compromise with truth and righteousness.

The verse concludes with the eternal destiny of those who exclude themselves from the life of the new covenant. Those who only appeared to profess Christ but were not truly saved will go to "the lake which burneth with fire and brimstone: which is the second death." This is not a statement of the destiny of the wicked, who have already been cast into the lake of fire (**20:15**). It is a warning to those who continually, deliberately, habitually practice sin (**1 John 3:9**). True salvation is evidenced by a transformed lifestyle, and with it, the promise of eternal security. True salvation is more than just words. It is how we live day to day. To believe and not obey is not yet to believe. The Bible warns, "Be not deceived" (**1 Corinthians 6:9**).

The water images of this passage form a stark contrast. In the end, believers will drink from the water of life. Unbelievers will be thrown into the lake of fire (**21:6**).

SEARCH THE SCRIPTURES

QUESTION 1
The location of the New Jerusalem is on earth (**Revelation 21:3**). How does this compare with popular perceptions of the afterlife?

The afterlife is popularly depicted as up high in the clouds, not on the earth.

QUESTION 2
In the new Heaven and new earth, everything will be made new (**v. 5**). If everything will be made new, can we neglect to take care of this present world?

No, we are responsible for God's creation.

LIGHT ON THE WORD
Water of Life
No one can survive without physical water. Christ uses the "water of life" metaphor to demonstrate the need for us to quench our spiritual thirst through Him (**John 4:10, 14**). For those who thirst for Him, He offers this water—eternal life. Those who belong to Him will be children of God and inherit all the blessings already mentioned: new Heaven and earth, eternal life free of pain, sorrow, and tears. In contrast, those who choose a sinful life apart from Him—fearful of a commitment to Him, rejecting Him, not believing, worshiping false gods, and living in sexual immorality—are destined for a place far worse, a place filled with pain and a second death.

BIBLE APPLICATION

AIM: Students will appreciate the vision of hope that God gives for their future life.

We are drawn to things that are new: new homes, new clothes, new jobs, new babies, and new cars (even a new car smell). There is something appealing about starting over; it provides hope, anticipation, a clearer outlook, and excitement. We appreciate newness. If such excitement exists in receiving new temporal things, which are here today and gone, broken, stolen, or old tomorrow, how much more excited should we be about the forthcoming new Heaven and new earth?

STUDENTS' RESPONSES

AIM: Students will anticipate God wiping away the tears from their eyes.

Life is full of suffering and difficulty, but this passage provides hope for a new, perfect world. We are often so focused on the present that we ignore that there is an eternity. When things are going well, we are content with the present. When we struggle, we strive to find a solution for the present. What challenges do you face now that viewing eternity helps you to put it into perspective? What decisions do you believe you need to make now in light of what is to come? Have you accepted Christ? Are you free of a lifestyle described in verse 8? If you have, are there people in your life that you need to tell about Jesus? Pray for courage to share your faith with others.

PRAYER

Father, You are a holy God who will one day judge the earth. We believe Your Word and abandon all excuses for practicing a lifestyle of sin. In the Name of Jesus we pray. Amen.

HOW TO SAY IT

Apocalyptic.   ah-pah-ka-**LIP**-tik.

Whoremongers.   **HOR**-mun-gers.

Abominable.   uh-**BAH**-mi-nuh-buhl.

DIG A LITTLE DEEPER

This section provides an additional research article to further your study of the lesson:

In this article, the author recounts that an African student studying in the States chose to preach about the joys of Heaven. The student explained why: "I've seen the great wealth that is here… I've listened to many sermons… But I've yet to hear one sermon about Heaven." His rationale? "Because everyone has so much in this country, no one preaches about Heaven. In my country most people have very little, so we preach on Heaven all the time." This article reminds the Christian of the call to be faithful, to be obedient, and to live with the expectation of spending eternity with Jesus Christ our Savior in a new Heaven and a new earth.

https://bible.org/seriespage/29-it-just-doesn-t-get-any-better-revelation-211-225

PREPARE FOR NEXT SUNDAY

Read **Revelation 21:9–14, 22–27** and "I See A New Jerusalem."

DAILY HOME BIBLE READINGS

MONDAY
God Will Dwell Among Them
(Exodus 29:42–46)

TUESDAY
Who May Live With God?
(Psalm 15)

WEDNESDAY
Life in the New Heaven and Earth
(Isaiah 65:20–25)

THURSDAY
Those Who Believe Have Eternal Life
(John 6:35–40)

FRIDAY
Mercy of Jesus Leads to Eternal Life
(Jude 20–25)

SATURDAY
God Will Wipe Away All Tears
(Revelation 7:13–17)

SUNDAY
Everything's Brand New
(Revelation 21:1–8)

COMMENTS / NOTES:

_____

_____

_____

_____

_____

_____

_____

_____

_____

_____

_____

_____

_____

_____

_____

_____

_____

_____

I SEE A NEW JERUSALEM

BIBLE BASIS: REVELATION 21:9–14, 22–27

BIBLE TRUTH: God has provided a new place for believers that is filled with His light and glory.

MEMORY VERSE: "And I saw no temple therein: for the Lord God Almighty and the Lamb are the temple of it. And the city had no need of the sun, neither of the moon, to shine in it: for the glory of God did lighten it, and the Lamb is the light thereof" (Revelation 21:22–23).

LESSON AIM: By the end of the lesson, we will: EXPLORE the possibility of living in a new place, even in another dimension of life; IMAGINE the richness and serenity of living in the New Jerusalem; and CELEBRATE God's provision of a new place for believers at the end of all things temporal and throughout eternity.

TEACHER PREPARATION

MATERIALS NEEDED: Quarterly Commentary/Teacher Manual, Adult Quarterly, Adult resources—charts, worksheets, and other teaching tools, paper, pens, pencils, Bibles (several different versions)

OTHER MATERIALS NEEDED / TEACHER'S NOTES:

_____

_____

LESSON OVERVIEW

LIFE NEED FOR TODAY'S LESSON
People have a hard time imaging living somewhere other than their home.

BIBLE LEARNING
God is always providing ways to give us peace and hope.

BIBLE APPLICATION
John gives us an opportunity to understand who will not enter into the New Jerusalem, the Holy City.

STUDENTS' RESPONSES
Believers can trust that God has already prepared a beautiful place for His people to live with Him for eternity.

LESSON SCRIPTURE

REVELATION 21:9–14, 22–27, KJV

9 And there came unto me one of the seven angels which had the seven vials full of the seven last plagues, and talked with me, saying, Come hither, I will shew thee the

REVELATION 21:9–14, 22–27, AMP

9 Then one of the seven angels who had the seven bowls filled with the seven final plagues came and spoke with me, saying, "Come here, I will show you the bride, the bride, the Lamb's wife.

10 And he carried me away in the spirit to a great and high mountain, and shewed me that great city, the holy Jerusalem, descending out of heaven from God,

11 Having the glory of God: and her light was like unto a stone most precious, even like a jasper stone, clear as crystal;

12 And had a wall great and high, and had twelve gates, and at the gates twelve angels, and names written thereon, which are the names of the twelve tribes of the children of Israel:

13 On the east three gates; on the north three gates; on the south three gates; and on the west three gates.

14 And the wall of the city had twelve foundations, and in them the names of the twelve apostles of the Lamb.

22 And I saw no temple therein: for the Lord God Almighty and the Lamb are the temple of it.

23 And the city had no need of the sun, neither of the moon, to shine in it: for the glory of God did lighten it, and the Lamb is the light thereof.

24 And the nations of them which are saved shall walk in the light of it: and the kings of the earth do bring their glory and honour into it.

25 And the gates of it shall not be shut at all by day: for there shall be no night there.

26 And they shall bring the glory and honour of the nations into it.

27 And there shall in no wise enter into it any thing that defileth, neither whatsoever worketh abomination, or maketh a lie: but

wife of the Lamb."

10 And he carried me away in the Spirit to a vast and lofty mountain, and showed me the holy (sanctified) city of Jerusalem coming down out of heaven from God,

11 having God's glory [filled with His radiant light]. The brilliance of it resembled a rare and very precious jewel, like jasper, shining and clear as crystal.

12 It had a massive and high wall, with twelve [large] gates, and at the gates [were stationed] twelve angels; and on the gates the names of the twelve tribes of the sons of Israel were written.

13 On the east side [there were] three gates, on the north three gates, on the south three gates, and on the west three gates.

14 And the wall of the city had twelve foundation stones, and on them the twelve names of the twelve apostles of the Lamb (Christ).

22 I saw no temple in it, for the Lord God Almighty [the Omnipotent, the Ruler of all] and the Lamb are its temple.

23 And the city has no need of the sun nor of the moon to give light to it, for the glory (splendor, radiance) of God has illumined it, and the Lamb is its lamp and light.

24 The nations [the redeemed people from the earth] will walk by its light, and the kings of the earth will bring into it their glory.

25 By day (for there will be no night there) its gates will never be closed [in fear of evil];

26 and they will bring the glory (splendor, majesty) and the honor of the nations into it;

27 and nothing that defiles or profanes or is unwashed will ever enter it, nor anyone who

they which are written in the Lamb's book of life.

practices abominations [detestable, morally repugnant things] and lying, but only those [will be admitted] whose names have been written in the Lamb's Book of Life.

LIGHT ON THE WORD

Rome. Rome was a society that practiced cultic worship of the emperor. They believed that this loyalty to the emperor assured Roman prosperity. The Christian proclamation that Jesus is Lord was viewed as a threat to Roman society and led to the persecution of Christians as a result of the Great Fire of Rome in AD 64. Rome was becoming more intolerant of other religions, leading to rebellion against Rome in Jerusalem.

The Apostle John was exiled to the island of Patmos as punishment for his outspoken beliefs about Christ that were contrary to the Roman empire. It is during his exile on Patmos that John received his revelation.

TEACHING THE BIBLE LESSON

LIFE NEED FOR TODAY'S LESSON

AIM: Students will agree that "home" is the best place to be.

INTRODUCTION

A Picture of Perfection

The heavenly city that John saw is a picture of perfection. It has perfect dimensions, beautifully adorned with precious gems and gold. The angel that spoke to John referred to the city as "the bride." In our lesson, we see the bride clothed in splendor and adorned in precious jewels. The heavenly city is protected with high, fortified walls. The twelve gates to the city are covered by twelve angels in order to ensure the city remains pure and unspoiled. The twelve gates echo the twelve gates in Ezekiel's new city, which represent the twelve tribes of Israel and the complete inclusion of God's people (**Ezekiel 48:30–35**).

BIBLE LEARNING

AIM: Students will agree that God is always providing ways to give us peace and hope.

I. THE RIGHT FOUNDATION (Revelation 21:9–14)

One of the most interesting facts about the city is that it is built on twelve foundations, each one bearing the name of one of the twelve apostles, the first bearers of the Gospel. This is because only through the Gospel can one become a citizen of this heavenly city. Revelation identifies the heavenly city as a place free from tears and heartaches, and ultimately free from sin. In the heavenly city, we can experience God's presence and glory without constraints. This can happen only through our belief in the Good News of Jesus Christ.

9 And there came unto me one of the seven angels which had the seven vials full of the seven last plagues, and talked with me, saying, Come hither, I will show thee the bride, the Lamb's wife.

The pouring out of the last plagues from these vials signifies the final series of God's judgment, the conclusion of His wrath. After these, John told us of the fall of Babylon (**Revelation 17–18**), the triumph of the heavenly army led by

Christ (**Revelation 19**), the binding, incarceration, and final judgment of Satan (**Revelation 20**), and then the passing away (the transformation) of the first Heaven and earth, which were replaced by a new Heaven and earth (**Revelation 21:1**). After this renewal, John beholds the Holy City, the New Jerusalem (**v. 2**).

In **verse 9**, the angel invites John to come, proposing to show him the Lamb's wife, the bride (Gk. *numphe*, **NOOM-fay**, a betrothed or newly married young woman). The "bride" usually in the New Testament refers to the Church, showing the close relationship between the Church and Christ, the bridegroom. Marriage imagery is used in the Old Testament to show a similar relationship between God and Israel; the word "bride" is one of the most important words used to refer to the Church. It normally signifies the relationship between Christ and the Church; here, however, we will see that the "bride" is the Holy City of the New Jerusalem.

10 And he carried me away in the Spirit to a great and high mountain, and shewed me that great city, the holy Jerusalem, descending out of heaven from God.

This verse runs parallel with **verse 2**, where John described this city using a personifying marital analogy, saying the city was "prepared as a bride adorned for her husband." This city is called "the bride" and "the Lamb's wife" (**21:2, 9**), just as the Church is also referred to as the Lamb's wife in **Revelation 19:7**. The fact that the same word is used for both the Church and the city points to a significant likeness. The earthly Jerusalem has been called to be the City of God (**Psalm 48:1–2**), the Holy City (**Isaiah 52:1; Matthew 4:5**), and the city where God has chosen to put His Name (**2 Chronicles 6:6**). Today it is the most famous holy city in the world and aptly called the "spiritual capital of the world." The earthly Jerusalem is a prefiguration of the New Jerusalem from Heaven.

11 Having the glory of God: and her light was like unto a stone most precious, even like a jasper stone, clear as crystal; 12 And had a wall great and high, and had twelve gates, and at the gates twelve angels, and names written thereon, which are the names of the twelve tribes of the children of Israel: 13 On the east three gates; on the north three gates; on the south three gates; and on the west three gates. 14 And the wall of the city had twelve foundations, and in them the names of the twelve apostles of the Lamb.

The holy Jerusalem is a city out of Heaven. It is not Heaven, but it possesses the features of Heaven. It is the dwelling place of the resurrected bodies of the Church (the redeemed bride), God, and Christ (**Revelation 21:3, 22:3**). In the Upper Room, Jesus promised to go prepare a place for His followers (**John 14:2–3**). This city is undoubtedly the promised prepared place for the redeemed bride. Our bodies are our temporary habitations for our spirits and souls (**2 Corinthians 5:1–8**). Our earthly homes are also temporary, but we have a final dwelling place: the Holy City, a wonderful place Jesus has prepared for us in Heaven.

When God called Abraham to leave his country, God promised him he would possess a foreign country. Although he never saw this promise fulfilled, in **Hebrews 11:10** the author infers that Abraham had a preview of the heavenly city, which sustained his faith. The heavenly city has been the destination of all those who live lives of faith.

SEARCH THE SCRIPTURES

QUESTION 1

Why is the New Jerusalem identified as the "bride" (**Revelation 21:9**)?

The city is prepared like a bride for her husband, and both the earthly Jerusalem and the New Jerusalem are the City of God.

LIGHT ON THE WORD

John's Vision of Heaven

John's vision of Heaven is told from two points of view: from Heaven and from earth. **Revelation 21:9** tells the narrative from the earthly viewpoint. Here John is approached by one of the seven angels who had the seven vials (or bowls) full of the seven last plagues. We are first introduced to these angels in **Revelation 15**, where one of the four beasts in Heaven gave them the seven golden vials full of the seven last plagues, which are also called the wrath of God.

II. LIVING IN GOD'S LIGHT (Revelation 21:22–27)

Our passage begins with the observation that the heavenly city has no temple. Initially, this seems odd. One would assume that the city that God created where He would dwell forever with humanity would have a temple dedicated for worship. However, the heavenly city is the place where God's presence is continually experienced fully and equally; no place in the Holy City will be more sacred or holy than any other. When we experience God's presence on earth, worship flows naturally. The only thing restricting this experience wherever we are is our own tendency to get distracted by earthly concerns. If we decide to seek out opportunities to focus on God and His goodness in our lives, we can gradually transform worship from a weekly experience to a daily lifestyle.

22 And I saw no temple therein: for the Lord God Almighty and the Lamb are the temple of it.

John tells us here that the city lacks a temple. What is translated as "temple" here is the Greek word *naos* (**nah-OS**). This refers to the inner sanctuary where only the priest could lawfully enter, and it is contrasted with *hieron* (**heer-ON**), which also means temple, but denotes the entire temple complex with all its courts and auxiliary buildings. Naos, the inner sanctuary or Holy of Holies, is the location of the Ark of the Covenant in the Mosaic tabernacle and Solomon's Temple. This is the place where God manifested His presence. This city does not need a temple because God's manifest presence would be experienced by all. There would be no need for a house, because the entire new creation would be His household. The Lord and the Lamb would be eternally worshiped in the heavenly city. There would be no need for rituals or sacrifices. It will be a place where everyone will experience the unmediated presence of God.

23 And the city had no need of the sun, neither of the moon, to shine in it: for the glory of God did lighten it, and the Lamb is the light thereof. 24 And the nations of them which are saved shall walk in the light of it: and the kings of the earth do bring their glory and honor into it.

John further tells us that the city has no need of the natural light of the sun and moon. While these two agents of light are the main illuminators of planet Earth, they can also cause some discomfort to the people below. God's desire to shield His people from the scorching effects of the light of the sun and moon is expressed by David: "the sun shall not smite thee by day, nor the moon by night. The LORD shall preserve thee from all evil: he shall preserve thy soul" (**Psalm 121:6–7**). This desire is ultimately fulfilled in the New Jerusalem.

The sun's light and heat will not be needed in the Holy City. In the New Jerusalem, the glory of God and the Lamb is declared here to be greater and more enduring and blissful than sunlight and moonlight. Sun and moon are features of the Heaven and earth that will pass away (**Revelation 21:1**). The Greek word translated "glory" is *doxa* (**DOX-ah**), used here to denote the supernatural brightness or splendor emanating from God; this is the brightness manifested in Christ when He was transfigured (**Matthew 17:1–2**). This glory will illuminate the city, and cause it to shine on the entire face of the earth; the saved nations shall "walk in the light of it." The nations will not need any light from heavenly bodies but only light from one source—God and the Lamb.

25 And the gates of it shall not be shut at all by day: for there shall be no night there. 26 And they shall bring the glory and honor of the nations into it.

The promise (actually a prophecy) in **Isaiah 60:11** continues here with the description of the city's gates. Open gates indicate admittance and readiness; here they mean constant coming and going, with no need to close.

The sun and moon will no longer impose a set time to shut the gates of the Holy City. Thus, the absence of these heavenly bodies means the absence of day and night. Here again is a reference to the nations, presumably through the agency of kings (**v. 24**), bringing glory and honor to the Holy City. The word "glory" here is the same word used to refer to God in **vv. 23–24**. Glory and honor here are associated with the nations, or the various peoples who are not from the tribes of Israel. What is most precious and esteemed from the peoples of the earth is now being brought into the holy city to join with the glory of God.

27 And there shall in no wise enter into it any thing that defileth, neither whatsoever worketh abomination, or maketh a lie: but they which are written in the Lamb's book of life.

By designation, the New Jerusalem is called "the Holy City," and in accordance to this name, there is a divine restriction against anything that defiles or causes abomination and lies. The Greek word translated "defileth," *koinoo* (**koy-NO-o**), means to render unholy, to make common, pollute, or make unclean. This refers to things and practices that would defile the city by rendering it common or ordinary. The Holy City assumes the status of the Holy of Holies; it is a place of great beauty, lavishly built with precious stones, so nothing unclean would enter it. The word translated "abomination" is *bdelugma* (**BDEL-oog-mah**), and it denotes an object of disgust or an idolatrous object. This term is used for idols. God and the Lord Jesus are the only objects of worship in the Holy City. No idol will be there. In Ezekiel's vision, he was made to see "where the idol that provokes to jealousy stood" at the entrance of the Temple's inner court facing the north (**Ezekiel 8:3**, NIV). The image of the beast is also called "the abomination that causes desolation." There will be no abomination in the Holy City.

The word translated "lie" is *pseudos* (**PSYOO-dos**), simply meaning falsehood or something not true. Jesus is the Truth; anything contrary to Him is a lie and will not enter the Holy City.

Any creature or act that is described as something that "defileth" or an "abomination" or a "lie" is forbidden entry into the Holy City. This divine restriction brings about an ultimate realization of a city devoid of evil. It is an end times fulfillment of God's prescribed course of conduct for human life. This prescribed course, prophesied in **Isaiah 35:8**, is laid down in its entirety in the faith we profess as Christians and will be perfectly realized in the Holy City.

SEARCH THE SCRIPTURES

QUESTION 2
John lists those who will be excluded from the heavenly city (**v. 27**). How do we evaluate whether we will be included in the heavenly city?

Nothing unclean or contrary to Jesus' holiness will not enter the city.

QUESTION 3

It is very easy for us to lose hope when our faith is tested or shaken. How does belief in the coming heavenly city help to strengthen our faith?

We have an eternal hope. Answers will vary.

LIGHT ON THE WORD

The Temple Destroyed

Jesus foretold the destruction of the Temple in **Matthew 24:2**. The Jewish historian Josephus provides us with a firsthand account of what happened. In response to the Jews' revolt, Rome laid siege to the city and captured the Fortress of Antonia just north of the Temple Mount in AD 70. Shortly thereafter they attacked the Temple and set fire to the gates. The Jews lost hope, and soon Jerusalem was in flames. After this time of civil unrest, persecution, and loss, John the apostle received a revelation from God. This revelation is of God being ultimately triumphant over the enemies of His people, and of the New Jerusalem, which will make the other one pale in comparison.

BIBLE APPLICATION

AIM: Students will agree that John gives us an opportunity to know who cannot enter into the New Jerusalem, the Holy City.

The heavenly city had 12 gates that were always open. This image serves as a reminder of God's desire for everyone to come into His presence and have a relationship with Him. As we strive to build our lives on a solid foundation, let us not forget to reach out to someone else and let them know that God is welcoming them to also come into His presence with open arms.

STUDENTS' RESPONSES

AIM: Students will have hope that God has already prepared a beautiful place for His people to live with Him for eternity.

It is very easy for us to lose hope when our faith is tested or shaken. How does belief in the coming heavenly city help to strengthen our faith?

PRAYER

O, Lord, how excellent is Your Name in all the universe! We marvel at the beauty of the New Jerusalem. Thank You for salvation that assures us we will live with You in the New Jerusalem! In the Name of Jesus we pray. Amen!

HOW TO SAY IT

Jasper.   jas-**PUR**.

Defileth.   di-**FY**-lith.

DIG A LITTLE DEEPER

This section provides an additional research article to further your study of the lesson:

This brief article paints a poignant picture of the end times. The author directs us to a time of corporal worship before God, a time when the Body of Christ will unify in worship and praise.

http://www.desiringgod.org/articles/
the-closing-ceremonies-and-the-end-of-history

PREPARE FOR NEXT SUNDAY

Read **Revelation 22:1–7** and "Living Waters."

DAILY HOME BIBLE READINGS

MONDAY
The First Heaven and Earth
(Genesis 1:28–2:3)

TUESDAY
The Glory of God Will Return
(Ezekiel 43:1–9)

WEDNESDAY
Dwellers in the New Jerusalem
(Revelation 3:10–12)

THURSDAY
Missing from the Holy City
(Revelation 21:1–4)

FRIDAY
City of the Alpha and Omega
(Revelation 21:5–8)

SATURDAY
The Architectural Splendor
of the New Jerusalem
(Revelation 21:15–21)

SUNDAY
I See a New Jerusalem
(Revelation 21:9–14, 22–27)

COMMENTS / NOTES:

LIVING WATERS

BIBLE BASIS: REVELATION 22:1–7

BIBLE TRUTH: In the new creation, God's power in the river of life has spiritual healing.

MEMORY VERSE: "And he shewed me a pure river of water of life, clear as crystal, proceeding out of the throne of God and of the Lamb" (Revelation 22:1).

LESSON AIM: By the end of the lesson, we will: RESEARCH the biblical references to the river of life to learn its spiritual and symbolic meaning; APPRECIATE that in the river of life is God's continual provision; and RESPOND to the river of life through acceptance, faith, and entrance into the fullness of the Kingdom.

TEACHER PREPARATION

MATERIALS NEEDED: Quarterly Commentary/Teacher Manual, Adult Quarterly, Adult resources—charts, worksheets, and other teaching tools, paper, pens, pencils, Bibles (several different versions)

OTHER MATERIALS NEEDED / TEACHER'S NOTES:

_____

_____

LESSON OVERVIEW

LIFE NEED FOR TODAY'S LESSON
People are aware that rivers give life and nourishment to the things that exist around them.

BIBLE APPLICATION
The river will nourish and heal everything in the city.

BIBLE LEARNING
God's power will be in the river.

STUDENTS' RESPONSES
Christians are assured of the ultimate happy ending—a triumphal procession in Christ.

LESSON SCRIPTURE

REVELATION 22:1–7, KJV

1 And he shewed me a pure river of water of life, clear as crystal, proceeding out of the throne of God and of the Lamb.

2 In the midst of the street of it, and on either side of the river, was there the tree of life, which bare twelve manner of fruits, and yielded her fruit every month: and the leaves of the tree were for the healing of the nations.

REVELATION 22:1–7, AMP

1 Then the angel showed me a river of the water of life, clear as crystal, flowing from the throne of God and of the Lamb (Christ),

2 in the middle of its street. On either side of the river was the tree of life, bearing twelve kinds of fruit, yielding its fruit every month; and the leaves of the tree were for the healing of the nations.

3 And there shall be no more curse: but the throne of God and of the Lamb shall be in it; and his servants shall serve him:

4 And they shall see his face; and his name shall be in their foreheads.

5 And there shall be no night there; and they need no candle, neither light of the sun; for the Lord God giveth them light: and they shall reign for ever and ever.

6 And he said unto me, These sayings are faithful and true: and the Lord God of the holy prophets sent his angel to shew unto his servants the things which must shortly be done.

7 Behold, I come quickly: blessed is he that keepeth the sayings of the prophecy of this book.

3 There will no longer exist anything that is cursed [because sin and illness and death are gone]; and the throne of God and of the Lamb will be in it, and His bond-servants will serve and worship Him [with great awe and joy and loving devotion];

4 they will [be privileged to] see His face, and His name will be on their foreheads.

5 And there will no longer be night; they have no need for lamplight or sunlight, because the Lord God will illumine them; and they will reign [as kings] forever and ever.

6 Then he said to me, "These words are faithful and true." And the Lord, the God of the spirits of the prophets, has sent His angel [as a representative] to show His bond-servants the things that must soon take place.

7 "And behold, I am coming quickly. Blessed (happy, prosperous, to be admired) is the one who heeds and takes to heart and remembers the words of the prophecy [that is, the predictions, consolations, and warnings] contained in this book (scroll)."

LIGHT ON THE WORD

Bride. The imagery of the bride is used widely in the Bible as a description of the people of God. In the Old Testament, the prophets presented Israel as a bride who had committed repeated adulteries (**Jeremiah 3; Ezekiel 16; Hosea 3**). The prophets also proclaimed that God was faithful to His unfaithful bride and would restore her (**Isaiah 61:10**). In the book of Revelation, bride imagery is used often for the church and her relationship to Christ. The bride belongs to Christ, who is the Bridegroom (**Matthew 9:15**). In Revelation, the church, as the bride of the Lamb, has prepared herself for marriage by performing righteous deeds (**19:7–8**). In **Revelation 21**, the great wedding is portrayed with the church prepared for her Bridegroom (**21:2, 9**). The bride pictured here has not earned her status through righteous deeds. These acts were the church's obedient response to God's saving grace. The garments of righteousness were given to her.

TEACHING THE BIBLE LESSON

LIFE NEED FOR TODAY'S LESSON

AIM: Students will agree that rivers give life and nourishment to the things that exist around them.

INTRODUCTION

Jesus Will Return

The first part of **Revelation 22** portrays, in visions and images, the wonderful future awaiting God's people in the new Heaven and the new earth. Drawing heavily on the book of Isaiah, John's vision concludes by showing the certainty of the promise. Just as the prophecies of the Old Testament have been fulfilled in Christ's first coming, so the prophecy of Revelation will be ultimately fulfilled through Christ's second coming. And just as Christ's first coming was great news for some (the poor in spirit, who believed in Him) and bad news for others (the proud of heart, who rejected Him), so also His unstoppable second coming will be wonderful news for those who belong to Christ, and woeful news for those who spurn the message of His Gospel.

BIBLE LEARNING

AIM: Students will evaluate the significance of the river of water of life in the Holy City.

I. THE GLORIOUS ABUNDANCE OF GOD'S PEOPLE (Revelation 22:1–5)

To paint a picture of the greatest possible abundance and blessing, John's vision returns to the place of God's original purpose: the Garden of Eden. Just as is true in Eden (**Genesis 2:10**), a life-giving river flows in the New Jerusalem; this "water of life" symbolizes the everlasting life given by God through the Spirit (see **John 7:37–39**) and the abundant life Jesus promises in **John 10:10**. Just as the tree of life stood in Eden (**Genesis 2:9**) as a sign of perfect fruitfulness and the provision of every human need, it will also stand in the New Jerusalem amidst the river, represented by twelve trees (a number symbolizing divine government and completeness).

1 And he shewed me a pure river of water of life, clear as crystal, proceeding out of the throne of God and of the Lamb.

John's vision in the Spirit continues (cf. **Revelation 21:10**). He is being made to have a panoramic view of the Holy City. He is shown a pure river containing the water of life. The Sons of Korah spoke prophetically of this river: "There is a river, the streams whereof shall make glad the city of God, the holy place of the tabernacles of the most High" (**Psalm 46:4**). The Greek word translated "river" is *potamos* (**pot-am-OS**), which means running water, like a stream, flood, or river. The Sons of Korah reveal to us in that passage that the river makes glad the city of God. It is the water of life that brings the life of God. This river had been foreshadowed by the river in the Garden of Eden (**Genesis 2:10**). The river from the millennial temple (**Ezekiel 47:1–12**) also foreshadows this river; it brings life to all creatures wherever it flows. Zechariah also prophesied the issuing out of "living waters" from Jerusalem (**Zechariah 14:8**). A figurative reference to this river that Jesus makes describes one of the greatest spiritual realities of the Christian faith: the outpouring, deposit, and flow of the Holy Spirit in the life of the believer (**John 7:38**).

2 In the midst of the street of it, and on either side of the river, was there the tree of life, which bare twelve manner of fruits, and yielded her fruit every month: and the leaves of the tree were for the healing of the nations.

The New Jerusalem is naturally prefigured by the Garden of Eden, the first place where humans lived in their innocence. Both have rivers, and Eden is the first place where the tree of life was mentioned. Everything in the Holy City is of the greatest proportion, being the most perfect reality compared to other references or similarities in the Bible, which are mere foreshadowings. For instance, the Bible talks about one tree of life in the middle of the Garden of Eden, but here numerous trees abound on both sides of the river. The tree of life conferred immortality on anyone who ate its fruit, hence its name (**Genesis 3:22**). In Ezekiel's vision, he revealed that the fruit of the tree of life was meant for food and healing (**Ezekiel 47:12**). Here John tells us the same thing: the fruits and leaves are for the healing of the nations. This tree is said to bear twelve kinds of fruit every month. As a tree of life, it bears fruit to confer immortality on its eater and maintain life in the Holy City. The Bible metaphorically calls four things the tree of life: wisdom (**Proverbs 3:18**), the fruit of righteousness (**Proverbs 11:30**), fulfilled desire (**Proverbs 13:12**), and a wholesome tongue (**Proverbs 15:4**). These things are all described as giving life to those who partake of them. The same can be said of this tree in Revelation, except that the life that this tree gives is eternal.

3 And there shall be no more curse: but the throne of God and the Lamb shall be in it: and his servants shall serve him: 4 And they shall see his face; and his name shall be in their foreheads.

The worst thing a person can say to someone else is a curse. The Greek word translated "curse" here is *katanathema* (**kah-tah-NAH-theh-mah**), meaning a wish that evil may befall a person. Curses served as protective and punitive measures against violating the terms of a treaty; they were intended to doom a person to calamity or destruction. The Curse in the Garden of Eden was a divine judgment against humankind's disobedience. But in the Holy City, curses have no place. The occupants of this city are not objects of divine wrath and punishment, so no disaster can come upon them. They are the redeemed who have qualified as occupants of the New Jerusalem by their faith in Christ and have distinguished themselves with lives above sin, curse, and calamity. The New Jerusalem will offer ultimate bliss to the believer, the greatest rewards and privileges that are not available in our present world. The throne of God and Christ will be there, bringing the habitation, presence, and direct government of God to the redeemed. Most blessedly of all, the "divine prohibition" will end. God's order that forbids humanity from seeing His face will no longer exist. This Old Testament order, communicated by God to Moses, stated: "Thou canst not see my face: for there shall no man see me, and live" (from **Exodus 33:20**). Over the ages the physical sight of God had been denied to humans, because the consequence was death. But in the New Jerusalem, there will be a new order: God's servants will serve Him, and they will see His face and behold Him physically. This is because those who live in the Holy City will be completely transformed to be like God (**1 John 3:2**). They will be absent of sin, and their bodies will be changed (**1 Corinthians 15:51–53**). His name (seal of ownership) will be on their foreheads.

5 And there shall be no night there; and they need no candle, neither light of the sun; for the Lord God giveth them light: and they shall reign for ever and ever.

In the beginning, God created light. This light came from the two main heavenly bodies (sun and moon), and came about on day four. One of their functions was to bring about day and night (**Genesis 1:14**). Here the passage says there shall be no night. Figuratively, the night stands for various periods and conditions in human life: a time of ignorance and helplessness (**Micah 3:6**), the depraved condition of humankind (**1 Thessalonians 5:5–7**), and also a time of inactivity or death (**John 9:4**). In the Holy City, there will be no ignorance, the depraved conditions of humankind will not exist, and death will be no more.

SEARCH THE SCRIPTURES

QUESTION 1

How will we benefit from the curse being removed from creation (**Revelation 22:3**)?

We will have ultimate bliss there, and be free from divine wrath and punishment.

QUESTION 2

How would you evaluate your awareness and expectancy that Jesus is coming soon (**v. 7**)?

Answers will vary.

LIGHT ON THE WORD

Spiritual Freedom

Paul refers to the "Jerusalem which is above" when pointing out the Christian's spiritual status of freedom from the law's curse. The author of Hebrews speaks of a "heavenly Jerusalem" (**Hebrews 12:22**) to denote the beauty and security of the New Covenant. The book of Revelation refers to "the holy city new Jerusalem" (**21:2**) and "that great city, the holy Jerusalem, descending out of heaven from God" (**v. 10**). Here the angel identifies the city with the bride, the church. The following description, in which Jerusalem is massive and radiant with jewels and perfect in symmetry, shows the wonderful destiny of God's people, when He will dwell among them forever.

II. THE GLORIOUS PROMISE OF GOD (vv. 6–7)

The words of the Bible can be hard to hang on to because the promises are so otherworldly and our sight is so limited. God in His mercy frequently gives added testimony to the certainty of what He reveals. To call the Lord the "God of the holy prophets" (**v. 6**) is to show that these words, just like the prophets' words, are breathed out by God and cannot be false. Just as the prophets were able to say, "Thus says the LORD," so also the angel, with the same authority, promises that these words are "faithful and true," and that these things "must shortly be done" (**v. 6**). Likewise, when John is commanded not to seal up the prophecy, but write it down, God shows us that the vision is true. The record of that vision is also inspired by Him, and utterly reliable.

6 And he said unto me, These sayings are faithful and true: and the Lord God of the holy prophets sent his angel to shew unto his servants the things which must shortly be done.

This is the second time the angel used the words "faithful and true" (**21:5, 22:6**), which also are applied directly to Christ (**Revelation 3:14, 19:11**). As Christ is faithful and true, so are His words sent via prophets or angels also faithful and true. Implied perhaps is an indictment on the predictable slowness of humankind to grasp each newly revealed facet of God's glory.

The same truth assurances could be said for both the book of Revelation and the entirety of God's Word. The apparent redundancy here must indicate the special importance to the church of these particular words—even while underscoring that God always has, in the same trustworthy manner, revealed the future through His prophets. The phrase translated as "the Lord God who inspires his prophets" in the NLT (cf. NIV) literally means that God is the prophets' very breath and spirit (Gk. *pneuma*, **puh-NEW-mah**; breath, spirit). This points to the authority of John's vision, connecting it to the prophets of the past as originating from God.

The hinge phrase "must shortly be done" (**v. 6**) has been translated many ways, yet all clearly concur that the Greek word *tachos* (**TAH-khos**) means quickness or speed. The original Greek did not intend "quickly" as commonly understood. Few would say 2,000 years is "quickly," but "suddenly" could happen at any time, even the distant future. This rendering also agrees with other verses that describe His coming as a thief in the night, taking a self-indulgent, self-absorbed world by surprise (**Matthew 24:38–41; 1 Thessalonians 5:4**).

7 Behold, I come quickly: blessed is he that keepeth the sayings of the prophecy of this book.

After reinforcing this element of surprise, the angel encourages believers, but subtly implies that those who don't "keep the sayings in this book" won't be "blessed" at Jesus' sudden appearance. In this Revelation beatitude, believers will be blessed, more likely ecstatic, as our time of vindication and the completion of our redemption will have come at long last.

In stark contrast, the unbelieving world will be judged and condemned. Here translated "sayings" but generally translated "words," John uses the Greek word *logos* (**LOG-os**), a word he used multiple times in thirty-six verses of his Gospel, to refer to the entire Word of God (see especially **John 1**).

Each succeeding generation must anticipate, prepare, watch, and be ready for Jesus' return. Nothing in our present world can give us enduring comfort and eternal joy; we must place all our hopes on Jesus Christ, serving Him wholeheartedly. He has prepared a wonderful and glorious future for those who put their trust in Him. Everything we do should be aimed at securing our places in the New Jerusalem, the place where God will dwell with His people.

SEARCH THE SCRIPTURES

QUESTION 3

Why is it often hard to have a true longing for Heaven?

Answers will vary.

LIGHT ON THE WORD

Imminent Hope

Ever since John penned his vision, these words of imminent hope have been available for all to see and react to as they choose. When Christ finally does return, no one will be able to claim total surprise, and they also will have no one to blame if His coming isn't welcome.

BIBLE APPLICATION

AIM: Students will appreciate that the river will nourish and heal everything in the city.

Think about circumstances or relationships in your life that leave you feeling bitter or resentful because of the way you've been treated. How do you respond when you feel slighted? Does a focus on making things right in this world keep you from longing for the next? Take this opportunity to repent of your misplaced hope and turn to Christ for forgiveness. In light of the incredible promises of God about your identity and your abundant inheritance, take time each day to intentionally rejoice and give thanks for the glory that awaits you in God's presence.

STUDENTS' RESPONSES

AIM: Students will agree that Christians are assured of the ultimate happy ending—a triumphal procession in Christ.

The promise is also given a specific urgency. Christ promises to come quickly, signaling to the believer that the words of the Book should be not only read but immediately obeyed. This admonishes all believers to expect Christ's return and the glorious fulfillment of God's promises.

PRAYER

Dear Lord, thank You for our triumphal walk with Christ! Thank You for the rivers of life that are healing, nourishing, and reflective of Your love, grace, and eternal bliss. In the Name of Jesus we pray. Amen.

HOW TO SAY IT

Shewed.   SHOOD.

Redundancy.   REE-dun-din-cee.

DIG A LITTLE DEEPER

This section provides an additional research article to further your study of the lesson:

Temporal imaginations can make an eternity with God seem boring and unfulfilling. The message in *The Daily Bread* should clarify the Christians heavenly perspective about eternity with God.

http://odb.org/2003/12/30/
what-will-we-do-in-heaven/

PREPARE FOR NEXT SUNDAY

Read **Revelation 22:12–21** and "Alpha and Omega."

DAILY HOME BIBLE READINGS

MONDAY
Wash and Be Healed
(2 Kings 5:10–14)

TUESDAY
Healing River Flows from the Temple
(Ezekiel 47:1–2, 12)

WEDNESDAY
God is Present and the City is Secure
(Psalm 46)

THURSDAY
The Sustaining Healing Water of Life
(Isaiah 41:17–20)

FRIDAY
The Lord Acts With Passion
(Isaiah 42:10–17)

SATURDAY
The Paralytic Walks Again
(Matthew 9:2–8)

SUNDAY
Living Waters
(Revelation 22:1–7)

COMMENTS / NOTES:

_____

_____

_____

_____

_____

_____

_____

_____

_____

_____

_____

_____

_____

_____

_____

_____

_____

_____

_____

_____

_____

_____

_____

ALPHA AND OMEGA

BIBLE BASIS: REVELATION 22:12–21

BIBLE TRUTH: Revelation affirms that God, who is the Alpha and Omega, controls all things.

MEMORY VERSE: "I am Alpha and Omega, the beginning and the end, the first and the last" (Revelation 22:13).

LESSON AIM: By the end of this lesson, we will: SURVEY the biblical references to the Second Coming to see the importance of this hoped-for reality; REJOICE that the invitation from Jesus to join the new community continues through the end of all things; and EMBRACE the call to become part of God's Kingdom.

TEACHER PREPARATION

MATERIALS NEEDED: Quarterly Commentary/Teacher Manual, Adult Quarterly, Adult resources—charts, worksheets, and other teaching tools, paper, pens, pencils, Bibles (several different versions)

OTHER MATERIALS NEEDED / TEACHER'S NOTES:

_____

_____

LESSON OVERVIEW

LIFE NEED FOR TODAY'S LESSON
People are aware that things have a beginning and an end.

BIBLE LEARNING
Walking in faith prepares us for Jesus' return.

BIBLE APPLICATION
Christians have the opportunity to spend eternity in God's Kingdom.

STUDENTS' RESPONSES
Believers have joy and anticipation in knowing that God's promise for a new life with Him is true.

LESSON SCRIPTURE

REVELATION 22:12–21, KJV

12 And, behold, I come quickly; and my reward is with me, to give every man according as his work shall be.

13 I am Alpha and Omega, the beginning and the end, the first and the last.

14 Blessed are they that do his commandments, that they may have right to the tree

REVELATION 22:12–21, AMP

12 "Behold, I (Jesus) am coming quickly, and My reward is with Me, to give to each one according to the merit of his deeds (earthly works, faithfulness).

13 I am the Alpha and the Omega, the First and the Last, the Beginning and the End [the Eternal One]."

of life, and may enter in through the gates into the city.

15 For without are dogs, and sorcerers, and whoremongers, and murderers, and idolaters, and whosoever loveth and maketh a lie.

16 I Jesus have sent mine angel to testify unto you these things in the churches. I am the root and the offspring of David, and the bright and morning star.

17 And the Spirit and the bride say, Come. And let him that heareth say, Come. And let him that is athirst come. And whosoever will, let him take the water of life freely.

18 For I testify unto every man that heareth the words of the prophecy of this book, If any man shall add unto these things, God shall add unto him the plagues that are written in this book:

19 And if any man shall take away from the words of the book of this prophecy, God shall take away his part out of the book of life, and out of the holy city, and from the things which are written in this book.

20 He which testifieth these things saith, Surely I come quickly. Amen. Even so, come, Lord Jesus.

21 The grace of our Lord Jesus Christ be with you all. Amen.

14 Blessed (happy, prosperous, to be admired) are those who wash their robes [in the blood of Christ by believing and trusting in Him— the righteous who do His commandments], so that they may have the right to the tree of life, and may enter by the gates into the city.

15 Outside are the dogs [the godless, the impure, those of low moral character] and the sorcerers [with their intoxicating drugs, and magic arts], and the immoral persons [the perverted, the molesters, and the adulterers], and the murderers, and the idolaters, and everyone who loves and practices lying (deception, cheating).

16 "I, Jesus, have sent My angel to testify to you and to give you assurance of these things for the churches. I am the Root (the Source, the Life) and the Offspring of David, the radiant and bright Morning Star."

17 The [Holy] Spirit and the bride (the church, believers) say, "Come." And let the one who hears say, "Come." And let the one who is thirsty come; let the one who wishes take and drink the water of life without cost.

18 I testify and warn everyone who hears the words of the prophecy of this book [its predictions, consolations, and admonitions]: if anyone adds [anything] to them, God will add to him the plagues (afflictions, calamities) which are written in this book;

19 and if anyone takes away from or distorts the words of the book of this prophecy, God will take away [from that one] his share from the tree of life and from the holy city (new Jerusalem), which are written in this book.

20 He who testifies and affirms these things says, "Yes, I am coming quickly." Amen. Come, Lord Jesus.

21 The grace of the Lord Jesus (the Christ, the Messiah) be with all [the saints—all believers, those set apart for God]. Amen.

LIGHT ON THE WORD

Revelation. The book of Revelation is considered apocalyptic writing. The term "apocalypse" refers to Jewish and Christian literature that uncovers or unveils future events or unseen realms of Heaven and Hell; conversationally, the word is applied to religious events surrounding the anticipated destruction of the world. Apocalyptic writing is viewed as mysterious language and imagery that could be perceived and interpreted in many different ways by the carnal mind. However, revelation is an unveiling through the Holy Spirit of the deep things and mysteries of God. In the Old and New Testaments, there are two full apocalypses (Daniel and Revelation), both of which speak cryptically of corrupt, human political realms in contrast to God's heavenly and eternal realm.

TEACHING THE BIBLE LESSON

LIFE NEED FOR TODAY'S LESSON

AIM: Students will agree that among the Apostles, John had a special relationship with Jesus.

INTRODUCTION

John

Specifically naming himself as the author of Revelation, John writes with authority to the church as a whole. From reading these Scriptures, it is apparent the son of Zebedee was a visionary and a prophet. He and his brother James were nicknamed by Jesus as the "Sons of Thunder." John had a seemingly special relationship with Jesus. In at least three instances, John accompanied Jesus apart from the majority of the twelve disciples (**Luke 8:51; Matthew 17:1; Mark 14:33**).

BIBLE LEARNING

AIM: Students will affirm that walking in faith prepares them for Jesus' return.

I. ALPHA AND OMEGA
(Revelation 22:12–13)

The significance of the "I am" statement stems from the book of Exodus (**3:13–15**), when God instructs Moses to tell the people of Israel that God sent him. Moses urges God for a specific name, and God's response is, "I AM WHO I AM," that is, "I am everything and whatever is required at any given moment." The term is all-encompassing. God further explains that this will be His name forever.

Jesus employs the "I am" statement as an assertion of His divinity and connection to God. He quotes God's declaration of being the first and the last who is the one true God (**Isaiah 44:6, 48:12**). Jesus utilizes the first and last letters of the Greek alphabet (alpha and omega) to further stress the point. The phrase occurs four times throughout Revelation (**1:8, 11; 21:6; 22:13**).

12 And, behold, I come quickly; and my reward is with me, to give every man according as his work shall be.

Although "quickly" is the standard interpretation of the Greek *tachus* (**tah-KOOS**), the more literal rendering is "suddenly." Both intend for the church, the bride of Christ, to prepare herself and be ready at any time for the return of her beloved Bridegroom because no one really knows when it will happen. The main point, repeated over and over in Scripture, is to be ready for Christ's return whenever it happens.

Passages such as **Matthew 16, James 2**, and **Revelation 22** remind us that we cannot expect to get away with corrupt behavior, mistreating one another intentionally. Hollow or shallow faith that does not lead to growth is not enough. A positive take on the verse is that Jesus will come with "rewards" (Gk. *misthos*, **mis-THOS**), like wages or payment for services, for those who have been faithful. While no one is saved by works, those who are saved will be rewarded according to their works (Gk. *ergon*, **ER-gon**, employment or labor).

13 I am Alpha and Omega, the beginning and the end, the first and the last.

Alpha is the first of twenty-four letters in the Greek alphabet and Omega is the last, thus making the connection between the beginning and the end, the first and the last. **Psalm 90:2** says God is from "everlasting to everlasting," and He is the same "yesterday, and today, and forever" (**Hebrews 13:8**). If Genesis and Revelation are the bookends of human history, Jesus is the holder of the bookends both pre-existing and post-existing our temporal time frame. This is true not only in the sense of existence, but in character and holiness, without beginning or end, and without change (**Malachi 3:6**). Alpha and Omega, moreover, is one of many self-proclaimed images of Christ found in Scripture. The same names are applied to God (cf. **Isaiah 41:4, 44:6; Revelation 1:8, 21:6**) and here specifically applied to Christ (cf. **Revelation 1:17, 2:8**), giving another insurmountable argument for His deity.

II. CITY GATES (vv. 14–15)

14 Blessed are they that do his commandments, that they may have right to the tree of life, and may enter in through the gates into the city. 15 For without are dogs, and sorcerers, and whoremongers, and murderers, and idolaters, and whosoever loveth and maketh a lie.

Revelation was written to churches in large cities. Thus John intentionally describes a particular place that contrasts with the metropolitan life the recipients are used to. **Chapter 3** introduces this city of God as the New Jerusalem (**3:12**), while **chapter 21** provides the description. The dimensions, ethos, foundation, building materials and jewels, walls, and character of its inhabitants are all detailed.

Jesus gives His blessing to those who obey God's commandments; this is their qualification for entering the gates of the heavenly city the New Jerusalem. These people have a right (*exousia*, **ek-ZOO-see-ah**) or authority to eat from the tree of life. Adam and Eve were banished from the garden so they wouldn't be able to eat this tree (**Genesis 3:22–24**), said to enable whoever ate its fruit to live forever. Now it is open to all who follow Jesus and obey God's commandments.

The people outside the city are those who do not keep God's commandments. Since the whole city is God's temple, then those who would defile it are kept outside. These people have disobeyed God to the point that their disobedience has become their identity. This list is very similar to the list in **Revelation 21:8**, with the addition of the category of dogs. Dogs were considered unclean animals in Judaism because they would eat carrion (**Leviticus 11:18; Deuteronomy 14:17**), and by extension in Greco-Roman and Jewish culture dogs sometimes represented immorality, including at times sexual immorality (**Deuteronomy 23:18; Matthew 7:6; Philippians 3:2**). The phrase "whosoever loveth and maketh a lie" is more than likely a further description of idolaters.

SEARCH THE SCRIPTURES
QUESTION 1
Jesus calls those who do His commandments blessed (**Revelation 22:14**). Write out a mission statement that details how you are going to live a blessed life.

Answers will vary.

LIGHT ON THE WORD
Enter into the Gates
John writes that those who have the right to the tree of life will enter the city by the gates. It is not known whether the gates are narrow as Jesus once asserted (**Matthew 7:14**), but there are twelve of them. Three gates face each

compass direction, and there is an angel and inscription of the twelve tribes at all the gates. The people outside the gates are those who are disobedient to God's commands. They would corrupt the city with their sin.

III. ROOT AND DESCENDANT OF DAVID (vv. 16–21)

Throughout the messianic prophecies is a motif that connects the expectant Savior to the lineage and legacy of King David. The Gospels continue the motif by casting Jesus as the fulfillment of the prophecies, and whatever remains void, the New Testament asserts will be accomplished once Jesus returns. Based on Scripture and because of their plight as a people, the initial followers of Christ longed for a Davidic king who would conquer the enemies of God in the same way that David did.

16 I Jesus have sent mine angel to testify unto you these things in the churches. I am the root and the offspring of David, and the bright and morning star.

Jesus places His stamp of approval on the testimony of the message of Revelation to the church (the word "you" in the Greek is plural), which includes our present age. No mortal could be both root (the Creator) and offspring (**Isaiah 11:1**); Jesus is both the Lord of David and the son of David (**Matthew 22:42–45**). The fallen angel Lucifer, once called a morning star (**Isaiah 14:12**; also day star in some versions), has from the beginning lied to mankind and falsely presented himself as an angel of light (**2 Corinthians 11:14**). Jesus affirms that He alone is the true Morning Star. Here three words associated with light are used to describe Jesus: star (Gk. aster, **ah-STAIR**; star, flame), bright (Gk. *lampros*, **lam-PROS**; white, radiant) and morning (Gk. *orthinos*, **or-thin-OS**; what is to the right, correct). Morning is associated with the re-introduction of light to the world. After a period of darkness, the star of the morning will appear, shining brightly.

17 And the Spirit and the bride say, Come. And let him that heareth say, Come. And let him that is athirst come. And whosoever will, let him take the water of life freely.

Both the Spirit of God, who indwells God's church, and the bride of Christ (the church and believers) invite those who have yet to decide for Christ to come to the water of life! We, along with the Spirit, wait expectantly, but we also serve as a testimony that the human heart is satisfied by coming to Jesus, and any who come to Him may freely drink of the water of life (**John 7:37–39; Revelation 22:1**), both now and forever.

18 For I testify unto every man that heareth the words of the prophecy of this book, If any man shall add unto these things, God shall add unto him the plagues that are written in this book: 19 And if any man shall take away from the words of the book of this prophecy, God shall take away his part out of the book of life, and out of the holy city, and from the things which are written in this book.

Matthew Henry observes that the words of warning resemble previous words of protection found in Scripture: "This sanction is like a flaming sword, to guard the canon of the Scripture from profane hands." Henry's words are reminiscent of the angel guarding the tree of life with a flaming sword (**Genesis 3:24**). God installed similar sanctions for the protection of the Law (see **Deuteronomy 4:2, 12:32; Proverbs 30:5–6**). God will judge offenders appropriately for their violation of His logos. The clearly promised curse balances the previous promised blessing offered to the faithful (**v. 12**) and together retain a familiar blessing/curse theme from the Old Testament as the New Testament closes.

20 He which testifieth these things saith, Surely I come quickly. Amen. Even so, come, Lord Jesus.

Christ's parting words are filled with mercy and hope. When Jesus ascended after His resurrection, He promised to be with them by His Spirit; now He promises He will soon return. His coming will be fulfilled as completely as the fulfillment of sending the Holy Spirit, the Comforter and Teacher of the church. The Greek word for "testify" is *martureo* (**mar-too-REH-oh**), meaning to give or bear witness, just as the apostles were witnesses throughout the New Testament. The primary message of the church is to be and remain ready.

21 The grace of our Lord Jesus Christ be with you all. Amen.

It is no coincidence that both the book and the Word end with a word of grace. Christ came to bring us grace. When His work on earth was finished, He left to prepare a place for us, and as surely as He first came according to His promise, He will return as promised for His bride. Until we are perfected in Him, we can find no better comfort, stronger peace, or more enduring hope than the presence of His grace to sustain us until His return.

SEARCH THE SCRIPTURES

QUESTION 2
Why is the punishment severe for anyone who adds or takes away from this book of prophecy (**Revelation 22:18–19**)?

This Scripture must be protected from rewriting or misinterpretation.

QUESTION 3
How relevant is the "second coming" to the way you live your life?

Answers will vary.

QUESTION 4
What does it mean to you personally that Jesus is the beginning and the end?

Answers will vary.

LIGHT ON THE WORD
Jesus' Return
Jesus is coming again! This biblical fact causes many questions about the event. In the most literal context, Jesus will rapture the Church and return to earth to satisfy unfulfilled prophecies (**I Corinthians 15:51; I Thessalonians 4:16**).

BIBLE APPLICATION

AIM: Students will agree that Christians will spend eternity in God's Kingdom.

Although Jesus graciously extends the invitation for us to enter the Kingdom and offers "waters of life," we cannot receive these gifts without obligation and investment. Sometimes we can be so preoccupied with the daily routine of life that we have no interest in questions of ultimate significance. We must not fail to consider and prepare for Jesus' return,

STUDENTS' RESPONSES

AIM: Students will express thanksgiving and praise for God's promise of a new life eternally with Him. Even so, come, Lord Jesus.

Verse 15 gives a few examples of actions and character flaws that can separate us from Jesus. Aside from what was mentioned, can you think of anything that may separate you from fully preparing yourself for Christ? The thoughts, words, or actions do not have to be what some consider "sin" in the conventional sense, but rather anything that could prevent you from dwelling in the closest proximity possible to Jesus.

PRAYER

Dear Lord, we look with hope and expectancy for Your return. May we as Your Church be the Bride who is eagerly awaiting the Bridegroom. We pray to be without spot or wrinkle, with our lamps trimmed and ready. Thank You for preparing a place for us to live with You eternally. In Jesus' Name. Amen.

HOW TO SAY IT

| Plagues. | **PLAYGZ.** |
| Testifieth. | **TES**-ti-**FEYE**-ith. |

DIG A LITTLE DEEPER

This section provides an additional research article to further your study of the lesson:

Jesus is coming again. All of our hope for the return of Jesus Christ will be fulfilled when "Heaven is emptied," as John Piper states. What a precious illustration as Christians eagerly await His return.

http://www.desiringgod.org/articles/all-the-angels-are-coming-with-him

PREPARE FOR NEXT SUNDAY

Read **Luke 1:26–38** and "God Promises a Savior."

DAILY HOME BIBLE READINGS

MONDAY
You Will Not Find Me
(John 7:32–36)

TUESDAY
This is the Messiah
(John 7:37–43)

WEDNESDAY
The Lord God, the Almighty
(Revelation 1:4b–8)

THURSDAY
Your First Work Rewarded
(Revelation 2:1–7)

FRIDAY
Worship Without End
(Revelation 7:9–12)

SATURDAY
Promised Redemption Fulfilled
(Isaiah 43:1–7)

SUNDAY
Alpha and Omega
(Revelation 22:8–21)

COMMENTS / NOTES:

_____
_____
_____
_____
_____
_____
_____
_____
_____
_____
_____
_____
_____
_____
_____
_____
_____
_____
_____
_____
_____
_____
_____

QUARTERLY COMMENTARY
CREATION: A DIVINE CYCLE
by Evangelist Yvonne Atkins

TEACHER'S TIPS
"SUNDAY SCHOOL TEACHING TIPS I"
by Jurisdictional Field Representative Sandra Daniel

"STOP THE INTERFERENCE
DISCOVERING THE HAZARDS OF INTERFERENCE
1 SAMUEL 3 (WITH FOCUS ON VERSES 1–11) (KJV)"
by Evangelist Betty J. Byrd

#TSSGTEACHINGTIP –
"CREATING THAT WINNING CLASS"
by Evangelist Waynell Henson

CREATION: A DIVINE CYCLE
BY EVANGELIST YVONNE ATKINS

The Gospel according to Luke, commonly shortened to the Gospel of Luke or simply Luke, is the third and longest of the four canonical Gospels. This quarter's lesson texts for December come from Luke. These Scriptures inform us of an angel's promise to Mary regarding the birth of Jesus. Who better to tell about the promised Savior than Dr. Luke? Luke announces the birth of Jesus Christ as if he was the attending physician at His birth (Luke 1:1–4, 13), giving us the most detailed account of Jesus' birth, childhood, and development. With a divine Father and a human mother, Jesus enters history—God in the flesh.

Luke reveals the origins, birth, ministry, death, resurrection, and ascension of Jesus Christ. A medical doctor and Greek Christian, Luke even accompanied the Apostle Paul on missionary journeys. The key phrase in the Gospel of Luke is "Son of Man" because He was a son of man—a human being—and the Son of God.

This book was written to record an accurate account, *"so that you may know the exact truth"* of the life of Jesus Christ as the perfect Savior of the world (Luke 1:4). Luke wrote to the Greeks to present Jesus in His perfect manhood as the "Son of Man," the Savior of all men.

UNIT 1 – THE SAVIOR IS BORN

The announcement to Mary of the birth of Jesus is parallel to the announcement to Zechariah of the birth of John the Baptist. In both accounts, the angel Gabriel appears to the parent, who is troubled by the vision and then told by the angel not to fear.

Gabriel appeared not only to Zechariah and Mary, but also to the prophet Daniel more than 500 years earlier. Only two of God's angels are directly named in the Bible—the archangel Michael, and Gabriel, God's special messenger. Gabriel often appears in Scripture as a messenger sent from God.

Gabriel is mentioned in both the Old and New Testaments of the Bible. His name means "man of God" or "strength of God." Gabriel scares people (Daniel 8:15–17; 9:21; Luke 1:12). He tells Mary, *"Fear not."* He also tells Mary that her son will be called *"the Son of the Most High."*

Luke specifies that God sent Gabriel to Nazareth, Joseph and Mary's hometown, a small Jewish village. There they gathered in the synagogue meeting for prayer and holidays.

Mary, a young, poor woman, was chosen by God. Being both young and poor would make Mary seem unusable by God for any major task. But God chose her for one of the most important acts of obedience He has ever demanded of anyone. God's favor did not automatically bring Mary instant success or fame. His blessing her to be the mother of Jesus would lead to much pain; her peers would ridicule her and her husband to be would come close to leaving her (Matthew 1:18–19). Mary's submission was part of God's plan to bring about our great salvation.

The birth of Jesus by a virgin is a miracle many people still find hard to believe. Considering that Luke was a medical doctor and knew how babies were conceived, one might think it would have been harder for him to believe, yet he believed. Luke was also a researcher and he based his Gospel on eyewitness accounts (Luke 1:1–2). Jewish tradition holds that he talked with Mary about the events he recorded in the first two chapters. This is Mary's story, not a fictional invention.

The virgin birth is important to the Christian faith. Jesus was born without the sin that entered the world through Adam. Jesus was born holy.

UNIT 2 – ALL CREATION PRAISES GOD

Sometimes we become overwhelmed by events in our world. Societal woes take their toll. Jobs, family structure, communities, government—many things make people worry, doubt, and search for a better understanding.

This quarter's lesson texts for January are from the book of Psalms. In Psalms, you hear believers crying out to God from the depths of despair, and hear them singing to God in the heights of celebration. Most importantly, you read about people sharing their honest feelings with God.

The book of Psalms was written in Palestine and Babylon from the time of Moses (about 1500 BC) to the time of Ezra (about 450 BC). Psalms was written by several different writers: Moses wrote Psalm 90, David wrote 73 psalms, Solomon wrote 2, Asaph the worship leader wrote Psalms 50 and 73–83, Heman the Ezrahite wrote Psalm 88, Ethan the Ezarhite wrote Psalm 89, and the sons of Korah (Exodus 6:24) wrote ten psalms. David and Solomon wrote several of the remaining 50 that did not include author's names. Authorship of other psalms cannot be determined, but Ezra is the collector and compiler of Psalms in its present form.

In the Hebrew Bible, Psalms is divided into 5 books: Book 1 is called the Genesis book (Psalms 1–41), Book II the Exodus book (Psalms 42–72), Book III the Leviticus book (Psalms 73–89), Book IV the Numbers book (Psalms 90–106), and Book V the Deuteronomy book (Psalms 107–150).

The book of Psalms has a special significance for understanding the religious life of ancient Israel. The prophets and sages provide some insight on what the Hebrews thought, but the psalms give us an indication of what the Hebrews felt.

People turn to the book of Psalms for comfort during times of struggle and distress. They find joy that takes them to heights unknown and they praise God as they discover the power of His everlasting love and forgiveness. "*Let every thing that hath breath praise the LORD. Praise ye the LORD*" (Psalm 150:6).

UNIT 3 – THE CHURCH IS BORN

The song writer writes about freedom, "No more shackles, no more chains, no more bondage, I am free." If you have ever been bound, restricted, or denied opportunities—whether from other people or yourself—then you can understand how exciting it is to be free.

This quarter's lesson texts for February, are from Galatians, the charter of Christian freedom. Galatians was written by Paul, an apostle to the Gentiles. This letter was addressed to all the churches of Galatia, a province of Asia Minor.

The churches in Galatia included converted Jews and Gentile converts. Paul wanted to confirm the Galatian churches in the faith of Christ, especially with respect to the importance of justification by God's grace through faith.

Galatians was written as a protest against corruption of the Gospel of Christ (Galatians 1:7). The essential truth of justification by faith rather than by the works of the law had been obscured by the Judaizers (extremist Jewish fraction within the church), insisting that believers had to submit to Jewish laws and tradition in addition to believing in Christ. This controversy tore apart the early church, and when Paul learned that this teaching had penetrated the Galatian churches and that they were not free in serving God, he wrote this epistle.

Galatians was written to refute the Judaizers and to call believers back to the pure Gospel. Paul defends his Gospel, arguing that it is the true message of salvation since he received it directly from Christ (Galatians 1 and 2).

Like Paul, we must defend the truth of the Gospel and reject all those who want to add their own truths. *"If the Son therefore shall make you free, ye shall be free indeed"* (John 8:36).

_____   _____

Evangelist Yvonne Atkins is the First Lady of Victory Temple Church of God in Christ in Tyler, TX, She is the Adult Women Sunday School Teacher for ages 40-50.
Texas Northeast Second Jurisdiction
Prelate, Bishop Dr. David R. Houston
Supervisor of Women, Mother Artie Morrow

SUNDAY SCHOOL TEACHING TIPS I

BY JURISDICTIONAL FIELD REPRESENTATIVE
SANDRA DANIEL

Change Curriculum Ignite Your Students With Change from the Ordinary

Throw away the workbooks and worksheets. Allow the "curriculum" to grow organically from current issues and themes that are important to your particular students. Connect biblical study to newspaper articles, current movies, TV shows, stories, or problems your students are facing in their daily lives. Generate a list of moral/ethical/"what if" questions and get them talking.

Create a Setting That is Conducive to Learning in a Relaxed Atmosphere

Students need a comfortable space where they feel free to share and talk.

Turn Your Students into Co-Teachers

Students who will never study on their own will be more than happy to teach on their own or when partnered. Partner interested students with one another and allow them to help. Set up a schedule of classes. They will likely learn more studying as teachers than they ever did as students.

Create an Atmosphere of Intergenerational Interaction

Invite various adults from the church to go to another class, the Youth class, Men's class, New Convert class, etc. Ask them to be interviewed about their faith. The class to be visited can come up with five questions about God, Jesus, Scripture, and the church, and each invited interviewee can talk for about 20 minutes. At the end of the time, the guest leaves and the rest of the hour is spent debriefing what was shared. This allows exposure to a variety of understandings of how others came to the faith. It also provides a chance to deepen relationships with others in the church.

Open Forum or Round Table Discussions

How about semi-regular Sunday morning forums for all ages, focused on social justice/cultural/theological topics of interest?

Use Variety in Presentation

Presentation variety invites the teacher and learner to focus on a single biblical text for several weeks in a row. This gives the learner an opportunity during each time of instruction to experience the story in a different way, such as drama, cooking, mission projects, movies, science, writing, art, etc. The teacher can incorporate events that allow experiences which will tap into their different intelligences and learning styles. One side benefit of this model is that you can involve as many participants as necessary to get the best results from the different workshops. You will also be able to tap the artists, musicians, scientists, and chefs in your congregation to come work.

Sunday School Community Evangelistic Partnership

Partner with one or two other churches. Plan to switch out Sunday School classes on one Sunday (after approval from your pastor). One quarter you might send the entire Sunday School class, and during another quarter you might just send some teachers. Work toward having the largest class and/or offering on that day by having the students invite people to one another's church for Sunday School. A special lesson on evangelism and/or missions will be shared. The results will manifest in the number of people that show up for Sunday School on the designated Sunday. Plan a Super Sunday School Day to give awards and recognition. Make the ecumenical move and see if other neighborhood churches would like to join you in developing a cooperative Sunday School Evangelism program.

Spiritual Discipline Training

Spiritual disciplines take practice. Consider offering opportunities each week for youth to experience a discipline, put it into practice, and report the results to the class on a designated Sunday. One event could be to establish prayer stations through the week. They would recruit two friends, make a list of seven items, and designate prayer stations where they would pray for seven minutes for seven days. Other suggestions to be carried out would be to observe the Sabbath through rest, speak only positive things for a week, and perform random acts of kindness for parents, teacher, neighbors, individuals in hospitals or nursing homes. Events would be Sunday School lesson-driven so that students would return with a testimony (report).

Short Term Reformation

Breaking routine can ignite a new fire in Sunday School. You might spend time in the fall focused on planning and carrying out mission projects. In Advent, turn the group into a drama team. The team should prepare a series of skits, practice with the class, ask other congregants to participate, and request to present the skits to augment a worship service. Alternatively, prepare for presentation on a special day, if so permitted. In the winter, become film critics. Ask the students to view faith-based films. Make a list so that everyone is viewing the same films. Tie your discussion to the movies selected and have the students explain what about the film is scripturally correct and what is inaccurate. When spring rolls around, study other faiths and denominations. Create posters specifically listing the doctrinal differences and what the Scripture says. In the summer, create a photography club, inviting students to create group photo shows based on "images of God" that they find. Divide them into teams and assign topics such as God and nature, God and water, God's miracles, God and people, etc.

Evangelist Sandra Daniel serves as the Jurisdictional Field Representative for the First Ecclesiastical Jurisdiction of Southern California under the leadership of Bishop Joe L. Ealy and General Assistant Supervisor/Jurisdictional Supervisor Mother Barbara McCoo Lewis. She is the Assistant Director of Leadership Ministry for the International Sunday School Department.

STOP THE INTERFERENCE
Discovering the Hazards of Interference
1 Samuel 3 (with focus on verses 1–11) (KJV)

BY EVANGELIST BETTY J. BYRD

One of our goals as a Sunday School teacher is to present teachings in a manner that would aid in bringing about <u>transformation</u> in our students. Therefore, we present and study Scriptures and study material that will aid in this transformation. The Bible study material, stories, and lessons should be presented in a way that will inspire and enable others to accept the life teachings and lessons to become who God has called us to be.

The lyrics of an old song say, *"Hush, hush, somebody's calling my name. Oh my Lord, Oh my Lord, what shall I do? What shall I do?"* The words indicate that someone is speaking and another is trying to hear what is being said to them, and another might be hampering or interfering with the receipt of this communication. We must alert our students that sometimes in our lives we encounter a problem with hearing God. I hear many ask the question, "Is that really You speaking, God?" Problems in our lives might make it difficult to have an adequate open line of communication with God. But through our study of the Scripture, we discover God's remedy to this interference.

Interference: Defining the Source. Interference is any unwanted signal that prevents you from watching television, listening to your radio/stereo, or talking on your cell phone. Interference might prevent reception totally, cause only a temporary loss of a signal, or affect the quality of the sound or picture produced by your equipment.

Common Causes of Interference. Before you can resolve an interference problem, **you must identify the source**. Interference can originate from many sources—internally or externally. Naturally, the problem could be the malfunctioning of your equipment or outside influences to your equipment. If you cannot locate the interference source in your own equipment, check because it must be outside sources affecting your reception.

Wherever we go, whatever we do, someone or something will interfere with our actions. Some interferences will come from someone we know, respect, or perhaps love. Some interferences come when we are not expecting it.

Some people have allowed interferences in our lives. We have allowed the cares of the world to suffocate us. We have allowed our co-workers to dictate when we can worship God. We have allowed sufferings to shatter our hopes. We have allowed the big waves of sin to smother the growth of our faith. Interferences are hazardous for us.

THE LORD CALLS SAMUEL

Samuel was called at a time of extremely limited prophetic activity, probably because so few Israelites were faithful and willing to listen (Judges 21:25). In 1 Samuel 3, three times Samuel mistook God's voice for the voice of Eli. Samuel had been assisting the prophet Eli in serving the tabernacle, but he did not yet know the Lord in an intimate and personal way. He had never heard God's voice. He had never received the Word of the Lord by divine revelation. Eli finally realized that God was speaking to Samuel and advised the young man what to do.

Sin makes our hearts less receptive to the promptings of the Holy Ghost. It makes us unable to feel and understand the voice of the Spirit.

By obeying God's Word and keeping the Commandments, we tune our Spiritual receiver. We need to make sure that our receiver is always fine-tuned to the right channel. Can we expect blessings from heaven when our lives are not in agreement with commandments from heaven? Sin makes our hearts less receptive to the promptings of the Holy Ghost.

Minimize Competition with the Voice of the Spirit. We must do all we can to minimize competing sounds—to tune them out. What makes you less likely to hear this still, small voice of the Spirit? Some could be gossiping, criticizing others, profane talk or music, pornography, illicit drug use, materialism, dishonesty, time wasting (such as excessively playing video games or watching television)—you get the picture. You and I must rid ourselves of anything in our lives that detracts from our ability to hear the voice of the Spirit.

What would have happened if the prophet Eli was not in tuned to the Lord God? His comments could have been interference to Samuel, but instead, it was a blessing to this young man of God.

Can't hear God through the cell phone, the kids, and the endless static of life? God speaks to us, and let us work and learn to "tune in" to the power of divine conversation.

Live so God can use you to be an extension of Him, and broadcast Him and His Word to others.

Evangelist Betty J. Byrd
Jurisdictional Young Women's Christian Council (YWCC) President
Alabama First Jurisdiction
Mother Mattie Taylor, Jurisdictional Supervisor
Bishop O. L. Meadows, Jurisdictional Prelate

#TSSGTEACHINGTIP – CREATING THAT WINNING CLASS

BY EVANGELIST WAYNELL HENSON

"The plans of the diligent lead surely to abundance…" – Proverbs 21:5

Perhaps it was a contour bottle filled with soda, a specialty coffee with a logo on the cup, or just a bottle of water, but I'm positive you enjoyed a specialty beverage of some kind this week. You were simply thirsty and picked up something that you would enjoy. But someone sat in a room for countless hours thinking of you, the moment you would make your choice, and just how to make that experience enjoyable. How do I know? I used to be that person!

Companies spend big dollars to get to know us as consumers. They know what we enjoy, how we behave, and how often we purchase/participate/engage with their brands. More than anything they know that we as consumers have the power of CHOICE! And they put together programs to connect with us. Super-savvy teachers who are winning with students have learned and employ the success strategies of many companies. The bottom line is purchases don't just happen, and students don't just happen. Just as companies compete for our business, we in very real ways as teachers/leaders compete with students for their valuable time! Recruiting, retaining, and growing your class must be a concerted and continuous effort… in other words, you have to PLAN to win!

1. DON'T BE AFRAID TO ASK!

To achieve meaningful success requires first having a goal! Lacking clarity on direction or desired outcomes leaves us falling short. Each quarter as a teacher/facilitator, think of the top one or two areas where you want to impact in your class. Is it regular attendance? I mean, numbers are great, but stability is far more powerful. Is it growth in attendance? Increase in offering? Increase in a particular knowledge area? Challenging students to daily reading? Whatever your desire is, don't be afraid to "put it out there!" Set high expectations! First, be vocal about your goal with your class, and then together you and the class can speak to God. You can be specific with Him, asking His guidance and direction.

2. USE WHAT YOU HAVE

Teamwork has value. Although you are the teacher/facilitator, so many resources are available to you. Take advantage of what your leadership offers. Remember, you do not have to create all of the solutions. Your most powerful mouthpieces are your current students! Ask them for ideas for creative recruitment efforts. Having their buy-in invests them more in the outreach and growth efforts. You win as a team! Make a specific target list. Keep it manageable. Perhaps start with five people. Challenge current students to take an active part of recruitment efforts through personal contact. Make social media work for you!

3. BE INTENTIONAL IN MANAGING VISITORS/PROSPECTIVE STUDENTS

Yes, as visitors, the truth is we all sort of cringe anticipating the (possibly embarrassing) moment that you get the "visitor stare." Establish a routine of welcoming visitors, perhaps with a small token from your class (great economical items can be found at your local Christian bookstore). Most of all have an intentional, but not "stalkerish," system of following up with visitors to say "Thank you for coming. We hope to see you again."

4. COMMUNICATE!

We all like to know that someone is concerned about us. Your class is your community! Create community—a sense of belonging and care. When someone is missing, never underestimate how important a quick "missed you today" text can be. Encourage your class to look out for one another. Also create social media pages to stay connected.

5. CREATE INCENTIVES

Inviting new students is everyone's job. Perhaps, once a quarter, develop an incentive day where students inviting guests who attend on that day are appreciated!

6. STAND OUT FROM THE CROWD!

Perhaps it is a monthly fellowship of donuts and juice. For my class, it was a personalized class coffee mug. Create a unifying item that is unique and special to your class. It distinguishes your class and brings the joy of "don't you wish your class was cool like mine?"

7. DON'T BE DISCOURAGED BY NUMBERS!

I am from a small family church. I now attend a moderate-size church. I have consulted with large churches. I share that to say that I can work with whatever you give me. I remember my first young adult class teaching assignment. For more than six months, my co-teacher and I had one student. But we had a determined attitude and motto to "Teach one like it was 100!" Sometimes God will watch us be faithful with what He has given us. And the real value of that time is developing systems that we can manage effectively when He sends the harvest. I believe we passed the test. In 15 months, that class of 1 became a class of 40. God rewards faithfulness!

8. CELEBRATE YOUR SUCCESS!

We desire, aspire, and set our plans before God, but we are not always great at stopping to celebrate the small milestones! When God created the earth at the end of the day, He paused and celebrate His own effort by saying, "That's good." Don't forget to pause for your own class "that's good" celebration!

"Commit your work to the Lord, and your plans will be established." – Proverbs 16:3

Evangelist Waynell Henson is a member of Dominion Word Ministries Church Of God In Christ, Elder Michael McWilliams, Pastor. She has a heartbeat for connecting in relevant and meaningful ways to inspire people to abundant living through the truth of God's Word. A gifted administrator and #MinistryLeaderCoach, she serves as the Executive Secretary of the International Sunday School Department (COGIC) and Co-Chairman of Auxiliaries in Ministry for the Kansas East Jurisdiction COGIC, Bishop L.F. Thuston, Prelate. With a heightened awareness of connecting with Gen-X'ers, G-Y'ers and millennials, she impacts a social media "Community" of more than 1,000 lovers of Sunday School. She shares the weekly lesson, growth strategies, and resources through platforms as Youtube, Facebook, Instagram, Pinterest, Twitter, and SnapChat. Have YOU joined "The Community"?

#HappyTeaching

Find more great ideas (#TeachingTipTuesday) on www.ThatSundaySchoolGirl.com.

QUARTERLY QUIZ

The questions on this page may be used in several ways: as a pretest at the beginning of the quarter; as a review at the end of the quarter; or as a review after each lesson. The questions are based on the Scripture text of each lesson (King James Version).

LESSON 1

1. Distinguish between God's favor (**Luke 1:30**) and the favor that we give to people.

_____

_____

2. What are some of the reasons that believers should trust that "nothing is impossible with God" (**v. 37**)?

_____

_____

LESSON 2

Mary's soul and spirit respond after Elisabeth's joyful words in **Luke 1:46–47**. How is Mary's response similar or different from when God fulfills His promise to you?

_____

_____

2. What can you infer from **vv. 39–56** regarding God's movement in our lives?

_____

_____

LESSON 3

1. Zacharias doubted God's Word. What are some of the reasons you doubt or have trouble fully believing God?

_____

_____

2. Create a mission program that shares the message of Christ based on speaking to believers who have turned away from Him.

_____

_____

LESSON 4

1. Compare the angel's response to the shepherds (**Luke 2:10**), Mary (**Luke 1:30**), and Zacharias (**Luke 1:13**). Why were the angel's words significant for each?

_____

_____

2. God moves in the lives of people in ordinary moments and unique ways. How do you test or confirm that He is directing you in a particular way?

_____

_____

LESSON 5

1. The psalmist highlights praising God through music and instruments (**Psalm 33:1–3**). Outline a worship litany that includes songs, music, and instruments to praise God.

_____

_____

2. Compare how your worship of God is impacted by His creative power in **vv. 6–9**.

_____

_____

QUARTERLY QUIZ

LESSON 6

1. If you praised God at least once a day, what impact might this have on your worship and praise of Him?

_____

_____

2. **Psalm 96:13** reminds us that God will judge the nations with His truth. Yet, how do you distinguish between God's truth, worldly truth, and our truth?

_____

_____

LESSON 7

1. Identify how some of the "dams" in your life prevent the active flow of the river of God (**Psalm 65:9**).

_____

_____

2. Critique the theme of this psalm and how it speaks to our relationship with God.

_____

_____

LESSON 8

1. The psalmist declares that the earth is built on God's foundation (**Psalm 104:5**). What are the reason(s) the foundation(s) in your relationship with God might have been weakened?

_____

_____

2. What are some of the underlying causes for nature praising God so freely?

_____

_____

LESSON 9

1. Do you agree or disagree that nature appreciates and praises God more than humanity? Explain your response.

_____

_____

2. Why do the dragons, hail, fire, and mountains praise God (**vv. 7–10**)?

_____

_____

LESSON 10

1. Is Paul's statement that before Christ, believers were like children (**Galatians 4:3**), evidenced in people today?

_____

_____

2. When you read the word "servant" in **verse 7**, are you agitated, calm, or uncomfortable? How are your feelings connected to a historical reality about slaves/slavery and God's love?

_____

_____

QUARTERLY QUIZ

LESSON 11

1. The Galatians turned to the weak and beggarly elements that led them into bondage again. As followers of Jesus, do you agree that "weak and beggarly elements" (**Galatians 4:9**) can potentially lead us into bondage?

_____

_____

2. Identify the reasons that you have felt uncomfortable sharing Jesus with others or praising God publicly.

_____

_____

LESSON 12

1. What are some of the means that believers use to work for salvation and why?

_____

_____

2. Analyze Paul's analogy between false teaching and yeast in **Galatians 5:9**.

_____

_____

LESSON 13

1. "Be not deceived; God is not mocked: for whatsoever a man soweth, that shall he also reap" (**Galatians 6:7**). What evidence can you provide to support how these statements are true today?

_____

_____

2. Select which fruit from the Holy Spirit is exhibited in your spiritual life and others that need more nurturing (**Galatians 5:22–23**).

_____

_____

Answers to Quarterly Quiz can be found on page 461

GOD PROMISES A SAVIOR

BIBLE BASIS: LUKE 1:26–38

BIBLE TRUTH: God is faithful to all His people.

MEMORY VERSE: "And, behold, thou shalt conceive in thy womb, and bring forth a son, and shalt call his name JESUS" (Luke 1:31).

LESSON AIM: By the end of this lesson, we will: VALIDATE God's faithfulness to Mary and ultimately to all His people; EXPERIENCE the joy of worshiping Jesus as God's promised Savior; and EXPRESS trust in God's promises by affirming His will for our lives.

TEACHER PREPARATION

MATERIALS NEEDED: Quarterly Commentary/Teacher Manual, Adult Quarterly, Adult resources—charts, worksheets, and other teaching tools, paper, pens, pencils, Bibles (several different versions)

OTHER MATERIALS NEEDED / TEACHER'S NOTES:

_____

_____

LESSON OVERVIEW

LIFE NEED FOR TODAY'S LESSON
Our actions, decisions, and even well-being are often based on our trust in the promises made by the Lord.

BIBLE LEARNING
Luke recounts the angel's announcement of the coming birth of Jesus, God's promised Savior.

BIBLE APPLICATION
Students can depend on God's promises.

STUDENTS' RESPONSES
Believers can trust in God's promises by affirming His will for our lives.

LESSON SCRIPTURE

LUKE 1:26–38, KJV

26 And in the sixth month the angel Gabriel was sent from God unto a city of Galilee, named Nazareth,

27 To a virgin espoused to a man whose name was Joseph, of the house of David; and the virgin's name was Mary.

28 And the angel came in unto her, and

LUKE 1:26–38, AMP

26 Now in the sixth month [of Elizabeth's pregnancy] the angel Gabriel was sent from God to a city in Galilee called Nazareth,

27 to a virgin betrothed to a man whose name was Joseph, a descendant of the house of David; and the virgin's name was Mary.

said, Hail, thou that art highly favoured, the Lord is with thee: blessed art thou among women.

29 And when she saw him, she was troubled at his saying, and cast in her mind what manner of salutation this should be.

30 And the angel said unto her, Fear not, Mary: for thou hast found favour with God.

31 And, behold, thou shalt conceive in thy womb, and bring forth a son, and shalt call his name JESUS.

32 He shall be great, and shall be called the Son of the Highest: and the Lord God shall give unto him the throne of his father David:

33 And he shall reign over the house of Jacob for ever; and of his kingdom there shall be no end.

34 Then said Mary unto the angel, How shall this be, seeing I know not a man?

35 And the angel answered and said unto her, The Holy Ghost shall come upon thee, and the power of the Highest shall overshadow thee: therefore also that holy thing which shall be born of thee shall be called the Son of God.

36 And, behold, thy cousin Elisabeth, she hath also conceived a son in her old age: and this is the sixth month with her, who was called barren.

37 For with God nothing shall be impossible.

38 And Mary said, Behold the handmaid of the Lord; be it unto me according to thy word. And the angel departed from her.

28 And coming to her, the angel said, "Greetings, favored one! The Lord is with you."

29 But she was greatly perplexed at what he said, and kept carefully considering what kind of greeting this was.

30 The angel said to her, "Do not be afraid, Mary, for you have found favor with God.

31 Listen carefully: you will conceive in your womb and give birth to a son, and you shall name Him Jesus.

32 He will be great and eminent and will be called the Son of the Most High; and the Lord God will give Him the throne of His father David;

33 and He will reign over the house of Jacob (Israel) forever, and of His kingdom there shall be no end."

34 Mary said to the angel, "How will this be, since I am a virgin and have no intimacy with any man?"

35 Then the angel replied to her, "The Holy Spirit will come upon you, and the power of the Most High will overshadow you [like a cloud]; for that reason the holy (pure, sinless) Child shall be called the Son of God.

36 And listen, even your relative Elizabeth has also conceived a son in her old age; and she who was called barren is now in her sixth month.

37 For with God nothing [is or ever] shall be impossible."

38 Then Mary said, "Behold, I am the servant of the Lord; may it be done to me according to your word." And the angel left her.

LIGHT ON THE WORD

Messianic Prophecies. Mary and Joseph went to the Temple and followed the religious customs (**Luke 2:21–41**). Given the information we know, just by reading scripture Mary would have been familiar with Messianic prophecies of the anticipated Savior (**Isaiah 7:14, 9:6–7, 11:1–5**). Living under Roman occupation, Mary understood the implication of the throne of David being re-established and, according to Gabriel, it would soon be manifested through her womb (**Luke 1:32**). More than anything, the promise she was given carried also political implications. This king was expected to regain control of the land, unify the people, and restore their relationship with God.

TEACHING THE BIBLE LESSON

LIFE NEED FOR TODAY'S LESSON

AIM: Students will decide that our actions, decisions, and even well-being are often based on our trust in the promises made by the Lord.

INTRODUCTION

God's Movement in Different Ways

The Bible presents Nazareth as a very unimportant town aside from being the birthplace of Jesus. It is often described as a ghetto of sorts. Being located in Lower Galilee, it was not bustling with business, and the inhabitants were not held in high regard. One of Jesus' future disciples raises the question, "Can anything good come out of Nazareth?" (**John 1:46**, AMP).

We evidence the move of God through the Holy Spirit in deciding where Jesus was to be born. God chose the obscure town of Nazareth! Just as something good can come out of any "ghetto" or urban area in America, the answer was "Yes!" to the question, "Can anything good come from Nazareth?" With the Spirit's empowerment, anyone can accomplish great things for God.

BIBLE LEARNING

AIM: Students will consider the significance of Luke's recounting the angel's announcement of the coming birth of Jesus, God's promised Savior.

I. GOD'S MESSENGER (LUKE 1:26–29)

The promise that Gabriel relayed to Mary on behalf of God is more than it appears at first reading. The promise is about the Davidic Messiah whom the Jews had been waiting for since the division of the Northern and Southern kingdoms—an heir to David's throne. The Old Testament prophets, who had foretold of a king, lived during periods of exile and oppression, and the Savior they spoke of was One who would deliver them from their political bondage and physical disenfranchisement. All of them expected a Messiah with attributes similar to David: military might, strong love for the Lord, and ability to lead the people. In the first century AD, not all Jews expected the Messiah to be a royal Messiah who would take up an earthly throne like David had, but because of the centrality of the prophetic tradition, many still hoped for such a Messiah who would overturn the corrupt political empire in their midst.

26 And in the sixth month the angel Gabriel was sent from God unto a city of Galilee, named Nazareth, 27 To a virgin espoused to a man whose name was Joseph, of the house of David; and the virgin's name was Mary. 28 And the angel came in unto her, and said, Hail, thou that art highly favoured, the Lord is with thee: blessed art thou among women. 29 And when she saw him, she was troubled at his saying, and cast in her mind what manner of salutation this should be.

The story of Mary and Joseph begins in the region of Galilee and the town of Nazareth where Jesus would grow up. In Elisabeth's sixth month of pregnancy, God sent Gabriel to Mary to announce that she would miraculously bear a child who would be Israel's Messiah. Luke calls Nazareth a *polis* (Gk. **POE-lees**), which is often translated as "city," but it was a small "town" (NIV) or "village." It's relatively unimportant size contrasts with Jerusalem, where Gabriel's previous appearance to Zacharias had taken place at the Temple (**v. 19**). In the eighth century BC, Assyria captured Galilee, causing it to be associated with Gentiles, but as a Roman region in the first century AD, it had strong Jewish and Gentile presences. Due to its small population, it was unlikely that anyone in the Roman Empire, whether Jew or Gentile, expected much from this sleepy town (**John 1:46**). The city and its citizens were disparaged and the object of deep prejudice by the Jews. Yet God had a vessel, by the name of Mary, in this unlikely place. Here we learn an important lesson: God is not a respecter of persons or places. Therefore, we must refrain from our quickness to judge other places, as we often do. God sent a message to a virgin (Gk. *parthenos*, **par-THEH-noce**) in Nazareth—Mary—as readily as he did to a priest in Jerusalem (Zacharias).

In the Greek translation of the Old Testament (commonly referred to as the Septuagint or LXX), *parthenos* means "girl," with chastity implied. Several verses stress chastity or virginity, such as **Leviticus 21:13–14**; **Deuteronomy 22:15, 28–29**; and **2 Samuel 13:2**. It also is used in the New Testament with the same understanding (**2 Corinthians 11:2; Revelation 14:4**). When used in describing Mary, it meant that she had not yet had sexual relations. Mary's question in verse 34, and the reference in verse 27 to her being "espoused" or pledged to be married, make this clear. Since betrothal often took place soon after puberty, Mary might have been a young teenager. Betrothal was similar to an engagement, but it was legally binding, and to break it was considered divorce (cf. **Matthew 1:19**). According to Jewish custom, only divorce or death could sever betrothal; and in the latter event, the girl, though unmarried, would be considered a widow. Mary had already committed to marry Joseph, but she had not had sexual relations with him. In the betrothal period, sexual contact was considered adultery and resulted in stoning.

II. FAVOR (vv. 30–34)

Today the word "favor" is overused in Christian speech to denote partiality or preference from God. The biblical definition of favor differs from favoritism. It is not rooted in partiality or exclusivity, but it is rooted in grace on the part of the giver by way of kindness.

30 And the angel said unto her, Fear not, Mary: for thou hast found favour with God. 31 And, behold, thou shalt conceive in thy womb, and bring forth a son, and shalt call his name JESUS. 32 He shall be great, and shall be called the Son of the Highest: and the Lord God shall give unto him the throne of his father David: 33 And he shall reign over the house of Jacob for ever; and of his kingdom there shall be no end. 34 Then said Mary unto the angel, How shall this be, seeing I know not a man?

Similar to an award ceremony, God has enough honor and grace for all of His people. Mary was the recipient of what some might consider the greatest honor among women, but it came with great cost. Although today we hold Mary in high esteem, she more than likely experienced a great deal of turmoil and backlash due to her out-of-wedlock pregnancy. We know for certain that she had to travel while pregnant and she gave birth in a less-than-ideal location.

Mary's question, "How shall this be?" probably arose from puzzlement rather than doubt or distrust. She did not ask for some sign or proof as Zacharias did (1:18), and her request was very different from Zacharias'. Hers stemmed from her faith; Zacharias' question stemmed from his lack of faith. She simply asked for more information. She was single and had never known a man sexually. How could she possibly bear a child? Mary's statement that she had not been with a man reveals the miraculous action of God that took place in Jesus' conception through the Holy Spirit. God's divine actions reveal that nothing is impossible for Him. If a woman can have a child despite not having any sexual relations, God can do anything.

III. WHAT'S MORE (vv. 35–38)

The specifics that Gabriel announces concerning the ministries of John the Baptist (**Luke 1:13–17**) and Jesus provide an interesting contrast. The mighty work God foretold He would do through John the Baptist's ministry would be surpassed by an even greater work through His Son's ministry. Whereas John would be "great in the sight of the Lord" (**1:15**), Jesus would be great without qualification (**v. 32**) and "called the Son of God" (**v. 35**). An even more important tie between the accounts is that the whole significance of John's ministry, as pointed out in **verse 17**, is found in his preparation for the One coming after him who was more powerful than he (**3:16**).

35 And the angel answered and said unto her, The Holy Ghost shall come upon thee, and the power of the Highest shall overshadow thee: therefore also that holy thing which shall be born of thee shall be called the Son of God. 36 And, behold, thy cousin Elisabeth, she hath also conceived a son in her old age: and this is the sixth month with her, who was called barren. 37 For with God nothing shall be impossible. 38 And Mary said, Behold the handmaid of the Lord; be it unto me according to thy word. And the angel departed from her.

To calm any lingering apprehensions that Mary might have had, the angel informed her of another seemingly impossible situation: Elisabeth's pregnancy in her old age. Elisabeth was in her sixth month of pregnancy, again bearing testimony to the fact that nothing is impossible with God. The actual Greek text says, "For with God no word shall be without power." The word translated as impossible is *adynateo* (**ah-doo-nah-TEH-oh**), which is a combination of *alpha* as a negative participle and *dunatos*, which means power, strength, ability, and, in this case, possibility. The translators of the KJV did not include a translation of the Greek word *rhema* (**RAY-ma**), in the original text. This simply means "word" or "thing" and could refer to the message God has sent as well as the events promised.

Mary's response to the angel was that she was only a servant of the Lord, which reveals her humility, perhaps one reason she had been chosen to bear the Messiah of Israel. Mary was a servant of God and would follow His words. No one could have asked for, or given, any better response. Her attitude of servanthood recalls that of Hannah, who also calls herself the Lord's *doule* (**DOO-lay**), meaning "servant" (**1 Samuel 1:11, LXX**). Mary's servanthood consisted of a submission to God that characterizes genuine believers in Scripture and should characterize all believers today (**cf. Luke 1:48**).

How do we respond to God's words even when they seem impossible? Do we accept them with faith, remembering that we are His humble servants? Or do we reject them as impossible? Mary's trusting submission is a worthy example for believers today.

SEARCH THE SCRIPTURES

QUESTION 1

A visit by an angel is most unusual, but it is not impossible. Have you ever thought that you had been visited by an angel?

Yes, when I was in the hospital and struggling between life and death. Answers will vary.

QUESTION 2

Write the important truth that the angel Gabriel shares with Mary in **verse 37**. Reflect on how this truth guides your life.

"For with God nothing shall be impossible (v. 37)." This truth is a reminder that I can make it because of God.

LIGHT ON THE WORD

Gabriel – God's Messenger

Luke consistently writes how angels are God's way of announcing, instructing, guiding and protecting (**1:11, 26, 2:8–15; Acts 8:26, 12:7**). In the Luke narrative, Gabriel not only delivers the news of the birth but can affirm and reassure Mary despite her doubts and questions. On assignment from God, Gabriel is dispatched with the express purpose of bringing good news. In earlier verses, he informs Zechariah that his prayers have been heard and his wife will give birth (**Luke 1:11–20**).

BIBLE APPLICATION

AIM: Students decide that Christians can depend on God's promises.

It is important to remember that no matter what we experience in life, God has made fundamental promises to all of us that we can hold on to, such as "I will never [under any circumstances] dESERT YOU [nor give you up nor leave you without support, nor will I in any degree leave you helpless], NOR WILL I FORSAKE or LET YOU DOWN or RELAX MY HOLD ON YOU

[assuredly not]!" (**Hebrews 13:5**) and "We know [with great confidence] that God [who is deeply concerned about us] causes all things to work together [as a plan] for good for those who love God, to those who are called according to His plan and purpose" (**Romans 8:28**). Whether or not we are seemingly barren like Elisabeth, or find ourselves in an unbelievable situation like Mary, Jesus is God's promised Savior on whom we can depend.

STUDENTS' RESPONSES

AIM: Students will validate that believers can trust in God's promises by affirming His will for our lives.

Whether intentional or unintentional, at some point our trust may have been betrayed. How we are affected depends on several different factors. Can we trust God after experiencing such disappointment? The answer is an unequivocal, "Yes!"

PRAYER

Dear gracious Lord, we are honored by Your love for us. Your gift to us, Jesus Christ, is an eternal gift that we are grateful for through eternity. We cherish and share this gift with others. In the Name of Jesus, we pray. Amen.

HOW TO SAY IT

Espoused.   eh-**SPOW**-d.

Salutation.   sal-you-**TAY**-shun.

DIG A LITTLE DEEPER

This section provides an additional research article to further your study of the lesson:

Mary, the mother of Jesus, embarked on a journey that no other woman had ever or will ever experience. Her remarkable trust in the Lord, and her willingness to be ashamed for His sake, speak volume about her character and trust in

God. Dr. Richard Strauss walks us through her emotional and triumphant journey.

https://bible.org/seriespage/11-do-you-trust-me-story-joseph-and-mary

PREPARE FOR NEXT SUNDAY

Read **Luke 1:39–56** and "The Affirmation of the Promise."

DAILY HOME BIBLE READINGS

MONDAY
Here Am I, Send Me
(Isaiah 6:1–8)

TUESDAY
Hannah's Womb Was Closed
(1 Samuel 1:1–11)

WEDNESDAY
I Asked Him of the Lord
(1 Samuel 1:15–20)

THURSDAY
Shall I Indeed Bear a Child?
(Genesis 18:9–15)

FRIDAY
Out of Nazareth
(John 1:43–46)

SATURDAY
A Young Woman Will Bear a Son
(Isaiah 7:10–14)

SUNDAY
Birth of Jesus Foretold
(Luke 1:26–38)

Sources:

Craddock, Fred B. *Luke: Interpretation, A Bible Commentary for Preaching and Teaching.* Edited by James Luther Mays, et al. Louisville, KY: John Knox Press, 1990.

Ferguson, Everett et al. ed. *Encyclopedia of Early Christianity* 2nd ed. New York, NY: Garland Publishing Inc, 1998.

Sakenfield, Katharine Dobb, ed. *New Interpreter's Dictionary of the Bible Me-R Vol. IV.* Nashville, TN: Abingdon Press, 2009.

Vine, W.E. *Expository Dictionary of New Testament Words.* Grand Rapids, MI: Zondervan Publishing House, 1981.

COMMENTS / NOTES:

THE AFFIRMATION OF THE PROMISE

BIBLE BASIS: LUKE 1:39–56

BIBLE TRUTH: Mary was humble and joyful at the promise of the coming of the Messiah.

MEMORY VERSES: "And Mary said, My soul doth magnify the Lord, And my spirit hath rejoiced in God my Saviour" (Luke 1:46–47).

LESSON AIM: By the end of the lesson, we will: ASSESS the ways Elisabeth and Mary celebrated God's promise of a Savior; ACKNOWLEDGE with gratitude the ways God is at work in the world; and creatively EXPRESS our confidence in God's promises.

TEACHER PREPARATION

MATERIALS NEEDED: Quarterly Commentary/Teacher Manual, Adult Quarterly, Adult resources—charts, worksheets, and other teaching tools, paper, pens, pencils, Bibles (several different versions)

OTHER MATERIALS NEEDED / TEACHER'S NOTES:

_____

_____

LESSON OVERVIEW

LIFE NEED FOR TODAY'S LESSON
It's vital to express praise to God for all that He has accomplished in our lives.

BIBLE APPLICATION
Christians can respond to God's promises with faith or skepticism, humility or pride.

BIBLE LEARNING
Luke tells of Elisabeth's affirmation of God's promise of the Savior and Mary's joyful praise for being the bearer of that divine promise.

STUDENTS' RESPONSES
Christians can creatively share their confidence in God's promises.

LESSON SCRIPTURE

LUKE 1:39–56, KJV

39 And Mary arose in those days, and went into the hill country with haste, into a city of Juda;

40 And entered into the house of Zacharias, and saluted Elisabeth.

41 And it came to pass, that, when Elisabeth heard the salutation of Mary, the babe

LUKE 1:39–56, AMP

39 Now at this time Mary arose and hurried to the hill country, to a city of Judah (Judea),

40 and she entered the house of Zacharias and greeted Elizabeth.

41 When Elizabeth heard Mary's greeting, her baby leaped in her womb; and Elizabeth

leaped in her womb; and Elisabeth was filled with the Holy Ghost:

42 And she spake out with a loud voice, and said, Blessed art thou among women, and blessed is the fruit of thy womb.

43 And whence is this to me, that the mother of my Lord should come to me?

44 For, lo, as soon as the voice of thy salutation sounded in mine ears, the babe leaped in my womb for joy.

45 And blessed is she that believed: for there shall be a performance of those things which were told her from the Lord.

46 And Mary said, My soul doth magnify the Lord,

47 And my spirit hath rejoiced in God my Saviour.

48 For he hath regarded the low estate of his handmaiden: for, behold, from henceforth all generations shall call me blessed.

49 For he that is mighty hath done to me great things; and holy is his name.

50 And his mercy is on them that fear him from generation to generation.

51 He hath shewed strength with his arm; he hath scattered the proud in the imagination of their hearts.

52 He hath put down the mighty from their seats, and exalted them of low degree.

53 He hath filled the hungry with good things; and the rich he hath sent empty away.

54 He hath helped his servant Israel, in remembrance of his mercy;

was filled with the Holy Spirit and empowered by Him.

42 And she exclaimed loudly, "Blessed [worthy to be praised] are you among women, and blessed is the fruit of your womb!

43 And how has it happened to me, that the mother of my Lord would come to me?

44 For behold, when the sound of your greeting reached my ears, the baby in my womb leaped for joy.

45 And blessed [spiritually fortunate and favored by God] is she who believed and confidently trusted that there would be a fulfillment of the things that were spoken to her [by the angel sent] from the Lord."

46 And Mary said, "My soul magnifies and exalts the Lord,

47 And my spirit has rejoiced in God my Savior.

48 "For He has looked [with loving care] on the humble state of His maidservant; for behold, from now on all generations will count me blessed and happy and favored by God!

49 "For He who is mighty has done great things for me; and holy is His name [to be worshiped in His purity, majesty, and glory].

50 "And His mercy is upon generation after generation toward those who [stand in great awe of God and] fear Him. From generation to generation.

51 "He has done mighty deeds with His [powerful] arm; He has scattered those who were proud in the thoughts of their heart.

52 "He has brought down rulers from their thrones, and exalted those who were humble.

55 As he spake to our fathers, to Abraham, and to his seed for ever.

56 And Mary abode with her about three months, and returned to her own house.

53 "He has filled the hungry with good things; and sent the rich away empty-handed.

54 "He has helped His servant Israel, in remembrance of His mercy,

55 Just as He promised to our fathers, to Abraham and to his descendants forever."

56 And Mary stayed with Elizabeth for about three months, and then returned to her home.

LIGHT ON THE WORD

Luke. The authorship of the book of Luke is practically undisputed. While his name does not appear in the book, evidence in the book of Acts suggests that Luke, a physician and companion of the Apostle Paul, was the author of both books. Luke was likely a Gentile by birth and well educated in Greek culture. In his writing, Luke emphasized joy at the announcement of the Good News of the Gospel. He is also known for his concern for the role of women and his interest in the have-nots of his day. Major themes in this book include feeding the hungry and ministering to the poor.

Servanthood. In biblical days, servants did not have any rights. They were expected to do what they were told without any expectation of thanks, promotion, or gratitude. Mary's self-defined "low estate" (**Luke 1:48**) parallels the servant theme of Jesus that we see illustrated throughout the Gospels as Jesus constantly took on the role of the humble servant.

TEACHING THE BIBLE LESSON

LIFE NEED FOR TODAY'S LESSON

AIM: Students will write a song of praise based on the Magnificat.

INTRODUCTION

Mary's Song

Mary's song in **Luke 1:46–55** is known as the Magnificat, which is the first word in the Latin translation of the song. This beautiful song has become an enduring hymn of the church, sung by millions of Christians down through the ages to this very day. It is not just a song of thanksgiving, but it has deep theological implications, prodding God's people to more fully understand His character. Among the topics addressed by this song are God's divine power (**vv. 49, 51–52**), holiness (**vv. 49, 51–52**), mercy (**v. 50**), and faithfulness (**vv. 53–55**).

This song was deeply rooted in the Scriptures of the Old Testament. It would not have been unusual for a pious Jew of this time period to have memorized many passages of Scripture, but it reflects well on Mary that she was apparently a pious and devout student of Scripture. The Magnificat also seems to be modeled after Hannah's prayer in **1 Samuel 2:1–10**. Mary would have known of Hannah's prayer of thanksgiving to God for giving her a long-prayed-for son, Samuel. Both women's songs present God as a champion of the poor, weak, and humble.

BIBLE LEARNING

AIM: Students will agree that the Holy Spirit speaks to us today through God's Word, the Bible.

I. MARY VISITS ELISABETH (LUKE 1:39–45)

Mary, filled with excitement and wonder at the angel's words, now hurried to visit her relative, Elisabeth. Though already related by blood, Mary and Elisabeth were now bound together by a common experience. Both women were to bear sons, but not just any sons—sons who were conceived under miraculous conditions. The births of these sons had been foretold and eagerly anticipated by the Jewish people for centuries!

39 And Mary arose in those days, and went into the hill country with haste, into a city of Judah; 40 And entered into the house of Zacharias, and saluted Elisabeth. 41 And it came to pass that, when Elisabeth heard the salutation of Mary, the babe leaped in her womb; and Elisabeth was filled with the Holy Ghost 42 And she spake out with a loud voice, and said, Blessed art thou among women, and blessed is the fruit of thy womb. 43 And whence is this to me, that the mother of my Lord should come to me? 44 For, lo, as soon as the voice of thy salutation sounded in mine ears, the babe leaped in my womb for joy. 45 And blessed is she that believed: for there shall be a performance of those things which were told her from the Lord.

Luke's use of the clause "and Mary arose in those days" seems to indicate that she took her journey immediately after the angel's visitation, probably one or two days later. That Mary took the trip fairly soon is apparent from the fact the angel Gabriel told her that Elisabeth was already six months pregnant (**v. 36**), and that Mary remained with Elisabeth for three months (**v. 56**). Mary returned home just before the birth of John (**v. 57**). The next clause "and went into the hill country with haste" also adds to the journey's urgency and immediacy. The word "haste," *spoude* (Gk. **spoo-DAY**), indicates a "speedy" dispatch and makes clear that she traveled immediately, adding excitement and a wondrous undertone to the story. Some commentators suggest that Mary went to Elisabeth because Joseph was about to put her away privately, or that she was being shunned by the inhabitants of Nazareth. However, this suggestion is baseless since her pregnancy was not evident before her travel, and Joseph and Mary had not started living together. The events recorded by **Matthew (1:18–25)** took place after her return from Elisabeth. By then, Mary would have been three months pregnant and beginning to show.

However, with excitement mixed with wonder and anxiety, Mary took the journey to see this miracle, which the angel had told her. She traveled from Nazareth in the north to a city in Judea. Some have suggested that the distance from Nazareth to Elisabeth and Zacharias' home was about 70 miles, and others suggest the journey took Mary between three and five days. This information and the city's name do not seem to matter much for Luke here, so he does not mention them. What is important to Luke is what took place as Mary enters the house of Zacharias and greets Elisabeth.

The Greek conjunction *hos* (**HOCE**) indicates a connection in time between two events, either at the same time or one right after the other. The underlying idea here is "as soon as" or "just as" Elisabeth heard Mary's greeting, a strange thing happened in her womb: the child inside "leaped" (Gk. *skirtao*, **skir-TAH-oh**, to jump). The word appears only two other times in the New Testament (**v. 44 and 6:23**) and is associated with joy. One can argue that it is natural for babies to move in the womb during the sixth month of pregnancy. Indeed, Elisabeth must have been experiencing such movements before now; however, she was able to differentiate this from other movements. This movement was extraordinary. The child, stirred by the power of the Holy Spirit, purposely revealed to Elisabeth the fulfillment of God's blessing and the prophesy of the Messiah. The child's leaping is the result of the filling of the Holy Spirit. Both events definitely happened simultaneously. The angel told Zacharias that the child born to Elisabeth would be filled with the Holy Spirit from his mother's womb (**v. 15**). Elisabeth is also filled with the Holy Spirit in the same way that the Spirit of God filled some people in the Old Testament as they prophesied, e.g., King Saul (**1 Samuel 11:6**), Saul's messengers (**1 Samuel 19:20**), and David (**2 Samuel 23:2**). This filling of the Holy Spirit is temporary and for specific purposes. It differs from the outpouring and the filling of the Holy Spirit, which started at Pentecost (**Acts 2**). Here the Holy Spirit uses Elisabeth to confirm to Mary the angel's prediction to her.

The statement "blessed art thou among women" echoes the angelic blessing from Gabriel (**v. 28**), and it means that Mary is the most blessed of all women. Her child is also blessed, which also echoes the angel's pronouncement concerning Jesus (**vv. 32–33**). Elisabeth's declaration through the Holy Spirit's power of blessings to both Mary and "the fruit of (her) womb" confirms to Mary that what God has spoken will surely happen. It also increases her faith and trust in God as the angel told her that with God, nothing is impossible (**v. 37**). The added lesson is that God uses different agents to speak to us: the Holy Spirit, angels, and humans.

Elisabeth praises Mary for her faith. This statement shows that Elisabeth is aware of God's prediction and promise to Mary. We are not told how she knew this. The natural view is that Mary might have told Elisabeth how the angel had visited and of God's promises to her. However, the supernatural view is that the Holy Spirit, as continuation of His work, probably revealed it to Elisabeth. The word "blessed" is the Greek *makarios* (**mah-KAH-ee-os**), which can also be translated as happy or fortunate, and can be used to pronounce blessing upon a person. Here Elisabeth pronounces blessing on Mary because of Mary's faith in accepting the Word of God (**cf. Psalm 1:1–2**). Why is Mary blessed? What does Elisabeth mean by the statement? We can look at this in two possible ways. The first way is to follow the King James Version translation—that she is blessed because of the assurance that God will definitely accomplish what He has spoken. Here is the premise for faith, and an urge to trust in God's faithfulness. He does not fail. Mary believed, so she is, and will be, happy. Finally, she is happy and blessed because she does not have to go through the same fate as Zacharias, who doubted God and could not speak as a result (**Luke 1:20**). Either of these two or a combination of both could explain Elisabeth's pronouncement of blessing on Mary.

II. MARY'S SONG OF PRAISE (vv. 46–56)

We first notice that Mary praises the Lord after Elisabeth, and by the Holy Spirit, confirms what the angel had told her earlier. Overwhelmed with joy and gratitude, and accepting God's promise, Mary reacts spontaneously and glorifies God.

46 And Mary said, My soul doth magnify the Lord, 47 And my spirit hath rejoiced in God my Saviour.

These verses indicate a total involvement of the whole self (emotional and spiritual) in praising God. The use of both "soul" and "spirit" underlies this fact. The word "soul" is a translation of the Greek *psuche* (**psoo-KHAY**), which generally means breath or life. It is the center of and makes up the whole being. The soul is the seat of feelings, emotion, desire, and affection.

The word "magnify" (Gk. *megaluno*, **meh-gah-LOO-no**) means to make great, extol, or esteem highly. "Spirit" (Gk. *pneuma*, **PNEW-mah**) oftentimes is synonymous with soul, and also refers to breath of life (that which gives a being existence). Mary employs the totality of her being (the soul and spirit) to glorify God in grateful worship of her Savior.

48 For he hath regarded the low estate of his handmaiden: for, behold, from henceforth all generations shall call me blessed. 49 For he that is mighty hath done to me great things; and holy is his name.

In **verses 48–49,** Mary gives the reason for her rejoicing and gratitude—God "hath regarded the low estate of his handmaiden." This means that God had looked upon her with respect, showing favor to her who was otherwise insignificant. Mary calls herself God's "handmaiden" (Gk. *doule*, **DOO-lay**), which means female slave—the lowest position one can have in the Greco-Roman culture. Women and slaves were regarded as the lowest class in the Ancient Near East, and they were often relegated to the background, the place of dishonor. To be both (woman and slave) makes her place even worse; the society has no regard for her. In contrast, God has regard for her. He has looked on her with favor, and given her a place of honor. The magnitude and extent of her elevation is brought to bear in the person who made it possible, the "mighty" and the "holy" **(v. 49).** Here Mary brings out what systematic theologians call the immutable (i.e., unchangeable) and incommunicable attributes of God—His omnipotence and holiness. Here we see God, who is so mighty and holy on one hand, able to look upon and have regard for Mary, who, on the other hand, is of the lowest class. Her low estate is not only because of her person, but also her heritage—Nazareth. Nazareth was one of the most insignificant and despised villages in Galilee **(cf. John 1:45–46).** In spite of these seeming disadvantages, God exalted and honored Mary. She has been tremendously blessed by God, she says. For "all generations shall call me blessed," which means every generation will acknowledge her as one blessed and most fortunate woman among all women **(cf. vv. 28, 42).** We have seen that the first strophe, or first structural division of Mary's poetic song, deals with God's blessing to Mary. She now turns to sing about what God has done in the life of the people of Israel **(vv. 50–53).**

51 He hath shewed strength with his arm; he hath scattered the proud in the imagination of their hearts. 52 He hath put down the mighty from their seats, and exalted them of low degree. 53 He hath filled the hungry with good things; and the rich he hath sent empty away.

These two pairs of contrasting parallels are the direct results of God's mighty act in the coming of the Messiah. By His show of strength, God has completely altered the human view of life in general. The "proud" (Gk. *huperephanos*, **hoo-pair-AY-fa-noce**), the haughty, or those who exalt themselves, are scattered. The verb "scattered" (Gk. *diaskorpizo*, **dee-ah-skor-PEED-zo**) is used figuratively here in either a military or agricultural sense. In its military sense, the strong, proud army that relies in its own strength without God is brought to nothing, driven and dispersed by a stronger force. In its agricultural sense, scattering refers to the winnowing process, where the chaff is separated from the wheat and blown away.

Not only are the proud scattered like chaff or put in disarray like an egoistic army, but God has also "put down the mighty from their seats." Here the mighty are synonymous with the proud—the "powers that be," the oppressors of the poor, the self-exalted who look down on and tyrannize others. The mighty are deprived of their self-exalted positions, while those who are truly humble ("them of low degree"), the insignificant, are exalted.

The next pair of parallels starts with the insignificant, "the hungry," which is synonymous with "them of low degree," and associated with poverty. Those who "fear Him" (**v. 50**) are fed (that is, "filled with good things") and shown mercy (**v. 50**). On the contrary, those who are "rich," proud, and self-sufficient without God, are sent "away empty." This is revolutionary indeed. It describes the purpose of Christ's coming into the world: to change the human view and principles of living. Christ spells out this principle in His Sermon on the Mount (especially **Matthew 5:3–6**), and He teaches the same to His disciples (**Matthew 23:12; Luke 18:14**).

54 He hath helped his servant Israel, in remembrance of his mercy; 55 As he spake to our fathers, to Abraham, and to his seed for ever. 56 And Mary abode with her about three months, and returned to her own house.

The third strophe of Mary's hymn reveals God's faithfulness in fulfilling His promises to Abraham by sending the Messiah. Here Mary celebrates God's mercy to Israel. Just as He promised Abraham and his descendants, God helps Israel, not forgetting His promise but remembering His mercy. This act of mercy is an old promise (covenant) God made to Abraham and all his generations after him. It is a living covenant to all humankind that is fulfilled in the incarnation of Jesus Christ—the Son of God.

Through this hymn of praise, Mary reveals the excellent nature of God: His divine power and authority over all things both spiritual and human (**vv. 49, 51**); His holiness (**v. 49**); His mercy and justice (**v. 50**); and His faithfulness and trustworthiness in fulfilling His promises (**vv. 54–55**). Through the incarnation of Christ, we realize the omnipotence, holiness, mercy, justice, and faithfulness of God. After this, Luke notes that Mary lived with Elisabeth and Zacharias for three more months. This was enough time to witness the birth of John. She remained to see the fulfillment of what God did in Elisabeth's life.

SEARCH THE SCRIPTURES

QUESTION 1

Share the importance of Mary's song for believers today. What verse resonates with your spiritual life? Why? How do you share God's truth with others?

Verse 47—my soul and heart speak praise and joy to God. I witness to others and assist them in difficult times. Answers will vary.

QUESTION 2

What does Mary's song say about God to you?

God is a provider and is true to God's Word. Answers will vary.

LIGHT ON THE WORD

The Humble and The Exalted

Mary's Song. Mary praises God's transformation of society, whereby the proud and powerful are brought low, while the lowly are brought up. Not only do Mary and Elisabeth represent the humble who have been exalted, but Nazareth signifies the revolutionary aspect of God's act through the coming of the Messiah. Historically, the Old Testament is full of examples of the proud and mighty whom God, by His infinite power and design, brought down: Pharaoh (**Exodus 15:1–11**), Haman (**Esther 6:6–7:10**), Nebuchadnezzar (**Daniel 4:24–37**), and other proud and haughty people (**1 Peter 5:5; James 4:6**). Similar examples of the humble being exalted by God are abundant: Joseph (**Genesis 41:38–45**), David (**1 Samuel 18; 2 Samuel 7**), Mordecai (**Esther 6:6–14**), Daniel (**Daniel 1:8–21**), and all the humble (**Matthew 23:12**).

BIBLE APPLICATION

AIM: Students will respond to God's promises by faith.

Even while living lives of thanksgiving for God's fulfillment of His promises in our lives, we sometimes neglect our responsibilities in His Kingdom. Mary's song points us to three practical applications of our faith. First, we are to live in great humility. A life lived in total surrender to Christ is the death of pride. Secondly, we can cast aside the world's emphasis on social status. God is at work destroying the social strata of the world, humbling the proud and exalting the humble, so we cannot live by the world's standards. Lastly, Mary's song reminds us that God's economy is not the same as ours. In our society of extreme consumerism and materialism, let us hold our possessions lightly and be generous to others.

STUDENTS' RESPONSES

AIM: Students will express how Christians can creatively share their confidence in God's promises.

When we are humble, like Mary, God will lift us up and give us a song to sing of His great works in our lives. This week, look for opportunities to praise God publicly for what He has done in your life, your family, or your community. Consciously search for ways you could bring His wonderful, "upside-down" justice into situations you encounter.

PRAYER

Dear magnificent God, Your blessings and goodness are too numerous to proclaim. Your mercy and joy are supreme. Your wisdom to choose those whom we would not choose is great news! We are chosen by You when others ignore us. Thank You Lord for keeping Your promises and loving us! In the Name of Jesus, we pray. Amen.

HOW TO SAY IT

Patriarch.   **PAY**-tree-ark.

Swaddling.   **SWAD**-ling.

DIG A LITTLE DEEPER

This section provides an additional research article to further your study of the lesson:

In Chapter 3 of *Exploring and Engaging Spirituality for Today's Children: A Holistic Approach* edited by Dr. La Verne Tolbert, Professor Joel Green (Fuller Theological Seminary) focuses on the fascinating "upside-down" comparison and contrast that Luke uses throughout his New Testament Gospel. Dr. Green enhances the reader's understanding of the metaphoric language throughout the Book of Luke and provides us with powerful insight into its meaning and purpose. Here is a chapter that is both educational and memorable.

http://www.worldcat.org/title/exploring-and-engaging-spirituality-for-todays-children-a-holistic-approach/oclc/880862090/viewport

PREPARE FOR NEXT SUNDAY

Read **Luke 1:8–20** and "The Forerunner of the Savior."

DAILY HOME BIBLE READINGS

MONDAY
The New Ruler from Bethlehem
(Micah 5:1–5)

TUESDAY
Joseph Takes Mary as His Wife
(Matthew 1:18–25)

WEDNESDAY
The Visit of the Wise Men
(Matthew 2:1–12)

THURSDAY
The Escape to Egypt
(Matthew 2:13–15)

FRIDAY
Journey from Nazareth to Bethlehem
(Luke 2:1–4)

SATURDAY
Mary Delivers Her Firstborn
(Luke 2:5–7)

SUNDAY
The Affirmation of the Promise
(Luke 1:39–56)

COMMENTS / NOTES:

THE FORERUNNER OF THE SAVIOR

BIBLE BASIS: LUKE 1:8–20

BIBLE TRUTH: Zacharias' feelings of doubt, apprehension, and joy are shared about his son John's birth.

MEMORY VERSE: "Thy wife Elisabeth shall bear thee a son, and thou shalt call his name John. And thou shalt have joy and gladness; and many shall rejoice at his birth" (from Luke 1:13–14).

LESSON AIM: By the end of the lesson, we will: EVALUATE the importance of faith as we consider Zacharias' role in the story of the birth of John; EXPLORE Zacharias' feelings of doubt and apprehension; and ACCEPT and FULFILL the tasks to which God has called us.

TEACHER PREPARATION

MATERIALS NEEDED: Quarterly Commentary/Teacher Manual, Adult Quarterly, Adult resources—charts, worksheets, and other teaching tools, paper, pens, pencils, Bibles (several different versions)

OTHER MATERIALS NEEDED / TEACHER'S NOTES:

_____

_____

LESSON OVERVIEW

LIFE NEED FOR TODAY'S LESSON
At times we are entrusted with incredible responsibilities beyond anything we might have imagined for ourselves.

BIBLE LEARNING
Luke tells of Zacharias' growing acceptance of his role as the father of John, the one called to be the forerunner of the Savior.

BIBLE APPLICATION
Despite our limitations, God's plan will go forth.

STUDENTS' RESPONSES
Believers agree that God answers our prayers in powerful and sometimes, unusual ways.

LESSON SCRIPTURE

LUKE 1:8–20, KJV

8 And it came to pass, that while he executed the priest's office before God in the order of his course,

9 According to the custom of the priest's office, his lot was to burn incense when he

LUKE 1:8–20, AMP

8 Now it happened while Zacharias was serving as priest before God in the appointed order of his priestly division,

9 as was the custom of the priesthood, he was chosen by lot to enter [the sanctuary of]

went into the temple of the Lord.

10 And the whole multitude of the people were praying without at the time of incense.

11 And there appeared unto him an angel of the Lord standing on the right side of the altar of incense.

12 And when Zacharias saw him, he was troubled, and fear fell upon him.

13 But the angel said unto him, Fear not, Zacharias: for thy prayer is heard; and thy wife Elisabeth shall bear thee a son, and thou shalt call his name John.

14 And thou shalt have joy and gladness; and many shall rejoice at his birth.

15 For he shall be great in the sight of the Lord, and shall drink neither wine nor strong drink; and he shall be filled with the Holy Ghost, even from his mother's womb.

16 And many of the children of Israel shall he turn to the Lord their God.

17 And he shall go before him in the spirit and power of Elias, to turn the hearts of the fathers to the children, and the disobedient to the wisdom of the just; to make ready a people prepared for the Lord.

18 And Zacharias said unto the angel, Whereby shall I know this? for I am an old man, and my wife well stricken in years.

19 And the angel answering said unto him, I am Gabriel, that stand in the presence of God; and am sent to speak unto thee, and to shew thee these glad tidings.

20 And, behold, thou shalt be dumb, and not able to speak, until the day that these things shall be performed, because thou believest not my words, which shall be fulfilled in their season.

the temple of the Lord and burn incense [on the altar of incense].

10 And all the congregation was praying outside [in the court of the temple] at the hour of the incense offering.

11 And an angel of the Lord appeared to him, standing to the right of the altar of incense.

12 When Zacharias saw the angel, he was troubled and overcome with fear.

13 But the angel said to him, "Do not be afraid, Zacharias, because your petition [in prayer] was heard, and your wife Elizabeth will bear you a son, and you will name him John.

14 You will have great joy and delight, and many will rejoice over his birth,

15 for he will be great and distinguished in the sight of the Lord; and will never drink wine or liquor, and he will be filled with and empowered to act by the Holy Spirit while still in his mother's womb.

16 He will turn many of the sons of Israel back [from sin] to [love and serve] the Lord their God.

17 It is he who will go as a forerunner before Him in the spirit and power of Elijah, TO TURN THE HEARTS OF THE FATHERS BACK TO THE CHILDREN, and the disobedient to the attitude of the righteous [which is to seek and submit to the will of God]—in order to make ready a people [perfectly] prepared [spiritually and morally] for the Lord."

18 And Zacharias said to the angel, "How will I be certain of this? For I am an old man and my wife is advanced in age."

19 The angel replied and said to him, "I am Gabriel; I stand and minister in the [very]

presence of God, and I have been sent [by Him] to speak to you and to bring you this good news.

20 Listen carefully, you will be continually silent and unable to speak until the day when these things take place, because you did not believe what I told you; but my words will be fulfilled at their proper time."

LIGHT ON THE WORD

Elisabeth. Priests could marry only a woman of pure Jewish lineage, with preference toward descendants of Aaron. Zacharias' wife, Elisabeth, met both qualifications. Nevertheless, Zacharias and Elisabeth lived in shame because they were unable to have children. In ancient times, to be barren was a tragedy. A childless couple would have no one to support them in their old age, but worse than that, barrenness was often considered a curse or divine judgment for sin. To nullify the idea that their barrenness was a result of God's judgment on Elisabeth, Luke clearly points out that both Zacharias and Elisabeth were "upright" and "blameless" in their relationship with God (**Luke 1:6**).

The Nazarite Vow. In **Numbers 6:1–21**, God delineated a special vow called the Nazarite vow. This was a vow of separation to God and involved consecrating oneself for a specific amount of time of special devotion to God. A person under the constraint of a Nazarite vow was prohibited from drinking any wine or other fermented drink. The Nazarite was also prohibited from eating or drinking anything that came from the grapevine—grapes, raisins, grape juice, and even the seeds and skins of grapes.

Nazarites were also prohibited from using a razor (i.e., cutting their hair) for the duration of their vow, and they could not go near a dead body. They were expected to be entirely devoted to God. At the completion of the vow, Nazarites went through a prescribed ceremony where they presented specific offerings to God.

TEACHING THE BIBLE LESSON

LIFE NEED FOR TODAY'S LESSON

AIM: Students will agree that they are entrusted with incredible responsibilities beyond anything they might have imagined for themselves.

INTRODUCTION

Priestly Duties

According to God's instructions, every male who was directly descended from Aaron was automatically a priest (see **Exodus 28:1**; **Leviticus 8**). Because of this, there were many more priests than there were jobs for them to do. The priests were divided into 12 divisions according to their lineage. Every priest would serve during the special holy days such as Passover, Pentecost, or the Feast of Tabernacles, but other than that, each division served two periods of one week each. The priests would draw lots to see who would serve each week. Priests who loved God and loved serving Him considered it the highlight of their life to be chosen to serve for a week. Within each division of nearly one thousand priests, the daily duties were also determined by lot. Daily duties included offering the morning or evening sacrifice for the nation of Israel, other assorted offerings of flour and oil, drink offerings, and burning incense.

BIBLE LEARNING

AIM: Students will evaluate Zacharias' growing acceptance of his role as the father of John, the one called to be the forerunner of the Savior.

I. THE CHANCE OF A LIFETIME (LUKE 1:8–10)

Zacharias was a priest of God from the division that had descended from Aaron through the line of Abijah (see **1 Chronicles 24:5–19**, esp. **v. 10**). He had not only been chosen to serve for his division's week, but he had been chosen to offer the incense. This was a day that any priest would have dreamed of!

Zacharias entered the Holy Place and began to pray near the heated altar of incense. The Bible does not say that Zacharias was praying for his own needs during this time. Perhaps he was praying for the coming of the Messiah, a prayer that was often prayed and the answer longed for. All people of Israel were constantly waiting in eager expectation for their Deliverer to come. Even now, as Zacharias interceded for the Jewish nation, they were outside mingling their prayers with his.

8 And it came to pass, that while he executed the priest's office before God in the order of his course, 9 According to the custom of the priest's office, his lot was to burn incense when he went into the temple of the Lord 10 And the whole multitude of the people were praying without at the time of incense.

After all his introductions, Luke uses verses 8–10 to describe the setting for the following story. The angel's appearance, Zacharias' response, and the angel's message all happened while the course of Abijah (the division in which Zacharias served, **Luke 1:5**) was engaged in its scheduled turn of Temple service.

Fortunately for Zacharias, he was assigned to perform the particular service of burning incense. Given the number of priests serving in each of the twenty-four divisions, and given that only one priest was required to offer incense at the daily sacrifices, this was a once-in-a-lifetime privilege for Zacharias. Moreover, it afforded him the opportunity to go into the Temple sanctuary (**v. 9**; Gk. *naos*, **nah-OSE**), which was comprised of the Holy Place and the Holy of Holies, as opposed to the entire Temple complex (cf. **Luke 2:27, 37, 46**; Gk. *hieron*, **hee-eh-RON**). Few priests were ever afforded this privilege. Because of the large number of priests, no ordinary priest was allowed to burn incense more than once in a lifetime. Consequently, this was the high point of Zacharias' priestly career.

II. VISITATION FROM AN ANGEL (vv. 11–20)

As Zacharias ministered before the Lord, an angel suddenly appeared to him and assured him that his prayers had been heard. God was going to send the Messiah! The personal prayers of Zacharias' heart were answered, too. He would become the father of a son—but not just any son. Zacharias' son would be a prophet, a Nazarite, a forerunner of the Messiah!

Zacharias was instructed to name his son John, meaning "God is gracious." This unexpected son, filled with and empowered by the Holy Spirit from birth, was destined to play an enormous role in God's plan of salvation and would bring joy to many.

11 And there appeared unto him an angel of the Lord standing on the right side of the altar of incense.

Luke further says that the angel was "standing on the right side of the altar of incense." To stand or be placed on the right side of someone or something suggests being favored (e.g, **Matthew 25:34**). In other words, the right side is the favored side—the side of joy and happiness and salvation. Here, when the angel of the Lord appeared "on the right side of the altar of incense," he was positioned to announce a blessing and bestow a favor upon the one who witnessed his appearance.

12 And when Zacharias saw him, he was troubled, and fear fell upon him.

When Zacharias saw the angel of the Lord, "he was troubled." Luke uses the Greek word *tarasso* (**tah-RAS-so**), which—when used in reference to people—expresses uneasiness mixed with fear, even to the point of shaking. Thus Luke adds, "and fear fell on him." Fear like this is the normal reaction of those who experience the supernatural presence of God.

13 But the angel said unto him, Fear not, Zacharias: for thy prayer is heard; and thy wife Elisabeth shall bear thee a son, and thou shalt call his name John.

Throughout the Bible, "fear not" is a common statement of reassurance upon witnessing or experiencing the supernatural activity and presence of God (see **Genesis 15:1**; **Mark 5:36**; **Luke 1:30**; **Revelation 1:17**).

The basis for the angel's words of reassurance is the good news that Zacharias' prayer has been heard. Exactly what Zacharias had been praying for is not clear. It is likely that he was praying for children. Luke is sure to set up (**v. 7**) that Zacharias and his wife, Elisabeth, are childless and beyond child-bearing age. It makes the angel's words more easily understood: "Your prayer [to have a baby] is answered: Elisabeth will have a baby."

Zacharias might also have been praying for the salvation of Israel. Thus the angel's declaration and instruction that "Elisabeth shall bear thee a son, and thou shalt call his name John," was enough to let Zacharias know that his son-to-be would, in some way, be involved in Israel's salvation.

In the social culture of Zacharias' day, the customary privilege was for the father to name his son. In this instance, the name John is divinely provided and therefore has significant meaning: "Jehovah has been gracious." Because of the Lord's grace, John's birth will bring heavenly and eternal joy, so the following verse is an affirmation.

14 And thou shalt have joy and gladness; and many shall rejoice at his birth.

This verse points to a special kind of joy that will come to Zacharias and Elisabeth, and then spread to many. Luke uses three words in connection with John's birth to describe this special kind of joy: *chara* (**khah-RAH**), translated "joy"; *agalliasis* (**ah-gall-LEE-ah-sees**), translated "gladness;" and *chairo* (**KHEYE-ro**). Luke wants his readers to know that God will do a special work through Zacharias and Elisabeth's son, John, that will benefit many in Israel. God will involve John in a plan for saving people.

15 For he shall be great in the sight of the Lord, and shall drink neither wine nor strong drink; and he shall be filled with the Holy Ghost, even from his mother's womb. 16 And many of the children of Israel shall he turn to the Lord their God. 17 And he shall go before him in the spirit and power of Elias, to turn the hearts of the fathers to the children, and the disobedient to the wisdom of the just; to make ready a people prepared for the Lord.

The angel prophesies to them of John's destiny. He will be a great man; note that he will be great in the sight of the Lord, not necessarily other people. John would also be restricted from drinking wine or any alcohol, similar to the lifelong Nazarite vow of Samson (**Judges 13:4–5, 7**). He would also be filled with the Holy Spirit from the his mother's womb.

This greatness would be the result of his life mission. John would turn many of the Children of Israel to the Lord. Next, the angel paraphrases **Malachi 4:5–6** in describing John's mission: he would be the forerunner of the new exodus as prophesied by Isaiah (**40:1–5**). John's role was to "make ready a people prepared for the Lord." The word for "make ready" (Gk. *hetoimazo*, **heh-toy-MAHD-zoh**) that Luke uses here is only used in the New Testament in an ethical or religious sense. John's life and message would be used to prepare the people spiritually for this new exodus.

18 And Zacharias said unto the angel, Whereby shall I know this? for I am an old man, and my wife well stricken in years. 19 And the angel answering said unto him, I am Gabriel, that stand in the presence of God; and am sent to speak unto thee, and to shew thee these glad tidings. 20 And, behold, thou shalt be dumb, and not able to speak, until the day that these things shall be performed, because thou believest not my words, which shall be fulfilled in their season.

Zacharias does not believe the angel's words. Similar to Abraham before him, he asks for confirmation (**Genesis 15:8**). The angel gives his qualifications as a messenger of God, but he also delivers some bad news: Zacharias would not speak until the birth of John, a sign that confirms the promise, but also rebukes Zacharias' lack of faith.

Zacharias was instructed to name his son John, meaning "God is gracious." This unexpected son, filled with and empowered by the Holy Spirit from birth, was destined to play an enormous role in God's plan of salvation and would bring joy to many.

SEARCH THE SCRIPTURES

QUESTION 1
You may have experienced barrenness in an area in your life. What might be your prayer during this time?

Dear Heavenly Father, please fill these spaces of emptiness with Your goodness and comfort. Thank you for working all things in my life for good. I continue to trust You. In the Name of Jesus, Amen. (Answers will vary.)

QUESTION 2
How might a discussion of the seriousness of the Nazarite vow help you plan a time of consecration for you and your family?

Set aside a particular time and have the family to prepare a favorite Scripture to share with one another. We would eat selected foods on certain days to show our discipline. Answers will vary.

LIGHT ON THE WORD

Voluntary Devotion
Though taking a Nazarite vow was usually voluntary, the Bible includes instances where people were apparently chosen by God to be Nazarites for life. Among these are Samson (see **Judges 13:2–5**), Samuel (see **1 Samuel 1:11**), and John the Baptist (**Luke 1:15**).

BIBLE APPLICATION

AIM: Students will agree that despite our limitations, God's plan will go forth.

Zacharias' request for proof from the angel contrasts sharply with Mary's request for details. Though as humans we tend toward skepticism, how might we more fully trust

God's promises and joyfully express our realization of His activity in our lives?

STUDENTS' RESPONSES

AIM: Students will agree that God answers our prayers in powerful and sometimes unusual ways.

No doubt in a daze, Zacharias silently finished his memorable week of service and went home. Elisabeth conceived a child, and Zacharias got the proof he had been seeking. It is noteworthy that Zacharias heard from God while he was in the Temple worshiping and serving God. He had placed himself in a position to hear from God. When we spend time in God's presence, we open up the door of communication. God speaks to those who listen for His voice.

PRAYER

Dear loving Lord, Your Holy Spirit fills us when we are empty. His presence in our lives gives us comfort. We love You and trust You no matter what our circumstances may be. Open our hearts even more to depend on and trust in You. In the Name of Jesus, we pray. Amen.

HOW TO SAY IT

Nazarite.   **NA**-zur-ite.

Jehovah.   juh-**HOE**-vah.

DIG A LITTLE DEEPER

This section provides an additional research article to further your study of the lesson:

Understanding the Old Testament's usage of vows is imperative to our biblical interpretation and application. In this article, the author explores the practice of making vows and the significance of vows that is specifically found in the book of Leviticus. The author concludes this study with practical insights about how vows are influencing the current lives of Christians, including benefits and drawbacks.

https://bible.org/seriespage/22-value-vow-leviticus-27

PREPARE FOR NEXT SUNDAY

Read **Luke 2:8–20** and "The Savior Has Been Born."

DAILY HOME BIBLE READINGS

MONDAY
Aaron and Sons, a Perpetual Priesthood
(Exodus 40:12–25)

TUESDAY
Tending the Altar of Incense
(Exodus 30:1–10)

WEDNESDAY
Chosen by Lot to Serve
(Acts 1:21–26)

THURSDAY
Zacharias and Elisabeth are Childless
(Luke 1:5–7)

FRIDAY
His Name is John
(Luke 1:57–66)

SATURDAY
Testimony of John the Baptist
(John 1:19–23)

SUNDAY
Birth of John the Baptist Foretold
(Luke 1:8–20)

COMMENTS / NOTES:

_____

_____

_____

_____

THE SAVIOR HAS BEEN BORN

BIBLE BASIS: LUKE 2:8–20

BIBLE TRUTH: Luke describes the circumstances of the birth announcement of Jesus to the shepherds.

MEMORY VERSE: "For unto you is born this day in the city of David a Saviour, which is Christ the Lord" (Luke 2:11).

LESSON AIM: By the end of this lesson, we will: EVALUATE the circumstances around Jesus' birth; EXPRESS joy at the Good News of God's fulfilled promise; and PROCLAIM the Good News of God's gift of the Messiah.

TEACHER PREPARATION

MATERIALS NEEDED: Quarterly Commentary/Teacher Manual, Adult Quarterly, Adult resources—charts, worksheets, and other teaching tools, paper, pens, pencils, Bibles (several different versions)

OTHER MATERIALS NEEDED / TEACHER'S NOTES:

_____

_____

LESSON OVERVIEW

LIFE NEED FOR TODAY'S LESSON
God elevates the humble.

BIBLE LEARNING
The shepherds, whose lives were difficult, received an announcement of God's fulfilled promise of the Messiah.

BIBLE APPLICATION
Believers can express joy at the Good News of God's fulfilled promise.

STUDENTS' RESPONSES
Christians must declare the Good News and share the blessings of Christ with others.

LESSON SCRIPTURE

LUKE 2:8–20, KJV

8 And there were in the same country shepherds abiding in the field, keeping watch over their flock by night.

9 And, lo, the angel of the Lord came upon them, and the glory of the Lord shone round about them: and they were sore afraid.

10 And the angel said unto them, Fear not: for, behold, I bring you good tidings of great

LUKE 2:8–20, AMP

8 In the same region there were shepherds staying out in the fields, keeping watch over their flock by night.

9 And an angel of the Lord suddenly stood before them, and the glory of the Lord flashed and shone around them, and they were terribly frightened.

10 But the angel said to them, "Do not be

joy, which shall be to all people.

11 For unto you is born this day in the city of David a Saviour, which is Christ the Lord.

12 And this shall be a sign unto you; Ye shall find the babe wrapped in swaddling clothes, lying in a manger.

13 And suddenly there was with the angel a multitude of the heavenly host praising God, and saying,

14 Glory to God in the highest, and on earth peace, good will toward men.

15 And it came to pass, as the angels were gone away from them into heaven, the shepherds said one to another, Let us now go even unto Bethlehem, and see this thing which is come to pass, which the Lord hath made known unto us.

16 And they came with haste, and found Mary, and Joseph, and the babe lying in a manger.

17 And when they had seen it, they made known abroad the saying which was told them concerning this child.

18 And all they that heard it wondered at those things which were told them by the shepherds.

19 But Mary kept all these things, and pondered them in her heart.

20 And the shepherds returned, glorifying and praising God for all the things that they had heard and seen, as it was told unto them.

afraid; for behold, I bring you good news of great joy which will be for all the people.

11 For this day in the city of David there has been born for you a Savior, who is Christ the Lord (the Messiah).

12 And this will be a sign for you [by which you will recognize Him]: you will find a Baby wrapped in [swaddling] cloths and lying in a manger."

13 Then suddenly there appeared with the angel a multitude of the heavenly host (angelic army) praising God and saying,

14 "Glory to God in the highest [heaven], and on earth peace among men with whom He is well-pleased."

15 When the angels had gone away from them into heaven, the shepherds began saying one to another, "Let us go straight to Bethlehem, and see this [wonderful] thing that has happened which the Lord has made known to us."

16 So they went in a hurry and found their way to Mary and Joseph, and the Baby as He lay in the manger.

17 And when they had seen this, they made known what had been told them about this Child,

18 and all who heard it were astounded and wondered at what the shepherds told them.

19 But Mary treasured all these things, giving careful thought to them and pondering them in her heart.

20 The shepherds returned, glorifying and praising God for all that they had heard and seen, just as it had been told them.

LIGHT ON THE WORD

The Good News. Luke's story differs from the story in Matthew, where the magi follow a star to Bethlehem to find the Savior in a manger. Luke's version describes humble local shepherds responding to a sign that a Savior has been born. In ancient days the occupation of shepherd was despised. Shepherds were disdained as lazy, deceitful people who grazed their flocks on the property of land owners. It is hard to imagine this kind of description bestowed upon shepherds. For today, the word shepherd conjures positive, pastoral images as Jesus is associated with such metaphors as the Good shepherd, protector, defender and guardian of His sheep; and we, the children of God, represent His sheep. The shepherds witness the radiance of the heavenly glory, showing how our daily lives can easily be interrupted with divine revelation. In this context, the message spoken by the angels announces the Good News to all people that no ordinary child is born; God's Son, the Savior of all humanity has entered the earthly realm.

TEACHING THE BIBLE LESSON

LIFE NEED FOR TODAY'S LESSON

AIM: Students will rejoice about the birth of our Savior.

INTRODUCTION

Angels of the Lord

An angel of the Lord is more properly translated as a "messenger" of God. Angels performed special functions at particular times in the history of Israel. Sometimes the angel of the Lord is depicted as acting for the Lord. Angels possess greater power than humans. The English word "angel" comes from the Greek word messenger. Some angels appear in human form. In certain passages the angel refers to God delivering His own message (**Genesis 18:2–15**).

Angels appear in the presence of God's people to announce good news (**Luke 2:9–11**), warn of danger (**Genesis 19:15**), guard from evil (**Deuteronomy 3:28; 6:22**), guide and protect (**Exodus 14:19**), nourish (**Genesis 21:14–20**), or instruct (**Acts 7:38**).

BIBLE LEARNING

AIM: Students will evaluate why God chose the shepherds, whose lives were difficult, to receive an announcement of God's fulfilled promise of the Messiah.

I. THE ANNOUNCEMENT: JESUS IS BORN (LUKE 2:8–9)

The title Messiah is derived from the Hebrew word *mashiakh*, a verbal adjective meaning "an anointed one." The New Testament writers describe and affirm Jesus' Messiahship in all four Gospel accounts. Jesus is described as the fulfillment of Israel's long expectation of a King who would deliver them from their oppressors. Jesus fulfilled those prophecies in a way that Israel didn't expect. He became the Savior of, not only the Jewish people, but also of the whole world, delivering humankind from sin and reconciling humanity's relationship with God.

8 And there were in the same country shepherds abiding in the field, keeping watch over their flock by night. 9 And, lo, the angel of the Lord came upon them, and the glory of the Lord shone round about them: and they were sore afraid.

In the following verses, Luke details the strange events that happened after the birth of Christ—the angelic announcement. Luke writes about shepherds living in the same country (or region), who were keeping their flock at night. The angel came to announce the birth of Christ. The fact that the shepherds were grazing their herd in the field by night contradicts the assumption that Christ was born in December.

Shepherds never kept flocks outside during the winter months because of the cold. It was customary to send flocks out after the Passover until the first rain in October or November. The actual month and year of Christ's birth is impossible to prove. Throughout the centuries, different Christian sects have given hundreds of suggestions for the date of His birth, but to no avail. However, we do not need to speculate. One thing is certain: He was born of a virgin in Bethlehem of Judea according to Scripture.

As the shepherds watch their flock, the angel suddenly appears to them. The glory of the Lord shines around them. The "glory" (Gk. *doxa*, **DOK-sah**) describes the radiating splendor and majesty of God's presence. In Scripture, glory always symbolizes the presence of God **(Exodus 24:16; 1 Kings 8:10; Isaiah 6:1–6)**, and it can be seen or felt in different forms.

God did not reveal His Son to the rich and powerful, but instead purposely made known our Messiah's arrival to lowly shepherds. Some biblical commentaries suggest these shepherds delivered the lambs for the Temple sacrifices performed for the forgiveness of sin. How humbling that God would choose these shepherds to greet His Son, the Majestic Lamb!

II. THE FULFILLMENT: JESUS IS GOD (vv. 10–15)

Luke's focus on the shepherds during that night carries a number of reasons and theological implications. The main reason is probably for the purpose of identification. Shepherding in the Jewish tradition was a lowly occupation usually reserved for slaves. Shepherds were not only considered poor at the time of Jesus, but also uneducated and therefore unlikely to be divine messengers or persons of any authority.

This story recaps how God invites us to join Him in His plans, not the other way around. Jesus established God's kingdom on earth,

healed humanity's physical impairments, and delivered us from sin. His birth gave humankind a new way to access God. Jesus' ultimate death on the Cross brought peace, everlasting life, hope, and permanent access to God. The story of Jesus' birth is a melody of hope, joy, and love that has enthused musicians for more than 2,000 years. The angel's song is an unparalleled favorite: "Glory to God in the Highest."

10 And the angel said unto them, Fear not: for, behold, I bring you good tidings of great joy, which shall be to all people. 11 For unto you is born this day in the city of David a Saviour, which is Christ the Lord.

Here again the reassuring words of the angel, "Fear not" (cf. **1:13, 30**), are echoed. The angel tells them not to fear and tells them why he is bearing good news. In Greek, this phrase is a single word, the verb *euaggelizo* (**ew-ang-gheh-LEED-zo**), which means to announce or declare good news. The English verb "evangelize" is a transliteration of the Greek, which can mean to preach, especially the Gospel. Hence, evangelism is the act of preaching, and evangelists are those who preach or proclaim the Good News of the Gospel. In the Greek translation of the Old Testament, *euaggelizo* referred to any type of happy news, but in the New Testament, it is used primarily for the Gospel of salvation. The angel qualifies the Good News that he announces to the shepherds; it will not only bring great joy, but is also for all people. The words "all people" (Gk. *pas laos*, **PAHS lah-OSE**) communicate the idea of all of God's people as a single group, which is then extended to all groups of peoples in **24:47**. Therefore, this Gospel is for all nationalities and intended by God to bring joy to all people universally. The angel announces the Good News, that the long-expected Messiah, the hope of Israel, the Savior, is born.

Notice how the angel describes this newborn babe. First, He is a "Saviour" (Gk. *soter*, so-TARE), meaning a deliverer, a preserver; this name was given by the ancients to deities, princes, kings, and men who had brought deliverance to their country. It is used repeatedly for both God and His Christ, the medium of God's salvation to humankind.

Secondly, He is Christ. The word "Christ" is a direct transliteration of the Greek word *Christos* (**khrees-TOCE**), which means anointed (the anointed one), an equivalent of the Hebrew word *Messiah*, both of which are descriptors of Jesus. For some Jews in the first century AD, the Messiah would be the King of the Jews, a political leader who would defeat their enemies and bring a golden era of peace and prosperity. In Christian thought, the term Messiah refers to Jesus' role as a spiritual deliverer, setting His people free from sin and death. In Old Testament times, anointing with oil was part of the ritual of commissioning a person for a special task; the phrase "anointed one" was applied to the person in such cases. The word "messiah" is used more than 30 times to describe kings (**2 Samuel 1:14, 16**), priests (**Leviticus 4:3, 5, 16**), and the patriarchs (**Psalm 105:15**). The Persian king Cyrus was referred to as a messiah (**Isaiah 45:1**). The word is also used for King David, who became the model of the messianic king who would come at the end of the age (**2 Samuel 22:51; Psalm 2:2**). During the time of Daniel, the word "Messiah" was used as an actual title of the future king (**Daniel 9:25–26**). Even later, as the Jewish people struggled against their political enemies, the Messiah came to be thought of as a political, military ruler. Because of political and military expectations attached to the Messiah as deliverer, many Jews did not accept Jesus as God's chosen Messiah. In the first and second centuries, those who did accept Jesus became part of the church, and today those who do either join Christian churches or Messianic Judaism.

Thirdly, He is the "Lord." The word is a translation of the Greek *kurios* (**KOO-ree-oce**), meaning master. It signifies ownership, one with supreme authority over another, or a group of people. It is a title of honor expressing respect and reverence by a servant to his or her master. The word was used in reference to princes, chiefs, and the Roman emperor. In the African context, servants, students, or apprentices call their owners, teachers, or instructors "master" as a sign of respect, never using their names. The Igbo call their master *Nna anyi ukwu* ("our big father" or "dad") or *Oga*. To them the owner, teacher, or instructor has the same responsibility and care over them as their real father while under their instruction. As such, they are obligated to respect them just like their birth father or mother. "Lord" is often used in the New Testament for God and the Christ. Here the angel's designation of the newborn babe as the Lord identifies Him as the possessor and supreme owner of all creation. Later in the Bible, the Apostle Peter declares that "God hath made ... Jesus ... both Lord and Christ" (**Acts 2:36**). While Christ refers to Jesus' humanity, Lord refers to His deity.

12 And this shall be a sign unto you; Ye shall find the babe wrapped in swaddling clothes, lying in a manger. 13 And suddenly there was with the angel a multitude of the heavenly host praising God, and saying, 14 Glory to God in the highest, and on earth peace, good will toward men.

As the angel announces the news to the shepherds, he is suddenly joined by "a multitude of the heavenly host praising God." The word "host" (Gk. *stratia*, **strah-tee-AH**) means an army or rank of soldiers. They are probably too many to count; hence Luke uses the adjective "multitude" (Gk. *plethos*, **play-THOS**) to describe them. This is a sign that something amazing is happening and that this child is no ordinary child.

The heavenly host fills the air with praises to God, singing, "Glory to God in the highest, and on earth peace, good will toward men."

With the phrase "glory to God in the highest," the angels seem to declare the purpose of the newborn child's birth. First, His birth brings the highest degree of glory to God. Here the angels foresee the ultimate purpose of Christ on earth—to glorify God through His death and resurrection. Second, Christ's birth ushers in peace on earth. This peace is between a holy God and sinful humanity—peace made possible by and purchased through the redemptive blood of Christ. This peace is offered freely to all who come to Him through faith, the perfect peace that starts inwardly and radiates out; it affects others, making it possible for people to live peaceably with one another. Isaiah said centuries before that He shall be called "the Prince of Peace" (Isaiah 9:6). Thirdly, the birth of Christ reveals God's "good will" for His creation. Right from the beginning, God has never willed otherwise. His desires for His children have always been for their good or well-being, and He seeks to convince us of that desire.

15 And it came to pass, as the angels were gone away from them into heaven, the shepherds said one to another, Let us now go even unto Bethlehem, and see this thing which is come to pass, which the Lord hath made known unto us.

After these spectacular and supernatural events, the shepherds decide to go to Bethlehem to see for themselves what the angels had told them. Their decision to go is not to verify the truth of what they were told—they never questioned or doubted it—but rather to see this strange event that the Lord has revealed to them through the angels. The clause "this thing which is come to pass" confirms the fact that they accepted the angels' message as truth from God.

III. THE RESPONSE: JESUS IS PRAISEWORTHY (vv. 16–20)

When the shepherds saw the child in the manager, they rejoiced. They recalled the angel's words and gladly shared all they had heard and seen about the child. Can you imagine how Joseph and Mary must have felt hearing such unbelievable revelatory announcements about their child? The only thing Mary could do is treasure these symphonic lyrics in her heart and consider the meaning of these wonderful events. All who heard the angelic announcement were amazed. In these verses, the author repeatedly emphasizes the theme of faithful witness to the Gospel. The shepherds now join the chorus of witnesses because they have seen and heard God's revelation. The result of the whole episode is the response that should arise from all God's people: the shepherds returned to their flocks glorifying and praising God.

16 And they came with haste, and found Mary, and Joseph, and the babe lying in a manger.

Hence, they hurried with excitement into Bethlehem to visit the newborn child. They find not only what the angel has told them concerning the child (v. 12), but they also find Mary and Joseph with the baby in the manger. What happened to their flocks, whether the shepherds left them by themselves under the protection of God, or under the care of some other people, the Bible does not tell us. How they found the right manger, the Bible does not say. However, the verb used here, "found" (Gk. *aneurisko*, **ah-new-RE-ES-ko**), implies that they searched before they found the child.

17 And when they had seen it, they made known abroad the saying which was told them concerning this child. 18 And all they that heard it wondered at those things which were told them by the shepherds. 19 But Mary kept all these things, and pondered them in her heart.

The shepherds were the first to hear the Good News of the birth of the Savior, and also the first to proclaim it to others. Their message was simple; they declared what the angels told them concerning the child, and what they had seen. Their message left the listeners with wonder and marvel. However, Mary's reaction is more subdued, as she "kept all these things, and pondered them in her heart." "All these things" includes the story the shepherds told—the appearance of the angel and the heavenly host.

20 And the shepherds returned, glorifying and praising God for all the things that they had heard and seen, as it was told unto them.

After visiting the newborn, and finding the child as the angels had told them, the shepherds return, glorifying and praising God. The object of their joyful praise is obvious—the long-expected Messiah is born and they have been witnesses. The birth of a Redeemer brings joy and peace to those who accept Him. Here the shepherds accepted the good tidings. Therefore, they praised and worshiped the Lord, and proclaimed to others the wonders of God's dealing with humankind. Like the shepherds, we are called to declare the birth of the Savior and its purpose to the world. Christ was born to bring peace and redemption to the world. This event occurred more than two thousand years ago, but it is as still relevant to us today as it was then. He came that we might have peace. He suffered that we might be healed, and He died that we might live. That is the message of Christmas.

SEARCH THE SCRIPTURES
QUESTION 1

If someone told you that an angel or the Lord told them good news, how would you respond?

I might be skeptical, but the Bible does say that we entertain angels unaware. Answers will vary.

QUESTION 2

Have you ever responded like Mary when you heard something special? If so, what was the outcome?

Mary kept everything in her heart. Even though some people thought I should have told them my good news, I am comfortable with my decision. Answers will vary.

LIGHT ON THE WORD
Shepherds Symbolize Care

In both the Old and New Testaments, shepherds symbolize those who care for God's people. Christ later identifies Himself in John's Gospel as the "good Shepherd" (**John 10:2, 11, 12, 14, 16**). The psalmist also writes, "The Lord is my shepherd" (**Psalm 23:1**). A number of passages in both testaments identify the Lord as the Shepherd of His people (**Isaiah 40:11; Jeremiah 23:1–4; Hebrews 13:20; 1 Peter 2:25, 5:2**).

BIBLE APPLICATION

AIM: Students will agree that believers can express joy at the Good News of God's fulfilled promise.

During the Christmas season, many people get into debt purchasing Christmas gifts. In all the hustle and bustle, we forget the real reason for the season. Christmas is more than just gifts under the tree. God has given us His Son, the greatest gift of them all. Jesus is the gift for all seasons and one we should share more readily than any other gift throughout the year. When is the last time you shared the Good News of Jesus?

STUDENTS' RESPONSES

AIM: Students will agree that Christians have a mandate to share the Good News and blessings of Christ with others.

179

How do we share the Good News of Jesus with our friends, family, and community? Be alert to the opportunities that may exist for you this week.

PRAYER

Dear Father, thank You for sending Your Son, Jesus Christ, as our Savior. We rejoice! Help us to share this Good News and the hope that Jesus brings, with someone this week. In Jesus' Name we pray, amen.

HOW TO SAY IT

Patriarch.   **PAY**-tree-ark.

Swaddling.   **SWAD**-ling.

DIG A LITTLE DEEPER

This section provides an additional research article to further your study of the lesson:

The Christmas season creates a variety of emotional responses. Whether these feelings are positive or negative depends upon each person's sense of emotional well-being. The joy of the celebration is often lost when the people decide to focus on their temporal situations. This brief message of hope reorients the Christian about the true reason for the season.

http://www.crosswalk.com/who-is-jesus/birth-of-jesus-christ/how-will-you-respond-to-the-birth-of-the-savior-jesus-christ-1454293.html

PREPARE FOR NEXT SUNDAY

Read **Psalm 33:1–9** and "Praising God the Creator."

DAILY HOME BIBLE READINGS

MONDAY
The New Ruler from Bethlehem
(Micah 5:1–5)

TUESDAY
Joseph Takes Mary as His Wife
(Matthew 1:18–25)

WEDNESDAY
The Visit of the Wise Men
(Matthew 2:1–12)

THURSDAY
The Escape to Egypt
(Matthew 2:13–15)

FRIDAY
Journey from Nazareth to Bethlehem
(Luke 2:1–4)

SATURDAY
Mary Delivers Her Firstborn
(Luke 2:5–7)

SUNDAY
The Savior Has Been Born
(Luke 2:8–20)

Sources:

Life Application Study Bible, New International Version. Wheaton, IL: Tyndale House Publishers, Inc., 1991. 1791-1792.

Jamieson, Robert, Fausset, A.R., Brown, David, *Commentary Practical and Explanatory on the Whole Bible*: Regency Reference Library, Grand Rapids, MI: Zondervan Publishing House, 1961. 991-992.

Strong, James. *Strong's Exhaustive Concordance of the Bible.* Nashville, TN: Thomas Nelson Publishers, 1990. 1027.

COMMENTS / NOTES:

_____
_____
_____
_____
_____
_____
_____
_____
_____
_____
_____

PRAISING GOD THE CREATOR

BIBLE BASIS: Psalm 33:1–9

BIBLE TRUTH: God is the Creator, Lord, Savior, and Deliverer; He alone is worthy of our trust and praise.

MEMORY VERSE: "By the word of the LORD were the heavens made; and all the host of them by the breath of his mouth" (Psalm 33:6).

LESSON AIM: By the end of this lesson, we will: RESOLVE that God is the Creator of all things and that He is in control of our lives; APPRECIATE His provisions and goodness; and COMMIT to making praise of God a major focus in our lives throughout the year.

TEACHER PREPARATION

MATERIALS NEEDED: Quarterly Commentary/Teacher Manual, Adult Quarterly, Adult resources—charts, worksheets, and other teaching tools, paper, pens, pencils, Bibles (several different versions)

OTHER MATERIALS NEEDED / TEACHER'S NOTES:

_____

_____

LESSON OVERVIEW

LIFE NEED FOR TODAY'S LESSON
People of faith acknowledge that life, and all that sustains it, comes from a steadfast and loving God.

BIBLE LEARNING
God is the Creator of all things.

BIBLE APPLICATION
Believers should commit to praising God as an important part of their lives.

STUDENTS' RESPONSES
Christians should never judge others on the basis for our their achievements.

LESSON SCRIPTURE

PSALM 33:1–9, KJV

1 Rejoice in the LORD, O ye righteous: for praise is comely for the upright.

2 Praise the LORD with harp: sing unto him with the psaltery and an instrument of ten strings.

3 Sing unto him a new song; play skillfully with a loud noise.

PSALM 33:1–9, AMP

1 Rejoice in the LORD, you righteous ones; praise is becoming and appropriate for those who are upright [in heart—those with moral integrity and godly character].

2 Give thanks to the LORD with the lyre; sing praises to Him with the harp of ten strings.

3 Sing to Him a new song; play skillfully [on the strings] with a loud and joyful sound.

4 For the word of the LORD is right; and all his works are done in truth.

5 He loveth righteousness and judgment: the earth is full of the goodness of the LORD.

6 By the word of the LORD were the heavens made; and all the host of them by the breath of his mouth.

7 He gathereth the waters of the sea together as an heap: he layeth up the depth in storehouses.

8 Let all the earth fear the LORD: let all the inhabitants of the world stand in awe of him.

9 For he spake, and it was done; he commanded, and it stood fast.

4 For the word of the LORD is right; and all His work is done in faithfulness.

5 He loves righteousness and justice; the earth is full of the lovingkindness of the LORD.

6 By the word of the LORD were the heavens made, and all their host by the breath of His mouth.

7 He gathers the waters of the sea together as in a wineskin; He puts the deeps in storehouses.

8 Let all the earth fear and worship the LORD; let all the inhabitants of the world stand in awe of Him.

9 For He spoke, and it was done; He commanded, and it stood fast.

LIGHT ON THE WORD

The Supremacy of the Lord. The word "Lord" in English Bibles is the rendering of the Hebrew *adonai* (**ah-doe-NIGH**) or the Greek *kurios* (**CURE-ee-os**). The Hebrew personal name for God, Yahweh, is usually translated "LORD" because God's actual name is not to be pronounced and adonai is read instead of Yahweh. God's rule and authority as Lord rests ultimately upon His creation and ownership of all things and people (**Psalm 24:1–2**). His total supremacy over nature is emphasized by His being called the Lord over earthquakes, wind, and fire (**1 Kings 19:10–14**), stars (**Isaiah 40:26**), beasts and sea monsters (**Job 40–41**), and primeval chaos (**Psalm 74:12–14, 89:8–10**).

TEACHING THE BIBLE LESSON

LIFE NEED FOR TODAY'S LESSON

AIM: Students will affirm that life and all that it sustains come from a gracious, just, steadfast, and loving God, and not by our own methods and works.

INTRODUCTION

Praise and Worship the Lord

At the center of the Bible is the book of Psalms. This book contains an assortment of songs and prayers that express the very heart and soul of humanity. Within the book we find a diversity of human experiences. The writers pour their hearts out to God. The psalmists confess their sins, doubts, and fears, and they ask God for assistance in times of trouble. The writers praise and worship the Lord.

BIBLE LEARNING

AIM: Students will agree that God is the Creator of all things and they will continue to trust Him with their future.

I. REJOICE IN PRAISE (Psalm 33:1–3)

This passage of Scripture illustrates how praise is the appropriate response to acknowledge our dependence on God. Praise is essentially offering ourselves to God, including our musical gifts. The first two verses suggest that what is important about praise is more the motive and goal of praise than the means. Instrumentation is appropriate, as is the human voice singing or shouting.

1 Rejoice in the LORD, O ye righteous: for praise is comely for the upright.

The psalmist begins Psalm 33 with a command to rejoice in the Lord. Unlike some other psalms, this command is not given to all of creation, but specifically to the righteous. Praise is comely (Heb. *na'veh*, **nah-VEH**), or suitable for the upright (Heb. *yashar*, **yah-SHAR**). The word "upright" literally means to be straight. When used for people, it is used to describe those who are righteous and pleasing in the sight of God.

2 Praise the LORD with harp: sing unto him with the psaltery and an instrument of ten strings.

Next, the psalmist points to the instruments and means of praise. The righteous are commanded to praise the Lord with the harp (*kinnor*, **keen-NOR**). The word in Hebrew literally means to twang. This instrument was possibly a zither with a large frame and gave tension to the strings when plucked. The next instrument mentioned is the psaltery, which was a lyre and shaped similar to a vase. They are also commanded to praise Him with the psaltery and an instrument of ten strings, which was an instrument similar to the lyre.

3 Sing unto him a new song; play skillfully with a loud noise.

People are to use their voices to sing a new song, inspired by the deliverance and mighty acts of God. They are also commanded to play skillfully and with a loud noise. The word "skillfully" (*yatav*, **yah-TAHV**) means to be good and pleasing. The sense used here is to play with high merriment and joy. This would also be accompanied by a loud noise (*teru'ah*, **teh-roo-AH**) or a shout of joy.

II. REASONS FOR PRAISE (vv. 4–5)

As is typical in the songs of praise, the invitation is followed by reasons for praise. God's "word" and "work" are manifestations of His own self. God is elsewhere described as "upright," which suggests that His people derive their identity from Him; in other words, our "godliness" is only a reflection of the characteristic of God, not deriving from our own fleshly goodness. In **verse 5**, we see the goal of God's speaking and acting in terms associated elsewhere with His character and rule: His righteousness and justice are manifested in His steadfast love for humankind. We must remember that as human beings, we are the result of a creative genius, God Almighty.

4 For the word of the LORD is right; and all his works are done in truth.

Next, the psalmist shifts to the underlying reasons for praise. The Word of the Lord is right, which is the same word used to describe the character of those giving praise. Instead, He adds that the Lord's works are done in truth (Heb. *'emunah*, **eh-moo-NAH**), which means more than just accuracy of facts; it means faithfulness. Everything He does is trustworthy and reliable.

5 He loveth righteousness and judgment: the earth is full of the goodness of the LORD.

Two things that the Lord loves are righteousness and judgment. Righteousness (*tsedaqah*, **tse-dah-KAH**) is adherence to a moral standard. Judgment (*mishpat*, **mish-PAHT**) is properly a verdict, here meaning justice or what is right and fair. Righteousness and justice are reasons for praising God because He has the best in mind for humanity.

III. REVERENCE IN PRAISE (vv. 6–9)

God is all-powerful and deserving of our reverence. Our society rarely thinks of personal or political achievements in terms of God's will. Some tend to think that their success is a result of hard work, rather than wisdom that is greater than their own. In fact, some people think that countries are rescued and security achieved by military might. People fail to recognize the limitations of their mortal capabilities, their limited resources, power, wisdom, and virtue. Can you imagine that there are people who do not realize that it is God who rules the world and we do not?

6 By the word of the LORD were the heavens made; and all the host of them by the breath of his mouth. 7 He gathereth the waters of the sea together as an heap: he layeth up the depth in storehouses.

This description of the act of creation focuses on the power of God's word. There was nothing until the Lord spoke! What a testimony to His creative power! It gives us another reason to praise him.

He also gathered the waters of the sea. This is a reference to either separating the waters from the dry land or possibly the Exodus. Either way, it shows that God is sovereign over His creation, including the watery depths. This is significant because in the ancient Near East, the sea was believed to be the home of powerful beings opposed to God and full of chaos.

The psalmist refutes this belief; God is sovereign over all.

8 Let all the earth fear the LORD: let all the inhabitants of the world stand in awe of him. 9 For he spake, and it was done; he commanded, and it stood fast.

The Lord should be feared on a universal level. He is not a territorial God resigned to one province. He should be feared (Heb. *yare'*, **yah-RAY**), or held in reverential awe. All the inhabitants of the world must stand in awe (Heb. *gur*, **GUR**) of Him. The first word for fear is common in the Old Testament to refer to fear, whether the object is a person (**Genesis 32:11**) or, more frequently, God (**Exodus 14:31**). The second word only occurs a few times, and here it is used for emphasis. By using two synonyms for fear in conjunction with two synonyms for the world, the psalmist describes the complete awe of God that all of creation should exhibit. This fear is a result of acknowledging the power of God in relation to His Word. When God speaks, it is done. Whatever He commands stands fast. If the Lord has this much power, then He is a God to be feared by the whole earth.

SEARCH THE SCRIPTURES

QUESTION 1
In what ways do you see God's righteousness and justice expressed today?

When people march and protest for justice. Better health care programs. Answers will vary.

QUESTION 2
How do believers demonstrate that they fear God?

By obeying God's Word and treating others with respect and true love. Answers will vary.

LIGHT ON THE WORD

The Steadfast Love of God

In light of God's sovereignty, the things and people that seem so obviously powerful—politicians, armies, and weapons—are exposed as mere illusions. The real power behind the universe, human history, and personal existence is the steadfast love of God which fills the earth and is revealed ultimately by His forgiveness of sin.

BIBLE APPLICATION

AIM: Students will commit to making praise of God a major focus in their lives.

Our society places great emphasis on individualism, self-promotion, and achievement. We are bombarded by media frenzy that models self-entitlement. God desires that we do hard work, remain vigilant, strive for excellence, and acquire some level of success. However, we must remain humble and faithful. So how do we accomplish success without becoming arrogant and ungrateful? What do we need to do to ensure that our focus remains centered on our Creator, who is our faithful provider?

STUDENTS' RESPONSES

AIM: Students will write out a praise to God and thank Him for being their ultimate Provider.

Start tomorrow morning and read Psalm 146. Get a notebook and write a sentence or two and respond to what you read. Make it a love letter, with your response in words of worship. Think about all the things you are thankful for God doing in your life. Praise God and share your outcome with the class next week.

PRAYER

Dear Lord, we rejoice in the steadfast love that we receive from You each and every day. Your majestic glory is greatly to be praised. We worship and adore You, O Lord. God, justice is what we want because You are holy and just. Create in us a clean heart to worship You. Let us make righteous decisions in our everyday lives. In the Name of Jesus, we pray. Amen.

HOW TO SAY IT

Comely.	**KUM**-lee.
Psaltery.	**SAL**-te-ree.

DIG A LITTLE DEEPER

This section provides an additional research article to further your study of the lesson:

With the advent of a New Year, the idea of hitting the "reset button" may be foremost in the minds of many. The author encourages readers to embrace an attitude of gratitude. Rather than focus on all the things that are missing that might make this year better than the last, this article challenges the reader to a paradigm shift that creates an "upward spiral" toward peace and fulfillment.

http://cct.biola.edu/blog/flowing-honey-gratitude-good-life/

PREPARE FOR NEXT SUNDAY

Read **Psalm 96:1–6, 10–13** and "All Creation Overflows with Praise."

DAILY HOME BIBLE READINGS

MONDAY
Praise, Worship, and Trust
(Psalm 146:1–4)

TUESDAY
Those Whose Help Is the Lord
(Psalm 146:5–10)

WEDNESDAY
The Limits of National Power
(Psalm 33:10–17)

THURSDAY
Hope in God's Steadfast Love
(Psalm 33:18–22)

FRIDAY
Creation a Witness to God's Plan
(Romans 1:16–20)

SATURDAY
Doing Justice and Kindness with Humility
(Micah 6:6–8)

SUNDAY
Praising God the Creator
(Psalm 33:1–9)

COMMENTS / NOTES:

ALL CREATION OVERFLOWS WITH PRAISE

BIBLE BASIS: PSALM 96:1–6, 10–13

BIBLE TRUTH: Psalm 96 speaks of God's greatness to be proclaimed by all nations.

MEMORY VERSE: "O sing to the Lord a new song; sing to the Lord, all the earth" (Psalm 96:1).

LESSON AIM: By the end of the lesson, we will: CONTEMPLATE creation's testimony to the majesty of God; EXPERIENCE awe in the presence of God's creation; and PRAISE God wholeheartedly in corporate and individual acts of worship.

TEACHER PREPARATION

MATERIALS NEEDED: Quarterly Commentary/Teacher Manual, Adult Quarterly, Adult resources—charts, worksheets, and other teaching tools, paper, pens, pencils, Bibles (several different versions)

OTHER MATERIALS NEEDED / TEACHER'S NOTES:

_____

_____

LESSON OVERVIEW

LIFE NEED FOR TODAY'S LESSON
We are awed by the beauty and grandeur of creation.

BIBLE LEARNING
The psalmist calls all creation to declare the glory of the Lord for His marvelous works.

BIBLE APPLICATION
Christians are encouraged to sing a new song unto the Lord as we remember His salvation, power, and intentional love for each of us.

STUDENTS' RESPONSES
We sometimes forget that God deserves praise for His marvelous works and glorious salvation.

LESSON SCRIPTURE

PSALM 96:1–6, 10–13, KJV

1 O sing unto the LORD a new song: sing unto the LORD, all the earth.

2 Sing unto the LORD, bless his name; shew forth his salvation from day to day.

3 Declare his glory among the heathen, his wonders among all people.

PSALM 96:1–6, 10–13, AMP

1 O sing to the LORD a new song; sing to the LORD, all the earth!

2 Sing to the LORD, bless His name; proclaim good news of His salvation from day to day.

3 Declare His glory among the nations, His marvelous works and wonderful deeds among all the peoples.

4 For the LORD is great, and greatly to be praised: he is to be feared above all gods.

5 For all the gods of the nations are idols: but the LORD made the heavens.

6 Honour and majesty are before him: strength and beauty are in his sanctuary.

10 Say among the heathen that the LORD reigneth: the world also shall be established that it shall not be moved: he shall judge the people righteously.

11 Let the heavens rejoice, and let the earth be glad; let the sea roar, and the fulness thereof.

12 Let the field be joyful, and all that is therein: then shall all the trees of the wood rejoice

13 Before the LORD: for he cometh, for he cometh to judge the earth: he shall judge the world with righteousness, and the people with his truth.

4 For great is the LORD and greatly to be praised; He is to be feared above all gods.

5 For all the gods of the peoples are [worthless, lifeless] idols, but the LORD made the heavens.

6 Splendor and majesty are before Him; strength and beauty are in His sanctuary.

10 Say among the nations, "The LORD reigns; indeed, the world is firmly and securely established, it shall not be moved; He will judge and rule the people with fairness."

11 Let the heavens be glad, and let the earth rejoice; let the sea roar, and all the things it contains;

12 Let the field be exultant, and all that is in it. Then all the trees of the forest will sing for joy

13 Before the LORD, for He is coming, for He is coming to judge the earth. He will judge the world with righteousness and the peoples in His faithfulness.

LIGHT ON THE WORD

Tell. The Israelites were expected to always sing the praises of the Lord and the salvation He brought. The word "tell" comes from the Hebrew word *basar*, which means to bear tidings or to bring news or good tidings. This announcement of good news is both fresh and full, and cheerfully proclaims God's salvation, which brings deliverance and freedom to the captives, and affirms that God rules with power and majesty.

Idols. Israel was commanded to have no other gods but the Lord because these worthless idols cannot be compared to the power and majesty of Israel's God. No crafted image made by human hands can compare with God,

enthroned above the earth with power and might (**Isaiah 40:22**). All gods are man-made and therefore incapable of creating anything. God is the Creator of everything, and therefore His generative power is unmatched.

TEACHING THE BIBLE LESSON

LIFE NEED FOR TODAY'S LESSON

AIM: Students will declare the beauty and grandeur of creation.

INTRODUCTION

Celebrate God's Divine Kingship

Psalm 96 is both a song of praise and more specifically an enthronement psalm, one that celebrates God's divine kingship over the earth. When kings are enthroned, a ritual celebration takes place at the coronation, but unlike human kings, all of creation is involved in God's divine enthronement. This new song for the Lord praises Him for His glory, salvation, and justice.

BIBLE LEARNING

AIM: Students will agree that all creation declares the glory of the Lord for His marvelous works.

I. A CALL TO PRAISE (PSALM 96:1–3)

The writer begins the hymn with a direct call to praise through singing a new song. This new song reflects an understanding of a new reality that points toward the transformation found in the Gospel. It speaks of God's greatness to be proclaimed by all nations. This reality is also a hope that contains the future promises that the Lord will fulfill in and through His people (**Isaiah 42:10**). The call to praise uses six dynamic imperatives—singing (three times), proclaiming, publishing, and telling—to affirm God's name, the Good News of salvation, His works in the world, and all the things that He does. Believers can sing a new hymn articulating their own gratefulness from a heart of thanksgiving and praise.

1 O sing unto the LORD a new song: sing unto the LORD, all the earth.

The psalm begins with a command to sing to the Lord a new song, telling the whole earth to sing. The command to the whole earth includes all of creation, as well as all people. Earth (Heb. *'erets*, **EH-rets**) can refer to creation, but in other contexts, earth refers to a group of people joined together in a common identity (i.e., political, religious, familial). Given that the psalm is filled with both creation (**vv. 5, 10–13**) and clan language (**vv. 3, 5, 7, 10, 13**), both meanings make sense here. Everyone and

everything that God has created must sing a new song to Him.

2 Sing unto the LORD, bless his name; shew forth his salvation from day to day. 3 Declare his glory among the heathen, his wonders among all people.

Verses 2–3 add the contents of the new song: blessings, daily testimonies of His salvation, recollections of His glory and wonders. The date of the psalm's composition is difficult to know because it does not include a superscript or reference to historical people or events, but the psalm commands that God's glory and salvation be proclaimed among the peoples (often "nations"). In other words, His people are to bring this news to everyone, day by day. In the context of the diaspora, where God's people are dispersed among other peoples, this psalm commands the faithful to declare their relationship with the Lord to everyone.

II. THE REASONS FOR PRAISE (vv. 4–6)

Praise flows out of the abundance of a grateful and joyful heart. The psalmist articulates the reasons one can praise as confirmation about who God is and why He should be worshiped. First, God should be feared above all other gods (**v. 4**) because all other deities are mere idols (**v. 5**) unworthy of value. Yahweh warned Israel (**Exodus 20:3**) against idol worship; no idol made with human hands could be more powerful than He.

4 For the LORD is great, and greatly to be praised: he is to be feared above all gods. 5 For all the gods of the nations are idols: but the LORD made the heavens. 6 Honour and majesty are before him: strength and beauty are in his sanctuary.

Verses 4–6 provide reasons for singing to the Lord and the language for doing so. Both **verses 4 and**

5 begin with the Hebrew word *ki* (**KEY**), which can mean "because" or introduce a direct quotation, and both meanings fit the context. Why should the whole earth sing to the Lord? Because He is great, powerfully praised, and feared over all gods. At times the Israelites could be tempted to worship other gods, especially if it seemed as if those gods were doing good things (cf. **Jeremiah 44**). The psalmist reminds the people that their God is the creator of all things. The gods of the peoples are weak, but the Lord made the heavens. The phrase "greatly to be praised" contains a participle in Hebrew, which indicates continuous action. In other words, creation constantly praises God because of His greatness and ability to create. **Verse 6** intensifies this praise by claiming that everything wonderful is connected to the Lord. The following verses are then a response to the intensity of God's glory and majesty.

III. A UNIVERSAL CALL TO WORSHIP (vv. 10–13)

The Lord reigns; He is the King! This declaration is the core of the Gospel message, centered in the truth that He is sovereign and has established the world. God is the creator, sustainer, and vindicator of the world. The psalmist has already proclaimed God's reign over the earth, but the climax of this hymn is the call for everything in the universe—all of Heaven, earth, the fields, and the sea—to rejoice and glorify its Creator.

10 Say among the heathen that the LORD reigneth: the world also shall be established that it shall not be moved: he shall judge the people righteously.

The command in **verses 7–10** to all the clans of the people continues: tell everyone about the Lord; He has established the land; it will never move; He will judge the people with equity. Here is a subtle critique of corrupt human rule along with vibrant praise. God is wholly perfect in His rule. He is aware of and will judge all earthly inequality.

11 Let the heavens rejoice, and let the earth be glad; let the sea roar, and the fullness thereof. 12 Let the field be joyful, and all that is therein: then shall all the trees of the wood rejoice 13 Before the LORD: for he cometh, for he cometh to judge the earth: he shall judge the world with righteousness, and the people with his truth.

After telling the people how to sing this new song to the Lord, the psalm shifts back to creation. The heavens are to rejoice, and the earth is to exult. The sea and its fullness are to roar. **Verse 11** mentions three major parts of creation as a way of including everything God has created—the heavens, the earth, and the sea. Then the fields and trees of the forest are added in **verse 12**. Nothing is left out in this song to the Lord. Moreover, their responses are loud: shouts of joy and exultation, roars like thunder, and cries of rejoicing. No part of creation will miss or be excluded from the song of praise to God. **Verse 13** provides both the location and reason for this new song of praise. It will happen in the Lord's presence, and this is possible because He is coming! When He comes, He will judge the earth with justice and the peoples with faithfulness. Righteousness is a translation of the Hebrew *tsedek* (**TSEH-dek**). In ancient Israel, there was no distinction between justice and righteousness; both meant to do what was right. God will judge rightly. The word rendered "truth" (*'emunah*, **eh-moo-NAH**) means faithfulness, honesty, and truth. In Hebrew, these ideas were inseparable. To be faithful was to be honest and true to the one you were in a relationship with. God will act rightly and honestly when He comes, and the response of all creation will be to sing a new song. The entire psalm can provide an opportunity for daily reminder of how to respond to God's glory and justice and how to be prepared for His coming. God's justice will turn the world right side up, and our proper response is for all of creation to praise Him!

SEARCH THE SCRIPTURES

QUESTION 1

Is God pleased by your attitude and worship?

Most of the time. Answers will vary.

QUESTION 2

Select a church hymn or Gospel song that describes why you praise God and give thanks to Him. How often do you sing or play this song? How often do you praise God individually and with others?

I sing, "Jesus is the Center of My Joy!" when I feel that I need to be reminded of Jesus' love. I praise God throughout the day. Answers will vary.

QUESTION 3

Psalm 96 is also found in **1 Chronicles 16:23–33.** This is King David's jubilant praise as he rejoices over the return of the Ark of the Covenant to Jerusalem. It is indicative of the daily praise that continued before the Lord. How intentional are we about praising God daily?

Answers will vary.

LIGHT ON THE WORD

Worship the True God

Worship is a key component of our daily communion with the Lord. We are reminded that God's sovereignty and glory are still active and present in a world that seems to focus solely on satisfying self. Through worship, we refocus our sometimes distracted and wandering hearts. Our majestic God made the heavens and the earth, and nothing is out of His reach or control, although the world seeks to convince us otherwise.

BIBLE APPLICATION

AIM: Students are encouraged to sing a new song unto the Lord as they remember His salvation, power, and intentional love for each of them.

We were created to praise and worship our majestic and powerful God. Ask for revelation about the areas of your life where you neglect to give God honor and glory. Make a commitment to spend time singing a new song of worship to the Lord each day. Finally, think of ways that your entire life could be a song of worship, a testimony of the faithfulness and majesty of your Creator.

STUDENTS' RESPONSES

AIM: Students will agree that pursuing injustice in our communities is one way to demonstrate praise to God.

This psalm is sometimes labeled a psalm of God's justice or judgment. The psalm has an end times tone, especially in the final verses, suggesting that the psalm hopes for God's eradication of human corruption as a final end to injustice.

PRAYER

Heavenly Father, You are our Redeemer and our Judge. You are sovereign and You rule above all and over all. Thank You for loving justice. Help us to be Your hands extended as we work on behalf of the poor and downtrodden in our communities. Thank You for the Holy Spirit's wisdom and guidance. We praise You in advance for the victory. In the Name of Jesus, we pray. Amen.

HOW TO SAY IT

Heathen.	HEE-thin.
Reigneth.	RAY-nith.

DIG A LITTLE DEEPER

This section provides an additional research article to further your study of the lesson: "We live in a moment, probably the most commodified, commercialized, marketized culture in the history of the world … every nook and cranny shot through with obsession with money-making and profit-taking." So says visiting scholar Dr. Cornel West during Biola University's seminar, The Table. Dr. West's vivid, provocative insight about the apathetic state of our culture challenges us to remember our Christian identity. Only then will we be sensitive and responsive to human suffering. He posits that the pervasiveness of consumerism has caused many of us to be callous about the needs of others. This thought-provoking dialogue is both intriguing and disturbing. Listen!

http://cct.biola.edu/blog/cornel-west-affluence-consumerism-spirituality-and-suffering/

PREPARE FOR NEXT SUNDAY

Read **Psalm 65:1–2, 9–13** and "Praise God the Provider."

DAILY HOME BIBLE READINGS

MONDAY
O Sing to the Lord
(1 Chronicles 16:23–34)

TUESDAY
Ascribe to the Lord, O Families
(Psalm 96:7–9)

WEDNESDAY
Justice Will Be Established
(Isaiah 42:1–4)

THURSDAY
Salvation is for All Peoples
(Isaiah 49:1–7)

FRIDAY
Sing Praises, O Gentiles
(Romans 15:7–13)

SATURDAY
Singing Around the Throne
(Revelation 5:11–14)

SUNDAY
All Creation Overflows with Praise
(Psalm 96:1–6, 10–13)

COMMENTS / NOTES:

_____

_____

_____

_____

_____

_____

_____

_____

_____

_____

_____

_____

_____

_____

_____

_____

_____

_____

_____

_____

_____

_____

PRAISE GOD THE PROVIDER

BIBLE BASIS: PSALM 65:1–2, 9–13

BIBLE TRUTH: Psalm 65 is a song of praise and thanksgiving for God's provisions for our well-being.

MEMORY VERSE: "By terrible things in righteousness wilt thou answer us, O God of our salvation; who art the confidence of all the ends of the earth, and of them that are afar off upon the sea" (Psalm 65:5).

LESSON AIM: By the end of the lesson, we will: CELEBRATE God's provision without complaint; EXPRESS gratitude for the ways God meets our physical needs; and PRAISE the Creator through good stewardship of our material blessings.

TEACHER PREPARATION

MATERIALS NEEDED: Quarterly Commentary/Teacher Manual, Adult Quarterly, Adult resources—charts, worksheets, and other teaching tools, paper, pens, pencils, Bibles (several different versions)

OTHER MATERIALS NEEDED / TEACHER'S NOTES:

_____

_____

LESSON OVERVIEW

LIFE NEED FOR TODAY'S LESSON
No matter how humble our circumstances, we often take for granted the exceptional blessings we enjoy.

BIBLE LEARNING
The psalmist declares that God is worthy of praise for both the physical and spiritual blessings He gives.

BIBLE APPLICATION
All are encouraged to praise God for the bounty that He provides.

STUDENTS' RESPONSES
Believers are reminded that God's blessings are provided for all to receive.

LESSON SCRIPTURE

PSALM 65:1–2, 9–13, KJV

1 Praise waiteth for thee, O God, in Sion: and unto thee shall the vow be performed.

2 O thou that hearest prayer, unto thee shall all flesh come.

9 Thou visitest the earth, and waterest it:

PSALM 65:1–2, 9–13, AMP

1 To You belongs silence [the submissive wonder of reverence], and [it bursts into] praise in Zion, O God; and to You the vow shall be performed.

2 O You who hear prayer, to You all mankind comes.

thou greatly enrichest it with the river of God, which is full of water: thou preparest them corn, when thou hast so provided for it.

10 Thou waterest the ridges thereof abundantly: thou settlest the furrows thereof: thou makest it soft with showers: thou blessest the springing thereof.

11 Thou crownest the year with thy goodness; and thy paths drop fatness.

12 They drop upon the pastures of the wilderness: and the little hills rejoice on every side.

13 The pastures are clothed with flocks; the valleys also are covered over with corn; they shout for joy, they also sing.

9 You visit the earth and make it overflow [with water]; You greatly enrich it; the stream of God is full of water; You provide their grain, when You have prepared the earth.

10 You water its furrows abundantly, You smooth its ridges; You soften it with showers, You bless its growth.

11 You crown the year with Your bounty, and Your paths overflow.

12 The pastures of the wilderness drip [with dew], and the hills are encircled with joy.

13 The meadows are clothed with flocks and the valleys are covered with grain; they shout for joy and they sing.

LIGHT ON THE WORD

Zion. This mountain in Jerusalem is where the Temple stood and where it was believed that God came down to dwell with His people. It is the place often used synonymously for Jerusalem.

Pasture. There was a scarcity of pasture and good land for feeding livestock in Palestine. This scarcity can be seen in the conflict between Abraham and Lot (**Genesis 13:5–13**). David would have been very familiar with the value of good pasture land through his humble beginnings as a shepherd (**1 Samuel 16:11–13, 17:15, Psalm 23**). This could have been motivation for his praying that God abundantly water the earth.

TEACHING THE BIBLE LESSON

LIFE NEED FOR TODAY'S LESSON

AIM: Students will agree that a heart of gratitude results in expressions of thanksgiving.

INTRODUCTION

Psalm of Thanksgiving

This psalm of David may have been sung in the sanctuary of Zion as a liturgical hymn at the time of a great harvest. It is believed that it may have been a national thanksgiving psalm for the abundant harvest and increasing livestock that Israel experienced at the end of a drought when a famine was averted. This confident hymn tells of the goodness and power of God that acknowledges God's spiritual (atonement for sin) and physical (tangible abundance on the earth) blessings on Israel.

BIBLE LEARNING

AIM: Students will agree that God is worthy of praise for both the physical and spiritual blessings He gives.

I. PRAISE FOR THE FORGIVENESS OF SINS (Psalm 65:1–2)

The psalm begins with a promise to fulfill a vow to praise Yahweh who is Israel's God. The praise is directed to God and is uttered in thanksgiving as a result of God's forgiveness of sin. The vow illustrated that people owed God their praise—they prayed for something and vowed to give God glory when He answered. There was a confident expectation that God would provide for the spiritual and physical needs of His people. God hears and answers the prayers of Israel (**Psalm 65:2**).

1 Praise waiteth for thee, O God, in Sion: and unto thee shall the vow be performed.

The psalm begins with reasons for praising God. The word for "praise" here (Heb. *tehillah*, **te-heel-LAH**) is a technical word for a song of praise, and the plural form is the name of the psalter in Hebrew (*tehillim*, **te-heel-LEEM**). Along with the song of praise is the fulfillment of a vow to God. In other words, God is worthy of a song of praise and a fulfilled vow. The images of the fullness of creation in the psalm point to this worthiness more clearly. If God fulfills His promises by filling the earth with life, we should keep our promises to Him as well.

2 O thou that hearest prayer, unto thee shall all flesh come.

Verses 2–8 provide a number of reasons for God's worthiness, beginning with the fact that He hears prayers. **Verse 2** praises the relationship between God and all living things—to God all flesh will come. The Hebrew word for "flesh" includes all living things, anything with blood and breath (*basar*, **bah-SAR**). The presence of all creatures in the midst of God echoes the heavenly throne room images in **Isaiah 6**, **Ezekiel 1–2**, and **Revelation 4**, each of which reveals all living things praising God at all times. **Verses 3–8** continue praising God for hearing prayers and forgiving sins, adding to His greatness the blessings of being in His presence and experiencing His salvation and justice through all the earth.

II. PRAISES FOR THE BLESSINGS OF THE LAND (vv. 9–13)

Israel's God cares for the land He loves, so He pours out an abundance of blessing upon it. The descriptions of how God cares for the land are all described in excess, in abundance and overflowing. There is praise and thanksgiving for God's provision of life and the flourishing harvest. God is powerful enough to take care of and provide the physical necessities of life. God is the giver of rain, grain and goodness. In response, the land joins in with singing praise to God.

9 Thou visitest the earth, and waterest it: thou greatly enrichest it with the river of God, which is full of water: thou preparest them corn, when thou hast so provided for it.

After praising God for His justice, righteousness, blessings, holiness, and power over creation, the psalm exults Him for caring for the land with water. "Thou visitest," the Hebrew verb (*paqad*, **pah-QAHD**), has a number of possible meanings, including visit, which conjures up images of a fully present God. It can also mean to set things up in correct order, suggesting that God has designed things appropriately, so that there are water systems that keep the earth nurtured, including a river of God that promises ample water. For those who have easy access to water and relatively few restrictions even during droughts, the power of this promise can be easily lost. In ancient Israel, flowing water supplies such as rivers were scarce, and the rainy season was vital for both the crops and the people. In addition to providing the necessary water, God also provides "corn," which stands for all grain, and was a staple for both humans and animals. These are basic necessities for creation to thrive, and the psalm calls us to reflect on the beauty of God's design and praise Him for providing for all of creation.

10 Thou waterest the ridges thereof abundantly: thou settlest the furrows thereof: thou makest it soft with showers: thou blessest the springing thereof.

Verse 10 continues the crop imagery by focusing on the process of sowing and the need for moist soil. God is so concerned for creation that He makes sure the plowed fields are watered, providing showers for them. The result is that God blesses the crops' growth in their most vulnerable time, when they are just sprouting. The word translated "springing" by the King James Version (Heb. *tsemach*, **TSEH-makh**) is a word for "sprout" or "branch," and it is related to a verb for growth, indicating that God is involved in the whole process of crop growth from the beginning.

11 Thou crownest the year with thy goodness; and thy paths drop fatness.

The crown symbolizes the highest honor, revealing that God holds creation in the highest esteem. The reference to crowning the year with goodness and God's paths dripping with fatness suggests the harvest season and its celebration. God blesses the entire year, but the culmination of celebration is at the harvest time when the crops He has blessed are ripe and ready to nourish creation. Just as God has given nature the highest honor and makes sure that all of creation is nurtured, so we should do likewise. We have been called to be God's stewards of creation (**Genesis 1:28, 2:15**), and this verse is a reminder of the importance of all of creation in His eyes.

12 They drop upon the pastures of the wilderness: and the little hills rejoice on every side. 13 The pastures are clothed with flocks; the valleys also are covered over with corn; they shout for joy, they also sing.

Verses 12–13 provide an all-encompassing picture of the extent of God's blessings. Both the wilderness and the hills, as well as the pastures and valleys, rejoice at His blessings. Flocks and grain are abundant, and creation itself shouts for joy and sings. This final verse closes with an image of an abundance of animals and crops, all of which join in the singing of God's praises!

Those of us who are removed from agricultural communities and always have enough clean water and food can too easily forget the extent to which we rely on the ecosystem for our own lives. God has created a global ecosystem that is intricately connected and interdependent, and the commands in Genesis for humans to fill the earth and rule it (**1:28**) and to tend to the garden (**2:15**) were intended as commands for us to take care of creation, just as God takes care of it here in this psalm (**v. 9**). How are we caring for creation? Are we truly thankful for God, creation, and everyone involved in making sure we have clean water and sufficient food? Do we have a tendency to waste resources provided by God for all of creation to thrive? This psalm is not just a call to praise God for His provision. We are also reminded of a creation that is well tended and lush. How can we be those stewards of creation who make sure that the earth looks like these thriving images in the psalm?

SEARCH THE SCRIPTURES

QUESTION 1
Are there any dams in your life that prevent the active flow of God's river of life?

Fears and life frustrations. Answers will vary.

QUESTION 2
Read **verses 1–2** and **9–10**. In what specific ways was God's care for you evidenced this past week?

When I was afraid, God sent someone to reassure me. Answers will vary.

LIGHT ON THE WORD

God and Creation

God is shown to be active in His creation as He "visited" (**v. 9**), "crowned" (**v. 11**) and "clothed" (**v. 13**) the land and the streams. God's divine provision of rain and a steady supply of water enabled the crops and livestock to flourish in the inexhaustible water. This water would be a reminder for Israel of God's provision and His role as the source of life. This water would come as a reminder that God's water can never run dry and His abundant provision gives life to everything (**Ezekiel 47:1–12**).

BIBLE APPLICATION

AIM: Students will praise God for the bounty that He provides.

We often think that God's blessings are exclusive to only His children but our gracious and merciful God desires for all humanity to come to know Him and be restored (**2 Peter 3:9**). He desires that none should perish but all come to salvation in Him as He willingly forgives sin. He uses creation as a demonstration of His goodness and grace toward us with the hope of drawing men and women to Himself (**Matthew 5:45**). Jesus is our Savior and the hope of all the peoples of the earth.

STUDENTS' RESPONSES

AIM: Students will seek the guidance of the Holy Spirit to help them bless someone during the week.

Jesus is the water of life to quench our thirsty souls. Ask God to saturate your heart with His love for your neighbor, to build relationships with them by stepping over boundaries of comfort, so that you can be a true witness of the love of Christ to those you would otherwise not consider. Pray for a stirring of your heart toward evangelism and discipleship of those around you as you find ways to share the Gospel.

PRAYER

Dear Lord, we praise You from the highest mountains to the lowest valleys. We are blessed in many ways by the purity of the beauty that You set before us, O God. From the sparkling waters to the soft snowflakes, we are reminded that You are in control of Heaven and earth. You are the sovereign God that we praise and worship. In the Name of Jesus, we pray. Amen.

HOW TO SAY IT

Sion   **SIE**-on.

Furrows   **FUR**-ohs.

DIG A LITTLE DEEPER

This section provides an additional research article to further your study of the lesson:

In contrast to the abundance experienced by many who live in the United States are those living in poverty, longing for God to answer their practical prayers for rain. Prayer is powerful, and everyone is invited to participate in calling on God to intervene in areas where there is hunger, strife, war, and turmoil. Copy and post this Prayer Guide as a reminder to pray for African countries that are in desperate need of daily provisions.

http://www.easternhills.org/files/prayer_guide_for_horn_of_africa.pdf

PREPARE FOR NEXT SUNDAY

Read **Psalm 104:1–4, 24–30** and "Praise God the Creator."

DAILY HOME BIBLE READINGS

MONDAY
Rejoice During the Festival of Booths
(Deuteronomy 16:13–15)

TUESDAY
God Forgives and Saves the People
(Psalm 65:3–4)

WEDNESDAY
God's Awesome Stabilizing Deeds
(Psalm 65:5–8)

THURSDAY
Let All the People Praise God
(Psalm 66:1–5)

FRIDAY
God's Restoration of All Humanity
(Isaiah 66:18–23)

SATURDAY
Sharing in God's New Community
(Acts 2:37–47)

SUNDAY
Praise God the Provider
(Psalm 65:1–2, 9–13)

Sources:
Alter, Robert. *The Book of Psalms: A Translation with Commentary*. New York, NY : W.W. Norton & Company., 2007.

deClaisse-Walford, Nancy, Jacobson, Rolf A. Jacobson, and Beth LaNeel Tanner. *The New International Commentary on the Old Testament: The Book of Psalms*. Grand Rapids, MI: Eerdmans, 2014.

Life Application Study Bible, New International Version. Wheaton, IL: Tyndale House Publishers, Inc., 1997. 2154–2155, 2170-2172.

Ross, Allen P. *A Commentary on The Psalms*. Vol. 2. Grand Rapids, MI: Kregel Publications, 2013. 42-89.

Waltner, James H. *Believers Church Bible Commentary Psalms* Scottdale, PA: Herald Press, 2006.

Wilson, Gerald H. *The NIV Application Commentary. Psalms Volume 1*. Grand Rapids, MI: Zondervan, 2002.

COMMENTS / NOTES:

PRAISE GOD THE CREATOR

BIBLE BASIS: PSALM 104:1–4, 24–30

BIBLE TRUTH: Psalm 104 is about how nature explicitly points to God as the Intelligent Creator.

MEMORY VERSE: "O Lord, how manifold are your works! In wisdom you have made them all; the earth is full of your creatures" (Psalm 104:24).

LESSON AIM: By the end of this lesson we will: PONDER the diversity and complexity of God's creation; AFFIRM God's wisdom in ordering the world as He did; and HONOR God by working to preserve the world's magnificent natural diversity.

TEACHER PREPARATION

MATERIALS NEEDED: Quarterly Commentary/Teacher Manual, Adult Quarterly, Adult resources—charts, worksheets, and other teaching tools, paper, pens, pencils, Bibles (several different versions)

OTHER MATERIALS NEEDED / TEACHER'S NOTES:

_____

_____

LESSON OVERVIEW

LIFE NEED FOR TODAY'S LESSON
When we experience the vast diversity of creation, we wonder how it is all held together and acknowledge our great God!

BIBLE LEARNING
The psalmist praises God for sustaining creation.

BIBLE APPLICATION
Christians can trust that God provides a multitude of amazing ways to know Him.

STUDENTS' RESPONSES
Believers are encouraged to honor and glorify the majesty of the Lord.

LESSON SCRIPTURE

PSALM 104:1–4, 24–30, KJV

1 Bless the LORD, O my soul. O LORD my God, thou art very great; thou art clothed with honour and majesty.

2 Who coverest thyself with light as with a garment: who stretchest out the heavens like a curtain:

PSALM 104:1–4, 24–30, AMP

1 Bless and affectionately praise the LORD, O my soul! O LORD my God, You are very great; You are clothed with splendor and majesty,

2 [You are the One] who covers Yourself with light as with a garment, Who stretches out the heavens like a tent curtain,

3 Who layeth the beams of his chambers in the waters: who maketh the clouds his chariot: who walketh upon the wings of the wind:

4 Who maketh his angels spirits; his ministers a flaming fire:

24 O LORD, how manifold are thy works! in wisdom hast thou made them all: the earth is full of thy riches.

25 So is this great and wide sea, wherein are things creeping innumerable, both small and great beasts.

26 There go the ships: there is that leviathan, whom thou hast made to play therein.

27 These wait all upon thee; that thou mayest give them their meat in due season.

28 That thou givest them they gather: thou openest thine hand, they are filled with good.

29 Thou hidest thy face, they are troubled: thou takest away their breath, they die, and return to their dust.

30 Thou sendest forth thy spirit, they are created: and thou renewest the face of the earth.

3 Who lays the beams of His upper chambers in the waters [above the firmament], who makes the clouds His chariot, who walks on the wings of the wind,

4 Who makes winds His messengers, flames of fire His ministers.

24 O LORD, how many and varied are Your works! In wisdom You have made them all; the earth is full of Your riches and Your creatures.

25 There is the sea, great and broad, in which are swarms without number, creatures both small and great.

26 There the ships [of the sea] sail, and Leviathan [the sea monster], which You have formed to play there.

27 They all wait for You to give them their food in its appointed season.

28 You give it to them, they gather it up; You open Your hand, they are filled and satisfied with good [things].

29 You hide Your face, they are dismayed; You take away their breath, they die and return to their dust.

30 You send out Your Spirit, they are created; You renew the face of the ground.

LIGHT ON THE WORD

Heavens. The firmament is God's palace or residence. It displays the radiance of His power and glory. There is no portion of the world, however minute, where it does not exhibit some glimmer of beauty, so distinct and bright that no one can use ignorance as an excuse to deny God's existence (**Psalm 19:1–4**).

Leviathan. A sea monster referenced in the Old Testament (**Job 41**). The word has become synonymous with any large sea creature. In literature it refers to great whales and in modern Hebrew it simply means "whale." In the Middle Ages, it was used as an image of Satan who attempted to destroy God's people and His creation. Some scholars associated it with the demon of envy. During the time of judgment it will be wiped out (**Isaiah 27:1**).

TEACHING THE BIBLE LESSON

LIFE NEED FOR TODAY'S LESSON

AIM: Students will experience the vast diversity of creation as we marvel that God holds it all together.

INTRODUCTION

God's Handiwork

Creation. Psalm 104 focuses on God's handiwork; it reviews the history of creation and magnifies the greatness of God. This psalm about nature explicitly points to God as the Intelligent Creator. The psalmist uses vivid imagery to emotionally move the reader, recreating this colorful wonder before their very eyes. Nature stays within its boundaries and does what God created it to do.

BIBLE LEARNING

AIM: Students will, like the psalmist, praise God for sustaining creation.

1. CREATION SHOWS GOD'S MAJESTY (Psalm 104:1–2)

Initially, the author spoke of himself blessing the Lord. The psalmist does so to express gratitude and respect. The "soul" is the entire being of a person who truly worships God. The personal blessing exalted God, who has robed Himself with glory and grandeur, yet the author acknowledged God personally as *My God*. The garment of authority and nobility is expressive of the character of God. Even the elegant array of King Solomon does not compare. The first thing on God's creation agenda was light. Like a garment, God wrapped Himself in the very light He created. It's unapproachable to any earthly living soul (**1 Timothy 6:16**).

1 Bless the LORD, O my soul. O LORD my God, thou art very great; thou art clothed with honour and majesty.

Starting and ending similar to Psalm 103 (a fact which underscores David's authorship), this psalm gives God the worship He is due. To "bless" (Heb. *barak*, **bah-ROCK**) means to wish good tidings or ascribe particular power (some versions render this word as "praise"). The word "great" in Hebrew is *gadal* (**gah-DOLL**), which means "to be or become great or strong" or "exalted" (see **Genesis 12:2; Exodus 2:10**). The word "very" in Hebrew is *me'od* (**meh-ODE**), which means "especially" or "exceedingly" (see **Genesis 1:31; Psalm 96:4**). Such added superlatives are appropriate within the context. Indeed, God is worthy of every superlative and expression of praise and blessing. We can't physically reach God, but by His visible glories we can see Him "darkly" (**1 Corinthians 13:12**); indeed, we, like Moses, couldn't survive the full brilliance of His person (**Exodus 34:29**). Thus, in part, because we could not bear His full appearance, God clothes Himself with the "fabric of the world," in the choice words of John Calvin. While earthly kings adorn themselves with royal finery of every kind, none can compare to God's infinitely greater "robes" of exceeding honor and majestic excellence (**Psalm 93:1; 1 Timothy 6:16**).

2 Who coverest thyself with light as with a garment; who stretchest out the heavens like a curtain:

In the previous verse, God clothed Himself with honor and majesty; in this verse His attire is light itself. If one of the garments in God's wardrobe is "light" (Heb. *'or*, **OR**, meaning daylight or a bright morning sun), one can't help but ask how bright His being is (**Habakkuk 3:4**).

"The heavens" (Heb. *shamayim*, **shah-MAH-yeem**) implies that either the visible arch in which the clouds move or the larger space where celestial bodies revolve is merely a curtain. The belief in the ancient Near East was that the sky was a dome or canopy that covered the earth like a disc. One can only wonder how grand God's royal pavilion—His heavenly tabernacle—is. Other verses such as **Isaiah 40:12, 54:2**, and **Job 37:18** refer to the heavens in a similar manner. **Isaiah 34:4** and **Revelation 6:14** refer to the sky (or heavens) being rolled up like a scroll.

II. GOD CREATES LIGHT AND HEAVEN (vv. 3–4)

The first three chapters of Genesis outlined God creating the earth. Here the psalmist poetically highlights the same information. This psalm focuses on God's handiwork; it reviews the history of creation and magnifies the greatness of God.

3 Who layeth the beams of his chambers in the waters: who maketh the clouds his chariot; who walketh upon the wings of the wind:

God's construction materials are vastly different from ours (**Amos 9:6**); everything is supported by His awesome power. His "beams" (Heb. *qara'*, **kah-RAH**, meaning something built from wood or having wooden beams) in footings of water are infinitely more stable than our strongest steel and concrete. Our great King doesn't require chariots or limousines to define His royalty; rather, He rides on the "clouds" (Heb. *'av*, **AHV**, meaning a thick cloud), and the "wind" (Heb. *ruakh*, **ROO-akh**, meaning spirit; also, breath or wind) is harnessed for His traveling needs. The sky itself obeys His every whim like a plane obeys its pilot. If the beams of His tabernacle are stabilized in the oceans, the clouds are His equally firm floorboards, and the wind provides His corridors.

4 Who maketh his angels spirits; his ministers a flaming fire:

Both "spirit(s)" and "wind" (**v. 3**) are translated from the same Hebrew word (*ruakh*). If "angels" (Heb. *mal'ak*, **mal-AHK**, meaning messenger) are made into spirits, they are also made into wind, upon which God is transported (see also **Hebrews 1:7**). In a real sense, God speaks words or breathes out life (wind), and angels (messengers) take His breath or words of life to deliver them (**Psalm 103:20**). We must remember the incredible power and importance of all God's countless angels (**Matthew 25:31; 2 Thessalonians 1:7; Hebrews 12:22; Revelation 5:11**), especially guardian angels (**Psalm 91:11**), cherubim (**Genesis 3:24; Exodus 25:20**), seraphim (**Isaiah 6:2, 6**), and the archangels (**1 Thessalonians 4:16; Jude 9**).

III. GOD CREATES CREATURES (vv. 24–27)

There are great creatures and small that live deep in the sea. The majesty of a dolphin or a stingray is amazing to see. The tiny—and tiniest—creatures with their unusual blend of colors, shapes, and habits make us wonder that God has a sense of humor. Consider this. God cares for and feeds them all. Why should we worry about whether or not God will take care of us? He will!

24 O LORD, how manifold are thy works! in wisdom hast thou made them all: the earth is full of thy riches.

This second portion of our lesson, **verses 24–30**, focuses on the animals of creation and the sustaining produce of the earth. In verses prior to this portion (**vv. 10–18**), the psalm writer elaborates on God's intentional interconnectedness of creation, e.g., water first finding its place and then becoming a resource for all of creation, sustaining life and fruitfulness, each cyclic facet of which in turn becomes food, seed, or supply for myriads of needs. Then everything is refreshed and replenished by rain. Everything God does—all His many "works" (cf. **v. 13**) are wonderful, magnificent, and excellent in every way; individually or collectively, they reveal His wisdom, power, creativity, and glory.

25 So is this great and wide sea, wherein are things creeping innumerable, both small and great beasts. 26 There go the ships: there is that leviathan, whom thou hast made to play therein.

From the perspective of ancient writers, both ships on the sea (**Proverbs 30:18–19**) and the great sea creatures (**Job 41:1; Psalm 74:14; Isaiah 27:1**) were marvels that particularly revealed to them God's boundless creative ability. This verse uses a literary device called hendiadys, which is when a part is used to represent the whole (e.g., from homeless box to penthouse suite, representing all residences). So it is that ships on the great sea and beasts of all kinds in the sea represent all of creation.

27 These wait all upon thee; that thou mayest give them their meat in due season.

God is the source and sustainer; He is the maker and the maintainer—everything comes from Him and everything depends on Him, including humankind. All of the living things expect that God will provide them with food when it's necessary. "Wait" here means to expect or hope for something to happen (Heb. *siber*, **see-BARE**). The picture is of God as nurturer–opening His very hand to feed.

IV. GOD PROVIDES FOR ALL ANIMALS (vv. 28–30)

Repeatedly God creates, preserves, and restores. It is His responsibility as Creator. As humans watching these phenomena in nature, it should give us assurance that in God's hands everyone is safe and secure. He is more than able to take care of the most difficult situation or circumstance in an individual's life.

28 That thou givest them they gather: thou openest thine hand, they are filled with good. 29 Thou hidest thy face, they are troubled: thou takest away their breath, they die, and return to their dust. 30 Thou sendest forth thy spirit, they are created: and thou renewest the face of the earth.

In Hebrew, "breath" is *ru'ach* (**RU-akh**), and means wind, breath, mind, or spirit. It is the same word used in **Genesis 1:2**: "The Spirit [*ruach*] of God moved upon the face of the waters." It is also the same word in **Genesis 7:22**, referring to all the creatures taken aboard the Ark: "All in whose nostrils was the breath [*ruach*] of life." *Ruach* also is used for both man and animals in **Ecclesiastes 3:21**. A quick look at the verbs in the last four verses (**vv. 27–30**) gives an overview of all that God does: He gives food to all, He opens His hand and fills creation with good things, He hides His face, He takes away breath/life [*ruach*], He sends His spirit [*ruach*], and He renews everything.

Interestingly, in **Genesis 2:7**, when God "breathed into his [man's] nostrils the breath of life," the Hebrew uses *neshamah* (**nesh-a-MA**), but it is essentially an interchangeable synonym for *ruach*. In **Isaiah 42:5**, "He that giveth breath [*neshemah*] unto the people … and spirit [*ruach*] to them." Also in **Job 34:14**, both Hebrew words are used side by side to indicate either man's life or death: "If he gather unto himself his spirit [*ruach*] and his breath [*neshamah*]." Both *neshamah* and *ruach* are used for the English "breath of life" in **Genesis 7:22**. The essence of the passage is that God is both giver and sustainer of the very breath and spirit within all living things—He alone gives, sustains, and takes life away.

SEARCH THE SCRIPTURES

QUESTION 1

What does it mean for you to bless the Lord with your soul (Psalm 104:1)?

To worship God in every area of my life. Answers will vary.

QUESTION 2

Read **Psalm 104:3–4**. How does this description of God guide your daily life?

God is bigger and more powerful than anything or anyone I can imagine. I wake up every day to serve this awesome God. Answers will vary.

LIGHT ON THE WORD

In God's Wisdom

In His wisdom, God provided mankind a wonderful universe in which to dwell. It communicates how God is powerful, majestic, creative, and totally in control of all things. Thinking deeply about these facts results in heartfelt worship. What problems in our lives threaten the belief that God is in control?

BIBLE APPLICATION

AIM: Students will celebrate that they can trust that God is omnipotent, yet gives us a multitude of ways to know Him.

We often take for granted what we are given. People help us out of the kindness of their hearts. Family and friends support us, and many of us have homes and jobs and access to heat and running water. But sometimes we dwell on the things we don't have, or spend too much time revisiting old slights or mistakes without appreciating all that has been provided for us.

It's easy to engage in one's usual routine without thanking God for His magnificent design. Ask God to help you daily recognize the benefits of His creation.

STUDENTS' RESPONSES

AIM: Students will honor and glorify the majesty of the Lord by caring for God's creation.

As a church or Sunday School class, locate a community organization that supports neighborhood gardens or educates youth about the earth's ecology. This fosters an appreciation for the wonders of God's creation.

Pray and write how God wants you to apply the teachings of this lesson to your life.

_____

_____

_____

PRAYER

Dear Lord, we bless You, praise You, and marvel at Your beauty. Only You can create a butterfly, or the mighty lion, beasts of the field, and sea creatures great and small. All of nature reminds us of Your awesomeness! Thank You for trusting us to care for Your world. In the Name of Jesus, we pray. Amen.

HOW TO SAY IT

Innumerable   in-oom-er-ah-**BULL.**

Renewest   **REE**-noo-wist.

DIG A LITTLE DEEPER

This section provides an additional research article to further your study of the lesson:

Whether watching the sunrise at dawn or gazing at stars at dusk, the majesty of God's creation is overwhelming and humbling. This devotional reflects the awe that inspired the biblical writers; their thoughts and their responses to creation are reflected in this brief article. In addition to singing, readers are challenged to explore other ways of praise—journaling, writing a poem, taking pictures, or creating a work of art.

http://www.todayintheword.org/titw_devotion.aspx?id=84139

PREPARE FOR NEXT SUNDAY

Read **Psalm 148** and "All Creation Praises God."

DAILY HOME BIBLE READINGS

MONDAY
God Sets Boundaries on the Earth
(Psalm 104:5–9)

TUESDAY
God Quenches the Thirsty Earth
(Psalm 104:10–18)

WEDNESDAY
God Establishes Times and Seasons
(Psalm 104:19–23)

THURSDAY
Joy and Wish for Perfect Harmony
(Psalm 104:31–35)

FRIDAY
God Gives Humanity Its Dignity
(Psalm 8)

SATURDAY
Do Not Worry, God Will Provide
(Matthew 6:25–34)

SUNDAY
Praise God the Creator
(Psalm 104:1–4, 24–30)

COMMENTS / NOTES:

ALL CREATION PRAISES GOD

BIBLE BASIS: PSALM 148

BIBLE TRUTH: The psalmist declares that all creation is created to worship God.

MEMORY VERSE: "Let them praise the name of the LORD; for he commanded, and they were created" (Psalm 148:5).

LESSON AIM: By the end of the lesson, we will: AGREE that creation exists primarily to praise God, not to meet our physical needs; EXULT in the wonders of God's creation; and RESPECT nature with an awareness of its divine purpose.

TEACHER PREPARATION

MATERIALS NEEDED: Quarterly Commentary/Teacher Manual, Adult Quarterly, Adult resources—charts, worksheets, and other teaching tools, paper, pens, pencils, Bibles (several different versions)

OTHER MATERIALS NEEDED / TEACHER'S NOTES:

_____

_____

LESSON OVERVIEW

LIFE NEED FOR TODAY'S LESSON
Nature exists for our benefit and for God's glory.

BIBLE APPLICATION
All of creation should worship and praise God for all that He has created.

BIBLE LEARNING
The psalmist asks every element of creation to join the chorus of praise for God.

STUDENTS' RESPONSES
Believers should respect and honor God's purposes for nature and humanity.

LESSON SCRIPTURE

PSALM 148, KJV

1 Praise ye the LORD, Praise ye the LORD from the heavens; praise him in the heights.

2 Praise ye him, all his angels: praise ye him, all his hosts.

3 Praise ye him, sun and moon; praise him, all ye stars of light.

4 Praise him, ye heavens of heavens, and ye waters that are above the heavens

PSALM 148, AMP

1 Praise the LORD! Praise the LORD from the heavens; praise Him in the heights!

2 Praise Him, all His angels; praise Him, all His hosts (armies)!

3 Praise Him, sun and moon: praise Him, all stars of light!

4 Praise Him, highest heavens, and the waters above the heavens!

5 Let them praise the name of the LORD; for he commanded, and they were created.

6 He hath also stablished for them forever and ever; he had made a decree which shall not pass.

7 Praise the LORD from the earth, ye dragons, and all deeps;

8 Fire, and hail; snow, and vapor; stormy wind fulfilling his word.

9 Mountains, and all hills; fruitful trees, and all cedars;

10 Beasts, and all cattle; creeping things, and flying fowl:

11 Kings of the earth, and all people; princes, and all judges of the earth:

12 Both young men, and maidens; old men, and children;

13 Let them praise the name of the LORD: for his name alone is excellent; his glory is above the earth and heaven.

14 He also exalteth the horn of his people, the praise of all his saints; even of the children of Israel, a people near unto him. Praise ye the LORD.

5 Let them praise the name of the LORD, for He commanded and they were created.

6 He has also established them forever and ever; He has made a decree which shall not pass away.

7 Praise the LORD from the earth, sea monsters and all deeps;

8 Lightning and hail, snow and fog; stormy wind, fulfilling His orders;

9 Mountains and all hills; fruitful trees and all cedars;

10 Beasts and all cattle; creeping things and winged birds;

11 Kings of the earth and all people; princes and all judges of the earth;

12 Both young men and virgins; old men and children.

13 Let them praise the name of the LORD, for His name alone is exalted and supreme; His glory and majesty are above earth and heaven.

14 He has lifted up a horn for His people [giving them strength, prosperity, dignity, and preeminence], praise for all His godly ones; for the people of Israel, a people near to Him. Praise the LORD! (Hallelujah!)

LIGHT ON THE WORD

Horn. The horn was a symbol of power and strength in ancient times, and the horn of God's people refers to the strength of God's people who praise Him.

TEACHING THE BIBLE LESSON

LIFE NEED FOR TODAY'S LESSON

AIM: Students will agree that nature exists as evidence of God's creation.

INTRODUCTION

A Passionate Heartfelt Praise

The writer of this psalm is unknown, but he definitely had a passionate heart filled with praise for God. The call is for more praise and worship, not merely an individual's expression but a call to the entire universe. The occasion for this psalm is unknown. Some point to a time of peace during King David's reign. He had rest from all of his enemies and the kingdom of Israel was settled and prospering. Others point to the time during the Temple rebuilding after the Babylonian exile.

BIBLE LEARNING

AIM: Students will agree that the psalmist asks every element of creation to join the chorus of praise for God.

I. HEAVENLY WORSHIP
(Psalm 148:1–6)

The author placed the theme of the psalm at the very beginning: *Praise the Lord*. The worshiping celebration starts with the heavens, the highest region of God's creation. One of the main groups in Heaven is the angelic host. Their duty is to praise God continually and to be available to do His bidding.

Sun, moon, and stars and all heavenly elements also join in praise to the Father. God designed them to shine night and day giving Him glory. The clouds carry within themselves an enormous amount of water. God makes sure only a certain amount is released for humanity's needs. This emphasizes God's orderly creation.

Why universal praise to God? He spoke and everything that exists in the world came into being at His command. The song is absolutely correct: *This is My Father's World*. Moreover, He's also sustains the world. Nothing will expire or run out; what He causes to rise up will stand forever.

1 Praise ye the LORD. Praise ye the LORD from the heavens: praise him in the heights. 2 Praise ye him, all his angels: praise ye him, all his hosts.

The psalmist gives the command to praise the Lord. In Hebrew, the phrase is "hallelujah," which means to celebrate or praise the Lord (*Yah* in Hebrew is a form of God's title "Lord"). This phrase is often repeated in **Psalms 145–150**, occurring more than ten times. Here we end with a crescendo of praise that encompasses the whole known world.

Next, the psalmist calls for praise from the inhabitants of Heaven (Heb. *shamayim*, **sha-MAH-yeem**); they can praise God in the heights (Heb. *marom*, **mah-ROME**). These two terms designate not just the sky or expanse above the earth but where the ancient Israelites believed God resided with His angels (Heb. *mal'ak*, **mall-AHK**) or messengers. Many of these angels, such as the seraphim, exist solely to worship and praise God.

3 Praise ye him, sun and moon: praise him, all ye stars of light. 4 Praise him, ye heavens of heavens, and ye waters that be above the heavens.

Now, the psalmist turns to the celestial bodies in the heavens, personifying the sun and moon and stars and making them capable of praising God. These celestial bodies were often objects of worship in the ancient Near East. The psalmist reverses what many would see as objects of reverence and puts them in their rightful place—they are made to revere God. They are not literally inanimate objects verbally boasting about God, but they are signs and evidence of His greatness. By performing their allotted tasks, they point to the power and wisdom of their Creator.

5 Let them praise the name of the LORD: for he commanded, and they were created. 6 He hath also stablished them for ever

and ever: he hath made a decree which shall not pass.

The reason for the heavens and their residents to praise God is His inherent power in creating the universe. The psalmist says that he commanded (Heb. *tsavah*, **tsa-VAH**), which means to charge someone to do something. God is sovereign over His creation. He speaks, and creation must obey. Furthermore, He creates *ex nihilo* or "out of nothing." He commanded, and they were created (Heb. *bara'*, **bah-RAH**). The word has the connotation of cutting out or carving out, meaning to be brought into existence. It is limited to the creative work of God alone, indicating the distinction and superiority of God's work. Nothing would exist without the power of the sovereign God. This is the reason for them to praise Him.

II. EARTHLY WORSHIP (vv. 7–10)

The author petitions the sea creatures to bring forth praise. This probably referred to extinct animals from the past, and everything present in the depths of the oceans. This likewise included the sea itself, pools, waves, tides, and any other water activity. The perfect harmony of these elements points to an intelligent, perfect Creator.

7 Praise the LORD from the earth, ye dragons, and all deeps:

The psalmist began in the heights, but now he descends to the depths. Whereas before he started the call to praise with the angels, supernatural beings of beauty and perfection, in this verse he points to the great sea creatures or dragons (Heb. *tannin*, **ta-NEEN**). These creatures were believed to dwell in the deeps (Heb. *tehom*, **teh-HOME**) or the ocean. These creatures were believed to oppose God and His people, and they were greatly feared. The psalmist says there is nothing to fear because even these creatures were created by God and are capable of praising Him.

Even the deeps or depths of the oceans and seas praise God. In ancient times, the sea was viewed as an unstable place. It was the great unknown and associated with chaos and darkness. As such, these places were to be avoided. The psalmist says that even these places are created by God and called to give Him praise.

8 Fire, and hail; snow, and vapours; stormy wind fulfilling his word: 9 Mountains, and all hills; fruitful trees, and all cedars: 10 Beasts, and all cattle; creeping things, and flying fowl:

Here the psalmist involves the whole span of creation. The Lord is sovereign over the elements; they fulfill (Heb. *'asah*, **ah-SAH**) or accomplish His Word. The sense is that they thoroughly and entirely put into effect the commands that are given. Nothing is outside the range of God and His sovereignty. The mountains, hills, and trees are called to praise Him. The beasts and cattle are called to praise Him. Even the creeping things (Heb. *remes*, **REH-mes**) or animals that crawl, such as reptiles are called to praise Him.

Both wild and tame animals and birds are supported by God; He supplies their food and drink. He also directs their course and activities so every one of them moves in harmony, even the smallest insect and snake. He beckons them to join with those who praise Him.

III. SPECIFIC WORSHIP (vv. 11–12)

The psalmist emphasizes the high ranking officials, then points out ordinary men, women and children. Youth in their prime of life, full of vigor and energy looking forward to plenty of life ahead, and the older generation thankful for their full life, both offer praise and thanksgiving to God. Even from children who do not have an extensive history with God, He still calls for praise (**Matthew 21:15**).

11 Kings of the earth, and all people; princes, and all judges of the earth: 12 Both young men, and maidens; old men, and children:

Next, the psalmist includes humanity in the chorus of praise, including those of high position such as kings, princes, and judges. The greatness of these rulers is outmatched by the glory of the Lord. He is King over everyone. He also directs the call toward the young men and the maidens. Those who are in the prime of life are called to praise Him. Both male and female, elders and children, in other words, all in the community, are called to praise God.

This is because the Lord's name alone is excellent (Heb. *sagav*, **sah-GAV**), meaning to be high and unattainable. The sense is that the Lord's name is exalted above all other names, and His glory, or *hod* (Heb. **HODE**), is above the heavens. The word for glory can be translated as majesty and has the same sense of weight, referring to the quality of awe or reverence it inspires in others. Clearly, the psalmist believes the Lord has no equal.

IV. EVERYONE WORSHIPS (vv. 13–14)

God specifically pointed out Israel at the end of this hymn. Some scholars believe the address to Israel is not the literal nation but a spiritual Israel which includes both Jew and Gentile, who looked to the coming Messiah (**Romans 2:28–29**). God's children realize their punishment for sin should have been eternal damnation, but God sent Jesus as a payment and this condemnation no longer hangs over their heads. This fact alone produces a humble worship-filled heart.

13 Let them praise the name of the LORD: for his name alone is excellent; his glory is above the earth and heaven. 14 He also exalteth the horn of his people, the praise of all his saints; even of the children of

Israel, a people near unto him. Praise ye the LORD.

The psalmist ends with an addendum to the reason for joining this chorus of praise. Not only is the Lord's name excellent and His glory above the heavens, but He also is praised for what He has done for His people. He "exalteth the horn of his people," which means He has honored His people for their strength. Although the word "horn" (Heb. *qeren*, **KEH-ren**) can simply refer to an animal horn, in poetry it carries with it the connotation of power and strength. The one who deserves all the glory and praise has lifted up His people.

This exalting of the horn also shows God's greatness and glory. This causes His saints (Heb. *chasid*, **kha-SEED**), or faithful and holy ones, to praise Him even more. This horn is the reason for the praise of the Children of Israel, a people who are near to Him. These people have experienced His majesty and power and have the most reason to praise the Lord.

SEARCH THE SCRIPTURES

QUESTION 1
In what way does nature (sun and moon, fire and hail, etc.) praise the Lord (**Psalm 148:1–14**)?

Nature praises God by doing what it has been commanded by Him to do. In this way nature displays God's glory.

QUESTION 2
The church advocates that people care for one another. How can the church assist people to better protect God's natural creation?

Plan special days for the church and the community to work together to clean the neighborhood, or plant a community garden. Answers will vary.

LIGHT ON THE WORD

The Final Confession

The Apostle Paul, in the book of Philippians, spoke of the coming season when every knee will bow and every tongue confess Jesus as Lord (**Philippians 2:5–11**). In the last days, this time of worship includes the involvement of all creation.

BIBLE APPLICATION

AIM: Students will appreciate that all of creation should worship and praise God for all that He has created.

People become Christians for various reasons. Some want to escape hell and go to Heaven. Others want benefits, like the wealthy of the biblical kings and patriarchs. Still others are people who are hurting and seek help for personal problems. But as you grow and mature in Christ, you understand you were created to be God's vessel of praise and ask Him how to become a daily worshiper. This should become a life priority.

STUDENTS' RESPONSES

AIM: Students will honor God's purposes for nature and humanity by praising Him in song.

Fill the pockets of your heart with praise. In the course of the day we have waiting time, down time, do nothing time. Is it possible for us to fill those pockets of time with a praise Scripture or song this week?

Think and respond to the following: What would a harmonious world look like that praises God together? Is that what we are thinking about and what we truly desire when we have praise and worship in our church? Does it look like **Psalm 148**?

PRAYER

Dear Lord, blessings, glory, and honor to You. We are to praise and worship You every day of our lives. Thank You for the sky, the universe, the fragrant flowers, the gentle breezes, and all of Your beauty and splendor of creation. In the Name of Jesus, we pray. Amen.

HOW TO SAY IT

Stablisheth.   **STA**-bli-shith.

Exalteth.   ek-**ZAL**-tith.

DIG A LITTLE DEEPER

This section provides an additional research article to further your study of the lesson:

"Learning to Lament: Giving Voice to the Winter Christian Experience" is a poignant analysis of practical ways to incorporate Scripture from the book of Psalms into our prayers during seasons of discouragement and loneliness. It is important to understand the balance between murmuring and complaining and talking to God via a lament. "When we fail to give voice to complaint, doubt, and lament, these experiences become internalized and privatized. We begin to feel alone and isolated in our spiritual struggles," says Dr. Richard Beck, Professor and Department Chair of Psychology at Abilene Christian University. He stresses that as in any relationship, these seasons are normal—as normal as are the seasons of winter, spring, summer, and fall. A psalm helps us pray when we don't know what to say.

http://cct.biola.edu/blog/learning-lament-giving-voice-winter-christian-experience/

PREPARE FOR NEXT SUNDAY

Read **Galatians 3:26–4:7** and "Re-Created to Live in Harmony."

DAILY HOME BIBLE READINGS

MONDAY
Praise the Lord!
(Psalm 150)

TUESDAY
Heavenly Beings Shout for Joy
(Job 38:1–7)

WEDNESDAY
Wisdom Present at Creation
(Proverbs 8:22–31)

THURSDAY
Angels Praise God
(Luke 2:8–14)

FRIDAY
Humans Continue God's Caring Ways
(Deuteronomy 24:17–22)

SATURDAY
God's Gracious Ways
(Psalm 145:13b–21)

SUNDAY
All Creation Praises God
(Psalm 148)

COMMENTS / NOTES:

RE-CREATED TO LIVE IN HARMONY

BIBLE BASIS: GALATIANS 3:26–4:7

BIBLE TRUTH: Paul states that all are one in Christ Jesus.

MEMORY VERSE: "There is neither Jew nor Greek, there is neither bond nor free, there is neither male nor female: for ye are all one in Christ Jesus" (Galatians 3:28).

LESSON AIM: By the end of the lesson, we will: EVALUATE the unity of Christians based on the saving work of Christ and the Holy Spirit; APPRECIATE that, through Christ, we are all one in the church; and EXAMINE ourselves for prejudiced attitudes against other believers.

TEACHER PREPARATION

MATERIALS NEEDED: Quarterly Commentary/Teacher Manual, Adult Quarterly, Adult resources—charts, worksheets, and other teaching tools, paper, pens, pencils, Bibles (several different versions)

OTHER MATERIALS NEEDED / TEACHER'S NOTES:

_____

_____

LESSON OVERVIEW

LIFE NEED FOR TODAY'S LESSON
Differences in race, class, and gender sometimes make it difficult for people to live in harmony.

BIBLE APPLICATION
Believers are to live in harmony with others regardless of ethnicity.

BIBLE LEARNING
Through Christ we have received the Spirit, bringing us into a community of oneness.

STUDENTS' RESPONSES
Christians are encouraged to live in harmony and peace with one another.

LESSON SCRIPTURE

GALATIANS 3:26–4:7, KJV

26 For ye are all the children of God by faith in Christ Jesus.

27 For as many of you as have been baptized into Christ have put on Christ.

28 There is neither Jew nor Greek, there is neither bond nor free, there is neither male nor female: for ye are all one in Christ Jesus.

GALATIANS 3:26–4:7, AMP

26 For you [who are born-again have been reborn from above—spiritually transformed, renewed, sanctified and] are all children of God [set apart for His purpose with full rights and privileges] through faith in Christ Jesus.

27 For all of you who were baptized into Christ [into a spiritual union with the Christ,

29 And if ye be Christ's, then are ye Abraham's seed, and heirs according to the promise.

4:1 Now I say, That the heir, as long as he is a child, differeth nothing from a servant, though he be lord of all;

2 But is under tutors and governors until the time appointed of the father.

3 Even so we, when we were children, were in bondage under the elements of the world:

4 But when the fulness of the time was come, God sent forth his Son, made of a woman, made under the law,

5 To redeem them that were under the law, that we might receive the adoption of sons.

6 And because ye are sons, God hath sent forth the Spirit of his Son into your hearts, crying, Abba, Father.

7 Wherefore thou art no more a servant, but a son; and if a son, then an heir of God through Christ.

the Anointed] have clothed yourselves with Christ [that is, you have taken on His characteristics and values].

28 There is [now no distinction in regard to salvation] neither Jew nor Greek, there is neither slave nor free, there is neither male nor female; for you [who believe] are all one in Christ Jesus [no one can claim a spiritual superiority].

29 And if you belong to Christ [if you are in Him], then you are Abraham's descendants, and [spiritual] heirs according to [God's] promise.

4:1 Now what I mean [when I talk about children and their guardians] is this: as long as the heir is a child, he does not differ at all from a slave even though he is the [future owner and] master of all [the estate];

2 but he is under [the authority of] guardians and household administrators or managers until the date set by his father [when he is of legal age].

3 So also we [whether Jews or Gentiles], when we were children (spiritually immature), were kept like slaves under the elementary [man-made religious or philosophical] teachings of the world.

4 But when [in God's plan] the proper time had fully come, God sent His Son, born of a woman, born under the [regulations of the] Law,

5 so that He might redeem and liberate those who were under the Law, that we [who believe] might be adopted as sons [as God's children with all rights as fully grown members of a family].

6 And because you [really] are [His] sons, God has sent the Spirit of His Son into our hearts, crying out, "Abba! Father!"

7 Therefore you are no longer a slave (bond-servant), but a son; and if a son, then also an heir through [the gracious act of] God [through Christ].

LIGHT ON THE WORD

Paul. At one time known as Saul (the Hebrew version of the name), Paul was born around the same time as Jesus Christ in Tarsus, the capital of Cilicia. His father was Jewish but a Roman citizen. There is not much mention of his mother. However, we can read about a sister and nephew and other relatives in Acts and Romans.

Galatia. Located in the central region of Asia Minor, Galatia has been referred to as Gallia of the East. In Roman times, Galatia was an ethnically mixed province due to its location in the empire.

TEACHING THE BIBLE LESSON

LIFE NEED FOR TODAY'S LESSON

AIM: Students will agree that the differences of race, class, and gender often create barriers that separate us from one another.

INTRODUCTION

Followers of Jesus

Followers of Jesus included Jews who adhered to Torah (Old Testament) tradition, as well as Gentile unbelievers of the Roman Empire. Galatians reflects, more strongly than most New Testament texts, the conflict among followers of Jesus regarding whether Gentiles needed to obey all of the Torah. Paul clearly supports Gentile freedom from such Torah commands as circumcision and Temple sacrifices. Unlike some of the Jewish leaders of the churches, Paul argued that Gentile converts should not be subject to certain mandates of the

Mosaic Law such as physical circumcision of the flesh since circumcision of the heart came through Jesus Christ. However, they should abide by God's Law (the Ten Commandments).

Under the Roman law, minors were considered slaves. A minor had to have a legal guardian. If the minor's father was dead, the guardian was chosen from the father's will. If the will was not available, the responsibility went to the nearest male relative. Galatians were freed from slavery or needed a guardian. God adopted them and made them His children, with a powerful inheritance.

BIBLE LEARNING

AIM: Students will evaluate the believers' oneness in Christ through the Holy Spirit.

I. ONE IN CHRIST (Galatians 3:26–29)

Believers in Christ are also Abraham's seed. Christ is the seed of Abraham, and being a Christian makes a person part of that seed, as well as an heir to the promise of Abraham. We are not just heirs, but we are also joint heirs with Christ Jesus (**Romans 8:15–17**)!

26 For ye are all the children of God by faith in Christ Jesus.

This verse expresses Paul's compassionate and pastoral heart. Though correct in his presentation of the Gospel, he says harsh things about the Galatians' failure to understand and learn the message of justification by faith. This is because some Jewish leaders of the church tried (and succeeded) in getting the Gentile Galatians to circumcise their males, which Paul thought unnecessary for participation in the promise of Christ (see **2:11–21**). Paul reminds the Galatians, however, that despite their failings, they are now "the children of God by faith in Christ Jesus." Paul teaches that we are made acceptable to God not because we fully understand the doctrine, but because we believe in the Lord Jesus Christ.

27 For as many of you as have been baptized into Christ have put on Christ.

Although this is Paul's only reference to Christian baptism in this letter to the Galatians, the reference is significant. The phrase "have been baptized into Christ" is Paul's way of calling out those who have accepted God's free grace through faith. The Greek word for "put on" (*enduo*, **en-DOO-oh**) means to be clothed, wear, or dress. Their water baptism, being a symbolic expression of their acceptance of Christ, affirms that they have indeed "clothed" themselves with Christ.

28 There is neither Jew nor Greek, there is neither bond nor free, there is neither male nor female: for ye are all one in Christ Jesus.

Paul uses three couplets to represent inequality. The first being ethnic: Jew/Greek; second, economic: bound/free; and third, gender: male/female. He states that all who, by faith, believe in the Lord Jesus Christ become one with each other. In a culture where Jews were a minority but viewed themselves as the children of God, free-born Gentiles who joined the church were in a precarious position. For non-Jews who had abandoned their official cults, slaves who had no rights, and women who were second-class citizens, Paul's claim of unity is a radical statement. It was good news for the Gentiles, slaves, and women who joined the family of faith.

29 And if ye be Christ's then are ye Abraham's seed, and heirs according to the promise.

With this point, Paul brings the reasoning from the last few verses back to the broader point he has been working through for the whole chapter, explaining how the Gentiles are welcomed into God's family through faith rather than works. Paul wants his Gentile readers to know that their relationship with Christ makes them Abraham's seed and qualifies them to be joint and equal heirs to the blessings outlined in God's promise to Abraham.

II. THE WORLD IN BONDAGE (4:1–3)

An heir has to wait for an appointed time to receive an inheritance. He (especially a male) would have the security of knowing that he was freeborn and due to receive his father's inheritance. The heir still has to be submissive to those over him until the set time comes. The comparison is made with us, as Christians. Before Christ, we were just like slaves, being controlled by the dominating forces of this world.

4:1 Now I say, That the heir, as long as he is a child, differeth nothing from a servant, though he be lord of all; 2 But is under tutors and governors until the time appointed of the father.

Paul recaps his comments in **Galatians 3:23–29**, where he presented the Galatians as being "heirs according to the promise." Although the Jews were heirs to the promise, some of them were held captive to the discipline of the Law, and treated like children living under the watchful, caring, and protective eye of a steward. This, Paul contended, was necessary because Jesus Christ had not yet come (**Galatians 3:23**). But after the coming of Christ (**Galatians 3:25**), believers were "no longer under" the Law. After the Incarnation, those who believe in Christ were now "sons of God," free to live their lives "unto God" (**Galatians 2:19**), "by the faith of the Son of God, who … gave himself for" them (**Galatians 2:20**).

Paul makes the point that although an heir has certain privileges and rights that a slave does not, as a child, the heir is still under the supervision of guardians and tutors. The heir's subjection to the tutors and governors is only "until the time appointed of the father." In other words, the heir will receive inheritance, but not until the day set by the father. This imagery recalls Paul's comment in **3:23**, and anticipates his comment in **4:4**. With great literary skill, Paul uses the legal language governing the inheritance law of his day to set the stage for his statements in **verses 3–5**.

3 Even so we, when we were children, were in bondage under the elements of the world:

In the next three verses, Paul applies the illustration set forth in **verses 1–2** to help explain the Galatians' experience. The question persists, however, about who the pronoun "we" refers to. Is this a reference to Jews or Gentiles, or both—including Paul? Given Paul's message of inclusiveness and his conviction that Christ came to rescue all people from enslavement to "the elements of the world" (of which the Law was one enslaving element), it is reasonable to believe that "we" refers to Jews, Gentiles, and Paul.

III. GOD DELIVERED THE WORLD (vv. 4–7)

By faith, God adopts believers through Christ, making them His children. God did not stop there; He also sent the Spirit of His Son. Every believer has the Spirit inside, bearing witness that the believer is part of God's holy family. God made it personal for believers, allowing the believer to refer to Him as Abba Father, indicating an intimacy with His children.

4 But when the fullness of the time was come, God sent forth his Son, made of a woman, made under the law.

The "fullness of time" recalls the "time appointed of the father" in Paul's illustration about the inheritance in **verse 2**. This analogy shows that where the Galatians were concerned, their inheritance was in the form of God sending "forth his Son." God's Son was human in that He was "made of a woman" and a Jew in that He was "made under the law." The Greek word for "made" used here is *ginomai* (**GHEE-no-my**), which can also be translated "born" (cf. NLT, NIV, ESV, etc.). In other words, Jesus was born of a woman, and born under the Law. Jesus, God's Son, came into the world like any other Jewish male child. But He came into the world with a mission.

5 To redeem them that were under the law, that we might receive the adoption of sons.

The mission of God's Son was to "redeem" or to emancipate from slavery to the Law those who were heirs to the promise, in order that they might receive the inheritance, namely "the adoption of sons." Paul uses adoption language here as a way of including the Gentiles who were not born Jews, in the inheritance that God has to offer. This brings Paul closer to the conclusion of his analogy. He has one more thing to say.

6 And because ye are sons, God hath sent forth the Spirit of his Son into your hearts, crying Abba, Father.

Before making his concluding statement, Paul reminds the Galatians that receiving their adoption as God's sons resulted also in His sending into their hearts "the Spirit of his Son." Not only did the sending of God's Spirit confirm the Galatians' new status and freedom as His sons, but it also empowered them to use their freedom responsibly.

7 Wherefore thou art no more a servant, but a son; and if a son, then an heir of God through Christ.

It is obvious from Paul's reasoning that he views each individual Galatian as being in a privileged position. The phrase "thou art" is singular, which indicates that Paul wants to direct his comment to each individual Galatian. It is as if he is saying, "You, you as an individual, are no longer a servant, but a child." The KJV continues, "...and if a son, then an heir of God through Christ." This translation is debatable primarily because the available Greek manuscripts do not all agree. (Some say "through Christ," some say "through God," others have minor variations on the phrasing.).However, the most commonly used Greek New Testament and the earliest manuscripts (one as early as the second century AD) read "through God." This translation makes the Galatians' status as heirs a work of God's grace, which supports Paul's message that salvation is not by works of the Law, but by God's grace freely given through faith in Jesus Christ.

One of the interesting contrasts that Paul makes throughout this section in Galatians is that of son versus servant. The familial language is very significant. The privileges of a son verses those of a servant help to illustrate the difference between having a relationship with God through the efficacious death and resurrection of Jesus Christ and trying to be righteous by obeying the Law. The difference is quite clear. The death of Christ and saving faith, bring a believer into the family of God as His adopted children who have an inheritance. As servants we were not part of the family and did not have any privileges. Why go back to such a system? For through Christ we are heirs! Through Christ we cry to God, "Abba, Father."

SEARCH THE SCRIPTURES

QUESTION 1

Why does God choose faith in Christ Jesus as the means of making us His children (Galatians 3:26)?

Faith makes us all equal. Everyone has a measure of faith (Romans 12:3). Without faith, it is impossible to please God (Hebrews 11:6).

QUESTION 2

How would you evaluate whether the Spirit of God was in your heart (4:6)?

By repenting of my sin and receiving Jesus Christ as Lord and Savior and being filled with the Holy Spirit.

LIGHT ON THE WORD

One Community

Some Greco-Roman cults did not honor social divisions because they were expensive, and could exclude everyone but the rich. However, the earlier Christians were resistant to division and formed bridges between the Jews and the Gentiles. The Jewish people were known as Abraham's seed, or offspring, with an inheritance to the promise.

Differences are often easier to point out than similarities. We should celebrate our commonalities when we encounter others in the faith. God has chosen to make us His children by faith, and this is worth celebrating.

BIBLE APPLICATION

AIM: Students will celebrate that they are recreated by God to live in harmony.

Being adopted by God as His child comes with great responsibility. As with the inheritance we receive, we also have a responsibility and commitment to live according to the way our Father has set for us. We are new creatures in Christ, and the way we live our lives should line up accordingly.

STUDENTS' RESPONSES

AIM: Students will agree that Christians are encouraged to live in harmony and peace

with one another by discussing their attitude toward law enforcement.

Ask yourself: Do I treat every believer in the faith as my brother and sister in Christ? If I do, how can I express love in a greater way? If not, try to make a conscious effort to ask God for help to see His children the way He does and to treat them as such.

PRAYER

Dear loving Lord, we have peace, joy, and mercy because of You. Grant us the courage and the wisdom to live with one another in ways that are pleasing to You. Thank You Lord for giving us Jesus and the Holy Spirit to guide us and live together as one in Christ Jesus. In the Name of Jesus, we pray. Amen.

HOW TO SAY IT

Abba.	**AH**-bah.
Differeth.	di-**FIR**-ith.

DIG A LITTLE DEEPER

This section provides an additional research article to further your study of the lesson:

"Savor the Flavor" is a brief discussion about the "melting pot" that is the Body of Christ. Christianity is sometimes defined by a particular group of people who neglect to include populations that are economically, socially, ethnically, and politically diverse. The testimony of the Gospel helps us to embrace these differences because of a paramount commonality: our Lord and Savior, Jesus Christ. Follow the link and listen to this devotional.

http://odb.org/2008/07/11/savor-the-flavor/

PREPARE FOR NEXT SUNDAY

Read **Galatians 4:8–20** and "New Birth Brings Freedom."

DAILY HOME BIBLE READINGS

MONDAY
The Spirit Made You a Believer
(Galatians 3:1–5)

TUESDAY
All Peoples are Blessed Through Abraham
(Genesis 22:15–18)

WEDNESDAY
Jesus Fulfills the Promise to Abraham
(Galatians 3:15–18)

THURSDAY
Baptized into One Body
(1 Corinthians 12:12–18)

FRIDAY
Know that You are Children of God
(1 John 2:28–3:3)

SATURDAY
Serve in the Name of Christ
(Colossians 3:12–17)

SUNDAY
Recruited to Live in Harmony
(Galatians 3:26–4:7)

COMMENTS / NOTES:

_____

_____

_____

_____

_____

_____

_____

_____

_____

_____

_____

NEW BIRTH BRINGS FREEDOM

BIBLE BASIS: GALATIANS 4:8–20

BIBLE TRUTH: Paul emphasizes freedom in Christ and not by observing special days and seasons.

MEMORY VERSE: "But now, after that ye have known God, or rather are known of God, how turn ye again to the weak and beggarly elements, whereunto ye desire again to be in bondage?" (Galatians 4:9).

LESSON AIM: By the end of this lesson, we will: EVALUATE those religious expectations and practices that diminish Christian freedom; EMPATHIZE with those who have been harmed by narrow religiosity; and CHALLENGE unhealthy attitudes toward religious practices or traditions.

TEACHER PREPARATION

MATERIALS NEEDED: Quarterly Commentary/Teacher Manual, Adult Quarterly, Adult resources—charts, worksheets, and other teaching tools, paper, pens, pencils, Bibles (several different versions)

OTHER MATERIALS NEEDED / TEACHER'S NOTES:

_____

_____

LESSON OVERVIEW

LIFE NEED FOR TODAY'S LESSON
People are tempted to sacrifice freedom in order to gain a sense of security.

BIBLE LEARNING
Paul rebuked the Galatians for trading their freedom in Christ.

BIBLE APPLICATION
Followers of Jesus need to be careful of the dangers of turning away from Him.

STUDENTS' RESPONSES
Students should know that in Christ there is freedom from slavery to religious legalism.

LESSON SCRIPTURE

GALATIANS 4:8–20, KJV

8 Howbeit then, when ye knew not God, ye did service unto them which by nature are no gods.

9 But now, after that ye have known God, or rather are known of God, how turn ye again to the weak and beggarly

GALATIANS 4:8–20, AMP

8 But at that time, when you did not know [the true] God and were unacquainted with Him, you [Gentiles] were slaves to those [pagan] things which by [their very] nature were not and could not be gods at all.

9 Now, however, since you have come to

elements, whereunto ye desire again to be in bondage?

10 Ye observe days, and months, and times, and years.

11 I am afraid of you, lest I have bestowed upon you labour in vain.

12 Brethren, I beseech you, be as I am; for I am as ye are: ye have not injured me at all.

13 Ye know how through infirmity of the flesh I preached the gospel unto you at the first.

14 And my temptation which was in my flesh ye despised not, nor rejected; but received me as an angel of God, even as Christ Jesus.

15 Where is then the blessedness ye spake of? for I bear you record, that, if it had been possible, ye would have plucked out your own eyes, and have given them to me.

16 Am I therefore become your enemy, because I tell you the truth?

17 They zealously affect you, but not well; yea, they would exclude you, that ye might affect them.

18 But it is good to be zealously affected always in a good thing, and not only when I am present with you.

19 My little children, of whom I travail in birth again until Christ be formed in you,

20 I desire to be present with you now, and to change my voice; for I stand in doubt of you.

know [the true] God [through personal experience], or rather to be known by God, how is it that you are turning back again to the weak and worthless elemental principles [of religions and philosophies], to which you want to be enslaved all over again?

10 [For example,] you observe [particular] days and months and seasons and years.

11 I fear for you, that perhaps I have labored [to the point of exhaustion] over you in vain.

12 Believers, I beg of you, become as I am [free from the bondage of Jewish ritualism and ordinances], for I have become as you are [a Gentile]. You did me no wrong [when I first came to you; do not do it now].

13 On the contrary, you know that it was because of a physical illness that I [remained and] preached the gospel to you the first time;

14 and even though my physical condition was a trial to you, you did not regard it with contempt, or scorn and reject me; but you received me as an angel of God, even as Christ Jesus Himself.

15 What then has become of that sense of blessing and the joy that you once had [from your salvation and your relationship with Christ]? For I testify of you that, if possible, you would have torn out your own eyes and given them to me [to replace mine].

16 So have I become your enemy by telling you the truth?

17 These men [the Judaizers] eagerly seek you [to entrap you with honeyed words and attention, to win you over to their philosophy], not honorably [for their purpose is not honorable or worthy of consideration]. They want to isolate you [from us who oppose them] so that you will seek them.

18 Now it is always pleasant to be eagerly sought after [provided that it is] for a good purpose, and not just when I am with you [seeking you myself—but beware of the others doing it].

19 My little children, for whom I am again in [the pains of] labor until Christ is [completely and permanently] formed within you—

20 how I wish that I were with you now and could change my tone, because I am perplexed in regard to you.

LIGHT ON THE WORD

Judaizers. Throughout the book of Galatians, Paul mounts an unrelenting argument against the Judaizers' beliefs and activities. They were teachers who believed that the way for Gentiles to be right with God was to obey the Law of Moses, including the rite of circumcision. We do not know who the Judaizers were by name, but we do know that they argued and debated Paul at the Jerusalem Council (**Acts 15**). The council ruled in favor of Paul and Barnabas and accepted the Gentiles as part of God's people on the basis of their belief in Christ, and not circumcision.

TEACHING THE BIBLE LESSON

LIFE NEED FOR TODAY'S LESSON

AIM: Students will agree that people are tempted to sacrifice freedom in order to gain a sense of security.

INTRODUCTION

Elemental Spirits

In ancient times, many believed in spirits that moved and operated the sun, moon, planets, and stars. These were worshiped as deities and believed to control the fate of individuals. This type of belief system is the origin of astrology, or knowledge of the stars. The astral spirits were associated with special days and rituals. Paul seems to believe that through customs and rituals involving calendar and dates, the Galatians were still in bondage to spiritual powers.

BIBLE LEARNING

AIM: Students will evaluate Paul's admonishment of the Galatians for their trading their freedom in Christ.

I. THE GALATIANS' DECEPTION (Galatians 4:8–11)

Compared to the true God to whom the Galatians have now surrendered, the "gods" they were turning to again, were to say the least, "weak and beggarly." Paul wondered why someone who had been delivered from such evil entities would choose to enter their control again. The Galatians probably did not know better at that time, but now they have no excuse. They knew the slavery they once lived under; in its place they found the liberty as children of God.

They were turning again to the observance of days, months, times, and years. Paul was not suggesting that it is improper to observe special days in the Jewish or Christian calendar, such as Passover, the Day of Atonement, Christmas, or Easter (Resurrection). Paul's teaching is that while circumcision itself is neither good nor evil, so too the observance of special days is neither mandatory nor inherently wrong. Paul's concern was that the Galatians might be drawn into a religious system where adherence to certain calendar celebrations was necessary to maintain a good standing with God.

4:8 Howbeit then, when ye knew not God, ye did service unto them which by nature are no gods. 9 But now, after that ye have known God, or rather are known of God, how turn ye again to the weak and beggarly elements, whereunto ye desire again to be in bondage? 10 Ye observe days, and months, and times, and years. 11 I am afraid of you, lest I have bestowed upon you labour in vain.

Paul lets the Galatians know that they had been set free from serving and worshiping idols. He then presents a rhetorical question to them, asking why they would return to bondage to the "weak and beggarly elements." The Galatians were concerned about special religious days, times, and years. They had been deceived into thinking this was the way to be right with God. These things only served to put them into bondage, while Christ came to set them free.

Paul says that observing these things was expected when they did not know God. However, now that they have heard the Gospel and known God, it is foolish to return to these practices. The Galatians were released from the bondage of pagan idolatry, but now the Judaizers were seeking to bring them into religious idolatry. They were using the Jewish religion as a mediator and not trusting in Christ to be their mediator. Paul laments that if this is the case, then he has labored in vain by preaching and teaching them the Gospel.

II. THE GOSPEL'S RECEPTION (vv. 12–16)

Paul proceeds to make a personal appeal to his Galatian converts. Using affectionate language, he calls the Galatians "brethren," which means "brothers and sisters," and then he pleads with them. Ministers, particularly pastors, must maintain a proper balance between theological teaching and pastoral concern. "Beseech" (Gk. *deomai*, **DEH-oh-my**) can mean to long for, or to beg. Paul was no longer arguing but imploring.

12 Brethren, I beseech you, be as I am; for I am as ye are: ye have not injured me at all. 13 Ye know how through infirmity of the flesh I preached the gospel unto you at the first. 14 And my temptation which was in my flesh ye despised not, nor rejected; but received me as an angel of God, even as Christ Jesus. 15 Where is then the blessedness ye spake of? for I bear you record, that, if it had been possible, ye would have plucked out your own eyes, and have given them to me. 16 Am I therefore become your enemy, because I tell you the truth?

He reminds them that for their sake, he had become a Gentile, cutting away from the traditions he was raised in and becoming what they are. Therefore, his appeal is that they should not seek to become Jews but become like himself. They should adopt an attitude like his own toward ceremonial Jewish law, which was the understanding that it was fine for Jews to continue to observe Torah tradition, but unnecessary for Gentiles who wanted to join the church. The Galatians have accepted the Christian faith, and they must not disown it for the Law, which Paul himself set aside in community with Gentiles. They should emulate Paul by remaining loyal to the truth of the Gospel (2:5, 14), by being dead to and not under the Law (2:19, 3:25), and by living out their faith in Christ (2:20, 3:26–29), and thereby not nullifying the grace of God (2:21), but enjoying all the benefits of the Gospel by means of faith in Christ (3:22). Paul concludes his imperative in **verse 12** by assuring them that his appeal is not based on some personal grievance or failure, but it is based on his genuine care and concern for them.

Paul follows up this assurance with the reminder of how they treated him while he was with them earlier. He recalls that he was with them due to an unspecified "weakness of the flesh," an "illness," on that first occasion. The exact nature of Paul's illness is undisclosed. Whatever the case, this illness caused Paul to change his plans and became the opportunity for his preaching the Gospel to the Galatians. The Galatians could have rejected Paul and his message on the basis of his illness, out of general superstition (cf. **Acts 28:3–6**), or as a result of perceiving his illness as caused by demonic activity (cf. **2 Corinthians 12:7**). Thus, Paul's sickness was indeed in some sense a "trial" for them, and yet in spite of that, the Galatians treated him with high regard and his message as the truth of God, as though he were "an angel" (Gk. *angelos*, **AHN-ge-los**) or even Jesus Christ Himself. This affection toward Paul, when the Galatians might have otherwise rejected him and his message makes all the more perplexing their treatment of him now, as they are apparently resisting Paul and his message, and following the infiltrators who were preaching "another gospel" among them.

Remembering the kind of welcome he had when he first visited Galatia, Paul could rightly now ask, "Where is then the blessedness ye spake of?" (**v. 15**). So genuine was their reception, commitment, selflessness, and generosity that Paul said that they would have plucked their own eyes for him (probably a figure of speech to indicate the willingness to meet his needs, rather than an indication that the sickness had to do with Paul's eyes). That affection has now gone. Once considered an angel of God, he is now an enemy because he had preached the true Gospel to them.

Next, the apostle appeals to them to become like him. He asks them to do this as a reciprocal action to his becoming like them (i.e., as a Gentile not under the Law). Paul exercised his freedom from the Law in order to contextualize the Gospel message from his Gentile audience in Galatia. Paul launches into his past history with the Galatians. He speaks of how he labored and preached the Gospel to them while suffering. Paul speaks of an infirmity of the flesh. We do not know exactly what this infirmity is, but we do know that the Galatians knew about it and Paul endured the pain of it while preaching to them. Paul states this to remind them of the truth they had committed themselves to previously. Prior to their turning to religion to make themselves righteous, they had received the Gospel that he preached and believed in the sufficiency of Christ and His righteousness. Paul speaks to them to remind them and alert them to the empty path they are on now.

III. PAUL'S EXPRESSION (vv. 17–20)

Paul changes his mood and expresses deep concern for the Galatians, in contrast to his opponents' superficial interest. He addresses his hoodwinked flock affectionately as "my little children" (**v. 19**). Although Paul usually addresses his converts as "brothers and sisters," he occasionally refers them as his "children" when he wants to draw attention to the fact that he was instrumental, as their spiritual father, in bringing them to the new birth of faith (**1 Corinthians 4:14; Philemon 10**). Here, however, the role of the father is not enough to capture his thought. Such is his personal investment that he compares himself to a mother who must go through the pangs of childbirth again for the sake of her children. This image witnesses to the deep personal anguish Paul felt over the defection of his spiritual offspring in Galatia.

17 They zealously affect you, but not well; yea, they would exclude you, that ye might affect them. 18 But it is good to be zealously affected always in a good thing, and not only when I am present with you. 19 My little children, of whom I travail in birth again until Christ be formed in you, 20 I desire to be present with you now, and to change my voice; for I stand in doubt of you.

There is no doubt that Paul is grieved as he asks if he is their enemy for speaking the truth. The Judaizers had influenced the Galatians with false teaching and effectively shut down Paul's influence on the young church. They wanted the Galatians to solely pay attention to them, not Paul. Paul says it is good to go after the right thing. The Judaizers were after the Galatians but for the wrong reasons: to preach strict Torah observance that they claimed would result in exclusion from the faith if transgressed.

The Galatians' turn toward a false religion is a move away from Christ. Paul's grief is intense. He states his desire that he would like to be present with the Galatians and change his tone, because now he doubts the authenticity of their faith.

SEARCH THE SCRIPTURES

QUESTION 1
The Galatians turned to the weak and beggarly elements that led them into bondage again. As followers of Jesus in the 21st century, what "weak and beggarly elements" can potentially lead us into bondage?

The idea that status or work is more important than worship. Answers will vary.

QUESTION 2
How did the Galatians receive Paul and his message (**v. 14**)? Share a time that you may have been rejected by others because of your relationship with Christ.

They initially received Paul with open arms, but are now rejecting him. Answers will vary.

QUESTION 3
Are there times in your life when you felt uncomfortable to share Jesus with others?

When I was afraid because people might laugh. Answers will vary.

LIGHT ON THE WORD

False Teachers - The Agitators
The agitators, who are causing the difficulties in Galatia, distorted the Gospel and damaged the relationship between Paul and the believers. Paul did not identify them by name, perhaps to not dignify them; he simply referred to them as "they." Paul accuses this group of earnestly pursing the Galatians, but not for good reasons. Paul sees them playing a mind game with the Galatians: excluding the Galatians so that the Galatians will earnestly pursue them. Paul concedes that it is good to be zealously affected or have someone concerned about them, but the motive and purpose are important. Paul sees that the Galatians' faith is still young, pointing out that they shouldn't just pursue good things when he is with them. It seems that whoever is with them, whether Paul or this zealous group, can easily influence the Galatians' faith.

BIBLE APPLICATION

AIM: Students will agree that salvation is more than ritual or tradition.

Many people in our society do not know what the Gospel is. They may say it is a style of music or going to church and getting yourself together. These things are not the same as the Gospel of Jesus Christ. We may not have to deal with the "weak and beggarly elements" the Galatians dealt with, but many things can trip us up and distract us from the true Gospel that sets us free. Wealth, power, relationships, and status can be used as a substitute for justification through Christ. Religion and going to church can be used as a substitute for a relationship with Jesus Christ. Sitting in a pew every Sunday does not make us right with God, nor does serving in the church justify us in His sight. How might religious tradition provide a false assurance of salvation, and what is the remedy?

STUDENTS' RESPONSES

AIM: Students will evaluate whether or not there is the potential of religious legalism in their own lives.

With the help of the Holy Spirit, prayer, introspection, and personal evaluation will put the spotlight on areas in our lives that need to be changed. Why not kneel in prayer (if you are able to do so), and have a little talk with Jesus?

PRAYER

Dear Lord, we seek to follow after Your ways and Your will. Sometimes we stray or walk away to do what we desire. Yet, Lord, You welcome us back into Your loving arms. Thank You for Your new mercies every day and for keeping us in spite of our thoughts and actions. In the Name of Jesus, we pray. Amen.

HOW TO SAY IT

Philemon.   **FI**-le-mon.

DIG A LITTLE DEEPER

This section provides an additional research article to further your study of the lesson:

In the pursuit of holiness, it is easy to be ensnared by the lure of good moral behavior as a means to make us justified before God. In this message by John Piper, the challenge is to identify the methods of the adversary, whose tactics are, though not new, restructured for this particular time in history. Piper warns the believer of the temptation to return to the enslaving mentality of self-righteousness and piety.

http://www.desiringgod.org/messages/dont-go-back-from-sonship-to-slavery

PREPARE FOR NEXT SUNDAY

Read **Galatians 5:1–17** and "Freedom In Christ."

DAILY HOME BIBLE READINGS

MONDAY
Becoming an Heir in God's Family
(Galatians 4:1–7)

TUESDAY
A Faithful Heir Will Succeed
(1 Kings 2:1–4)

WEDNESDAY
Power and Strength through Weakness
(2 Corinthians 12:7b–10)

THURSDAY
The Cost of Being a Disciple
(Luke 9:23-27, 57–62)

FRIDAY
The Spirit Brings Life
(Romans 8:1–11)

SATURDAY
Led by the Spirit of Christ
(Romans 8:12–17)

SUNDAY
New Birth Brings Freedom
(Galatians 4:8–20)

Sources:
Carson, D. A., R. T. France, J. A. Motyer, and G. J. Wenham, eds. *New Bible Commentary.* Downers Grove, IL: InterVarsity Press, 1994.
Keener, Craig S. *The IVP Bible Background Commentary: New Testament.* Downers Grove, IL: InterVarsity Press, 1993.

FREEDOM IN CHRIST

BIBLE BASIS: GALATIANS 5:1–17

BIBLE TRUTH: Paul tells the Galatians to become slaves to one another through love.

MEMORY VERSE: "For, brethren, ye have been called unto liberty; only use not liberty for an occasion to the flesh, but by love serve one another" (Galatians 5:13).

LESSON AIM: By the end of the lesson, we will: EVALUATE Paul's teaching about life in the Spirit as foundational for Christian holiness; CELEBRATE the Holy Spirit's presence in their lives; and EMBRACE new ways of creating openness to the Spirit's leading.

TEACHER PREPARATION

MATERIALS NEEDED: Quarterly Commentary/Teacher Manual, Adult Quarterly, Adult resources—charts, worksheets, and other teaching tools, paper, pens, pencils, Bibles (several different versions)

OTHER MATERIALS NEEDED / TEACHER'S NOTES:

_____

_____

LESSON OVERVIEW

LIFE NEED FOR TODAY'S LESSON
God's grace frees believers from trusting in their own efforts for salvation.

BIBLE LEARNING
Paul urges the Galatians to stand firm in Christian freedom.

BIBLE APPLICATION
Christian freedom offers the opportunity of a Spirit-led life.

STUDENTS' RESPONSES
Followers of Christ are sometimes easily caught up in various legalistic practices.

LESSON SCRIPTURE

GALATIANS 5:1–17, KJV

1 Stand fast therefore in the liberty wherewith Christ hath made us free, and be not entangled again with the yoke of bondage.

2 Behold, I Paul say unto you, that if ye be circumcised, Christ shall profit you nothing.

GALATIANS 5:1–17, AMP

1 It was for this freedom that Christ set us free [completely liberating us]; therefore keep standing firm and do not be subject again to a yoke of slavery [which you once removed].

2 Notice, it is I, Paul, who tells you that if you receive circumcision [as a supposed requirement of salvation], Christ will be of

3 For I testify again to every man that is circumcised, that he is a debtor to do the whole law.

4 Christ is become of no effect unto you, whosoever of you are justified by the law; ye are fallen from grace.

5 For we through the Spirit wait for the hope of righteousness by faith.

6 For in Jesus Christ neither circumcision availeth any thing, nor uncircumcision; but faith which worketh by love.

7 Ye did run well; who did hinder you that ye should not obey the truth?

8 This persuasion cometh not of him that calleth you.

9 A little leaven leaveneth the whole lump.

10 I have confidence in you through the Lord, that ye will be none otherwise minded: but he that troubleth you shall bear his judgment, whosoever he be.

11 And I, brethren, if I yet preach circumcision, why do I yet suffer persecution? then is the offence of the cross ceased.

12 I would they were even cut off which trouble you.

13 For, brethren, ye have been called unto liberty; only use not liberty for an occasion to the flesh, but by love serve one another.

14 For all the law is fulfilled in one word, even in this; Thou shalt love thy neighbour as thyself.

15 But if ye bite and devour one another, take heed that ye be not consumed one of another.

16 This I say then, Walk in the Spirit, and ye shall not fulfil the lust of the flesh.

no benefit to you [for you will lack the faith in Christ that is necessary for salvation].

3 Once more I solemnly affirm to every man who receives circumcision [as a supposed requirement of salvation], that he is under obligation and required to keep the whole Law.

4 You have been severed from Christ, if you seek to be justified [that is, declared free of the guilt of sin and its penalty, and placed in right standing with God] through the Law; you have fallen from grace [for you have lost your grasp on God's unmerited favor and blessing].

5 For we [not relying on the Law but] through the [strength and power of the Holy] Spirit, by faith, are waiting [confidently] for the hope of righteousness [the completion of our salvation].

6 For [if we are] in Christ Jesus neither circumcision nor uncircumcision means anything, but only faith activated and expressed and working through love.

7 You were running [the race] well; who has interfered and prevented you from obeying the truth?

8 This [deceptive] persuasion is not from Him who called you [to freedom in Christ].

9 A little leaven [a slight inclination to error, or a few false teachers] leavens the whole batch [it perverts the concept of faith and misleads the church].

10 I have confidence in you in the Lord that you will adopt no other view [contrary to mine on the matter]; but the one who is disturbing you, whoever he is, will have to bear the penalty.

11 But as for me, brothers, if I am still preaching circumcision [as I had done before I met

17 For the flesh lusteth against the Spirit, and the Spirit against the flesh: and these are contrary the one to the other: so that ye cannot do the things that ye would.

Christ; and as some accuse me of doing now, as necessary for salvation], why am I still being persecuted [by Jews]? In that case the stumbling block of the cross [to unbelieving Jews] has been abolished.

12 I wish that those who are troubling you [by teaching that circumcision is necessary for salvation] would even [go all the way and] castrate themselves!

13 For you, my brothers, were called to freedom; only do not let your freedom become an opportunity for the sinful nature (worldliness, selfishness), but through love serve and seek the best for one another.

14 For the whole Law [concerning human relationships] is fulfilled in one precept, "You shall love your neighbor as yourself [that is, you shall have an unselfish concern for others and do things for their benefit]."

15 But if you bite and devour one another [in bickering and strife], watch out that you [along with your entire fellowship] are not consumed by one another.

16 But I say, walk habitually in the [Holy] Spirit [seek Him and be responsive to His guidance], and then you will certainly not carry out the desire of the sinful nature [which responds impulsively without regard for God and His precepts].

17 For the sinful nature has its desire which is opposed to the Spirit, and the [desire of the] Spirit opposes the sinful nature; for these [two, the sinful nature and the Spirit] are in direct opposition to each other [continually in conflict], so that you [as believers] do not [always] do whatever [good things] you want to do.

229

LIGHT ON THE WORD

Galatia. The Galatia of the New Testament was an area in what is now north central Turkey, where people of many different cultural backgrounds lived together. The Gauls, a Celtic people, had invaded the Asia Minor peninsula upon invitation of the king of Bithynia, who enlisted their help in fighting civil wars. They eventually settled in parts of the region formerly known as Cappadocia and Phrygia. The area became a Roman province in 25 BC. Because of Rome's tendency to rezone its provinces, the Galatians, Paul addressed in his letter would not have only been inhabitants of Galatia proper, but they were also citizens of other nearby regions.

Circumcision. Circumcision is a symbol of God's covenant with Abraham (**Genesis 17**). Every male among Abraham's people (blood relatives and servants) was to be circumcised. Although circumcision was common in ancient societies, the Abrahamic covenant's circumcision was unique in that after the initial group of men was circumcised, the ritual was from then on practiced on eight-day-old infant boys. When circumcision was written down as part of the Law (**Leviticus 12:3**), Moses shared the procedure's spiritual understanding by "instructing the Israelites to circumcise their hearts" (**Deuteronomy 10:16**), which meant that in addition to the physical sign, they were also under God's covenant and had to follow His instructions. As Judaism grew, circumcision also became a symbol of Jewish identity, especially in the Greco-Roman Empire when the dominant culture did not circumcise their males.

TEACHING THE BIBLE LESSON

LIFE NEED FOR TODAY'S LESSON

AIM: Students will agree that living a circumcised life begins with the work of the Holy Spirit in our hearts.

INTRODUCTION

Division Among Believers

At the time Paul wrote this letter to the Galatians, a group of Jewish Christians, known as Judaizers, was teaching that Gentile converts needed to be circumcised both as a sign of their covenant with God and a means of justification or being made right with God. They also insisted the Gentile Christians observe other parts of Mosaic Law. Paul and others of like mind found the demand for circumcision in contradiction to salvation by the grace of Jesus Christ. The debate about circumcision and the Law in the growing Christian community had created such division among believers that it threatened to implode Christianity. In **chapter 4**, Paul reminds the Galatians that before they knew God, they had been slaves to pagan gods, and he asks them why they would want to be slaves once again now that God knows them (**Galatians 4:8–9**). Paul tells them they are not the children of bondage, but of freedom (**4:31**).

BIBLE LEARNING

AIM: Students will agree to stand firm in their Christian freedom.

I. BE NOT ENTANGLED
(Galatians 5:1–6)

This is a connecting verse; it summarizes all that has been said and anticipates what will be said. There is greater clarity of thought when this verse is read as two separate statements. First is a statement emphasizing the purpose of God's saving act in Christ: "For freedom Christ has set us free" (NIV). Second is a statement of entreaty, a plea or an appeal based upon the purpose of God's saving activity: "Stand firm, therefore, and do not let yourselves be burdened again by a yoke of slavery."

The "yoke of slavery" was more than the "yoke" of the Jewish Law. The Gentile Christians were never under the "yoke" of the Jewish Law, but they were under paganism. Therefore, Paul uses the phrase "yoke of slavery" to mean "the elements of the world" (**4:3**) that he calls "weak and beggarly" (**4:9**). Both the Jewish Law and paganism were included in "the elements of the world" that rob people of their freedom in Christ. Another word to examine is "entangled"; the Greek word for "entangled" is *enecho* (**en-EH-koh**), meaning to be subject to or loaded down with. Paul says to not be loaded down or subjected again to the yoke of bondage.

1 Stand fast therefore in the liberty wherewith Christ hath made us free, and be not entangled again with the yoke of bondage. 2 Behold, I Paul say unto you, that if ye be circumcised, Christ shall profit you nothing. 3 For I testify again to every man that is circumcised, that he is a debtor to do the whole law. 4 Christ is become of no effect unto you, whosoever of you are justified by the law; ye are fallen from grace. 5 For we through the Spirit wait for the hope of righteousness by faith. 6 For in Jesus Christ neither circumcision availeth any thing, nor uncircumcision; but faith which worketh by love.

Today's text begins in the middle of Paul's efforts to persuade the Galatians to not follow false teachers who want them to be subject to Mosaic Law. Paul urges the Galatians to stand firm in the freedom Christ has set before them. The yoke of bondage, a metaphor for the Law, is meant to illustrate that the Law stands in contrast to the yoke of Christ, which is easy and light (**Matthew 11:29–30**). Anyone who accepts circumcision must observe the entire Law, "for whosoever shall keep the whole law, and yet offend in one point, he is guilty of all" (**James 2:10**). In this regard, those under the Law are in constant debt, because keeping all the statutes without fail is impossible. Paul writes that anyone seeking to be right with God through observing the Law has in fact "fallen from grace" (**Galatians 5:4**).

In essence, for those intending to follow the Law, the grace of Jesus Christ is useless to them because they have forsaken the advantages of His free gift of grace. To persuade the Galatians to not be entangled by the Law, Paul explains that it is the Holy Spirit and faith, not the Law, that make their relationships with God right (**v. 5**). He adds that in Christ, it is of no consequence whether or not one is circumcised because what matters is faith manifested in love.

II. STAY ON THE RIGHT COURSE (vv. 7–12)

Paul knows the Judaizers were guilty of "cutting in," a phrase translating the Greek word *anakopto* (**ah-nah-COP-to**). This word is also used to refer to runners who come across their prescribed course and throw other participants off the track. Additionally, it was also a military term used to refer to breaking up a road or erecting an obstacle to hinder or prevent the opposing army's progress. The Galatians were familiar with these images and therefore understood Paul's question. Paul anticipates and affirms their answer in the following verse.

Paul reminds the Galatians that God calls them and He is not the author of their confusion. It is interesting that Paul does not blame Satan for the Galatians' confusion. It appears that Paul wants to keep the focus upon the false brethren who cut in and broke up the road that the Galatians were successfully traveling on.

7 Ye did run well; who did hinder you that ye should not obey the truth? 8 This persuasion cometh not of him that calleth you. 9 A little leaven leaveneth the whole lump. 10 I have confidence in you through the Lord, that ye will be none otherwise minded: but he that troubleth you shall bear his judgment, whosoever he be. 11 And I, brethren, if I yet preach circumcision, why do I yet suffer persecution? then is the offence of the cross ceased. 12

I would they were even cut off which trouble you.

In **verse 7**, Paul reminds the Galatians that when they were new believers, they were striving in the faith. However, false teachers wanted to divert them from truth. These people's plans are not the work of God, and their teachings do not reflect the foundation of Christianity: "by grace are ye saved through faith; and that not of yourselves: it is the gift of God: Not of works, lest any man should boast" (**Ephesians 2:8–9**). To illustrate the harm these false teachings could cause, Paul compares them to yeast, a fungus which, when a small amount is used, can spread throughout the whole dough. If these teachers' tongues were left unfettered, they could infect the whole church. However, Paul is confident God will keep the Galatians.

To say the least, **verse 11** is problematic, primarily because we do not know the context of Paul's statement "if I yet preach circumcision." It may be that he is parenthetically responding to a specific charge from his opponents. The Judaizers, for example, were not above pointing out Paul's association with Timothy's circumcision (**Acts 16:3**). They could also reference Paul's having been circumcised himself (**Philippians 3:5**). Moreover, it may be that Paul preached circumcision during his pre-Christian days. In any event, he refutes the suggestion that he now preaches circumcision. In fact, he adds, to do so would be an "offence" to the cross of Christ.

In **verse 12**, the tone of the Greek is harsh. What Paul says is a terrible thing to wish on anyone, "As for those who are troubling you, O that they would go the whole way and castrate themselves." F.F. Bruce translates it, "I wish that those who are upsetting you would complete their cutting operation—on themselves." Additionally, Sam K. Williams has called our attention to **Deuteronomy 23:1**, where "the severing of the penis would … cut a man off from the people of God."

Assuming that the Galatians were familiar with this Scripture, they would have heard Paul's harsh comment as a wish that the Judaizers remove or sever themselves from the Christian community. The harshness of Paul's language helps us to understand the depth of his disagreement with the Judaizers' message.

III. CALLED TO BE FREE (vv. 13–17)

The Apostle Paul was concerned about the threat of the Judaizers and the threat of the flesh, or the Galatians' misuse of their Christian freedom. Paul frames his concern by saying two things about the Galatian Christians: first, that they "have been called," and second, that that calling is "unto liberty." Previously, Paul has spoken about the Galatians' "call" with the emphasis on the "call of God" (**Galatians 1:6, 5:8**). The meaning is the same here: "you have been called by God unto liberty." The liberty the Galatians have been called to is Christian freedom. In other words, God has called the Galatians to be free from the elements of the world so as to be free to live for the Lord.

13 For, brethren, ye have been called unto liberty; only use not liberty for an occasion to the flesh, but by love serve one another. 14 For all the law is fulfilled in one word, even in this; Thou shalt love thy neighbour as thyself. 15 But if ye bite and devour one another, take heed that ye be not consumed one of another. 16 This I say then, Walk in the Spirit, and ye shall not fulfil the lust of the flesh. 17 For the flesh lusteth against the Spirit, and the Spirit against the flesh: and these are contrary the one to the other: so that ye cannot do the things that ye would.

Today's text ends with Paul again reminding the Galatians that they were called to be free and should not use their freedom as an opportunity to sin, but instead serve each other in love. For those still concerned with the Law,

Paul writes that the whole Law is summed up in the command "Thou shalt love your neighbor as thyself" (**Leviticus 19:18**). Engaging in conflict would only destroy their community. Paul beseeches the Galatians to live lives led by the Holy Spirit so they will not give in to their sinful nature. He explains that the desires of the flesh and the Spirit are constantly warring within believers, preventing us from doing what is right (cf. **Romans 7:15–24**).

Paul highlights the consequences of failure to make doing God's will and loving others the aim of Christian living. Paul uses a conditional clause saying that if you do such and such, this might happen. He warns the church not to bite and devour one another. The Greek word for bite here is generally used for snakes. The word for devour is *katesthio* (Gk. **kah-tess-TH-EE-oh**), meaning to eat up, consume, or tear to pieces; this word is often used for animals. In other words, Paul is warning them that they were fighting like wild animals, and if they did not stop, they would all be consumed—thus the preceding admonition to love one another, fulfilling the law (**v. 14**).

SEARCH THE SCRIPTURES

QUESTION 1
What are some ways we try to work for salvation? Why?

Money, our jobs, status in the church, family. Answers will vary.

QUESTION 2
Walking or living in the Spirit in **verse 16** is essential for every believer. Walking in the Spirit is the opposite of fulfilling the lust of the flesh. Discuss some ways that a believer walks in the Spirit.

The believer walks in the Spirit by praying and depending upon the leading of the Holy Spirit, obeying God's Word, and living a lifestyle that is pleasing to God demonstrating

the fruit of the Spirit (Galatians 5:22). **Answers will vary.**

LIGHT ON THE WORD

Waiting on the Lord
Paul identifies with the faithful in Galatia, including himself in the "we" here. A paraphrase of Paul's words here would be, "We wait for the full realization of our salvation in the faith that we already have it." This is implied by Paul's use of the word "hope" from *elpis* (Gk. **el-PIS**), which means to an expectation for what has not happened yet. Another image helps to understand the full meaning of **verse 5**. The word "wait" is translated from *apekdechomai* (Gk. **ahp-ek-DEH-kho-meye**) and carries the meaning of awaiting eagerly. This kind of waiting does not suggest sitting around with our arms folded doing nothing. Rather, it conjures the image of a waiter in a restaurant, who is "on the case" patiently and attentively serving, discharging the expectations of the job. It is also important to note that this waiting is "through the Spirit"; we must continue to be on the job, empowered by the Spirit, patiently serving our Lord with pleasure—in anticipation of the day when God "will render to every man according to his deeds" (**Romans 2:6**). At that time, true followers of Christ will be declared righteous by their faith, fulfilling their hope.

BIBLE APPLICATION

AIM: Students will decide that Christian freedom is only possible with a Spirit-led life.

It's a blessing to have the Holy Spirit to guide us in the right direction. In your daily devotion, before sharing your petitions, ask God to help you to be sensitive to the Holy Spirit's leading. Study scriptural accounts of those who were Spirit-led to understand the ways He speaks to us. As you learn to recognize the urging of the Spirit, commit to following His guidance, even if it means you will be traveling outside of your comfort zone. It will be worth it.

STUDENTS' RESPONSES

AIM: Students will agree that followers of Christ are sometimes easily caught up in various legalistic traditions or catering to their fleshy desires.

Our society is merit-based, meaning we perform to get rewards. We perform certain duties at work to get a raise. We must meet certain requirements to get A's in school. Some even make grand gestures to win the heart of someone they love. On the other hand, there are times we receive something special—a gift. The beautiful fact about grace is this: it's a gift! Grace is a gift we can never earn and will never deserve. Grace is God's unmerited favor to undeserving man. This definition is worth memorizing.

PRAYER

Dear God, teach us how not to be caught up in extreme political, social, religious, and other experiences that take us away from You. Our selfish desires and misinformation, or false teachings, will take us to places and with people who are not of You. Protect us from our harmful thoughts and those who will do us harm. In the Name of Jesus, we pray. Amen.

HOW TO SAY IT

Entangled.   in-**TANG**-ild.

Leaveneth.   **LE**-vin-ith.

DIG A LITTLE DEEPER

This section provides an additional research article to further your study of the lesson:

In this article, Ravi Zacharias discusses the futility in dogmatically approaching unbelievers. With the advent of access to a variety of ideological systems and varied views about God, the manner in which Christians engage in discussion can speak just as loudly as the truth that is being conveyed.

http://rzim.org/just-thinking/reaching-the-happy-thinking-pagan

PREPARE FOR NEXT SUNDAY

Read **Galatians 5:18–6:10** and "Christ Creates Holy Living."

DAILY HOME BIBLE READINGS

MONDAY
Christ, the Wisdom of God
(1 Corinthians 1:18–25)

TUESDAY
The Lord is God Alone
(Deuteronomy 6:4–9)

WEDNESDAY
You Shall Love Your Neighbor
(Leviticus 19:13–18)

THURSDAY
Rescued from Death
(Romans 7:15–24)

FRIDAY
Keep Focused and Pure
(1 Corinthians 5:1–2, 6–9)

SATURDAY
Produce the Fruit of the Spirit
(Galatians 5:22–26)

SUNDAY
Freedom in Christ
(Galatians 5:1–17)

Sources:
Commentary on Galatians. Grand Rapids: Eerdmans Publishing Co., 1982, p. 233. (Galatians Nashville: Abingdon Press, 1997, p. 142).

CHRIST CREATES HOLY LIVING

BIBLE BASIS: GALATIANS 5:18–6:10

BIBLE TRUTH: Believers who are in relationship with the Spirit are no longer subject to the Law, nor condemned by it.

MEMORY VERSES: "But the fruit of the Spirit is love, joy, peace, longsuffering, gentleness, goodness, faith, meekness, temperance: against such there is no law" (Galatians 5:22–23).

LESSON AIM: By the end of the lesson, we will: AGREE that the characteristics Paul lists as the fruit of the Spirit are the evidence of God's presence within us; VOLUNTEER to meet the needs of others in the church; and COMMIT, by the Holy Spirit's empowerment, to work for the good of everyone, especially those in the family of faith.

TEACHER PREPARATION

MATERIALS NEEDED: Quarterly Commentary/Teacher Manual, Adult Quarterly, Adult resources—charts, worksheets, and other teaching tools, paper, pens, pencils, Bibles (several different versions)

OTHER MATERIALS NEEDED / TEACHER'S NOTES:

_____

_____

LESSON OVERVIEW

LIFE NEED FOR TODAY'S LESSON
The fruit of the Spirit is essential for holy living.

BIBLE LEARNING
Paul sharply contrasts a Spirit-filled life with life in the flesh.

BIBLE APPLICATION
Students can develop the characteristics of an authentic Christian lifestyle.

STUDENTS' RESPONSES
Believers with the evidence of the fruit of the Spirit experience a closer relationship with Jesus Christ.

LESSON SCRIPTURE

GALATIANS 5:18–6:10, KJV

18 But if ye be led of the Spirit, ye are not under the law.

19 Now the works of the flesh are manifest, which are these; Adultery, fornication, uncleanness, lasciviousness,

GALATIANS 5:18–6:10, AMP

18 But if you are guided and led by the Spirit, you are not subject to the Law.

19 Now the practices of the sinful nature are clearly evident: they are sexual immorality, impurity, sensuality (total irresponsibility, lack of self-control),

20 Idolatry, witchcraft, hatred, variance, emulations, wrath, strife, seditions, heresies,

21 Envyings, murders, drunkenness, revellings, and such like: of the which I tell you before, as I have also told you in time past, that they which do such things shall not inherit the kingdom of God.

22 But the fruit of the Spirit is love, joy, peace, longsuffering, gentleness, goodness, faith,

23 Meekness, temperance: against such there is no law.

24 And they that are Christ's have crucified the flesh with the affections and lusts.

25 If we live in the Spirit, let us also walk in the Spirit.

26 Let us not be desirous of vain glory, provoking one another, envying one another.

6:1 Brethren, if a man be overtaken in a fault, ye which are spiritual, restore such an one in the spirit of meekness; considering thyself, lest thou also be tempted.

2 Bear ye one another's burdens, and so fulfil the law of Christ.

3 For if a man think himself to be something, when he is nothing, he deceiveth himself.

4 But let every man prove his own work, and then shall he have rejoicing in himself alone, and not in another.

5 For every man shall bear his own burden.

6 Let him that is taught in the word communicate unto him that teacheth in all good things.

7 Be not deceived; God is not mocked: for whatsoever a man soweth, that shall he also reap.

20 idolatry, sorcery, hostility, strife, jealousy, fits of anger, disputes, dissensions, factions [that promote heresies],

21 envy, drunkenness, riotous behavior, and other things like these. I warn you beforehand, just as I did previously, that those who practice such things will not inherit the kingdom of God.

22 But the fruit of the Spirit [the result of His presence within us] is love [unselfish concern for others], joy, [inner] peace, patience [not the ability to wait, but how we act while waiting], kindness, goodness, faithfulness,

23 gentleness, self-control. Against such things there is no law.

24 And those who belong to Christ Jesus have crucified the sinful nature together with its passions and appetites.

25 If we [claim to] live by the [Holy] Spirit, we must also walk by the Spirit [with personal integrity, godly character, and moral courage—our conduct empowered by the Holy Spirit].

26 We must not become conceited, challenging or provoking one another, envying one another.

6:1 Brothers, if anyone is caught in any sin, you who are spiritual [that is, you who are responsive to the guidance of the Spirit] are to restore such a person in a spirit of gentleness [not with a sense of superiority or self-righteousness], keeping a watchful eye on yourself, so that you are not tempted as well.

2 Carry one another's burdens and in this way you will fulfill the requirements of the law of Christ [that is, the law of Christian love].

3 For if anyone thinks he is something [special] when [in fact] he is nothing [special

8 For he that soweth to his flesh shall of the flesh reap corruption; but he that soweth to the Spirit shall of the Spirit reap life everlasting.

9 And let us not be weary in well doing: for in due season we shall reap, if we faint not.

10 As we have therefore opportunity, let us do good unto all men, especially unto them who are of the household of faith.

except in his own eyes], he deceives himself.

4 But each one must carefully scrutinize his own work [examining his actions, attitudes, and behavior], and then he can have the personal satisfaction and inner joy of doing something commendable without comparing himself to another.

5 For every person will have to bear [with patience] his own burden [of faults and shortcomings for which he alone is responsible].

6 The one who is taught the word [of God] is to share all good things with his teacher [contributing to his spiritual and material support].

7 Do not be deceived, God is not mocked [He will not allow Himself to be ridiculed, nor treated with contempt nor allow His precepts to be scornfully set aside]; for whatever a man sows, this and this only is what he will reap.

8 For the one who sows to his flesh [his sinful capacity, his worldliness, his disgraceful impulses] will reap from the flesh ruin and destruction, but the one who sows to the Spirit will from the Spirit reap eternal life.

9 Let us not grow weary or become discouraged in doing good, for at the proper time we will reap, if we do not give in.

10 So then, while we [as individual believers] have the opportunity, let us do good to all people [not only being helpful, but also doing that which promotes their spiritual well-being], and especially [be a blessing] to those of the household of faith (born-again believers).

LIGHT ON THE WORD

Fruit. Most of the time, we cannot recognize a fruit from the look of its seed. Only after seeds are planted in the ground and start sprouting do we know what type of fruit has been planted. Fruit is used metaphorically in Scripture to illustrate this fact. We do not know the power at work in people's lives until we see the fruit that power produces. In Scripture, fruit (works or deeds) is the sign of God's power moving within a person. Sin produces fruit (works) of the flesh, but the Holy Spirit produces the fruit of the Spirit in the lives of believers.

Sowing and Reaping. Agrarian societies, like that of the first-century church, relied on sowing and reaping crops for subsistence. For this reason, agricultural metaphors were often used to illustrate biblical truths. The farming process was grueling. Farmers had to properly till (break up the soil) land that was hard and rocky in order to get a healthy harvest. After the seeds were sown, the land had to be watered and the sprouting crops pruned. Watering was not an easy task. Although fields were located near water sources, farmers mostly relied on the rainy season twice a year (fall and spring) to water their crops. While waiting patiently to reap the harvest, farmers had to contend with drought, weeds, and all manner of pests. Because they did not live on farms but in nearby villages, farmers had to worry about thieves stealing crops while they were away. Although the farmer's life was arduous, his or her prize was finally reaping the harvest. The Galatians truly understood the patience it took to "not be weary in well doing for in due season we shall reap if we faint not" (**Galatians 6:9**).

TEACHING THE BIBLE LESSON

LIFE NEED FOR TODAY'S LESSON

AIM: Students will agree that believers can live holy by being led by the Spirit.

INTRODUCTION

Followers of the Way

The Roman government viewed first-century Christianity as merely a sect of Judaism because the church was still searching for its identity, and many in the first century churches identified as Jewish (Jews who followed Jesus). Many Christians in fact still worshiped in the Jewish synagogues. The first believers did not even call themselves Christians, but "followers of the Way." Antioch was where the term "Christian" was first used (**Acts 11:26**).

BIBLE LEARNING

AIM: Students will compare and contrast the Spirit-filled life with a life of the flesh by listing the characteristics of the fruit of the Spirit in one column and the works of the flesh in the other column.

I. WORKS OF THE FLESH (Galatians 5:18–21)

Paul alerts the Galatians to the possibilities inherent in their new life in Christ. If they let themselves be led by the Spirit, they will not feel obligated to a legal system that can command but is powerless to enforce obedience. By choosing to follow the Spirit's leading, they will be free from the Law and empowered by the Spirit to pursue the things of the Spirit.

The word for "led" in the Greek is *ago* (**AH-go**), used in the passive voice to mean to be brought along or taken along. Therefore, being led by the Spirit means submitting our will to Him, which leads us to do God's will. However, following the Spirit is not passive; the believer is still responsible for performing obligations. The sense of the original language is that believers must continue to take responsibility and consciously let the Spirit lead them.

18 But if ye be led of the Spirit, ye are not under the law. 19 Now the works of the flesh are manifest, which are these; Adultery, fornication, uncleanness, lasciviousness, 20 Idolatry, witchcraft, hatred, variance, emulations, wrath, strife, seditions, heresies, 21 Envyings, murders, drunkenness, revellings, and such like: of the which I tell you before, as I have also told you in time past, that they which do such things shall not inherit the kingdom of God.

Today's lesson begins in the midst of Paul's attempt to convince the Galatians to not become enslaved by the Law, which—unlike the Holy Spirit—was not intended to save, but rather to shed light on sin (**Romans 3:20**). Paul informs that those led by the Spirit (i.e., those who are under the continual guidance of and in abiding relationship with the Spirit) are no longer subject to the Law, nor can be condemned by it (**Romans 8:1**). Paul switches focus for a moment to describe the works of the flesh (the sinful state of people). He uses this vice list, a convention of Greco-Roman moral rhetoric, to emphasize that those who continually practice these sins will not inherit the Kingdom of God.

As increasing numbers of Gentiles became believers, due largely to Paul's endeavors, the necessity of observing the Mosaic Law came into question. Paul's insistence that our righteousness is based on Christ's righteousness and received as a gift became the foundation of the Christian faith. This marked the separation of Christianity from Judaism. In Paul's letter to the Galatians, he consistently emphasizes the difference between being enslaved by the Law and being free in the Holy Spirit as a means to teach the true Gospel and solidify the church's identity.

These verses clearly define fleshly and improper behavior for Christians called to exercise freedom in Christ. In fact, Paul adds emphatically what he has said on numerous occasions: "they which do such things (i.e., habitually practice such behaviors) shall not (i.e., shall in no way) inherit the kingdom of God." The Greek translates this as a solemn warning for us today.

II. THE FRUIT OF THE SPIRIT (vv. 22–26)

The works of the flesh contrast the fruit of the Spirit. The word "fruit" denotes an organic growth that stems from the believer's relationship with Christ. The first fruit listed is love. It is also the virtue upon which all the other fruit are based (**1 Corinthians 13:1–3**).

22 But the fruit of the Spirit is love, joy, peace, longsuffering, gentleness, goodness, faith, 23 meekness, temperance: against such there is no law. 24 And they that are Christ's have crucified the flesh with the affections and lusts.

Paul identifies the qualities evident in those believers who walk in the Spirit. He contrasts the singular fruit of the Spirit with the plural works of the flesh. The singular form of the Greek word *karpos* (**kar-POCE**), meaning fruit, indicates that the Spirit is capable of producing this fruit in every believer. They are not fruits, but fruit. The Spirit produces character and righteous behavior, which do not need laws and make obedience to the Law obsolete. The "works" produced by the flesh need the Law to keep them in check, so those who try to live by those works (obedience to the Law) always fall short. Those who walk in the Spirit put to death the flesh and its desires, and they allow the Spirit of God to lead them and produce fruit that does not need legislation.

In other words, those who have identified themselves with Christ and belong to Him "have crucified" or put to death everything in opposition to Him, and are free to produce the fruit of the Spirit through their behavior.

25 If we live in the Spirit, let us also walk in the Spirit.

This concisely summarizes what Paul has already said. It states what is true "since we live in the Spirit." It reflects the logical consequence of the reality of living in the Spirit: "let us also walk in the Spirit." Since we live in the Spirit, we must line up with the Spirit. Believers who claim to live in the Spirit must also express behavior resulting from the Spirit's control.

26 Let us not be desirous of vain glory, provoking one another, envying one another.

This verse seems to suggest that Paul does not want his readers to become overconfident about their position in Christ. A person who is in Christ and led by the Spirit will always reflect His spirit and attitude. Sometimes good behavior can provoke and stir up jealousy in others, particularly when done in ways that attract attention.

It is reasonable to think that Paul saw the Galatians arguing among themselves from this vantage point. Those who correctly understood salvation may have acted in ways that provoked others or stirred up envy. Consequently, they conducted themselves worse than those who were wrong. The implication is that believers have an obligation to manage their conduct so as not to tempt others to do wrong.

The attitude that seeks to prove one's rightness at the expense of another's spiritual well-being borders on "vain glory." This does not speak well of the Holy Spirit's leading.

III. CARRY ANOTHER'S BURDENS (Galatians 6:1–6)

Chapter 6 begins with Paul imploring the spiritually stronger Galatians to help strengthen those among them who are overtaken by sin. Overtaken does not mean continually sinning (**Galatians 6:1**), but having their guard down. Stronger believers should help meekly, being careful to not also be tempted to sin. Paul then requests they shoulder the burdens of the weak as a way to fulfill the Law of Christ, which is to love one another (**Galatians 5:14**). Those who try to judge the weaker, thinking themselves above helping others, deceive themselves. They should examine their own work because all must carry their own burdens. The burden in verse 5 refers to the believer's work, which we will all be held accountable for on Judgment Day. This is different from the burden in **verse 2**, which refers to daily trials faced by every Christian.

1 Brethren, if a man be overtaken in a fault, ye which are spiritual, restore such an one in the spirit of meekness; considering thyself, lest thou also be tempted.

The word "overtaken" (Gk. *prolambano*, **pro-lam-BAH-no**) can mean to be entrapped, taken, caught by surprise, or to take a false step. This gives the meaning that the man "overtaken in a fault" was not intentionally doing wrong, but he suddenly became aware that his actions were wrong. In such cases, Paul counsels, believers should have a spirit of meekness and a view toward restoration. They must not satisfy the lust of the flesh by using the situation to gossip, feel superior, or exact overly harsh punishment on those at fault. The antidote to such fleshly behavior is to "consider thyself, lest thou also be tempted." As we correct our fellow Christians, we should keep in mind the famous saying, "There but for the grace of God go I."

2 Bear ye one another's burdens, and so fulfil the law of Christ.

Those led by the Spirit are called to be willing and available to help carry one another's loads. Paul's sense makes this behavior the style of living in Christian fellowship. The verb "bear" is from the Greek word *bastazo* (**bahs-TAHD-zo**), meaning to take up, carry, or endure, suffer, or undergo. The word for "burdens" is *baros* (Gk. **BAH-roce**), meaning weight or, as in this case, hardship. We should support one another by helping to bear heavy hardship. Bearing each other's burdens should not be occasional, but it should be a way of living and behaving in Christian community. With this behavior, we, like Christ, will have fulfilled the Law.

3 For if a man think himself to be something, when he is nothing, he deceiveth himself.

This verse helps believers understand how vulnerable they are to the influence of the flesh. Every believer is a stone's throw away from thinking too highly of himself or herself. This is particularly true today, when many factors—economic position, racial and ethnic identity, comparing ourselves to others on social media—make it easy to feel better than others. Properly and legitimately estimating our own value is an expression of the Spirit-led life. When **verse 2** is connected to verse 3, the message is clear: those who overvalue themselves are unlikely to bear another's burdens.

4 But let every man prove his own work, and then shall he have rejoicing in himself alone, and not in another.

Paul's concern in this verse is that followers compare themselves only to what the Spirit calls them to become. Those led by the Spirit don't need to compare themselves with other believers; self-evaluation comes from proving their work in the light of God's Word. In fact, rejoicing because you think you are better than someone else betrays life in Christ. It is not the way of the Spirit. Given this interpretation of **verse 4**, **verse 5** is a logical restatement.

5 For every man shall bear his own burden.

This might appear to contradict verse 2, where Paul says we should help share each other's burdens. Here he says to bear your own burden. The difference is apparent in the Greek. The Greek word for burden here is *phortion* (**for-TEE-on**). It is different from verse 2; the meaning is better conveyed as "load," referring to everyone "pulling their own weight" in responsibilities. In other words, you should do your work and not expect someone else to do it for you. In this way, the work of ministry is shouldered by everyone and not by a few. We each have a responsibility to carry part of the burden of ministry, such as evangelism, teaching, praising, or showing hospitality. This is quite different from helping someone who is burdened down with problems; in this case we come to their aid to help shoulder their pain. Laziness is not a virtue in Scripture; our Christian responsibility is to carry our own weight and help bear the others' misfortunes.

6 Let him that is taught in the word communicate unto him that teacheth in all good things.

Paul continues the line of thought that illustrates the interconnectedness of the body of Christ. Those taught in the Word should communicate (Gk. *koinoneo*, **koi-no-NEH-oh**), or share, and partner with those who teach the Word. In other words, those who receive spiritual blessings should share their material blessings with those who labor over them. This is a relationship of mutual reciprocity, and it is the type of relationship the Lord wants to be maintained between leaders and followers in the church.

IV. WHAT THEY REAP, THEY WILL SOW (vv. 7–10)

Now that Paul has explained the difference between the flesh and the Spirit and implored them to support one another, he tells the Galatians to not be fooled because anyone can turn away from God's justice. Whatever they reap, they will sow. If someone pleases their sinful nature, they will perish, but if they please the Spirit, they will have eternal life. Paul says to not get tired of doing right, because if they hold on, they will reap blessings at the appointed time. In the meantime, the Galatians should take advantage of every opportunity to do good for all, especially for fellow believers.

7 Be not deceived; God is not mocked: for whatsoever a man soweth, that shall he also reap. 8 For he that soweth to his flesh shall of the flesh reap corruption; but he that soweth to the Spirit shall of the Spirit reap life everlasting.

Using the metaphor of a farmer who sows and reaps the harvest, Paul says that what a believer sows determines what he or she harvests—our choices determine our consequences. Whether we choose to live in the Spirit or in the flesh, consequences will follow. Believers are encouraged to sow to the Spirit, and refuse to become discouraged. This explains the need for Paul's note of encouragement in **verse 9.**

9 And let us not be weary in well doing: for in due season we shall reap if we faint not.

The admonition is to not become "weary" nor "faint." The Greek word for weary is *ekkakeo* (**ek-kah-KEH-oh**), meaning to lose heart or become tired. The word for faint in the Greek is *ekluo* (**ek-LOO-oh**), meaning to faint or give up. These words are synonymous. Paul encourages the Galatians not to give up, because there will be a reward after all is said and done.

10 As we have therefore opportunity, let us do good unto all men, especially unto them who are of the household of faith.

Paul concludes this section with the primary directives for the Christian faith. He points toward the expectation that whenever an opportunity (Gk. *kairos*, **kye-ROCE**) or divine moment presents itself, the believer has already made up his or her mind to act. Believers must do good, and the scope of their good works includes all people, but especially those of the household (Gk. *oikeios*, **oy-KAY-oce**) of faith. This term was used for everybody who was part of a Roman household—all the people connected to the father or *pater familias*, who was the head of the household. As the people of God, we form the same type of community with Him as our head. In other words, those related to us through faith in Jesus should be the first and foremost recipients of our good deeds.

SEARCH THE SCRIPTURES

QUESTION 1
Why does Paul compare and contrast the works of the flesh with the fruit of the Spirit (Galatians 5:19–26)?

Paul wants to show believers what their lifestyle should be in comparison to a life controlled by the flesh. Answers will vary.

QUESTION 2
Paul gives abstract concepts for the fruit of the Spirit (i.e., love, joy, peace). What are specific concrete actions that exhibit the fruit of the Spirit (vv. 22–23)?

Peace and love in how I participate in helping others in need and supporting justice actions in political settings. Answers will vary.

QUESTION 3
Christians have the responsibility to bear one another's burdens. How might this relate to seeking justice in your community?

Participate in protest marches or attend meetings that discuss policy, health issues, and educational and community funding. Answers will vary.

LIGHT ON THE WORD

Our Lives Must Reflect the Fruit

From the moment we're born, laws govern our lives. Babies must have birth certificates. Children must go to school. Walk on green. Stop on red. Most people try to follow the law to the letter. It's easy for us to look at the fruit of the Spirit as more laws to follow. But manifesting the fruit of the Spirit in our lives is not something we do. It's who we are. Confession, prayer and fasting, and turning from a lifestyle of sin are the ingredients for a fruitful, Spirit-led life. The result? Our lives will be an outpouring of our love for Christ and our desire will be to serve one another.

BIBLE APPLICATION

AIM: Students will agree that Christians can develop the characteristics of an authentic Christian lifestyle when they are led by the Holy Spirit.

The Holy Spirit is love manifested in believers' lives. There is no law against love. Followers of Christ may struggle with sinful desires, but Paul reminds us that there is victory in a life that is filled with the Spirit (**Galatians 5:16**). Practicing a lifestyle of sin is in stark contrast to living in the Spirit. Jesus Christ died to set us free from a lifestyle of sin. Is there room for excuses?

STUDENTS' RESPONSES

AIM: Students will agree to live by the fruit of the Spirit and experience a closer relationship with Christ.

Walking implies relationship with Christ. Starting out the day with prayer and reading the Bible are important steps to developing and maintaining a relationship with the Lord. In the quiet of the morning, why not bring your Bible to your favorite spot and have a cup of coffee with Jesus?

PRAYER

Dear Heavenly Father, thank You for Your Word. Forgive us for any excuses we may have that keep us from obeying You. Today, we commit to walking in the Spirit so that we may experience the peace and joy that only a relationship with You brings. May our love for You be demonstrated by our obedience to You. Thank You for the precious gift of the Holy Spirit who guides our lives. In the Name of Jesus, we pray. Amen.

HOW TO SAY IT

Lasciviousness   lah-**SI**-vee-us-nes.

Variance   **VA**-ree-ens.

Emulations   em-yoo-**LAY**-shuns.

DIG A LITTLE DEEPER

This section provides an additional research article to further your study of the lesson:

What does authentic Christian faith look like in the life of the believer? In this article from Charisma Magazine, authentic faith is described as reflecting God's love, first and foremost. Authentic faith comes when spiritual disciplines are coupled with self-examination. The author explores how this process manifests itself in the life of the believer.

http://www.charismamag.com/spirit/spiritual-growth/18839-are-we-authentic-christian-believers-or-just-faking-it

PREPARE FOR NEXT SUNDAY

Read **1 John 4:7–19** and "The Source of All Love."

DAILY HOME BIBLE READINGS

MONDAY
Walk in Newness of Life
(Romans 6:1–11)

TUESDAY
The Sower and the Seed
(Luke 8:4–15)

WEDNESDAY
Gifts that Lead to Faithfulness
(1 Peter 1:3–9)

THURSDAY
Wholeness by Prayer and Action
(James 5:13–20)

FRIDAY
Practice Mutual Discipline
(Matthew 18:15–20)

SATURDAY
Support Ministers Generously
(1 Corinthians 9:3–12)

SUNDAY
Christ Creates Holy Living
(Galatians 5:18–6:10)

COMMENTS / NOTES:

QUARTERLY COMMENTARY
GOD LOVES US
IT "AIN'T" LOVE IF IT ISN'T OF GOD!
by Superintendent Larry L. Polk

TEACHER'S TIPS

"SUNDAY SCHOOL TEACHING TIPS II"
by Jurisdictional Field Representative Sandra Daniel

"SUNDAY SCHOOL TEACHING TIPS BY APPLYING EPHESIANS 5:14–17"
by Evangelist Quin R. Westbrook

#TSSGTEACHINGTIP –
"QUESTIONS, QUESTIONS AND MORE QUESTIONS!"
by Evangelist Waynell Henson

GOD LOVES US
IT "AIN'T" LOVE IF IT ISN'T OF GOD!

BY SUPERINTENDENT LARRY L. POLK

According to the Global Language Monitor, as of 2015, the number of words in the English language is 1,033,322. This same source confirms that a new word is created every 98 minutes, or about 14.7–16 words per day. Such an extensive vocabulary might make it seem as though any word could be easily defined. However, the most commonly used word in the English language—love—is also the most difficult to define. The ancient Greeks were a sophisticated society and had a different way of talking about love; they recognized six different varieties of love and would be shocked by our crudeness, if you will, in using one single word to express our emotions toward an individual or an inanimate object.

Love undeniably plays an enormous and unavoidable role in our culture, discussed in song, film, and novels, humorously or seriously; it is a constant theme of maturing life and a vibrant theme for youth. The nature of love has, since the time of the ancient Greeks, been a mainstay in philosophy, producing theories that range from the materialistic conception of love as purely a physical phenomenon (an animalistic or genetic urge that dictates our behavior) to theories of love as an intensely spiritual affair that in its highest form, permits us to touch divinity (Alexander Moseley).

Perhaps it is difficult to define because society has corrupted its meaning by confusing it with lust or by overusing the term. Part of the word's unique character is also understood within the linguistics of the Greek language. Unlike the English dialect, the Greek usage describes shades of meanings between types of love. In English, we might use the single word "love" to describe affection for a person ("I love my wife/husband"), as well as affection for an inanimate object ("I love my car"). We inherently understand that though the same word is used, the meanings are different. Greek, one of the primary languages of the New Testament, uses six different words to describe love. One portrays sexual love, **Eros**. This form of love was named after the Greek god of fertility, and represents the idea of sexual passion and desire. By the way, it was not always seen as something positive. Another means to express an interpersonal loving or liking based on receiving pleasure or enjoyment is **Philia or friendship**. The Greeks valued Philia far more than Eros. Philia concerned the deep comradely friendship that developed between brothers-in-arms who had fought together on the battlefield. Still another type of love describes familial love: **Pragma**. This type of love was the deep understanding that developed between long, mature relationships. Pragma was about making compromises to help the relationship work over time, and showing patience and tolerance. The fourth type of love, **Philautia**, or love of the self, had two types. One was an unhealthy love of self—narcissism—where one became self-obsessed and focused on personal fame and fortune. A healthier version of philautia enhances one's wider capacity to love. The fifth type is called **Ludus**, or playful love. The kind of affection adults have for children or the playful "flirtatious" activity with adult strangers is an example of ludus. The final and sixth type of love described by the Greeks is Agapao or Agape. In the biblical texts, the term **Agapao** stands out as a unique manifestation of love. It is a noble word expressing the highest form of the concept. What makes Agape the highest form of the concept of love is because it is "selfless." This form of love is extended to all people, whether they are family or strangers.

Of course, **Agapao** is the love that God possesses for man, which flows from His character. This was a novel and supreme concept to those in the first century, who first heard of this characteristic of God as expressed by Jesus and the writings of the New Testament. The Greeks understood that man might die for God—but could hardly grasp that God would die for man. Agape was later translated into Latin as "caritas," which is the origin of the word "charity."

We often hear the phrase "love is a verb," therefore love is "caring in action." Love isn't what we feel or what we think, but rather what we do! "For God so loved the world, that he gave his only begotten Son, that whosoever believeth in him should not perish, but have eternal life" (John 3:16). Our quarterly lessons will focus on this context. We will see, through this quarter, God's undeniable love for man as we see Him as the source, His overflowing love for us, how He manifested that love, and His restoration powers because of His love.

The lessons in this quarter will require us to ask ourselves questions that go beyond the shallow and glib definition of love so we can clearly understand the word in both the conceptual and practical aspects. We will find in the first unit God's eternal, preserving, and renewing love. Here, we must ask the question, "Is love a collection of 'feelings' (falling in love) or is it a mental decision (choosing to love)?" It is neither, but rather the character of God, who He is (1 John 4:8). Therefore, if we are to love with the love of God, then it must become part of our character.

UNIT 1 – GOD'S ETERNAL, PRESERVING, RENEWING LOVE

Because it is His character, God's love is eternal as He is eternal. Earlier it was stated that God is love, and if this is true, then love must inform our decision-making. In Genesis 2, we read about the specific creation of Adam—formed from the dust of the ground, which comprises the elements—into whose nostrils God breathed life so that he became a living and breathing soul (v. 7). God wasn't emotional toward man as He "made" him; He made the decision to make him. It wasn't by happenstance that woman was made from man, but rather a decision made by God (vv. 21–22). Therefore, we come to understand that the source of all love is God. If we are going to love, then we must abide in God and He in us.

Scripture tells us that God created mankind for the purpose of expressing His divine, unconditional, all-satisfying love. Because of the fall of man and his disobedience, we walked away from God as described in the concept of Philautia (self-love). We allow our eyes to cause us to lust and 1 John 2:16 clearly tells us, *"For all that is in the world, the lust of the flesh, and the lust of the eyes, and the pride of life, is not of the Father, but is of the world."* Often our eyes cause us to look for love in all the wrong places. What people look for and need is support and reassurance of their worth as individuals, not because of what they do or do not have, what their last name is or isn't, etc.

However, one of the most devastating failures in a Christian's life is the inability to embrace the pure love of God because of four things.

- First, the way we love each other can distort how we perceive God's love. As imperfect people, we exhibit imperfect love. Our wrong motives, hurts, and emotional lows have tainted His unconditional love.

- Secondly, our guilt over sinful behavior often causes us to feel unworthy of God's love. This is obviously a trick of the devil. We are reassured of this in Romans 5:8: "*But God commendeth his love toward us, in that, while we were yet sinners, Christ died for us.*"

- Thirdly, the reason we find it hard to accept God's love is because of our legalistic attitudes. Many people see the Bible as simply a book of rules, a collection of do's and don'ts. If you are basing your view of divine love on your ability to uphold every biblical principle or precept, you are doomed to failure. God gave us His Word for instruction and inspiration, not as a measuring stick by which He dispenses love.

- Finally, we misinterpret God's divine discipline. We must understand that God does discipline His children; however, He is a trustworthy Father, and His discipline and love are inextricably connected. (Hebrews 12:5–6 says, " *And ye have forgotten the exhortation which speaketh unto you as unto children, My son, despise not thou the chastening of the Lord, nor faint when thou art rebuked of him: For whom the Lord loveth he chasteneth, and scourgeth every son whom he receiveth.*") Therefore, spiritual discipline is an act of love.

UNIT 2 – GOD'S CARING, SAVING AND UPHOLDING LOVE

The second unit assures us that God cares, saves, and is there to lift us up, continually. In spite of what we have done, we will see God as Protector, Healer, Comforter, and Savior. In this unit, we will examine God's caring, saving and upholding love.

Living in a world filled with turmoil, dissent, and chaos creates an ever-increasing need to help people find peace and comfort. These concepts can be difficult to find in a skeptical and suspicious world, and can cause a lonely existence. As we share the love of God through His Word, we must assure those who have not yet learned to love that they were created in the image of God and therefore a part of Him. To find true happiness and peace, one must come to accept Jesus Christ as the Son of God and to realize that He is the only way to have peace and communion with a Holy God—since God is love (1 John 4:8).

Living in a world where senseless killings, terrorist attacks, and street violence are the order of the day, it is understandable that people feel detached and often isolated. As the Lord is our Shepherd, we too must shepherd others as we spread the Good News to a dying world. Because God loves us, we can face the obstacles and challenges of the world knowing that we are victorious in Him.

If we are sincere in our mission, then we must leave the shallow waters and launch into the deep, where our catch is great. However, we must be prepared to "deal with the catch," often found only in deep waters. In the shallow waters, most of the fish are the same. They look, talk, act, and dress like us. However, in the deep waters are all kinds of fish. They might not look, act, dress, or believe like you, but we must be able to suspend judgment, rid ourselves of our prejudices, and extend the love of God to all. Too often we are quick to look at someone with tattoos, piercings, or a sordid background and judge them without getting to know them. However, we must minister to them and show God's love; remember, it wasn't that long ago that we were that person. The love of God is so great that it covers a multitude of sins (1 Peter 4:8). We too must exercise this type of love as we help others to identify with and establish an intimate relationship with God.

Too many people are joining cults, gangs, and the drug culture because they need and want to be accepted as part of a "family." We must expand our definition of "family." It no longer made up of Mom, Dad, and 2.5 children, but rather involves loving relationships where individuals feel connected, supported, and valued. Through the love of God, we are able to move beyond our limited definitions and move to a much broader concept of family—the church and community. We need a paradigm shift as we are thrust into the 21st century and a now-global community. To combat this phenomenon and the limited definition of family, we must share with the world the spiritual concept of love—God's love, where all people can feel connected and have a sense of belonging. They can become a part of the family of God, and we must be clear the path to His family.

UNIT 3 – GOD'S PERVASIVE AND SUSTAINING LOVE

Finally, we will come to understand God's pervasive and sustaining love as we examine several situations where His love was extended to those who were disobedient (as He extends His love today, toward us). Ephesians 2:8 says it all: *"For by grace are ye saved through faith; and that not of yourselves: it is the gift of God."* Because we are a part of God, His desire is to unite us with Him again, as before the Fall in Genesis. Just as God continually showed His love for Israel, He does the same for us. We were not only saved by grace but also through faith which God gave to each of us at conception. It shows the divine love of God for us to have a "reunion" with Him. What love! Because of love, we reach out to others and share the Good News of Jesus Christ who is the Author of love; it is what we do!

Because "love is what we do," we will explore the power of love as we consider wholesome relationships that lead to restoration after our spiritual relationship with God is damaged. We will come to understand God's unconditional love for mankind. As stated earlier, love is intrinsic to God's nature; it is who He is (John 4:8). Contrary to the world's mindset, the fact that "God is love" does not mean He winks at or excuses our sin (Romans 6:23), but forgives us if we are humble enough to ask. Because of His love, He has compassion on believers and unbelievers. While on earth, Jesus befriended "tax collectors and sinners" (Luke 7:34). These two groups were despised and avoided by godly Jews of Jesus' day because tax collectors often exploited their fellow countrymen by requiring more money than was actually due. "Sinners" were those who sneered at God's Law and failed to participate in Temple worship. Let's not sneer at the "sinners" but rather understand we are being called to share the Word with those thought to be "unacceptable."

Finally, we see God's love as being sacrificial. Jesus Christ surrendered His life on the Cross so that we might have eternal life and enjoy fellowship with God both while here on earth and eternally. His only motivation for this was love for mankind. John 15:13 says, "Greater love hath no man than this, that a man lay down his life for his friends." When we truly love God, we find that His love is contagious. When we walk in close fellowship with Christ, God's love flows through us to those around us. The Holy Spirit fills us so that we can extend unconditional love to others.

In each of the units in this quarter, see if you can identify the different types of love being experienced and how you can strive to employ agape love in your call to perform the Great Commission. How can you show love as you go "deep sea fishing"? How did Jonah get past his hatred for Nineveh and show God's love? How can you practice this unconditional (agape) love?

Superintendent Larry L. Polk is the Senior Pastor of St. Emmanuel Church Of God In Christ, Denison, Texas. Jurisdictionally, he serves as Examiner for the Ministerial Education Ordination Committee and State Sunday School Superintendent for Texas Northeast First Jurisdiction. Polk also serves as the Superintendent of the Southwest Region of the International Sunday School Department, member of the International Sunday School Leadership Ministry Team, and recently was appointed as Co-Director of the Sunday School Church Growth Academy. He was selected in 2015 as *"Mr. Sunday School"* at the Holy Convocation Sunday School Breakfast in St. Louis, MO.

Professionally, Superintendent Polk is a former professor of Human Development and Speech Communication, having taught college for more than 39 years, and is presently retired. He has also worked as a substance abuse counselor.

He is a graduate of Texas A&M University, Commerce where he completed his Bachelor of Arts Degree in Sociology and Psychology, amd a Master of Science Degree in Student Personnel and Counseling with a Psychology emphasis. He has completed more than 60 credit hours of post-graduate work in Speech Communications, Psychology, Marriage and Family Therapy, Counseling, and Sociology.

Superintendent Polk serves under the leadership of Bishop James E. Hornsby, Prelate, and Mother Pia Haynes Williams, Supervisor.

Superintendent Polk is married to Mrs. Carolyn Davis Polk for almost 45 years and is the father of two daughters and a proud grandfather. Supt. Polk believes that *"knowledge is worthless if it isn't shared."*

SUNDAY SCHOOL TEACHING TIPS II
BY JURISDICTIONAL FIELD REPRESENTATIVE
SANDRA DANIEL

Prepare Your Classes in Advance

- Don't wait until Saturday night to start thinking about your Sunday morning class.

- Set aside quality time each day to make plans and find relevant materials.

- Lessons will have more impact when they are not rushed through at the last minute.

Avoid Passing the Buck

- Don't be lazy.

- Plan, study, prepare, and be creative, using as many interactive activities as you can.

- It is OK to periodically schedule small breathing periods for yourself by using a video or work-book activity. Be careful to not substitute and depend on the activity to curtail your actual teaching time.

- Your lessons should be focused and Bible-based, always keeping your students in mind and creatively stimulating your students to a point where they desire to be active participants.

- The lesson should be a life-changing experience.

Constructively Criticize Yourself

- Be realistic with yourself about how the class is going.

- Observe the students as they enter. Are they excited for class? How is your attendance level?

- If you are sure that you could be doing better, but unsure of how, ask the Superintendent, other teachers, and /or church members to sit in on a few of your Sunday School classes.

- Ask them to give you an informal evaluation.

- Be open to accepting critiques and working on ways to improve your lessons and class.

Delegate

- It is OK to allow your students to assist with attendance, offering, handing out books, etc.

- There is no reason why delegation should not be a subtle part of your teaching.

- The more work you are able to assign to others, the more time you will have to focus on your main objective of Sunday School—teaching.

Be Positive and Stay Updated

- Sunday School is an enriching part of our spiritual journey that should not be overlooked. Your role as an instructor is a critical one, and you should be accepting all of the help being offered to you. Books, training sessions, workshops, Sunday School seminars, and other resources will allow you the time and energy you need to prepare valuable, effective, and relevant lesson plans that your students will take with them for life.

Evangelist Sandra Daniel Evangelist Sandra Daniel serves as the Jurisdictional Field Representative for the First Ecclesiastical Jurisdiction of Southern California under the leadership of Bishop Joe L. Ealy and General Assistant Supervisor/Jurisdictional Supervisor Mother Barbara McCoo Lewis. She is the Assistant Director of Leadership Ministry for the International Sunday School Department.

SUNDAY SCHOOL TEACHING TIPS BY APPLYING EPHESIANS 5:14–17

BY EVANGELIST QUIN R. WESTBROOK

Nowadays our churches are filled with a wide range of members: the newly converted as well as those who have attended Sunday School since they were in their mother's womb. While it is important to keep certain traditions and customs alive, as Jeremiah reminded us to "*Stand ye in the ways, and see, and ask for the old paths, where is the good way, and walk therein, and ye shall find rest for your souls*" (Jeremiah 6:16), it is also very important to examine some teaching practices and examine areas for flexibility and incorporation of new ideas to help retain groups that have had difficulty maintaining attendance in prior years. Now is the time to really take a look at what can be done differently during Sunday School time, whether you are a superintendent or teacher.

Paul tells us in Ephesians 5:14–17, that those who are sleeping need to awaken, that we are to be wise, and we must make the best use of our time because the days are evil. These classes are integral in shedding light on the Word of God, so our students can understand what the will of the Lord is.

1. DON'T BE TOO PREDICTABLE. WAKE UP! CAN YOUR STUDENTS SET THEIR WATCH BY YOU?

As the saying goes, "if it ain't broke, don't fix it," but examine where you are and ensure that you are not operating your Sunday School and its classes by the phenomenon known as *Muscle Memory*. According to Wikipedia, *Muscle Memory* has been used synonymously with motor learning, a form of procedural memory that involves consolidating a specific motor task into memory through repetition. When a movement is repeated over time, a long-term muscle memory is created for that task, eventually allowing it to be performed without conscious effort. This process decreases the need for attention and creates maximum efficiency within the motor and memory systems. While muscle memory might create an efficient system, it can also be inattentive and inflexible.

After prayerfully asking the Lord to guide you (a good place to start in determining if your class or Sunday School is running by long-term muscle memory), think about when was the last time you received actionable, constructive feedback specifically related to your Sunday School. Consider feedback from two groups: Sunday School students and non-Sunday School students.

Survey your current students to obtain their feedback on what can be improved. Ask your students if they are interested in volunteering to work, and also the areas they are interested in serving in.

Have you ever conducted a survey of your church's members to find out the reasons why they do not attend Sunday School or your class? If the answer is "yes," what did you learn from that survey? If the answer is "no," think about why not, and what you can do to change that.

You can choose to employ a few different survey methodologies, and a little research on the Internet can provide many different resources to help choose the appropriate survey structure.

2. RELATABILITY/PRACTICAL APPLICATION. BE WISE!

For some of the newer converts, they might find biblical fundamentals not only new, but the King James Version of the Bible might seem extremely out of their grasp.

Behold! Thou mayest know the difference between ye and yea, or thou and thee, but everyone else is having flashbacks to high school English class and might feel intimidated and discouraged when they lack familiarity with 16th-century English, reading aloud in unison, or some of our other class/Sunday School customs. Please ensure that one of the seasoned brothers or sisters in your class takes the time to explain some of the customs to the new members.

As teachers, remember where you were before setting foot in Sunday School, and while you never stop learning, always remember those who are at a different phase in their study of God's Word.

Small group instruction, a question-and-answer period, and breakout sessions are important to teach students to read and understand the meaning of the Scriptures.

3. PERIODIC STUDENT ASSESSMENTS – MAKE GOOD USE OF THE TIME!

52 lessons each year

13 lessons each quarter

4–5 lessons each month

Do you know what your students want to achieve? Yes, the lessons can be so rich and deep that we often find ourselves longing for more time in class. In addition to the weekly concepts, unit, quarterly and yearly concepts should be shared, taught, and reviewed. But checking in with your students to learn what they want to achieve, or hear their personal vision for the year, quarter, or month can be a way to gain a sustained student-teacher relationship.

Has this personal vision been discussed and shared in class or during fellowship time? Consider allowing time for decreeing, declaring, and agreeing in prayer with one another. Have you encouraged students to take a look around and notice the positive impact that regular Sunday School attendance has had on their lives?

Ephesus was known as a center of pagan worship, and drew many who worshiped the Roman goddess Diana. The church at Ephesus experienced similar challenges to those the church faces today, and existed in an environment rife with distractions that threatened to take the focus away from God. Before advising the Christian to put on the whole armor of God in Ephesians 6, the reader was reminded to imitate God in Ephesians 5. We serve a wise, omniscient God who has gifted you to share His Word. Our duty is to awake, be wise, and properly use the time that God has given us.

Evangelist Quin R. Westbrook is a member of Grace Chapel Church Of God In Christ in Los Angeles, CA, where she serves as local Sunday School Superintendent. Elder Elton E. Hooker is her pastor. Jurisdictionally, she serves as the District Sunday School Superintendent for the Central District within the First Ecclesiastical Jurisdiction of Southern California. Bishop Joe L. Ealy is her Jurisdictional Prelate and Mother Barbara McCoo Lewis, Assistant General Supervisor, is her Jurisdictional Supervisor. Nationally, she serves as a member of the International Sunday School Department PR & Marketing Team and Executive Assistant to Vice President Althea Sims. She is a graduate of the University of Southern California with a B.A. in Political Science and a minor in Spanish Literature. Professionally, Evangelist Westbrook is employed as a Human Resources Manager.

#TSSGTEACHINGTIP – QUESTIONS, QUESTIONS AND MORE QUESTIONS!

BY EVANGELIST WAYNELL HENSON

I love Sunday School. I love Sunday School like I love a sunny day, chocolate ice cream, and the beach at sunset. I hope that didn't sound too trite. But I seriously love it! I am constantly in recruitment mode. There is not a week that I am not inviting someone to join class. While I am not the person who will hound prospective students with a wake-up call, once I set my sights on a new Sunday School friend, I simply tell them, "I'm saving the seat next to me and I'll be watching the door for you next week!"

I have a friend who was "won" to Sunday School and now wears her "I Love Sunday School" T-shirt as proudly as I do. A couple of weeks ago, I listened as she talked about how much she enjoys class, the fellowship, and in her words, "I can ask my dumb questions there." In my mind I immediately thought, "There are no dumb questions." But then I thought that coming in as a new student must be a bit overwhelming when everyone seems to know it all. Her statement slowed me down just a bit to think about just how many people sit with ideas and questions and don't have the courage to speak up.

Incidentally, my friend happens to be a Gen-Y'er. I am a Gen-X'er. Winning with students is a delicate balance of teaching and creating meaningful interaction. Students certainly come to receive, but look for opportunities to give just the same.

Questions… questions… and more questions.

It has been said among educators that "to question well is to teach well." Questions are an effective way to teach. Asking questions might seem simple, but they are among the most powerful tools we have as teachers/facilitators! The right question at the right time can create an energy that sets the tone for the time of learning or it could be the inspiration for new learning in a student.

Good questions can:

- Motivate student learning and fuel curiosity

- Foster intellectual development and stimulate critical thinking

- Gauge/assess student understanding

- Guide discussion and shape a positive learning environment

The Purpose of Questions

Questions serve different functions. Some questions have more benefit for the teacher than the student. Other questions are an opportunity to help students learn—perhaps pushing students to think about how to apply what has been taught, or expanding thinking on the lesson.

Questions check for:

- Knowledge – Does the student recognize or recall the info?

- Comprehension – More than just recitation, does or can the student explain in their own words, demonstrating understanding?

- Application – How does the lesson work? Can they demonstrate it in their own real-life scenario?

- Analysis – Can you break it down and explain the lesson or message?

- Synthesis – Can you take the learning and creatively solve a new problem?

I understand that as teachers/facilitators, we are often armed with full arsenals of information to share. But remember to **PAUSE** and ask specific questions. Avoid questions that are closed-ended—those answered with a simple yes or no. Also for adult learners, push past the surface reading of the Scripture and develop questions that push reflection, personal sharing, and life application. Push students to "higher-order thinking"! Challenge yourself to develop three life application questions each week from the lesson study. Get the conversation going!

QUESTIONS GO BOTH WAYS!

Never close off a subject. Our minds are moving throughout the lesson. My pastor says, "There are things that you don't know. And there are things that you don't know you don't know." Perhaps questions will arise as more light is shed on the lesson that will draw you into discussion for clarity or insight.

Model teachers create environments where students are self-feeding on the lesson all week! The daily readings are an amazing and easy devotional habit to encourage. It is incredible when we ALL show up ready to engage! And the value of our class time skyrockets! Warren Berger gave a winning strategy to encouraging questions in the classroom!

1. Make It Safe!

2. Make It "Cool"!

3. Make It Fun!

4. Make It Rewarding!

5. Make It Stick!

<u>*Be intentional*</u> about creating an environment for questions. Be open! Your students will surprise you with their own insights from the lesson.

Evangelist Waynell Henson is a member of Dominion Word Ministries Church Of God In Christ, Elder Michael McWilliams, Pastor. She has a heartbeat for connecting in relevant and meaningful ways to inspire people to abundant living through the truth of God's Word. A gifted administrator and #MinistryLeaderCoach, she serves as the Executive Secretary of the International Sunday School Department (COGIC) and Co-Chairman of Auxiliaries in Ministry for the Kansas East Jurisdiction COGIC, Bishop L.F. Thuston, Prelate. With a heightened awareness of connecting with Gen-X'ers, G-Y'ers, and millennials, she impacts a social media "Community" of more than 1,000 lovers of Sunday School. She shares the weekly lesson, growth strategies, and resources through platforms as YouTube, Facebook, Instagram, Pinterest, Twitter, and SnapChat. Have YOU joined "The Community"?

#HappyTeaching

Find more great ideas (#TeachingTipTuesday) on www.ThatSundaySchoolGirl.com.

QUARTERLY QUIZ

The questions on this page may be used in several ways: as a pretest at the beginning of the quarter; as a review at the end of the quarter; or as a review after each lesson. The questions are based on the Scripture text of each lesson (King James Version).

LESSON 1

1. According to **1 John 4:9**, God's love for us is revealed through His Son, Christ. Compare John's message with how believers choose to love God, themselves, and one another.

_____

_____

2. How can some of the problems that affect the community of faith change, if believers truly implemented love in their approach to discipleship?

_____

_____

LESSON 2

1. Paul reminds his audience of their transgressions and sins (**Ephesian 2:1**). Why was it important for the Ephesians and for believers today to remember Christ in our transgressions and sins?

_____

_____

2. What evidence can you share that supports the devil in verse 2 as the prince of the air?

_____

_____

LESSON 3

1. What are some of the tools that might be used to prune the vine for more fruit to grow on the branch of Christ (**John 15:2**)?

_____

_____

2. If you had to give your life for a friend, would you hesitate? Is your response consistent with Jesus' statement that "greater love hath no man than" to lay down one's life for one's friend (**v. 13**)?

_____

_____

LESSON 4

1. Joel moves from prophecy of judgment to the forgiveness and blessings God will outpour to His people. What does Joel's new declaration to the people tell you about God?

_____

_____

2. What are the possible blessings and outcomes that the people will receive in **Joel 2:28–32**? After reading these verses, how are you encouraged to live in the love and hope we have in Christ?

_____

_____

QUARTERLY QUIZ

LESSON 5

1. God still seeks to lead, protect, and provide for His people. As believers, we must submit to His leading as our Shepherd. Can you defend why you relate to God as your Shepherd?

_____

_____

2. Even believers have problems and enemies as David did. How does God's guidance provide protection when we find ourselves in dark places and enemy territories?

_____

_____

LESSON 6

1. Which events in your life reflect how your thoughts and ideas about Christ were like Nicodemus'?

_____

_____

2. If a believer is not born again by water and only of the Spirit, can they enter into the kingdom of God (**John 3:3, 5**)? Explain your response.

_____

_____

LESSON 7

1. What people do you think Mary is referring to by "they" have taken Him and "we" cannot find him (**John 20:2**)? Why is it sometimes good to have others share in your spiritual discoveries?

_____

_____

2. All who looked into the tomb saw that Jesus was not there. Analyze the significance of what items were left and where (**vv. 5–7**).

_____

_____

LESSON 8

1. According to **Romans 5:8**, God shows His love for us by giving Christ, who died for us. Is this enough for believers to worship God when things are not going their way?

_____

_____

2. Select three ways that God loves us and compose a short thank You note to God for His love.

_____

_____

LESSON 9

1. Jesus is the Good Shepherd and His followers are the sheep (**John 10:11**). Critique the qualities of our Good Shepherd, Jesus, and five qualities of the sheep.

_____

_____

2. Distinguish the reason(s) Jesus' statement, "I lay down my life for the sheep," is important for believers to embrace (**v. 15**).

_____

_____

QUARTERLY QUIZ

LESSON 10

1. Why do some believers, like Jonah, run away from what God wants us to do? What are some consequences that can happen when believers do not do what God wants them to do?

_____

_____

2. What characteristics of a dove did Jonah display?

_____

_____

LESSON 11

1. Jonah knew to call to the Lord for help (**Jonah 2:1**). How can you encourage others to have hope and not give up?

_____

_____

2. Compose a prayer based on the Scripture text that resonates with where you are emotionally and spiritually in your life. Explain your response.

_____

_____

LESSON 12

1. What was the turning point as to why Jonah's preaching and prophecy from the Lord prevailed and the people from Nineveh repented (**Jonah 3:10, 4:1**)?

_____

_____

2. Complete the following: When Jonah ran away from God, I was reminded of when I ran from God because I felt that God had _____ me. What was the motive for your feelings?

_____

_____

LESSON 13

1. What is the relationship between the qualities of God and His protection of Jonah and of us when we are not doing what we want to do?

_____

_____

2. In your opinion, why were Jonah's priorities out of order (**Jonah 4:9–10**)? Explain how your priorities might be out of order with God's way.

_____

_____

Answers to Quarterly Quiz can be found on page 463

THE SOURCE OF ALL LOVE

BIBLE BASIS: 1 JOHN 4:7–19

BIBLE TRUTH: John declares that loving one another demonstrates the spiritual heritage of love that is born of God.

MEMORY VERSE: "Beloved, if God so loved us, we ought also to love one another" (1 John 4:11).

LESSON AIM: By the end of the lesson, we will: EVALUATE the differences and similarities between God's love and human love; REFLECT on how His perfect love casts out fear in the believer's life; and AFFIRM what it means to love others the way God loves us.

TEACHER PREPARATION

MATERIALS NEEDED: Quarterly Commentary/Teacher Manual, Adult Quarterly, Adult resources—charts, worksheets, and other teaching tools, paper, pens, pencils, Bibles (several different versions)

OTHER MATERIALS NEEDED / TEACHER'S NOTES:

_____

_____

LESSON OVERVIEW

LIFE NEED FOR TODAY'S LESSON
Many people search in all the wrong places for a perfect love they can trust.

BIBLE APPLICATION
When we are persuaded of God's love for us, it casts away all fear and leaves us free to love.

BIBLE LEARNING
John reminds us that God is love and those who abide in God's love have His love perfected in them.

STUDENTS' RESPONSES
Even believers can find it difficult to give and to receive love.

LESSON SCRIPTURE

1 JOHN 4:7–19, KJV

7 Beloved, let us love one another: for love is of God; and every one that loveth is born of God, and knoweth God.

8 He that loveth not knoweth not God; for God is love.

9 In this was manifested the love of God toward us, because that God sent his only

1 JOHN 4:7–19, AMP

7 Beloved, let us [unselfishly] love and seek the best for one another, for love is from God; and everyone who loves [others] is born of God and knows God [through personal experience].

8 The one who does not love has not become acquainted with God [does not and never did know Him], for God is love. [He is

begotten Son into the world, that we might live through him.

10 Herein is love, not that we loved God, but that he loved us, and sent his Son to be the propitiation for our sins.

11 Beloved, if God so loved us, we ought also to love one another.

12 No man hath seen God at any time. If we love one another, God dwelleth in us, and his love is perfected in us.

13 Hereby know we that we dwell in him, and he in us, because he hath given us of his Spirit.

14 And we have seen and do testify that the Father sent the Son to be the Saviour of the world.

15 Whosoever shall confess that Jesus is the Son of God, God dwelleth in him, and he in God.

16 And we have known and believed the love that God hath to us. God is love; and he that dwelleth in love dwelleth in God, and God in him.

17 Herein is our love made perfect, that we may have boldness in the day of judgment: because as he is, so are we in this world.

18 There is no fear in love; but perfect love casteth out fear: because fear hath torment. He that feareth is not made perfect in love.

19 We love him, because he first loved us.

the originator of love, and it is an enduring attribute of His nature.]

9 By this the love of God was displayed in us, in that God has sent His [One and] only begotten Son [the One who is truly unique, the only One of His kind] into the world so that we might live through Him.

10 In this is love, not that we loved God, but that He loved us and sent His Son to be the propitiation [that is, the atoning sacrifice, and the satisfying offering] for our sins [fulfilling God's requirement for justice against sin and placating His wrath].

11 Beloved, if God so loved us [in this incredible way], we also ought to love one another.

12 No one has seen God at any time. But if we love one another [with unselfish concern], God abides in us, and His love [the love that is His essence abides in us and] is completed and perfected in us.

13 By this we know [with confident assurance] that we abide in Him and He in us, because He has given to us His [Holy] Spirit.

14 We [who were with Him in person] have seen and testify [as eye-witnesses] that the Father has sent the Son to be the Savior of the world.

15 Whoever confesses and acknowledges that Jesus is the Son of God, God abides in him, and he in God.

16 We have come to know [by personal observation and experience], and have believed [with deep, consistent faith] the love which God has for us. God is love, and the one who abides in love abides in God, and God abides continually in him.

17 In this [union and fellowship with Him], love is completed and perfected with us, so that we may have confidence in the day of judgment [with assurance and boldness to face Him]; because as He is, so are we in this world.

18 There is no fear in love [dread does not exist]. But perfect (complete, full-grown) love drives out fear, because fear involves [the expectation of divine] punishment, so the one who is afraid [of God's judgment] is not perfected in love [has not grown into a sufficient understanding of God's love].

19 We love, because He first loved us.

LIGHT ON THE WORD

One of the hand-picked Apostles of Jesus, John, was in the inner circle and was invited by Jesus to experience His power firsthand. Jesus gave John and his brother, James, the nickname "Boanerges" or "sons of thunder" (**Mark 3:17**). The nickname is indicative of their hot tempers and great ambition (**Luke 9:51–56; Mark 10:35–41**). John's Gospel provides an intimate portrait of God's love in Christ. He refers to himself as "the disciple whom Jesus loved" (**John 13:23, 20:2**).

TEACHING THE BIBLE LESSON

LIFE NEED FOR TODAY'S LESSON

AIM: Students will agree that many people search in all the wrong places for a perfect love they can trust.

INTRODUCTION

John's Letter of Reassurance

The Apostle John wrote his epistles (the Johannine letters) to a group of churches in Asia Minor to combat heretical doctrine and false teachings regarding Jesus Christ, most notably about His deity and Resurrection, as they awaited His return. Using his authority as an Apostle with knowledge and experience with the risen Christ, John wrote his letters to reassure believers of their commitment and to provide moral standards to live by as a reflection of their transformation.

BIBLE LEARNING

AIM: Students will decide that God is love and those who abide in God's love, have His love perfected in them.

I. GOD'S COMMAND TO LOVE ONE ANOTHER (1 John 4:7–11)

The Apostle John gives hearers and readers of his letter the key indicator of a follower of Jesus Christ—love. Just as God through Moses commanded the Israelites to love Him with all their heart, mind, and strength (**Deuteronomy 6:4**), Jesus continued in this vein to love God and one another (**Leviticus 19:18; Matthew 22:36–39**). John emphasizes what it means to be born of God: love is the principal quality that identifies someone who has been saved. Writing to what is probably a Gentile audience, he appeals to their logic by arguing that the one who does not love does not know God because He is love (**v. 8**).

7 Beloved, let us love one another: for love is of God; and every one that loveth is born of God, and knoweth God.

After dealing with the matter of discerning the spirits, John here returns to the discussion on love that he began in chapter 3. He now calls Christians to demonstrate what he identifies as one of the distinguishing marks of a true believer: to love one another, because God is the source of love.

This statement is not meant to stand alone. John is not engaging in deep philosophical and theological discussion. He tells the early Church that God is the source of love because he wants to emphasize what it means to be in a true relationship with Him. In other words, John wants to distinguish between those in a right relationship with God and those who are not. Those who love "have been born of God" (NIV), John says. They are God's children, and He is their Father. This is why John tells us that God is the source of love, because if we truly love as God loves, we demonstrate that we are His children by manifesting His love toward others.

Expressing love toward one another is one method of demonstrating that we know God. The Greek word for "knoweth," *ginosko* (**ghin-OCE-ko**) denotes knowledge from personal experience beginning with salvation. John uses the present tense of the verb here to emphasize that this knowledge is ongoing, not temporary. Thus the person who loves can say that he or she truly knows God and will continue to know Him.

8 He that loveth not knoweth not God; for God is love.

Since love is a distinguishing mark of a true Christian, John says that the one who does not love has not come to know God. He puts this statement in the past tense to indicate that regardless of the orthodoxy of their profession of faith, someone who does not love has never entered into a relationship with God. John's point is not that love must be perfectly demonstrated at all times, but his point is that a believer who claims to be a child of God should show some sign of the practice of true love in his or her life.

John reveals God's character by simply stating, "God is love." Just as God is Light (**1 John 1:5**) or Spirit (**John 4:24**), so God is love, too. Since God is love, claiming that we know God but not expressing love is inconsistent.

9 In this was manifested the love of God toward us, because that God sent his only begotten Son into the world, that we might live through him.

Next, John turns to the supreme example of God's love—His Son, Jesus Christ who died for our sins. God's love experienced through salvation is then expressed in our lives. This true love acts on behalf of and for the sake of others through our intentional actions, not just mere feelings or emotions.

This is not to say that emotions are exempt, but they are not primary. John says that the supreme demonstration of love is that God sent His only Son into the world to give His life for as many as receive Him—those who acknowledge their sin, repent, and receive Jesus as Savior. Yes, God sent His Son that we might truly live and by so doing, He concretely demonstrated the reality of His love toward us.

10 Herein is love, not that we loved God, but that he loved us, and sent his Son to be the propitiation for our sins. 11 Beloved, if God so loved us, we ought also to love one another.

God sent His one and only Son into the world to demonstrate His love so that we who were spiritually dead might have life. Scripture tells us that while we were still sinning and rebelling, God demonstrated His love toward us by sending His Son to die for us (**Romans 5:8**).

In verse 10, the word "propitiation" is the Greek word *hilasmos* (**hil-as-MOS**), which is related to removing sin through atonement or sacrifice. Propitiation means that God's righteous wrath toward sinful man was placated or pacified through the death of Jesus on the Cross. In other words, God did for us what we could not do for ourselves. The requirement for sin, a perfect sacrifice, had been set by God the Father and was met by God the Son. Says theologian James Boice, "the price paid is not really a price paid by another to God but rather a price God pays to Himself. It is God paying our bill so that salvation for us might be truly free." Herein lies the supreme example of love. While we were in a state of disobedience toward God because of our sins, God gave up His Son to remove our sin and guilt and calls us to Himself to receive eternal life. Now that's love!

In light of this supreme example of love, how can we not love one another? Only by repenting and accepting the death of Jesus Christ as our way of salvation can we truly comprehend God's perfect love. Christians ought to become the proverbial "chip off the old block." We must become loving and caring toward others just as God is with us. Christ's sacrifice on the Cross reminds us of God's great love for us. We cannot produce this kind of love in our own strength—it comes from God. When the love that God placed in our hearts is ignited, only then are we able to fulfill His command to love one another.

SEARCH THE SCRIPTURES
QUESTION 1
How can you defend the fact that Christians are to always love others regardless of the circumstances according to **1 John 4:7–8**?

I can defend that we should show love, because love is not weak and will ultimately overcome obstacles. Dr. Martin Luther King Jr.'s life is an example of love in action even in the worst circumstances. Answers will vary.

QUESTION 2
Explain the sinner's role and God's role in propitiation. What did sinners do for God? What did God do for sinners?

Sinners were sinning and did nothing to propitiate the wrath of God. Because of His great love, God Himself set the requirement for sin—a perfect sacrifice—and then God Himself met the requirement for sin when Jesus Christ died on the Cross.

LIGHT ON THE WORD
Steadfast in God's Love
John encouraged those challenged in their faith to remain steadfast in their confession of and fidelity to Jesus Christ and not to succumb to the pressures of the world around them (**1 John 2:15–27**). Writing from Ephesus, John gives explicit instruction in this letter to not entertain false teachings and to stay away from deceptive spirits, and tells us how to recognize an antichrist—one who does not believe that Jesus Christ is the Son of God (**1 John 4:1–6**).

II. GOD'S LOVE PERFECTED (vv. 12–15)

God's love is "perfected," that is, completed or accomplished, when we trust Jesus Christ for salvation and love our brothers and sisters. We live in community with love as the motive. John reminds us that no one has ever seen God, but we know He is real, especially when we love unselfishly, preferring others to ourselves. We replicate God in the earth and make Him visible to the world.

12 No man hath seen God at any time. If we love one another, God dwelleth in us, and his love is perfected in us.

It is fundamentally true that no one has actually seen God with their natural eyes. Thus the question emerges, "How does one truly see God?" Ultimately, we see God the Father in His

Son, Jesus Christ, and we see God in everyday life as believers demonstrate true love toward one another. He is the source of love. When we show love toward one another, we bear witness to the world of the reality of God's divine presence within us.

The word "perfected" is the Greek verb *teleioo* (**teh-lay-OH-oh**), which means to accomplish, complete, or bring to an end. Therefore, when we love others, we perfect or complete God's command to love as He, through Christ, has loved us.

13 Hereby know we that we dwell in him, and he in us, because he hath given us of his Spirit.

God lives in His people through the Holy Spirit as an assurance of the reality of the relationship we have with Him. The term "dwell" (Gk. *meno*, **MEN-o**) means to abide or remain. Thus, John affirms that the same Spirit of the living God that taught Jesus also abides within every believer. When couples marry, a ring is used as a symbol of their commitment to one another. Every time the husband or wife looks at his or her ring, it is a reminder of their commitment to abide with one another throughout this life. God has demonstrated His commitment to us by giving us something that is much greater than a ring—the Holy Spirit!

14 And we have seen and do testify that the Father sent the Son to be the Saviour of the world. 15 Whosoever shall confess that Jesus is the Son of God, God dwelleth in him, and he in God.

John notes that eyewitnesses have seen and given testimony that God sent His Son into the world to be our Savior. It is worth mentioning that John's statement should not be taken out of context. At first glance, it would appear that the word "we" refers to the disciples who walked and talked with Jesus (see **1 John 1:1–4**). However, some scholars indicate that John is referring to the entire Church community because of their abiding faith in God, rather than the original eyewitnesses of Jesus' earthly ministry. Whatever the case, John wants his readers to know that "whosoever" believes can experience God's indwelling. John states that anyone who will "confess" (Gk. *homologeo*, **ho-mo-lo-GEH-oh**, to acknowledge, profess, or agree) that Jesus Christ is the Son of God will dwell with God and He in them.

Salvation—confession of faith that Jesus is the Son of God according to **John 3:16**, the presence of the Holy Spirit within, obedience to God's Word, and loving one another—provides the assurance that God abides in us and we in Him.

III. GOD'S LOVE HAS NO FEAR (vv. 16–19)

It was believed that Christ's return would occur at any moment, but John encouraged believers to rest and be confident no matter the day of His return, and that they are eternally secure as they continue in love. They had no reason to fear judgment or punishment because of the complete love of God in Christ. God's love would drive out any fear or torment.

The same is true for us today. Jesus promises as we abide in Him that the Triune God would dwell with us (**John 15:4–10**). Because of God's abiding presence with us by our faith in Jesus Christ, we are reassured too.

16 And we have known and believed the love that God hath to us. God is love; and he that dwelleth in love dwelleth in God, and God in him.

John tells us that God is love. This does not mean love is God. Instead it means that love is an inseparable aspect of God's character and God shows us what love is supposed to look like. He restates what he has suggested throughout this passage, that those who "dwelleth" (Gk.

meno) or abide in God have the benefit of a personal relationship with Him. As a result, those whose lives demonstrate true Christian love are assured that God will continue to live in them and they in Him.

17 Herein is our love made perfect, that we may have boldness in the day of judgment: because as he is, so are we in this world.

The reality of God's love among believers is a means of confidence on the Day of Judgment. The Greek word used here for "boldness" is *parrhesia* (**par-rhay-SEE-ah**), which means outspokenness, frankness, and confidence, especially among those of high rank. John reintroduces the theme of boldness here, which he mentioned earlier (**1 John 2:28, 3:21–22**). He reminds readers how God's love is made "perfect" (Gk. *teleioo*) or complete within us. Once we allow God's love to control our lives, it will grow and become complete. As a result, we will be able to come boldly before God's throne of judgment, confident that He will not cast us away.

18 There is no fear in love; but perfect love casteth out fear: because fear hath torment. He that feareth is not made perfect in love.

Having just encouraged the community of believers to have confidence in God's love, John reminds them that true love does not have any fear. In this verse, John shows the disparity between fear (Gk. *phobos*, **FO-bos**), meaning dread or terror, and love (Gk. *agape*, **ah-GAH-pay**), meaning affection, benevolence, or goodwill—the two cannot coexist. The word "torment" is the Greek word *kolasis* (**KO-lah-seese**), which means correction, punishment, or penalty. John says that it is not God's will that any of His children be tormented. When we fear, we are not considering the perfect love God has for us, and the fear in turn prohibits us from demonstrating love toward others (cf. **2 Timothy 1:7**).

19 We love him, because he first loved us.

Expressing love for one another is an outward sign of love for God. We cannot see God, but we can see other human beings around us.

LIGHT ON THE WORD
Day of Judgment

The Day of Judgment is referred to in **verse 17**. Early Church believers waited with eager anticipation for Christ's return. They knew not the day or the time but were told by Jesus Himself to be ready (**Matthew 24:44**). Jesus will set up His Kingdom on earth. Everyone will give an account for their lives and will receive either their reward or punishment (cf. **2 Corinthians 5:10; 2 Thessalonians 2:1–8; Revelation 22:12**). Also known as the "Day of the Lord" or the "second coming of Christ" (**1 Thessalonians 4:16–17**), this day will be one of great joy for those who are in Christ. But to those who do not receive God's redemption through His Son, it is a day of judgment.

BIBLE APPLICATION

AIM: Students will understand that when we are persuaded of God's love for us, it casts away all fear, and leaves us free to love.

God's love is intense, intentional, believes the best (not the worst), and is not selfish. Pray and ask Him to reveal opportunities to reflect His love in the earth, particularly by how you love in the faith community. If you have to start in your own home, start there. Seek to move outside your comfort zone and reach across barriers to radically love. Make love contagious.

STUDENTS' RESPONSES

AIM: Students will agree that believers were encouraged to love one another.

These believers were challenged by philosophical questions about Christ, which caused lots of confusion, particularly about His return. John reminded these believers that they must remain in God and that He is able to complete their love for Him and each other.

As Christians we are commanded by God to love, starting first and foremost with our faith community. Are there relationships with people in your family and community of faith in which you need to reexamine how you love them or how you are loved? If so, when will you start, and how?

PRAYER

Dear God of love and wonder, we are indebted to the excellent and perfect love that You give to us. Shower Your love on all of creation as reminders that with Your love, the impossible moments become realities of hope. In the Name of Jesus, we pray. Amen.

DIG A LITTLE DEEPER

This section provides an additional research article to further your study of the lesson:

The discussion among many believers centers on the return of Christ, affirms Dr. Larry Eskridge, Associate Director of the Institute for the Study of American Evangelicals at Wheaton College. In this article, he examines the doctrine of the end times through historical events that seem to line up with biblical prophecies.

http://www.wheaton.edu/ISAE/Defining-Evangelicalism/End-Times

HOW TO SAY IT

Propitiation   pro-pih-she-**AY**-shun.

Dwelleth   **DWEH**-lith.

PREPARE FOR NEXT SUNDAY

Read **Ephesians 4:1–6** and "God's Overflowing Love."

DAILY HOME BIBLE READINGS

MONDAY
Christ Died for Us
(1 John 3:11–17)

TUESDAY
Jesus and the Father's Love
(John 14:18–24)

WEDNESDAY
Believe in Jesus, Love One Another
(1 John 3:18–24)

THURSDAY
The Spirit of God Confesses Jesus
(1 John 4:1–6)

FRIDAY
Loving God and Brothers and Sisters
(1 John 4:20–5:5)

SATURDAY
Thankful for God's Steadfast Love
(Psalm 40:1–10)

SUNDAY
The Source of All Love
(1 John 4:7–19)

Reference:
Boice, James Montgomery. Foundations of the Christian Faith: A Comprehensive & Readable Theology. 1986 ed. Downers Grove, IL: InterVarsity Press, 1986. p. 325.

COMMENTS / NOTES:

_____

_____

_____

_____

_____

_____

_____

GOD'S OVERFLOWING LOVE

BIBLE BASIS: EPHESIANS 2:1–10

BIBLE TRUTH: Believers are called to live in unity and maturity as one body in Christ.

MEMORY VERSE: "Even when we were dead in sins, hath quickened us together with Christ, (by grace ye are saved;)" (Ephesians 2:5).

LESSON AIM: By the end of the lesson, we will: VALIDATE that God's love addresses the separation of sin; GIVE thanks for His grace, which offers new possibilities for living in human community; and PROCLAIM God's love in the world and in our communities.

TEACHER PREPARATION

MATERIALS NEEDED: Quarterly Commentary/Teacher Manual, Adult Quarterly, Adult resources—charts, worksheets, and other teaching tools, paper, pens, pencils, Bibles (several different versions)

OTHER MATERIALS NEEDED / TEACHER'S NOTES:

_____

_____

LESSON OVERVIEW

LIFE NEED FOR TODAY'S LESSON
Belivers are dead to sin and do not habitually practice sin.

BIBLE LEARNING
Out of His great love for us, God saved us by grace through faith.

BIBLE APPLICATION
God will show the immense richness of His grace to those who have faith in Christ Jesus.

STUDENTS' RESPONSES
Believers know that the grace of God transforms us into the image of His Son.

LESSON SCRIPTURE

EPHESIANS 2:1–10, KJV

1 And you hath he quickened, who were dead in trespasses and sins;

2 Wherein in time past ye walked according to the course of this world, according to the prince of the power of the air, the spirit that now worketh in the children of disobedience:

3 Among whom also we all had our

EPHESIANS 2:1–10, AMP

1 And you [He made alive when you] were [spiritually] dead and separated from Him because of your transgressions and sins,

2 in which you once walked. You were following the ways of this world [influenced by this present age], in accordance with the prince of the power of the air (Satan), the spirit who is now at work in the disobedient [the unbelieving, who fight against the purposes of God].

conversation in times past in the lusts of our flesh, fulfilling the desires of the flesh and of the mind; and were by nature the children of wrath, even as others.

4 But God, who is rich in mercy, for his great love wherewith he loved us,

5 Even when we were dead in sins, hath quickened us together with Christ, (by grace ye are saved;)

6 And hath raised us up together, and made us sit together in heavenly places in Christ Jesus:

7 That in the ages to come he might shew the exceeding riches of his grace in his kindness toward us through Christ Jesus.

8 For by grace are ye saved through faith; and that not of yourselves: it is the gift of God:

9 Not of works, lest any man should boast.

10 For we are his workmanship, created in Christ Jesus unto good works, which God hath before ordained that we should walk in them.

3 Among these [unbelievers] we all once lived in the passions of our flesh [our behavior governed by the sinful self], indulging the desires of human nature [without the Holy Spirit] and [the impulses] of the [sinful] mind. We were, by nature, children [under the sentence] of [God's] wrath, just like the rest [of mankind].

4 But God, being [so very] rich in mercy, because of His great and wonderful love with which He loved us,

5 even when we were [spiritually] dead and separated from Him because of our sins, He made us [spiritually] alive together with Christ (for by His grace—His undeserved favor and mercy—you have been saved from God's judgment).

6 And He raised us up together with Him [when we believed], and seated us with Him in the heavenly places, [because we are] in Christ Jesus,

7 [and He did this] so that in the ages to come He might [clearly] show the immeasurable and unsurpassed riches of His grace in [His] kindness toward us in Christ Jesus [by providing for our redemption].

8 For it is by grace [God's remarkable compassion and favor drawing you to Christ] that you have been saved [actually delivered from judgment and given eternal life] through faith. And this [salvation] is not of yourselves [not through your own effort], but it is the [undeserved, gracious] gift of God;

9 not as a result of [your] works [nor your attempts to keep the Law], so that no one will [be able to] boast or take credit in any way [for his salvation].

10 For we are His workmanship [His own master work, a work of art], created in Christ

Jesus [reborn from above—spiritually transformed, renewed, ready to be used] for good works, which God prepared [for us] beforehand [taking paths which He set], so that we would walk in them [living the good life which He prearranged and made ready for us].

LIGHT ON THE WORD

Ephesus. A major epicenter of trade in the province of Asia, which is now modern-day Turkey. It was considered one of the major ports for commerce and religion, most notably because of its many temples and marketplace. The temple of Diana (her Roman name; Artemis to the Greeks) was a place of pilgrimage for Greek and Roman deities and generated much trade (**Acts 19:29–30**). God did extraordinary miracles in Ephesus through Paul to the point that "even handkerchiefs or aprons that had touched his skin were carried away to the sick, and their diseases left them and the evil spirits came out of them" (**Acts 19:12**, ESV).

TEACHING THE BIBLE LESSON

LIFE NEED FOR TODAY'S LESSON

AIM: Students will agree that God ordained Paul to be a witness to the Gentiles.

INTRODUCTION

Paul

Known as the Apostle to the Gentiles, Paul was specifically called out by Jesus to a special ministry to bring reconciliation between God and humanity, between Jew and Gentile, bond and free (**Acts 9:15, 13:46–47, 20:24; Galatians 3:28**). God precisely equipped Paul with the ability to reach all kinds of people for the sake of the Gospel (**1 Corinthians 9:21–23**). He was born into a rich heritage as a descendant of the tribe of Benjamin, a Pharisee with Roman citizenship, and is believed to be a member of the Sanhedrin. Paul spoke multiple languages and was considered a scholar.

BIBLE LEARNING

AIM: Students will agree that out of His great love for us, God saved us by grace through faith.

I. DEAD BEFORE CHRIST (Ephesians 2:1–3)

The Apostle Paul reminds readers of where they came from before they followed Christ. Writing to a Gentile audience, he uses the word "dead" to mean spiritual separation from God. He emphasizes the fallen state of humanity, prone to sin because of satanic influence and the sin nature. He encourages these Gentile believers that they are no longer bound to their former way of life because they have been "quickened" (made alive) in their spirit, awakened to God's loving presence, raised up and seated in heavenly places with Christ Jesus (**Ephesians 2:6**).

1 And you hath he quickened, who were dead in trespasses and sins;

By using an extreme word like "dead," the author emphasizes the helplessness of unbelievers. A dead man can do nothing for himself. He needs a miracle—divine intervention—to live again. And that is what God has done for us.

"Trespasses" (Gk. *paraptoma*, **pah-ROP-toe-mah**) are lapses or deviations from the right way of living. "Sins" (Gk. *hamartia*, **ha-mar-TEE-ah**) are acts in which we "miss the mark"—as an archer sometimes misses the target. These terms overlap and reinforce each other, to show us the magnitude of the problem of sin.

2 Wherein in time past ye walked according to the course of this world, according to the prince of the power of the air, the spirit that now worketh in the children of disobedience:

"Wherein" is translated "in which" by modern translations. Grammatically, it refers only to the "sins" from verse 1. However, according to the logic of the passage, it also refers to the "trespasses."

Paul now uses familiar imagery: Life is a journey. Every person must travel in one of two directions. Either we walk the broad, easy path that leads to destruction or the difficult, narrow path that leads to life (**Matthew 7:13–14**).

Instead of "course," the usual translation of the Greek word there is "age" (Gk. *aion*, **eye-ON**), which normally refers to a period of time and retains that meaning here. Before our conversion, we lived not for eternity but temporary pleasure—the same way everyone else does. We were corrupted by the false beliefs and debased values that permeate this world.

"The prince of the power of the air" is a reference to Satan, who the Bible teaches is real, powerful, and actively trying to subvert God's purposes in this world. The ancients thought of the "air" (Gk. *aer*, **ah-AYR**) as the space between the earth and the moon; the Greeks used this term to refer to the lower, impure air where spirits live. Paul, while not endorsing this pagan view of the spirit world, uses the terminology to make the point that Satan wrongly claims the right to exercise his will

in the physical universe. The children of God are characterized by obedience to His will (**1 Peter 1:14**). However, those who disobey reveal themselves to be children of the devil (**Matthew 13:38; 1 John 3:10**); they are called "children of disobedience."

3 Among whom also we all had our conversation in times past in the lusts of our flesh, fulfilling the desires of the flesh and of the mind; and were by nature the children of wrath, even as others.

In Greek, the phrase "among whom" is nearly identical to the phrase "in which" from verse two, which draws our attention to the way the two verses complement each other. Verse two describes our former life characterized by sinful actions; verse three points out our former alliance with sinful people.

Paul is describing a situation in which we were not only surrounded by sinful people, but we were influenced by them and did the same things. The phrase "had our conversation" does not refer to simply talking together among unbelievers; in the Greek (*anastrepho*, **ah-nah-STRE-foe**), it is a metaphor that means "conducted or behaved ourselves." The desires that dominated us in that previous walk of life were "of the flesh." The "flesh" (Gk. *sarx*, **SARKS**) in Pauline writings refers to the sinful nature that continues to think, speak, and act out of depravity (cf. **Galatians 5:19–21**). Christians are called to put this nature within them to death by living in the power of the Holy Spirit (**Romans 8:13**).

"Fulfilling the desires of the flesh and of the mind" intensifies the idea of the previous clause. Apart from Christ, sin not only influenced us, but it dominated our entire being. In Paul's description, we did not choose to repeatedly sin out of free will, but we were bound involuntarily to sin and driven compulsively by it. A tragic destiny awaits those whose lives are held captive by sinful desire.

"Children of wrath" speaks to an eternal destiny full of God's just punishment for our rebellion. "Wrath" (Gk. *orge*, **or-GAY**) is anger or indignation; in the Bible, it is also used to mean "judgment" or "punishment."

II. MADE ALIVE IN CHRIST (vv. 4–7)

Paul again emphasizes the believer's identity and position—marked in Christ and seated in heavenly places with Him (**v. 6**). The Church's presence on earth must bear witness to the truth that Jesus lives. The Church has a wide impact, as Paul implies when he declares that the whole world would know the immeasurable riches of God's love and grace (i.e., His unmerited favor expressed through Jesus). The only way for the whole world to know this is by the Church telling them the Good News. What Paul conveys is so profoundly life-changing that if embraced, it will forever alter how believers live in community. It was important for these Gentile believers to know that they are accepted and that God has lavished His love on them, so they did not revert to their former ways.

4 But God, who is rich in mercy, for his great love wherewith he loved us,

The conjunction "but" introduces a stark contrast. Out of gloom and despair comes hope and light. God has seen the plight of His people and decided to do something to deliver them. "Rich" (Gk. *plousios*, **PLOO-see-os**) tells us that He has an abundant supply of what we need. "Mercy" (Gk. *eleos*, **EL-eh-os**) is God's compassion and pity for us in our helpless condition.

"For" is translated "because of" in other English versions and helps the modern reader see Paul's line of reasoning a little bit more clearly. The reason behind God's merciful act of deliverance is His love (affection) for His people. The author intensifies the description of this love with repetition by saying, in essence, that God "loved us with love."

5 Even when we were dead in sins, hath quickened us together with Christ, (by grace ye are saved;)

God's love is magnified when we understand that, after we were already dead in sin, He had mercy on us. The phrase "dead in sins" uses the exact same Greek words as **verse 1**. Before we had even taken our first breath, how could we be "dead in sin"? The answer: Because of Adam's sin, everyone is born into sin or born a sinner.

"Quickened together with" (Gk. *suzoopoieo*, **sood-zo-op-oy-EH-o**) is a phrase formed by adding the preposition "with" to the verb "made alive." It is the first of three consecutive "together with" verbs (the other two come in **v. 6**).

Since the next verb speaks to our resurrection, this word seems to refer mainly to the new condition of spiritual life we currently experience in Christ—the opposite of the spiritual death described earlier in the passage. Since Christ was born and lived without sin, we have spiritual life when we repent and are saved. Christ Jesus is our source of spiritual vitality.

"Ye are saved" (Gk. *sozo*, **SODE-zo**) is in the perfect tense, which denotes a past action with continuing consequences—"Ye have been saved" would be a more literal translation. We experience our salvation in the present, but it is rooted in God's real-life intervention in time and eternity past. Sozo has a range of possible meanings, all of which illuminate our understanding of what God has done for us in Christ: rescue, liberate, keep from harm, heal, preserve.

6 And hath raised us up together, and made us sit together in heavenly places in Christ Jesus:

This verse strongly echoes **1:20**, which uses nearly the exact same words to tell us that God raised Jesus from the dead and set Him at His right hand in Heaven. The similarity of both theme and vocabulary is a powerful reinforcement of the "in Christ" motif. What God did for all His children, He did first in Christ. We experience our salvation, through faith, by becoming partakers in Christ's experience.

"Raised up together" (Gk. *sunegeiro*, **soon-eh-GAY-roh**) is a compound word made out of the verb "to raise" and the preposition "with." Other New Testament passages speak of the resurrection of the dead with the verb "to raise." By using "raised with," Paul is emphasizing the fact that our resurrection is a sharing with Christ in His resurrection. Paul even goes so far as to say that if Christ has not been raised, "our preaching is vain, and your faith is also vain" (from **1 Corinthians 15:14**). If Jesus had remained in the grave, we would have no hope of life after death. This is why Paul speaks of our resurrection, even though it is in the future, as a past event. Because we can look back in history to the foundational event of Christ's Resurrection, we have the assurance that our resurrection is a certainty. Christ is the "firstfruits" from the grave (**1 Corinthians 15:20, 23**).

The promises of life and resurrection are not all that we receive in our union with Christ. We also receive the promise of great privilege and responsibility. "Made us sit together with" (Gk. *sugkathizo*, **soon-kah-THEED-zoh**) is the final "together with" verb of the sentence. A compound of "with" and "sit down," the verb can mean "to sit down with" or "to cause to sit down with." Since the subject of the sentence is God and we are the objects of His action, the latter is the obvious meaning here. The "sitting down" together with Christ is a direct reference to Jesus' promise. He promised that His true followers will be seated with Him on thrones as rulers in the eternal Kingdom of God (**Luke 22:29–30; Revelation 3:20–21**).

"Heavenly places" (Gk. *epouranios*, **ep-oo-RAN-ee-os**) is the same phrase used earlier to designate the spiritual realm in which God has blessed His children and in which Christ is currently seated. It is also where we encounter Satan and other spiritual opponents of God's plan of redemption (**Ephesians 1:3, 20, 3:10**).

Since "with Christ," in verse five, already made it perfectly clear whom we are joined "together with" in these different aspects of our salvation, "in Christ" is repetitive and emphatic. Paul is consumed by his enthusiasm for what Jesus has done for us.

7 That in the ages to come he might shew the exceeding riches of his grace in his kindness toward us through Christ Jesus.

Now, we come to see the reason for God's merciful acts that are described in **verses 5 and 6**: for all of eternity, God wants to lavish His kindness on His children. An "age" (Gk. *aion*, **eye-OWN**) is an era, duration, or period of time in God's plan of redemption. Paul is not instructing us on the precise number or order of the "ages." This is evident when we consider that in **1:21**, he speaks of the present "age" and one (singular) "age to come."

Rather, the author is speaking of eternity as the endless future era, which will begin when Christ returns. The "riches of his grace" describes the means by which God could afford to do all that He has done for His people. The fact that He plans to continue to show us His riches for all of eternity reminds us that God is infinitely wealthy—not in terms of material wealth but in spiritual power. The love He shows to His people is also never-ending (**Psalm 103:17**).

III. CREATE IN CHRIST (vv. 8–10)

Having focused on how our salvation ends in grace, Paul reminds us of the point he made in his **verse 5** interjection: our salvation also begins and continues in grace. In **verse 5**, the exact same statement helped us to see that grace miraculously accomplishes our salvation, in spite of our spiritually dead condition. Here we see that grace generously gives us what we do not deserve.

8 For by grace are ye saved through faith; and that not of yourselves: it is the gift of God: 9 Not of works, lest any man should boast.

The words "through faith" do not appear in verse 5. "Faith" (Gk. *pistis*, **PIS-tis**) is belief or conviction. True saving faith is that which trusts or relies on what God has done for our salvation. Paul uses the term "works" (Gk. *ergon*, **ER-gon**) to mean "obedience to God's law." Salvation through works is the opposite of salvation through faith.

Faith relies on Christ's perfect obedience to the law of God. Faith trusts that Christ's sacrifice completely paid for our sin and that His perfect righteousness is fully credited to our account. But those who rely on their own works hope that their obedience earns them God's favor. This is why salvation is a gift. If it were something that we could earn or demand, it would be a right—a "wage" or a "debt" in the terms of **Romans 4:4–5**.

Moreover, salvation is a gift in the fullest sense—unrequested, unexpected, and undeserved. The only way in which the recipient of a gift is involved in the giving process is in the receipt or rejection of the gift and expression of either gratitude or contempt toward the giver.

Another aspect of this gift becomes clear when we consider the demonstrative pronoun "that." In the English, it seems to refer most naturally to "faith," which means faith would be the gift of God. However, in the Greek, this is highly unlikely because "faith" is a feminine noun and "that" appears in the neuter. Instead "that" matches with "gift" (also neuter), both of which refer to the first part of verse 8: "by grace are ye saved through faith." God, not humankind, is the source of everything that is necessary for salvation to be accomplished (**1 Corinthians 1:30**).

This passage challenges our pride. We would like to think that even if we can't take credit for earning our salvation, at least we can take credit for trusting in Christ to save us. When we understand the Gospel, though, we see that no one has any grounds to boast. To "boast" (Gk. *kauchaomai*, **kow-KHAH-oh-meye**) means "to glory in or on account of something." Some Jews (especially some of the Pharisees and Sadducees) boasted that their faithful obedience to the Mosaic Law would earn them righteous standing before God. In fact, Paul himself formerly boasted about such things (**Philippians 3:4–6**).

10 For we are his workmanship, created in Christ Jesus unto good works, which God hath before ordained that we should walk in them.

This passage ends with a touch of irony. We are not saved by our works, but our salvation means that we are God's workmanship. "Workmanship" (Gk. *poiema*, **POY-ay-mah**) means "what is made, creation." Elsewhere in Scripture, God uses the metaphor of pottery to help us understand this concept. He is the master potter; we are the clay (**Isaiah 64:8; Jeremiah 18:6**).

Good works are not optional for Christians. The Scriptures teach us they are not just a calling but also an identifying mark of true faith. **James 2:17** warns us that "faith, if it hath not works, is dead." The commands and laws of the Old and New Testaments can't save us, but they help us to tell good works from evil. Good works are those that flow from love for God and love for our fellows (**Matthew 22:37–40; Romans 13:8**).

Good works are such an integral part of our new identity in Christ that God has "before ordained" them (Gk. *proetoimazo*, pro-eh-toy-MAD-zo), meaning He has "prepared (them) beforehand." All that remains for us, is to "walk in them"—to follow the path He has laid out for us. The preparation of our good works includes such blessings as the perfect example of Christ (**Ephesians 5:2**), the power of the Holy Spirit to live a holy life (**Galatians 5:16**), the understanding of what God's will is for our life (**Romans 12:2**), the pouring out of God's own love into our hearts (**Romans 5:5**), and spiritual gifts that enable us to build up the body of Christ in unique and meaningful ways (**1 Corinthians 12:7**). Paul was so consumed with living the life the Lord had ordained for him that he said,"it is no longer I who live, but Christ lives in me," (from **Galatians 2:20**, AMP).

SEARCH THE SCRIPTURES

QUESTION 1

Read **verse 8**. Create a three- to four-word tagline or phrase that explains "the gift of God."

God's gift—grace. (Answers will vary.)

QUESTION 2

Discuss the relationship between sinners who were separated from Christ (**Ephesians 2:1**) and believers who have obtained mercy (**Ephesians 2:4**).

Mercy is when God doesn't give us what we deserve. (Grace is when God gives us what we don't deserve.) Sinners separated from Christ deserve death, but God, in His mercy, provides salvation and makes spiritually alive all who trust in Jesus Christ as Savior.

LIGHT ON THE WORD

Rich in Theology

The book of Ephesians is one of God's masterful works through Paul, rich in theology, designed to form and strengthen faith in God's love and acceptance through Jesus Christ. Paul spent a considerable amount of time in Ephesus, which proved to be a worthy investment. The church at Ephesus became one of the leading centers of Christianity.

BIBLE APPLICATION

AIM: Students will agree that God shows His immense richness of His grace in kindness to those who are in Christ Jesus.

God's love for us is extravagant and endless. Out of His great love and mercy, He rescued us through His Son so that we may have life more abundantly in unbroken fellowship. We are compelled to give the love we receive, and we should help people realize they are accepted and loved. We can give thanks to God for His indescribable gift by intentionally loving those who are broken, hurting, and marginalized. They are not forgotten nor forsaken as we express our faith in love.

STUDENTS' RESPONSES

AIM: Students will agree that the grace of God transforms us into the image of His Son.

Examine your relationship with God. Do you appreciate His grace or take it for granted? This week, pay attention and note God's grace at work in your life. Ask God how you can be an extension of that grace to someone else, especially someone you find hard to love. Radically love someone this week, starting in your own household.

PRAYER

Dear Precious Lord, if it had not been for You loving us first, continuing to love us, and giving us Jesus for the forgiveness of our sins, where would we be? We lift Your name and give thanks for Your mercy. We love You more and more. You are the Alpha and the Omega of our lives. In the Name of Jesus, we pray. Amen.

DIG A LITTLE DEEPER

This section provides an additional research article to further your study of the lesson:

Tragedy struck a Bible study group in Charleston, South Carolina on June 17, 2015. A group of Christians included in their worship setting a young man who seemed to wander into their church. Sadly, this young man took many lives. To the amazement of many, family members, church members, and the community did not respond in anger or violence. The love of Christ was demonstrated. Captured on tape is a musician singing "Amazing Grace." Enjoy this rendition of the Christian hymn authored by English clergyman Charles Newton. Its message: There is no sin so great that it is beyond the reach of God's amazing grace!

http://thesouthernweekend.com/darius-rucker-honors-charleston-church-shooting-victims-with-amazing-grace/

HOW TO SAY IT

Ordained.   or-**DAYND**.

Deviation.   dee-vee-**AY**-shun.

PREPARE FOR NEXT SUNDAY

Read **John 15:1–17** and "God's Love Manifest."

DAILY HOME BIBLE READINGS

MONDAY
God, Be Merciful for Us Sinners
(Luke 18:9–14)

TUESDAY
Justified by Faith
(Romans 3:21–31)

WEDNESDAY
Christ Died for Sinners
(Romans 5:6–11)

THURSDAY
Raised with Christ
(1 Corinthians 15:12–25)

FRIDAY
Know the Love of Christ
(Ephesians 3:14–21)

SATURDAY
Live Worthy of Your Calling
(Ephesians 4:1–6)

SUNDAY
God's Overflowing Love
(Ephesians 2:1–10)

COMMENTS / NOTES:

_____
_____
_____
_____
_____
_____
_____
_____
_____
_____
_____
_____
_____
_____
_____
_____
_____
_____
_____
_____

GOD'S LOVE MANIFESTED

BIBLE BASIS: JOHN 15:1–17

BIBLE TRUTH: God's love is joy and power made for all of Creation.

MEMORY VERSE: "This is my commandment, That ye love one another, as I have loved you" (John 15:12).

LESSON AIM: By the end of the lesson, we will: EVALUATE the role of love in human life and explore how God's love empowers and changes human love; EXPRESS the joy that is found in keeping God's commandments to love others; and PRACTICE the love of God in ministries and lifestyles that grow from being called to be disciples.

TEACHER PREPARATION

MATERIALS NEEDED: Quarterly Commentary/Teacher Manual, Adult Quarterly, Adult resources—charts, worksheets, and other teaching tools, paper, pens, pencils, Bibles (several different versions)

OTHER MATERIALS NEEDED / TEACHER'S NOTES:

_____

_____

LESSON OVERVIEW

LIFE NEED FOR TODAY'S LESSON
People search for what enables them to love and be loved by others.

BIBLE APPLICATION
God's love empowers us to love Him and one another.

BIBLE LEARNING
The Apostle John says that God's love is an all-encompassing love.

STUDENTS' RESPONSES
Believers are commanded to love one another.

LESSON SCRIPTURE

JOHN 15:1–17, KJV

1 "I am the true vine, and my Father is the husbandman.

2 Every branch in me that beareth not fruit he taketh away: and every branch that beareth fruit, he purgeth it, that it may bring forth more fruit.

JOHN 15:1–17, AMP

1 "I am the true Vine, and My Father is the vinedresser.

2 Every branch in Me that does not bear fruit, He takes away; and every branch that continues to bear fruit, He [repeatedly] prunes, so that it will bear more fruit [even richer and finer fruit].

3 Now ye are clean through the word which I have spoken unto you.

4 Abide in me, and I in you. As the branch cannot bear fruit of itself, except it abide in the vine; no more can ye, except ye abide in me.

5 I am the vine, ye are the branches: He that abideth in me, and I in him, the same bringeth forth much fruit: for without me ye can do nothing.

6 If a man abide not in me, he is cast forth as a branch, and is withered; and men gather them, and cast them into the fire, and they are burned.

7 If ye abide in me, and my words abide in you, ye shall ask what ye will, and it shall be done unto you.

8 Herein is my Father glorified, that ye bear much fruit; so shall ye be my disciples.

9 As the Father hath loved me, so have I loved you: continue ye in my love.

10 If ye keep my commandments, ye shall abide in my love; even as I have kept my Father's commandments, and abide in his love.

11 These things have I spoken unto you, that my joy might remain in you, and that your joy might be full.

12 This is my commandment, That ye love one another, as I have loved you.

13 Greater love hath no man than this, that a man lay down his life for his friends.

14 Ye are my friends, if ye do whatsoever I command you.

15 Henceforth I call you not servants; for the servant knoweth not what his lord doeth: but I have called you friends; for all things

3 You are already clean because of the word which I have given you [the teachings which I have discussed with you].

4 Remain in Me, and I [will remain] in you. Just as no branch can bear fruit by itself without remaining in the vine, neither can you [bear fruit, producing evidence of your faith] unless you remain in Me.

5 I am the Vine; you are the branches. The one who remains in Me and I in him bears much fruit, for [otherwise] apart from Me [that is, cut off from vital union with Me] you can do nothing.

6 If anyone does not remain in Me, he is thrown out like a [broken off] branch, and withers and dies; and they gather such branches and throw them into the fire, and they are burned.

7 If you remain in Me and My words remain in you [that is, if we are vitally united and My message lives in your heart], ask whatever you wish and it will be done for you.

8 My Father is glorified and honored by this, when you bear much fruit, and prove yourselves to be My [true] disciples.

9 I have loved you just as the Father has loved Me; remain in My love [and do not doubt My love for you].

10 If you keep My commandments and obey My teaching, you will remain in My love, just as I have kept My Father's commandments and remain in His love.

11 I have told you these things so that My joy and delight may be in you, and that your joy may be made full and complete and overflowing.

12 "This is My commandment, that you love and unselfishly seek the best for one another, just as I have loved you.

that I have heard of my Father I have made known unto you.

16 Ye have not chosen me, but I have chosen you, and ordained you, that ye should go and bring forth fruit, and that your fruit should remain: that whatsoever ye shall ask of the Father in my name, he may give it you.

17 These things I command you, that ye love one another.

13 No one has greater love [nor stronger commitment] than to lay down his own life for his friends.

14 You are my friends if you keep on doing what I command you.

15 I do not call you servants any longer, for the servant does not know what his master is doing; but I have called you [My] friends, because I have revealed to you everything that I have heard from My Father.

16 You have not chosen Me, but I have chosen you and I have appointed and placed and purposefully planted you, so that you would go and bear fruit and keep on bearing, and that your fruit will remain and be lasting, so that whatever you ask of the Father in My name [as My representative] He may give to you.

17 This [is what] I command you: that you love and unselfishly seek the best for one another.

LIGHT ON THE WORD

In this discourse, John uses the metaphor of the vine and its branches to show the interconnection between the disciples and Jesus, as well as their connection with one another. As the "husbandman," the Father exercises just as much care for the branches as He does the vine.

TEACHING THE BIBLE LESSON

LIFE NEED FOR TODAY'S LESSON

AIM: Students will agree that people search for love and desire to be loved by others.

INTRODUCTION

Jesus, the Disciples, and the Vineyard

Jesus is just a few hours away from the Cross, and He and His disciples are walking through a vineyard. He shares a profound message with them in parallelism: The Father is the vinedresser (the owner of the vineyard); Jesus is the vine (the trunk of the grapevine); and believers are the branches (the part that produces fruit). The branches cannot live or produce unless connected to the vine. The vinedresser sees that the branches are taken care of and produce fruit. Similarly, the vinedresser prunes the branches that bear fruit so that they will produce even more.

BIBLE LEARNING

AIM: Students will discover how the Apostle John says that God's love is an all-encompassing love.

I. JESUS THE VINE (John 15:1–3)

Husbandman is a general term for farmer. In the case of **John 15**, the word specifically refers to those who cultivate vineyards, or vinedressers. The husbandman or vinedresser would tend to the plants by pruning and repositioning branches to bear more fruit. The vinedresser would also remove dried-up branches that hinder the health of the vine.

1 I am the true vine, and my Father is the husbandman.

This is the seventh of Jesus' self-referenced "I am" statements, the complete list of which is found only in John's Gospel. It is interesting to note that Jesus chose the word "true" in tandem with "vine" in speaking to people intimately familiar with farming language and imagery. The odd language clearly implies that "true" is in contrast to all that is false or untrue. Jesus is the only "true vine" in a world of false or untrue vines. Indeed, the Word often warns of false prophets and teachers (**Matthew 7:15; Mark 13:22; 1 John 4:1**).

The fruitful branches are synonymous with true believers who, by their living union with Christ, are tenderly and lovingly cared for to produce more fruit. But sometimes a branch yields no fruit at all. As a result, the Father cuts off every branch that is unproductive. Likewise, one's spiritual life can become barren and unfruitful, causing disconnection from the vine (Jesus), by not studying God's Word, not witnessing, or having an undeveloped prayer life (**2 Peter 1:8**). When this happens, the husbandman (God) will remove the unproductive branch, which is an ineffective witness. But those branches (believers) that have been pruned (allowed the Word of God to shape them) become more productive (fruitful) Christians, and Jesus promises to abide with them.

2 Every branch in me that beareth not fruit he taketh away: and every branch that beareth fruit, he purgeth it, that it may bring forth more fruit.

Some controversy exists in the interpretation of "taketh away" (Gk. *airo*, **EYE-roh**), and also of "purgeth" (Gk. *kathairo*, **kath-AH-ee-ro**). The two words are similar enough to constitute a play on words or a rhyme, lost in translation. The latter word, from which we get the word "catharsis," is used only twice in the New Testament (**Hebrews 10:2**). One of the possible meanings of *airo* is "to raise up, elevate, or lift up," as in raising up a fish when catching it. The "taketh away" interpretation is also legitimate, as in "to take off from something attached, remove, or carry away." In context with the entire vine/branch/fruit metaphor, "lifting up" is acceptable in the sense that an unproductive branch might be lifted and cleaned to enhance its productivity (grapevines are tied up). However, when combined with the syntax of the rest of the verse, the sense of "removing" seems stronger.

The husbandman lifts and cleans the vine (washing with the Word, see **verse 3**; see also **Ephesians 5:26**) of all that is unproductive (impure, sinful), removing those parts so the good parts (fruit-bearing branches) that remain will have maximum nourishment and become even more productive. Especially in light of later verses that speak of judgment and unproductive branches being cut off, this seems a more contextually faithful rendering. If anything, a gentle, loving but thorough cleansing rather than a harsh, bloody pruning emerges.

3 Now ye are clean through the word which I have spoken unto you.

If "purgeth" doesn't capture the cleansing sense of the Greek word *kathairo*, the more explicit phrase "clean through the word" used immediately afterward should steer the interpreter toward it. Following a thorough scrubbing that removes unproductiveness and impurities, "now ye are clean," a spiritual cleansing that comes only through the Word—the result of which is now being more productive. This is also more in line with reality, rather than straining to make every literal aspect of a metaphor fit human life.

II. CONDITIONS FOR FRUIT-BEARING (vv. 4–8)

Christians struggle with abiding versus not abiding—and how critical it is to their very survival in Christ. Even when Christ draws an explicit parallel with a physical branch and repeats Himself numerous times on the importance of abiding, how many have yet to transfer the weight of the metaphor to their lives? Just as a branch on a fruit vine doesn't exist just to be a branch but to produce fruit, so we exist not for ourselves, but to produce God's fruit. This is possible only with His nourishment, which we receive only when we abide in Him.

4 Abide in me, and I in you. As the branch cannot bear fruit of itself, except it abide in the vine; no more can ye, except ye abide in me. 5 I am the vine, ye are the branches: He that abideth in me, and I in him, the same bringeth forth much fruit: for without me ye can do nothing. 6 If a man abide not in me, he is cast forth as a branch, and is withered; and men gather them, and cast them into the fire, and they are burned. 7 If ye abide in me, and my words abide in you, ye shall ask what ye will, and it shall be done unto you. 8 Herein is my Father glorified, that ye bear much fruit; so shall ye be my disciples.

A branch cannot produce fruit unless it is connected to the root. Just as Jesus depends on His Father, believers need to abide or remain in Him (Jesus) to stay connected to the root. Abiding, for the disciples and for all believers today, means to make a constant, moment-by-moment decision to depend on Christ. And we must not be passive—believers can't just sit and "remain" until they die. Instead, we must be actively abiding which produces fruit.

A vine that produces much fruit glorifies God. True disciples, then, do more than just believe what Jesus says; they let His words abide in them. When a believer abides in Christ and holds His Word inside, their prayers will be answered (**v. 7**). This does not mean that all prayers are granted. In order to pray and get results, a believer must remain in Christ. When we remain in Him, our thoughts and desires conform to His, and we can pray "in Jesus' name," knowing that our requests please God.

While the primary meaning of "fruit" is that of the vine or tree, the word also refers to works (Gk. *karpos*, **kar-POS**). Just as a grape does the grapevine no personal good, our fruit is not for ourselves but for others and the glory of God (**Philippians 1:11**).

III. ABIDING IN LOVE (vv. 9–11)

We are never asked to do what Christ would not do. In the book of John, it is well-established that Christ proved His love for His Father by His obedience to Him (**John 8:29, 12:49, 14:31, 17:4**). Following suit, the disciples proved their love by their obedience, and we, in turn, prove our love for Christ by our obedience to Him, and receive His promise of abiding in Him.

9 As the Father hath loved me, so have I loved you: continue ye in my love. 10 If ye keep my commandments, ye shall abide in my love; even as I have kept my Father's commandments, and abide in his love. 11 These things have I spoken unto you, that my joy might remain in you, and that your joy might be full.

Jesus zeroes in on what has been called the ultimate fruit—love. Repeatedly, we are told of God's love for His Son, such as in **2 Peter 1:17**, which recalls the pronouncement at Jesus' baptism: "This is my beloved Son, in whom I am well pleased." Jesus loved His disciples with His Father's love, even though, unlike them (and us), He alone was worthy of such great love.

We learn that the basis for "abiding" with Jesus is the love that God and Jesus share with each other. Jesus, then, likens His love for the disciples to the type of love He has for His Father. The highest expression of Jesus' love was expressed on the Cross: He loved us enough to give His life for us. Although we have not been called to die for one another, we must learn to love each other sacrificially as Jesus loved us.

In **verse 10**, Jesus comes to the essence of His message to the disciples: the only way the disciples (or any believer) will continue to abide in God's love is if they, like Him, practice obedience and keep His Father's commandments. Jesus is delighted to do the will of the Father. He tells us that the basis of Christian joy can be found only in Christ.

IV. I AM A FRIEND OF GOD (vv. 12–17)

Jesus called the disciples "friends" because of the revelation He disclosed to them. It made them close to Jesus. It wasn't the Father's will that everything that could be known should be made known, but everything that God wanted known was communicated through Christ (**Matthew 11:27, 24:36**). While servants were common in first-century Israel— and still are in some parts of the world—it is easier for most of us to relate to the concept of employees. Bosses don't confide everything to their employees as a rule, but life would certainly be different in corporate America if CEOs suddenly started calling their employees friends and began a policy of total information disclosure.

12 This is my commandment, That ye love one another, as I have loved you. 13 Greater love hath no man than this, that a man lay down his life for his friends. 14 Ye are my friends, if ye do whatsoever I command you. 15 Henceforth I call you not servants; for the servant knoweth not what his lord doeth: but I have called you friends; for all things that I have heard of my Father I have made known unto you. 16 Ye have not chosen me, but I have chosen you, and ordained you, that ye should go and bring forth fruit, and that your fruit should remain: that whatsoever ye shall ask of the Father in my name, he may give it you. 17 These things I command you, that ye love one another.

Jesus called the disciples His friends. However, becoming His friend was not without a condition: They had to obey His commandments. Jesus told the disciples everything He had heard from His Father. He expected them to lay down their lives if necessary (**v. 14**). If they followed this command, they would no longer be servants but friends of God. What an awesome thing to be chosen as a friend of God!

Once again, we see Jesus referring to God's own unselfish sacrifice in coming as the Incarnation to die on the Cross (**John 3:16**). By calling the disciples His friends, Jesus showed that He trusted them, and that He expected them to spread the Gospel and produce fruit for God's Kingdom. Jesus chose and ordained the disciples. He chose them for a mission, and His Father would answer their requests to accomplish that mission. Today, the Lord continues to choose believers for specific missions. Are we being fruitful?

According to **2 Peter 1:5–7**, we start with faith and add the fruit of the Spirit, finally adding love, as if it were the highest attainment of the faith that the Master intended from the beginning. It is almost as though all the other fruit is easier to acquire or produce; indeed, this is possible, since, in the New Testament, so much emphasis is placed on exhorting believers to love, to learn to love, to seek love, to become love. Because it is the highest, it is the hardest; because it most closely resembles Christ, it requires greater surrender and sacrifice. Yet we are virtually surrounded with Scriptures that exhort us to make love our highest priority, to pursue love, and to let love transform us into the very image of Christ, who is love (**Romans 12:2; 1 Timothy 6:11; 2 Corinthians 3:18; 2 Timothy 2:22**).

SEARCH THE SCRIPTURES

QUESTION 1

Compare the word "purge" in **1 John 15:2**, **2 Chronicles 34:3**, and **Matthew 3:12**.

These three Scriptures refer to the pruning of trees and vines from useless shoots and to cleansing from impurity. Answers will vary.

QUESTION 2

Compose a short prayer that reflects abiding in Christ that you can share with someone (**v. 10**).

Answers will vary.

LIGHT ON THE WORD

Abiding in Christ

Christ reminds His disciples (His friends) that He chose them and has given them a task. As with them, when we abide in Christ, we receive His nourishment, we are fruitful, we fulfill our purpose as branches, we please the Gardener, we feed and nourish others, we produce seeds for planting, and we become eligible for pruning (**John 6:27**). Such a believer has fulfilled the qualifications for prayers being answered, just as God answered His people's prayers in times past: "He granted their entreaty because they relied on and trusted in Him," (from **1 Chronicles 5:20**, AMP).

BIBLE APPLICATION

AIM: Students will affirm that God's love empowers us to love Him and one another.

A plant used for the cultivation of grapes, the vine is often used in the Bible literally and figuratively. The vine is a symbol of prosperity, as the cultivation of grapes was primarily for wine. It is also a symbol of a sedentary life (**1 Kings 4:25**), which was the ideal for the once nomadic nation of Israel. The vine was used by Jesus and others as a picture of God's people (**John 15:2; Psalm 80:8; Isaiah 5:2**). What type of fruit is growing from your spiritual vine because of your connection with Christ?

STUDENTS' RESPONSES

AIM: Students will agree that believers are commanded to love one another.

In today's society, many Christians believe that obeying God begins and ends with going to church once a week. While God commands us to meet with the "body," He expects us to continue to walk in His light daily. A part of that walk should include spreading the Gospel so that nonbelievers may be saved and weak Christians may be strengthened. We must be actively sharing, reaching out, and building godly relationships that glorify our Father and bear fruit for God's Kingdom. How does knowing God's plan for His people change your life?

PRAYER

Dear God, thank You for abiding in us and loving us. You are faithful! We cannot say thank You enough for who You are for all of creation. Your love is steadfast and unmovable. Purge Your humble servants from all unrighteousness to serve You with clean hearts. In the Name of Jesus, we pray. Amen.

DIG A LITTLE DEEPER

This section provides an additional research article to further your study of the lesson:

Are you saved, sanctified, and filled with the Holy Ghost? If your answer is "Yes!" then the evidence of your salvation must be a life that's bearing fruit. Follow this COGIC nine-day Bible study and blog that examines the fruit of the Spirit beginning with this question: "What fruit are you producing?"

http://www.cogic.org/blog/devotions/what-fruit-are-you-producing/

HOW TO SAY IT

Purgeth   per-**JITH.**

Abide   uh-**BYDE.**

PREPARE FOR NEXT SUNDAY

Read **Joel 2:12–13, 18–19, 28–32** and "God's Love Restores."

DAILY HOME BIBLE READINGS

MONDAY
Restore Your Vine, O Lord
(Psalm 80:8–19)

TUESDAY
Love, a New Commandment
(John 13:31–35)

WEDNESDAY
Self-Discipline for Holy Living
(1 Peter 1:13–21)

THURSDAY
Walking in Truth and Love
(2 John 4–11)

FRIDAY
Becoming One in Christ
(Ephesians 2:11–21)

SATURDAY
Abiding in God's Love
(1 John 4:16b–19)

SUNDAY
God's Love Manifested
(John 15:1–17)

COMMENTS / NOTES:

_____
_____
_____
_____
_____
_____
_____
_____
_____
_____
_____
_____
_____
_____
_____
_____
_____
_____
_____
_____
_____
_____
_____
_____
_____
_____

GOD'S LOVE RESTORES

BIBLE BASIS: JOEL 2:12–13, 18–19, 28–32

BIBLE TRUTH: Joel prophesies to God's people to repent and give their hearts to Him.

MEMORY VERSE: "And rend your heart, and not your garments, and turn unto the LORD your God: for he is gracious and merciful, slow to anger, and of great kindness, and repenteth him of the evil" (Joel 2:13).

LESSON AIM: By the end of the lesson, we will: ANALYZE what motivates people to repent and seek restoration; APPRECIATE the love of God that enables prophecy, dreams, and visions; and SEEK restored relationships in personal and community life.

TEACHER PREPARATION

MATERIALS NEEDED: Quarterly Commentary/Teacher Manual, Adult Quarterly, Adult resources—charts, worksheets, and other teaching tools, paper, pens, pencils, Bibles (several different versions)

OTHER MATERIALS NEEDED / TEACHER'S NOTES:

_____

_____

LESSON OVERVIEW

LIFE NEED FOR TODAY'S LESSON
The rewards of wholesome relationships may be shattered by unloving and unfaithful actions.

BIBLE APPLICATION
Believers can decide to repent and live in the love and grace of God.

BIBLE LEARNING
Joel recounts the benefits that emanate from a restored relationship with God.

STUDENTS' RESPONSES
Christians are encouraged to turn from their selfish desires and follow after God.

LESSON SCRIPTURE

JOEL 2:12–13, 18–19, 28–32, KJV

12 Therefore also now, saith the LORD, turn ye even to me with all your heart, and with fasting, and with weeping, and with mourning:

13 And rend your heart, and not your garments, and turn unto the LORD your God: for he is gracious and merciful, slow to

JOEL 2:12–13, 18–19, 28–32, AMP

12 "Even now," says the LORD, "Turn and come to Me with all your heart [in genuine repentance], with fasting and weeping and mourning [until every barrier is removed and the broken fellowship is restored];

13 Rip your heart to pieces [in sorrow and contrition] and not your garments." Now

anger, and of great kindness, and repenteth him of the evil.

18 Then will the LORD be jealous for his land, and pity his people.

19 Yea, the LORD will answer and say unto his people, Behold, I will send you corn, and wine, and oil, and ye shall be satisfied therewith: and I will no more make you a reproach among the heathen:

28 And it shall come to pass afterward, that I will pour out my spirit upon all flesh; and your sons and your daughters shall prophesy, your old men shall dream dreams, your young men shall see visions:

29 And also upon the servants and upon the handmaids in those days will I pour out my spirit.

30 And I will shew wonders in the heavens and in the earth, blood, and fire, and pillars of smoke.

31 The sun shall be turned into darkness, and the moon into blood, before the great and terrible day of the LORD come.

32 And it shall come to pass, that whosoever shall call on the name of the LORD shall be delivered: for in mount Zion and in Jerusalem shall be deliverance, as the LORD hath said, and in the remnant whom the LORD shall call.

return [in repentance] to the LORD your God, for He is gracious and compassionate, slow to anger, abounding in lovingkindness [faithful to His covenant with His people]; and He relents [His sentence of] evil [when His people genuinely repent].

18 Then the LORD will be jealous for His land [ready to defend it since it is rightfully and uniquely His] and will have compassion on His people [and will spare them].

19 The LORD will answer and say to His people, "Behold, I am going to send you grain and new wine and oil, and you will be satisfied in full with them; and I will never again make you an object of ridicule among the [Gentile] nations.

28 "It shall come about after this that I shall pour out My Spirit on all mankind; and your sons and your daughters will prophesy, your old men will dream dreams, your young men will see visions.

29 "Even on the male and female servants I will pour out My Spirit in those days.

30 "I will show signs and wonders [displaying My power] in the heavens and on the earth, blood and fire and columns of smoke.

31 "The sun will be turned into darkness and the moon into blood before the great and terrible day of the LORD comes.

32 "And it shall come about that whoever calls on the name of the LORD will be saved [from the coming judgment] for on Mount Zion and in Jerusalem there will be those who escape, as the LORD has said, even among the remnant [of survivors] whom the LORD calls.

LIGHT ON THE WORD

Joel. Joel's name means "whose God is Jehovah." Little is known of Joel except that he was the son of a man named Pethuel. It is believed that Joel wrote the book named after him during the time of Judah's return from exile. Others believe that it was written right before the death of King Josiah, just one generation before the exile.

Remnant. In the Scriptures, "remnant" refers to those who survived a disaster or judgment. This remnant would continue the population of humankind or the people of God. They would be holy and devoted to God and constitute the faithful. This concept is found throughout the Old and New Testaments (**1 Kings 19:15–18, Amos 5:15, Romans 11:5**). A remnant is a sign of God's grace to humanity in light of His stern judgment on unrepentant sin.

TEACHING THE BIBLE LESSON

LIFE NEED FOR TODAY'S LESSON

AIM: Students will agree that the rewards of wholesome relationships may be shattered by unloving and unfaithful actions.

INTRODUCTION

Joel's Prophecy Then and Now

Yehud (formerly Judah) was a small province under the power of the Babylonian Empire. During a prior period of unification, Judah was the Southern Kingdom, composed of two of the twelve tribes of Israel with its capital at Jerusalem (**1 Kings 12–2 Kings 25**). Joel's message comes to Judah as a matter of urgency. It will mean the life or death of Judah, and all future generations.

For Christians, the prophecy of Joel extends to us and to Christ's Church even today. The Apostle Peter, speaking to the newly born Church on the day of Pentecost, delivers a sermon with the exact prophetic words of this passage from Joel (**Joel 2:28–32; Acts 2:17–21**). Prophecy functions to teach us God's desires for our lives. It is a warning, a teaching, and a call to action. The prophet must deliver the message to the people, notwithstanding any of their own internal conflicts and hesitations. The prophet should receive no personal gain or recognition. All of the attention resulting from a prophecy should be focused upon God. The responsibility of the hearer of the prophecy is to take heed, transform their lives, and spread the word to those who are unaware of it.

BIBLE LEARNING

AIM: Students will evaluate how Joel recounts the benefits that emanate from a restored relationship with God.

I. GOD'S PEOPLE TURN BACK TO HIM (Joel 2:12–13)

Repentance must be in Judah's heart. The "heart" in Hebrew idiom symbolizes the human will and intellect. God is gracious (Heb. *khannun*, **kha-NOON**), giving the total goodwill of a superior to an inferior. He is also merciful (Heb. *rakhum*, **ra-KHOOM**), imparting the kind of love as a parent for his or her child. God is slow to anger in that He does not immediately punish, but rather He always patiently provides an opportunity for people to repent and turn back to Him. God is patient, forgiving, gracious, and merciful, because of His steadfast love (Heb. *khesed*, **KHE-sed**) and the loving faithfulness to the covenant promise with His people.

12 Therefore also now, saith the LORD, turn ye even to me with all your heart, and with fasting, and with weeping, and with mourning: 13 And rend your heart, and not your garments, and turn unto the LORD your God: for he is gracious and merciful, slow to anger, and of great kindness, and repenteth him of the evil.

The prophet Joel describes Judah being devastated by locusts and scorching heat—the judgment Yahweh inflicts upon the people. The prophet answers the question of who will be able to endure this judgment by the Lord when it happens. The only way someone can expect to endure it is to repent, which simply means to turn to God and away from evil. God only wants His people to repent, but this repentance must be a move in the heart. To repent is to turn toward God with all of your heart and away from your current direction of sin.

The prophet leaves an opening for the possibility that as their hearts change, our Lord has the capacity to relent from inflicting horrific consequences on us because of His compassionate heart. Joel asks the question, "Who knows whether God will change from the pronounced judgment?" God is sovereign, with the infinite ability to do whatever He wishes. This unpredictable nature of God is not a cause for us to doubt His promises. When God pronounces goodwill to us, we can count on His stable, strong word. That is the compassion of God, the ability to suffer with His people and feel sorrow for them that He has shown repeatedly in Israel's history. God will relent from punishing us, if He desires to do so. We have upon us the requirement to relent, repent, and change to move our hearts into His direction.

II. GOD TURNS BACK TO HIS PEOPLE (vv. 18–19)

The Lord's care for His people would be represented by provision. His blessing would be seen in their harvest. Prosperity would come to Judah. Their barns and vats would be full of produce. This wouldn't be their own doing, but a result of their relationship with God and His mercy on them.

18 Then will the Lord be jealous for his land, and pity his people. 19 Yea, the Lord will answer and say unto his people, Behold, I will send you corn, and wine, and oil, and ye shall be satisfied therewith: and I will no more make you a reproach among the heathen:

The Lord responds to His people's repentance. He desires to be in relationship with them, expressed in the word "jealous" (Heb. *qanne'*, **kah-NAY**), which denotes desire for exclusivity in relationship. The Lord wants Judah to be His people exclusively and not tied to another. This jealousy is a key part of God's identity (cf. **Exodus 20:5**). He also will take pity (Heb. *khamal*, **chah-MAL**) on His people. The word means to spare or show leniency. These are not just compassionate feelings; they are backed by compassionate action.

Next, Joel speaks to the totality of God's merciful response. Not only would He spare them from judgment, but also He would send wine, oil, and corn (which is better translated "grain"). These are symbols of a rich agricultural harvest and a sign of prosperity. The Lord would cause them to prosper, and they would be filled with satisfaction as their reproach would be removed. They would no longer be a shame and disgrace to the surrounding nations. This language can be used as argument for the book of Joel being written in the post-exilic period, as this was the time for Judah's disgrace as they are taken into captivity among the nations.

III. WHOEVER TURNS TO GOD WILL BE SAVED (vv. 28–32)

God's promise of the gift of the Spirit extends to all flesh. Both men and women, both young and old, and even servants will receive this gift. The lowliest person in God's household would be a candidate for God to pour out His Spirit upon.

28 And it shall come to pass afterward, that I will pour out my spirit upon all flesh; and your sons and your daughters shall prophesy, your old men shall dream dreams, your young men shall see visions: 29 And also upon the servants and upon the handmaids in those days will I pour out my spirit.

The manifestation of certain powerful signs of the fulfillment of God's promise is evident. God will pour out the Spirit on "all flesh," much like one pours out a fluid. The action to "pour out" is the Hebrew *shafak* (**shah-FAWK**) to spill forth. Figuratively, it also means to expend life, sprawl, or gush out. The Spirit of God is always depicted as a gift of power, given to enable the recipient to fulfill a specific role for God (**Exodus 31:2–5; Judges 6:34; Micah 3:8; Haggai 1:14**). The parallel for this text in Joel is found in the New Testament, **Acts 2:4**. There the newly appointed Apostle Peter declares that the outpouring of the Spirit upon the disciples enables them to become effective witnesses for Christ "to the ends of the earth" (**Acts 1:8; 2:4**).

30 And I will shew wonders in the heavens and in the earth, blood, and fire, and pillars of smoke. 31 The sun shall be turned into darkness, and the moon into blood, before the great and terrible day of the LORD come. 32 And it shall come to pass, that whosoever shall call on the name of the LORD shall be delivered: for in mount Zion and in Jerusalem shall be deliverance, as the LORD hath said, and in the remnant whom the LORD shall call.

These days would be accompanied by wonders (Heb. *mopet*, **MO-feth**), nonverbal actions or gestures that encode a message. Given the context, they are better interpreted as signs. These signs are the sun turning to darkness and the moon turning to blood. These cosmic events would signal the coming of the Day of the Lord. The first wonders are blood, fire, and pillars of smoke, which are all signs of death and destruction. Then the Lord promises the sun will be turned into darkness and the moon into blood. The word for "turned" in Hebrew in fact indicates a 180-degree change, or overturning (Heb. *haphak*, **hah-FAWK**). What were created as sources of light according to Genesis (**1:14–18**), are now sources of doom and destruction (darkness and blood). The juxtaposition of darkness and light, as in the creation account in Genesis, should not be missed. The Day of the Lord will bring a complete overturning of the normal patterns of life and growth that God established in the beginning. It will be great and terrible.

SEARCH THE SCRIPTURES

QUESTION 1
How is **Joel 2:12–13** similar to events in our society today?

Both represent people choosing their own way instead of God's way. (Answers will vary.)

QUESTION 2

Joel admonished the people to tear their hearts and not their clothes in **verse 13**. What is the underlying reason for this and how do we apply this principle today?

Tearing of the clothes represented an outward appearance of repentance rather than true repentance of the heart. Today, we repent by confessing our sins, making changes, and being obedient to God. (Answers will vary.)

LIGHT ON THE WORD
A Promise is Given
In the midst of catastrophic judgment, a promise is given. Those who call on the Lord will be saved. Their repentance and dependence on God would be a refuge from His wrath. The sun, moon, and heavens would be affected as signs of the coming day of the Lord. Darkness would sweep over the earth, and the moon would turn red like blood. This judgment would not affect God's people who turn to Him in faith.

BIBLE APPLICATION

AIM: Students will learn that Joel recounts the benefits that emanate from a restored relationship with God.

God is a God of second chances. Many people don't turn to Him for a variety of reasons. Some are too proud, while others see themselves as unworthy and their lives as unredeemable. These are all lies. The truth is that God longs to hear the cries of those who repent. With this repentance comes restoration. God desires to restore His people to a right relationship with Him. As they turn to Him, they can be assured of His love and mercy to meet them where they are. A humble and broken heart of repentance is the key to restoration. Do you have a heart of repentance?

STUDENTS' RESPONSES

AIM: Students will decide to turn from their selfish desires and obey God.

Reread the Scripture lesson. Permit the prophecy given to Joel for repentance to infuse your spirit. Is there an area in your life that demands repentance? Pray and ask the Holy Spirit to reveal any sin from which you need to turn. Now, in groups of two or three, share what God has revealed and one step you will take to obey God.

PRAYER

Dear Lord, we need You each and every day in our lives. Thank you for empowering us through the Holy Spirit to live obediently to your Word. We give You our will and repent from our sinful ways. In the Name of Jesus, we pray. Amen.

DIG A LITTLE DEEPER

This section provides an additional research article to further your study of the lesson:

In *Repentance: The Most Misunderstood Word in the Bible* (Grace Gospel Press, Milwaukee, 2010) the true meaning of repentance is clearly defined. Pastor Michael Corcoris, who earned a Doctor of Divinity from Talbot School of Theology, explains that the word "repent" appears over 50 times in the Bible. In his book, each instance of its usage, context, and practical application is

explored. Read this in-depth book review and perhaps add *Repentance* to your personal library.

http://www.dts.edu/reviews/g-michael-cocoris-repentance

HOW TO SAY IT

Reproach   ree-**PROCH**.

Repenteth   ree-**PEN**-tith.

PREPARE FOR NEXT SUNDAY

Read **Psalm 23** and "God as Our Shepherd."

DAILY HOME BIBLE READINGS

MONDAY
The Prophesied Day of the Lord
(Joel 2:1–11)

TUESDAY
The People Called to Repent
(Joel 2:15–17)

WEDNESDAY
God Restores Land and People
(Joel 2:20–27)

THURSDAY
Day of the Lord at Pentecost
(Acts 2:14–21)

FRIDAY
The Final Day of the Lord
(2 Peter 3:1–10)

SATURDAY
God Judges Nations, Proclaims Judah's Future
(Joel 3:1–3, 18–21)

SUNDAY
Our Gracious and Merciful God
(Joel 2:12–13, 18–19, 28–32)

GOD AS OUR SHEPHERD

BIBLE BASIS: PSALM 23

BIBLE TRUTH: God cares for us, protects us, and loves us.

MEMORY VERSE: "The Lord is my shepherd, I shall not want" (Psalm 23:1).

LESSON AIM: By the end of the lesson, we will: EVALUATE Psalm 23's use of shepherding for trusting in God; APPRECIATE ways that God's love provides goodness and mercy to people when they face challenges; and CHOOSE to trust God's leading, which transforms challenges and difficulties.

TEACHER PREPARATION

MATERIALS NEEDED: Quarterly Commentary/Teacher Manual, Adult Quarterly, Adult resources—charts, worksheets, and other teaching tools, paper, pens, pencils, Bibles (several different versions)

OTHER MATERIALS NEEDED / TEACHER'S NOTES:

_____

_____

LESSON OVERVIEW

LIFE NEED FOR TODAY'S LESSON
Life has challenges that may seem too difficult to endure but for the power of the Holy Ghost.

BIBLE APPLICATION
Followers of Christ experience the comfort and protection of the Lord.

BIBLE LEARNING
The psalmist reminds us that the Lord cares for His people and provides for all their needs.

STUDENTS' RESPONSES
Believers can find support and reassurance for life challenges when we accept the love and promises of God.

LESSON SCRIPTURE

PSALM 23, KJV

1 The LORD is my shepherd; I shall not want.

2 He maketh me to lie down in green pastures: he leadeth me beside the still waters.

3 He restoreth my soul: he leadeth me in the paths of righteousness for his name's sake.

4 Yea, though I walk through the valley of the shadow of death, I will fear no evil: for

PSALM 23, AMP

1 The LORD is my Shepherd [to feed, to guide and to shield me], I shall not want.

2 He lets me lie down in green pastures; He leads me beside the still and quiet waters.

3 He refreshes and restores my soul (life); He leads me in the paths of righteousness for His name's sake.

thou art with me; thy rod and thy staff they comfort me.

5 Thou preparest a table before me in the presence of mine enemies: thou anointest my head with oil; my cup runneth over.

6 Surely goodness and mercy shall follow me all the days of my life: and I will dwell in the house of the LORD for ever.

4 Even though I walk through the [sunless] valley of the shadow of death, I fear no evil, for You are with me; Your rod [to protect] and Your staff [to guide], they comfort and console me.

5 You prepare a table before me in the presence of my enemies. You have anointed and refreshed my head with oil; My cup overflows.

6 Surely goodness and mercy and unfailing love shall follow me all the days of my life, And I shall dwell forever [throughout all my days] in the house and in the presence of the LORD.

LIGHT ON THE WORD

David. David was the youngest son of Jesse of the tribe of Judah, and the second king of Israel. David is also the author of many hymns, including **Psalm 23**. He was brought up to be a shepherd, and in this occupation he learned the courage he would later demonstrate in battle.

As a shepherd, David was charged with caring for the sheep. He had to provide food and water, protect the sheep from predators, and return any sheep that may have strayed from the fold. David's was a rugged, outdoor life that demanded he protect and lead his flock. These skills were valuable tools for developing his leadership skills and relationship with God.

TEACHING THE BIBLE LESSON

LIFE NEED FOR TODAY'S LESSON

AIM: Students will agree that the Holy Ghost gives us power to overcome situations that may seem too difficult to endure.

INTRODUCTION

An Earthly Shepherd

The role of shepherd goes back to the days of Abel. **Psalm 23** is a psalm of David, who was raised in that very occupation. As a shepherd, he fought with lions and bears to protect his sheep (**1 Samuel 17:34–35**). He was well-acquainted with all the responsibilities of a shepherd. David uses his experience as a shepherd to illustrate the love and care of God. In ancient Middle Eastern culture, sheep were prized symbols of wealth. Their wool was used to make yarn. Also, sheep were a common animal for sacrifice or food, which made them especially precious.

BIBLE LEARNING

AIM: Students will accept that the Lord cares for His people and provides for all their needs.

I. GOD AS SHEPHERD (Psalm 23:1–4)

Psalm 23 presents God as the Shepherd who loves and cares for His sheep. Sheep are unable to survive on their own, so they depend completely on the shepherd. **Psalm 23** elaborates on God's providential care as He cares for, guides, and gives refreshment to His people.

David opens by affirming the Lord as his shepherd, and that he has everything he needs. First, he delights in God's care, providing everything he needed. As his shepherd, the Lord also guided him. He led David beside the still waters, which may be interpreted as a resting place. Like a shepherd who knows the right paths to lead the sheep home, the Lord led David down the right path to bring glory to His name.

1 The LORD is my shepherd; I shall not want.

Immediately, **verse 1** affirms Yahweh as Shepherd. This concept originated in the early life of the Israelites, particularly during the time of Jacob. The traditions of Israel's time in the desert seem to have given rise to the thought of God as their Shepherd. This concept became a favorite idiom throughout Israelite history. Several biblical passages highlight God as Shepherd and Protector (**Genesis 49:24; Jeremiah 13:17; Micah 7:14**).

Traditionally, the shepherd theme is interpreted communally. The shepherd has a relationship with his flock. The pronoun "my" makes this portion of the psalm distinct in that it speaks of one individual's personal relationship with the shepherd. The speaker confirms that a relationship with the shepherd brings about wonderful results. The needs of the sheep are met and God (the Shepherd) becomes the ultimate source of provision. This verse establishes that God is loyal and devoted to each individual sheep.

2 He maketh me to lie down in green pastures: he leadeth me beside the still waters. 3 He restoreth my soul: he leadeth me in the paths of righteousness for his name's sake.

The verses extend the metaphor of a loving and devoted shepherd, illustrating the nature of the shepherd's guidance and provision. The psalmist speaks of God guiding him through the ups and downs of life. Green pastures and still waters are significant elements in the beginning of the psalm. Grassy pastures indicate tender grass, young herbage, and abundance. God puts the psalmist in the midst of plenty to enjoy it with ease and comfort. The shepherd leading the sheep by still waters portrays the Lord showing the psalmist to a resting place where he could be refreshed safely.

This not only confirms the duties of the shepherd, but also affirms that he is prepared to keep the sheep nourished in every way. It is important to note that it was the shepherd's job to supply the sheep with water either at a running stream or at troughs attached to the wells (**Genesis 29:7, 30:38; Exodus 2:16**).

4 Yea, though I walk through the valley of the shadow of death, I will fear no evil: for thou art with me; thy rod and thy staff they comfort me.

This verse uses several metaphors to specify the relationship between the Shepherd and His sheep. First, the phrase "valley of the shadow of death" might have a few different meanings. The term might refer to the hill country of Judah, which consisted of narrow valleys that were often dark, gloomy, and difficult to climb. Also, the valleys had deep caves where wild beasts and robbers resided. This made the journey for the pilgrim extremely dangerous as he passed through the hill country. Literally, the peril of death could occur in the valleys of the hill country. Second, the phrase might also be used figuratively. The author could be comparing the deep shadow of death's valley to Egyptian slavery or the Israelites' long time in the wilderness.

The Great Shepherd protects His people during their exodus and wandering in the wilderness.

Triumphantly, the Good Shepherd leads the sheep out of the wilderness into the Promised Land (**Jeremiah 2:6**). Such language could also be used as a tool of encouragement to the exiled Israelites later. Certainly God, who led the ancestors out of bondage, will liberate these captives. Whatever the psalmist's intent, he emphasizes that there is divine protection in the midst of danger or death.

In keeping with the image of God as Shepherd, the psalmist highlights a rod and a staff. Shepherds used rods to count the sheep, care for the sheep, and check the condition of the sheep. It was also a symbol of power and authority. Staffs were used to aid the shepherd in climbing hills and beating away bushes and reptiles in the area. These symbols imply that the shepherd is capable of protecting his flock as well as leading them.

II. GUESTS IN GOD'S HOUSE (vv. 5–6)

The psalm shifts to God as gracious host and provider. God offers safety and protection, even spreading a table of lavish hospitality. Even in the presence of David's enemies, the Lord made provision for him. God's abundant care can be symbolized by the anointing with oil and the overflowing cup. The psalm ends with David affirming that God gives him victory over death and that he will spend eternity with Him.

5 Thou preparest a table before me in the presence of mine enemies: thou anointest my head with oil; my cup runneth over. 6 Surely goodness and mercy shall follow me all the days of my life: and I will dwell in the house of the LORD forever.

Here, the image changes from a shepherd to a host. The intimate relationship between God and His people are like that of a host and his guests. God as the gracious host protects the guests from any enemy. In the ancient East, the host would customarily protect the guest from his enemies at all costs. A man pursued by enemies could seek another man's tent for refuge. The owner of that tent would be obligated to protect his guest from the enemy. Additionally, the host would sprinkle the guests with perfume as a way of welcoming them into his fellowship.

Such a loving and gracious host gives pure satisfaction and security to the guests ("my cup overflows"). These images provide us with more detail about God's nature. God is a gracious host who protects His guests from all enemies. He is our shield and protector. Our enemies stand outside the tent door glaring, but they are not allowed to destroy us. Their plans are frustrated while our God makes a statement. He is truly a Friend.

God also prepares a great banquet and longs for our fellowship. Feasting in His presence nourishes our souls and prepares us for greatness. The psalm ends with some future expectation. A relationship with the Divine Shepherd or the Gracious Host will result in goodness, mercy, and God's everlasting presence. The psalmist is convinced that God's wise guidance will lead to a promising future.

SEARCH THE SCRIPTURES
QUESTION 1
Critique who David was and how his occupation as shepherd enabled him as king and warrior.

David was a king, father, husband, and strategist. As a shepherd, his skills allowed him to anticipate and solve problems while he was tending the sheep. This would assist him as a king and warrior as he made decisions and had to learn how to protect himself, his family, and his kingdom. (Answers will vary.)

QUESTION 2
Compare and contrast God as the Shepherd and an earthly shepherd.

God is forever the Shepherd who made all of creation and will continue to protect and care for us. An earthly shepherd responsible for sheep has limits on the time spent with and methods of caring for the flock. (Answers will vary.)

LIGHT ON THE WORD

God Cares

As in **Psalm 23**, God graciously protects and provides for believers today. Believers have enemies and experience stressful and dangerous situations, as David did. He offers us sanctuary in times of difficulty. God can transform our situations and our lives. As with David, God's blessing is always on His people. We can dwell with the Lord and experience full communion with Him forever.

BIBLE APPLICATION

AIM: Students will agree that followers of Christ experience the comfort and protection of the Lord.

Meditate on God's Word and reflect on the Lord as your shepherd. Ask Jesus to lead you as a shepherd leads and cares for His sheep. Rest in the truth that the Lord will protect and provide for you. Finally, thank Jesus for His love and providential care in your life.

STUDENTS' RESPONSES

AIM: Students will decide that the love and promises of God provide support and reassurance for life's challenges.

Adults face difficult situations. We face danger, anxiety, and fear as we journey through life. We can turn to God as our shepherd to lead, protect, and provide for us. We must understand that He is our Shepherd and Leader, and submit to His leadership. We must trust Him as our provider, asking and thanking Him for making provision for our needs. We must run to Him as our refuge in times of trouble. Finally, we must maintain a vital union with God for life.

PRAYER

Dear Lord, You are our Shepherd who provides us the comfort, love, protection, and guidance that we need. You lead us through our valleys and to our mountaintops. You keep us even when we wander away. Praises and blessings to You, now and forever. In Jesus' Name, we pray. Amen.

DIG A LITTLE DEEPER

This section provides an additional research article to further your study of the lesson:

In this video presentation, Pastor Mike Fabarez discusses the practical implications of living without fear and putting complete confidence in God. There's encouragement here as Psalm 23 is applied to daily life.

http://open.biola.edu/resources/trust-in-the-lord-and-be-not-afraid

HOW TO SAY IT

Pastures.	**PAS**-chers.
Anointest	ah-**NOYNT**-ist.

PREPARE FOR NEXT SUNDAY

Read **John 3:1–16** and "God's Saving Love in Christ."

DAILY HOME BIBLE READINGS

MONDAY
God's People Seek a Resting Place
(Numbers 10:29–36)

TUESDAY
God the True Shepherd
(Ezekiel 34:11–16)

WEDNESDAY
The Lord Brings the People Home
(Jeremiah 23:1–8)

THURSDAY
Jesus Sacrifices for the Flock
(John 10:11–18)

FRIDAY
Shepherds in God's Household Today
(Hebrews 13:17, 20–21)

SATURDAY
Tending the Flock of God
(1 Peter 5:1–11)

SUNDAY
God as Our Shepherd
(Psalm 23)

COMMENTS / NOTES:

GOD'S SAVING LOVE IN CHRIST

BIBLE BASIS: JOHN 3:1–16

BIBLE TRUTH: Jesus offers new birth and eternal life to those who believe.

MEMORY VERSE: "For God so loved the world, that he gave his only begotten Son, that whosoever believeth in him should not perish, but have everlasting life" (John 3:16).

LESSON AIM: By the end of the lesson, we will: EVALUATE the story of Nicodemus who learned from Jesus what it means "to be born from above"; APPRECIATE how God's love offers salvation rather than condemnation; and PROCLAIM the Gospel so that men and women who are lost will be saved.

TEACHER PREPARATION

MATERIALS NEEDED: Quarterly Commentary/Teacher Manual, Adult Quarterly, Adult resources—charts, worksheets, and other teaching tools, paper, pens, pencils, Bibles (several different versions)

OTHER MATERIALS NEEDED / TEACHER'S NOTES:

_____

_____

LESSON OVERVIEW

LIFE NEED FOR TODAY'S LESSON
Those who are lost are seeking salvation and may be curious about who Jesus is.

BIBLE LEARNING
God proved His love for the world through the ultimate sacrifice of His only Son.

BIBLE APPLICATION
For all who believe in Christ, there are wonderful promises that will last for eternity.

STUDENTS' RESPONSES
Students have a responsibility to share the Gospel with those who are seeking answers to life's difficult questions.

LESSON SCRIPTURE

JOHN 3:1–16, KJV

1 There was a man of the Pharisees, named Nicodemus, a ruler of the Jews:

2 The same came to Jesus by night, and said unto him, Rabbi, we know that thou art a teacher come from God: for no man can do these miracles that thou doest, except God be with him.

JOHN 3:1–16, AMP

1 Now there was a certain man among the Pharisees named Nicodemus, a ruler (member of the Sanhedrin) among the Jews,

2 who came to Jesus at night and said to Him, "Rabbi (Teacher), we know [without any doubt] that You have come from God as a teacher; for no one can do these signs [these wonders,

3 Jesus answered and said unto him, Verily, verily, I say unto thee, Except a man be born again, he cannot see the kingdom of God.

4 Nicodemus saith unto him, How can a man be born when he is old? can he enter the second time into his mother's womb, and be born?

5 Jesus answered, Verily, verily, I say unto thee, Except a man be born of water and of the Spirit, he cannot enter into the kingdom of God.

6 That which is born of the flesh is flesh; and that which is born of the Spirit is spirit.

7 Marvel not that I said unto thee, Ye must be born again.

8 The wind bloweth where it listeth, and thou hearest the sound thereof, but canst not tell whence it cometh, and whither it goeth: so is every one that is born of the Spirit.

9 Nicodemus answered and said unto him, How can these things be?

10 Jesus answered and said unto him, Art thou a master of Israel, and knowest not these things?

11 Verily, verily, I say unto thee, We speak that we do know, and testify that we have seen; and ye receive not our witness.

12 If I have told you earthly things, and ye believe not, how shall ye believe, if I tell you of heavenly things?

13 And no man hath ascended up to heaven, but he that came down from heaven, even the Son of man which is in heaven.

14 And as Moses lifted up the serpent in the wilderness, even so must the Son of man be lifted up:

15 That whosoever believeth in him should

these attesting miracles] that You do unless God is with him."

3 Jesus answered him, "I assure you and most solemnly say to you, unless a person is born again [reborn from above—spiritually transformed, renewed, sanctified], he cannot [ever] see and experience the kingdom of God."

4 Nicodemus said to Him, "How can a man be born when he is old? He cannot enter his mother's womb a second time and be born, can he?"

5 Jesus answered, "I assure you and most solemnly say to you, unless one is born of water and the Spirit he cannot [ever] enter the kingdom of God.

6 That which is born of the flesh is flesh [the physical is merely physical], and that which is born of the Spirit is spirit.

7 Do not be surprised that I have told you, 'You must be born again [reborn from above—spiritually transformed, renewed, sanctified].'

8 The wind blows where it wishes and you hear its sound, but you do not know where it is coming from and where it is going; so it is with everyone who is born of the Spirit."

9 Nicodemus said to Him, "How can these things be possible?"

10 Jesus replied, "You are the [great and well-known] teacher of Israel, and yet you do not know nor understand these things [from Scripture]?

11 I assure you and most solemnly say to you, we speak only of what we [absolutely] know and testify about what we have [actually] seen [as eyewitnesses]; and [still] you [reject our evidence and] do not accept our testimony.

12 If I told you earthly things [that is, things that happen right here on earth] and you do

not perish, but have eternal life.

16 For God so loved the world, that he gave his only begotten Son, that whosoever believeth in him should not perish, but have everlasting life.

not believe, how will you believe and trust Me if I tell you heavenly things?

13 No one has gone up into heaven, but there is One who came down from heaven, the Son of Man [Himself—whose home is in heaven].

14 Just as Moses lifted up the [bronze] serpent in the desert [on a pole], so must the Son of Man be lifted up [on the cross],

15 so that whoever believes will in Him have eternal life [after physical death, and will actually live forever].

16 "For God so [greatly] loved and dearly prized the world, that He [even] gave His [One and] only begotten Son, so that whoever believes and trusts in Him [as Savior] shall not perish, but have eternal life.

LIGHT ON THE WORD

Nicodemus. A Pharisees and member of the Sanhedrin, Nicodemus was both a religious and a political leader. He came to Jesus by night. Perhaps he was afraid to let the other Pharisees know about his interest in Jesus' teachings.

TEACHING THE BIBLE LESSON

LIFE NEED FOR TODAY'S LESSON

AIM: Students will agree that those who are lost are seeking salvation and may be curious about Jesus.

INTRODUCTION

A Secret Meeting

Jesus encounters Nicodemus near the Passover. He had recently cleared out the Temple, which caused some commotion. The religious leaders demanded to know what authority Jesus had to do these things, and they demanded to see

a sign. He told them that He would destroy the Temple and raise it again in three days. The religious leaders were furious.

At the same time, John tells us that Jesus performed many miracles during the Passover celebration and that many believed in Him because of these signs (**John 2:23**). Word about Jesus began to spread.

Among those who heard about Jesus was Nicodemus, a Pharisee who was very educated in the Scriptures. He secretly visited Jesus to learn more about Him. Why? Nicodemus recognized that Jesus would be unable to perform miracles "unless God is with him" (**John 3:2**, AMP). Apparently, there were others who felt the same as did Nicodemus. But not everyone agreed. There were differing opinions about Jesus, His identity, and His power to do such mighty acts. Nicodemus decided to go to Jesus and find out for himself.

BIBLE LEARNING

AIM: Students will agree that God proved His love for the world through the ultimate sacrifice of His only Son.

I. JESUS IS FROM GOD (John 3:1–2)

Nicodemus was a member of the Sanhedrin, the highest court of the Jews. He came to Jesus one night to speak to Him.

The reason for the timing of Nicodemus' visit is uncertain. Some scholars suggest that Nicodemus came to Jesus by night because he was fearful. Others scholars have suggested that Nicodemus came at night because he desired privacy, since Jesus was usually engaged in public ministry during the day. Whatever his reason, Nicodemus recognized that Jesus might be the Messiah, and he wanted to find out more about Jesus.

1 There was a man of the Pharisees, named Nicodemus, a ruler of the Jews.

The Pharisees were regarded as the most devout keepers of the Law among the Jews. They guarded the standards and judged the actions of the Jewish community. By the first century AD, the Pharisees were the most popular of the three main Jewish sects. The other two sects were the Essenes and the Sadducees. Although Pharisees were extremely detailed in all matters of the commandments, their religion was often an outward show based on self-righteousness. Throughout Jesus' ministry, the Pharisees were bitter enemies of our Lord and sought to destroy His influence among the people.

The phrase "ruler of the Jews" means that Nicodemus also served on the Sanhedrin Council, which was comprised of seventy priests, elders, and scribes, along with the high priest. Nicodemus was a very powerful, well-educated Jewish leader.

2 The same came to Jesus by night, and said unto him, Rabbi, we know that thou art a teacher come from God: for no man can do these miracles that thou doest, except God be with him.

Under the cover of darkness, this man of religious authority sought out Jesus. He addressed Jesus as "Rabbi," a title of honor used by the Jews to address distinguished religious teachers. By using this title, Nicodemus was giving honor and recognition to the divine authority of Jesus' teachings and the acts that He was performing.

The "we" that Nicodemus speaks for is unclear. It would appear that he was speaking for the Pharisees and/or the Sanhedrin Council. But the Pharisees' behavior would seem to oppose any notion that they sincerely believed Jesus' work was God-inspired. Nicodemus was more likely referring to a group of Pharisees who was beginning to believe in Jesus.

II. BORN OF THE SPIRIT (vv. 3–9)

Jesus begins to teach Nicodemus. He explains that one must be born again to enter the Kingdom of God. Nicodemus was thinking only of a natural birth, but Jesus says that one must be born again or born "from above" (AMP) to enter the Kingdom of God. Nicodemus would have seen no need for this since, according to Pharisaism, to be born a Jew was enough to qualify him for entrance into God's Kingdom.

3 Jesus answered, and said unto him, Verily, verily, I say unto thee, Except a man be born again, he cannot see the kingdom of God.

Verse 3 begins by saying Jesus "answered" (Gk. *apokrinomai*, **ah-poe-KREE-no-my**), which means to answer a question or to speak in response to something that is said or done. Nicodemus had not yet asked a question; however, Jesus knowing his intent, proceeded to tell Nicodemus that he must be born again.

4 Nicodemus saith unto him, How can a man be born when he is old? Can he enter the second time into his mother's womb, and be born?

Nicodemus' question was a logical response. Notice that he didn't ask, "How can a man be born again," but "How can a man be born, when he is old?" According to Messianic scholar Dr. Arnold Fruchtenbaum of Ariel Ministries, Pharisaic Judaism had six different ways of being born again: (1) when Gentiles converted to Judaism; (2) when a man was crowned king; (3) when a Jewish boy becomes a bar mitzvah (son of the Law) at age 13; (4) when a Jewish man married; (5) when a Jew was ordained as a rabbi; and (6) when a Jew became the head of a rabbinical school. Except for the first two examples, Nicodemus had experienced all of the other rebirths. "He had done everything right, but now he was being told that something else was lacking in his life. What disequilibrium!" writes Dr. La Verne Tolbert, a former seminary professor.

5 Jesus answered, Verily, verily, I say unto thee, Except a man be born of water and of the Spirit, he cannot enter into the kingdom of God.

To "be born of water" is natural birth. To be born of the Spirit is a different matter. This has to come from God. Jesus explains to Nicodemus that to enter God's Kingdom, a different birth is required—a spiritual birth or being born from above. To be "born again" is the beginning of new, eternal life that only comes from God. Faith in Jesus Christ is the only way to being saved or born again (**John 14:6**).

6 That which is born of the flesh is flesh; and that which is born of the Spirit is spirit.

The Greek word for "flesh" (*sarx*, **SARKS**) denotes both the physical body and fallen human nature apart from divine influence. This word is also translated as "carnal" (**Romans 8:7**). The Bible teaches that the flesh is prone to sin and selfishness, and it is therefore in opposition to the Spirit of God (**Romans 8:5–9**). Being "in the flesh" means being unrenewed; to live "according to the flesh" is to live and act sinfully (**Romans 7:5; Ephesians 2:3**).

7 Marvel not that I said unto thee, Ye must be born again.

In **Psalm 51:5**, David acknowledges, "Behold, I was shapen in iniquity; and in sin did my mother conceive me." In **verse 10**, he prays: "Create in me a clean heart, O God; and renew a right spirit within me." Like David, we inherited a sin nature from Adam (cf. **Romans 5:12**). Similarly, in **John 3:7**, it is as if Jesus is saying to Nicodemus, "Do not be surprised that something drastic must happen to transform the human nature."

The word "must" (Gk. *dei*, **day-EE**) indicates that the new birth is an absolute necessity. Our God represents holiness in the highest sense (cf. **Isaiah 6:3; Revelation 15:4**). To enter His Kingdom and become His children, we must be radically transformed through the salvation experience (see **1 Peter 1:16; Hebrews 12:14**). Those who have been "born of the flesh" must also be "born of the Spirit" (**John 3:16**).

8 The wind bloweth where it listeth, and thou hearest the sound thereof, but canst not tell whence it cometh, and whither it goeth: so is every one that is born of the Spirit.

In Greek, as well as in Hebrew, the same word (*pneuma*, **PNEW-ma**) is used for both "spirit" and "wind." The wind cannot be controlled because God directs it. Though the source of the wind is invisible, the effect, or evidence, of its activity is plain. So it is with everyone who is born of the Spirit.

9 Nicodemus answered and said unto him, How can these things be?

Nicodemus questioned the process of being born again. Jesus explains that there are two requirements for entering the Kingdom of God. One requirement would be fulfilled by God; the other requirement was man's responsibility.

III. BELIEVING IN THE SON OF MAN (vv. 10–15)

Jesus challenges Nicodemus' lack of understanding. The Old Testament prophets foresaw a time when people would be regenerated by the Spirit. As a religious leader and skilled interpreter of the Law, Nicodemus should have understood about God's Spirit.

10 Jesus answered and said unto him, Art thou a master of Israel, and knowest not these things?

Jesus uses the word "master" (Gk. *didaskalos*, **dee-DAS-ka-lohs**) to describe Nicodemus as one who is expertly qualified to teach, because as the head of a rabbinical school, teaching is what Nicodemus did. But at present, he could not possibly teach what he does not understand. After Jesus is crucified, we see indications that Nicodemus did, indeed, place his faith in Jesus as Messiah (**John 19:39**).

11 Verily, verily, I say unto thee, We speak that we do know, and testify that we have seen; and ye receive not our witness.

Jesus makes it clear that His followers know the truth about who He is through firsthand experience (**John 7:16, 8:38, 1 John 1:3**). Yet the Jewish authorities refused to believe.

12 If I have told you earthly things, and ye believe not, how shall ye believe, if I tell you of heavenly things?

When Jesus talks about "earthly things" (Gk. *epigeios*, **eh-PEE-gay-oce**), He is referring to the things that occur on earth or His analogies related to birth, wind, and water. The phrase "heavenly things" (Gk. *epouranios*, **ep-oo-RAH-nee-os**) refers to things that exist or take place in Heaven.

13 And no man hath ascended up to heaven, but he that came down from heaven, even the Son of man which is in heaven.

Here, Jesus provides in detail the steps to being born again. As God the Son, Jesus came down from Heaven. He had a purpose, to pay the price for the sin of the world.

The phrase "Son of man" appears in the Old Testament primarily to specify a member of humanity (cf. **Psalm 8:4**). It was also used to refer to the prophet in the book of Ezekiel (e.g., **Ezekiel 2:1**). Later in the apocalyptic book of Daniel, one sees a new development in the use of the phrase (**Daniel 7:13**): the "Son of man" takes on the character of a divine agent who will carry out judgment and deliverance.

In the New Testament, John the Baptist testified that Jesus is the Son of God (**John 1:34**). Also, he stated that this "Son" was the Word become flesh (**1:14**). Moreover, this Word was in the beginning with God, and was God (**1:1**).

Therefore, Jesus is the Word of God, who became flesh and dwelt in the world as a man, the "Son of man." The Word of God is the Son of God who became the Son of man, our Lord Jesus Christ.

14 And as Moses lifted up the serpent in the wilderness, even so must the Son of man be lifted up: 15 That whosoever believeth in him should not perish, but have eternal life.

In the wilderness when the Israelites murmured against God, He sent fiery (i.e., poisonous) serpents among the people to bite them, and many Israelites died. When the people repented, the Lord told Moses to make a bronze serpent, and set it upon a pole. Then if anyone who was bitten would look at that bronze serpent, they would live (**Numbers 21**). Our just and merciful God provided a means of salvation for a disobedient people, so that they might survive divine judgment.

The phrase "lifted up" is translated from the Greek word *hupsoo* (**hoop-so'-o**), which means to lift up on high or to exalt; both definitions apply in this verse. Jesus tells Nicodemus about His death. Nicodemus is among the first to learn that Jesus will be crucified—lifted up physically on the Cross of Calvary—to become the source of salvation for all who will look to Him in faith. Here is God's initiative. God is meeting His own requirement for sin by providing the perfect sacrifice, Jesus Christ.

IV. JESUS CAME TO SAVE (v. 16)

Faith in Jesus takes us from condemnation to salvation and from death to life. Eternal life does not refer to length alone, but also a quality of life in the Kingdom of God. God, in love, sent Jesus to make this new life possible.

16 For God so loved the world, that he gave his only begotten Son, that whosoever believeth in him should not perish, but have everlasting life.

John 3:16 is one of the most beloved verses in all of Scripture. However, in this study, we must also remember that it is found in the context of a conversation between Jesus and Nicodemus. This verse presents the Gospel in short. God, motivated by love, gave His Son to bring salvation. His love was not just for a certain people group, but to anyone who would receive Him throughout the whole world. By His death, Jesus brought sinners, the enemies of God, into right relationship with God.

SEARCH THE SCRIPTURES

QUESTION 1
How is the Jewish custom of being "born again" similar to the African-American tradition of a Rites of Passage program for boys?

At each stage of being "born again," a Jewish person has a new identity. A Rites of Passage program gives boys a new identity when they re-enter the "village" as young men.

QUESTION 2
How might you be similar to Nicodemus in your spiritual life or in your every day life?

Nicodemus was not afraid to ask questions. When we ask questions, we acquire answers. Nicodemus set aside time to spend with Jesus. Believers need private time (devotions) with Jesus. (Answers will vary.)

LIGHT ON THE WORD
The Shadow of Uncertainty
Out of the darkness of night, under the shadow of uncertainty, Nicodemus came to Jesus, the Light of the world. It is in **John 3:16** that Nicodemus (and each of us) finds the answer: God takes away our sins and grants us new birth, or "everlasting life," because of His unmerited love for us, which is manifested by the sacrifice of His Son and our Savior Jesus Christ.

BIBLE APPLICATION

AIM: Students will validate that for everyone who believes in Jesus Christ for salvation, eternal life is guaranteed.

Like Nicodemus, there are men and women who are seeking answers to life's disillusionment. Many become "religious," thinking that just going to church is enough. But salvation is more than religion or following a set of rules. Christ Jesus desires a personal relationship with everyone who believes in Him. Will you share the truth of this Good News? Jesus is still the answer for the world today.

STUDENTS' RESPONSES

AIM: Students should decide to spend time talking with others about salvation through Jesus Christ.

When asked about their faith, people will often remark that their mother is a Christian or that a grandparent is a pastor. But being born into families that believe in Jesus doesn't make a person a Christian any more than sitting in a garage makes a person a car. Like Nicodemus, everyone must be born again, "reborn from above" (AMP) through faith in Jesus Christ.

PRAYER

Dear Heavenly Father, thank You for salvation through our Lord and Savior, Jesus Christ. Thank You that Jesus died on the Cross for our sin. Thank You for the Holy Spirit who empowers us to live holy and share this Good News with others. Lead us to someone this week who may be lost and who needs to know about Your love for them. In the Name of Jesus, we pray. Amen.

DIG A LITTLE DEEPER

This section provides an additional research article to further your study of the lesson:

Contextual analysis is crucial to proper biblical interpretation. In **John 3:1–16**, the references to Jewish culture and traditions can be easily overlooked if not examined through the proper lens. Dr. Arnold Fruchtenbaum provides insightful cultural context for a thorough unpacking of Jesus' dialogue with Nicodemus. He clarifies Nicodemus' conflict with being "born again" and provides a sound hermeneutic that is enlightening.

https://webcache.googleusercontent.com/search?q=cache:sHsQm7PBX3AJ:https://missionventureministries.files.wordpress.com/2010/04/nicodemus-and-yeshua-jesus1.doc+&cd=5&hl=en&ct=clnk&gl=us

HOW TO SAY IT

Nicodemus	ni-co-**DEE**-mus.
Listeth	lis-**TITH**.

PREPARE FOR NEXT SUNDAY

Read **John 20:1–10** and "God's Love as Victory Over Death."

DAILY HOME BIBLE READINGS

MONDAY
God's Salvation is for the World
(John 3:17–21)

TUESDAY
Don't Love the World's Things
(1 John 2:15–17)

WEDNESDAY
Nicodemus Pleads "Give Jesus a Hearing"
(John 7:45–52)

THURSDAY
The Serpent in the Wilderness
(Numbers 21:4–9)

FRIDAY
Nicodemus Brings Spices for Burial
(John 19:38–42)

SATURDAY
Rebirth and Renewal by Water and Spirit
(Titus 3:1–7)

SUNDAY
God's Saving Love in Christ
(John 3:1–16)

Sources:
Fruchtenbaum, Arnold. "Nicodemus and Yeshua (Jesus). Jewish salvation God's way." https://webcache.googleusercontent.com/search?q=cache:sHsQm7PBX3AJ:https://missionventureministries.files.wordpress.com/2010/04/nicodemus-and-yeshua-jesus1.doc+&cd=5&hl=en&ct=clnk&gl=us. Accessed February 9, 2016.
Tolbert, La Verne. *Teaching like Jesus: A Practical Guide to Christian Education in Your Church.* Grand Rapids, MI: Zondervan, 2000. p. 162.

GOD'S LOVE AS VICTORY OVER DEATH

BIBLE BASIS: JOHN 20:1–10

BIBLE TRUTH: Jesus rose from the dead. This fulfilled God's promise for salvation for all.

MEMORY VERSE: "Then went in also that other disciple, which came first to the sepulchre, and he saw, and believed" (John 20:8).

LESSON AIM: By the end of the lesson, we will: JUDGE the events of the Resurrection and the power of God to overcome death; CELEBRATE the saving power of new life offered in the Resurrection; and PROCLAIM to others the power of God's love and the Good News of the Resurrection.

TEACHER PREPARATION

MATERIALS NEEDED: Quarterly Commentary/Teacher Manual, Adult Quarterly, Adult resources—charts, worksheets, and other teaching tools, paper, pens, pencils, Bibles (several different versions)

OTHER MATERIALS NEEDED / TEACHER'S NOTES:

_____

_____

LESSON OVERVIEW

LIFE NEED FOR TODAY'S LESSON
Some life events are beyond the realm of our imagination.

BIBLE APPLICATION
The Resurrection of Jesus offers hope and trust in the promises of God.

BIBLE LEARNING
The disciples were confounded when they entered the empty tomb.

STUDENTS' RESPONSES
Believers can rejoice and share the Good News that Christ has risen from the dead!

LESSON SCRIPTURE

JOHN 20:1–10, KJV

1 The first day of the week cometh Mary Magdalene early, when it was yet dark, unto the sepulchre, and seeth the stone taken away from the sepulchre.

2 Then she runneth, and cometh to Simon Peter, and to the other disciple, whom Jesus loved, and saith unto them, They have taken away the LORD out of the sepulchre, and we know not where they have laid him.

JOHN 20:1–10, AMP

1 Now on the first day of the week Mary Magdalene came to the tomb early, while it was still dark, and saw the stone [already] removed from the [groove across the entrance of the] tomb.

2 So she ran and went to Simon Peter and to the other disciple (John), whom Jesus loved (esteemed), and said to them, "They have

3 Peter therefore went forth, and that other disciple, and came to the sepulchre.

4 So they ran both together: and the other disciple did outrun Peter, and came first to the sepulchre.

5 And he stooping down, and looking in, saw the linen clothes lying; yet went he not in.

6 Then cometh Simon Peter following him, and went into the sepulchre, and seeth the linen clothes lie,

7 And the napkin, that was about his head, not lying with the linen clothes, but wrapped together in a place by itself.

8 Then went in also that other disciple, which came first to the sepulchre, and he saw, and believed.

9 For as yet they knew not the scripture, that he must rise again from the dead.

10 Then the disciples went away again unto their own home.

taken away the Lord out of the tomb, and we do not know where they have laid Him!"

3 So Peter and the other disciple left, and they were going to the tomb.

4 And the two were running together, but the other disciple outran Peter and arrived at the tomb first.

5 Stooping down and looking in, he saw the linen wrappings [neatly] lying there; but he did not go in.

6 Then Simon Peter came up, following him, and went into the tomb and saw the linen wrappings [neatly] lying there;

7 and the [burial] face-cloth which had been on Jesus' head, not lying with the [other] linen wrappings, but rolled up in a place by itself.

8 So the other disciple, who had reached the tomb first, went in too; and he saw [the wrappings and the face-cloth] and believed [without any doubt that Jesus had risen from the dead].

9 For as yet they did not understand the Scripture, that He must rise from the dead.

10 Then the disciples went back again to their own homes.

LIGHT ON THE WORD

Mary Magdalene. Also called Mary of Mandala, she traveled with Jesus as one of His followers. She witnessed both Jesus' crucifixion and resurrection (**Matthew 27:56, 28:1; Mark 15:20, 16:1; John 19:25, 20:1**). Jesus cast seven demons out of her (**Luke 8:2; Mark 16:9**).

Peter. Peter was one of the disciples in Jesus' inner circle. He is perhaps the most outspoken

of the Twelve. He often boldly asserts his devotion to Christ with an abundance of zeal, Jesus will then correct him, and Peter will then just as boldly accept his Master's correction. For example, when Jesus washes His disciples' feet before the Last Supper, Peter objects to Christ taking so lowly a role. But when Jesus explains the meaning of the gesture, Peter offers to let Jesus wash all of him. In today's Lesson Scripture, we see Peter running to Jesus' tomb and boldly entering it, in hopes of fully understanding this unique event.

TEACHING THE BIBLE LESSON

LIFE NEED FOR TODAY'S LESSON

AIM: Students will agree that some life events may be beyond the realm of our imagination.

INTRODUCTION

The Best Report

After Mary's report to the disciples, John (the author of the book, humbly referring to himself as the other disciple) and Peter went to observe the empty tomb for themselves. They immediately "went forth" (v. 3). They had to see it with their own eyes. John outran Peter and made it to the tomb first. Their love and honor for their Rabbi caused them to run to discover the empty tomb. Soon they would discover that He was more than just a Rabbi; He was the resurrected Son of God.

BIBLE LEARNING

AIM: Students will evaluate the disciples amazement when they entered the empty tomb.

I. THE DECLARATION (John 20:1–4)

Faithful to Jesus, even after His death, John presents Mary Magdalene rising early and going to Jesus' tomb to anoint His body with precious ointments and spices, as was the custom of the day. Both Mark (15:47) and Luke (23:55) record that Mary and the other women had watched Jesus' burial and the sealing of the tomb. So, while we are not surprised that Mary could locate the tomb in the dark of the early morning hours, it is not clear how Mary expected to remove the huge stone placed at the entrance of the tomb. Perhaps she expected the Roman soldiers who were guarding the tomb to roll the stone for her. In any case, when Mary

Magdalene arrives at the burial site, the giant stone has already been removed.

1 The first day of the week cometh Mary Magdalene early, when it was yet dark, unto the sepulchre, and seeth the stone taken away from the sepulchre.

Mary Magdalene's association with Jesus most likely began when He cured her and other women of demon possession (**Luke 8:2**) early in His ministry. She is not mentioned before then. Her name indicates that she either came from or was a resident of the town of Magdala, situated on the western shore of the Sea of Galilee. She is often identified as a prostitute, especially by American Catholics and in many western European countries where homes for unwed mothers are routinely named "Magdalene" homes. This notion is, however, unfounded and bears no scriptural evidence to support it.

2 Then she runneth, and cometh to Simon Peter, and to the other disciple, whom Jesus loved, and saith unto them, They have taken away the LORD out of the sepulchre, and we know not where they have laid him. 3 Peter therefore went forth, and that other disciple, and came to the sepulchre.

At this point in John's narrative, Mary Magdalene runs to tell Peter and the other disciples that Jesus' body is missing. John does not tell us that Mary has yet to even enter the tomb. In John's account, Mary does not enter the tomb until after the men leave (**20:11–12**). Matthew's account tells of a "great earthquake" (Matthew 28:2) and has the angel rolling back the stone, making the announcement to the women, and inviting them inside the tomb to see for themselves (**28:2–6**). The narratives of both Mark and Luke indicate that the women enter the tomb and encounter an angel who announces that Jesus has risen. John's difference does not imply any disharmony in the Gospels, but it suggests a differing view of the more significant points to the account. We must also remember that of the four Gospel writers, only John was actually an eyewitness to this event (Matthew was among the Twelve, but he is not mentioned as going to the tomb). He possibly prioritized the notification of Peter and himself and simply chose to leave out details that occurred before his arrival at the grave site. This is logical in light of the fact that his Gospel is written after the other three; he knows they have already included those details.

4 So they ran both together: and the other disciple did outrun Peter, and came first to the sepulchre.

Only John's Gospel records that the other disciple outran Peter to the sepulcher. Again, this does not indicate disharmony, but rather the privileging of certain details by the writer, who also happens to be a central character. John is relating the sense of excitement he surely must have felt at that time. He was speculated to be younger than Peter, and certainly would have been able to outdistance the older man as they raced to the tomb.

II. THE CONFRONTATION (vv. 5–10)

Peter and John had heard Jesus talk about His resurrection, but they still did not understand the connection between His teaching, the Old Testament prophecies, and this phenomenal event (e.g., **Psalm 16:10**). The confused men returned to either their meeting place or their homes. They didn't have all the answers, but they definitely understood something unique and wonderful had taken place.

5 And he stooping down, and looking in, saw the linen clothes lying; yet went he not in.

Although John outruns Peter and arrives at the sepulcher first, he does not go in. Some have argued that perhaps John was afraid to enter the tomb alone. A more likely reason is that he simply defers to the older apostle. It is probably out of respect for Peter's position as leader of the apostles that John allows him to enter the tomb first.

6 Then cometh Simon Peter following him, and went into the sepulchre, and seeth the linen clothes lie, 7 And the napkin, that was about his head, not lying with the linen clothes, but wrapped together in a place by itself.

John seems to emphasize the supernatural implications concerning the fact that the burial linens were intentionally folded and put aside. Jesus was no longer dead. He had conquered death by His resurrection! He took off the burial clothing. Only the Son of the One and Only God could defeat death and seal the victory over sin and death, thereby securing our own salvation.

8 Then went in also the other disciple, which came first to the sepulchre, and he saw, and believed.

John's Gospel alone records that upon seeing the empty grave and the discarded grave clothes, John "believed." This is understandable since the writer, better than anyone else, would know this to be a fact. It is interesting to note that in Luke's account, Peter, upon seeing the discarded burial clothing, "wonder[ed] in himself at that which was come to pass" (**Luke 24:12**).

While Peter, the elder statesman, puzzles over the occurrence, the younger disciple believes. John uses the Greek word *pisteuo* (**peas-TEW-oh**), which means to have faith or conviction.

9 For as yet they knew not the scripture, that he must rise again from the dead. 10 Then the disciples went away again unto their own home.

Verse 9 offers a fuller explanation for Peter's puzzlement and John's subsequent belief by emphasizing how unexpected these events were to both of them. Although they were closer to Jesus than any of the other apostles, these events still take these men by surprise. It had only been days earlier when Jesus had spoken to His disciples, telling them "a little while, and ye shall not see me: and again, a little while and ye shall see me" (John 16:19). The Apostles were unsure of what Jesus meant. That He would defy the laws of nature and be physically raised from the dead had not occurred to them. Therefore, in verse 10, they simply went to their homes again, pondering all that they had seen and heard.

SEARCH THE SCRIPTURES

QUESTION 1

Mary Magdalene was a follower of Christ. Based on how John presents her in the Scripture, what qualities does she possess that allowed her to remain faithful to Christ?

Mary Magdalene is consistent, determined, and faithful to Christ. Most of all, she loves the Lord. (Answers will vary.)

QUESTION 2

Mary Magdalene, John, and Peter were perplexed by Jesus' Resurrection. Explain how you responded in the past to news about an event in your life that was unexpected or alarming.

(Answers will vary.)

LIGHT ON THE WORD

Confused and Perplexed!

The men witnessed the napkin from around Christ's head laid in a place by itself and the other wrappings in another place. A body could not have gotten out of wrappings from head to toe without being cut or unwound. But the wrappings were not cut or in disarray, but neatly folded. God made sure to highlight these details to offset any lies about a stolen body. If a thief stole a dead body, it's highly unlikely robbers would take the time to unwrap it and fold the wrapping clothes in different places.

BIBLE APPLICATION

AIM: Students will proclaim that the Resurrection of Jesus offers hope and trust in the promises of God.

God's power demonstrated by Christ being raised from the dead should give all believers the hope and assurance that this will also occur at the time of their death. Jesus' Resurrection is a showcase of what lies in store for those who have faith in Christ. How does knowing we will partake both in Christ's death and His Resurrection (Philippians 3:10–11) affect our daily lives as believers?

STUDENTS' RESPONSES

AIM: Students will appreciate that they can rejoice and share the Good News that Christ has risen from the dead!

It's early; Resurrection Sunday has just begun. Put aside some time and pray about the true meaning of Jesus' Resurrection. Ask God to bring to mind anyone—your family, church, group of friends or co-workers—who does not understand salvation in connection to Jesus and the empty tomb. Ask God to give you an opportunity to speak with them about this lesson.

PRAYER

Dear God, we give You all praises and glory for sacrificing Your life for us. Thank You for forgiving us of our sins and allowing us to experience the depth of Your love in many ways. Jesus, You are the joy that is the center of all that we do and need to do in our lives and for all of creation. We bless You and love You! In Your Name, we pray. Amen.

DIG A LITTLE DEEPER

This section provides an additional research article to further your study of the lesson:

The Resurrection of Christ has been scrutinized for over 2,000 years, and the discussion continues today. Skeptics doubt its veracity and historicity. However, the Resurrection is a crucial element of biblical theology and a foundational historical event that must be defended. In this article, Dr. William Lane Craig provides a sound defense affirming that Jesus Christ did, indeed, rise from the dead.

http://www.reasonablefaith.org/the-resurrection-of-jesus

HOW TO SAY IT

Seeth   **SEE**-ith.

Sepulchre   se-**PUL**-ker.

PREPARE FOR NEXT SUNDAY

Read **Romans 5:6–11, 8:31–39** and "God's Reconciling Love."

DAILY HOME BIBLE READINGS

MONDAY
Jesus' Side is Pierced
(John 19:31–37)

TUESDAY
The Spirit, Water, and Blood Agree
(1 John 5:6–12)

WEDNESDAY
The Lord Breaks No Bones
(Psalm 34:15–20)

THURSDAY
Soldiers Cast Lots for Jesus' Clothing
(John 19:23–25a)

FRIDAY
Jesus' Final Words to His Mother
(John 19:26–27)

SATURDAY
The Women and Peter Were Amazed
(Luke 24:1–12)

SUNDAY
God's Love as Victory Over Death
(John 20:1–10)

COMMENTS / NOTES:

_____

_____

_____

_____

_____

_____

_____

_____

_____

_____

_____

_____

_____

_____

_____

_____

_____

_____

_____

_____

_____

_____

_____

_____

_____

GOD'S RECONCILING LOVE

BIBLE BASIS: ROMANS 5:6–11, 8:31–39

BIBLE TRUTH: Nothing can separate God's love in Christ Jesus from His people.

MEMORY VERSE: "Nor height, nor depth, nor any other creature, shall be able to separate us from the love of God, which is in Christ Jesus our Lord" (Romans 8:39).

LESSON AIM: By the end of the lesson, we will: EVALUATE the meaning of justification by faith; EXPERIENCE the joy of God's reconciling love; and LIVE OUT God's reconciling love in the world.

TEACHER PREPARATION

MATERIALS NEEDED: Quarterly Commentary/Teacher Manual, Adult Quarterly, Adult resources—charts, worksheets, and other teaching tools, paper, pens, pencils, Bibles (several different versions)

OTHER MATERIALS NEEDED / TEACHER'S NOTES:

_____

_____

LESSON OVERVIEW

LIFE NEED FOR TODAY'S LESSON
Hardship, distress, and separations of all kinds are common life experiences.

BIBLE LEARNING
Paul is convinced that nothing in all of creation can separate us from the love of God in Jesus Christ.

BIBLE APPLICATION
God's love conveys His sovereignty over all of His creation.

STUDENTS' RESPONSES
Students are able to share the love of God with others through words and actions.

LESSON SCRIPTURE

ROMANS 5:6–11, 8:31–39, KJV

5:6 For when we were yet without strength, in due time Christ died for the ungodly.

7 For scarcely for a righteous man will one die: yet adventure for a good man some would even dare to die?

8 But God commendeth his love toward us,

ROMANS 5:6–11, 8:31–39, AMP

5:6 While we were still helpless [powerless to provide for our salvation], at the right time Christ died [as a substitute] for the ungodly.

7 Now it is an extraordinary thing for one to willingly give his life even for an upright man, though perhaps for a good man [one

in that, while we were yet sinners, Christ died for us.

9 Much more then, being now justified by his blood, we shall be saved from wrath through him.

10 For if, when we were enemies, we were reconciled to God by the death of his Son, much more, being reconciled, we shall be saved by his life.

11 And not only so, but we also joy in God through our Lord Jesus Christ, by whom we have now received the atonement.

8:31 What shall we then say to these things? If God be for us, who can be against us?

32 He that spared not his own Son, but delivered him up for us all, how shall he not with him also freely give us all things?

33 Who shall lay anything to the charge of God's elect? It is God that justifieth.

34 Who is he that condemneth? It is Christ that died, yea rather, that is risen again, who is even at the right hand of God, who also maketh intercession for us.

35 Who shall separate us from the love of Christ? shall tribulation, or distress, or persecution, or famine, or nakedness, or peril, or sword?

36 As it is written, For thy sake we are killed all the day long; we are accounted as sheep for the slaughter.

37 Nay, in all these things we are more than conquerors through him that loved us.

38 For I am persuaded, that neither death, nor life, nor angels, nor principalities, nor powers, nor things present, nor things to come,

39 Nor height, nor depth, nor any other

who is noble and selfless and worthy] someone might even dare to die.

8 But God clearly shows and proves His own love for us, by the fact that while we were still sinners, Christ died for us.

9 Therefore, since we have now been justified [declared free of the guilt of sin] by His blood, [how much more certain is it that] we will be saved from the wrath of God through Him.

10 For if while we were enemies we were reconciled to God through the death of His Son, it is much more certain, having been reconciled, that we will be saved [from the consequences of sin] by His life [that is, we will be saved because Christ lives today].

11 Not only that, but we also rejoice in God [rejoicing in His love and perfection] through our Lord Jesus Christ, through whom we have now received and enjoy our reconciliation [with God].

8:31 What then shall we say to all these things? If God is for us, who can be [successful] against us?

32 He who did not spare [even] His own Son, but gave Him up for us all, how will He not also, along with Him, graciously give us all things?

33 Who will bring any charge against God's elect (His chosen ones)? It is God who justifies us [declaring us blameless and putting us in a right relationship with Himself].

34 Who is the one who condemns us? Christ Jesus is the One who died [to pay our penalty], and more than that, who was raised [from the dead], and who is at the right hand of God interceding [with the Father] for us.

35 Who shall ever separate us from the love of Christ? Will tribulation, or distress, or persecution, or famine, or nakedness, or danger, or sword?

creature, shall be able to separate us from the love of God, which is in Christ Jesus our Lord.

36 Just as it is written and forever remains written, "For Your sake we are put to death all day long; we are regarded as sheep for the slaughter."

37 Yet in all these things we are more than conquerors and gain an overwhelming victory through Him who loved us [so much that He died for us].

38 For I am convinced [and continue to be convinced—beyond any doubt] that neither death, nor life, nor angels, nor principalities, nor things present and threatening, nor things to come, nor powers,

39 nor height, nor depth, nor any other created thing, will be able to separate us from the [unlimited] love of God, which is in Christ Jesus our Lord.

LIGHT ON THE WORD

Love (**Romans 5:8**) *agape* (Gk.)—Deep love and affection, as for a family member or friend; divine love that God proffers.

Justified (**v. 9**) *dikaioo* (Gk)—To endorse legally, to show what is right; conformed to a proper standard or upright.

Reconcile (**v. 10**) *katallasso* (Gk)—Two parties changing to the same position; the redemptive sense of a sinner's relationship with the Lord being repaired.

TEACHING THE BIBLE LESSON

LIFE NEED FOR TODAY'S LESSON

AIM: Students will agree that hardship, distress, and separations of all kinds are common life experiences.

INTRODUCTION

Reconciliation

Through Christ, God reconciled the world to Himself. Once a person trusts Christ for salvation, their sin is no longer counted against them; they are in right relationship with God. Because of Christ's death and resurrection, we experience peace with God (**Colossians 1:20–21**).

Reconciliation with God is needed because unbelievers' relationship with Him is broken through sin. God is never at fault. Unlike human relationships, where both parties must admit their sin before reconciliation can take place, God never has to admit incorrect behavior, because He is holy, perfect, and blameless. The sinner must admit their sin before God, confessing their inability to save themselves or fix this relationship on their own.

BIBLE LEARNING

AIM: Students will agree that nothing in all of creation can separate us from the love of God in Jesus Christ.

I. NOTHING GREATER
(Romans 5:6–11)

Paul vividly describes the love of God. The holy, almighty God generously and freely gives His love to those who are ungodly, undeserving, unlovable, and unlovely. When God decided the time was right, He sent Jesus to die on behalf of the people just described—which is everyone (**Galatians 4:4**).

6 For when we were yet without strength, in due time Christ died for the ungodly.

At the appointed time, Christ offered Himself as our eternal sacrifice "when we were yet without strength"—that is, when we were powerless to save ourselves and thus ready to die. Christ's death reveals three properties of God's love. First, He did this for the "ungodly," those whose character and sinful nature are repulsive in God's eyes. Second, He did this when they were "without strength"—nothing stood between humanity and damnation but divine compassion. Third, He did this "in due time," when it was most appropriate that it should take place. Throughout, Paul uses the language of "we," indicating that he considers himself also to have been without strength, ungodly and a sinner (**v. 8**).

7 For scarcely for a righteous man will one die: yet peradventure for a good man some would even dare to die. 8 But God commendeth his love toward us, in that, while we were yet sinners, Christ died for us.

The Apostle Paul now proceeds to illustrate God's compassion. Few people would be willing to sacrifice their lives for a "righteous man" of exceptional character. A few more might be willing to die for a person who, besides being exceptional, was also distinguished as a benefactor to society. But God, in glorious contrast to what people might do for each other, displayed His love "while we were yet sinners"—that is, in a state of absolute rebellion. Although most people would not be willing to die to save a wicked or evil person, Christ died for us.

9 Much more then, being now justified by his blood, we shall be saved from wrath through him. 10 For if, when we were enemies, we were reconciled to God by the death of his Son, much more, being reconciled, we shall be saved by his life.

Having been "justified by his blood," we shall be saved from wrath through Christ's sacrifice. Christ's death restored our relationship with God while we were in open rebellion against Him. Since we are now reconciled, "we shall be saved by his life." If Christ's sacrifice was offered for people incapable of the least appreciation for God's love or Christ's labors on their behalf, how much more will He do for those who receive salvation? To be "saved from wrath through him" refers to the entire work of salvation and justification by faith. Those who reject Jesus as Savior will stand before the Great White Throne Judgment (**Revelation 20:11–15**) to account for their sin. The wrath of God will be revealed to all who ignored the Gospel of Jesus. Believers will not be in this judgment. The Apostle Jude best described Christ's continuing work of salvation when he said that Christ "is able to keep you from falling, and to present you faultless before the presence of his glory with exceeding joy" (from **Jude 24**).

11 And not only so, but we also joy in God through our Lord Jesus Christ, by whom we have now received the atonement.

"And not only so" refers to the blessing Paul

mentioned previously. We not only find joy in our newfound peace, standing, and salvation, but we rejoice in God Himself. We find joy in our God for what He has done and who He is. Our joy comes from our union with Christ, who brought about our atonement.

"Atonement" (Gk. *katallage*, **kah-tah-lah-GAY**) is the noun form of the verb for "reconcile" in **verse 10**. It indicates a shift from a negative relationship to a positive one, or a broken relationship to a healthy one. Paul here focuses on the restored relationship provided by Christ's atoning death. This restored relationship with God brings about joy, or more literally boasting (see **v. 2**, "rejoice").

II. NOTHING SEPARATING (8:31–39)

In the first part of Romans, Paul records all that God has accomplished for our salvation through faith in Jesus Christ. After Paul discusses foundational doctrinal issues, in **Romans 8:31**, he asks: "If God be for us, who can be against us?" Most people assume that God is in their corner whether they are Christians or not. But one little word should instill some doubt—if. Just because a man thinks God is with him does not make it so. God is only for an individual if that person is reconciled to God through Jesus Christ.

8:31 What shall we then say to these things? If God be for us, who can be against us? 32 He that spared not his own Son, but delivered him up for us all, how shall he not with him also freely give us all things?

As a result of this knowledge of divine sovereignty, Paul exults in the comfort that God is for His people. He asks and answers his own question: "If God be for us, who can be against us?" The concept of God being for His people runs throughout the Old Testament (**Psalm 56:9, 105:12–15; Isaiah 54:17**). What makes Paul's words unique is that now through the lens of Christ, we even see the hard times as under God's control. We face trials and opposition to conform us to Christ's image. God is for us in all things good or bad. With that in mind, Paul says no one is a formidable foe.

This understanding of God's gracious act in giving Jesus "for us all" is the grounds by which Paul asks rhetorically, "How shall he not with him also freely give us all things?" The two words "freely give" (Gk. *charizomai*, **khah-REED-zoh-meye**) are actually one word in Greek, meaning to give as a sign of one's goodwill toward another. Paul emphatically states that when we see all that God has accomplished for us in Christ, which Paul details in the first 7 chapters of Romans, we can be assured that God has nothing but good will toward those who believe.

33 Who shall lay anything to the charge of God's elect? It is God that justifieth. 34 Who is he that condemneth? It is Christ that died, yea rather, that is risen again, who is even at the right hand of God, who also maketh intercession for us.

The argument continues with Paul's rhetorical question. He proceeds with legal terminology and asks, "Who shall lay anything to the charge of God's elect?" The phrase "lay anything to the charge" (Gk. *egkaleo*, **eng-kah-LEH-oh**) means to accuse or file a formal legal complaint against someone. For Paul, the answer is obviously "no one"; God "justifieth" (Gk. *dikaioo*, **dee-kie-OH-oh**), or makes or pronounces a believer righteous—in right standing and right relationship with God. There is no one to condemn (Gk. *katakrino*, **kah-tah-KREE-no**) the believer. The word "condemn" means to pronounce guilt and punishment for a crime in a legal context. Paul's answer to the question, "Who is he that condemneth?" has the implied answer, "No one," because of the work of Christ. This work is not limited to Jesus' death and Resurrection, but it also continues with Jesus sitting at the right hand of God, making intercession (Gk. *entugchano*, **en-toon-KHAH-noh**) for us.

35 Who shall separate us from the love of Christ? shall tribulation, or distress, or persecution, or famine, or nakedness, or peril, or sword? 36 As it is written, For thy sake we are killed all the day long; we are accounted as sheep for the slaughter. 37 Nay, in all these things we are more than conquerors through him that loved us.

Next Paul raises the question of possible separation from Christ's love. The different earthly woes of God's people are listed. Tribulation (Gk. *thlipsis*, **THLEEP-seese**) is the first problem listed; this word comes from *thlibo*, which means to press or squash and metaphorically has the sense of oppression or affliction. The next is distress (Gk. *stenochoria*, **ste-no-kho-REE-ah**), which has the sense of being in constricted conditions, where it seems the world is falling down on someone. The third problem is persecution (Gk. *diogmos*, **dee-og-MOCE**), the systematic hunting down of believers for torture and execution in an effort to destroy the religion. This was a real threat for Paul, who faced much persecution in his lifetime.

Famine is the shortage of food, resulting in acute hunger and death. The word for nakedness is *gumnotes* (Gk. **goom-NO-tes**), which in this context means insufficient clothing, not total exposure. Peril (Gk. *kindunos*, **KEEN-doo-noce**) is danger from any circumstance; Paul used this word in reference to his being in danger as an apostle (**2 Corinthians 11:26**). The believer also faces the reality of the sword (Gk. *machaira*, **MAH-kheye-rah**), which is the word for the small sword as opposed to a large one. This designation causes some to question whether Paul intends the official "sword" of the state. However, this word is also used in **Romans 13:4** in connection with the state's authority to punish. Here, Paul may have described official state execution. The general sense is that the believers face death at any moment.

Paul then quotes from **Psalm 44:22**. This psalm was often quoted by rabbis in the second century AD with martyrdom in view, and Paul may have had this in view here. In contrast to this dismal fate, **verse 37** has triumph and hope. Although the Christian's life is similar to a sheep prepared for the slaughter, Paul says this is not the whole story. Believers are more than conquerors through Christ. The KJV translates the Greek as "we are more than conquerors" (*hypernikao*, **hoo-per-nee-KAH-oh**). The Greek term is a single word, with the basic verb for conquering with an intensifying prefix that tells the Church this will be no normal victory—it will be the ultimate victory. To think of ultimate victory as persecuted subjects only magnifies God's power to reward the faithful.

38 For I am persuaded, that neither death, nor life, nor angels, nor principalities, nor powers, nor things present, nor things to come, 39 Nor height, nor depth, nor any other creature, shall be able to separate us from the love of God, which is in Christ Jesus our Lord.

Paul is totally convinced. Nothing physical, social, or spiritual can separate us from the love of God in Christ Jesus. Paul speaks of everything in the three categories that would have the capacity to separate us from God's love and declares that nothing can separate us. Paul gets specific and notes the opposites: life nor death, heights nor depths, things present nor things to come with all of their abilities to frighten, paralyze, or make us turn away. None of these can separate us from the love of God. What hope and comfort for us!

SEARCH THE SCRIPTURES

QUESTION 1

How do you celebrate the freedom that living a life in the Spirit brings as a result of justification and reconciliation?

There is no fear. God lets me know that I am forgiven and in right standing with Him. I have hope in the Lord through Christ. (Answers will vary.)

QUESTION 2

Why is it important for us to know that nothing can separate us from God's love in Jesus?

We are reminded that God is in control and His love is more powerful than any other force or person. By the same token, we should have so much love for God that we do not let anything stop us from serving Him.

LIGHT ON THE WORD

God's Best for Our Sin

God did not spare (Gk. *pheidomai*, **FAY-doh-meye**) His own Son when it came to our good. The word *spare* means to refrain or keep from harm. The sense in this verse is that God did not hold Him back as a treasure. God delivered (Gk. *paradidomi*, **pah-rah-DEE-doh-me**) Him, which means to hand over or give up. The word is often used for betrayal, as in Judas' betrayal of Jesus (**Mark 14:10**), as well as for the Sanhedrin turning Jesus over to Pilate (**Mark 15:1**), and Pilate giving Jesus to the crowd in Jerusalem and to the Roman soldiers for crucifixion (**Luke 23:25**). In this sense, Paul is showing that God was sovereignly guiding the entirety of events surrounding Jesus' death on the Cross. God the Father had ordained that Jesus Christ, God the Son, would be crucified for our sin before the creation of the world (**Revelation 13:8**).

BIBLE APPLICATION

AIM: Students will decide that God's love conveys God's sovereignty over creation.

All over the Internet are articles about how to have a better relationship with your spouse, children, friends, and co-workers. People desire to improve their interpersonal relationships. However, the foundation of that desire is easy to ignore; a good relationship with others starts with God. As His examples and spokespeople to the world, Christians must ensure that their personal walk with God is loving and intimate. Then, with that overflow of love, we can teach the world how to love each other and improve all relationships.

STUDENTS' RESPONSES

AIM: Students will express ways that believers can share the love of God with others through words and actions.

Find a quiet place for a little personal retreat, just you and the Lord. Spend some time there to review the Scripture and insights in this lesson: God loves me! God proved His love for me by sending Jesus to die for my sin. God wants a close relationship with me; where am I? Do I need to confess? (Admit to God what He's showing you.)

PRAYER

Dear Lord, it is with glad hearts and reassuring minds that we thank You, God. We praise You, Jesus, for loving us more than we love ourselves. In the Name of Jesus, we pray. Amen.

DIG A LITTLE DEEPER

This section provides an additional research article to further your study of the lesson:

What is the status of Israel in light of the Gospel? Are they still considered God's chosen people? This article in the *Master's Seminary Journal* unpacks biblical passages surrounding Israel's status. By focusing on three views, Pastor Matt Waymeyer examines the variations in the polemic against the nation of Israel.

http://www.tms.edu/m/tmsj16c.pdf

HOW TO SAY IT

Commendeth   ku-**MEN**-dith.

Peradventure   per-ad-**VEN**-chur.

PREPARE FOR NEXT SUNDAY

Read **John 10:1–15** and "God's Preserving Love."

DAILY HOME BIBLE READINGS

MONDAY
Mutually Sharing the Gospel of Christ
(Romans 1:1–15)

TUESDAY
Fruit of Justification by Faith
(Romans 5:1–5)

WEDNESDAY
Grace Abounded through Jesus Christ
(Romans 5:18–21)

THURSDAY
Believers' Present Suffering and Future Glory
(Romans 8:18–25)

FRIDAY
God's Will Shapes Human Direction
(Romans 8:26–30)

SATURDAY
Paul's Faithful Ministry Despite Suffering
(2 Corinthians 11:21b–27)

SUNDAY
God's Reconciling Love
(Romans 5:6–11, 8:31–39)

COMMENTS / NOTES:

GOD'S PRESERVING LOVE

BIBLE BASIS: JOHN 10:1–15

BIBLE TRUTH: Jesus, who is our Good Shepherd, cares for us, and gave the ultimate sacrifice, His life.

MEMORY VERSES: "I am the good shepherd, and know my sheep, and am known of mine. As the Father knoweth me, even so know I the Father: and I lay down my life for the sheep" (John 10:14–15).

LESSON AIM: By the end of this lesson, we will: EVALUATE the understanding of Jesus as the Good Shepherd who protects His sheep; AFFIRM the love of God expressed in the life and ministry of Jesus, the Good Shepherd; and RESPOND to God's persevering love by loving others.

TEACHER PREPARATION

MATERIALS NEEDED: Quarterly Commentary/Teacher Manual, Adult Quarterly, Adult resources—charts, worksheets, and other teaching tools, paper, pens, pencils, Bibles (several different versions)

OTHER MATERIALS NEEDED / TEACHER'S NOTES:

_____

_____

LESSON OVERVIEW

LIFE NEED FOR TODAY'S LESSON
Some people are looking for a leader who will solve all the problems of the world.

BIBLE LEARNING
Jesus, as the Good Shepherd, is the leader who shows and imparts God's love to those who follow Him.

BIBLE APPLICATION
We can look to Jesus as the example of a great leader because He shows love to all who follow Him.

STUDENTS' RESPONSES
Christians can depend on Jesus to shepherd them in God's way.

LESSON SCRIPTURE

JOHN 10:1–15, KJV

1 Verily, verily, I say unto you, He that entereth not by the door into the sheepfold, but climbeth up some other way, the same is a thief and a robber.

2 But he that entereth in by the door is the

JOHN 10:1–15, AMP

1 "I assure you and most solemnly say to you, he who does not enter by the door into the sheepfold, but climbs up from some other place [on the stone wall], that one is a thief and a robber.

shepherd of the sheep.

3 To him the porter openeth; and the sheep hear his voice: and he calleth his own sheep by name, and leadeth them out.

4 And when he putteth forth his own sheep, he goeth before them, and the sheep follow him: for they know his voice.

5 And a stranger will they not follow, but will flee from him: for they know not the voice of strangers.

6 This parable spake Jesus unto them: but they understood not what things they were which he spake unto them.

7 Then said Jesus unto them again, Verily, verily, I say unto you, I am the door of the sheep.

8 All that ever came before me are thieves and robbers: but the sheep did not hear them.

9 I am the door: by me if any man enter in, he shall be saved, and shall go in and out, and find pasture.

10 The thief cometh not, but for to steal, and to kill, and to destroy: I am come that they might have life, and that they might have it more abundantly.

11 I am the good shepherd: the good shepherd giveth his life for the sheep.

12 But he that is an hireling, and not the shepherd, whose own the sheep are not, seeth the wolf coming, and leaveth the sheep, and fleeth: and the wolf catcheth them, and scattereth the sheep.

13 The hireling fleeth, because he is an hireling, and careth not for the sheep.

14 I am the good shepherd, and know my sheep, and am known of mine.

2 But he who enters by the door is the shepherd of the sheep [the protector and provider].

3 The doorkeeper opens [the gate] for this man, and the sheep hear his voice and pay attention to it. And [knowing that they listen] he calls his own sheep by name and leads them out [to pasture].

4 When he has brought all his own sheep outside, he walks on ahead of them, and the sheep follow him because they know his voice and recognize his call.

5 They will never follow a stranger, but will run away from him, because they do not know the voice of strangers."

6 Jesus used this figure of speech with them, but they did not understand what He was talking about.

7 So Jesus said again, "I assure you and most solemnly say to you, I am the Door for the sheep [leading to life].

8 All who came before Me [as false messiahs and self-appointed leaders] are thieves and robbers, but the [true] sheep did not hear them.

9 I am the Door; anyone who enters through Me will be saved [and will live forever], and will go in and out [freely], and find pasture (spiritual security).

10 The thief comes only in order to steal and kill and destroy. I came that they may have and enjoy life, and have it in abundance [to the full, till it overflows].

11 I am the Good Shepherd. The Good Shepherd lays down His [own] life for the sheep.

12 But the hired man [who merely serves for wages], who is neither the shepherd nor the

15 As the Father knoweth me, even so know I the Father: and I lay down my life for the sheep.

owner of the sheep, when he sees the wolf coming, deserts the flock and runs away; and the wolf snatches the sheep and scatters them.

13 The man runs because he is a hired hand [who serves only for wages] and is not concerned about the [safety of the] sheep.

14 I am the Good Shepherd, and I know [without any doubt those who are] My own and My own know Me [and have a deep, personal relationship with Me]—

15 even as the Father knows Me and I know the Father—and I lay down My [very own] life [sacrificing it] for the benefit of the sheep.

LIGHT ON THE WORD

Pharisees. The Pharisees were religious leaders who practiced the strict observation of the Mosaic Torah. Their power provided them great influence among the people, especially in the synagogues. They thought it was very important to follow God's will. The Pharisees believed, like Jesus, in the resurrection of the dead. However, they did not believe Jesus was the Messiah because He constantly violated their accepted interpretations of the Law of Moses.

TEACHING THE BIBLE LESSON

LIFE NEED FOR TODAY'S LESSON

AIM: Students will agree that some people are looking for a leader who will solve all the problems of the world.

INTRODUCTION

Jesus Causes Conflict

The Pharisees had established 39 categories of actions forbidden on the Sabbath, based on their own interpretation of God's Law and on Jewish custom. No work was permitted on the Sabbath. They frequently accused Jesus of breaking the Sabbath. Jesus never permitted their interpretation of the Law to hinder Him from His ministry on earth.

Jesus' ministry caused conflict with the religious leaders, especially the Pharisees. John records two times Jesus healed on the Sabbath (**5:1–17, 9:1–7**). On both occasions the Pharisees accused Him of violating the Law. In John 9, the blind man whom Jesus healed was taken to the Pharisees who questioned him. He told them Jesus was "a prophet" (**9:17**). The religious leaders were divided in their understanding of who Jesus was. However, it had already been predicted that the Messiah would give sight to the blind (**Isaiah 29:18, 35:5, 42:7**). Jesus had proven once again that He was the Messiah.

BIBLE LEARNING

AIM: Students will agree that Jesus, as the Good Shepherd, is the leader who shows and imparts God's love to those who follow.

I. THE GATEKEEPER (John 10:1–10)

In this discourse, Jesus employs the familiar analogy of a shepherd and his flock to teach an important lesson about Himself and His relationship with believers. Applying the imagery of the shepherd to kings and priests was a common practice in Middle Eastern culture. In the Old Testament, the shepherd was often used to symbolize a royal caretaker of God's people (cf. **2 Samuel 5:2; Isaiah 44:28**). God Himself was referred to as the "Shepherd of Israel" (see **Genesis 49:24; Psalm 23:1–4, 80:1**). The "sheepfold" (Gk. *probaton*, **PRO-bah-tone**) or herd of sheep were kept in a walled enclosure with one entrance. Usually, a sheepfold would hold several flocks. The "shepherd" (Gk. *poimen*, **poy-MANE**), or gatekeeper, set up sleeping posts near the entrance to ward off wild beasts, thieves, and other intruders.

1 Verily, verily, I say unto you, He that entereth not by the door into the sheepfold, but climbeth up some other way, the same is a thief and a robber.

The parable depicts the shepherd as the only one allowed access to the flock. The shepherd is in stark contrast to a "thief" (Gk. *kleptes*, **KLEP-tace**) or a "robber" (Gk. *lestes*, **lace-TACE**), who must sneak into the fold. Unlike the stranger, from whom the sheep run away, the shepherd has established a relationship with the sheep. The welfare of his sheep is uppermost in his mind.

2 But he that entereth in by the door is the shepherd of the sheep. 3 To him the porter openeth; and the sheep hear his voice: and he calleth his own sheep by name, and leadeth them out.

The shepherd was allowed access to the sheep, as evidenced by the "porter" (Gk. *thuroros*, **thoo-row-ROCE**, meaning "gatekeeper") opening the door for him. The shepherd rose in the mornings to call out his sheep by name. He rightfully entered the fold because the sheep were his, and their best interest was his primary concern. He had no intention of bringing harm to them. Regardless of the number of flocks in the fold, the shepherd called out to his own by name, and they recognized and responded to his familiar "voice" (Gk. *phone*, **fo-NAY**, meaning "sound").

4 And when he putteth forth his own sheep, he goeth before them, and the sheep follow him: for they know his voice.

The shepherd went ahead of the sheep instead of driving them from behind. Their bond was so strong and intimate that the sheep willingly followed him out of the sheepfold as he went ahead of them. They knew the sound of his voice, which reassured them. His presence and his rod and staff brought comfort to the sheep (cf. **Psalm 23:4**).

5 And a stranger will they not follow, but will flee from him: for they know not the voice of strangers.

Jesus used this parable to teach how the shepherd formed his flock. As in **verses 3 and 4**, the imagery used in **verse 5** communicates a sense of intimacy. Note the role the shepherd's "voice" (Gk. *phone*) plays in this discourse. The sheep followed because they knew the shepherd's voice, but they would never follow a stranger whose voice they did not recognize. The sheep that stayed safe recognized the voice of the shepherd. They came to the shepherd because he called them—the proper response for sheep.

6 This parable spake Jesus unto them: but they understood not what things they were which he spake unto them. 7 Then

said Jesus unto them again, Verily, verily, I say unto you, I am the door of the sheep.

Up to this point, Jesus has spoken figuratively about the Pharisees' situation. He realized His audience would certainly understand the analogy of the shepherd/sheep relationship; unfortunately, they missed His intended spiritual lesson. So, Jesus shifts metaphors and declares, "I am the door of the sheep." Again, His hearers would be familiar with the figure of a shepherd as a "door" (Gk. *thura*, **THOO-rah**) of the sheep. Since shepherds habitually lie down across the entrance of the sheepfold with their bodies, forming a barrier to thieves and wild beasts, they speak of themselves as the door to let the flock in or out and to protect it from intruders. Through the door, the flock goes in and out to graze and to rest. If attacked or frightened, the sheep can retreat into the security of the fold.

Several times in the Gospel of John, Jesus describes Himself using the phrase "I am" (Gk. *ego eimi*, **eh-GO ay-ME**; cf. **6:35, 8:12, 9:5, 11:25, 14:6, 15:1, 5**). Christ's usage of the phrase in this manner leaves no question about His claim to deity. In fact, to a perceptive Jew who understood the term *ego eimi* as a reference to Exodus 3:14, Jesus was declaring Himself equal to God (cf. **John 10:33**).

8 All that ever came before me are thieves and robbers: but the sheep did not hear them.

This verse is not a reference to Old Testament prophets, but to all Messianic pretenders and religious charlatans, like many of the Pharisees and chief priests of the time. Jesus describes them as "thieves" (Gk. *kleptes*) who divest the unwary of their precious possessions, and "robbers" (Gk. *lestes*) who plunder brazenly by violence. They did not care about the spiritual good of the people, only themselves. As a result, the sheep (i.e., those who are faithful) would not heed their voice.

9 I am the door: by me if any man enter in, he shall be saved, and shall go in and out, and find pasture.

Christ claims to be *the* door, not just *a* door. Jesus is explicitly identifying Himself as the means to salvation (cf. **Psalm 118:19–21**). As the Shepherd, Jesus provides safety and sustenance for His flock. He is the only way of salvation. Through Him, believers find "pasture" (Gk. *nome*, **no-MAY**), or provision for all of their daily needs.

10 The thief cometh not, but for to steal, and to kill, and to destroy: I am come that they might have life, and that they might have it more abundantly.

The thief's motive is diametrically opposed to the shepherd. His interest is selfish. He steals the sheep in order to kill them and feed himself, thus destroying part of the flock. In this description, we see a veiled glimpse into the character of the Pharisees and religious authorities who opposed Jesus. In contrast, Christ is the Life-Giver and Life-Sustainer. His interest is the welfare of the sheep. He enables the sheep to have full and secure lives. The thief takes life, but conversely Christ gives life.

II. THE GOOD SHEPHERD (vv. 11–15)

When the sheep turn to Him, the Shepherd offers guidance. Whatever their needs, He provides (**Psalm 23**). The Shepherd is trustworthy because He proved His love for the sheep by laying down His life (**v. 15**). Jesus' sacrifice on the Cross was based on His love for the world and His desire to save us. This was pure love.

11 I am the good shepherd: the good shepherd giveth his life for the sheep.

The adjective "good" (Gk. *kalos*, **ka-LOCE**) carries the meaning of being a true or a model shepherd. Here, Jesus is referring to the model of a shepherd found in **Ezekiel 34:11–16**.

According to Ezekiel, the good shepherd gathers, feeds, and protects the sheep. A strong bond exists between sheep and shepherd. It was not unusual for Palestinian shepherds to risk their lives for their flocks. Wild beasts, lions, jackals, wolves, and bears were on the prowl. In David's experience as a shepherd, his fights with a lion and a bear over the life of his flock convinced him that God was also able to give Goliath into his hands (**1 Samuel 17:34–37**). When Jesus says, "I am the good shepherd" (i.e., the true Shepherd), He is expressing how He carries out His mission of salvation.

12 But he that is an hireling, and not the shepherd, whose own the sheep are not, seeth the wolf coming, and leaveth the sheep, and fleeth: and the wolf catcheth them, and scattereth the sheep.

A "hireling" (Gk. *misthotos*, **mees-tho-TOCE**), or hired servant, is someone who is willing to do a specific task for a price. He might not be personally invested in the sheep, but instead he's only willing to do exactly what he is told and not take on additional risks or responsibilities. Therefore, if a wolf shows up, he runs to save his own life, leaving the sheep to fend for themselves. The result is devastating for the sheep. The hireling's self-interest exposes the flock to fatal danger. Israel had many false religious leaders, selfish kings, and imitation messiahs; as a result, the flock of God suffered constantly from their abuse. This is still the case today, as the Church suffers from false teachers and hypocritical leadership.

13 The hireling fleeth, because he is an hireling, and careth not for the sheep. 14 I am the good shepherd, and know my sheep, and am known of mine.

The "good" (Gk. *kalos*, **kal-OS**, meaning "noble" or "true") shepherd cares for the sheep—so much so that he is willing to lay down his life for them. It is important again to note the bond of intimacy between the shepherd and his sheep, as indicated by the phrase "I know" (Gk. *ginosko*, **ghee-NOCE-ko**). The use of the Greek word *ginosko* implies Christ's ownership and watchful oversight of the sheep. The reciprocal point that the sheep know their shepherd identifies the sheep's response to Christ's love and intimate care. Moreover, the use of *ginosko* indicates that this knowledge is of high value to the shepherd.

15 As the Father knoweth me, even so know I the Father: and I lay down my life for the sheep.

The deep mutual knowledge between Christ (the Shepherd) and His sheep is likened to the relationship between the Father and the Son. The "knowing" between God the Father and Jesus, His Son, is a uniquely intimate relationship. The connection between the sheep and the shepherd who knows his sheep and lays down his life for them shows unity of purpose between the Father and the Son. Jesus is more than the Good Shepherd; He is the fulfillment of God's promises to His people. Christ voluntarily laid down His life for us. His death was not an unfortunate accident, but part of the planned purpose of God.

SEARCH THE SCRIPTURES

QUESTION 1
Verses 7 and 10 describe the purpose of the gate in relationship to the thief. How do you protect yourself from the thief?

Prayer, talking with other Christians, and reading God's Word. (Answers will vary.)

QUESTION 2

Is Jesus your Good Shepherd? How do you know His voice? How do others see Him in your life?

The Bible is God's voice. Others see that I depend upon God for direction through prayer.

LIGHT ON THE WORD

Jesus is the Good Shepherd

Jesus declared, "I am the good shepherd" (**v. 11; cf. Matthew 18:12–13; Luke 15:4–6**). Shepherds often risk dangers to save the sheep, which are loved and worthy of protection. The hired hand is paid to take care of the sheep, so when danger comes, he abandons them (**vv. 12–13**); it is just a job to him. They have no personal interest, just like some religious leaders (**Jeremiah 23:1–3; Ezekiel 34:5–10; Zechariah 11:15–17**).

BIBLE APPLICATION

AIM: Students agree that Jesus' love is demonstrated to all who follow Him.

Jesus offers life in abundance "to the full, till it overflows" (**v. 10, AMP**). The decision to receive this life rests on the individual.

STUDENTS' RESPONSES

AIM: Students will affirm that Christians can depend on Jesus to shepherd them in God's way.

Pray for the leaders in your church, community, and nation. Remember that no matter who is in charge, God is always and ultimately in control.

PRAYER

Dear Gracious God, You remind us in many ways that we are our brother and sister's keepers. Keep us and lead us during harsh winters and joyous summers. In Your Name, we pray. Amen.

DIG A LITTLE DEEPER

This section provides an additional research article to further your study of the lesson:

The usage of the term "shepherd" in John is juxtaposed with its usage in Ezekiel. Jesus' compassion toward those who have been rejected reveals the heart of God to shepherd His people. And what a Good Shepherd!

https://bible.org/seriespage/23-good-shepherd-john-101-18

HOW TO SAY IT

Hireling	**HIRE**-leeng.
Fleeth	**FLEE**-ith.

PREPARE FOR NEXT SUNDAY

Read **Jonah 1:7–17** and "God's Sustaining Love."

DAILY HOME BIBLE READINGS

MONDAY
Why You Don't Understand
(Matthew 13:10–17)

TUESDAY
God Will Rescue the Endangered Sheep
(Ezekiel 34:1–10)

WEDNESDAY
The Shepherd Cares for the Lost
(Matthew 18:1–5, 10–14)

THURSDAY
Pastors Shepherd the Church of God
(Acts 20:25–28)

FRIDAY
Peter, Tend My Sheep
(John 21:15–19)

SATURDAY
The Blind See
(John 9:35–41)

SUNDAY
God's Preserving Love
(John 10:1–15)

GOD'S SUSTAINING LOVE

BIBLE BASIS: JONAH 1:7–17

BIBLE TRUTH: God's great power was witnessed by many.

MEMORY VERSE: "Then were the men exceedingly afraid, and said unto him, Why hast thou done this?" (Jonah 1:10a).

LESSON AIM: By the end of the lesson, we will: EVALUATE the nature of God's love in the story of Jonah; SENSE how people feel when faced with calamity and how they respond when others think they have caused the calamity; and PRAY for assurance of the presence of God's love in the midst of calamity.

TEACHER PREPARATION

MATERIALS NEEDED: Quarterly Commentary/Teacher Manual, Adult Quarterly, Adult resources—charts, worksheets, and other teaching tools, paper, pens, pencils, Bibles (several different versions)

OTHER MATERIALS NEEDED / TEACHER'S NOTES:

_____

_____

LESSON OVERVIEW

LIFE NEED FOR TODAY'S LESSON
When disaster comes, people ask, "Why?"

BIBLE LEARNING
Jonah's selfish decision led to calamity; however, he discovered that God's love still surrounded him.

BIBLE APPLICATION
Bad choices can affect others and cause more harm than expected.

STUDENTS' RESPONSES
Trusting God allows us to make better decisions.

LESSON SCRIPTURE

JONAH 1:7–17, KJV

7 And they said every one to his fellow, Come, and let us cast lots, that we may know for whose cause this evil is upon us. So they cast lots, and the lot fell upon Jonah.

8 Then said they unto him, Tell us, we pray thee, for whose cause this evil is upon us; What is thine occupation? and whence comest thou? what is thy country? and of what people art thou?

JONAH 1:7–17, AMP

7 And they said to another, "Come, let us cast lots, so we may learn who is to blame for this disaster." So they cast lots and the lot fell on Jonah.

8 Then they said to him, "Now tell us! Who is to blame for this disaster? What is your occupation? Where do you come from? What is your country?"

9 And he said unto them, I am an Hebrew; and I fear the LORD, the God of heaven, which hath made the sea and the dry land.

10 Then were the men exceedingly afraid, and said unto him, Why hast thou done this? For the men knew that he fled from the presence of the LORD, because he had told them.

11 Then said they unto him, What shall we do unto thee, that the sea may be calm unto us? for the sea wrought, and was tempestuous.

12 And he said unto them, Take me up, and cast me forth into the sea; so shall the sea be calm unto you: for I know that for my sake this great tempest is upon you.

13 Nevertheless the men rowed hard to bring it to the land; but they could not: for the sea wrought, and was tempestuous against them.

14 Wherefore they cried unto the LORD, and said, We beseech thee, O LORD, we beseech thee, let us not perish for this man's life, and lay not upon us innocent blood: for thou, O LORD, hast done as it pleased thee.

15 So they took up Jonah, and cast him forth into the sea: and the sea ceased from her raging.

16 Then the men feared the LORD exceedingly, and offered a sacrifice unto the LORD, and made vows.

17 Now the LORD had prepared a great fish to swallow up Jonah. And Jonah was in the belly of the fish three days and three nights.

9 So he said to them, "I am a Hebrew, and I [reverently] fear and worship the LORD, the God of heaven, who made the sea and the dry land."

10 Then the men became extremely frightened and said to him, "How could you do this?" For the men knew that he was running from the presence of the LORD, because he had told them.

11 Then they said to him, "What should we do to you, so that the sea will become calm for us?"—for the sea was becoming more and more violent.

12 Jonah said to them, "Pick me up and throw me into the sea. Then the sea will become calm for you, for I know that it is because of me that this great storm has come upon you."

13 Nevertheless, the men rowed hard [breaking through the waves] to return to land, but they could not, because the sea became even more violent [surging higher] against them.

14 Then they called on the LORD and said, "Please, O LORD, do not let us perish because of taking this man's life, and do not make us accountable for innocent blood; for You, O LORD, have done as You pleased."

15 So they picked up Jonah and threw him into the sea, and the sea stopped its raging.

16 Then the men greatly feared the LORD, and they offered a sacrifice to the LORD and made vows.

17 Now the LORD had prepared (appointed, destined) a great fish to swallow Jonah. And Jonah was in the stomach of the fish three days and three nights.

LIGHT ON THE WORD

Tarshish. Tarshish was a city or territory west of the Mediterranean Sea with which the Phoenicians traded (**2 Chronicles 9:21; Psalm 72:10**). It is believed to be the modern city of Tartessus, in the southern part of Spain near Gibraltar. Tarshish was famous for its ships (**Psalm 48:7; Isaiah 2:16**), which carried exotic animals and precious and industrial materials (**1 Kings 10:22; Jeremiah 10:9**). Because the ships of Tarshish carried such great riches, they became symbols of wealth, power, and pride.

Nineveh. Nineveh was a famous ancient city situated on the eastern bank of the Tigris River opposite the modern city of Mosul. It was built by Nimrod and eventually made the capital of Assyria, until its fall in 612 BC. It was more than 500 miles from Jonah's hometown of Gath Hepher in Israel. The prophet Nahum speaks at length about the city's sins, including evil plots against the Lord (**Nahum 1:9**), prostitution and witchcraft (**3:4**), and commercial exploitation (**3:16**).

TEACHING THE BIBLE LESSON

LIFE NEED FOR TODAY'S LESSON

AIM: Students will agree that when disaster comes, people ask, "Why?"

INTRODUCTION

Jonah Preferred to Die

Why does Jonah prefer to die rather than carry out God's instruction? His patriotism and love for his people—which he could not comprehend how his God could have mercy on the Ninevites—and (theologically speaking) his ignorance had blinded his spiritual eyes and clouded his mind so that he could not understand God's eternal salvation plan for all peoples (**Jonah 4:1–3**). Jonah's confession, "I fear the LORD, the God of heaven, which hath made the sea and the dry land," is contradicted by his actions. If he truly feared God, he would have obeyed Him, rather than trying to die.

BIBLE LEARNING

AIM: Students will agree that Jonah's selfish decision almost led to calamity, but God's love still surrounded him.

I. JONAH'S DISOBEDIENCE EXPOSED (Jonah 1:7–10)

Jonah's name means "dove." He was the son of Amittai, who came from Gath-hepher, which was three miles northeast of Nazareth. Jonah's prophetic ministry took place before the reign of Jeroboam II (782–753 BC). He predicted the victory over the Syrians and the largest extension of the Israelite border (**2 Kings 14:25**).

Jonah was commissioned by God to go and prophesy to the people of Nineveh. Like other Israelites, he hated the Assyrians, and so he decided to flee by ship instead. He hopped on board a ship headed to Tarshish in Joppa. That is when the trouble began for all on board. God sent a storm with strong, gusty winds to create havoc. The sailors called on their false gods to calm the sea and nothing happened. They woke up Jonah and implored him to pray to his God for help.

7 And they said every one to his fellow, Come, and let us cast lots, that we may know for whose cause this evil is upon us. So they cast lots, and the lot fell upon Jonah. 8 Then said they unto him, Tell us, we pray thee, for whose cause this evil is upon us; What is thine occupation? and whence comest thou? what is thy country? and of what people art thou?

Casting lots was a common practice in ancient times used for decision making. People would throw or pick stones, sticks, or animal bones to determine what steps or course to take next.

Even through the casting of lots, God is in control. Jonah thought that he could hide from the Lord, but even now he is exposed as disobedient. The sailors ask him questions to determine the cause of the storm and what part he had to play in bringing it about.

9 And he said unto them, I am an Hebrew; and I fear the LORD, the God of heaven, which hath made the sea and the dry land. 10 Then were the men exceedingly afraid, and said unto him, Why hast thou done this? For the men knew that he fled from the presence of the LORD, because he had told them.

Jonah begins by stating his nationality and theological beliefs. He fears the God of Heaven who created the sea and the dry land. He lets the sailors know that God is the cause of their predicament. The ship's crew members are incredulous when they find out that he tried to run away from a God you can't run away from. God made the sea and the dry land, so He has control over all of it. Jonah stands convicted in the presence of those who do not even know the Lord.

II. JONAH'S FATE (vv. 11–17)

Jonah goes into the sea, and the sailors' ordeal ends as the storm stops. Here again, as in the previous verses, the sea is personified (**vv. 11–12**); the reaction of the sea is idiomatically expressed as "the sea ceased from her raging." The word "raging" (Heb. *za'aph*, **ZAH-aff**), i.e., "indignation" or "wrath," is used elsewhere in the Bible to denote emotions attributed to kings and God. The boisterous movement of the sea is restricted, which shows that it is the Lord, the Creator of Heaven and earth, the sea and all that is in them, who controls the waves and the sea (cf. **Mark 4:37–39**).

11 Then said they unto him, What shall we do unto thee, that the sea may be calm unto us? for the sea wrought and was tempestuous. 12 And he said unto them, Take me up, **and cast me forth into the sea; so shall the sea be calm unto you: for I know that for my sake this great tempest is upon you.**

The people on the ship ask Jonah what they should do with him to calm the storm, because it was now becoming worse, and the sea was very turbulent. Jonah tells them to throw him overboard in order to pacify the raging sea.

13 Nevertheless the men rowed hard to bring it to the land; but they could not: for the sea wrought, and was tempestuous against them. 14 Wherefore they cried unto the LORD, and said, We beseech thee, O LORD, we beseech thee, let us not perish for this man's life, and lay not upon us innocent blood: for thou, O LORD, hast done as it pleased thee.

Here, the crew decides to return to the port of Joppa so that Jonah can get off the ship alive. By now, they were probably far out to sea and were a great distance from the shore when the storm began. Under normal circumstances, it is suicidal to try to row a boat to shore in a heavy storm like the one described here.

Note that in **verse 5**, the sailors and everyone in the ship "cried every man unto his god," but now they turn to Yahweh. In their prayer, they acknowledge two facts about the sovereignty of the Lord. First, simply by going ahead with the plan to throw Jonah into the sea, they acknowledge that no human efforts can save them from the fierce storm through which God is exhibiting His authority and anger. Second, they acknowledge that God in His sovereignty does what He pleases. They recognize the hand of God at work.

The clause "lay not upon us innocent blood" indicates their reluctance to carry out Jonah's wish, as does their request that, since they have no other alternative than to throw Jonah overboard, they should not be held accountable for the action they are about to take. They are begging for God's understanding in regards to the crime they are about to commit. There is, however, one positive outcome of the whole situation: the people who hitherto never knew the Lord God of Israel are able to confess Him as the only sovereign God.

15 So they took up Jonah, and cast him forth into the sea: and the sea ceased from her raging.

The verb "took" is the Hebrew word *nasa'* (**nah-SAH**).

16 Then the men feared the LORD exceedingly, and offered a sacrifice unto the LORD, and made vows.

The author gives three reactions of the sailors: (1) they "feared the LORD exceedingly," (2) they "offered a sacrifice to the LORD," and (3) they "made vows." Rather than being punished further for what is a potentially murderous act, the sailors receive calm and peace, prompting a different reaction than before. We note that in **verse 9** as he confesses to the sailors, Jonah says to them, "I am a Hebrew and I worship the LORD, the God of heaven, who made the sea and the land" (NIV). Although they are terrified by that confession, they do not seem totally convinced by Jonah's word. Now, however, they recognize the Lord's greatness by the instantaneous calm that follows the moment Jonah touches the waters of the sea. They begin to fear the Lord. The verb "fear" (Heb. *yare'*, **yah-RAY**) has a number of connotations, including "to be afraid" or "to be frightened, to be dreadful" as in verse 10, where it is used to describe the reaction of the sailors upon hearing Jonah's confession. It also means "to revere, to be astonished, or to stand in awe." It is a fear that inspires reverence and godly awe, as we see here (**v. 16**). Jonah's confession in **verse 9**, "I fear the Lord," is accurately translated "worship" (NIV). Also, *yare* is to be understood in the same light—they stand in reverence and awe and worship the Lord.

Astounded by what they have just experienced, the sailors not only "feared the LORD exceedingly;" they show their reverence for Him by an act of worship: they offer a sacrifice to the Lord followed by vows. We do not know of the type of sacrifice the sailors offered to the Lord from the ship. However, the author's use of both the verb *zabach* (**za-BAKH**, to offer) and its noun derivative *zebach* (**zeh-BAKH**, a sacrifice) suggests that they killed an animal as an offering to the Lord. Therefore, animals were likely on board as part of the ship's cargo, or perhaps reserved for sacrifices to the sailors' gods (a common practice at the time whether at the beginning or end of a journey, or during a crisis). Here, the sailors offer the animal in a legitimate way as a mark of their worship, no more to their own individual gods, but instead to the living God of Israel.

The third thing the author tells us is that the sailors made vows, connoting the act of verbal consecration or promise that is often associated with devotion and service to God. Overwhelmed by the instant quieting of the sea, the sailors make a pledge, not under compulsion or duress, but in appreciation and thanksgiving to the Almighty God. The author is silent, however, about whether the sailors become proselytes and follow the true God later.

17 Now the LORD had prepared a great fish to swallow up Jonah. And Jonah was in the belly of the fish three days and three nights.

As Jonah falls into the sea, the Lord prepares a great fish to swallow him up. The word "now" serves here as both a conjunction and as a transition from where we left Jonah (**v. 15**) before reading about the sailors' reaction. With this word, the author brings our mind back to the main character and continues the account from there. The statement about God's preparation indicates that even before Jonah touches the sea, even before the sailors throw him overboard, the Lord had already appointed a great fish to swallow him. The verb "prepared" (Heb. *manah*, **ma-NAH**) also means "to appoint, assign, tell, or ordain." We note here that God has control of all His creatures and that He can use anything to serve His purpose.

SEARCH THE SCRIPTURES

QUESTION 1

What are some of the possible reasons why Jonah was initially willing to risk the lives of others?

He was selfish. (Answers will vary.)

QUESTION 2

What questions do you ask someone who has intentionally involved you in a problem or some type of trouble?

Why have you done this? What is your problem? You do have a way to get me out of this, right? (Answers will vary.)

LIGHT ON THE WORD

God and Jonah

The book of Jonah is a story about a personal encounter between God and His servant Jonah, who tried to avert His plan. On the other hand, it is also about an encounter for a wicked people to whom He decides to show mercy. These encounters arise from God's call to Jonah to go and preach to the wicked nation—Nineveh—so that they can repent from their evil ways and be saved. The title, "the book of Jonah," tends to suggest that Jonah was the author, but this is misleading; the author is unknown. The book is about Jonah and his encounter with God.

BIBLE APPLICATION

AIM: Students will agree that God has compassion on those who repent.

God loves all people, even our enemies and those whom we view as different. We have to be obedient to God's commands even if we dislike the task. If we do not, others might be hurt. Repentance is necessary when our words and actions inflict harm on ourselves or others. Prayer is key when we face trials and suffering. God will hear us and have compassion.

STUDENTS' RESPONSES

AIM: Students are assured that trusting God enables them to make better decisions.

In our lives, we might experience trials and misfortune. It could be our own fault or the fault of others. We might have to acknowledge our wrongdoing to restore relationships and begin the process of healing. We might also have to forgive and show love to those who have caused us harm. No matter what the circumstances, we can be assured that God is present. If we pray and seek God, we will find He is compassionate, loving, and merciful.

PRAYER

Dear Father, thank You for not allowing others to be affected by some of our bad decisions and selfish choices. Thank You, Lord, for loving us when are wrong and for helping us correct our ways through the power of the Holy Spirit. In the Name of Jesus, we pray. Amen.

DIG A LITTLE DEEPER

This section provides an additional research article to further your study of the lesson:

The call for Christians to be actively engaged in ministry, regardless of education or ethnicity, is clearly outlined in Scripture. Yes, obeying God's call to ministry can be complex, as seen in the book of Jonah, but the willingness to be obedient fulfills God's ordained purpose in every Christian's life. In this reflective article, read the collective voices from students at Yale Divinity School who have been called to ministry. Their perspective is inspiring and refreshing.

http://reflections.yale.edu/article/seize-day-vocation-calling-work/right-where-i-m-supposed-be-thoughts-vocation

HOW TO SAY IT

Wrought   **RAWT**.

Tempestuous   tim-pes-**CHOO**-us.

PREPARE FOR NEXT SUNDAY

Read **Jonah 2** and "God's Love Preserved Jonah."

DAILY HOME BIBLE READINGS

MONDAY
Can I Flee from God's Presence?
(Psalm 139:1–12)

TUESDAY
The Lord's Voice in the Storm
(Psalm 29:1–9)

WEDNESDAY
Compassion After Rejection
(Isaiah 54:1–10)

THURSDAY
God's Wrath Against Nineveh
(Nahum 1:1–8)

FRIDAY
Fleeing from God's Call
(Jonah 1:1–5)

SATURDAY
A Stormy Confession
(Jonah 1:6–12)

SUNDAY
God's Sustaining Love
(Jonah 1:7–17)

COMMENTS / NOTES:

GOD'S LOVE PRESERVED JONAH

BIBLE BASIS: JONAH 2

BIBLE TRUTH: God is faithful to His Word.

MEMORY VERSE: "But I will sacrifice unto thee with the voice of thanksgiving; I will pay that that I have vowed. Salvation is of the LORD" (Jonah 2:9).

LESSON AIM: By the end of the lesson, we will: EVALUATE that God's love protects and preserves us when we make decisions to do His will; EXPRESS gratitude that God rescues and protects us; and EXPLORE how God's love is expressed when we accept the mission He gives us.

TEACHER PREPARATION

MATERIALS NEEDED: Quarterly Commentary/Teacher Manual, Adult Quarterly, Adult resources—charts, worksheets, and other teaching tools, paper, pens, pencils, Bibles (several different versions)

OTHER MATERIALS NEEDED / TEACHER'S NOTES:

_____

_____

LESSON OVERVIEW

LIFE NEED FOR TODAY'S LESSON
People are thankful when they are rescued from dire circumstances.

BIBLE APPLICATION
Students are grateful to God for caring for them when they are in challenging situations.

BIBLE LEARNING
Jonah acknowledges with thanksgiving that God's love protects and offers deliverance.

STUDENTS' RESPONSES
Students can trust that God is with them during times of danger.

LESSON SCRIPTURE

JONAH 2, KJV

1 Then Jonah prayed unto the LORD his God out of the fish's belly,

2 And said, I cried by reason of mine affliction unto the LORD, and he heard me; out of the belly of hell cried I, and thou heardest my voice.

3 For thou hadst cast me into the deep, in the midst of the seas; and the floods

JONAH 2, AMP

1 Then Jonah prayed to the LORD his God from the stomach of the fish,

2 and said, "I called out of my trouble and distress to the LORD, and He answered me; out of the belly of Sheol I cried for help, and You heard my voice.

3 "For You cast me into the deep, into the [deep] heart of the seas, and the currents compassed me about: all thy billows and thy waves passed over me.

4 Then I said, I am cast out of thy sight; yet I will look again toward thy holy temple.

5 The waters compassed me about, even to the soul: the depth closed me round about, the weeds were wrapped about my head.

6 I went down to the bottoms of the mountains; the earth with her bars was about me for ever: yet hast thou brought up my life from corruption, O LORD my God.

7 When my soul fainted within me I remembered the LORD: and my prayer came in unto thee, into thine holy temple.

8 They that observe lying vanities forsake their own mercy.

9 But I will sacrifice unto thee with the voice of thanksgiving; I will pay that that I have vowed. Salvation is of the LORD.

10 And the LORD spake unto the fish, and it vomited out Jonah upon the dry land.

surrounded and engulfed me; all Your breakers and billowing waves passed over me.

4 "Then I said, 'I have been cast out of Your sight. Nevertheless I will look again toward Your holy temple.'

5 "The waters surrounded me, to the point of death. The great deep engulfed me, seaweed was wrapped around my head.

6 "I descended to the [very] roots of the mountains. The earth with its bars closed behind me [bolting me in] forever, yet You have brought up my life from the pit (death), O LORD my God.

7 "When my soul was fainting within me, I remembered the LORD, and my prayer came to You, into Your holy temple.

8 "Those who regard and follow worthless idols turn away from their [living source of] mercy and lovingkindness.

9 "But [as for me], I will sacrifice to You with the voice of thanksgiving; I shall pay that which I have vowed. Salvation is from the LORD!"

10 So the LORD commanded the fish, and it vomited Jonah up onto the dry land.

LIGHT ON THE WORD

The seas. The seas were known in the ancient world as the realm of chaotic, powerful beings. The sea itself was considered a power in opposition to the gods. Many of the Psalms show that the sea far from being opposed to God, is under His rule. He is in control of it (**Psalm 104:7–9**) and it gives praise to Him (**Psalm 148:7**). This is because the Lord created the sea (**Genesis 1:9**) and declared that it was good.

TEACHING THE BIBLE LESSON

LIFE NEED FOR TODAY'S LESSON

AIM: Students will express gratitude that they are rescued from dire circumstances.

INTRODUCTION

A True Fish Story

In the previous chapter, Jonah disobediently went in the opposite direction from where God had commanded him to go. He did not want to preach to the Assyrian people of Nineveh, so he decided to board a ship headed for Tarshish. The Assyrians were a conquering nation at the time and known for their cruel methods of subjugation. Jonah, instead of hearing and obeying God's voice, gave in to fear and prejudice. As a result, God sent a storm to stop Jonah's ship and a fish to swallow him.

BIBLE LEARNING

AIM: Students will evaluate Jonah's acknowledgment, with thanksgiving, that God's love protects and offers deliverance.

I. JONAH'S PREDICAMENT (Jonah 2:1)

Some argue that Jonah was not miraculously kept alive in the belly of the fish, but rather that he died and was resurrected after three days as a copy of Christ's death, burial, and Resurrection (**Matthew 12:40**). Christ's reference to Jonah here does not indicate that Jonah died or was dead for three days, but that he was in the fish's belly for three days. It signifies that Jonah was alive while in the fish's belly.

1 Then Jonah prayed unto the LORD his God out of the fish's belly,

Jonah has gotten himself into a very terrible situation. His disobedience has caused him to be swallowed by a fish. This predicament prompts him to pray. Jonah faces death inside the belly of a fish and has no other option but to cry out to God.

He does not pray from the Temple or the comfort of his home. He prays to God in an impossible and very uncomfortable position. This situation calls for prayer. He is stuck inside a fish and imprisoned. Some would wait out their fate and resign themselves to die, but Jonah has hope in God. He believes that God can hear him no matter where he is and no matter what situation he is in.

II. JONAH'S PRAYER (vv. 2–8)

Jonah's prayer is a mixture of recounting his immediate circumstances, the horror of what it means to be trapped inside a sea creature, and heartfelt repentance. It is a plea for mercy, but also much more than that—a poetic description of his circumstances. As you read the prayer, you can imagine the seaweed wrapped around his head. You can see the waters overwhelming him. Jonah is intimately familiar with his suffering.

2 And said, I cried by reason of mine affliction unto the LORD, and he heard me; out of the belly of hell cried I, and thou heardest my voice.

Jonah says that he cried "by reason of mine affliction." The word for affliction is taken from a root word meaning enemy or adversary. In other words, Jonah cried to the Lord because of the opposition against him. We do not know whether Jonah referred to the waves while he struggled to survive in the open sea or the wetness and stench in the belly of the fish.

The word translated "hell" (Heb. *she'ol*, **sheh-OLE**) is the Hebrew word for the place of the dead. This is how Jonah describes his brush with death. Sheol was thought to be under the seas, so to be in danger in the sea would be akin to being trapped in the "belly" (Heb. *beten*, **beh-TEN**) or the "depths" of hell.

3 For thou hadst cast me into the deep, in the midst of the seas; and the floods compassed me about: all thy billows and thy waves passed over me.

The language here is similar to language in the Psalms (e.g., **18:4, 42:7, 88:17**). Some speculate that this prayer is not really from Jonah but someone else. This might be the case, but Jonah might also be utilizing the language of the hymns and prayers that he knows. Whether using his own words or the words of a familiar prayer/psalm, Jonah's grief is so great that he equates God with the sea itself. God has thrown Jonah into the heart of the sea, and now all of God's breaking and heaping waves are passing over Jonah. The Hebrew for billows (*mishbar*, **mish-BAR**) is from the verb that means to break or even shatter, referring specifically to the moment when waves are most powerful because they are breaking. Likewise, the word for waves (Heb. *gal*, **GALL**) is from the verb meaning to roll over and over, indicating the constant motion of the waves, even as they are breaking all around Jonah. Only the power of God can equate with the power of the sea in this moment.

4 Then I said, I am cast out of thy sight; yet I will look again toward thy holy temple.

Jonah describes his situation. As he is in the belly of the fish, he is cast away from God's sight. The word for "cast out" is *garash* (Heb. **gahr-OSH**), which is often seen in the Scriptures for banishing God's enemies from the Promised Land, as well as divorce in the sense of a husband driving out his divorced wife from his home. This is not a slight to God's omniscience, but a description of Jonah's spiritual state. At this moment, he is out of God's favor and separated from His presence. Contrasted to this, Jonah states that he will "look again toward thy holy temple," confident that he would one day be able to pray in the Temple.

5 The waters compassed me about, even to the soul: the depth closed me round about, the weeds were wrapped about my head. 6 I went down to the bottoms of the mountains; the earth with her bars was about me for ever: yet hast thou brought up my life from corruption, O LORD my God.

Here Jonah describes his predicament. The waters surrounded him even to his soul (Heb. *nefesh*, **NEH-fesh**). The word for soul in its most basic meaning refers to the throat (where one's very breath fills the lungs and where one's

accurate cut can kill), as well as to life itself. In other words, the waters were up to his throat and threatening his very life. Jonah was at the brink of death and needed a reversal of fortune.

The phrase "I went down to the bottom of the mountains" also describes Jonah's life-threatening situation. The mountains were thought to be rooted in the depths of the earth. In other words, he was in the deepest parts of the ocean with no hope of help or rescue. As he describes the "earth with her bars," the sense is that there is no turning back. He would drown in the depths of the sea and have no access to the earth.

7 When my soul fainted within me I remembered the LORD: and my prayer came in unto thee, into thine holy temple.

Now, we see a turn in Jonah's prayer. Before, he describes the pain and agony of his predicament. He was in danger and distress. Now, we see a turning point where he knows his prayer has been heard, and can hope for salvation and deliverance. Before he hoped to be in the Temple praying, but now Jonah declares that his prayer reached the Temple where God's presence resided. Although he was far from God and cast out of His sight, his prayer reached His ears.

Being assured that his prayer was heard probably reinforces for Jonah what he recently learned from the storm at sea. He tried to run away from God, fleeing toward Tarshish. When God sent the storm, however, Jonah knew he could not outrun Him. Now in the depths of the sea, Jonah again thought he was beyond God's power, but again finds that he was wrong. God's power stretches across the farthest sea and to the bottom of the deepest ocean.

8 They that observe lying vanities forsake their own mercy.

The Hebrew word here translated "observe" (*shamar*, **sha-MAR**) is also translated "keep" or "heed." Jonah contrasts himself with those who heed "vanities" (Heb. *hebel*, **HEH-vel**), a word often used to refer to idols and false gods. Those worshiping false gods will neglect their "mercy" (Heb. *khesed*, **KHE-sed**), which is a key theological idea in the Old Testament, referring to covenant love and faithfulness between God and His children, but also just kindness toward others (cf. **Genesis 24:49; Zechariah 7:9**).

III. JONAH'S PRAISE AND PRESERVATION (vv. 9–10)

Vows were promises and pledges to God to fulfill an obligation. This usually included offering a sacrifice at the end of a vow. Vows were not mandatory and were done on a volunteer basis. They were usually given in response to God as a form of gratitude (**Psalm 56:12**), a way to gain the Lord's favor (**1 Samuel 1:11, 27–28**), or to display total dedication to the Lord (**Numbers 6:1–8**). The Law provided regulations to making vows, reminding the Israelites that vows were to be taken seriously (**Deuteronomy 23:21–23**).

9 But I will sacrifice unto thee with the voice of thanksgiving; I will pay that that I have vowed. Salvation is of the LORD.

Jonah is so expectant of God's deliverance that he is already praising Him. His voice of thanksgiving will be his sacrifice to the Lord. He has made a vow to God and will fulfill that vow. This is the attitude of someone fully committed to God no matter what the future holds. Jonah exclaims, "Salvation belongs to the Lord," meaning he will not turn to anyone or anything else for salvation.

10 And the LORD spake unto the fish, and it vomited out Jonah upon the dry land.

After three days and three nights, the Lord speaks to the fish (again) and commands it to vomit Jonah onto shore—and it obeys. Once Jonah realizes where his help must come from, he receives it. Jonah does not specifically ask God to save him from the belly of the fish. Instead, he comes to realize that God is the only One who can save him, and that is all the acknowledgment God wants before setting His prophet free to fulfill His will again.

Jonah was correct to place his complete trust in God. He is sovereign, and even the creatures of the deep obey His voice. Jonah's life was preserved because he cried out to God in repentance. He was then free to serve the God who saved him.

SEARCH THE SCRIPTURES

QUESTION 1

How were the seas described in ancient world? Select two Psalms that reflect who rules the seas.

Chaotic and powerful, ruled by God; Psalm 104 and Psalm 148. (Answers will vary.)

QUESTION 2

Jonah declares what in **verse 9**? What have you promised to the Lord in exchange for His deliverance? Have you kept your promise? Explain.

Jonah promised to offer sacrifices and praises, and he promised to fulfill all his vows. We make promises, too. (Answers will vary.)

LIGHT ON THE WORD

Strange Place for Repentance

There in the belly of the fish, Jonah repents for his actions. This seed of repentance is expressed in his prayer for deliverance from this predicament. Jonah's prayer is significant, since it is a request for deliverance as well as a hymn of praise. Jonah is finally committed to obeying God and he desperately wants to be released from this situation. God heard his prayer. He'll hear your prayer, too. Now, praise Him!

BIBLE APPLICATION

AIM: Students will agree that believers can thank God for caring for them when they are in challenging situations.

List three ways God has come to your aid in an impossible situation, and thank Him. If there is an impossible situation in your life now, pray a prayer like Jonah's, knowing that God will hear and answer. Tell three people how God delivered you after you repented of your sins.

STUDENTS' RESPONSES

AIM: Students will trust that God is with them during times of danger.

Jonah knew where his help came from. So many today do not know where or to whom to turn when things do not turn out well. Many refuse to go to God in hard times, even if their trouble was caused by their disobedience. The Lord is always willing to show us mercy. There is no sin He will not forgive. As long as we have breath in our lungs, we have the opportunity to pray to Him and seek Him out. There are no impossible cases with God.

PRAYER

Dear God, we are grateful for a second chance, a third chance, and more. Help us to give friends and family another chance. You are a just God who expects us to be just and loving toward others and ourselves. In the Name of Jesus, we pray. Amen.

DIG A LITTLE DEEPER

This section provides an additional research article to further your study of the lesson:

"Jonah was a racist, a hyper-nationalist. He did not want to go to Nineveh because he knew God would have mercy on his enemies." So writes Dr. John Piper about the prophet Jonah, who chose his national pride over the call to preach a message that would lead his enemies to repent. Piper compares Jonah's racism to the ethnic racism he experienced growing up in the Bible Belt in Greenville, South Carolina.

http://www.desiringgod.org/messages/the-education-of-a-prophet-jonah

HOW TO SAY IT

Affliction   uh-**FLICK**-shun.

Corruption   ku-rup-**SHUN**.

PREPARE FOR NEXT SUNDAY

Read **Jonah 3** and "God's Love for Nineveh."

DAILY HOME BIBLE READINGS

MONDAY
Thanks for Deliverance from Death
(Psalm 116:1–14)

TUESDAY
Who Can Be Safe with the Leviathan?
(Job 41:1–11)

WEDNESDAY
The Lord Will Strike, Then Heal
(Isaiah 19:19–22)

THURSDAY
Answer Me, O Lord
(Psalm 69:13–18)

FRIDAY
Something Greater Than Jonah is Here
(Luke 11:29–32)

SATURDAY
Make Disciples of All Nations
(Matthew 28:16–20)

SUNDAY
God's Love Preserved Jonah
(Jonah 2)

GOD'S LOVE FOR NINEVEH

BIBLE BASIS: JONAH 3

BIBLE TRUTH: God wants the people of Nineveh to repent and trust only in Him.

MEMORY VERSE: "And God saw their works, that they turned from their evil way; and God repented of the evil, that he had said that he would do unto them; and he did it not" (Jonah 3:10).

LESSON AIM: By the end of the lesson, we will: VALIDATE that repentance is related to God's love; SENSE the joy that comes when we are forgiven for our sins; and SHARE examples of times when wholeness and peace are the result of God's intervening love.

TEACHER PREPARATION

MATERIALS NEEDED: Quarterly Commentary/Teacher Manual, Adult Quarterly, Adult resources—charts, worksheets, and other teaching tools, paper, pens, pencils, Bibles (several different versions)

OTHER MATERIALS NEEDED / TEACHER'S NOTES:

_____

_____

LESSON OVERVIEW

LIFE NEED FOR TODAY'S LESSON
Communities today are wracked with separation and violence.

BIBLE LEARNING
When the people of Nineveh repented, God showed divine love to the people.

BIBLE APPLICATION
When people choose to follow God's demand for righteousness, compassion, and justice, they can live in wholeness and peace.

STUDENTS' RESPONSES
Students can learn to live in God's peace and justice and lead others to a life for Christ.

LESSON SCRIPTURE

JONAH 3, KJV

1 And the word of the LORD came unto Jonah the second time, saying,

2 Arise, go unto Nineveh, that great city, and preach unto it the preaching that I bid thee.

3 So Jonah arose, and went unto Nineveh, according to the word of the LORD. Now

JONAH 3, AMP

1 Now the word of the LORD came to Jonah the second time, saying,

2 "Go to Nineveh the great city and declare to it the message which I am going to tell you."

3 So Jonah went to Nineveh in accordance with the word of the LORD. Now Nineveh

Nineveh was an exceeding great city of three days' journey.

4 And Jonah began to enter into the city a day's journey, and he cried, and said, Yet forty days, and Nineveh shall be overthrown.

5 So the people of Nineveh believed God, and proclaimed a fast, and put on sackcloth, from the greatest of them even to the least of them.

6 For word came unto the king of Nineveh, and he arose from his throne, and he laid his robe from him, and covered him with sackcloth, and sat in ashes.

7 And he caused it to be proclaimed and published through Nineveh by the decree of the king and his nobles, saying, Let neither man nor beast, herd nor flock, taste any thing: let them not feed, nor drink water:

8 But let man and beast be covered with sackcloth, and cry mightily unto God: yea, let them turn every one from his evil way, and from the violence that is in their hands.

9 Who can tell if God will turn and repent, and turn away from his fierce anger, that we perish not?

10 And God saw their works, that they turned from their evil way; and God repented of the evil, that he had said that he would do unto them; and he did it not.

was an exceedingly great city, a three days' walk [about sixty miles in circumference].

4 Then on the first day's walk, Jonah began to go through the city, and he called out and said, "Forty days more [remain] and [then] Nineveh will be overthrown!"

5 The people of Nineveh believed and trusted in God; and they proclaimed a fast and put on sackcloth [in penitent mourning], from the greatest even to the least of them.

6 When word reached the king of Nineveh [of Jonah's message from God], he rose from his throne, took off his robe, covered himself with sackcloth and sat in the dust [in repentance].

7 He issued a proclamation and it said, "In Nineveh, by the decree of the king and his nobles: No man, animal, herd, or flock is to taste anything. They are not to eat or drink water.

8 But both man and animal must be covered with sackcloth; and every one is to call on God earnestly and forcefully that each may turn from his wicked way and from the violence that is in his hands.

9 Who knows, God may turn [in compassion] and relent and withdraw His burning anger (judgment) so that we will not perish."

10 When God saw their deeds, that they turned from their wicked way, then God [had compassion and] relented concerning the disaster which He had declared that He would bring upon them. And He did not do it.

LIGHT ON THE WORD

Fasting. Very little is dictated about fasting in Old Testament law, with only the fast of the Day of Atonement, Yom Kippur, explicitly ordained (**Leviticus 16:29–34, 23:27–32**). In fact, the Old Testament includes instances of fasting in ancient Israel for purposes such as repentance (**Jonah 3:5**), petition (**2 Samuel 12:16**), and mourning (**1 Samuel 31:13**). Fasting served numerous purposes (**Isaiah 58:6**), but in each instance, the individual or community humbled themselves before God by refraining from food and drink.

Sackcloth and ashes. Sackcloth was a coarse garment of poor quality, usually made of goat hair. These garments were worn by those in mourning or by prophets as a sign of their earnestness. Ashes were worn on the head as a sign of mourning as well. They served as a reminder of the fragility of life and that humanity will all go to dust, or the earth.

TEACHING THE BIBLE LESSON

LIFE NEED FOR TODAY'S LESSON

AIM: Students agree that communities today are wracked with separation and violence.

INTRODUCTION

Jonah Goes to Nineveh

In last week's lesson, we saw examples of God's grace. Jonah disobeyed God, attempted to run away from His service, and finally was ready to die rather than submit to God's will. In spite of all this, when Jonah's situation appeared hopeless, God prepared a great fish to rescue him.

Jonah was saved from death by grace. God not only saved his life, but also restored him to his position as prophet. Jonah failed God, but God did not give up on Jonah. God had a job that He wanted Jonah to do, and his failure did not disqualify him for the mission.

BIBLE LEARNING

AIM: Students will agree that when the people of Nineveh repented, God gave them divine love.

I. JONAH'S REPENTANCE (Jonah 3:1–4)

Jonah obeys the Lord and goes to Nineveh as God commissioned him. The author now mentions again that Nineveh was "an exceeding great city of three days' journey," referring to its size. The estimated size of the city of Nineveh measured three miles in length and less than a mile and a half in breadth, and the city wall was about eight miles in length. This does not seem very big; however, when the other surrounding cities that make up the metropolitan area are included, we find that it was an "exceeding great (large) city." The expression "exceedingly great" literally means "great to God" or "great before God" and describes the magnitude of the city in the unique way of expressing a superlative.

1 And the word of the LORD came unto Jonah the second time, saying, 2 Arise, go unto Nineveh, that great city, and preach unto it the preaching that I bid thee. 3 So Jonah arose, and went unto Nineveh, according to the word of the LORD. Now Nineveh was an exceeding great city of three days' journey. 4 And Jonah began to enter into the city a day's journey, and he cried, and said, Yet forty days, and Nineveh shall be overthrown.

After his experience on the boat and in the belly of the great fish, Jonah was finally ready to submit to God's will. And God gave the reluctant prophet a second chance. Once again God commanded Jonah to go to Nineveh and announce His judgment against the city. This time Jonah readily obeyed God and made the 500-mile journey to Nineveh. When the prophet arrived in the city, he immediately began to proclaim the message of God's judgment to the inhabitants. The city of Nineveh itself was about 8 miles in circumference, and a pace straight through the city would not have taken three days, even starting outside the city itself, but Jonah was expected to spend three days in the city. Jonah walked through the city shouting out God's message, "In forty days Nineveh will be destroyed." The people of Nineveh heard Jonah's words, believed his report, and repented of their sin.

The immense task is soon reduced to a day's journey (or a day's work rather than three), as the inhabitants of the city fall on their knees in repentance as soon as Jonah declares the Lord's message.

The expression "And Jonah began to enter into the city a day's journey" tends to suggest that he entered the city, probably Nineveh proper the first day, and started proclaiming the message of doom awaiting them. The message is simple: "Yet forty days, and Nineveh shall be overthrown." This is the only prophecy in the book and means, "In forty more days, Nineveh will be completely changed." The prophecy here was conditional, and the condition is implicit; the prophecy will be fulfilled if the people do not repent. Had the prophecy been unconditional, they would have received no mercy. God would have overthrown or destroyed the city without warning or notice. It would have been unnecessary to send Jonah or any other messenger to the city to preach to them.

II. NINEVEH'S REPENTANCE (vv. 5–8)

As they heard Jonah's preaching (announcement of doom), they repented and believed God, and declared a national day of fasting and prayer, asking for forgiveness. Note the things Nineveh did to obtain mercy. First, they believed God (v. 5), meaning they accepted His verdict against them and trusted Him for salvation. Simply put, they repented of their evil ways and put their trust in God. Second, they declared a fast

and "put on sackcloth, from the greatest ... to the least of them," which showed an attitude of sorrow, remorse, and mourning—the marks of genuine repentance for their sin. The king, the nobles, and all the people, including all domestic animals, joined in the national mourning and called on the Lord for forgiveness (vv. 6–9).

5 So the people of Nineveh believed God, and proclaimed a fast, and put on sackcloth, from the greatest of them even to the least of them. 6 For word came unto the king of Nineveh, and he arose from his throne, and he laid his robe from him, and covered him with sackcloth, and sat in ashes. 7 And he caused it to be proclaimed and published through Nineveh by the decree of the king and his nobles, saying, Let neither man nor beast, herd nor flock, taste any thing: let them not feed, nor drink water: 8 But let man and beast be covered with sackcloth, and cry mightily unto God: yea, let them turn every one from his evil way, and from the violence that is in their hands. 9 Who can tell if God will turn and repent, and turn away from his fierce anger, that we perish not?

As an external sign of their repentance, all the people fasted (cf. **1 Samuel 7:6**). They clothed themselves in sackcloth (cf. **Genesis 37:34**). Everyone from the king to the lowest beggar participated in these acts of repentance (**Jonah 3:5–6**). The people hoped that God would show compassion and turn away from His fierce anger (**v. 9**). Even the animals were not allowed to eat or drink.

Some have wondered why these pagan people would have responded to an Israelite prophet. Jewish rabbis explain it this way: The Ninevites had heard of Jonah's miraculous deliverance from the fish's belly, and believed that God must be very powerful for His reach to extend so far. This argument is very likely since Jesus said, "For as Jonah was a sign to the Ninevites, so also will the

Son of man be to this generation" (Luke 11:30). In the ancient Near Eastern mind, gods ruled over different regions. In the minds of the Ninevites the God who was worshiped in Israel and still threatened Nineveh was powerful indeed.

III. GOD'S REPENTANCE (V. 10)

The conversion of Nineveh is the high point of the book of Jonah. The Ninevites not only heard the Word of God, they also believed. God forgave Nineveh just as He forgave Jonah. He is ready to forgive anyone and everyone who is willing to turn away from their sins and submit to His will.

10 And God saw their works, that they turned from their evil way; and God repented of the evil, that he had said that he would do unto them; and he did it not.

Recognizing the genuineness of their repentance from their evil ways, the Lord changes His mind and forgives them. They "turned (Heb. *shub*, **SHOOV**) from their evil," which means that they turned back from what they were doing before, or turned from their evil ways. It carries the idea of changing course and turning back, or changing from one way of life to a new way of life, usually either positive or negative. In this case, the Ninevites' change was positive and pleasing to God. Thus, God "repented" (Heb. *nakham*, **nah-KHAM**), i.e., changed His mind about destroying the city. This has nothing to do with God turning from a wrong. Instead, the word used for repent, "*nakham*," carries the idea of having compassion, easing oneself of anger, or being moved to pity. Moved by compassion and by the evidence of sorrow and repentance from the city, the Lord is no longer angry and He spares them the punishment, which He had pronounced on them. Here, we see what we have assumed throughout the book of Jonah: God is merciful. God relents from carrying out His judgments against people who turn to Him with their whole heart in repentance.

The Prophet Joel declares, "Rip your heart to pieces in sorrow and contrition and not your garments. Now return in repentance to the LORD your God, for He is gracious and compassionate, slow to anger, abounding in lovingkindness faithful to His covenant with His people; And He relents His sentence of evil when His people genuinely repent," (**Joel 2:13–14**, AMP; see also **Jeremiah 18:6–10**). However, God does not arbitrarily avert the punishment He has planned to execute against a sinful nation or people without evidence of genuine repentance. The question that faces us is this: "Should the Lord have compassion on Nineveh?" Jonah did not think so.

SEARCH THE SCRIPTURES

QUESTION 1

The people wore sackcloth to symbolize their mourning. Explain how the church provides ways for people to express their repentance collectively before God.

Answers will vary.

QUESTION 2

What are some things that you believe your neighborhood/community needs to repent from or do differently before God?

Speak up more for those who are voiceless or marginalized. (Answers will vary.)

LIGHT ON THE WORD

Headed in God's Direction

When God saw that the people of Nineveh had turned from their evil ways, He turned from destroying the city. The Lord extended His mercy to them by not executing the destruction they so richly deserved. He extended His grace by giving them what they could never deserve: forgiveness. He changed His mind about the judgment they were to receive.

BIBLE APPLICATION

AIM: Students will agree that when people choose to follow God's demands for righteousness, compassion, and justice, they can live together in peace.

Many people find it hard to stop doing something they know is wrong. Whether they are addicted or just stubborn, some people continue to persist in heading in the wrong direction. God's call to repentance is a call to head in the right direction. It is not intended to stop all enjoyment and fun, but rather to help people experience God's love. This can only happen when we turn from our evil ways.

STUDENTS' RESPONSES

AIM: Students will decide to show others how to live in God's peace and justice.

God's love is available to all, but not everyone experiences it. Write in your journal the reason you decided to repent and experience God's love. Next, discuss this with another believer.

PRAYER

Dear God, You forgive us and provide a way for us to return to You. You bless us with our dignity and a chance to do right by others. Grant us Your peace and mercy in all the places and spaces that we need You. In the Name of Jesus, we pray. Amen.

DIG A LITTLE DEEPER

This section provides an additional research article to further your study of the lesson:

How will they know unless someone tells them? In this article, Dr. Celestin Musekura, a scholar from Rwanda, shares his captivating story of the transformative power of God, which took him from being the village priest offering sacrifices and blood to the ancestors, to a pastor who changed his entire village.

http://www.dts.edu/read/oh-what-a-savior-celestin-musekura/

HOW TO SAY IT

Exceeding   ek-**SEE**-deeng.

Overthrown   oh-vur-**THRONE**.

PREPARE FOR NEXT SUNDAY

Read **Jonah 4** and "God's Pervasive Love."

DAILY HOME BIBLE READINGS

MONDAY
Destined to Prophesy to the Nations
(Jeremiah 1:4–10)

TUESDAY
"Return to Me," Says the Lord
(Zechariah 1:1–6)

WEDNESDAY
With Repentance Comes Joy
(Luke 15:8–10)

THURSDAY
Woes to the Unrepentant Communities
(Matthew 11:20–24)

FRIDAY
Proclaiming Repentance, Faith Lives
(Acts 20:18b–24)

SATURDAY
Gentiles Repent and Experience New Life
(Acts 11:11–18)

SUNDAY
Turn from Evil Ways
(Jonah 3)

GOD'S PERVASIVE LOVE

BIBLE BASIS: JONAH 4

BIBLE TRUTH: Jonah was angry at God's compassion.

MEMORY VERSE: "And should not I spare Nineveh, that great city, wherein are more than sixscore thousand persons that cannot discern between their right hand and their left hand; and also much cattle?" (Jonah 4:11).

LESSON AIM: By the end of the lesson, we will: EVALUATE God's loving compassion for those who are disobedient; EMPATHIZE with God's larger perspective and plan for the salvation of all people; and PRACTICE compassion with those who are far from God.

TEACHER PREPARATION

MATERIALS NEEDED: Quarterly Commentary/Teacher Manual, Adult Quarterly, Adult resources—charts, worksheets, and other teaching tools, paper, pens, pencils, Bibles (several different versions)

OTHER MATERIALS NEEDED / TEACHER'S NOTES:

_____

_____

LESSON OVERVIEW

LIFE NEED FOR TODAY'S LESSON
People become displeased and angry when things do not go their way.

BIBLE LEARNING
Jonah discovers the wide breadth of God's pervasive love.

BIBLE APPLICATION
Students can learn how to love as we experience the pervasive, all-inclusive love of God.

STUDENTS' RESPONSES
Followers of Christ are expected to show compassion for others.

LESSON SCRIPTURE

JONAH 4, KJV

1 But it displeased Jonah exceedingly, and he was very angry.

2 And he prayed unto the LORD, and said, I pray thee, O LORD, was not this my saying, when I was yet in my country? Therefore I fled before unto Tarshish: for I knew that thou art a gracious God, and merciful,

JONAH 4, AMP

1 But it greatly displeased Jonah and he became angry.

2 He prayed to the LORD and said, "O LORD, is this not what I said when I was still in my country? That is why I ran to Tarshish, because I knew that You are a gracious and compassionate God, slow to anger and great

slow to anger, and of great kindness, and repentest thee of the evil.

3 Therefore now, O LORD, take, I beseech thee, my life from me; for it is better for me to die than to live.

4 Then said the LORD, Doest thou well to be angry?

5 So Jonah went out of the city, and sat on the east side of the city, and there made him a booth, and sat under it in the shadow, till he might see what would become of the city.

6 And the LORD God prepared a gourd, and made it to come up over Jonah, that it might be a shadow over his head, to deliver him from his grief. So Jonah was exceeding glad of the gourd.

7 But God prepared a worm when the morning rose the next day, and it smote the gourd that it withered.

8 And it came to pass, when the sun did arise, that God prepared a vehement east wind; and the sun beat upon the head of Jonah, that he fainted, and wished in himself to die, and said, It is better for me to die than to live.

9 And God said to Jonah, Doest thou well to be angry for the gourd? And he said, I do well to be angry, even unto death.

10 Then said the LORD, Thou hast had pity on the gourd, for the which thou hast not laboured, neither madest it grow; which came up in a night, and perished in a night:

11 And should not I spare Nineveh, that great city, wherein are more than sixscore thousand persons that cannot discern between their right hand and their left hand; and also much cattle?

in lovingkindness, and [when sinners turn to You] You revoke the [sentence of] disaster [against them].

3 Therefore now, O LORD, just take my life from me, for it is better for me to die than to live."

4 Then the LORD said, "Do you have a good reason to be angry?"

5 Then Jonah went out of the city and sat east of it. There he made himself a shelter and sat under its shade so that he could see what would happen in the city.

6 So the LORD God prepared a plant and it grew up over Jonah, to be a shade over his head to spare him from discomfort. And Jonah was extremely happy about [the protection of] the plant.

7 But God prepared a worm when morning dawned the next day, and it attacked the plant and it withered.

8 When the sun came up God prepared a scorching east wind, and the sun beat down on Jonah's head so that he fainted and he wished to die, and said, "It is better for me to die than to live."

9 Then God said to Jonah, "Do you have a good reason to be angry about [the loss of] the plant?" And he said, "I have a [very] good reason to be angry, angry enough to die!"

10 Then the LORD said, "You had compassion on the plant for which you did not work and which you did not cause to grow, which came up overnight and perished overnight.

11 Should I not have compassion on Nineveh, the great city in which there are more than 120,000 [innocent] persons, who do not know the difference between their right and left hand [and are not yet accountable for sin], as well as many [blameless] animals?"

LIGHT ON THE WORD

Assyrians. Assyrians were known for their fierce cruelty. By today's borders, their empire would span the countries of Iraq, Iran, Syria, and Turkey. **Isaiah 36** tells us that when the Assyrians were about to attack Jerusalem, they began with a campaign of fear. For example, they sometimes captured their enemies and skinned them alive or cut off their heads and piled them in a pyramid to terrify those still alive in the city.

Nineveh. Nineveh was located along the eastern bank of the Tigris River. **Genesis 10:11** identifies Nimrod, great-grandson of Noah, as the founder of both Nineveh and Babylon. It was the capitol of the Assyrian empire for many years. The inhabitants were described as wealthy, warlike, highly civilized merchants who worshiped Ishtar (Astarte) the fertility goddess. The city was eventually attacked by the Medes and fell around 606 BC.

TEACHING THE BIBLE LESSON

LIFE NEED FOR TODAY'S LESSON

AIM: Students will agree that people become displeased and angry when things do not go their way.

INTRODUCTION

Jonah's Contemporaries

The king of Israel during Jonah's ministry was Jeroboam II (**2 Kings 14:23–29**). He ruled for forty-one years. He succeeded Jeroboam, the first king of Israel, an Ephraimite "who had made Israel to sin" by introducing the worship of golden calves at Bethel and Dan. Jeroboam II conquered Hamath, Damascus, and all of the region east of the Jordan down to the Dead Sea. Jonah prophesied this extension of Israel's territory (**2 Kings 14:25**). Jeroboam II's long reign allowed him to increase his luxury through oppression and vice. Israel prospered while iniquity flourished (**Amos 2:6–8; Hosea 4:12–14**). Jonah's contemporaries include Hosea (**1:1**) and Amos (**1:1**).

BIBLE LEARNING

AIM: Students will agree that Jonah discovers the wide breadth of God's pervasive love.

I. JONAH'S COMPLAINT
(Jonah 4:1–4)

Here we see a man who is so patriotic that he puts his love for his people above the will of God and the salvation of 120,000 people of Nineveh. Jonah becomes so angry and enraged at the saving of 120,000 people from destruction—people he converted to God through his preaching—and so angry at the goodness of God that he prefers to die. "It is better for me to die than to live," he says. Is he justified in being so angry?

1 But it displeased Jonah exceedingly, and he was very angry.

Rather than being excited over the success of his mission to Nineveh, Jonah is exceedingly displeased with God's action. He is "very angry" that God forgave the inhabitants of the city of Nineveh and spared them the punishment, which He had declared early against them. Here, Jonah explicitly confesses the reason, previously unexplained, for his attempt to escape from the command of God. He does not think that the Ninevites deserved mercy from Yahweh. Consequently, he is extremely angry when the city is spared rather than destroyed. The Hebrew construction and wordplay describing the emotional state of Jonah at this point does not carry over to the English translation. The verb "displeased" is the Hebrew word *ra'a'* (**rah-AH**), immediately linked with its noun *ra'* and modified by the adverb "exceedingly" or "greatly" (Heb. *gadol*, **gah-DOLE**). The word *ra'a'* with the noun *ra'* carries the idea of being evil or wicked, or of being injurious or hurt. Jonah was extremely and greatly hurt, to the extent that he became furious, probably with God: "He was very angry" (Heb. *kharah*, **khah-RAH**). *Kharah* means "to glow, to be hot, or to blaze up." The literal translation of the verse would read something like, "Jonah was greatly displeased with displeasure and he became furious." He was more than upset. He burned with anger. He was enraged and dejected that God's mercy had been extended to the people of Nineveh, the enemy of his people Israel.

2 And he prayed unto the LORD, and said, I pray thee, O LORD, was not this my saying, when I was yet in my country? Therefore I fled before unto Tarshish: for I knew that thou art a gracious God, and merciful, slow to anger and of great kindness, and repentest thee of the evil. 3 Therefore now, O LORD, take, I beseech thee, my life from me; for it is better for me to die than to live.

With anger and frustration, Jonah complains to God, accusing Him of "injustice" for being merciful to the city of Nineveh. He knows who God is and knows His character. He knows that God is gracious, merciful, kind, and compassionate, and that He forgives those who repent of their sin and come to Him. Jonah is aware of the possible outcome of the message that he is called to preach in Nineveh: they would repent and God would forgive them.

Now that Nineveh has repented, the anger of God against the city is averted, and the people are spared. Jonah cannot handle this; it was for this very reason he had tried to flee to Tarshish. In his "selfish" prayer, he rhetorically questions God's character by asking, "Was not this my saying, when I was yet in my country?" Is he expecting a positive answer from the Lord? Of course not. His attempt to flee to Tarshish is because of his knowledge of God's unchanging character: "For I knew that thou art a gracious

God, and merciful, slow to anger, and of great kindness, and repentest thee of the evil." He cannot reconcile himself with this knowledge.

He therefore begs the Lord to take away his life. The conjunction "therefore now," from the Hebrew word *'attah* (**at-TAH**), reflects the reason Jonah seeks to die. The use of this conjunction here also implies that the time for discussion of the matter is over. There is nothing else to do but to fulfill the request. Jonah seems to say, "Since I know you are a gracious God, and merciful, slow to anger, and of great kindness, and repentest thee of the evil, and I know you cannot change, let me die. It is better for me that way than to see these people forgiven." This statement clearly indicates the extent and degree of his anger and displeasure at what God has done (**v. 1**). He is so furious that for the second time he would prefer to die (see **1:12**).

4 Then said the LORD, Doest thou well to be angry?

The Lord confronts Jonah in **verse 4** and poses the same question to him: "Doest thou well to be angry?" This question can be framed in a variety of ways: "What right have you to be angry?" "Are you right to be angry?" "What justifies your anger?" and so on. In other words, the Lord is, on one hand, asking what gives Jonah authority to question Him or to meddle with His own authority and plan. By questioning Jonah, the Lord implicitly establishes His sovereignty and authority. God alone is the Lord and Creator of all things, and Jonah has no right to question His sovereignty and authority. What God does with His creation is within His control and power. Jonah seems to have forgotten that the Lord says, "I will ... be gracious to whom I will be gracious, and will shew mercy on whom I will shew mercy" (**Exodus 33:19**). Through this question to Jonah, the Lord implicitly makes it clear that no person merits His grace or His acts of mercy, but that His will is the basis for bestowing His blessings.

II. JONAH'S GOURD (vv. 5–8)

Jonah is outraged. He expresses the same kind of anger and frustration as he did when he realized the grace the people of Nineveh experienced. God spared the people of Nineveh but He wouldn't spare this plant. Jonah actually wants to die after he experiences the heat without the plant's shade.

5 So Jonah went out of the city, and sat on the east side of the city, and there made him a booth, and sat under it in the shadow, till he might see what would become of the city. 6 And the LORD God prepared a gourd, and made it to come up over Jonah, that it might be a shadow over his head, to deliver him from his grief. So Jonah was exceeding glad of the gourd.

The Lord caused a plant to grow up over Jonah and give him shade. The word "gourd" is *qiqayon* (Heb. **ki-kah-YONE**), and most commentators believe this to be the castor oil plant. This plant has an abundance of large leaves as well as small gourds on the branches. It is more than able to give shade to the traveler in the Near East.

Jonah's reaction to the plant is one of joy. Not only is he glad (Heb. *samach*, **sa-MOK**), which means to rejoice and sometimes religiously, but he is exceedingly (Heb. *gadol*) glad, which describes Jonah's strong intensity. This is an unusual amount of emotion for a plant that gives shade.

7 But God prepared a worm when the morning rose the next day, and it smote the gourd that it withered. 8 And it came to pass, when the sun did arise, that God prepared a vehement east wind; and the sun beat upon the head of Jonah, that he fainted, and wished in himself to die, and said, It is better for me to die than to live.

Next, God prepares a worm to eat the plant. This worm is the coccus ilicis. The Hebrew word for this worm (Heb. *tola'*, **toe-LAH**) is also used for the scarlet dye, which was taken from the decayed shell of the female of the species. Throughout the night, the worm smote (Heb. *nakah*, **na-KAH**) the plant. The literal meaning of the word is to kill or wound. The sense here is to blight with disease.

After this, God sends a vehement (Heb. *kharishi*, **kha-ree-SHE**) or hot east wind to blow on Jonah. It was intolerable enough for Jonah to become tired and wish that he was dead. It is this same phrase he used in **verse 3**. This exposes Jonah's twisted emotions as he wrestles with life. He is upset about the plants withering as much as he is upset about the Lord sparing Nineveh.

III. JONAH'S REBUKE (vv. 9–11)

The Lord rebukes Jonah. Jonah feels sorry about the plant that he did nothing to cause to grow. This plant had a short life span and Jonah is upset about it. God allows Jonah to see a larger picture when he declares that there are 120,000 in Nineveh who don't know their left from their right and also animals. God wants to show mercy to His creation. He has compassion and His love ranges wide over humanity.

9 And God said to Jonah, Doest thou well to be angry for the gourd? And he said, I do well to be angry, even unto death. 10 Then said the LORD, Thou hast had pity on the gourd, for the which thou hast not laboured, neither madest it grow; which came up in a night, and perished in a night:

Next, the Lord questions Jonah's priorities. Jonah responds with justification for his anger. The Lord says that Jonah had pity (Heb. *khus*, **KHOOS**) on the gourd. The word means "to spare and to have compassion on someone or something." Jonah had not invested any effort in causing the plant to grow. The Lord also points out that the plant had a short life span and shows that Jonah's angry fits are petty.

11 And should not I spare Nineveh, that great city, wherein are more than sixscore thousand persons that cannot discern between their right hand and their left hand; and also much cattle?

The Lord's question stemmed from Jonah's reaction to the withering of the plant (vv. 6–10). How could Jonah be concerned about the death of the gourd but remain unconcerned, and indeed angry, about the well-being of the people of Nineveh? Here again is another rhetorical question. The author emphasizes the contrast between Jonah's relation to the plant and God's relation to the people of Nineveh. The Lord questions Jonah, saying, "If you are so concerned about the well-being of one ordinary plant, do you have any reason I should not have mercy on 120,000 "persons that cannot discern between their right hand and their left hand" and their animals? Why do you wish that they should perish?"

The expression, "persons that cannot discern between their right hand and their left hand" is an idiomatic expression that tends to refer to the ignorance of the people of Nineveh regarding the Law as compared with the Israelites. The expression can also refer to innocent children; in that case, the 120,000 persons do not refer to the entire population of Nineveh at the time, but to the number of children in the city. In either case, the expression directly corresponds in meaning with its Igbo (Nigerian) equivalent. In Igbo, the idiom runs "innocent children who cannot differentiate their left hand from their right," and for children, it has a positive connotation. If used for adults, though, the connotation is negative and expresses ignorance or stupidity. In either case, it also denotes the helplessness of the people in question.

SEARCH THE SCRIPTURES

QUESTION 1
Why are some Christians jealous of others or upset with God when others receive particular blessings and they do not?

Some Christians believe they are more deserving than others. (Answers will vary.)

QUESTION 2
How do you respond when God blesses you and then takes it away?

Upset, frustrated with God, or feeling that maybe something better is coming. (Answers will vary.)

LIGHT ON THE WORD

God's Kindness to Jonah's Anger
Jonah, fuming in anger, walks outside the city. As he sits in his makeshift shelter, God causes a large, leafy plant to provide shade for Jonah. At this act of kindness, Jonah is thankful to God. The plant provides shade to ease his discomfort. Then God causes the leafy plant to dry up and wither.

BIBLE APPLICATION

AIM: Students will agree that Christians must learn how to love as they experience the pervasive, all-inclusive love of God.

Opportunities to confront wrong beliefs, in ourselves and in others, present themselves to us daily. Jonah's callous heart prevented him from caring for others. Like Jonah, we too may need a fresh love for God's truth to genuinely care for others. When offended, we can challenge others in love. God's loving challenge is often in the form of blunt questions. For instance, God challenged Jonah to repent by providing for him while pressing him to examine his motives.

STUDENTS' RESPONSES

AIM: Students will decide that followers of Christ are expected to show compassion for others.

When offended, Christians might respond in anger or frustration. Like Jonah, we may fail to remember God's mercy to us. Our short-sightedness limits our ability to extend mercy to others. This week, commit to doing one act of kindness for someone with whom you are having conflict, or to a stranger. Pray to see the needs of others as God sees them.

PRAYER

Dear gracious God, when we struggle with showing compassion to others, remind us of Your compassion toward us. Let us rejoice in Your faithfulness to each of us and guide us to be more like Christ. In the Name of Jesus, we pray. Amen.

DIG A LITTLE DEEPER

This section provides an additional research article to further your study of the lesson:

Experiencing anger with God over life's struggles is common. Whether the anger is expressed like Jonah's or buried deep in the heart, it is something that is real. In this article, a young athlete who had the potential to become an Olympic champion sacrificed her dreams to care for her schizophrenic mother. Her anger seemed justified, but God had a redemptive plan for her life.

http://www.apu.edu/athletics/trackandfield/stories/12405/

HOW TO SAY IT

Vehement.   **VEE**-hi-mint.

Beseech.   bi-**SEECH**.

PREPARE FOR NEXT SUNDAY

Read **Judges 4:1–10** and "Deborah and Barak."

DAILY HOME BIBLE READINGS

MONDAY
The Lord's Proclamation
(Exodus 34:4–9)

TUESDAY
The Lord Forgives Iniquity
(Numbers 14:10b–11, 17–20)

WEDNESDAY
The Lord Did Not Forsake
(Nehemiah 9:16–21)

THURSDAY
Bless the Lord, O My Soul
(Psalm 103:1–14)

FRIDAY
A Prayer to the Lord for Help
(Psalm 86:1–7)

SATURDAY
Nations Will Bow Before the Lord
(Psalm 86:8–13)

SUNDAY
God's Pervasive Love
(Jonah 4)

COMMENTS / NOTES:

QUARTERLY COMMENTARY
GOD'S URGENT CALL
by Dr. William C. McCoy

TEACHER'S TIPS

"SUNDAY SCHOOL TEACHING TIPS III"
by Jurisdictional Field Representative Sandra Daniel

#TSSGTEACHINGTIP –
"THE EFFECTIVE USE OF CLOSURE"
by Evangelist Waynell Henson

GOD'S URGENT CALL

BY DR. WILLIAM C. MCCOY

On the first Sunday in September 2007, I sat on the steps of the pulpit with my head buried in my hands—alone. It was early, and service was not slated to start for another 90 minutes. It was the first official day of service for the new ministry, my first Sunday as pastor of a church. Waves of doubt rushed over my mind…

"And Moses said unto God, Who am I?"
Exodus 3:11

Who was I to start a church? I wasn't qualified in the least to do this job. Furthermore, I really didn't want to do it. I had served as an assistant pastor of a church long enough to realize pastoring was not for the faint of heart. Through my pastor and mentor, I witnessed the good, the bad, and the ugly, so I really didn't want to be a pastor. I would have been content being an ordained elder without charge.

But there was no denying that God had called me. I ran from it as long as I could, but I always knew pastoring was a part of my destiny. I had learned early in life that God had great things in store for me, so I heeded God's call and told Him, "Yes, Lord."

"For unto whomsoever much is given, of him shall be much required…"
Luke 12:48

The overarching theme for this quarter serves to remind us of God's urgent call, and His penchant for using people from every walk of life to fulfill His sovereign mission to bring us closer to Him and to an expected end.

UNIT 1 – CALLED TO BE STRONG

Unit 1 deals with the judges God called to demonstrate His ability to deliver His people from their enemies. Judges were national figures who heeded the voice of God and were used by Him in supernatural ways. The root meaning of the word "judge" is to govern or to decide what is right or wrong. It also means to vindicate or to deliver, which is the most appropriate version for this group of lessons.

In the 12th century BC, Deborah (Heb. "Bee") and Barak (Heb. "Lightning") were called upon to deliver the Children of Israel out of the hands of the Canaanites—an oppression that lasted at least 20 years (Lesson 1). Deborah, the prophetess and wife of Lappidoth, was judging (deciding right and wrong before the people), but heeded the voice of the Lord in helping Barak to acknowledge his call to lead the nation in a victorious uprising. Understanding Deborah's role in impending victory, Barak refused to fight without her at his side. This created an unlikely union with a positive outcome. It was in the Plain of Esdraelon (commonly known as the "Emek"—the "Valley") that this war would be waged. Despite overwhelming odds, Barak and Deborah, with God on their side, put the enemy to flight and led the nation in victory.

From time to time, one might question the voice of God and desire a sign of confirmation. What God requires of us can be simple or complex, but it takes someone of mental and spiritual fortitude to carry it out. The first step is identifying God's voice and proceeding with confidence and assurance on what He commands. Such was the case of Gideon (Heb. "Hewer"), who in the 12th century BC, after hearing God's call through an angel sitting under an oak tree, requested God's ambassador to tarry until he returned with a sacrifice to prove His will (Lesson 2). God in no way is bound by human doubt and certainly does not have to prove Himself to man, but He understands where we are in our journey and meets us where we are. By honoring the conditions, God strengthened His chosen one to carry out the task set before him. Gideon, the youngest son of Joash, knew that the message he received was authentic, which erased all doubts and fears.

Lesson 3 introduces us to Jephthah (Heb. "Set Free"), a figure who strengthens the idea that God enjoys utilizing the marginalized population to fulfill His divine will. Born in the land of Gilead by a man named Gilead and a harlot, Jephthah was ostracized by his half-brothers and the entire community because of his mother and was forced to flee in haste and despair. Interestingly enough, his leadership qualities were utilized while away from his native land, as he became the leader of a band of robbers, but God had a different plan. Like so many of us, those who caused the trouble were forced to circle back around and request the assistance of the very one they despised and had driven away. In order to prevail against the children of Ammon, the elders had to rely on Jephthah, so they convinced him to return and become the head of their forces. By answering Israel's call, Jephthah reclaimed his rightful place among the Children of Israel.

As many of these lessons describe, the judges of Israel were raised during times of national waywardness and sin. God would allow various nations to invade Israel when she was not following His way, but He would not allow the invasion to last forever; instead, God would eventually raise a judge to deliver His people from their oppression. In the 12th century BC, Samson (Heb. "Man of the Sun") was called from the womb of his mother, a barren woman who received special instructions for a special child destined to begin Israel's deliverance process out of the hands of the Philistines (Lesson 4). This lesson is an important example of God's predestined call to those have a unique and special purpose in His divine will. This lesson is also a good reminder of the importance of dedicating our children after birth and reminding them of the special place they have in carrying God's will forward.

UNIT 2 – CALLING OF THE PROPHETS

God's call is never manifested more thoroughly and emphatically than His call to those who will serve as His mouthpiece. Generation after generation has witnessed preachers divinely assigned to address a nation, and in some cases, the entire world on behalf of God. Such work is never easy, and the assignee will definitely pay a decisive cost, but the reward for obeying God's commands will always outweigh the trouble. The next group of lessons (Unit 2) demonstrates that God calls specific people at specific times for specific purposes.

Lesson 5 deals with the very familiar story of the call of Moses (Heb. "To Draw Out"). We know Moses was destined for greatness from birth, but he himself had to accept that fact. Even when he fled Egypt and eventually settled down into a "normal" existence, Moses found himself called by God for a specific purpose. On Mount Horeb (or Sinai), God called Moses to a greater, more encompassing work than being a shepherd. Full of doubt and probably some fear, Moses questioned God's line of reasoning for choosing him, but for every excuse, God had a rebuttal wrapped in love, power, and assurance. This lesson also provides a glimpse of God's ability to take an ordinary occurrence and create a divine situation out of it, for from a burning bush (not uncommon where Moses was) He caught the attention of one of the greatest leaders in the Bible.

The call of God is not always low-key. As a matter of fact, He delights in speaking to us in ways that leave us awestruck and humbled. Such was the case with Isaiah (Heb. "God's Salvation"), whose vision at the age of 25 was like none other (Lesson 6). Given a glimpse of His glory, Isaiah knew that human frailty left him lacking in all areas of divine assignments. A supreme act of love and grace bridged the gap between God's assignment and Isaiah's readiness, but God has a way of preparing His people for their task. By the time God delivered the question of "who will accept the assignment," Isaiah is more than ready for the task and utters the famous words, "Here am I; send me." From that day forward, Isaiah devoted himself to the vocation of prophecy.

In a very similar act, God assured Jeremiah (Heb. "God Will Elevate") that he, too, was called before he was born (Lesson 7). In fact, the substance of Jeremiah's call mirrored that of Samson, for both men were sanctified (set apart for a divine purpose) while in their mother's womb. Like Moses, Jeremiah was resistant at first, questioning the validity of God's message coming from someone so young; yet God's response was reminiscent of the way He dealt with Isaiah (the two prophets were only a century apart)—He touched his mouth and gloriously imparted His Word into Jeremiah. The prophet was not only to speak for Him, but his words would have a powerful effect on the future of the nation. Jeremiah was to "root out, pull down, and destroy"; but his God-given word would also build back up to bring life back into the people. His task, around 627 BC, was to parallel the national cleansing of King Josiah, who carried out sweeping religious reformation and restored the Temple in Jerusalem.

The call of Ezekiel ("The Strength of God") in late 500 BC served as an ardent plea for the people to turn their hearts to God without reservation (Lesson 8). This was an exceptionally difficult call because God Himself declared that the people would reject the prophet because they had already rejected his God. How must Ezekiel have felt knowing that the people would reject him before he uttered one word! The essence of this lesson is that God's will must be fulfilled, even when the message is not pleasant to hear and is all but doomed from the start. Why continue with such a message? Because God's mercy and grace dictate that He will give us a chance regardless of our circumstances and mindset. God erased Israel's opportunity to say, "If you had given me a chance, I would have done what you wanted me to do." God's preparation of the prophet was also unique and compelling, a lesson important for us to remember as we share what God has given to us in perilous times. God commands Ezekiel to "eat the scroll," signifying that His Word would be with him even while dealing with hard-headed and stubborn people.

So what do we do when we are divinely assigned to speak a message that is not pleasant to hear? What do we do when God pronounces edicts that foretell a person's fall or a nation's captivity? We must do like Amos (Heb. "Burden") and say what God tells us to say (Lesson 9). In Amos' case, the priest Amaziah, around 775 BC, tried to dissuade the king from listening to the prophetic utterings of Amos, who at that time was a sheep-farmer who gathered the fruit from sycamore trees. Amaziah then tried to persuade Amos to leave the land he was destined to prophesy against. This call was unique because of the relative calm in the region, but the luxurious living spurred Amos to rail against the establishment. Determined to do the will of God, Amos continued to utter the message of doom against Israel, and even against Amaziah and his family. God's messages are not always pleasant, but they are necessary to capture the attention of His people to convince them to turn from their wicked ways.

UNIT 3 – CALLS IN THE NEW TESTAMENT

God's calls continued through the New Testament and even through today. The next series of lessons takes us through the early church and the men God entrusted His Word to while setting the stage for growth through proclamation of the Gospel and conversion.

It is important to note that church growth does not occur without a certain amount of pain and discomfort, as was the case in the early days of the church. As murmuring and complaints rose due to neglect of the widows, the disciples wisely introduced structure to the fledgling church so that business would be dealt with in a timely and complete manner (Lesson 10). They looked for individuals who were honest, full of the Holy Ghost, and wise to deal with the church's business. This practice should be upheld even today, because the church's vitality depends on it. The church must be served by those anointed by God, so that His work can be made manifest in the lives of those individuals, as demonstrated by Stephen (Gk. "Crown or Wreath") in this lesson. Stephen's call came through his faithfulness and the special anointing placed on his life. He was one of the seven Greek-speaking or Hellenist (a student of Greek civilization, language, or literature) disciples chosen to deal with the business of the early church.

Lesson 11 expands on the point that the Gospel is for everyone. How curious it must have been for Philip (Gk. "Lover of Horses") to be told where to go without being told why! It is always amazing to do what God tells you to do, even when He doesn't tell you the whole story. This exercises our faith in powerful ways! Through blind faith and obedience, Philip (who was also one of the seven men appointed to deal with the business of the early church, along with Stephen) was introduced to an Ethiopian eunuch who just happened to be reading God's Word and was ready for exposure to the call of salvation. What a message this must have been to Philip—to know that God's call was extended to everyone who would accept His Son as Lord and Savior!

Lesson 12 reminds me of a song we used to sing in church years ago:

> *"Just keep on praying for the Lord is nigh*
> *Just keep on praying, He'll hear your cry*
> *For He has promised, and His word is true*
> *Just keep on praying, He'll answer you"*

This lesson deals with the call of Saul (Heb. "Asked of God") and the involvement of Ananias (Heb. "Jehovah Has Been Gracious") in that call. This particular call by God assures us that He can call anyone He so chooses. A person's background is of little consequence with the Almighty, and their present circumstance is only of slight consequence to God. If He calls, you must answer! Like with Ananias, He might even appoint you to be His spokesperson. Ananias probably had difficulty agreeing to go, as Saul had a ferocious reputation among the saints for his atrocious, defiant behavior, but Saul would make changes that would affect the church in ways only God could orchestrate. His conversion led to the name change from Saul to Paul (Lat. "Little").

How fitting that we end this quarter with a reminder that God has no respect for persons in His call for salvation. Peter (Gk. "Rock"), whose surname was Simon (Gk. "Hearing"), was under the impression that God's call was only for one group of people—Israel—but God informed him that the call of salvation was for everyone. Lesson 13 recounts Cornelius' request through divine revelation for Peter to come speak to him and his household. This request would also confirm to Peter the meaning of a subsequent vision God gave him declaring, "What God hath cleansed, that call not thou common." God, in His infinite wisdom, was preparing the way for explosive church growth and vast expansion of His Word. Ultimately, as we consider God's will and reflectively look back at this quarter's lessons, we must realize that we are called for a specific purpose to fulfill a specific plan orchestrated by Him. The songwriter said it best:

> I'm Yours Lord
> With everything I've got
> With everything I am
> And everything I'm not
> Try me now and see
> See if I can be
> Completely Yours!

Dr. William C. McCoy serves as the Sunday School Superintendent for Wisconsin 1st Jurisdiction under the leader ship of Bishop Sedgwick Daniels, general board member. He also serves as the Co-Pastor of Greater New Unity Church Of God In Christ in Rockford, IL.

Professionally, Dr. McCoy works as Director of the BELIEF Program, the nationally-ranked Ethics program for Northern Illinois University's (NIU) College of Business. He also serves as the President of the Black Faculty and Staff Association, Treasurer of the Presidential Commission on the Status of Minorities, and member of the Presidential Commission on Interfaith.

Dr. McCoy was recently awarded the 2016 Supportive Professional Services (SPS) Presidential Award for Excellence at NIU, the highest award possible for that position classification. His dissertation centered on teaching adult Sunday School teachers how to teach better.

SUNDAY SCHOOL TEACHING TIPS III

BY JURISDICTIONAL FIELD REPRESENTATIVE
SANDRA DANIEL

If You Don't Know It, They Won't Learn It

You can't teach what you don't know. In other words, if you don't know it, they won't learn it. Students will lose their motivation when they learn you didn't care enough about them to thoroughly study what you are attempting to teach. That doesn't mean you have to be able to answer every off-topic question they ask; it's okay and a great example to say, "I'll have to look up the answer to that." But if it's part of the lesson you expect them to learn, you'd better know it.

Get Your Mind Thinking Early

Start early in preparing. Not just because it's easier, but because you give God an opportunity to bring ideas to your mind about the lesson, even when you're not actively working on it. Preparing a lesson and can't think of an appropriate interactive activity? You can work on that all week. If you start the night before, it's too late.

Have Them Live It

Another great way to instill the life application of a lesson is to have students act it out. This incorporates movement, makes the lesson more real, and helps reinforce it in their minds.

Have a Point

Keep the application firmly in mind when creating lesson activities. Make sure the lesson teaches it, the memory verse reinforces it, the activities review it, and the students know it. Focus. Don't try to include everything related to the issue. Concentrate on the discussion points. This gives them a chance to ask application questions.

Set Expectations

Let the students know up front what the class will entail. Give students a reason to listen. Inform them that you will be reviewing. Encourage active listening. Ask questions during the lesson. Encourage discussion.

Depend on God

Remember that God will support you. You are to do His work with excellence. He will provide the resources, time, and talent, since you have offered your will.

Evangelist Sandra Daniel serves as the Jurisdictional Field Representative for the First Ecclesiastical Jurisdiction of Southern California under the leadership of Bishop Joe L. Ealy and General Assistant Supervisor/Jurisdictional Supervisor Mother Barbara McCoo Lewis. She is the Assistant Director of Leadership Ministry for the International Sunday School Department.

#TSSGTEACHINGTIP –
THE EFFECTIVE USE OF CLOSURE

BY EVANGELIST WAYNELL HENSON

You've heard many lessons and sermons over your life. Is there one that really sticks out in your mind? For me, it is a Family and Friends Day message preached by my pastor. His message title was "Making It on Broken Pieces." He fully shared the story of Paul in Acts 27 being transported by ship as a prisoner. The ship struck what some translations call a reef or sandbar. The ship was incapacitated and the stern broken to pieces. "*But the centurion, willing to save Paul, kept them from their purpose; and commanded that they which could swim should cast themselves first into the sea, and get to land: And the rest, some on boards, and some on broken pieces of the ship. And so it came to pass, that they escaped all safe to land*" (Acts 27:43–44). I remember a visual of several connected wooden planks. Each plank reflected a life circumstance. Like the water crashing against the stern, breaking it, life's situations hit us. And often the forces and difficulties in our own lives are forceful enough to break pieces away. Holding one board, he reminded us that the people made it to land—a safe place—not on the ship, but simply holding on to "A Broken Piece."

Sunday School certainly is not the Sunday morning sermon, but what I shared was the effective use of CLOSURE! What is a closure? Think of it like a Pentecostal preacher who says at least three times at the end of a message, "I'm getting ready to close." In other words, I am about to wrap up the discussion and share something that will leave a lasting impact with you. Think of teaching like a book—there is a front and back cover! Every lesson needs a "closure."

Great Sunday School teachers/facilitators use closure to:

- Ensure that students understood the lesson content

- Place emphasis on key information or headlines from the material

- Address any open discussion from the class; here you can also clarify any misunderstanding

- Challenge each student to find a way to make the lesson active in the upcoming week

Closure is helpful for the students to:

- Summarize and synthesize their understanding of major lesson points

- Link the ideas and discussion to their own real world

- Find ways to stretch themselves as a result of the lesson study

Closure is just that extra "boost" a teacher/facilitator gives to the lesson. After you have reviewed the lesson content and discussed the lesson, challenge yourself to find an effective close. It doesn't have to be dramatic, like broken pieces, but it should be effective!

A few thoughts for Closure Activities:

1. **Summary/Share**

   Place a colorful notecard on each student's chair at the beginning of class. Challenge students to write their three key lesson learning points. At the end of class, have students to share aloud one learning point, or partner with a neighbor for 4 minutes (2 minutes each).

   a. This concept also works as a "Gallery Walk," using sticky notes and allowing students affix their thoughts/learning/praise reports to a wall or designated area! Imagine the "Wall of Learning" at the end of a quarter!

2. **The "Elevator Speech"**

   "It's just a minute… 60 seconds in it." Ask students to create a 1-minute summary of the lesson. It's going to happen—dining after church, work, the store; someone will ask a student, "How was church today?" Your great students will have an answer!

3. **STATUS: Share it!**

   This is a social age! Sharing is especially impactful for young adult learners. It is as empowering for the one sharing as it is the reader! Truth is, their "gadgets" are out anyway, so challenge students to share a key lesson point on their social pages. Create a hashtag for your church or Sunday School class. This will allow you to quickly find and group postings from your students and could be a great outreach method!

4. **Six Word Summary!**

   Challenge your class to create a headline about the lesson impact in six words.

5. **The Modern-Day Version**

   Allow students to re-write the lesson in modern-day language and perform a skit, or take a modern-day scenario and challenge students to product an outcome based on the lesson and or learnings.

6. **Craft/Snack**

   For primary classes, utilizing a craft or snack is a great way to tie the lesson and help young learners to connect lesson points.

Evangelist Waynell Henson is a member of Dominion Word Ministries Church Of God In Christ, Elder Michael McWilliams, Pastor. She has a heartbeat for connecting in relevant and meaningful ways to inspire people to abundant living through the truth of God's Word. A gifted administrator and #MinistryLeaderCoach, she serves as the Executive Secretary of the International Sunday School Department (COGIC) and Co-Chairman of Auxiliaries in Ministry for the Kansas East Jurisdiction COGIC, Bishop L.F. Thuston, Prelate. With a heightened awareness of connecting with Gen-X'ers, G-Y'ers and millennials, she impacts a social media "Community" of more than 1,000 lovers of Sunday School. She shares the weekly lesson, growth strategies and resources through platforms as Youtube, Facebook, Instagram, Pinterest, Twitter, and SnapChat. Have YOU joined "The Community"?

#HappyTeaching

Find more great ideas (#TeachingTipTuesday) on www.ThatSundaySchoolGirl.com.

QUARTERLY QUIZ

The questions on this page may be used in several ways: as a pretest at the beginning of the quarter; as a review at the end of the quarter; or as a review after each lesson. The questions are based on the Scripture text of each lesson (King James Version).

LESSON 1

1. Why do believers sometimes choose to depend on others more than we depend on God?

_____

_____

2. Think of the Deborah in your life and share how you needed this person to help you through a challenging time. Explain when you have experienced a Barak moment and how God's Word helped you.

_____

_____

LESSON 2

1. Gideon was unsure about God supporting the Israelites because of how they had suffered at the hands of the Midians (**Judges 6:11**). Compare Gideon's doubt to when you have questioned God's choices or doubted His active presence in your life.

_____

_____

2. God accepted Gideon's challenge to prove that He was speaking to him in **verses 17–18**. What does God's response to Gideon reveal about their relationship?

_____

_____

LESSON 3

1. What gifts did the Spirit of God use to anoint leaders (**Judges 11:29**)? Summarize how your special gifts are included in your ministry.

_____

_____

2. According to Isaiah, people thought that they could hide from God (**v. 27**). Do you agree that this is true in the church today and for you personally? Explain.

_____

_____

LESSON 4

1. God makes promises to unexpected people (**Judges 13:3–7**). When God has given you an unexpected promise, how did you respond?

_____

_____

2. Manoah and his wife would have the major responsibility of raising their son Samson. Evaluate how your church assists parents with raising a child.

_____

_____

LESSON 5

1. When God calls you to a particular task outside your comfort zone, explain your responses and limitations.

_____

_____

QUARTERLY QUIZ

2. **Exodus 3:5** describes God telling Moses to take off his shoes because he is standing on holy ground. Why is it important for Moses and believers to recognize and respond to God's holiness?

_____

_____

LESSON 6

1. Reflect on the images and symbols used to describe God's power and majesty. How do these images impact and uplift whom God is to you and to the world?

_____

_____

2. Isaiah's lips were touched and his sin purged in **Isaiah 6:7**. Complete the following: "God, purify my _____ and allow me to serve You with greater excitement and depth when I _____." Explain your responses.

_____

_____

LESSON 7

1. Compare Jeremiah's response to God's call and a time you were reluctant or hesitant to share or listen to the Gospel.

_____

_____

2. Develop a meditation based on God's response to Jeremiah throughout the lesson (**Jeremiah 1:4–10**).

_____

_____

LESSON 8

1. Ezekiel declares that the people of Israel are "impudent and hardhearted" (**Ezekiel 3:7**). Identify reasons why people who refuse to listen to God's Word will not hear you speak of repentance and returning to God. How can believers speak or share Christ with those who refuse to hear God's Word?

_____

_____

2. God encourages and strengthens Ezekiel to prophesy to the obstinate people (**vv. 8–11**). Ezekiel received God's truth and reassurance. Select three Scriptures that remind you of God's truth and assurance to share Him with someone you do not know.

_____

_____

LESSON 9

1. Amos prophesied because of his faith and relationship with God. Share your purpose for connecting people with Christ.

_____

_____

2. Choosing to obey God can be a challenging discipline. Summarize how you discipline yourself to obey God.

_____

_____

QUARTERLY QUIZ

LESSON 10

1. We are called to tell the story of Christ. Which methods or approaches do you use to tell others about Christ? How often do you witness to others?

_____

_____

2. The apostles needed to prioritize and divide the work so that the widows' needs were met. Evaluate how you use your time. How can you reconsider and change how you spend your time?

_____

_____

_____

LESSON 11

1. The eunuch was baptized by Philip and was very happy (**Acts 8:38–39**). Do you remember your baptism? Which church hymn, gospel song, or poem would you use to express the significance of your baptism?

_____

_____

2. The eunuch made time to read God's Word, and wanted someone to teach him so that he could understand it (**vv. 28–32**). Who has had the greatest impact on your Bible study, and why?

_____

_____

LESSON 12

1. Why are believers reluctant to listen to someone who claims repentance and proclaims Christ, but has lived a life that was not Christ-like?

_____

_____

2. Christ tells Ananias in **Acts 9:16** that Paul will suffer "great things" for His sake. Have you ever suffered for the sake of Christ? How has this changed your witness to others?

_____

_____

LESSON 13

1. Design a prayer with themes of obedience, respect, honor, and joy (**Acts 10:19–25**).

_____

_____

2. Cornelius fasted and prayed, and his prayer was answered. Have your church and personal life made fasting and praying necessary components of spiritual development? Why or why not?

_____

_____

Answers to Quarterly Quiz can be found on page 465

DEBORAH AND BARAK

BIBLE BASIS: JUDGES 4:1–10

BIBLE TRUTH: God's plan was fulfilled through Deborah's leadership and support.

MEMORY VERSE: "And she said, I will surely go with thee: notwithstanding the journey that thou takest shall not be for thine honour; for the Lord shall sell Sisera into the hand of a woman" (from Judges 4:9).

LESSON AIM: By the end of this lesson, we will: AGREE that there were changing leadership dynamics during the time of Deborah; CONTRAST Barak's sense of inadequacy and Deborah's sense of confidence; and ASSESS godly counsel and be willing to share such wisdom with others.

TEACHER PREPARATION

MATERIALS NEEDED: Quarterly Commentary/Teacher Manual, Adult Quarterly, Adult resources—charts, worksheets, and other teaching tools, paper, pens, pencils, Bibles (several different versions)

OTHER MATERIALS NEEDED / TEACHER'S NOTES:

_____

_____

LESSON OVERVIEW

LIFE NEED FOR TODAY'S LESSON
People who are called to be leaders may doubt their capabilities.

BIBLE LEARNING
Barak willingly went into battle after the prophetess Deborah agreed to accompany him.

BIBLE APPLICATION
God challenges us to do extraordinary things.

STUDENTS' RESPONSES
Believers can trust that even in our doubt, God will provide.

LESSON SCRIPTURE

JUDGES 4:1–10, KJV

1 And the children of Israel again did evil in the sight of the LORD, when Ehud was dead.

2 And the LORD sold them into the hand of Jabin king of Canaan, that reigned in Hazor; the captain of whose host was Sisera, which dwelt in Harosheth of the Gentiles.

JUDGES 4:1–10, AMP

1 But the Israelites again did evil in the sight of the LORD, after Ehud died.

2 So the LORD sold them into the hand of Jabin king of Canaan, who reigned in Hazor. The commander of his army was Sisera, who lived in Harosheth-hagoyim.

3 And the children of Israel cried unto the LORD: for he had nine hundred chariots of iron; and twenty years he mightily oppressed the children of Israel.

4 And Deborah, a prophetess, the wife of Lapidoth, she judged Israel at that time.

5 And she dwelt under the palm tree of Deborah between Ramah and Bethel in mount Ephraim: and the children of Israel came up to her for judgment.

6 And she sent and called Barak the son of Abinoam out of Kedeshnaphtali, and said unto him, Hath not the LORD God of Israel commanded, saying, Go and draw toward mount Tabor, and take with thee ten thousand men of the children of Naphtali and of the children of Zebulun?

7 And I will draw unto thee to the river Kishon Sisera, the captain of Jabin's army, with his chariots and his multitude; and I will deliver him into thine hand.

8 And Barak said unto her, If thou wilt go with me, then I will go: but if thou wilt not go with me, then I will not go.

9 And she said, I will surely go with thee: notwithstanding the journey that thou takest shall not be for thine honour; for the LORD shall sell Sisera into the hand of a woman. And Deborah arose, and went with Barak to Kedesh.

10 And Barak called Zebulun and Naphtali to Kedesh; and he went up with ten thousand men at his feet: and Deborah went up with him.

3 Then the Israelites cried out to the LORD [for help], for Jabin had nine hundred iron chariots and had oppressed and tormented the sons of Israel severely for twenty years.

4 Now Deborah, a prophetess, the wife of Lappidoth, was judging Israel at that time.

5 She used to sit [to hear and decide disputes] under the palm tree of Deborah between Ramah and Bethel in the hill country of Ephraim; and the Israelites came up to her for judgment.

6 Now she sent word and summoned Barak the son of Abinoam from Kedesh-naphtali, and said to him, "Behold, the LORD, the God of Israel, has commanded, 'Go and march to Mount Tabor, and take with you ten thousand men [of war] from the tribes of Naphtali and Zebulun.

7 I will draw out Sisera, the commander of Jabin's army, with his chariots and his infantry to meet you at the river Kishon, and I will hand him over to you.'"

8 Then Barak said to her, "If you will go with me, then I will go; but if you will not go with me, I will not go."

9 She said, "I will certainly go with you; nevertheless, the journey that you are about to take will not be for your honor and glory, because the LORD will sell Sisera into the hand of a woman." Then Deborah got up and went with Barak to Kedesh.

10 And Barak summoned [the fighting men of the tribes of] Zebulun and Naphtali to Kedesh, and ten thousand men went up under his command; Deborah also went up with him.

LIGHT ON THE WORD

Deborah. Her name means "honeybee." She was a leader, wife, prophetess, and poet. Deborah's responsibilities included settling disputes and offering advice and guidance to leaders like Barak. She was a woman of influence and power, whose decision-making was a marked contrast to that of Jephthah, Gideon, and Samson, who judged Israel after her. Jephthah's vow forced his daughter to a lifetime of singleness(**Judges 11:29–40**); Samson struggled with lust and devoted himself to a prostitute (**Judges 16:1**). As a woman, Deborah demonstrated fidelity to her husband and integrity with those whom she led. The Bible gives no reason as to why she judged from under a palm tree. Moses sat under the oak of Mamre to judge, and Saul sat under a pomegranate in Migron. Scripture simply clarifies that the position of the palm tree gave Deborah access to be judge over both the nations of Israel and Judah.

Barak. His name means "lightning." Initially hesitant to accept his call to fight against Sisera. Barak later led ten thousand warriors from the tribes of Naphtali and Zebulun into battle against the Canaanites. However, he accepted the Lord's call to battle only after Deborah agreed to accompany him. Regardless, he is listed in **Hebrews 11:32** as a hero of faith.

TEACHING THE BIBLE LESSON

LIFE NEED FOR TODAY'S LESSON

AIM: Students will agree that leaders may doubt their capabilities.

INTRODUCTION

Deborah - A Fearless Leader

Israel lived comfortably in peace after Ehud's triumph over Moab (**Judges 3:12–30**). Then they were forced into survival mode by Canaanite troops. Cities previously destroyed by Joshua had been rebuilt as the Canaanites grew stronger. People previously conquered by the Israelites now ruled and demanded the payment of tribute.

Deborah stood to speak for God during challenging times. Without a similar model or mentor, she assumed a role generally filled by men and rose up to initiate a fight, motivate an army, and encourage a leader. Barak did not allow Deborah's gender to cloud his response. He answered the call and partnered with Deborah to lead the army.

BIBLE LEARNING

AIM: Students will agree that Barak willingly went into battle with the prophetess Deborah accompanying him.

I. SISERA'S OPPRESSION (Judges 4:1–3)

Sisera was the general of Jabin's soldiers; Jabin was the Canaanite king. Sisera was possibly a Hurrian, a people known as expert chariot-fighters in the Late Bronze Age. Well-prepared and equipped, he relied on his nine hundred chariots of iron and a host of soldiers.

The Consequences of Disobedience (Judges 4:1–3)

1 And the children of Israel again did evil in the sight of the LORD, when Ehud was dead. 2 And the LORD sold them into the hand of Jabin king of Canaan, that reigned in Hazor the captain of whose host was Sisera, which dwelt in Harosheth of the Gentiles. 3 And the children of Israel cried unto the LORD: for he had nine hundred chariots of iron; and twenty years he mightily oppressed the children of Israel.

God "sold" Israel, or handed Israel over as one would a slave, because of their disobedience.

The word translated "sold" (Heb. *makar*, **mah-KAR**) is a common word, also used for selling things like oxen or slaves. Thus, the people became merchandise, liable to be sold if no longer useful to their owner. This could also be read to mean that God surrendered them to the enemy or sent them away from His presence. He sold them "into the hand" of a human being, implying dominion, forced fellowship, or labor joined with pain caused by misuse of power. Note the progression: They left the hand of God, were sold or transferred into a human hand, and were given over into the hands of the nations. In other words, God would allow Jabin and his people to oppress Israel as punishment for sin. This action is the essence of what the Bible means by reaping what you sow (**Galatians 6:7–8**). Whenever we disobey God, we voluntarily place ourselves outside of His will. Thus, without God's protection, we will suffer from harmful situations as natural consequences or from His punishment (see **Hebrews 12:5–7**).

The city of Hazor was located within the land of the tribe of Naphtali. Hazor was near the eastern border of the territory of Napthali west of the Jordan River. The land of the tribe of Zebulun was adjacent to the southwest border of Naphtali. Both of these tribal territories were in the northern area of the Promised Land. Obviously, non-Hebrew people lived on the land which had been captured by Israel under Joshua. Therefore, Sisera's base of operations in Harosheth was located among the northern tribes of Israel, and he could easily reach out to torment them. The king named Jabin in this text is a descendant of another king, also named Jabin, who had previously been defeated by Joshua (see **Joshua 11:1, 10**). This passage is a continuation of the cycle of rebellion, punishment, and restoration recurring throughout the book of Judges.

Once again, after a brief time of peace and safety, the Israelites had gone back to worshiping the gods of their neighbors. This would result in their being oppressed by those same people. God would not tolerate their idolatry and unfaithfulness. They were His people, and He expected them to be loyal to Him. After Ehud died, the Israelites fell into the hands of Jabin, the king of Hazor. He oppressed the Israelites through his general Sisera, who had nine hundred iron chariots at his command. This definitely placed him at an advantage as the Israelites had no chariots or iron weapons. To go against Sisera would be suicide.

II. DEBORAH'S INSPIRATION (vv. 4–7)

The Lord would not break His covenant with His people. He raises up an unlikely leader in Deborah. Considering the patriarchal culture of the time, Deborah's leadership as a woman is unusual. She is a prophetess and a judge, speaking God's Word and enforcing His laws and wisdom. Deborah was a formidable leader during this time of oppression and chaos.

God's Plan for Barak (vv. 4–7)

4 And Deborah, a prophetess, the wife of Lapidoth, she judged Israel at that time. 5 And she dwelt under the palm tree of Deborah between Ramah and Bethel in mount Ephraim: and the children of Israel came up to her for judgment. 6 And she sent and called Barak the son of Abinoam out of Kedeshnaphtali, and said unto him, Hath not the LORD God of Israel commanded, saying, Go and draw toward mount Tabor, and take with thee ten thousand men of the children of Naphtali and of the children of Zebulun? 7 And I will draw unto thee to the river Kishon Sisera, the captain of Jabin's army, with his chariots and his multitude; and I will deliver him into thine hand.

Deborah is introduced to us right away as a "prophetess" (Heb. *'ishshah nebi'ah*, **ish-SHAH** ne-vee-YAH), literally "a woman prophet." A prophet spoke on behalf of God to the people (cf. **Deuteronomy 18:15–22**). Up to this point in Israel's history, Moses was the most eminent of the prophets. Joshua was never referred to as a prophet, since his work was not to reveal new words from the Lord but to lead Israel in obedience to what the Lord had commanded through Moses. Deborah begins the prophecy to Barak by asking a question, "Hath not...?"

The word rendered "hath not" (Heb. *halo*, **ha-LOH**) is probably better understood as "behold" or "indeed." Deborah is not assuming that Barak has already heard from God about what he is supposed to do. By every indication, this is the first time Barak has received this message. Deborah gives him the message, however, in a way that prophets commonly gave messages from God: with words that carry authority and demand a resolute answer.

Mount Tabor rises steeply 1,843 feet above sea level at the northeast corner of the Jezreel Valley, and forces stationed on it could easily control one of the most important crossroads in the region. Tabor also offered the advantage of being a prominent landmark, and the forces Barak summoned would have no confusion about where to make their stand. Essentially, God was telling Barak to use his forces to defiantly take control of the strategic high ground, forcing the enemy to come to him. Note that God provided the leader as well as the strategy.

Naphtali and Zebulun were regions subject to the oppressive rule of Jabin, king of Hazor. Hazor (Jabin's capital city) and Harosheth Hagoyim (Sisera's home city) straddled these two areas—Hazor to the northeast of Naphtali, and Harosheth Hagoyim to the southwest of Zebulun.

III. BARAK'S INSPIRATION (vv. 8–10)

Barak lets Deborah know that he will go only if she does. His faith is not in God, but Deborah's

leadership. He doesn't realize that God is the deciding factor; his advantage over Sisera is not Deborah, but that God will be with him. As a result, Deborah informs him that because of his hesitation and fear, the honor of victory will go to a woman, not to him. His personal lack of faith resulted in being dishonored by God and not receiving personal victory.

Barak Depends on Deborah (vv. 8–10)

8 And Barak said unto her, If thou wilt go with me, then I will go: but if thou wilt not go with me, then I will not go. 9 And she said, I will surely go with thee: notwithstanding the journey that thou takest shall not be for thine honour; for the LORD shall sell Sisera into the hand of a woman. And Deborah arose, and went with Barak to Kedesh. 10 And Barak called Zebulun and Naphtali to Kedesh; and he went up with ten thousand men at his feet: and Deborah went up with him.

Barak hesitated at the task given to him. Even with 10,000 men in his army, the Canaanite force was clearly superior. Barak was not the first or last leader God chose for Israel who hesitated to obey: recall Moses (**Exodus 3:11**) and Gideon (**Judges 6:15**).

Deborah's promise to go with Barak at this place in the story is astounding because it comes at the point when God normally promises His presence with the leader He is sending (cf. **Exodus 3:12; Joshua 1:5; Judges 6:16**). It seems best to understand the promise of her presence as the promise of God's presence, given to help Barak in his weakness.

God has repeatedly shown that He is willing to accommodate the weakness of His chosen instruments (cf. **Deuteronomy 7:7, 9:4–6**). Nevertheless, Barak should have known that God had promised to drive out the Canaanites for the Israelites if only they were faithful to continue to fight (cf. **Joshua 13:6, 23:5**). Deborah's displeasure with Barak's hesitation is obvious in her prediction that Barak will not gain glory on this mission.

Ten thousand might sound like a large number of troops to the modern reader. By comparison, however, the Canaanite army had 900 chariots, each manned by two soldiers, and most likely an infantry to boot. The implication is that the Canaanite infantry was vast—several times the size of Barak's force. Indeed, when Joshua first conquered Hazor, its king conscripted troops from the many outlying cities and villages in his realm. He succeeded in assembling an army "as numerous as the sand on the seashore" (**Joshua 11:4**). Note also that Gideon was able to muster 32,000 men—three times more than Barak—when he prepared for his attack on the armies of Midian (**Judges 7:3**). From this we can surmise that more people could have joined in the fight against Sisera, but God made it a point that He only called for a force of 10,000 against a technologically superior force—and He won.

SEARCH THE SCRIPTURES

QUESTION 1
What things in our lives can make us feel inadequate to respond to God's call?

Answers will vary.

QUESTION 2
What examples might we see in our nation's leaders of confidence in God or the opposite, self-reliance?

Answers will vary.

LIGHT ON THE WORD

A Unique Judge
Deborah is unique among the judges in that she is identified as not whom God chose to be

a deliverer, but the messenger to that deliverer, Barak. Deborah's location under the palm tree could mean several different things. Her home might have been located at that certain spot, or she could have held court outdoors there. The Hebrew word translated "dwelt" (*yashab*, **yah-SHAV**) can mean either "to sit" or "to dwell." Deborah spent a lot of time under the tree listening and serving as a judge.

BIBLE APPLICATION

AIM: Students will value that God challenges us to do extraordinary things.

Christian leadership begins with a call—a sense that God has a specific role or task for each Christian to accomplish (**Romans 12:2**). God prepared Barak for his battle with Sisera and raised him up to be a general. Similarly, He prepares each believer to accomplish specific tasks. What role has God prepared you for? The call originates with God, and confidence to accomplish the task begins in us. We grow in confidence by making time to meditate on the Bible's promises, even just by repeating them over and over to ourselves and sharing God's Word.

STUDENTS' RESPONSES

AIM: Students will justify that believers can trust that even in our doubt, God will provide.

Victory over Sisera did not end the battle. Israel later pursued King Jabin until they destroyed him. Christians engaged in spiritual warfare can sometimes follow a cycle of apostasy, oppression, repentance, and deliverance. The cycle occurs when Christians value their own strength and capabilities over dependence on God. Doubt and over-reliance on something other than God will eventually cause Christians to fall, becoming ensnared in bondage.

Times for courage can be instances where we have to deliver bad news, such as: you did not get the job, you are fired, I'm taking away your cell phone for a week. Focusing on ourselves or the situation rather than God's promises can lead to anxiety, doubt, and even panic. Instead, choose to believe God's message, reach out for fellowship, and accept good advice when it is offered.

PRAYER

Dear Almighty God, we sometimes doubt Your Word, and what You have called us to do. Grant us the courage and the wisdom to move forward and build Your Kingdom. Thank You for providing us with help when we are afraid and the strength to help others who need encouragement. In the Name of Jesus, we pray. Amen.

HOW TO SAY IT

Sisera.   **SI**-sur-ah.

Hashoreth.   ha-**SHOW**-reth.

Lapidoth.   la-pee-**DOTE**.

DIG A LITTLE DEEPER

This section provides an additional research article to further your study of the lesson:

The biblical account of the prophetess Deborah provides qualifications for any leader. In this article, Liz Curtis Higgs highlights significant attributes that leaders today can emulate. In Deborah's leadership, she allowed God to guide her decision-making and trusted Him to fulfill His Word. And in the end, when God destroyed those who sought to oppose His army, Deborah gave all praise and honor back to Him.

http://www.todayschristianwoman.com/articles/2007/march/9.22.html

PREPARE FOR NEXT SUNDAY

Read **Judges 6:11–18** and "Gideon's Call."

DAILY HOME BIBLE READINGS

MONDAY
An Angel Rebukes Israel's Faithlessness
(Judges 2:1–5)

TUESDAY
Joshua's Death Ends an Era
(Judges 2:6–10)

WEDNESDAY
The People Lose God's Protection
(Judges 2:16–23)

THURSDAY
Ode to Israel's Faithful Judges
(Hebrews 11:29–40)

FRIDAY
Victory Song of the Divine Warrior
(Judges 5:1–5)

SATURDAY
Jael Defeats the Enemy Leader, Sisera
(Judges 5:24–27)

SUNDAY
Deborah and Barak
(Judges 4:1–10)

COMMENTS / NOTES:

_____
_____
_____
_____
_____
_____
_____
_____
_____
_____
_____
_____
_____

GIDEON'S CALL

BIBLE BASIS: JUDGES 6:11–18

BIBLE TRUTH: God chooses wisely to fulfill His plans.

MEMORY VERSE: "And the angel of the LORD appeared unto him, and said unto him, The LORD is with thee, thou mighty man of valour" (Judges 6:12).

LESSON AIM: By the end of the lesson, we will: DECIDE that God's criteria for choosing leaders differ from those set by humans; ACCEPT when we feel unqualified for a task because of perceived inadequacies; and CONFIRM the appropriateness of voicing doubts about personal capabilities and requesting signs in a twenty-first-century context.

TEACHER PREPARATION

MATERIALS NEEDED: Quarterly Commentary/Teacher Manual, Adult Quarterly, Adult resources—charts, worksheets, and other teaching tools, paper, pens, pencils, Bibles (several different versions)

OTHER MATERIALS NEEDED / TEACHER'S NOTES:

_____

_____

LESSON OVERVIEW

LIFE NEED FOR TODAY'S LESSON
People sometimes view their circumstances as obstacles to becoming effective leaders.

BIBLE APPLICATION
God will equip those whom He calls for leadership.

BIBLE LEARNING
Gideon voiced his doubts to God and requested a miraculous sign from Him.

STUDENTS' RESPONSES
Christians appreciate that God can work through our doubts.

LESSON SCRIPTURE

JUDGES 6:11–18, KJV

11 And there came an angel of the LORD, and sat under an oak which was in Ophrah, that pertained unto Joash the Abiezrite: and his son Gideon threshed wheat by the winepress, to hide it from the Midianites.

12 And the angel of the LORD appeared unto him, and said unto him, The LORD is with thee, thou mighty man of valour.

JUDGES 6:11–18, AMP

11 Now the Angel of the LORD came and sat under the terebinth tree at Ophrah, which belonged to Joash the Abiezrite, and his son Gideon was beating wheat in the wine press [instead of the threshing floor] to [hide it and] save it from the Midianites.

13 And Gideon said unto him, Oh my Lord, if the LORD be with us, why then is all this befallen us? and where be all his miracles which our fathers told us of, saying, Did not the LORD bring us up from Egypt? but now the LORD hath forsaken us, and delivered us into the hands of the Midianites.

14 And the LORD looked upon him, and said, Go in this thy might, and thou shalt save Israel from the hand of the Midianites: have not I sent thee?

15 And he said unto him, Oh my Lord, wherewith shall I save Israel? behold, my family is poor in Manasseh, and I am the least in my father's house.

16 And the LORD said unto him, Surely I will be with thee, and thou shalt smite the Midianites as one man.

17 And he said unto him, If now I have found grace in thy sight, then shew me a sign that thou talkest with me.

18 Depart not hence, I pray thee, until I come unto thee, and bring forth my present, and set it before thee. And he said, I will tarry until thou come again.

12 And the Angel of the LORD appeared to him and said to him, "The LORD is with you, O brave man."

13 But Gideon said to him, "Please my lord, if the LORD is with us, then why has all this happened to us? And where are all His wondrous works which our fathers told us about when they said, 'Did not the LORD bring us up from Egypt?' But now the LORD has abandoned us and put us into the hand of Midian."

14 The LORD turned to him and said, "Go in this strength of yours and save Israel from the hand of Midian. Have I not sent you?"

15 But Gideon said to Him, "Please Lord, how am I to rescue Israel? Behold, my family is the least [significant] in Manasseh, and I am the youngest (smallest) in my father's house."

16 The LORD answered him, "I will certainly be with you, and you will strike down the Midianites as [if they were only] one man."

17 Gideon replied to Him, "If I have found any favor in Your sight, then show me a sign that it is You who speaks with me.

18 Please do not depart from here until I come back to You, and bring my offering and place it before You." And He said, "I will wait until you return."

LIGHT ON THE WORD

The Midianites were a group of people who descended from Abraham's fourth son through his concubine Keturah (**1 Chronicles 1:32**). The Midianites, who settled in northeast Arabia, would adopt Arabian customs and cultures. Their name appears in Genesis and Exodus with the stories of Joseph and Moses because of their close proximity to the Israelites. The Midianites were just one of the many nations that would rise against Israel while in the Promised Land.

TEACHING THE BIBLE LESSON

LIFE NEED FOR TODAY'S LESSON

AIM: Students will respect that people sometimes view their circumstances as obstacles to being effective leaders.

INTRODUCTION

Leadership is Needed

In an effort to guide the Israelites, God appointed judges to assist them in following His Law, but the Israelites still wanted to follow their own agendas and worship false gods. God desired for the Israelites to remember their ancestors' experiences—traveling through the wilderness so that they would learn how to honor God. But every time God delivered them from their evil ways, the Israelites disobeyed God and returned to idolatry.

BIBLE LEARNING

AIM: Students will agree that Gideon voiced his doubts to God and requested a miraculous sign from Him.

I. DOING WHAT YOU CAN
(Judges 6:11–12)

When the angel of the Lord visited Gideon, he was threshing wheat at the bottom of a wine-press to avoid drawing attention to himself. During biblical times, people would often thresh wheat at the top of the hill so that the chaff of the wheat could be carried away in the wind, leaving only the useful part of the wheat behind. Gideon threshed the wheat in a winepress, usually located in a pit, so that the flying chaff wouldn't give away his location to the Midianites who had taken over the land. By working there, he could hide his produce from those who might try to steal it. Gideon continued doing what he could to live through the oppression. Though Gideon was performing a common task in fear, the angel of the Lord reassures him that God was with him, even before Gideon could verbalize his fears. This reassurance would be the first of many confirmations for Gideon that he would be victorious against the enemy.

An Angel Finds Gideon
(Judges 6:11–12)

11 And there came an angel of the LORD, and sat under an oak which was in Ophrah, that pertained unto Joash the Abiezrite: and his son Gideon threshed wheat by the wine-press, to hide it from the Midianites.

The Israelites were in hiding from their enemies and could not fend for themselves. The Midianites invaded their land, destroyed their farms, and took away all their livestock, leaving them helpless (**Judges 6:3–6**). Gideon is threshing wheat in a very secluded place, probably so the family could survive. The fact that Gideon threshed wheat by the winepress expresses the degree of distress and humiliation the people are undergoing. Under normal circumstances, cattle were used to thresh grains on a threshing floor. Gideon is working in an unusual place—in a wine press (Heb. *gath*, **GATH**), which was a circular pit hollowed out of rock—most likely to avoid discovery by the invaders.

Instead of using the winepress for processing wine, Gideon is using it for threshing grain because the Israelites do not have any grapes left to make wine. Their adversaries have taken over all their vineyards. The people were living under great fear.

12 And the angel of the LORD appeared unto him, and said unto him, The LORD is with thee, thou mighty man of valour.

As Gideon is working in this secret place, the angel appears to him. We are not told how the angel appears—most likely in a human form, as a prophet. After the angel's disappearance, Gideon realizes he has been talking with the angel of the Lord (**vv. 21–22**). The angel appears and approaches Gideon and addresses him in an unusual manner: "The LORD is with thee, thou mighty man of valour." The phrase "mighty man of valour" comes from two Hebrew words (*gibbor*, **ghib-BORE**, and *khayil*, **KHAH-yeel**) that can be interpreted as "great or powerful warrior; a strong and valiant man." It also can be translated as "man of standing," which makes sense considering Gideon's reasoning in **verse 15**.

Gideon naturally replies with a series of questions: Given Israel's circumstances, if God is with us, and in view of what He has done in the past, why are we in such a mess? Why won't He help us like He did when we were in Egypt? Why has God turned us over to our adversaries? The answer to these questions is obvious—sin. Israel has forsaken their God, and He reciprocates by allowing their enemies to conquer and oppress them in accordance with His covenant and warning (**Leviticus 26; Deuteronomy 28**). He is only fulfilling this part of the covenant just as He has in the past, and on many occasions, He kept the other part of the promise by blessing them when they were obedient to Him.

II. REMEMBERING THE PAST (v. 13)

Because Israel had faced many trials in the Promised Land, Gideon was skeptical that God could be with him and the Israelites. He has several questions that he wants answered. Yet, Gideon neglects to reflect on how the people's disobedience led them to their troubles; instead he asks why God did not deliver them.

Gideon's Concern (v. 13)

13 And Gideon said unto him, Oh my Lord, if the LORD be with us, why then is all this befallen us? and where be all his miracles which our fathers told us of, saying, Did not the LORD bring us up from Egypt? but now the LORD hath forsaken us, and delivered us into the hands of the Midianites.

Gideon expresses his concerns by questioning the angel's words: "If the LORD is with us, then why has all this happened to us?" He recalls a time when his ancestors spoke of a God who delivered and redeemed them from troubles in times past; Gideon questioned whether or not God would do the same for them now.

III. QUALIFYING THE CALL (vv. 14–16)

God responds to Gideon to remind him of his own abilities to do what was necessary to save the Israelites: "Go in this strength of yours and save Israel from the hand of Midian. Have I not sent you?" Gideon questions whether he is qualified to do what God has asked of him because he is the "least" of his tribe. Gideon thought that because he was the smallest in stature and status, he would not be able to defeat the army of Midianites. God qualifies us to do His work. Whenever God calls us to His work, He knows that we are capable. Because God can see the end from the beginning, He already knows we can be successful at whatever He asks us to do—if we do it in His strength.

God Reassures Gideon (vv. 14–16)

14 And the LORD looked upon him, and said, Go in this thy might, and thou shalt save Israel from the hand of the Midianites: have not I sent thee?

While Gideon is pondering all his inadequacies, lack of qualifications, and probably doubting his abilities, "the LORD looked upon him" and orders him to go and save his people from the Midianites. We notice that Gideon addresses the angel regarding "the LORD," but it is God Himself that looks upon Gideon and speaks. The word "looked" comes from the Hebrew word *panah* (**pah-NAH**), which means "to turn, to face, to look at." That means the Lord turns and looks (facing him squarely) and commissions him to action. It is a look of confidence and emphatic assurance.

The Lord tells Gideon to go in the strength he has and rescue the people. In other words, "You have enough power; you don't need more, because the Lord is with you." Here God commissions Gideon in the same way as He did Moses and Joshua (**Exodus 3:10, Joshua 1:5**). The rhetorical question, "Have not I sent thee?" (**Judges 6:14**), is another way of reconfirming His calling and certifying the mission. In other words, the Lord says, "I am the One sending you; you need not fear or be afraid, for I am with you." Gideon did not have to worry about being strong enough, because as Paul says, God's strength is perfected in our weakness (**2 Corinthians 12:9–10**).

15 And he said unto him, Oh my Lord, wherewith shall I save Israel? behold, my family is poor in Manasseh, and I am the least in my father's house. 16 And the LORD said unto him, Surely I will be with thee, and thou shalt smite the Midianites as one man.

Gideon gives the excuse that his family is poor and he is the least in his father's house. In saying this, he acknowledges that he has no authority. To call soldiers together was the ability of someone of influence. He had no influence over his own family, nor any other families or tribes.

The Lord gives reassurance that He will be with Gideon. God does not reassure Gideon with anything else but His presence. The Israelites will come together to fight under Gideon's leadership and defeat the Midianites. In other words, Gideon will defeat every single one of the Midianites in one fell swoop (as he does).

IV. WORSHIPING AND WAITING (vv. 17–18)

God reassures Gideon that He will not only give him a sign, but He will also wait for him to return with a sacrificial meal. This exchange between God and Gideon is the affirmation that Gideon needed to get over his fears and go in obedience—and a sign that Gideon was willing to go forward in obedience despite his fears. This beautifully demonstrates how God is caring, loving, and concerned about the things we are concerned about; He was willing to wait on Gideon so he could be reassured through this act of worship. God often meets us with the same kind of loving patience. He knows we are prone to worry and fear.

GIDEON'S CONFIRMATION (vv. 17–18)

17 And he said unto him, If now I have found grace in thy sight, then shew me a sign that thou talkest with me. 18 Depart not hence, I pray thee, until I come unto thee, and bring forth my present, and set it before thee. And he said, I will tarry until thou come again.

Gideon wants to confirm this amazing encounter and offer of grace (Heb. *khen*, **KHEN**). This word means a feeling of favorable emotional regard, always given from a person in higher social standing to one of lower rank. Gideon wanted to know for sure whether God would be with him. He asks for a sign, and the angel of the Lord indulges him. He promises to wait for Gideon's present (Heb. *minkhah*, **meen-KHAH**), which is another word for sacrifice, most often a grain offering. Gideon's desire is to truly confirm that the Lord has sent this messenger by giving a worship offering that only the Lord would receive.

What a great turnaround for Gideon, who must have been contemplating his weaknesses, but now would lead an army. How could he be chosen for such an enormous assignment: delivering his people from such a powerful and cruel people like the Midianites? Gideon could not fathom being the one to lead his people to face such a mighty army.

But the Lord had other plans. Here we learn that God uses not the famous, the strong, or the most eloquent, but rather ordinary people: the weak and the feeble, the less eloquent, and the seemingly insignificant to carry out His purposes.

SEARCH THE SCRIPTURES

QUESTION 1

How can we be reassured that whatever God brings to us, He will also give us the tools to be successful?

Answers will vary.

QUESTION 2

Have you rejected a leader, and have you ever been rejected as a leader? What were the results in both situations?

Answers will vary.

LIGHT ON THE WORD

Repeated Disobedience

The Israelites were repeatedly disobedient. Other nations that resided in the Promised Land began fighting against the Israelites. They refused to depend on God. The Israelites remind us to trust God and not lean to our own understanding. Things may look impossible, but God handles our impossibilities with ease.

BIBLE APPLICATION

AIM: Students will validate that God will equip those whom He calls for leadership.

Because we live in a society that emphasizes being "qualified," we can lose sight of what it means to be gifted and called by God, even if we do not meet man-made qualifications. We often miss an opportunity for God to use us because we think we do not have the qualifications to complete what He's asked us to do. Gideon rose to the occasion because he was willing to trust God more than his personal skills and abilities.

STUDENTS' RESPONSES

AIM: Students will appreciate that God can work through our doubts.

You might be thinking about something God has called you to do, but don't feel capable because you don't have the experience, education, resources, or know-how. Today, write down what God has asked you to do. Then, write down the steps it will take to achieve that goal. Find one thing that you feel you can do to start the process of obedience. Pray for God to continue to give you the courage to obey the plan, even if you feel unequipped to do so.

PRAYER

Dear God of wisdom, continue to bless us with leaders who will advance Your Kingdom and guide Your people. Allow each of us to know Your voice through the power of the Holy Spirit and to respond as doers of Your Word. In the Name of Jesus, we pray. Amen.

HOW TO SAY IT

Abiezrites.   ah-bee-**EZ**-rites.

Midianites.   **MI**-dee-uh-nites.

Mannasseh.   muh-**NA**-suh.

DIG A LITTLE DEEPER

This section provides an additional research article to further your study of the lesson:

The dynamic call of God to become a leader can be both frightening and overwhelming. Biblical leaders often found it difficult to accept the responsibility. Along with Gideon, this article compares two others who struggled with the call to lead the people of God. Through their honesty, we witness the power of God to overcome personal fears and seemingly impossible circumstances.

https://www.biblegateway.com/blog/2012/08/three-bible-heroes-who-doubted/

PREPARE FOR NEXT SUNDAY

Read **Judges 11:4–11, 29–31** and "Jephthah Answers the Call."

DAILY HOME BIBLE READINGS

MONDAY
Oppression Results from Disobedience
(Judges 6:1–10)

TUESDAY
May God Judge Enemies Harshly
(Psalm 83:1–12, 18)

WEDNESDAY
Gideon Sees the Angel of the Lord
(Judges 6:19–24)

THURSDAY
Fleece Confirms Victory Over Midianites
(Judges 6:36–40)

FRIDAY
Midianites Defeated Without Weapons
(Judges 7:19–23)

SATURDAY
Gideon Dies, Israel Forgets God's Ways
(Judges 8:29–35)

SUNDAY
Gideon's Call
(Judges 6:11–18)

COMMENTS / NOTES:

_____

_____

_____

_____

_____

_____

_____

_____

_____

_____

_____

_____

_____

_____

_____

_____

_____

_____

_____

_____

_____

_____

_____

JEPHTHAH ANSWERS THE CALL

BIBLE BASIS: JUDGES 11:4–11, 29–31

BIBLE TRUTH: God is no respecter of persons when choosing someone to do His work.

MEMORY VERSE: "And Jephthah said unto the elders of Gilead, If ye bring me home again to fight against the children of Ammon, and the LORD deliver them before me, shall I be your head?" (Judges 11:9).

LESSON AIM: By the end of the lesson, we will: DECIDE that people who have had disagreements can unite to defeat a common foe; VALUE the difference in others; and EVALUATE the importance of reaching "a meeting of the minds" on motives and expected outcomes before accepting a leadership role.

TEACHER PREPARATION

MATERIALS NEEDED: Quarterly Commentary/Teacher Manual, Adult Quarterly, Adult resources—charts, worksheets, and other teaching tools, paper, pens, pencils, Bibles (several different versions)

OTHER MATERIALS NEEDED / TEACHER'S NOTES:

_____

_____

LESSON OVERVIEW

LIFE NEED FOR TODAY'S LESSON
People who are called to be leaders might question their supporters.

BIBLE LEARNING
Jephthah discussed the inconsistencies in the behavior of his supporters and established conditions for leadership.

BIBLE APPLICATION
Believers should decide that when others reject us, God will prepare a place for us to feel appreciated.

STUDENTS' RESPONSES
Believers can evaluate and enhance their leadership skills.

LESSON SCRIPTURE

JUDGES 11:4–11, 29–31, KJV

4 And it came to pass in process of time, that the children of Ammon made war against Israel.

5 And it was so, that when the children of Ammon made war against Israel, the elders

JUDGES 11:4–11, 29–31, AMP

4 Now it happened after a while that the Ammonites fought against Israel.

5 When the Ammonites fought against Israel, the elders of Gilead went to get Jephthah from the land of Tob;

of Gilead went to fetch Jephthah out of the land of Tob:

6 And they said unto Jephthah, Come, and be our captain, that we may fight with the children of Ammon.

7 And Jephthah said unto the elders of Gilead, Did not ye hate me, and expel me out of my father's house? and why are ye come unto me now when ye are in distress?

8 And the elders of Gilead said unto Jephthah, Therefore we turn again to thee now, that thou mayest go with us, and fight against the children of Ammon, and be our head over all the inhabitants of Gilead.

9 And Jephthah said unto the elders of Gilead, If ye bring me home again to fight against the children of Ammon, and the LORD deliver them before me, shall I be your head?

10 And the elders of Gilead said unto Jephthah, The LORD be witness between us, if we do not so according to thy words.

11 Then Jephthah went with the elders of Gilead, and the people made him head and captain over them: and Jephthah uttered all his words before the LORD in Mizpeh.

29 Then the Spirit of the LORD came upon Jephthah, and he passed over Gilead, and Manasseh, and passed over Mizpeh of Gilead, and from Mizpeh of Gilead he passed over unto the children of Ammon.

30 And Jephthah vowed a vow unto the LORD, and said, If thou shalt without fail deliver the children of Ammon into mine hands,

31 Then it shall be, that whatsoever cometh forth of the doors of my house to meet me, when I return in peace from the children of Ammon, shall surely be the LORD's, and I will offer it up for a burnt offering.

6 and they said to Jephthah, "Come and be our leader, so that we may fight against the Ammonites."

7 But Jephthah said to the elders of Gilead, "Did you not hate me and drive me from the house of my father? Why have you come to me now when you are in trouble?"

8 The elders of Gilead said to Jephthah, "This is why we have turned to you now: that you may go with us and fight the Ammonites and become head over all the inhabitants of Gilead."

9 So Jephthah said to the elders of Gilead, "If you take me back [home] to fight against the Ammonites and the LORD gives them over to me, will I [really] become your head?"

10 The elders of Gilead said to Jephthah, "The LORD is the witness between us; be assured that we will do as you have said."

11 So Jephthah went with the elders of Gilead, and the people made him head and leader over them. And Jephthah repeated everything that he had promised before the LORD at Mizpah.

29 Then the Spirit of the LORD came upon Jephthah, and he passed through Gilead and Manasseh, and Mizpah of Gilead, and from Mizpah of Gilead he passed on to the Ammonites.

30 Jephthah made a vow to the LORD and said, "If You will indeed give the Ammonites into my hand,

31 then whatever comes out of the doors of my house to meet me when I return in peace from the Ammonites, it shall be the LORD's, and I will offer it up as a burnt offering."

LIGHT ON THE WORD

Jephthah. A skilled negotiator and warrior, Jephthah was chosen as a leader to defeat the Ammonites because of his ability to negotiate with both the Israelites and the Ammonite king. Although he was ostracized by his family for being the illegitimate child of his father, Gilead, and a prostitute, Jephthah rose as a leader to become Israel's judge. Jephthah's history and family line could not change his destiny—God would still use him. He would, however, make a vow that would cost him dearly—which teaches us caution before making a covenant with God without counting the cost.

TEACHING THE BIBLE LESSON

LIFE NEED FOR TODAY'S LESSON

AIM: Students will relate to leaders questioning their supporters.

INTRODUCTION

The Ammonites

The Ammonites were a group of people who descended from Ammon, who was conceived by Lot's younger daughter (**Genesis 19:30–38**). This is important to note because Ammon was an ally to Moab, another nation conceived through the incestuous relationship between Lot and his daughters. In the time of the judges, the nation of Ammon was at war with Israel. After defeating the tribes of Judah, Benjamin, and Ephraim, Ammon was an impenetrable enemy that Israel had a slim chance of defeating; victory would require uncanny wisdom and much faith in God.

BIBLE LEARNING

AIM: Students will assess Jephthah's reasoning as he discussed the inconsistencies in the request and his community's previous behavior.

I. FEELING OF REJECTION
(Judges 11:4–8)

Because his brothers and the community rejected him, Jephthah entered into a position of leadership with emotional baggage. He carried this resentment with him as he navigated his position as judge and soon-to-be leader of the Israelites. Jephthah reminds the elders of Gilead that although they needed his help, they had also been the ones who rejected him. The elders admitted their guilt and begged Jephthah to lead them into victory over the Ammonites.

Rejection and Victory (Judges 11:4–8)

4 And it came to pass in process of time, that the children of Ammon made war against Israel.

The phrase "And it came to pass" introduces a new scene related to the previous scene or event. It can also indicate the passing of time. Another way of saying this is "After a while," implying that some distance has passed between the events that came before the current episode, but that they are related. As such, **Judges 11:4** establishes that the current state of war with the Ammonites (literally "sons of Ammon" or "descendants of Ammon") is related to the preceding threat of war by the Ammonites against Israel in **Judges 10:17**. Up to this point in the story, the Israelites had been under Ammonite subjugation, but now tensions have broken into war between the two nations.

5 And it was so, that when the children of Ammon made war against Israel, the elders of Gilead went to fetch Jephthah out of the land of Tob: 6 And they said unto Jephthah, Come, and be our captain, that we may fight with the children of Ammon.

Gilead was both a personal name and the name of the northern Transjordanian territory occupied by the Israelite tribes of Reuben, Gad, and the half-tribe of Manasseh (**Numbers**

34:14–15). The Ammonites, who occupied central Transjordan, were on the march to engage Israel in Gilead. The theological justification for the war was that the Israelites were facing the consequences of worshiping foreign gods (**Judges 10:6–7, 13**). They had rebelled against God, so He allowed them to be oppressed by the Ammonites. When the Israelites could stand their affliction no longer, they cried out to God for deliverance (**v. 15**), and He took pity on them (**v. 16**). Their unlikely hero was Jephthah, a mighty warrior and son of Gilead. The text is ambiguous about whether his father's name was Gilead or he was descended from the line of Gilead. Jephthah's story follows a popular motif in the Old Testament narratives of the least becoming the first (e.g., **Genesis 25:22–23; Judges 6:15; 1 Samuel 16:13**). He was unlikely because his mother was a prostitute (Heb. *'ishsha zonah*, **eesh-AH zoh-NAH; Judges 11:1**). It is unclear whether she was a woman whose status as an unmarried mother placed her outside social boundaries, since the term used here often refers to a woman having extramarital sex (cf. **Hosea 1:2**).

Jephthah lived with his father, Gilead, and was raised within his father's household. Gilead provided for him, and he included Jephthah in his inheritance. The fact that a father is not married to his child's mother does not equate to absenteeism. Nevertheless, his father also had sons from his legal wife, and when they grew older, they forced Jephthah to depart from Gilead to keep him from receiving part of their father's inheritance. Jephthah fled to the land of Tob, where he built a reputation as the leader of a band of outlaws (**v. 3**). The elders traveled to Tob to bring Jephthah back to Gilead to be their military leader.

7 And Jephthah said unto the elders of Gilead, Did not ye hate me, and expel me out of my father's house? and why are ye come unto me now when ye are in distress? 8 And the elders of Gilead said unto Jephthah, Therefore we turn again to thee now, that thou mayest go with us, and fight against the children of Ammon, and be our head over all the inhabitants of Gilead.

It must have surprised Jephthah when members of the same extended family who had expelled him from Gilead came to bring him back from Tob to lead the military campaign against Ammon. He responded skeptically, reminding them of how they had mistreated him when it suited them. Jephthah accuses the elders of being complicit in his being separated from his family line and inheritance (cf. **v. 2**). The elders seem to realize that Jephthah will not comply with their request. In response, using a more conciliatory tone, they up the ante; they will make him the head (Heb. *ro'sh*, **ROASH**) of all Gilead. The elders' initial offer was for Jephthah to take the temporary position of military leader or ruler (Heb. *qatsin*, **kat-SEEN**). However, now if he would come with them and lead them in battle against the Ammonites, they would also make him head of the Gileadites, as the military captains had originally planned (**Judges 10:18**).

II. SEEING THE BIGGER PICTURE (vv. 9–11)

Once Jephthah accepted his position as leader, he had to begin to see the bigger picture: though his family and community had rejected him because of the circumstances of his birth, he now had to take on the role and responsibility of being their leader. The city where he accepts this role, Mizpeh, means "lookout" or "watchtower." This is symbolic of Jephthah's role as ruler, as he will "lookout" for the people of Israel and negotiate on their behalf.

Jephthah's Offer to the Elders (vv. 9–11)

9 And Jephthah said unto the elders of Gilead, If ye bring me home again to fight

against the children of Ammon, and the LORD deliver them before me, shall I be your head? 10 And the elders of Gilead said unto Jephthah, The LORD be witness between us, if we do not so according to thy words.

Jephthah was likely aware of the captains' offer and feigned reluctance as a negotiating tactic to get the elders to offer to make him both captain and head. The position of military leader was temporary and ceased once the battle was won. However, the offer to make him the head or leader of the Gileadites was a permanent civil position. Jephthah proffered that if God gave him the victory, then they should make him their head. The elders agreed to these terms, reversing Jephthah's fortunes: the cast-out son who was made the least among his brothers would become the first as their ruler. The formula, "The LORD be witness between us," was used by two or more parties entering into an agreement or covenant to invoke God as a witness to compel the parties to comply with the terms of the agreement (cf. **Genesis 31:49**). The oath uttered by Laban, "The Lord watch between me and thee, when we are absent one from another," has been turned into a sentimental benediction. However, it was a covenant made between two adversaries, Laban and Jacob, and was a thinly disguised threat from Laban to bring harm to Jacob if he mistreated Laban's daughters, Rachel and Leah.

11 Then Jephthah went with the elders of Gilead, and the people made him head and captain over them: and Jephthah uttered all his words before the LORD in Mizpeh.

The relationship between Jephthah and the elders was not unlike the one between Laban and Jacob. An element of distrust required them to call on God as a witness to their covenant. Jephthah and the elders departed for Mizpeh, where they ratified the agreement to make Jephthah their military and civilian head after the conflict ceased. Mizpeh was a sanctuary located on the border of Gilead between Ephraim and Benjamin. Laban had named it Mizpeh ("watchpost") because it was the place where he invoked God to watch between Jacob and him. Now, after having successfully negotiated the leadership position with the elders, Jephthah was installed as captain and head over all the Gileadites. He concluded the ceremony by affirming his agreement before God.

III. MAKING A VOW TO THE LORD (vv. 29–31)

By accepting the physical responsibility as leader of the people, Jephthah also has to accept the spiritual responsibility of leadership. His vow to God to make a burnt sacrifice of the first thing that greeted him after victory over the Ammonites seemed like a noble vow, but Jephthah had no way of knowing what—or who—would greet him after the war. Offering a sacrifice to God as a thank you for blessings was part of the culture. As a leader, however, Jephthah had to be mindful that being overzealous in his pursuit to reclaim his status might cause him to make a hasty vow.

WATCH WHAT YOU PROMISE (vv. 29–31)

29 Then the Spirit of the LORD came upon Jephthah, and he passed over Gilead, and Manasseh, and passed over Mizpeh of Gilead, and from Mizpeh of Gilead he passed over unto the children of Ammon.

God did not raise Jephthah up to be the deliverer in Gilead. However, God appears to tacitly approve the decision by the elders by bestowing His Spirit on Jephthah. Certain judges in the book of Judges were endowed with the Spirit of God, which granted them power and authority to accomplish the task before them, with sometimes mixed results (**Judges 3:10; 6:34; 13:25**).

Endowed with the Spirit, Jephthah goes out to meet the Ammonites. The reader expects that Jephthah will meet with success on account of God's Spirit being upon him.

30 And Jephthah vowed a vow unto the LORD, and said, If thou shalt without fail deliver the children of Ammon into mine hands, 31 Then it shall be, that whatsoever cometh forth of the doors of my house to meet me, when I return in peace from the children of Ammon, shall surely be the LORD's, and I will offer it up for a burnt offering.

"If…" These two letters can wield such tremendous power. Jephthah makes a vow to God that included a conditional clause foreboding terrible events to come. Before engaging the Ammonites in war, Jephthah vows that if God gives them into his hand, then whatever came out from his house to meet him, he would offer up to God as a burnt offering. Jephthah's vow interrupts the flow of the narrative. The normal sequence should have been the coming of God's Spirit upon the judge, who goes out to meet the enemy, who is delivered into his hand as a result of the judge being endowed with God's Spirit. However, there is a departure from this pattern before the reporting of the battle resumes in **v. 32**. This signals that the focus is less on God delivering the enemy into Jephthah's hand than on the vow.

When Jephthah returned home, his only child, a daughter, ran to congratulate him with singing and dancing. Jephthah was devastated! Since sacrificing humans is against God's Law (**Leviticus 18:21, 20:2–5; Deuteronomy 12:31, 18:10**), Jephthah's anxiety to ensure his personal victory meant that his daughter's life would be dedicated to religious service. She would remain a virgin and never marry. She bemoaned her fate by spending two months in the mountains (**Judges 11:37–40**).

SEARCH THE SCRIPTURES

QUESTION 1
Thinking ahead, how might Jephthah's vow to God be detrimental to him in the future (**vv. 30–31**)?

Jephthah was denied the joy of having grandchildren.

QUESTION 2
Read **verse 31** and share why we sometimes do not think before we speak. Do you think that Jephthah was too confident when making his vow? Or, was Jephthah's vow an attempt to manipulate God to give him the victory?

Answers will vary.

LIGHT ON THE WORD
The Power of Words
Most scholars agree that the vow was an impetuous and faithless move by Jephthah. Jephthah's endowment with God's Spirit had already guaranteed him victory. However, it is more likely that Jephthah acted out of fear. His previous rejection by his kin had made him insecure. He needed this victory to cement his people's choice of him as their leader.

BIBLE APPLICATION

AIM: Students will agree that when others reject us, God will prepare a place for us to feel appreciated.

Have you even been in trouble and said to God, "Lord, if you just get me out of this situation, I promise to (fill in the blank)?" We often make promises to God and each other that are often times impossible to keep, even if we mean well when we make the promise. Scripture reminds us that we should let our "yes" be "yes" and our "no" be "no" (**Matthew 5:37**), for to promise anything beyond that can lead us down a path of broken promises.

STUDENTS' RESPONSES

AIM: Students will evaluate their own leadership skills.

In a world where we are pulled in many directions to commit ourselves to people and causes, it can be easy to step into roles of leadership that require more of us than we're willing to give. Often, it is our desire to reclaim our position in community. So we take on more responsibilities than we should, making it hard to keep our promises. This week, remember Jephthah's story and find ways to lead people without overpromising.

PRAYER

Dear Heavenly Father, our guide and our leader, show us how to lead, when to follow, and what to say. Give us the presence of mind and spirit to support our leaders. Your chosen ones may not always be who we think should lead, so open our hearts to walk in the path of leadership that You have given us. In the Name of Jesus, we pray. Amen.

HOW TO SAY IT

Gilead.   **GI**-lee-ad.

Ammon.   ah-**MOAN**.

Mizpeh.   miz-**PEH**.

DIG A LITTLE DEEPER

This section provides an additional research article to further your study of the lesson:

Judges is a thought-provoking book that can also be troubling at times. Jephthah's vow is disturbing, but this account underscores the importance of reading the Bible in its entirety. Here is an outline of the book of Judges that provides insight into the sin of the nation of Israel as well as the continual call of God for

His people. It's a sobering reminder that there are consequences for disobedience.

https://bible.org/seriespage/15-israel-s-dark-ages-judges

PREPARE FOR NEXT SUNDAY

Read **Judges 13:1–7, 24–25** and "Samson's Call."

DAILY HOME BIBLE READINGS

MONDAY
Jephthah, Rejected by His Family, Flees
(Judges 11:1–3)

TUESDAY
Jephthah Resolves a Dispute with Edom
(Judges 11:12–18)

WEDNESDAY
Jephthah Reveals God's Aid of Israel
(Judges 11:19–22)

THURSDAY
Ammonite King Rejects Jephthah's Claims
(Judges 11:23–28)

FRIDAY
Jephthah Sacrifices His Daughter
to Fulfill His Vow
(Judges 11:34–40)

SATURDAY
Leaders Discern the Way Forward
(Acts 15:6–21)

SUNDAY
Jephthah Answers the Call
(Judges 11:4–11)

SAMSON'S CALL

BIBLE BASIS: JUDGES 13:1–7, 24–25

BIBLE TRUTH: God's leaders are called and prepared to do His will in ways that may be challenging.

MEMORY VERSE: "For, lo, thou shalt conceive, and bear a son; and no razor shall come on his head: for the child shall be a Nazarite unto God from the womb: and he shall begin to deliver Israel out of the hand of the Philistines." (Judges 13:5).

LESSON AIM: By the end of this lesson, we will: EVALUATE the details of Samson's birth and calling; EMPATHIZE how the emotions Samson probably experienced regarding lifestyle restrictions imposed on him by others; and ACKNOWLEDGE that unforeseen circumstances prepare people for leadership roles today.

TEACHER PREPARATION

MATERIALS NEEDED: Quarterly Commentary/Teacher Manual, Adult Quarterly, Adult resources—charts, worksheets, and other teaching tools, paper, pens, pencils, Bibles (several different versions)

OTHER MATERIALS NEEDED / TEACHER'S NOTES:

_____

_____

LESSON OVERVIEW

LIFE NEED FOR TODAY'S LESSON
Preparation for leadership may involve life circumstances not of one's own choosing.

BIBLE LEARNING
Samson's call was assured as shown by the instructions the Lord's angel gave to his mother.

BIBLE APPLICATION
As God set Samson apart to become one of Israel's judges, He also sets us apart for leadership roles.

STUDENTS' RESPONSES
God will provide blessings in impossible situations.

LESSON SCRIPTURE

JUDGES 13:1–7, 24–25, KJV

1 And the children of Israel did evil again in the sight of the LORD; and the LORD delivered them into the hand of the Philistines forty years.

2 And there was a certain man of Zorah, of the family of the Danites, whose name was

JUDGES 13:1–7, 24–25, AMP

1 Now Israel again did what was evil in the sight of the LORD, and the LORD gave them into the hands of the Philistines for forty years.

2 And there was a certain man of Zorah, of the family of the Danites, whose name was

Manoah; and his wife was barren, and bare not.

3 And the angel of the LORD appeared unto the woman, and said unto her, Behold now, thou art barren, and bearest not: but thou shalt conceive, and bear a son.

4 Now therefore beware, I pray thee, and drink not wine nor strong drink, and eat not any unclean thing:

5 For, lo, thou shalt conceive, and bear a son; and no razor shall come on his head: for the child shall be a Nazarite unto God from the womb: and he shall begin to deliver Israel out of the hand of the Philistines.

6 Then the woman came and told her husband, saying, A man of God came unto me, and his countenance was like the countenance of an angel of God, very terrible: but I asked him not whence he was, neither told he me his name:

7 But he said unto me, Behold, thou shalt conceive, and bear a son; and now drink no wine nor strong drink, neither eat any unclean thing: for the child shall be a Nazarite to God from the womb to the day of his death.

24 And the woman bare a son, and called his name Samson: and the child grew, and the LORD blessed him.

25 And the Spirit of the LORD began to move him at times in the camp of Dan between Zorah and Eshtaol.

Manoah; and his wife was infertile and had no children.

3 And the Angel of the LORD appeared to the woman and said to her, "Behold, you are infertile and have no children, but you shall conceive and give birth to a son.

4 Therefore, be careful not to drink wine or [any other] intoxicating drink, and do not eat anything [ceremonially] unclean.

5 For behold, you shall conceive and give birth to a son. No razor shall come upon his head, for the boy shall be a Nazirite [dedicated] to God from birth; and he shall begin to rescue Israel from the hands of the Philistines."

6 Then the woman went and told her husband, saying, "A Man of God came to me and his appearance was like the appearance of the Angel of God, very awesome. I did not ask Him where he came from, and he did not tell me his name.

7 But He said to me, 'Behold, you shall conceive and give birth to a son, and now you shall not drink wine or [any other] intoxicating drink, nor eat anything [ceremonially] unclean, for the boy shall be a Nazirite to God from birth to the day of his death.'"

24 So the woman [in due time] gave birth to a son and named him Samson; and the boy grew and the LORD blessed him.

25 And the Spirit of the LORD began to stir him at times in Mahaneh-dan, between Zorah and Eshtaol.

LIGHT ON THE WORD

Philistines. One of the Aegean "Sea Peoples," the Philistines migrated to Palestine in approximately the twelfth century BC and established themselves in five city states called the Philistine Pentapolis: Gaza, Ashkelon, Ashdod, Ekron, and Gath. The Philistines' military superiority, economic strength, and administrative capabilities enabled them to be dominant over the Israelites (**1 Samuel 13**). The Philistine threat to Judah is first seen in the account of Samson (**Judges 13–16**).

TEACHING THE BIBLE LESSON

LIFE NEED FOR TODAY'S LESSON

AIM: Students will agree that preparation for leadership may involve life circumstances not of one's own choosing.

INTRODUCTION

Sin, Rebellion, Mercy, and Grace

The book of Judges describes a period in Israelite history characterized by idolatry, debauchery, sin, rebellion, and oppression on one hand, and repentance, mercy, grace, and peace on the other. The book spans the period between the death of the Israelite leader Joshua and the chaotic infighting of Israelite tribes before the rise of the monarchy. The Children of Israel did not heed God's instruction and failed to remove the inhabitants completely from the land (**Judges 1:19–36, 2:1–2**). Repeatedly throughout the book is this sad commentary: "In those days [when the judges governed] there was no king in Israel; every man did what was right in his own eyes" (Judges 21:25, AMP; see also Judges 17:6). Because of Israel's disobedience, God allowed the Canaanites, Sidonians, Hivites, and Philistines to remain in the land and become snares to the Israelites (**Judges 2:3, 3:1–7**).

BIBLE LEARNING

AIM: Students will decide that Samson's call was assured as shown by the instructions the Lord's angel gave to his mother.

I. THE PROBLEM OF SIN AND OPPRESSION (Judges 13:1)

Judges 13:1 begins another cycle of oppression as God hands Israel over to the Philistines, who would rule over them for forty years. This is the sixth time the phrase "And the children of Israel did evil again..." is used in the book of Judges (**3:7, 12, 4:1, 6:1, 10:6**). While the judge-deliverer was alive, the Children of Israel had relative peace. With the judge's death, the Israelites reverted back to their rebellion and rejection of God's commandments. Because of their disobedience and rejection, they were given over to Philistine oppression (**Judges 10:6–7, 13:1**). In this cycle of oppression, the pattern of repentance was broken: there was no indication that the Children of Israel cried out to God in repentance, as they had done in the past (**3:15, 4:3, 6:6, 10:10**).

1 And the children of Israel did evil again in the sight of the LORD; and the LORD delivered them into the hand of the Philistines forty years.

Since the Israelites continued to do evil in the sight of God, He punished them—they experienced His wrath—and God used the Philistines to carry out His punishment on His own people. **Judges 13:1** tells us that the Israelites chose sin, "evil" (Heb. *ra'*, **RAH**), meaning "wickedness, wrong," in the sight of the omnipresent (all-present), holy (set apart from sin) Lord. He deemed that their actions were sinful; He "delivered" them (Heb. *natan*, **nah-TAHN**), which means He "gave" them into the hands of their enemies for forty years.

II. GOD'S PROMISE OF DELIVERANCE (vv. 2–7)

Just as the all-powerful, true, and living God was in charge by allowing the Philistines to take the Children of Israel into bondage, He was in charge in delivering them from bondage.

Looking at their continual cycle of sin, the Israelites now began to cry out to God for deliverance. God raised up their deliverer through a barren (Heb. 'aqar, **ah-KAR,** sterile, childless, fruitless) woman. This is a clear case of God doing the impossible. The man whose name was Manoah lived in Zorah, which was a town in Dan. The phrase "a certain man" should also remind us that God uses ordinary—often totally inadequate—people to do His work. Through these people, God can get all the glory due to Him for the outcomes He has caused.

A Special Announcement (vv. 2–7)

2 And there was a certain man of Zorah, of the family of the Danites, whose name was Manoah; and his wife was barren, and bare not. 3 And the angel of the LORD appeared unto the woman, and said unto her, Behold now, thou art barren, and bearest not: but thou shalt conceive, and bear a son.

The Israelites did not cry out in repentance under the weight of oppression, and God made no announcement that He would raise up a judge-deliverer (**2:16, 18, 3:9, 15**). **Judges 13:2–7** functions as a birth and calling narrative for the final judge, Samson. In **Judges 13:2**, Manoah is introduced, and his tribal affiliation and geographical location are given. In contrast, his wife is introduced as the unnamed and barren woman. In **verse 3**, the angel of the Lord appears to the woman and announces to her that she will become pregnant and give birth to a child. Like Sarah, Rachel, and Hannah before her, this woman would bear a son because of the Lord. There is no context for where Manoah's wife was when the angel came to her or whether she had been pleading to God regarding her infertility. However, her barrenness was not unnoticed by God, who is not bound by impossible circumstances. He can and does work in and through what seems impossible in man's eyes to accomplish His purposes.

4 Now therefore beware, I pray thee, and drink not wine nor strong drink, and eat not any unclean thing: 5 For, lo, thou shalt conceive, and bear a son; and no razor shall come on his head: for the child shall be a Nazarite unto God from the womb: and he shall begin to deliver Israel out of the hand of the Philistines.

The boy's conception and birth were God's doing and came with special restrictions (**Judges 13:4**). The mother was to maintain a strict diet—no wine, no strong alcoholic beverages, and no unclean food—during the time of her pregnancy. The restriction of unclean food was not a new restriction for an Israelite, but given the spiritual state of the people and their rejection of God, this mother had to be reminded about what He required (**Leviticus 11; Deuteronomy 14**). In **verse 5**, the restrictions expanded to include postnatal care of the baby: his hair was never to be cut. The reason for the restrictions became evident, as the boy was to be dedicated to God as a Nazarite. He would begin to deliver his people from the Philistines. **Numbers 6:1–21** outlines the provisions of the Nazarite vow. Normally, a person would make this vow voluntarily to show his dedication to God for a period of time. In this case, God divinely imposed the vow upon the boy for the duration of his life. The boy had been called by God and was appointed for a specific task.

6 Then the woman came and told her husband, saying, A man of God came unto me, and his countenance was like the countenance of an angel of God, very terrible: but I asked him not whence he was, neither told he me his name: 7 But he said unto me, Behold, thou shalt conceive, and bear a son; and now drink no wine nor strong drink, neither eat any unclean thing: for the child shall be a Nazarite to God from the womb to the day of his death.

In response to the angel's announcement, the wife ran to her husband to tell him what had happened (**Judges 13:6**). Her report first described the angel as a man of God who looked like an angel of God. Only after describing this heavenly visitor did she recount the message she received. She told her husband that they would have a son, and told him about the dietary restrictions. Their son would be dedicated to God as a Nazarite from birth.

III. FULFILLMENT OF THE PROMISE (vv. 24–25)

At the end of **chapter 13**, the author reiterates that the promise given to the woman was not just a figment of her imagination; it was fulfilled. Manoah's wife did bear a son and she named him Samson. God's call was evident in the boy's life because he grew up and was blessed by the Lord, and the Lord's Spirit began to impel him. God, in His mercy, did not leave His people without deliverance. They did not cry out to Him in repentance nor turn from their wicked ways. Still, God raised up someone whom He would use to begin to deliver His people.

24 And the woman bare a son, and called his name Samson: and the child grew, and the LORD blessed him.

There is a song the lyrics of which read "All God's promises are true." This part of the text demonstrates that God fulfills His promises. Yes, His promises are indeed true! The woman who was barren for so many years gave birth to a son "and called his name Samson" (**v. 24**). In Hebrew, "Samson" is Shimshon (**sheem-SHONE**) and means "like the sun." Samson was also blessed (Heb. *barak*, **bah-ROCK**), which means "saluted, adored"; his blessings flowed from God. In other words, when Samson obeyed God and did His will, his life was blessed.

25 And the Spirit of the LORD began to move him at times in the camp of Dan between Zorah and Eshtaol.

God's Spirit denotes His presence with His people. The word "Spirit" (Heb. *ruakh*, **ROO-akh**) means "wind, breath, mind, spirit," but here it refers to God's presence and power at work in Samson. The one true God was preparing Samson to deliver His people from the hands of their enemies. So God began to prepare Samson for his role as judge of Israel, where he would reign twenty years. After forty years, the Israelites were going to be set free from the Philistines' bondage, and all that they could do was yield to the power of Almighty God.

Samson's tenure as judge was marked by moments of foolishness and tragedy. Even though Samson sinned terribly and often used poor judgment, God still accomplished much through him. Frail humanity cannot hinder His plans. Whatever He decrees will certainly come to fruition. The bigger picture is that in spite of Samson's behavior, God wanted to free His chosen people from bondage, and He did just that. The destiny of the Children of Israel and God's purpose for their lives were always in His hands. In comparison, Samson was like the nation of Israel: he was called by God to be a judge, and just as the nation thrived when they obeyed God, Samson thrived as long as he obeyed God. We, too, will thrive as long as we obey God and follow His inerrant Word.

SEARCH THE SCRIPTURES

QUESTION 1
Samson was called to be a Nazarite (**Judges 13:5, Numbers 6:1–21**). Is this particular calling applicable to Christians living in the 21st century?

Answers will vary.

QUESTION 2
The text says that the Spirit of the Lord began to move Samson (**v. 25**). How do we know when the Spirit of the Lord is moving us?

Answers will vary.

LIGHT ON THE WORD

A Right Relationship

From the book of Judges and this lesson, we should learn that a holy God hates sin and punishes it as well. Sin has dire consequences. The ultimate penalty for sin is death, and God sets before us the way of life and the way of death (**Jeremiah 21:8**). At the other end of the spectrum is the fact that He also works out miraculous redemption plans and forgives sin; those who repent (turn from sin and turn to God) can be restored to a right relationship with Him.

BIBLE APPLICATION

AIM: Students will affirm that God set Samson apart for Himself to become one of Israel's judges, and sets us apart for leadership roles.

Parents have a huge responsibility as the ones who must teach and lead their children in a growing relationship with Christ. In a culture becoming increasingly non-Christian, parenting has become a huge challenge for those seeking a godly family. Parents must find creative ways to teach their children about who God is and model for them how to have a relationship with Him. Parents are not perfect; neither are kids. We are all flawed. But, God can and will use us when we surrender to Him.

STUDENTS' RESPONSES

AIM: Students will decide that God provides blessings in impossible situations.

God uses a variety of things in our lives—our childhood, family situations, personalities, strengths, weaknesses, talents, environments, experiences—for His glory. Nothing that we go through in our lives is wasted, but we must be open and allow the Lord to use these situations to mold and shape us. Prayerfully reflect on your life this week. List three things the Lord might have been doing in your life that you may have overlooked. What are some circumstances He has used to shape you that have influenced your life today?

PRAYER

Dear Heavenly Father, thank You for Your faithfulness. Forgive us when we ignore Your warnings and persist in actions and attitudes that grieve the Holy Spirit. We repent and turn from our sin. May we be worthy that You choose us as leaders to deliver Your Word to Your people. In the Name of Jesus, we pray. Amen.

HOW TO SAY IT

Ekron.   ek-**RAHN**.

Manoah.   ma-**NO**-uh.

Ashkelon.   ash-ku-**LAHN**.

DIG A LITTLE DEEPER

This section provides an additional research article to further your study of the lesson:

In this article recounting an archaeological dig, the account of Samson unfolds into a beautiful mosaic. This was an unlikely discovery, because it was previously thought to be located in an area where Jewish people were highly persecuted. This scientific article demonstrates the continuity of Scripture and the preservation of the integrity of biblical accounts.

http://www.livescience.com/21331-ancient-mosaic-bible-story-samson.html

PREPARE FOR NEXT SUNDAY

Read **Exodus 3:1–12** and "Moses and the Burning Bush."

DAILY HOME BIBLE READINGS

MONDAY
Announcement of Samson's Birth to Manoah
(Judges 13:8–18)

TUESDAY
The Angel Accepts Manoah's Sacrifice
(Judges 13:19–23)

WEDNESDAY
Vow of Separation to the Lord
(Numbers 6:1–8, 13–17)

THURSDAY
Samson Marries a Woman of Timnah
(Judges 14:1–9)

FRIDAY
Samson Conquers the Philistines
(Judges 15:1–8)

SATURDAY
In Death, Samson Defeats the Philistines
(Judges 16:23–31)

SUNDAY
Samson's Call
(Judges 13:1–7, 24–25)

COMMENTS / NOTES:

MOSES AND THE BURNING BUSH

BIBLE BASIS: EXODUS 3:1–12

BIBLE TRUTH: God speaks to His people in creative ways.

MEMORY VERSES: "Now therefore, behold, the cry of the children of Israel is come unto me: and I have also seen the oppression wherewith the Egyptians oppress them. Come now therefore, and I will send thee unto Pharaoh, that thou mayest bring forth my people the children of Israel out of Egypt" (Exodus 3:9–10).

LESSON AIM: By the end of this lesson, we will: EVALUATE the remarkable details of how Moses was called by God; RESPECT God's disdain for injustice and His desire to correct it; and COMMIT to eradicate injustice in ways that honor God's identity, purpose, and presence.

TEACHER PREPARATION

MATERIALS NEEDED: Quarterly Commentary/Teacher Manual, Adult Quarterly, Adult resources—charts, worksheets, and other teaching tools, paper, pens, pencils, Bibles (several different versions)

OTHER MATERIALS NEEDED / TEACHER'S NOTES:

_____

_____

LESSON OVERVIEW

LIFE NEED FOR TODAY'S LESSON
People desire effective ways to address injustice.

BIBLE APPLICATION
Believers are called to challenge injustice and advocate for social equity in an unjust world.

BIBLE LEARNING
God calls Moses to redeem the lives of His people.

STUDENTS' RESPONSES
Christians are expected to choose justice and care for those who are oppressed.

LESSON SCRIPTURE

EXODUS 3:1–12, KJV

1 Now Moses kept the flock of Jethro his father in law, the priest of Midian: and he led the flock to the backside of the desert, and came to the mountain of God, even to Horeb.

2 And the angel of the LORD appeared

EXODUS 3:1–12, AMP

1 Now Moses was keeping the flock of Jethro (Reuel) his father-in-law, the priest of Midian; and he led his flock to the west side of the wilderness and came to Horeb (Sinai), the mountain of God.

2 The Angel of the LORD appeared to him

unto him in a flame of fire out of the midst of a bush: and he looked, and, behold, the bush burned with fire, and the bush was not consumed.

3 And Moses said, I will now turn aside, and see this great sight, why the bush is not burnt.

4 And when the LORD saw that he turned aside to see, God called unto him out of the midst of the bush, and said, Moses, Moses. And he said, Here am I.

5 And he said, Draw not nigh hither: put off thy shoes from off thy feet, for the place whereon thou standest is holy ground.

6 Moreover he said, I am the God of thy father, the God of Abraham, the God of Isaac, and the God of Jacob. And Moses hid his face; for he was afraid to look upon God.

7 And the LORD said, I have surely seen the affliction of my people which are in Egypt, and have heard their cry by reason of their taskmasters; for I know their sorrows;

8 And I am come down to deliver them out of the hand of the Egyptians, and to bring them up out of that land unto a good land and a large, unto a land flowing with milk and honey; unto the place of the Canaanites, and the Hittites, and the Amorites, and the Perizzites, and the Hivites, and the Jebusites.

9 Now therefore, behold, the cry of the children of Israel is come unto me: and I have also seen the oppression wherewith the Egyptians oppress them.

10 Come now therefore, and I will send thee unto Pharaoh, that thou mayest bring forth my people the children of Israel out of Egypt.

11 And Moses said unto God, Who am I, that I should go unto Pharaoh, and that I

in a blazing flame of fire from the midst of a bush; and he looked, and behold, the bush was on fire, yet it was not consumed.

3 So Moses said, "I must turn away [from the flock] and see this great sight—why the bush is not burned up."

4 When the LORD saw that he turned away [from the flock] to look, God called to him from the midst of the bush and said, "Moses, Moses!" And he said, "Here I am."

5 Then God said, "Do not come near; take your sandals off your feet [out of respect], because the place on which you are standing is holy ground."

6 Then He said, "I am the God of your father, the God of Abraham, the God of Isaac, and the God of Jacob." Then Moses hid his face, because he was afraid to look at God.

7 The LORD said, "I have in fact seen the affliction (suffering, desolation) of My people who are in Egypt, and have heard their cry because of their taskmasters (oppressors); for I know their pain and suffering.

8 So I have come down to rescue them from the hand (power) of the Egyptians, and to bring them up from that land to a land [that is] good and spacious, to a land flowing with milk and honey [a land of plenty]—to the place of the Canaanite, the Hittite, the Amorite, the Perizzite, the Hivite, and the Jebusite.

9 Now, behold, the cry of the children of Israel has come to Me; and I have also seen how the Egyptians oppress them.

10 Therefore, come now, and I will send you to Pharaoh, and then bring My people, the children of Israel, out of Egypt."

11 But Moses said to God, "Who am I, that I should go to Pharaoh, and that I should

should bring forth the children of Israel out of Egypt?

12 And he said, Certainly I will be with thee; and this shall be a token unto thee, that I have sent thee: When thou hast brought forth the people out of Egypt, ye shall serve God upon this mountain.

bring the children of Israel out of Egypt?"

12 And God said, "Certainly I will be with you, and this shall be the sign to you that it is I who have sent you: when you have brought the people out of Egypt, you shall serve and worship God at this mountain."

LIGHT ON THE WORD

Mount Sinai. This mountain was a very important landmark for the Israelites. Also called Horeb, it has huge significance in Judaism. Mount Sinai is both the site of Moses receiving his call from God (**Exodus 3:1**) and the Children of Israel receiving God's Law and covenant (**Exodus 19–20**). After the Israelites were rescued from Egypt, they crossed the Red Sea into the wilderness; there they camped at the foot of Mt. Sinai while Moses climbed the mountain to enter God's presence. God revealed Himself to Moses and gave to him His Law and covenant affirming Israel as His holy nation. God would be their leader (**Exodus 19:3–6**).

TEACHING THE BIBLE LESSON

LIFE NEED FOR TODAY'S LESSON

AIM: Students will agree that people desire effective ways to address injustice.

INTRODUCTION

God Will Deliver His People

Jacob's family moved to Egypt at the invitation of Joseph, who had been reunited with his family after being raised to a position of prominence in Egypt. During the famine, Joseph had control of Egypt's stores and resources as one of Pharaoh's rulers. Seventy of Jacob's direct descendants moved with him to Egypt.

In time, Jacob, Joseph, and Joseph's brothers died; Jacob's descendants grew in number, and the Egyptians began to fear them. The pharaoh, who came to power after Joseph's death, did not know Joseph or the Israelites' history in Egypt. He worried that this growing group of people would one day rise up to conquer his kingdom. So, in an effort to repress the Hebrews, the Egyptians made them slaves and forced them into hard and oppressive labor. God was aware of His people's troubles, because He told Abraham that His people would be strangers in a foreign land and oppressed as slaves for four hundred years. However, He would rescue His people and punish the oppressor (**Genesis 15:13–16**).

BIBLE LEARNING

AIM: Students will validate that God called Moses to redeem the lives of His people.

I. GOD APPEARS (Exodus 3:1–4)

Moses was carrying out his usual work as a shepherd. The verb translated "kept" is more literally "was shepherding" in the Hebrew (*hayah roʻeh*, **hah-YAH ro-EH**). This participle expresses the continuance of the occupation; it was his habitual occupation.

Moses had become the shepherd of Jethro, his father-in-law. Jethro, called Reuel (**Exodus 2:18–20**), is probably a title meaning "eminence" or "highness." The story takes place many years after Moses fled from Egypt to Midian because he killed an Egyptian who was oppressing an Israelite. Pharaoh ordered Moses' arrest, but he escaped to Midian. Moses, now a fugitive, went from being a prince in Pharaoh's court to being God's shepherd in the wilderness. According to **Acts 7:30**, it was forty years later.

An Unexpected Visit (vv. 3–4)

1 Now Moses kept the flock of Jethro his father in law, the priest of Midian: and he led the flock to the backside of the desert, and came to the mountain of God, even to Horeb. 2 And the angel of the LORD appeared unto him in a flame of fire out of the midst of a bush: and he looked, and, behold, the bush burned with fire, and the bush was not consumed. 3 And Moses said, I will now turn aside, and see this great sight, why the bush is not burnt. 4 And when the LORD saw that he turned aside to see, God called unto him out of the midst of the bush, and said, Moses, Moses. And he said, Here am I.

The text begins by locating Moses in Midian and providing background to demonstrate that his life had changed. Once an Egyptian prince, Moses was now involved in the life of his own people. He was a shepherd, an occupation that he would have thought demeaning as an Egyptian, because Egyptians despised shepherds (**Genesis 46:34**).

Moses was out tending his father-in-law's flock, which suggests that he had not accumulated a flock of his own. He was located far away from Midian, because "he led the flock far into the wilderness and came to Sinai, the mountain of God." As a shepherd, he would have traveled to ensure he had good grazing pasture for his flock. Out in the wilderness at Sinai, God, in the form of the angel of the Lord, suddenly appears to Moses in a blazing fire from the bush. Moses saw the bush, that it was on fire but did not burn. Through this unusual encounter, God captures Moses' attention and reveals Himself. The Lord also does this in the life of the believer; in the midst of everyday life, He gets our attention as He draws us to Himself.

The Lord not only reveals Himself, but speaks and calls Moses by name, suggesting that this encounter was personal. In ancient Near Eastern culture, repeating the name signified endearment. This encounter must have disarmed Moses, because he immediately answers, "Here I am!" suggesting his readiness to listen.

II. THE PRESENCE OF GOD (vv. 5–6)

Moses was told not to come near. The phrase "draw not nigh hither" can be translated in modern language as "stop coming near, as you are doing." Moses did not recognize the presence or nature of God. Later, after his experience with the Lord, he would be ready to draw near Him and intercede for others (see **Exodus 32:30**).

Take Off Your Shoes (vv. 5–6)

5 And he said, Draw not nigh hither: put off thy shoes from off thy feet, for the place whereon thou standest is holy ground. 6 Moreover he said, I am the God of thy father, the God of Abraham, the God of Isaac, and the God of Jacob. And Moses hid his face; for he was afraid to look upon God.

Without disclosing His identity, God commands Moses not to come any closer, but to remove his sandals. He immediately reveals to Moses the holy nature of His presence. The ground itself was not holy, but it became holy because God was there. God is holy, and we cannot enter into His presence lightly or in any way that does not recognize the magnitude of His holiness. In acknowledgment of God's holiness, Moses takes off his sandals. Then, God discloses His identity, saying that He is the God of the patriarchs—Abraham, Isaac, and Jacob. God connects Moses to his heritage. Moses realizes that he is in the presence of God and responds by hiding his face because he was afraid to look at Him. In ancient Near Eastern culture, it was believed that if someone looked at a god, his life was in danger. Moses knew that looking at God could have meant death (**Genesis 32:30; Exodus 33:20; Judges 13:22**), because he understood that God is holy.

III. GOD ENGAGES MOSES (vv. 7–10)

God Himself, virtually in bodily form, had come down to deliver His people out the hands of the Egyptians. He would lead them to the land promised to their fathers: a good, large land, flowing with milk and honey. The expression "milk and honey" describes a land with abundant food—a prosperous and fertile land. It is a proverbial description of Canaan symbolizing continuity, stability, and identity, which only God can provide.

God's Rescue Plan (vv. 7-10)

7 And the LORD said, I have surely seen the affliction of my people which are in Egypt, and have heard their cry by reason of their taskmasters; for I know their sorrows; 8 And I am come down to deliver them out of the hand of the Egyptians, and to bring them up out of that land unto a good land and a large, unto a land flowing with milk and honey; unto the place of the Canaanites, and the Hittites, and the Amorites, and the Perizzites, and the Hivites, and the Jebusites. 9 Now therefore, behold, the cry of the children of Israel is come unto me: and I have also seen the oppression wherewith the Egyptians oppress them. 10 Come now therefore, and I will send thee unto Pharaoh, that thou mayest bring forth my people the children of Israel out of Egypt.

In **Exodus 2:23–25**, the Israelites cried out to God for deliverance. He heard their cry and remembered the covenant He made with Abraham, Issac, and Jacob (**Genesis 15:4–6, 26:1–5, 35:9–12**). God keeps His promises. The interaction between God and Moses continues in **verse 7**. God tells Moses He has seen, heard, and is aware of the suffering of His people in Egypt. In fact, the Hebrew text emphatically indicates that God certainly had seen His people's affliction. The emphasis in the text implies God's personal interest in His people's suffering. As believers, we must not forget that God is not blind to our suffering nor unconcerned with His people's afflictions (**Matthew 10:29–31**). We must trust Him in the midst of whatever we face, knowing that He will deliver in due time.

In **verse 8**, God shares His rescue plan with Moses: He has come down to deliver His people from their slavery. God was going to do something about their suffering. He would not only remove them from oppression, but also lead them to a good land, fertile and spacious but inhabited (**Genesis 12:1–3**). In **verse 9**, God reiterates that He has seen their oppression and has heard the cries of His people (**Exodus 2:23–25, 3:7**).

In **verse 10**, God tells Moses that He has chosen him to be an instrument in His hand. Moses will go to Pharaoh and will lead the people of Israel out of Egypt. In **Exodus 2:11–12**, Moses had rescued a Hebrew, killed an Egyptian, and fled. That time, Moses operated in his own strength. This time, his rescue mission was ordained by God.

Sometimes we move ahead of the Lord, taking on tasks in our strength rather than waiting to be empowered by the Lord. God called Moses to partner with Him to redeem His people from slavery.

IV. GOD COMMISSIONS MOSES (vv. 11–12)

The Lord, in answer to Moses' fear, told him that He Himself would be with him. Where Moses' abilities might fail would be a God of unlimited abilities. What Moses desired was assurance that God had truly sent him.

God Empowered Moses (vv. 11–12)

11 And Moses said unto God, Who am I, that I should go unto Pharaoh, and that I should bring forth the children of Israel out of Egypt? 12 And he said, Certainly I will be with thee; and this shall be a token unto thee, that I have sent thee: When thou hast brought forth the people out of Egypt, ye shall serve God upon this mountain.

Moses, who earlier said "Here I am," now responds to God's call with questions. "Who am I, that I should go to Pharaoh, and that I should bring the children of Israel out of Egypt?" (**Exodus 3:11, AMP**). God assures Moses that He would be with him. God's call and presence would give Moses the authority and power he would need to stand before Pharaoh and lead the people. God would not only be with Moses but also give him a sign that would prove to him that he would be fulfilling God's assigned task. The people would successfully leave Egypt, come to Mount Sinai, and worship before their God. The sign would only be seen after Moses was obedient.

No matter how Moses felt about what God had called him to do, what was important was that God empowered him and would be with him to execute His plan. Moses' success was not dependent on who he was nor his ability, but his obedience and trust in God. God equips and empowers those whom He calls to do His work.

We must be obedient to the call and faithful to the tasks He has called us to do, knowing that He will enable us to accomplish them.

SEARCH THE SCRIPTURES

QUESTION 1

Moses had an unusual experience with God that quickly captured his attention. What experience have you had with God that has captured your attention to serve His people (**Exodus 3:2–4**)?

The burning bush. Answers will vary.

QUESTION 2

What does the account of Moses' call tell about God? What characteristics of God are highlighted (**vv. 1–12**)?

God is extremely creative, prepares His leaders, is patient, and chooses various types of leaders. Answers will vary.

LIGHT ON THE WORD

Theophany

The term "theophany" does not occur in the Bible, but is used to describe a narrative in which God's presence is made visible to either individuals or groups. The word is derived from two Greek words: *theos*, "God," and *phainein*, "to appear." In the Old Testament, God's appearance takes various forms. In **Exodus 3:1–12**, God appears to Moses as the angel of the Lord in the blazing fire in the bush.

BIBLE APPLICATION

AIM: Students will validate that believers are called to challenge injustice and advocate for justice in an unjust world.

The Israelites were oppressed foreigners in Egypt. Moses understood God's holiness and obeyed His call to help redeem the Israelites whom God called to Himself. As believers, we have to see injustice through the lens of who God is and we must get involved. Today, in our country and all over the world, people are being oppressed. Statistics show that approximately 27 million people are in some form of slavery worldwide. There are an equally overwhelming number of people who are slaves to sin. Here in the United States, sex trafficking of foster children and other kinds of injustices are apparent in our society. How can the church get involved to help fight against such atrocities? How can you get involved to fight against injustice? God used Moses to deliver slaves from Egypt. How can you help deliver from bondage those who are slaves to sin?

STUDENTS' RESPONSES

AIM: Students will decide that Christians are expected to choose justice and care for those who are oppressed.

Commit to pray this week, asking God to reveal to you specifically where and how you can become involved in helping those suffering and in need. Here a few suggestions:

- Write two ways God may be signaling you to get more involved at church, in the community, or with charity to help those in need. Decide on your plan of action to respond.

- Partner with your church, and select one place to volunteer for a few hours.

- Partner with a foster care agency to begin a Covenants for Kids program in your area (see Dig a Little Deeper).

- Partner with your church outreach team and help the homeless, seniors, and others by sharing the Gospel of Jesus Christ.

PRAYER

Dear Lord, You call us in the most unexpected times, and in the most unexpected ways. Yet, when we are afraid to follow You or to believe that we can do what You have called us to do, You continue to encourage us and give us strength for the journey. Thank You Lord for reassuring us. Help us to make a difference in our community. In the Name of Jesus, we pray. Amen.

HOW TO SAY IT

Midian.   **MI**-dee-an.

Theos.   theh-**AHS**.

Phainein.   **FEYE**-nane.

DIG A LITTLE DEEPER

This section provides an additional research article to further your study of the lesson:

When children are emancipated from foster care, they do so without caring connections to adults. Within months, many are homeless, hooked on drugs or alcohol, or become victims of the sex-trafficking trade. African American children represent a disproportionate number of children who are being raised in foster care, and they remain in the system the longest—an average of 10 years or more. Churches have the capacity to change this outcome by starting a Covenants for Kids program. Through a partnership with the local social service agency, volunteers from churches can drive children who are living in foster care to church. This program began in California and has proven to be successful. For more information, read this research article and visit the website: www.covenantsforkids.info.

http://www.covenantsforkids.info/orphans-cont.html

PREPARE FOR NEXT SUNDAY

Read **Isaiah 6:1–8** and read "Isaiah in the Temple."

DAILY HOME BIBLE READINGS

MONDAY
Insist on Justice for All
(Exodus 23:1–9)

TUESDAY
Eternal Cost of Not Offering Justice
(Matthew 25:41–46)

WEDNESDAY
No Perversion of Justice Allowed
(2 Chronicles 19:4–7)

THURSDAY
Persist until Justice is Done
(Luke 18:1–8)

FRIDAY
Deacons Called to Ministry of Justice
(Acts 6:1–7)

SATURDAY
Israelites Meet God at Mount Sinai
(Exodus 19:1–9)

SUNDAY
Moses and the Burning Bush
(Exodus 3:1–12)

COMMENTS / NOTES:

ISAIAH IN THE TEMPLE

BIBLE BASIS: ISAIAH 6:1–8

BIBLE TRUTH: God's presence is powerful and transforming.

MEMORY VERSE: "Also I heard the voice of the Lord, saying, Whom shall I send, and who will go for us? Then said I, Here am I; send me" (Isaiah 6:8).

LESSON AIM: By the end of the lesson, we will: EVALUATE the circumstances of Isaiah's call and his reaction to it; EXAMINE the reasons for Isaiah's emotions as he reacted to his call; and DECIDE to answer God's call to service.

TEACHER PREPARATION

MATERIALS NEEDED: Quarterly Commentary/Teacher Manual, Adult Quarterly, Adult resources—charts, worksheets, and other teaching tools, paper, pens, pencils, Bibles (several different versions)

OTHER MATERIALS NEEDED / TEACHER'S NOTES:

_____

_____

LESSON OVERVIEW

LIFE NEED FOR TODAY'S LESSON
Unexpected circumstances can lead us into paths we don't anticipate.

BIBLE APPLICATION
Christians will develop a relationship with God that deepens their confidence.

BIBLE LEARNING
Isaiah's confidence is rooted in the unusual events of his call.

STUDENTS' RESPONSES
Believers will prioritize their decisions in life based on trusting God.

LESSON SCRIPTURE

ISAIAH 6:1–8, KJV

1 In the year that king Uzziah died I saw also the LORD sitting upon a throne, high and lifted up, and his train filled the temple.

2 Above it stood the seraphims: each one had six wings; with twain he covered his face, and with twain he covered his feet, and with twain he did fly.

ISAIAH 6:1–8, NIV

1 In the year that King Uzziah died, I saw [in a vision] the Lord sitting on a throne, high and exalted, with the train of His royal robe filling the [most holy part of the] temple.

2 Above Him seraphim (heavenly beings) stood; each one had six wings: with two wings he covered his face, with two wings he covered his feet, and with two wings he flew.

3 And one cried unto another, and said, Holy, holy, holy, is the LORD of hosts: the whole earth is full of his glory.

4 And the posts of the door moved at the voice of him that cried, and the house was filled with smoke.

5 Then said I, Woe is me! for I am undone; because I am a man of unclean lips, and I dwell in the midst of a people of unclean lips: for mine eyes have seen the King, the LORD of hosts.

6 Then flew one of the seraphims unto me, having a live coal in his hand, which he had taken with the tongs from off the altar:

7 And he laid it upon my mouth, and said, Lo, this hath touched thy lips; and thine iniquity is taken away, and thy sin purged.

8 Also I heard the voice of the Lord, saying, Whom shall I send, and who will go for us? Then said I, Here am I; send me.

3 And one called out to another, saying, "Holy, Holy, Holy is the LORD of hosts; the whole earth is filled with His glory."

4 And the foundations of the thresholds trembled at the voice of him who called out, and the temple was filling with smoke.

5 Then I said, "Woe is me! For I am ruined, because I am a man of [ceremonially] unclean lips, and I live among a people of unclean lips; for my eyes have seen the King, the LORD of hosts."

6 Then one of the seraphim flew to me with a burning coal in his hand, which he had taken from the altar with tongs.

7 He touched my mouth with it and said, "Listen carefully, this has touched your lips; your wickedness [your sin, your injustice, your wrongdoing] is taken away and your sin atoned for and forgiven."

8 Then I heard the voice of the Lord, saying, "Whom shall I send, and who will go for Us?" Then I said, "Here am I. Send me!"

LIGHT ON THE WORD

Judah and Israel. During the time Isaiah was called to serve as a prophet (around 740 BC), the nations of Judah and Israel were being disobedient to God, living lives displeasing to Him. These nations worshiped idols and depended on the "power" and abilities of sorcerers and magicians, while turning their backs on God and forgetting all He had done for their ancestors. The Lord used warnings of judgment to help lead His people to repentance, salvation, and dependence on Him.

TEACHING THE BIBLE LESSON

LIFE NEED FOR TODAY'S LESSON

AIM: Students will agree that unexpected circumstances can lead them into paths they don't anticipate.

INTRODUCTION

A Broken Covenant

Throughout biblical history, God's people have been inconsistent in their allegiance to Him. Whether creating golden images for idol worship, taking His love and mercy for granted, or constantly complaining, His people had a history of disobedience. When God made Isaiah a prophet, the same pattern continued. In God's eyes, Judah and Israel had broken a covenant agreement with Him. They did this by oppressing the poor, worshiping pagan idols, and turning to sorcerers and magicians. As a result, God sent words of judgment to His people to explain their sins against Him. If they continued to defy God or break their contract with Him, destruction of the two nations would result.

BIBLE LEARNING

AIM: Students will examine the unusual events of Isaiah's call that led to his confidence.

I. A GOD EXPERIENCE (Isaiah 6:1–4)

Isaiah explains in detail an experience he had with God. Isaiah saw God in His rightful place, sitting on a throne, representing God's position as king and ruler of all. In Isaiah's experience with God, he saw God wearing a robe, the appropriate attire for His position as King. Isaiah then notices beings called seraphim, which served as helpers for God. Isaiah saw firsthand that God uses others to fulfill His purpose. These seraphim displayed how Isaiah should approach a holy God, covering their face and feet in His presence as a sign of respect and lowliness. Then, the seraphim approached God with a spirit of worship (**v. 3**). When in the presence of God, we must worship Him with all we have like the seraphim (**v. 4**) and not hold anything back. Isaiah's God-experience prepared him for his ultimate calling.

God's Throne Room (Isaiah 6:1–4)

1 In the year that king Uzziah died I saw also the LORD sitting upon a throne, high and lifted up, and his train filled the temple.

For years Israel had traveled a path of its own choosing and was now in spiritual and moral darkness. The king had helped the people's departure from God. Now that leader was dead. A righteous God would be justified in pronouncing the same judgment of death upon the rebellious nation and all of its inhabitants. This was Isaiah's state of mind as he stood observing God upon His "throne" (Heb. *kisse'*, **kis-SAY**), "high" (Heb. *rum*, **ROOM**) and "lifted up" (Heb. *nasa'*, **naw-SAW**). The Holy of Holies in the Temple was considered to be God's throne room. To see God as "high and lifted up" carries the sense that He is exalted. In the ancient Near East, kings' thrones were set atop a series of steps. So it is natural for Isaiah to see God the divine king in the same way. A temple was thought to be the connection between God's heavenly house and earth; in this case, it connects His heavenly throne and earth. As that connection point, some of the throne room spills over to the Temple. But what spills over? Just the "train" (Heb. *shul*, **SHOOL**), which is the long back section of a gown or robe. This is enough to fill up the entire Temple because God is that awesome!

2 Above it stood the seraphims: each one had six wings; with twain he covered his face, and with twain he covered his feet, and with twain he did fly.

The scene is all the more frightening to Isaiah as he sees the "seraphims" (Heb. *serafim*, **seh-rah-FEEM**, literally "the burning ones") standing in God's presence worshiping and serving Him. The Hebrew word used for God's messengers places an emphasis on the fact that God is utterly holy. The seraphim must appear to Isaiah like living fire, standing above the throne waiting to serve God. With one pair of wings ("twain"), the seraphim cover their eyes lest they peer into the divine, and with another pair, they cover their feet in humble acknowledgment that they stand upon holy ground. Isaiah now sees himself all the more clearly as an unclean creature, dwelling amid unclean and rebellious humanity.

3 And one cried unto another, and said, Holy, holy, holy, is the LORD of hosts: the whole earth is full of his glory. 4 And the posts of the door moved at the voice of him that cried, and the house was filled with smoke.

Every utterance of the seraphs confirms for Isaiah that God is "holy" (Heb. *kadosh*, **kah-DOASH**). God is utterly transcendent, so far above and distinct from His created beings that none is truly worthy to be in His presence. God's holiness is central to His identity. Some scholars argue that it is His primary attribute that permeates all of the others (such as love, sovereignty, omnipotence, etc.). Amid those characteristics of God, His "glory" (Heb. *kavod*, **kah-VODE**) fills the whole earth, making it impossible to escape His presence. The scene must have been overwhelming and frightening, as not only were the seraphim proclaiming God's holiness and glory, but also the Temple itself shook. Then there was smoke, which may be analogous to the Shekinah cloud that represented God's presence with the Israelites in the desert (**Exodus 40:38**). Shekinah is from the Hebrew word for dwelling and refers specifically to the cloud of God's presence that followed the Israelites through the wilderness. The smoke itself is representative of God's presence with the people.

II. ISAIAH'S RESPONSE (v. 5)

God handpicked this unique group of people to be His messengers. Prophets were considered to be God's special representatives. They confronted the leaders during periods of disobedience (cf. **2 Samuel 12**, Nathan confronting David) and verbally warned God's people when they were disobedient. Prophets were not the most popular people because of their message, but they were respected due to their closeness to God. The prophet's message was intended to help God's people get back in line with Him and give them hope for reconciliation. Isaiah was chosen by God to deliver His message when the people did not want to listen or change.

A Prophet's Confession (v. 5)

5 Then said I, Woe is me! for I am undone; because I am a man of unclean lips, and I dwell in the midst of a people of unclean lips: for mine eyes have seen the King, the LORD of hosts.

Once Isaiah has an experience with God, he then does what we should do—respond. His response has several components—fear, confession, and admiration. As followers of God, we should have a healthy fear (reverence or respect) of Him. Isaiah was so in awe with God's presence, that he thought it was the end for him ("Woe is me! for I am undone," Isaiah responds).

Isaiah then confessed himself as a sinful man with filthy or unclean lips. He realized that since he was in God's presence, he should confess and repent for anything displeasing to Him. He responded in admiration for being able to experience God's presence even in his current condition. We must remember to respond like Isaiah did when we are in God's presence.

III. GOD'S RESPONSE (vv. 6–7)

Since God loved His people and continued to have mercy on them, He continued to give hope. God told His people that He would be with them and still deliver them from their enemies if they would repent of their sins. God had so much compassion for His people that He called a person to give these warnings: Isaiah, one of their own. Through calling Isaiah as a prophet, God used someone to whom the people could relate to portray a message of repentance, salvation, and caution. God handpicked Isaiah to give the people a choice of continuing to break their covenant or repairing the breach.

The Seraphim and Isaiah's Cleansing (vv. 6–7)

6 Then flew one of the seraphims unto me, having a live coal in his hand, which he had taken with the tongs from off the altar: 7 And he laid it upon my mouth, and said, Lo, this hath touched thy lips; and thine iniquity is taken away, and thy sin purged.

As God prepares and transforms Isaiah, He gives Isaiah the experience of forgiveness (**v. 7**). God removes any guilt Isaiah may feel so he can freely operate in his calling. As God calls us to work for Him, we cannot allow anything to stand in the way, including our own guilt. God will respond to us when we respond to Him.

IV. ISAIAH'S COMMITMENT (v. 8)

When Isaiah responded to God by accentuating all his faults, God exhibits to him what He wants for Israel and Judah: forgiveness. God uses the seraphim (His helpers) to repair Isaiah's condition, using burning coal to touch the location of his iniquity: his mouth. Through this act, God symbolically prepared Isaiah for his assignment. God will always prepare you for an assignment He gives. In this symbolic preparation, God is transforming Isaiah, and He will transform us so we can be prepared for the task at hand.

God Prepares and Forgives Isaiah (v. 8)

8 Also I heard the voice of the Lord, saying, Whom shall I send, and who will go for us? Then said I, Here am I; send me.

After God prepares and forgives Isaiah, He then asks, "Whom shall I send, and who will go for us?" Isaiah now makes a commitment to God to accept His assignment. Isaiah could have easily ignored the question and refused to accept God's call, but he gave of himself for God to use however necessary.

Isaiah remembered his God experience and interaction. He remembered that God forgave him and honored him with His presence. So in return, Isaiah becomes committed to God by accepting His calling. Commitment to God is giving ourselves to Him for His use. No matter what God calls us to do—and it might not be pleasant (cf. **Isaiah 6:9–13**)—like Isaiah we say, "Here am I Lord. Send me."

SEARCH THE SCRIPTURES

QUESTION 1
Explain why God may want to purify us before beginning certain assignments. Have you experienced God's purification process?

Answers will vary.

QUESTION 2
In **v. 8**, God was looking for a messenger. What assignment might God have for you?

Answers will vary.

LIGHT ON THE WORD

God's Faithfulness
A seraph heads in his direction, and like any awe-struck human being, Isaiah may have felt that it was about to carry out God's judgment against him. Isaiah still had not realized the depth of God's commitment to His chosen people, Israel. The nation had broken faith with the living God, but He did not break faith with them.

BIBLE APPLICATION

AIM: Students will develop a deeper relationship with God.

Many people say they are ready to go to new levels in different areas of their lives. But when given the opportunity to do so, they do not want to go through necessary challenges to get there. When Isaiah faced God, he could have ignored what God asked him to do, but because he responded and made a commitment to God, he was one of the greatest prophets in history.

STUDENTS' RESPONSES

AIM: Students will prioritize their decisions in life based on trusting God.

Isaiah stepped up to help his people avoid destruction. What can you do in your community to step up and make a difference? Additionally, it is very easy for us to get so wrapped up in what we believe we cannot do that we ignore God's assignment for our lives. How can we operate now in the assignment He gives us?

PRAYER

O Lord of wisdom, by the power of the Holy Spirit, grant us listening ears to hear Your voice and to accept when You have called us to take action. Prepare our hands, hearts, minds, and bodies to step out in faith. As we trust You, Lord, let us remember to bless You and praise who You are in us. In the precious Name of Jesus, we pray. Amen.

HOW TO SAY IT

Seraphim.   sa-ra-**FIM**.

Twain.   **TWANE**.

DIG A LITTLE DEEPER

This section provides an additional research article to further your study of the lesson:

Understanding and properly fulfilling the call of God is often challenging and discouraging. We read in biblical accounts about the failures and missteps of those who seemingly "hear" from God. Key to living successfully is understanding the distinction between calling and vocation. What are the distinctions? How is one to practically apply this knowledge and become settled in his or her current situation?

Dr. Scott Rae provides an intuitive analysis to a difficult topic.

http://www.talbot.edu/talbot-talks/vocation-calling/

PREPARE FOR NEXT SUNDAY

Read **Jeremiah 1:4–10** and "Jeremiah's Call and Commission."

DAILY HOME BIBLE READINGS

MONDAY
Reign of King Uzziah
(2 Chronicles 26:1–10, 15)

TUESDAY
True Worship in Action
(Isaiah 58:6–12)

WEDNESDAY
Holiness Befits God's House
(Psalm 93)

THURSDAY
Gentiles Will Hear the Good News
(Acts 28:23–29)

FRIDAY
Perfect Your Holiness Living
(2 Corinthians 6:14–7:1)

SATURDAY
Practice Holiness While Waiting
(2 Peter 3:11–16)

SUNDAY
Isaiah in the Temple
(Isaiah 6:1–8)

COMMENTS / NOTES:

_____

_____

_____

_____

JEREMIAH'S CALL AND COMMISSION

BIBLE BASIS: JEREMIAH 1:4–10

BIBLE TRUTH: God's promises are true.

MEMORY VERSE: "Be not afraid of their faces: for I am with thee to deliver thee, saith the LORD" (Jeremiah 1:8).

LESSON AIM: By the end of the lesson, we will: EVALUATE the details of the promises God made to Jeremiah; AFFIRM the intensity of Jeremiah's call and his emotional reaction to it; and ACCEPT a call from God with eagerness.

TEACHER PREPARATION

MATERIALS NEEDED: Quarterly Commentary/Teacher Manual, Adult Quarterly, Adult resources—charts, worksheets, and other teaching tools, paper, pens, pencils, Bibles (several different versions)

OTHER MATERIALS NEEDED / TEACHER'S NOTES:

_____

_____

LIFE NEED FOR TODAY'S LESSON

Each of us has some fear or insecurity that might convince us that we have nothing to give others.

BIBLE LEARNING

Jeremiah's response was based on God's promise to be with him.

BIBLE APPLICATION

Christians will strengthen their belief that God always keeps promises.

STUDENTS' RESPONSES

Believers affirm that God encourages believers even when they lack confidence.

LESSON SCRIPTURE

JEREMIAH 1:4–10, KJV

4 Then the word of the LORD came unto me, saying,

5 Before I formed thee in the belly I knew thee; and before thou camest forth out of the womb I sanctified thee, and I ordained thee a prophet unto the nations.

JEREMIAH 1:4–10, AMP

4 Now the word of the LORD came to me, saying,

5 "Before I formed you in the womb I knew you [and approved of you as My chosen instrument], and before you were born I consecrated you [to Myself as My own]; I have appointed you as a prophet to the nations."

6 Then said I, Ah, Lord GOD! behold, I cannot speak: for I am a child.

7 But the LORD said unto me, Say not, I am a child: for thou shalt go to all that I shall send thee, and whatsoever I command thee thou shalt speak.

8 Be not afraid of their faces: for I am with thee to deliver thee, saith the LORD.

9 Then the LORD put forth his hand, and touched my mouth. And the LORD said unto me, Behold, I have put my words in thy mouth.

10 See, I have this day set thee over the nations and over the kingdoms, to root out, and to pull down, and to destroy, and to throw down, to build, and to plant.

6 Then I said, "Ah, Lord GOD! Behold, I do not know how to speak, for I am [only] a young man."

7 But the LORD said to me, "Do not say, 'I am [only] a young man,' because everywhere I send you, you shall go, and whatever I command you, you shall speak.

8 "Do not be afraid of them [or their hostile faces], for I am with you [always] to protect you and deliver you," says the LORD.

9 Then the LORD stretched out His hand and touched my mouth, and the LORD said to me, "Behold (hear Me), I have put My words in your mouth.

10 "See, I have appointed you this day over the nations and over the kingdoms, to uproot and break down, to destroy and to overthrow, to build and to plant."

LIGHT ON THE WORD

Judgment. The prophet would give warnings to God's people when they were disobedient. If the people did not heed the warnings, then God would issue a judgment on them. Judgment was a punishment that God would give to the people for disobedience and breaking their covenant. It would only occur after God had given His people multiple chances to repent from their disobedience. The hope was that the people would return to obeying and following God.

TEACHING THE BIBLE LESSON

LIFE NEED FOR TODAY'S LESSON

AIM: Students will affirm that fear or insecurity might cause them to think that they have nothing to offer to others.

INTRODUCTION

Jeremiah's Warning

Jeremiah tried to warn the people what would happen if they continued to break their covenant. He tried to urge the people to repent from their sin and disobedience. Instead of heeding the warnings, they became angry at him. The people of Judah and Jerusalem ignored God's message through Jeremiah. Jeremiah prophesied that they would be in exile for seventy years because of their hardened hearts and Jerusalem would be destroyed by their enemy, the Babylonians.

Judah and Jerusalem were completely oblivious to God's anger toward them. They forgot about all the times God had showed them love and support, and focused only on themselves. Unfortunately, some people were innocent victims of their brothers' and sisters' sins, but they too suffered. God gave many chances, but it was up to them to take action.

BIBLE LEARNING

AIM: Students will justify that Jeremiah's response was based on God's promise to be with him as he lived out his calling.

I. BORN FOR THIS (Jeremiah 1:4–5)

When God called Jeremiah to be a prophet, He wanted to reassure him that he was born to do this. God tells Jeremiah that before he was born, before he was formed in the womb, He knew what Jeremiah was going to do. God had already set him apart to be a prophet. Jeremiah had no need to worry because his path was set. When God sets up something, it will succeed because He can never fail at anything He does. We also learn that God is omniscient, or all-knowing. He already knew that Jeremiah was going to be successful for Him. Whatever God called you to do, you were born to do it also. Jeremiah did not have to be nervous in this new chapter of his life because God created him to be a prophet. He was born for this.

God's Plan for Jeremiah (Jeremiah 1:4–5)

4 Then the word of the LORD came unto me, saying, 5 Before I formed thee in the belly I knew thee; and before thou camest forth out of the womb I sanctified thee, and I ordained thee a prophet unto the nations.

Jeremiah 1:4–10 is commonly referred to as the call of Jeremiah. The call narrative here follows the prophetic call formula in the Old Testament: (1) divine confrontation; (2) introductory word; (3) commission; (4) objection; (5) reassurance; (6) sign (**Exodus 3:1–4:9, Judges 6:11–24**). Jeremiah's call begins with a divine encounter presented here as a dialogue between him and God: "The word of the LORD came unto me" (**Jeremiah 1:4**). God's appearance is followed by an introductory word that establishes that the choice of Jeremiah as a prophet (Heb. *navi'*, **nah-VEE**) was no arbitrary decision, but that God had set him apart (Heb. *kadash*, **kah-DASH**, consecrate, make holy), before he was even born. A prophet was a spokesperson called by God to serve as an intermediary between Him and the people. God commissioned Jeremiah to preach His Word to the nations (Heb. *goyim*, **goy-EEM**). At this time "nations" still referred especially to a group within a certain territory other than Israel or Judah. However when God's people were under Assyrian, Babylonian, Persian, Greek, and Roman rule, it referred more to a group with particular ancestral heritage other than the Jews. This word implies His message will be not just for Israel, but for all the world.

II. CHANGE FOCUS (vv. 6–7)

As Jeremiah became nervous, God again reassured him by reminding him that age and experience are not factors when it comes to His work. Regardless, Jeremiah had to go wherever God sent him (**v. 7**).

Jeremiah Focuses on God (vv. 6–7)

6 Then said I, Ah, Lord GOD! behold, I cannot speak: for I am a child. 7 But the LORD said unto me, Say not, I am a child: for thou shalt go to all that I shall send thee, and whatsoever I command thee thou shalt speak.

Once God shares with Jeremiah that he was created for his calling, Jeremiah loses focus. Instead of celebrating the fact that God was in control, Jeremiah begins dwelling on his inadequacies. He says he is unable to speak because he is too young. Jeremiah feels that he does not have enough experience to do what God called him to do. Jeremiah briefly forgets that when God calls a person to do something, human experience or ability is irrelevant because He gives people the ability to do His work. Though we should always prepare ourselves through education and other avenues, we should not rely on these preparations when it comes to our Heavenly Father's business. When Jeremiah thought the job was too much for him, he focused on himself and not on the One who called him.

III. EQUIP (vv. 8–9)

God knew that the task would bring about different challenges, so He tells Jeremiah not to worry about other people harming him because He will be there to protect him. Whatever God calls us to do, His presence will always be with us through the anointing of the Holy Spirit who empowers us. He will never abandon us (**Hebrews 13:5**).

God's Presence is with Jeremiah (vv. 8–9)

8 Be not afraid of their faces: for I am with thee to deliver thee, saith the LORD. 9 Then the LORD put forth his hand, and touched my mouth. And the LORD said unto me, Behold, I have put my words in thy mouth.

Despite Jeremiah's doubts about being up to the challenge, and his fears of the opposition he will face, he need not worry because God reassures him. God will accompany him and deliver him from his adversaries (cf. **Exodus 3:12**). The desire for God to accompany us through dangers and trials and the faith that He will deliver us is our fervent prayer.

At the funeral of Rev. Dr. Martin Luther King, the gospel singer Mahalia Jackson sang the words to King's favorite song "Precious Lord":

Precious Lord, take my hand
Lead me on, let me stand

The well-renowned gospel singer and composer Thomas A. Dorsey was inspired to pen the hymn "Precious Lord" upon the death of his wife, who died giving birth to their son, who died shortly after. For both Dorsey and King, the confidence that God would accompany them and lead them on gave them the reassurance to continue to deliver God's message to a nation hostile to His Word.

God promised to equip Jeremiah with His presence, but then also equip him in the same way He equipped Isaiah: by touching his mouth. God touching Jeremiah's mouth was His way of showing him that He will be talking through him. God equipped Jeremiah with all he needed to operate in his calling.

IV. COMMISSIONED (v. 10)

After showing Jeremiah he was born to be a "prophet to the nations" (AMP) and equipping him, God then commissions him for service (**v. 10**). He commissions Jeremiah to stand up against nations and kingdoms, and build up those willing to repent. God commissions Jeremiah not only to preach to Jerusalem, but also to preach to everyone. This commissioning means God entrusts Jeremiah to act as an agent for Him. Jeremiah would speak for God, giving people another chance to keep their covenant with Him. Sometimes the words would tear down and destroy, if Jerusalem did not comply. God's Words and actions could also build up, though, for those who come to Him with a repentant heart. God entrusts Jeremiah with the calling of His spokesperson or prophet. God will always give you your assignment when He feels you are ready to accept it.

Born to Be a Prophet (v. 10)

10 See, I have this day set thee over the nations and over the kingdoms, to root out, and to pull down, and to destroy, and to throw down, to build, and to plant.

Having assured Jeremiah that God will accompany him and has equipped him for the task, He reiterates the task for which He has commissioned Jeremiah: to be a prophet "over the nations and over the kingdoms" (cf. **v. 5**). Jeremiah's mission on one hand is to act as a sword: "to root out," "pull down," "destroy," and "throw down." It is no wonder that Jeremiah's messages moved the recipients to such aggression toward him—he preached a message of doom and destruction to rulers and nations, kings and kingdoms, even his own. On the other hand, he offered a message of hope of renewal: "to build, and to plant." The latter message of reconstruction was harder to receive in the aftermath of the judgment God wrought on the nations and kingdoms.

SEARCH THE SCRIPTURES

QUESTION 1
Jeremiah was young and not confident of being God's messenger. How might your excuses prevent you from experiencing God's purpose in your life?

You can miss out on the blessings God has for you and what you were to share with others. Answers will vary.

QUESTION 2
Have you ever been accused of being too emotional like Jeremiah or too passionate about doing God's work? How did that make you feel?

Answers will vary.

LIGHT ON THE WORD

Taking a Risk
Some people refuse to take on new challenges because they are afraid of taking a risk. However, they realize that sometimes we have to take a risk. Think of someone you know who has a hard time taking on new challenges. How would you help encourage that person to take on a challenge?

BIBLE APPLICATION

AIM: Students will consider stepping outside their comfort zones.

People tend to only rely on what they can see. It is hard for us to step outside our comfort zone, especially when we allow fear to guide us. God will challenge us to step outside of our comfort zone to see if we are willing to trust Him. Jeremiah was willing to step out of his comfort zone to serve as God's spokesperson because he understood that God was with him.

STUDENTS' RESPONSES

AIM: Students will affirm that God encourages believers even when they lack confidence.

When we are given a task that appears too much for us to handle, we sometimes focus on our weaknesses as reasons to refuse. How did God dispel Jeremiah's excuse about his weaknesses? How does God dispel your excuses?

PRAYER

Dear Loving Lord, who is compassionate and never failing, You are always there for us. Without You to walk with us and carry us every step of the way, we would stumble. When we are doubtful, You know how to help us trust You to take another step. Thank You God. In Jesus' Name we pray. Amen.

HOW TO SAY IT

Abiathar.   Uh-**BY**-uh-ther.

Hilkiah.   Hill-**KIE**-uh.

Jehoiakim.   Jeh-**HOI**-a-kim.

DIG A LITTLE DEEPER

This section provides an additional research article to further your study of the lesson:

In recent times, it seems that speaking the truth, even in love, is risky and controversial. How can God's Word be proclaimed under such duress? In this article from *The Master's Seminary*, John McArthur provides an exhaustive discussion on the preservation of God's Word in light of cultural trends.

http://www.tms.edu/m/17a.pdf

PREPARE FOR NEXT SUNDAY

Read **Ezekiel 3:1–11** and read "Ezekiel's Call."

DAILY HOME BIBLE READINGS

MONDAY
A Prophet like Moses
(Deuteronomy 18:15–22)

TUESDAY
By Almond Branch and Boiling Pot
(Jeremiah 1:11–19)

WEDNESDAY
Assured of the Lord's Deliverance
(Jeremiah 15:10–21)

THURSDAY
Prophetic Message from the Potter
(Jeremiah 18:1–11)

FRIDAY
Egypt Punished; Israel Saved
(Jeremiah 46:25–28)

SATURDAY
Jesus Calls Disciples
(Mark 1:16–20)

SUNDAY
Jeremiah's Call and Commission
(Jeremiah 1:4–10)

COMMENTS / NOTES:

EZEKIEL'S CALL

BIBLE BASIS: EZEKIEL 3:1–11

BIBLE TRUTH: God expects His followers to share His Word.

MEMORY VERSES: "Moreover he said unto me, Son of man, all my words that I shall speak unto thee receive in thine heart, and hear with thine ears. And go, get thee to them of the captivity, unto the children of thy people, and speak unto them, and tell them, Thus saith the Lord GOD; whether they will hear, or whether they will forbear" (Ezekiel 3:10–11).

LESSON AIM: By the end of the lesson, we will: EVALUATE God's call of Ezekiel in terms of his eating a scroll; ACCEPT that like Ezekiel, we have an obligation to speak to people who obstinately refuse to listen; and ADOPT ways to be "harder than flint" in obeying God's call to be His messengers.

TEACHER PREPARATION

MATERIALS NEEDED: Quarterly Commentary/Teacher Manual, Adult Quarterly, Adult resources—charts, worksheets, and other teaching tools, paper, pens, pencils, Bibles (several different versions)

OTHER MATERIALS NEEDED / TEACHER'S NOTES:

_____

_____

LESSON OVERVIEW

LIFE NEED FOR TODAY'S LESSON
Discouragement and doubt can hinder what we hope to achieve.

BIBLE APPLICATION
God gives us what we need to strengthen and protect us in the challenges we face.

BIBLE LEARNING
Ezekiel's call involved his eating a scroll that sweetened the bitter taste of his mission.

STUDENTS' RESPONSES
Believers can examine how God guides them to deliver His Word to various types of people.

LESSON SCRIPTURE

EZEKIEL 3:1–11, KJV

1 Moreover he said unto me, Son of man, eat that thou findest; eat this roll, and go speak unto the house of Israel.

2 So I opened my mouth, and he caused me to eat that roll.

EZEKIEL 3:1–11, AMP

1 He said to me, "Son of man, eat what you find [in this book]; eat this scroll, then go, speak to the house of Israel."

2 So I opened my mouth, and He fed me the scroll.

3 And he said unto me, Son of man, cause thy belly to eat, and fill thy bowels with this roll that I give thee. Then did I eat it; and it was in my mouth as honey for sweetness.

4 And he said unto me, Son of man, go, get thee unto the house of Israel, and speak with my words unto them.

5 For thou art not sent to a people of a strange speech and of an hard language, but to the house of Israel;

6 Not to many people of a strange speech and of an hard language, whose words thou canst not understand. Surely, had I sent thee to them, they would have hearkened unto thee.

7 But the house of Israel will not hearken unto thee; for they will not hearken unto me: for all the house of Israel are impudent and hardhearted.

8 Behold, I have made thy face strong against their faces, and thy forehead strong against their foreheads.

9 As an adamant harder than flint have I made thy forehead: fear them not, neither be dismayed at their looks, though they be a rebellious house.

10 Moreover he said unto me, Son of man, all my words that I shall speak unto thee receive in thine heart, and hear with thine ears.

11 And go, get thee to them of the captivity, unto the children of thy people, and speak unto them, and tell them, Thus saith the Lord GOD; whether they will hear, or whether they will forbear.

3 He said to me, "Son of man, eat this scroll that I am giving you and fill your stomach with it." So I ate it, and it was as sweet as honey in my mouth.

4 Then He said to me, "Son of man, go to the house of Israel and speak My words to them.

5 For you are not being sent to a people of unintelligible speech or difficult language, but to the house of Israel,

6 not to many peoples of unintelligible speech or difficult language, whose words you cannot understand. But I have sent you to them who should listen to you and pay attention to My message;

7 yet the house of Israel will not be willing to listen to you and obey you, since they are not willing to listen to Me and obey Me, for the entire house of Israel is stubborn and obstinate.

8 Behold, I have made your face as hard as their faces and your forehead as hard as their foreheads.

9 I have made your forehead like emery (diamond), harder than flint. Do not be afraid of them or be dismayed before them, though they are a rebellious house."

10 Moreover, He said to me, "Son of man, receive into your heart all My words which I will speak to you and hear with your ears (listen closely).

11 Go to the [Jewish] exiles [in Babylon], to the children of your people, and speak to them, whether they listen or not, and tell them, 'Thus says the Lord GOD.'"

LIGHT ON THE WORD

Ezekiel. The prophet's name meant "God is my strength." He was a Zadokite priest, the son of a priest named Buzi. Ezekiel lived 600 miles from Jerusalem before being taken captive to Babylon where he lived near the Kebar River during the fifth year of King Jehoiachin's captivity. He was given a message and a vision of God's magnificence and power to fortify him to preach the Word to the first Jewish exiles relocated in Babylon where they would spend seventy years in oppression. He also prophesied warnings of judgment to surrounding enemy nations.

TEACHING THE BIBLE LESSON

LIFE NEED FOR TODAY'S LESSON

AIM: Students will agree that trusting God's sovereignty propels us into fulfilling His purpose in our lives.

INTRODUCTION

The Prophet Ezekiel

Ezekiel was a priest in Jerusalem at the end of the kingdom of Judah, as well as a contemporary of Jeremiah. Because he had authority, he was exiled to Babylon along with King Jehoiachin in 597 BC at the age of 25. His first vision (**Chapter 1**) is reported to have taken place five years later (592) while in exile along the Chebar Canal, which connected to the Euphrates in the Nippur region. When his beloved wife died suddenly, he focused on his priestly duties instead of bereavement to demonstrate that God's will over our lives takes precedence over every other duty, including mourning for a loved one, building, city, or past life (**Ezekiel 24:15–24**). The death of the prophet's wife was a sign of the destruction of Jerusalem by the Chaldeans and the loss of the Temple.

BIBLE LEARNING

AIM: Students will evaluate the reason that Ezekiel's call involved his eating a scroll.

I. GOD'S CALL TO EZEKIEL (Ezekiel 3:1)

The ministry of Ezekiel, the son of Buzi, extended from 593 to 571 BC, and mostly took place around Tel Abib, near the Chebar Canal in Babylon (modern-day Iraq), during the Babylonian Captivity (605 to 538 BC). He was one of approximately 10,000 inhabitants of Judah exiled to Babylon in 597 BC when Nebuchadnezzar invaded Jerusalem. King Jehoiachin and many of his subjects, including warriors, artisans, and many members of the royal and priestly families, were taken away to captivity in Babylon (**2 Kings 24:14–16**). Five years after this mass deportation, when Ezekiel turned 30, the heavens opened and he saw visions of God (**Ezekiel 1:1**), beginning his prophetic calling.

The Faithful Eat of God's Word (v. 1)

1 Moreover he said unto me, Son of man, eat that thou findest; eat this roll, and go speak unto the house of Israel.

"Eating the Word of God" is an expression found in Ezekiel and in the New Testament book of Revelation, as John is called to eat the book that was in the hands of the angel (**Revelation 10:9–10**). Those chosen to eat the Word were also chosen because of their faithfulness to deliver God's message no matter the opposition. Several verses use the word "scroll" in Old Testament prophecy (e.g. Jeremiah, Ezekiel, Zechariah) as the conveyance of God's Word. God's instructions are to fully chew on the Word, and experience the sweetness of His Word in preparation to confront the bitter hardness of human hearts.

God's Word must be digested and consumed. We digest His Word with full recognition that we are "sons of man," frail and humble dust without the sustaining Word of God. After the command to eat, Ezekiel was commanded to go and speak. We too are called, like Ezekiel, to eat God's Word, then go and speak truth and light to a dying world.

II. EZEKIEL'S RESPONSE (vv. 2–3)

Ezekiel followed the instruction to open his mouth. Only after opening his mouth was he given the scroll. Obeying God is a step-by-step journey. God is usually patient, and waits for us to obey at step one before taking us to step two. Any reluctance on our part only delays the journey, causing God to repeat instructions until we finally obey.

Again, Ezekiel was told to eat the scroll—the third and final repetition. This time, the request had an extension: "fill thy bowels with this roll that I give thee" Ezekiel had to eat the scroll until it filled his stomach with the Word of God, the bread of heaven. He must fill himself with God's Word until there is no room for his own words.

Obedience to God's Command (vv. 2–3)

2 So I opened my mouth, and he caused me to eat that roll. 3 And he said unto me, Son of man, cause thy belly to eat, and fill thy bowels with this roll that I give thee. Then did I eat it; and it was in my mouth as honey for sweetness.

There is only one acceptable response to a divine message and vision: obedience. Ezekiel did two things: he opened his mouth, and he ate the scroll. Now that Ezekiel proved faithful and allowed the Lord to prepare him, he was given his assignment to speak. His response to obey is immediate; he doesn't hesitate to obey the voice of God.

The scroll Ezekiel is commanded to eat contains "lamentation, mourning, and woe" (**2:10**). This kind of message might be thought to be bitter or sour, but in Ezekiel's mouth, it is as sweet as honey.

In several passages, written documents have the power to affect the course of human events (**2 Samuel 11:14–15; 1 Kings 21:8–9, 11; Esther 8:8, 10**). By eating the scroll, Ezekiel becomes one with the words on the scroll. In doing so, he symbolically takes into his inner being the fate of his people. Ezekiel is more than just a messenger detached from his assignment; he has now become the message.

III. EZEKIEL'S MISSION (vv. 4–9)

The Lord sends Ezekiel to speak to the house of Israel, encouraging him because the task ahead was daunting. He is not sent to a foreign nation of difficult languages, not the Chaldeans or Babylonians, but to the Israelites, to reprove them for their sins. An instruction that Ezekiel had received earlier is also repeated here: "speak with my words to them" (**3:4**). Thus, Ezekiel must speak to the Israelites all that God had spoken to him, and only that. However, the people will not listen, not because they do not understand him or his language, but because they are impudent and hard-hearted.

The Lord Encourages Ezekiel (vv. 4–9)

4 And he said unto me, Son of man, go, get thee unto the house of Israel, and speak with my words unto them. 5 For thou art not sent to a people of a strange speech and of an hard language, but to the house of Israel; 6 Not to many people of a strange speech and of an hard language, whose words thou canst not understand. Surely, had I sent thee to them, they would have hearkened unto thee. 7 But the house of Israel will not hearken unto thee; for

they will not hearken unto me: for all the house of Israel are impudent and hard-hearted. Behold, I have made thy face strong against their faces, and thy fore-head strong against their foreheads. 9 As an adamant harder than flint have I made thy forehead: fear them not, neither be dismayed at their looks, though they be a rebellious house.

God's command to Ezekiel requires that he put the sweetness of the Word to urgent use. Go to Judah and tell them now. Right after Ezekiel had eaten the Word of God, tasted its sweetness, been filled with the Spirit, and personally seen God's glory, God commanded him to go right now and tell the people of Judah the consequences of their sin. Ezekiel was able to do this because he had first submitted to the Word of God and yielded his heart. He was equipped to boldly go and tell his fellow Israelites what God said. Ezekiel is to speak God's words, not his own words. When we evangelize or minister to others, we must be careful to speak God's words, not our opinion or interpretation. Memorize and meditate on His Word, fast and pray in the Spirit, and then speak His Word in hostile environments and offer hope to those in distress.

IV. THE PEOPLE'S RESPONSE (vv. 10–11)

God admonishes Ezekiel to pay careful attention to everything He says. Ezekiel has to receive what God says with his heart and hear with his ears—he must listen carefully to what God will continue to say. He has to assimilate the Word of God until it becomes a part of him. Then he can speak it with confidence and conviction. His mission was to tell the Israelites what the Lord had said and that the Lord had said it. He had to speak to them whether they listened or not—and they will not listen. Judging solely by whether the people listened, it would seem that Ezekiel's ministry failed

miserably. However, this is not true. His task was only to speak what God told him. Whether the people changed was not Ezekiel's business. All he had to do was speak the Word.

Hardened Hearts (vv. 10–11)

10 Moreover he said unto me, Son of man, all my words that I shall speak unto thee receive in thine heart, and hear with thine ears. 11 And go, get thee to them of the captivity, unto the children of thy people, and speak unto them, and tell them, Thus saith the Lord GOD; whether they will hear, or whether they will forbear.

Ezekiel was called to preach in his own country, to his own people, in his own language—to fellow Israelites, not the Babylonians. God explained that if He had sent him to minister to the Babylonian captors, they would listen! In other words, Israel was more hardened than the worst of the nations around them.

Language barriers can be overcome; but a hardened head and heart are another matter. Ezekiel was not to take it personally when his message from God was rejected; Israel's spiritual deafness was acquired over many years of turning away from His Word. Time after time in the Scriptures, we read of Israel choosing to reject God. This is no different. Regardless of their lack of spiritual receptivity, Ezekiel is called to preach to the people of Judah.

SEARCH THE SCRIPTURES

QUESTION 1

Ezekiel eats the scroll in **verse 2**. How does this symbolizes his obedience to God and His mission for him?

Ezekiel obeys God step-by-step to taste that His Word is sweet. He prophesies God's Word, which is now a part of him.

QUESTION 2

God's demand on Ezekiel had a big impact. How does having a relationship with God impact your everyday life? Do you share God's Word with others?

Answers will vary.

LIGHT ON THE WORD

Listening and Obeying God

Ezekiel humbly submitted and followed God's instructions. He could then speak God's Word, and his example generated great respect among the Hebrew exiles and confirmed him as a prophet of God. His message was that the real spiritual temple is in the hearts of God's people; they must be willing to obey, listen, and be broken for a greater eternal hope.

BIBLE APPLICATION

AIM: Students will decide to read their Bible daily and "digest" the sweet Word of God.

Many adults remember times when a positive experience "sweetened" their lives in the midst of discouragement and doubt. Many times we doubt our ability to overcome hindrances and feel alone in standing up for what is right. We can easily become discouraged when obstacles prevent us from reaching our goals. God wants us to read, study, memorize, pray, and discuss His Word so that we become bold when we speak before a person or crowd.

STUDENTS' RESPONSES

AIM: Students will appreciate God's guidance as they proclaim God's Word to various types of people.

When we reflect on God's unfailing promises and the many examples He has presented in His Word, we should be encouraged to overcome hostile situations. List the different potentially hostile situations you could face personally as a witness for Christ. Ask God to make you hard as flint in order to obey Him when the time comes.

PRAYER

Sweet Heavenly Father, we truly appreciate that You protect us and show us how to live out Your Word. As we share and help others to know You, we thank You for the wisdom of the Holy Spirit to speak only what you want us to say. In the loving Name of Jesus, we pray. Amen.

HOW TO SAY IT

Adamant. ah-**DUH**-mant.

Hearkened. **HAR**-kend.

DIG A LITTLE DEEPER

This section provides an additional research article to further your study of the lesson:

Bible reading and memorization is a necessary spiritual discipline that allows us to internalize the Word of God so that it may reach the very bone and marrow of our human souls. In Ezekiel, this descriptive action of eating the scroll from the Lord is prescriptive in the life of the believer. This article is a practical guide to "eating" God's Word: "Here's something you know instinctively. You can memorize every bit of cereal box information about ingredients and nutritional value. But for that cereal to do you any good, you have to pour it out, top it with milk or cream, and eat it."

http://worship.calvin.edu/resources/resource-library/eugene-peterson-on-god-s-standing-invitation-eat-this-book/

PREPARE FOR NEXT SUNDAY

Read **Amos 7:10–17** and "Amos' Call."

DAILY HOME BIBLE READINGS

MONDAY
Ezekiel, the Lord's Messenger
(Ezekiel 2:1–7)

TUESDAY
Words of Lamentation, Mourning, and Woe
(Ezekiel 2:8–10)

WEDNESDAY
Eat the Scroll and Prophesy
(Revelation 10:8–11)

THURSDAY
Written Edict Stops Jewish Calamity
(Esther 8:7–10)

FRIDAY
Sentinel Must Convey God's Message
(Ezekiel 3:12–21)

SATURDAY
Israel Exalted at Last
(Ezekiel 17:22–24)

SUNDAY
Ezekiel's Call
(Ezekiel 3:1–11)

COMMENTS / NOTES:

AMOS' CALL

BIBLE BASIS: AMOS 7:10–17

BIBLE TRUTH: God's prophets experienced difficult times.

MEMORY VERSES: "Then answered Amos, and said to Amaziah, I was no prophet, neither was I a prophet's son; but I was an herdman, and a gatherer of sycomore fruit: And the LORD took me as I followed the flock, and the LORD said unto me, Go, prophesy unto my people Israel" (Amos 7:14–15).

LESSON AIM: By the end of the lesson, we will: EVALUATE the challenges Amaziah and Jeroboam presented to Amos' prophetic ministry; ACCEPT that like Amos, we are called to serve in unfamiliar places and capacities; and SHARE examples of our commitment to serving God in spite of opposition.

TEACHER PREPARATION

MATERIALS NEEDED: Quarterly Commentary/Teacher Manual, Adult Quarterly, Adult resources—charts, worksheets, and other teaching tools, paper, pens, pencils, Bibles (several different versions)

OTHER MATERIALS NEEDED / TEACHER'S NOTES:

_____

_____

LESSON OVERVIEW

LIFE NEED FOR TODAY'S LESSON
At times, we are torn between obeying God's direction and what others think we should do.

BIBLE APPLICATION
Believers can demonstrate their faithfulness to God in spite of the circumstances.

BIBLE LEARNING
Amos committed to serving even in the face of negativity.

STUDENTS' RESPONSES
Believers have the opportunity to choose to listen and obey God.

LESSON SCRIPTURE

AMOS 7:10–17, KJV

10 Then Amaziah the priest of Bethel sent to Jeroboam king of Israel, saying, Amos hath conspired against thee in the midst of the house of Israel: the land is not able to bear all his words.

AMOS 7:10–17, AMP

10 Then Amaziah, the priest of Bethel [site of the golden calf shrine], sent word to Jeroboam king of Israel, saying, "Amos has conspired against you in the midst of the house of Israel; the land is unable to endure all his words.

11 For thus Amos saith, Jeroboam shall die by the sword, and Israel shall surely be led away captive out of their own land.

12 Also Amaziah said unto Amos, O thou seer, go, flee thee away into the land of Judah, and there eat bread, and prophesy there:

13 But prophesy not again any more at Bethel: for it is the king's chapel, and it is the king's court.

14 Then answered Amos, and said to Amaziah, I was no prophet, neither was I a prophet's son; but I was an herdman, and a gatherer of sycomore fruit:

15 And the LORD took me as I followed the flock, and the LORD said unto me, Go, prophesy unto my people Israel.

16 Now therefore hear thou the word of the LORD: Thou sayest, Prophesy not against Israel, and drop not thy word against the house of Isaac.

17 Therefore thus saith the LORD; Thy wife shall be an harlot in the city, and thy sons and thy daughters shall fall by the sword, and thy land shall be divided by line; and thou shalt die in a polluted land: and Israel shall surely go into captivity forth of his land.

11 For in this way Amos has said, 'Jeroboam will die by the sword and Israel will certainly go from its land into exile.'"

12 Then Amaziah said to Amos, "Go, you seer, run for your life [from Israel] to the land of Judah [your own country] and eat bread and live as a prophet there!

13 But do not prophesy any longer at Bethel, for it is the king's sanctuary and a royal residence."

14 Then Amos replied to Amaziah, "I am not a prophet [by profession], nor am I a prophet's son; I am a herdsman and a grower of sycamore figs.

15 But the LORD took me as I followed the flock and the LORD said to me, 'Go, prophesy to My people Israel.'

16 Now therefore, listen to the word of the LORD: You say, 'You shall not prophesy against Israel nor shall you speak against the house of Isaac.'

17 Therefore, thus says the LORD, 'Your wife shall become a prostitute in the city [when the Assyrians capture Samaria] and your sons and your daughters shall fall by the sword, and your land shall be divided by a measuring line; you yourself shall die in an unclean and defiled [pagan] land, and Israel shall certainly go from its land into exile.'"

LIGHT ON THE WORD

Amos. His personal name means "one who is carried," and he was a prophet from Judah who ministered in Israel around 750 BC. Some might describe the prophet Amos as a "burden bearer." He carried a heavy burden for his people, or rather, his people were a burden he carried. As a prophet, Amos was a primary figure among the series of courageous men known as the minor prophets. They are called "minor" only because their books are far shorter than the major prophets, such as Isaiah, Jeremiah, and Ezekiel. In Judaism, the minor prophets' writings are commonly known as the "Book of the Twelve" because there are twelve of them and they fit onto one scroll (i.e., book).

TEACHING THE BIBLE LESSON

LIFE NEED FOR TODAY'S LESSON

AIM: Students will agree that obeying God's direction supersedes what others think we should do.

INTRODUCTION

God's Judgment

Amos documented the reasons for God's judgment against Israel, such as legal injustice, economic exploitation, religious hypocrisy, luxurious indulgence, and boastful complacency. The violations resulted in the nation being doomed, but individuals who repented were spared. This did not sit well with those in power. These sins exposed their spiritual state and called them to account. Amos continued to show not only the sins of the rich and powerful but also the fate of Israel as the people continued to practice sin and injustice.

BIBLE LEARNING

AIM: Students will relate to Amos' commitment to serving even in the face of negativity.

I. THE ANGRY PRIEST (Amos 7:10–13)

Amaziah was a priest at Bethel who led the people of Israel into idolatry. Bent on worshiping idols, he is threatened by Amos' prophecy against the Israelites. Because of this, he tells the king of Israel, Jeroboam, that Amos' message is not good for the kingdom.

A Rejected Prophecy (vv. 10–13)

10 Then Amaziah the priest of Bethel sent to Jeroboam king of Israel, saying, Amos hath conspired against thee in the midst of the house of Israel: the land is not able to bear all his words.11 For thus Amos saith, Jeroboam shall die by the sword, and Israel shall surely be led away captive out of their own land. 12 Also Amaziah said unto Amos, O thou seer, go, flee thee away into the land of Judah, and there eat bread, and prophesy there: 13 But prophesy not again any more at Bethel: for it is the king's chapel, and it is the king's court.

The Bible does not tell of any response from Jeroboam to Amaziah. Probably, he paid no attention to the message at all, thinking it came from a visionary unworthy of serious consideration. However, Amaziah found it necessary to order Amos to return to the land of Judah: "O thou seer, go, flee thee away into the land of Judah." The Hebrew word *khozeh* (**kho-ZEH**) is used for "seer" here. It means "one who has visions." When used elsewhere in the Old Testament, it is a powerful word of respect, but it seems to be used contemptuously here, in reference to Amos' visions recorded earlier in the chapter. In a rather patronizing manner, Amaziah attempted to advise Amos to flee for his own safety back to the land of Judah. Of course, if Jeroboam had taken the treason accusations seriously, Amos' life would be in danger. So, it would be in Amos' best interests to escape the punishment. Amaziah assumed that, just like himself, Amos was a professional prophet who earned his living as the women mentioned by Ezekiel who were ready to say whatever pleased their hearers, however false, for "handfuls of barley and pieces of bread" (**Ezekiel 13:19**). When he said to Amos, "There eat bread and prophesy," he meant, "You can earn a comfortable livelihood there." He presumed that Amos was in it for the money. It would, thus, be more sensible for Amos to go back to safety in Judah where he would continue to live as a prophet and make better money. This is the climax of Amos' message. Jeroboam, king of a thriving kingdom that took pride in its military strength, was to die by the sword in battle. As if this is not enough, the whole of Israel would be taken captive from their own land. Threats like this are spread throughout the book of Amos (**4:2–3; 5:27; 6:7; 7:17; 9:4**), but the mention of the sword here takes Amos' prophecies to a higher level. The sword that is drawn at **7:9** as the Lord rises against the house of Jeroboam shall not return to its sheath until Jeroboam himself (**7:11**) and the sons and daughters of Amaziah have fallen (**7:17**). Jeroboam did not deserve to rule over Israel any longer, nor did the idolatrous nation of Israel deserve any more chances. God's judgment would come and not fail.

Amaziah had no understanding that Amos was inspired and motivated by a different Spirit. It seems safety and earning a livelihood were very important to Amaziah. Probably he got his security from his relationship with Jeroboam, which could explain Amaziah's defense of the throne and the shrine, calling it the "king's chapel." He presumed the same of Amos—that he would be safe and be able to earn his living back in Judah. The scene of this confrontation, the shrine at Bethel, was both a royal chapel and national cathedral where calf worship took place. It was probably preferred by Jeroboam to Dan and the other shrines as it was nearer to Samaria, the capital. It was also the king's court—a seat of the kingdom—where the king's nobles gathered to discuss kingdom business. It was no place for unknown and uninvited priests and prophets. A place of such significance deserved reverence, and a foreign commoner like Amos was not welcome. His preaching and message in the vicinity of such a place would threaten his own life.

II. THE CALLED PROPHET (vv. 14–15)

Amos was content as a shepherd. God had called him away from his flock so that he could speak the truth to God's wayward flock, Israel. Amos was called to prophesy and did not do this out of self-will; God sent him to speak the truth to Israel and call them to repentance.

Amos Keeps Talking (vv. 14–15)

14 Then answered Amos, and said to Amaziah, I was no prophet, neither was I a prophet's son; but I was an herdman, and a gatherer of sycomore fruit: 15 And the LORD took me as I followed the flock, and the LORD said unto me, Go, prophesy unto my people Israel.

Amos then lets Amaziah know the details of his call. Unlike some who were trained as prophets (perhaps at the school of the prophets mentioned in **1 Samuel 10, 19; 2 Kings 2, 6**), Amos was a shepherd and farmer. He had no sights on making a name for himself; he had not planned this nor put it into motion. To put it simply, for Amos, being a prophet was not a career move.

III. THE FATEFUL PROPHECY (vv. 16–17)

Amos' response to Amaziah's message is full of doom and gloom. He not only continues with the message that Amaziah refused to listen to but he also spells out the people's fate in detail. Not only will the Israelites be taken into exile, but also Amaziah's own wife will be a prostitute and his sons and daughters will be killed. Amos' words expound on the message and make it personal for Amaziah.

God's Faithful Protection (vv. 16–17)

16 Now therefore hear thou the word of the LORD: Thou sayest, Prophesy not against Israel, and drop not thy word against the house of Isaac. 17 Therefore thus saith the LORD; Thy wife shall be an harlot in the city, and thy sons and thy daughters shall fall by the sword, and thy land shall be divided by line; and thou shalt die in a polluted land: and Israel shall surely go into captivity forth of his land.

It would seem that Amaziah had told Amos not to prophesy against Israel and the House of Isaac, invoking the names of their common ancestors as a channel of authority, but Amos turned his attempts against him. He addressed Amaziah regarding his defense of the king and the shrine. Because Amaziah had tried to stop Amos from prophesying against Israel, and had also advised him to return to Judah, he too had to be judged. Instead of reducing the force of his words to ease the fire of his condemnation of Amaziah and Israel, or even withdrawing his prophecy, Amos reaffirms them. Amaziah had to hear the true Word of the real Lord whom he contradicted while pretending to serve Him. Indeed, Amaziah had sought to silence Amos, but when his judgment comes, he would be silenced by God's fury. His own family would be destroyed. His wife would be abused and treated as a harlot by the victorious Assyrian army (see **Isaiah 13:16; Zechariah 14:2**). In addition, his children would be killed by the sword. His land would be divided among the new occupants. Amaziah himself would die in exile in a strange land. To conclude it all, Israel would be taken into exile.

God protects the servants who engage in His work faithfully. The prophet is only required to speak the Word no matter the circumstance. After that, he must trust and obey, expecting God's next direction.

SEARCH THE SCRIPTURES

QUESTION 1

How might **Amos 5:4** apply to our communities today?

Answers will vary.

QUESTION 2

Amaziah considered that earning a living was all that mattered to Amos. Is there any danger today that ministry might be considered more of a "job" than a calling?

Answers will vary.

LIGHT ON THE WORD

Amaziah Refuses to Listen

Amaziah refused to listen to Amos' message that he would die in a foreign land. His wife and children would be oppressed and killed by invaders. Their temple of idolatry would not be a sanctuary. Although they believed that Bethel and Israel were under their jurisdiction, the Israelites were mistaken; they were under God's jurisdiction and He would judge them for their sins.

BIBLE APPLICATION

AIM: Students will agree that believers can demonstrate their faithfulness to God in spite of the circumstances.

God called Amos to prophesy in a land that was not his own. He was called to do something that he was not trained to do. Many times God calls us to situations where we are not properly trained and where we have not been before. In order to get through the backlash and rejection that comes with that, you must be secure in your call. The call of God is what qualifies you and not your training. Training is helpful, but the call is what keeps you going when everyone and everything is against you.

STUDENTS' RESPONSES

AIM: Students will decide that they have the opportunity to choose to listen and obey God.

Have you ever experienced the call of God on your life? Talk to three pastors or missionaries and ask them how they received the call. Also ask them whether it has helped them through tough times to remember God's calling on their life. Bring your answers back to the class to discuss.

PRAYER

Dear God, thank You for choosing us and for using us. The more we draw closer to You and know Your voice, the more we are eager to follow You. Thank You for Your divine presence in our lives that strengthens us by the power of the Holy Spirit to obey you. We love You! In the Name of Jesus, we pray. Amen.

HOW TO SAY IT

Amaziah.	a-mah-**ZEYE**-uh.
Jeroboam.	je-ru-**BO**-um.

DIG A LITTLE DEEPER

This section provides an additional research article to further your study of the lesson:

Amos was a lowly man of no royal heritage. But he was called to do a great work, so his origin of birth was not an issue with God. This CBN article and video discusses the call of missionaries who are sent to dangerous places. These were not celebrities or politicians, just regular people fulfilling the call of God on their lives.

http://www.cbn.com/cbnnews/world/2009/june/danger-rises-for-american-missionaries-in-yemen/?mobile=false

PREPARE FOR NEXT SUNDAY

Read **Acts 6:1–7** and "Called to Witness."

DAILY HOME BIBLE READINGS

MONDAY
The Elect Keep the Commandments
(Deuteronomy 7:7–11)

TUESDAY
Hananiah Opposes the Prophetic Message
(Jeremiah 28:12–16)

WEDNESDAY
Oracle Against Israel
(Amos 1:1–2, 3:12–15)

THURSDAY
Seek Good and Live
(Amos 5:10–15)

FRIDAY
Let Justice Roll Down Like Waters
(Amos 5:18–24)

SATURDAY
David's Kingdom Restored
(Amos 9:11–15)

SUNDAY
Amos' Call
(Amos 7:10–17)

COMMENTS / NOTES:

_____

_____

_____

_____

_____

_____

_____

_____

_____

_____

_____

_____

_____

_____

_____

_____

_____

_____

CALLED TO WITNESS

BIBLE BASIS: ACTS 6:1–7

BIBLE TRUTH: Workers are essential to meet the many needs of people.

MEMORY VERSE: "Wherefore, brethren, look ye out among you seven men of honest report, full of the Holy Ghost and wisdom, whom we may appoint over this business" (Acts 6:3).

LESSON AIM: By the end of the lesson, we will: EVALUATE the ministry challenges of evangelism and benevolence in the first-century church; COMPARE how the church today balances efforts of outreach with other needs; and APPRECIATE the specific ministry call to meet the needs in your community.

TEACHER PREPARATION

MATERIALS NEEDED: Quarterly Commentary/Teacher Manual, Adult Quarterly, Adult resources—charts, worksheets, and other teaching tools, paper, pens, pencils, Bibles (several different versions)

OTHER MATERIALS NEEDED / TEACHER'S NOTES:

_____

_____

LESSON OVERVIEW

LIFE NEED FOR TODAY'S LESSON
We are called to take the Gospel to all the corners of the world.

BIBLE LEARNING
The Apostles addressed the concern to make the best use of God's gifts.

BIBLE APPLICATION
Believers must experience and practice sharing the love of God with various types of people.

STUDENTS' RESPONSES
Followers of Christ must prioritize their time and resources for effective life and ministry practices.

LESSON SCRIPTURE

ACTS 6:1–7, KJV

1 And in those days, when the number of the disciples was multiplied, there arose a murmuring of the Grecians against the Hebrews, because their widows were neglected in the daily ministration.

ACTS 6:1–7, AMP

1 Now about this time, when the number of disciples was increasing, a complaint was made by the Hellenists (Greek-speaking Jews) against the [native] Hebrews, because their widows were being overlooked in the daily serving of food.

2 Then the twelve called the multitude of the disciples unto them, and said, It is not reason that we should leave the word of God, and serve tables.

3 Wherefore, brethren, look ye out among you seven men of honest report, full of the Holy Ghost and wisdom, whom we may appoint over this business.

4 But we will give ourselves continually to prayer, and to the ministry of the word.

5 And the saying pleased the whole multitude: and they chose Stephen, a man full of faith and of the Holy Ghost, and Philip, and Prochorus, and Nicanor, and Timon, and Parmenas, and Nicolas a proselyte of Antioch:

6 Whom they set before the apostles: and when they had prayed, they laid their hands on them.

7 And the word of God increased; and the number of the disciples multiplied in Jerusalem greatly; and a great company of the priests were obedient to the faith.

2 So the Twelve called the disciples together and said, "It is not appropriate for us to neglect [teaching] the word of God in order to serve tables and manage the distribution of food.

3 Therefore, brothers, choose from among you seven men with good reputations [men of godly character and moral integrity], full of the Spirit and of wisdom, whom we may put in charge of this task.

4 But we will [continue to] devote ourselves [steadfastly] to prayer and to the ministry of the word."

5 The suggestion pleased the whole congregation; and they selected Stephen, a man full of faith [in Christ Jesus], and [filled with and led by] the Holy Spirit, and Philip, Prochorus, Nicanor, Timon, Parmenas, and Nicolas (Nikolaos), a proselyte (Gentile convert) from Antioch.

6 They brought these men before the apostles; and after praying, they laid their hands on them [to dedicate and commission them for this service].

7 And the message of God kept on growing and spreading, and the number of disciples continued to increase greatly in Jerusalem; and a large number of the priests were becoming obedient to the faith [accepting Jesus as Messiah and acknowledging Him as the Source of eternal salvation].

LIGHT ON THE WORD

Palestinian and Hellenestic Jews. The growing number of believers who were turning to the disciples' teachings were comprised primarily of Palestinian and Hellenistic Jews. This was an odd pairing since the two groups were known to have long-standing friction between them. One of the differences that was easily noticeable was their languages. Palestinian Jews spoke Aramaic for everyday conversation and Hebrew during worship at the synagogues and Temple. The Hellenistic Jews, who had been dispersed and mixed with cultures along the Mediterranean shores, were accustomed to speaking Greek. These Greek-speaking Jews were often looked at as an inferior class by Jews in Palestine. The conversion of a large number of Greek-speaking Jews on the day of Pentecost now brought these two groups into community as God was drawing people from all cultures, backgrounds, ethnic groups, and socioeconomic statuses to Christ.

TEACHING THE BIBLE LESSON

LIFE NEED FOR TODAY'S LESSON

AIM: Students will agree that we are called to take the Gospel to all corners of the world.

INTRODUCTION

A Good Reputation

To alleviate any hint of partiality, the apostles allowed the community of believers to select the individuals who would oversee the dispute regarding the food distribution. The criteria for selecting these individuals were their reputation, wisdom, and obedience to the Holy Spirit. The apostles selected seven new administrators, all converts of Greek descent. All seven selected had Greek names. One of the seven, Nicolas, was not even Jewish by birth, but a proselyte, converting from paganism to Judaism and then becoming a believer in Christ. For the apostles, the integrity of the seven was more important than their ethnic or cultural backgrounds.

BIBLE LEARNING

AIM: Students will validate that the apostles addressed the concern of the congregation in an effective manner.

I. PROBLEM AND PRIORITY
(Acts 6:1–2)

Starting on the day of Pentecost with Peter's compelling message about a risen Savior, the apostles had been vigilant about sharing the Gospel message. Huge numbers of individuals were identifying themselves as believers and formed a community where they shared their life and possessions. Jewish believers from outside Jerusalem started to complain about unfair distribution of resources in the community. Such a criticism could not be overlooked if the apostles wanted to maintain unity and build bonds of peace among all believers. Yet, the apostles knew that their primary call was to share the Gospel.

Addressing the Problems in the Church (Acts 6:1–2)

1 And in those days, when the number of the disciples was multiplied, there arose a murmuring of the Grecians against the Hebrews, because their widows were neglected in the daily ministration. 2 Then the twelve called the multitude of the disciples unto them, and said, It is not reason that we should leave the word of God, and serve tables.

Like all good church leadership, "the twelve" assembled the followers of Christ—Greeks and Hebrews—in order to prevent further problems. "The twelve" refers to the original men who followed Jesus during His earthly ministry. They were Jesus' original disciples with the exception of Judas (not Iscariot), who was replaced by Matthias (**Acts 1:23–26**).

The twelve leaders suggested to the congregation that it was better for them (the leaders) to spend their time praying and proclaiming the Gospel than spend time with the other daily services of the church, such as passing out food (i.e., "serving tables"). This was wise thinking, because there were not many men at that early point in church history who knew as much about Jesus as those original disciples. So, it was better for them to spend time passing on what they knew, rather than acting as waiters.

Though it may not always be possible for pastors to minister full-time today, a church that can support its pastor and family puts itself in a better position to get the full devotion to study, prayer, and the delivery of God's Word. Dedicated pastors who are true to the Bible certainly deserve to be supported by those they serve (**1 Corinthians 9:7–14**). The disciples recognized the importance of a pastor's total dedication to ministry. A wise church today, which is financially able, will do the same.

II. SOLUTION AND SELECTION (vv. 3–5)

The Apostles realized that they couldn't do everything themselves, but they could get everything done by recruiting the gifts and talents of those in their community. The people within the community knew the true character of the individuals among them and chose seven men whom they trusted to be the administrators. The early church was not without its problems, but its answers were also provided within the community.

Choosing the Best to Serve (vv. 3–5)

3 Wherefore, brethren, look ye out among you seven men of honest report, full of the Holy Ghost and wisdom, whom we may appoint over this business. 4 But we will give ourselves continually to prayer, and to the ministry of the word. 5 And the saying pleased the whole multitude: and they chose Stephen, a man full of faith and of the Holy Ghost, and Philip, and Prochorus, and Nicanor, and Timon, and Parmenas, and Nicolas a proselyte of Antioch.

The Twelve then delegated to the congregation the responsibility of selecting seven men to whom they would, in turn, delegate responsibility for the proper distribution of daily church services. The ability to properly delegate responsibility and authority is another hallmark of good leadership. In this case, it served the function of promoting the most efficient use of time by the leaders. One good reason for delegation of duties is to get better results due to expertise in a given area. The Holy Spirit distributes various "spiritual gifts" to everyone in the body of Christ (**1 Corinthians 12:4, 11**). Thus, some believers are more gifted in certain areas than others. They are the ones who should be given duties in the area of their gift(s).

Delegation also can serve the function of sharing the workload so that leaders are not prematurely burned out. Moses was one of the first Israelite leaders to delegate work to prevent an overload (**Exodus 18:17–26**).

Finally, the twelve leaders stated the qualifications for the seven men who were to be selected by the congregation. They had to be "of honest report," or have good reputations, so that the people would respect and trust them. Furthermore, they had to be "full of the Holy Ghost" so that they had the proper servant's heart and were led by God's Spirit in their work. Last, they had to be men of "wisdom," so that they had sound judgment and made godly decisions.

III. GROWTH AND GREATNESS (vv. 6–7)

Through prayer and the bestowment of blessings, the apostles confirmed the people's selection of the seven administrators. These seven men managed the daily affairs of the community and the apostles preached with unhindered consciences, knowing that any new converts would enter a community that was prepared to serve them. The community continue to grow; even Jewish priests were being converted to the faith. In addition, the seven were not limited by their roles and assigned tasks. Stephen, one of the seven, was given by God the ability to perform miracles and signs. His knowledge of Scripture, his skill as a debater and his submission to the Holy Spirit were examples for church leaders then and now. Like those individuals who preach and teach, those who hold other positions in ministry have a responsibility to be competent, devoted, and sober-minded servants for Christ.

The Disciples Multiplied (vv. 6–7)

6 Whom they set before the apostles: and when they had prayed, they laid their hands on them.

The congregation presented the seven men whom they had selected to the Twelve. Those seven men were the forerunners of what now are called "deacons" (see **1 Timothy 3:10–13**), and, "the twelve" here are identified as the first "apostles." At that time, the seven deacons were installed in their office in a ceremony before God. The apostles prayed for them and their new undertaking, and "laid their hands on them." This practice was similar to the ordination ceremonies many churches hold now.

The laying on of hands by the apostles was similar to the way that the Old Testament prophet Samuel anointed Saul and David with oil when God installed them in office as king (see **1 Samuel 10:1; 16:13**). It stems from the Old Testament practice laying hands on an animal to cover sins (see **Leviticus 1:4; 3:2, 8, 13; 4:4**). The practice was symbolic of a transfer of one's sins to the sacrificial offering. So, too, the apostles in our study text were anointing the seven deacons for the Lord's service and inviting the flow of God's power through the Holy Spirit into their lives.

7 And the word of God increased; and the number of the disciples multiplied in Jerusalem greatly; and a great company of the priests were obedient to the faith.

With the potential split in the church having been averted, everything was in the proper order. As a result of this newfound peace, order, and efficiency within the church at Jerusalem, tremendous fruit was borne by its ministry. Since the apostles were focused only on prayer and preaching, we are told that "the word of God increased." The apostles taught others the Gospel and preached with more power. Furthermore, "the number of the disciples multiplied in Jerusalem." The preaching of the Gospel produced many new converts. It was a phenomenon similar to Jesus' parable of sowing seed which produced "fruit, some an hundredfold, some sixtyfold, some thirtyfold" (**Matthew 13:8**).

In modern times, we can look around our community and see thousands of people who are lost and under the heavy yoke of spiritual oppression. We see them on the street corners, in bars and dope houses, and in our jails. As Jesus said, "The harvest truly is plenteous" (from **Matthew 9:37**). There are enough lost souls in our communities across urban America to bust the seams of every church in sight. But, just as the apostles and the early church, we must spread the Gospel message with Holy Ghost power. Therefore, we must focus on our mission and devote ourselves to our spiritual gifting, whether that be preaching, teaching, studying, or evangelizing.

Finally, many of the religious leaders who formerly opposed the spread of the Gospel began to accept it. This change of heart shows the awesomeness of God and His Word. The Bible says, "Through the greatness of thy power shall thine enemies submit themselves unto thee" (from **Psalm 66:3**). Truly the conversion of "a great company of the priests" confirms the truth of Scripture.

SEARCH THE SCRIPTURES

QUESTION 1

We evidenced the wisdom of the apostles to preach and teach while the deacons focused on church administration. Are there any changes that might need to take place in your church to allow the pastor to focus more on teaching and preaching?

Answers will vary.

QUESTION 2
What criteria should we use today to select church leaders?

Answers will vary.

LIGHT ON THE WORD
The Growth of the Church
God caused the church to grow tremendously in the early days of its existence. Such growth was a sign of God's presence, power, and truth. The unbelieving world had to admit, if nothing else, that something out of the ordinary was at work. Of course, believers today understand that the church, and its growth, is fueled by the presence and power of God through the Holy Spirit, and by the truth found in Christ (see **1 Corinthians 12:13; Acts 1:8**).

BIBLE APPLICATION

AIM: Students will experience and practice sharing the love of God with various types of people.

The twentieth-century theologian Howard Thurman once said, "Don't ask yourself what the world needs. Ask yourself what makes you come alive and then go do that. Because what the world needs is people who have come alive." What makes you come alive? What gifts and talents do you enjoy? What are some ways your joyous talents can meet the needs of your community and world?

STUDENTS' RESPONSES

AIM: Students will deduce that the followers of Christ must prioritize their time and resources for effective life and ministry practices.

Highly effective people know that they must put first things first to accomplish the tasks they have been given. They also know that to live in community they must not only care about themselves but also be concerned about the needs of others. To do that, they think win-win. They listen with open minds to the concerns of others and create safe and creative spaces for people to find workable and mutually beneficial solutions to problems. By incorporating the strengths and resources of the group, they accomplish more than they could by themselves. Problems, whether in our homes, at work, or church, are often opportunities to learn new skills and develop new relationships, experiences needed for both personal and spiritual growth.

PRAYER

Dear Heavenly Father, You have blessed us to share Your Word. As we are chosen by the Holy Spirit to serve as leaders, let us all be doers of Your Word. Bless us to be faithful servants. Bless those who serve in the church and help us to reach the lost in our community. Bless our pastor and his family. Grant him wisdom as he studies and teaches this congregation. In Your glorious Name, we pray. Amen.

HOW TO SAY IT

Proselyte.   prah-suh-**LITE**.

Prochorus.   prah-**KO**-rus.

DIG A LITTLE DEEPER

This section provides an additional research article to further your study of the lesson:

Dallas Willard, a philosophical and theological scholar from the University of Southern California, unpacks a conversational method for evangelism. This question-and-answer dialogue walks the reader through a brief discussion that addresses common concerns many have about accepting the Christian faith.

http://www.dwillard.org/articles/artview. asp?artID=14

PREPARE FOR NEXT SUNDAY

Read **Acts 8:26–39** and "Called to Break Down Barriers."

DAILY HOME BIBLE READINGS

MONDAY
Jesus Commissions Disciples
(Acts 1:1–11)

TUESDAY
Matthias Chosen to Replace Judas
(Acts 1:15–17, 20–26)

WEDNESDAY
The Holy Spirit Descends upon the Disciples
(Acts 2:1–13)

THURSDAY
First Converts Called to the Faith
(Acts 2:37–44)

FRIDAY
Stephen Arrested While Serving
(Acts 6:8–15)

SATURDAY
Stephen Stoned to Death While Praying
(Acts 7:54–81a)

SUNDAY
Called to Witness
(Acts 6:1–7)

COMMENTS / NOTES:

_____
_____
_____
_____
_____
_____
_____
_____
_____
_____
_____
_____
_____
_____
_____
_____
_____
_____
_____
_____
_____
_____
_____
_____
_____
_____
_____
_____
_____
_____
_____
_____
_____
_____

CALLED TO BREAK DOWN BARRIERS

BIBLE BASIS: ACTS 8:26–39

BIBLE TRUTH: The Gospel is for all to hear and receive.

MEMORY VERSE: "Then Philip opened his mouth, and began at the same scripture, and preached unto him Jesus" (Acts 8:35).

LESSON AIM: By the end of the lesson, we will: EVALUATE that the encounter between Philip and the Ethiopian represented a cross-cultural recognition of Jesus' identity; VALUE the need for cross-cultural evangelism; and PLAN to participate in cross-cultural outreach.

TEACHER PREPARATION

MATERIALS NEEDED: Quarterly Commentary/Teacher Manual, Adult Quarterly, Adult resources—charts, worksheets, and other teaching tools, paper, pens, pencils, Bibles (several different versions)

OTHER MATERIALS NEEDED / TEACHER'S NOTES:

_____

_____

LESSON OVERVIEW

LIFE NEED FOR TODAY'S LESSON
We are called to cross-cultural engagement and evangelism.

BIBLE APPLICATION
Believers are baptized in obedience to Scripture.

BIBLE LEARNING
Philip was willing to share the Gospel with someone from a different cultural background.

STUDENTS' RESPONSES:
As Christians nurture their relationship with Christ, they become stronger in their testimony about Him.

LESSON SCRIPTURE

ACTS 8:26–39, KJV

26 And the angel of the Lord spake unto Philip, saying, Arise, and go toward the south unto the way that goeth down from Jerusalem unto Gaza, which is desert.

27 And he arose and went: and, behold, a man of Ethiopia, an eunuch of great authority under Candace queen of the Ethiopians, who had the charge of all her treasure, and

ACTS 8:26–39, AMP

26 But an angel of the Lord said to Philip, "Get up and go south to the road that runs from Jerusalem down to Gaza." (This is a desert road).

27 So he got up and went; and there was an Ethiopian eunuch [a man of great authority], a court official of Candace, queen of the Ethiopians, who was in charge of all

had come to Jerusalem for to worship,

28 Was returning, and sitting in his chariot read Esaias the prophet.

29 Then the Spirit said unto Philip, Go near, and join thyself to this chariot.

30 And Philip ran thither to him, and heard him read the prophet Esaias, and said, Understandest thou what thou readest?

31 And he said, How can I, except some man should guide me? And he desired Philip that he would come up and sit with him.

32 The place of the scripture which he read was this, He was led as a sheep to the slaughter; and like a lamb dumb before his shearer, so opened he not his mouth:

33 In his humiliation his judgment was taken away: and who shall declare his generation? for his life is taken from the earth.

34 And the eunuch answered Philip, and said, I pray thee, of whom speaketh the prophet this? of himself, or of some other man?

35 Then Philip opened his mouth, and began at the same scripture, and preached unto him Jesus.

36 And as they went on their way, they came unto a certain water: and the eunuch said, See, here is water; what doth hinder me to be baptized?

37 And Philip said, If thou believest with all thine heart, thou mayest. And he answered and said, I believe that Jesus Christ is the Son of God.

38 And he commanded the chariot to stand still: and they went down both into the water, both Philip and the eunuch; and he baptized him.

her treasure. He had come to Jerusalem to worship,

28 and he was returning, and sitting in his chariot he was reading [the scroll of] the prophet Isaiah.

29 Then the [Holy] Spirit said to Philip, "Go up and join this chariot."

30 Philip ran up and heard the man reading the prophet Isaiah, and asked, "Do you understand what you are reading?"

31 And he said, "Well, how could I [understand] unless someone guides me [correctly]?" And he invited Philip to come up and sit with him.

32 Now this was the passage of Scripture which he was reading: "LIKE A SHEEP HE WAS LED TO THE SLAUGHTER; AND AS A LAMB BEFORE ITS SHEARER IS SILENT, SO HE DOES NOT OPEN HIS MOUTH.

33 "IN HUMILIATION HIS JUDGMENT WAS TAKEN AWAY [justice was denied Him]. WHO WILL DESCRIBE HIS GENERATION? FOR HIS LIFE IS TAKEN FROM THE EARTH."

34 The eunuch replied to Philip, "Please tell me, about whom does the prophet say this? About himself or about someone else?"

35 Then Philip spoke and beginning with this Scripture he preached Jesus to him [explaining that He is the promised Messiah and the source of salvation].

36 As they continued along the road, they came to some water; and the eunuch exclaimed, "Look! Water! What forbids me from being baptized?"

37 [Philip said to him, "If you believe with all your heart, you may." And he replied, "I do believe that Jesus Christ is the Son of God."]

39 And when they were come up out of the water, the Spirit of the Lord caught away Philip, that the eunuch saw him no more: and he went on his way rejoicing.

38 And he ordered that the chariot be stopped; and both Philip and the eunuch went down into the water, and Philip baptized him.

39 When they came up out of the water, the Spirit of the Lord [suddenly] took Philip [and carried him] away [to a different place]; and the eunuch no longer saw him, but he went on his way rejoicing.

LIGHT ON THE WORD

Philip the Evangelist. The Philip who shares the Gospel with the Ethiopian eunuch is not the Apostle Philip. This Philip was one of the seven men selected in **Acts 6** to help ensure that widows and the poor, whether from Hebrew and Greek backgrounds, would be treated fairly. He was chosen because of his integrity and obedience to the guidance of the Holy Spirit. Philip, along with the other six men, are often referred to as the first deacons of the church. They cared for the material needs of the growing group of believers so that the apostles could continue preaching and teaching the Gospel without distraction.

TEACHING THE BIBLE LESSON

LIFE NEED FOR TODAY'S LESSON

AIM: Students will agree that believers are called to take the Gospel to all the corners of the world.

INTRODUCTION

A Special Assignment

When believers started to be persecuted in Jerusalem, Philip, like many new Christ followers, fled that city. He went to Samaria and began sharing the Gospel of Jesus Christ there. Philip's speaking was accompanied by miraculous signs from God, and people from diverse walks of life turned to Christ because of his words. While in the midst of this successful evangelistic crusade, Philip responded to a prompting from God to leave the success of the city for a special assignment on a desert road. There he found a man, different from him in many ways, who was trying to understand prophetic writings about the Messiah found in the book of Isaiah. So clear and compelling must have been Philip's words that the man decided to become a believer, asking Philip to baptize him. The man left Philip rejoicing, and Philip left the desert road knowing that God could use him to share the Gospel in varied situations and places.

BIBLE LEARNING

AIM: Students will evaluate why Philip was willing to share the Gospel with one person.

I. LEAVING THE FAMILIAR (Acts 8:26–29)

Jerusalem was built on a hill; any departure was considered "go[ing] down" from the city. Gaza was one of the five cities occupied by the Philistines in southwest Palestine from approximately 1200-600 BC. After it was captured by Nebuchadnezzar and later the Greeks and Romans, it remained an important city of commerce due to its location near the sea. At the time Luke writes, it was on a caravan route leading to Egypt that someone traveling from Jerusalem to Ethiopia would naturally take.

The Lord's Angel Speaks to Philip (Acts 8:26–29)

26 And the angel of the Lord spake unto Philip, saying, Arise, and go toward the south unto the way that goeth down from Jerusalem unto Gaza, which is desert.

There he met an Ethiopian who was traveling back to his country. Ethiopia, located south of Egypt, was known to Jews from ancient days (**Psalm 68:31; Jeremiah 38:7**). The man, a eunuch and officer for the queen of Ethiopia, had traveled a long distance to Jerusalem to worship. Still hungry and thirsty to know God, the eunuch was reading the Scriptures, trying to understand its meaning when Philip came alongside his chariot. While Philip's religious upbringing might have dismissed this man from being worthy of God's grace and mercy, Philip acknowledged God's saving work was for all people, even Gentiles and eunuchs (**Isaiah 56:3–8**), by engaging him in a conversation.

27 And he arose and went: and, behold, a man of Ethiopia, an eunuch of great authority under Candace queen of the Ethiopians, who had the charge of all her treasure, and had come to Jerusalem for to worship. 28 Was returning, and sitting in his chariot read Esaias the prophet. 29 Then the Spirit said unto Philip, Go near, and join thyself to this chariot.

Ethiopia, now the area called Sudan, was often among the Gentile nations that were named in the Bible as being subject to God's judgment for their corruption (**Isaiah 20:3–5; 43:3; Ezekiel 30:1–9; Nahum 3:9; Zephaniah 2:11–12**). The Ethiopian eunuch held a high position in the Ethiopian government. He was in charge of the entire treasury of the Candace. According to ancient writers such as Pliny the Elder and Callisthenes, Candace, queen of the Ethiopians, was a dynastic rather than a personal name. That is, it was used to refer to a royal line of queens over various generations (e.g., "the Candace").

The Ethiopian eunuch, as other Ethiopians, had come to Jerusalem to worship. The narrative does not indicate whether he was a Jew or a proselyte (i.e., a Gentile who has converted to Judaism). He may have been a God-fearing person (i.e., a non-Jew who, although sympathetic to Judaism, did not submit to circumcision or observe the Torah in its entirety, but did agree with the ethical monotheism of the Jews and sometimes attended their synagogue services). If he was a eunuch not only by position but also physically, it would not have been possible for him to participate in the worship in the Temple. In this regard, his status was like that of other foreigners who came to the Temple, in spite of being excluded from it.

II. INCLUDING OTHERS (vv. 30–35)

The eunuch wanted to know who this person was he was reading about in Isaiah. Was it Isaiah, the Jewish people, or someone else? Philip used this passage and many others to share the Good News about Jesus Christ and God's redemptive plan of salvation that included everyone. For someone who might have felt marginalized and excluded from full access to God's presence this certainly would have been good news.

Philip Meets the Unnamed Ethiopian (vv. 30–35)

31 And he said, How can I, except some man should guide me? And he desired Philip that he would come up and sit with him.

The eunuch admits he won't be able to understand the text unless someone "guide[s]" him.

"Guide" (Gk. *hodegeo*, **ho-day-GEH-oh**) literally means to lead along a road (see Jesus' use of the term "blind leaders" and "blind lead the blind" in **Matthew 15:14**). Here "guide" gains the transferred sense of "leading" in righteousness or wisdom similar to its use in passages such as **Psalms 5:8, 73:24; John 16:13**. Thus, the eunuch invited Philip to get in and sit with him under the assumption that he would be able to explain the passage in Isaiah. Traditionally, the Jews applied the concepts of suffering and humiliation in **Isaiah 52:13–53:12** to the nation of Israel or to the unrighteous Gentile nations. Thus, the idea of a suffering Messiah was not a common idea among Jews of the time. This passage, then, must have been unclear to the eunuch.

32 The place of the scripture which he read was this, He was led as a sheep to the slaughter; and like a lamb dumb before his shearer, so opened he not his mouth. 33 In his humiliation his judgment was taken away: and who shall declare his generation? for his life is taken from the earth.

The passage the eunuch is reading is **Isaiah 53:7–8**. The Greek word for "humiliation" (*tapeinosis*, **ta-PAY-no-sees**) provides a possible allusion both to Luke's theme of humbling the haughty and exalting the humble (**Luke 1:52; 3:5, 14:11, 18:14**), and to the humility of Jesus becoming incarnate and finally His humiliation on the Cross (cf. **Philippians 2:7–8**).

34 And the eunuch answered Philip, and said, I pray thee, of whom speaketh the prophet this? of himself, or of some other man? 35 Then Philip opened his mouth, and began at the same scripture, and preached unto him Jesus.

The eunuch's question is the pertinent one. The traditional understanding of this passage did not address his deep spiritual hunger. After having been invited into the Ethiopian's chariot, Philip explained the Isaiah passage by beginning with the same text, and showed him that Jesus was the focus of the Scriptures. In a similar scene (**Luke 24:13–35**), the risen Jesus teaches the two on the road to Emmaus how to understand the Scriptures: "O fools, and slow of heart to believe all that the prophets have spoken: Ought not Christ to have suffered these things, and to enter into his glory? And beginning at Moses and all the prophets, he expounded unto them in all the scriptures the things concerning himself" (from **vv. 25–27**).

The Scripture passage in Isaiah that the eunuch was reading focused on the humiliation and exaltation of the Messiah. The application of the passage to Jesus is clear, to His humiliation and exaltation in particular ("his judgment was taken away," **v. 33**). This type of interpretation of the prophecy of Isaiah is also seen in other New Testament Scriptures (**Romans 10:16, John 12:38**).

III. REJOICING IN GOD'S SALVATION (vv. 36–39)

In his discourse, Philip must have shared the importance of baptism in signifying a relationship with Christ and His body, the church. As soon as the Ethiopian saw a body of water, he wanted to be baptized. He confessed his faith in Christ and then he and Philip went down to the water where Philip baptized him. The Ethiopian continued his journey rejoicing in his newfound salvation. Philip was sent by God to Azotus, an ancient Philistine capital, to another ethnic group that needed to hear the Gospel (**v. 40**).

Philip Baptizes the Ethiopian Eunuch (vv. 36–39)

36 And as they went on their way, they came unto a certain water: and the eunuch said, See, here is water; what doth hinder me to be baptized? 37 And Philip said, If

thou believest with all thine heart, thou mayest. And he answered and said, I believe that Jesus Christ is the Son of God. 38 And he commanded the chariot to stand still: and they went down both into the water, both Philip and the eunuch; and he baptized him.

After hearing the Scripture explained and being shown how it pointed to Jesus, the eunuch asked, "What doth hinder me to be baptized?" "Hinder" (Gk. *koluo*, **ko-LOO-oh**) is also used in **Luke 11:52**, where Jesus accuses the lawyers of preventing ("hinder[ing]") others from entering the Kingdom. Because there was no reason for his exclusion from full inclusion among the followers of Jesus, the Ethiopian eunuch ordered the chariot to stop; Philip and the eunuch both went down to the water, and Philip baptized him.

39 And when they were come up out of the water, the Spirit of the Lord caught away Philip, that the eunuch saw him no more: and he went on his way rejoicing.

The Old Testament often portrays the Spirit moving prophets around in this fashion, catching them up and away to another location instantly (cf. **1 Kings 18:12; 2 Kings 2:16; Ezekiel 11:24**). The Greek word used for caught away is *harpazo* (**har-POD-zo**) which can also mean "snatch." After his conversion experience, the eunuch continued on his way "rejoicing" (Gk. *chairo*, **KIGH-row**), an appropriate response to salvation. Frequently in the books of Luke and Acts, joy or rejoicing is a noted response to God's work in the world (**Luke 1:14, 6:23; Acts 5:41**).

SEARCH THE SCRIPTURES

QUESTION 1

Do you believe with all your heart that Jesus Christ is the Son of God? Have you been baptized?

Answers will vary.

QUESTION 2

What important lesson about evangelism do we learn in Philip's approach to the Ethiopian eunuch? What Scripture might you reference?

Peter started with the eunuch's question, so we should start by answering questions people are asking. "Always be ready to give a [logical] defense to anyone who asks you to account for the hope and confident assurance [elicited by faith] that is within you, yet [do it] with gentleness and respect" (1 Peter 3:15b, AMP). Answers will vary.

LIGHT ON THE WORD

Sharing the Gospel often starts by listening and learning where others are in their understanding of Scripture, God, or core Bible teachings. On our jobs, in our communities, or while shopping at the store, we will meet individuals from different nations, religions, and socioeconomic backgrounds. Like Philip, listen and share the Gospel as you are guided by the Lord, and the Holy Spirit.

BIBLE APPLICATION

AIM: Students will plan opportunities to witness about Jesus to others.

We encounter various types of people as we share the message of Christ. Many might dress differently, speak with an accent, and have preferences unfamiliar to us. It's easy to ignore those we see as different, missing opportunities to share the Good News. We become Christ's hands and feet when we are willing to cross any boundary for the Gospel's sake.

STUDENTS' RESPONSES

AIM: Students will value how they become stronger in their testimony about Christ as their relationship in Him grows.

Many times we are uncomfortable with people who are different from us. Go to a store or restaurant where people speak a different language from yours. Volunteer to teach an English as a Second Language class. Talk to a neighbor who is of a different ethnicity and ask him or her to tell about his or her country of origin.

PRAYER

Dear Lord, we celebrate who You are. Because of You, we have the joy of sharing the Gospel with others. We need to break down barriers that keep us from witnessing to our family, strangers, and friends. Open our mouths and prepare our hearts to proclaim the goodness of Your love and justice for all. In the wonderful Name of Jesus, we pray. Amen.

HOW TO SAY IT

Eunuch.   **YOO**-nik.

Candace.   **CAN**-dis.

DIG A LITTLE DEEPER

This section provides an additional research article to further your study of the lesson:

In this interview, Dr. Lawrence O. Richards, a prolific Christian teacher and author, discusses his daily discipline and the call for continued education. He encourages believers to sharpen their cognitive abilities through reading and reflection. God's Word will shape the answers to the questions that are most important.

http://www.christianwritingtoday.com/talking-with-dr-larry-richards/

PREPARE FOR NEXT SUNDAY

Read **Acts 9:10–20** and "Called to Preach."

DAILY HOME BIBLE READINGS

MONDAY
Jesus Heals Canaanite Daughter
(Matthew 15:21–28)

TUESDAY
Good News for All Peoples
(Galatians 3:23–29)

WEDNESDAY
All Who Call Will Be Saved
(Romans 10:9–15)

THURSDAY
Persecution Scatters the Church
(Acts 8:1b–3)

FRIDAY
Converts in Samaria Baptized
(Acts 8:4–13)

SATURDAY
Simon Repents of Selfish Power Grab
(Acts 8:14–25)

SUNDAY
Called to Break Down Barriers
(Acts 8:26–39)

COMMENTS / NOTES:

_____

_____

_____

_____

_____

_____

_____

_____

_____

_____

_____

CALLED TO PREACH

BIBLE BASIS: ACTS 9:10–20

BIBLE TRUTH: God calls and prepares people to proclaim His Word.

MEMORY VERSE: "And straightway he preached Christ in the synagogues, that he is the Son of God" (Acts 9:20).

LESSON AIM: At the end of the lesson, we will: AGREE that God calls preachers and sends them out so that His Word is proclaimed; APPRECIATE the love that God shows for the world through the preaching of His Word; and ENCOURAGE every preacher we know to study, preach, and do God's Word.

TEACHER PREPARATION

MATERIALS NEEDED: Quarterly Commentary/Teacher Manual, Adult Quarterly, Adult resources—charts, worksheets, and other teaching tools, paper, pens, pencils, Bibles (several different versions)

OTHER MATERIALS NEEDED / TEACHER'S NOTES:

_____

_____

LESSON OVERVIEW

LIFE NEED FOR TODAY'S LESSON
What would today's world look like if there were no preachers sharing the Word of Jesus Christ?

BIBLE LEARNING
Although Ananias was hesitant, he obeyed God and Saul's sight was restored.

BIBLE APPLICATION
As believers, we are willing to go where the Holy Spirit sends us.

STUDENTS' RESPONSES
Believers value developing a relationship with Christ.

LESSON SCRIPTURE

ACTS 9:10–20, KJV

10 And there was a certain disciple at Damascus, named Ananias; and to him said the Lord in a vision, Ananias. And he said, Behold, I am here, Lord.

11 And the Lord said unto him, Arise, and go into the street which is called Straight, and enquire in the house of Judas for one called Saul, of Tarsus: for, behold, he prayeth,

ACTS 9:10–20, AMP

10 Now in Damascus there was a disciple named Ananias; and the Lord said to him in a vision, "Ananias." And he answered, "Here I am, Lord."

11 And the Lord said to him, "Get up and go to the street called Straight, and ask at the house of Judas for a man from Tarsus named Saul; for he is praying [there],

12 And hath seen in a vision a man named Ananias coming in, and putting his hand on him, that he might receive his sight.

13 Then Ananias answered, Lord, I have heard by many of this man, how much evil he hath done to thy saints at Jerusalem:

14 And here he hath authority from the chief priests to bind all that call on thy name.

15 But the Lord said unto him, Go thy way: for he is a chosen vessel unto me, to bear my name before the Gentiles, and kings, and the children of Israel:

16 For I will shew him how great things he must suffer for my name's sake.

17 And Ananias went his way, and entered into the house; and putting his hands on him said, Brother Saul, the Lord, even Jesus, that appeared unto thee in the way as thou camest, hath sent me, that thou mightest receive thy sight, and be filled with the Holy Ghost.

18 And immediately there fell from his eyes as it had been scales: and he received sight forthwith, and arose, and was baptized.

19 And when he had received meat, he was strengthened. Then was Saul certain days with the disciples which were at Damascus.

20 And straightway he preached Christ in the synagogues, that he is the Son of God.

12 and in a vision he has seen a man named Ananias come in and place his hands on him, so that he may regain his sight."

13 But Ananias answered, "Lord, I have heard from many people about this man, especially how much suffering and evil he has brought on Your saints (God's people) at Jerusalem;

14 and here [in Damascus] he has authority from the high priests to put in chains all who call on Your name [confessing You as Savior]."

15 But the Lord said to him, "Go, for this man is a [deliberately] chosen instrument of Mine, to bear My name before the Gentiles and kings and the sons of Israel;

16 for I will make clear to him how much he must suffer and endure for My name's sake."

17 So Ananias left and entered the house, and he laid his hands on Saul and said, "Brother Saul, the Lord Jesus, who appeared to you on the road as you came [to Damascus], has sent me so that you may regain your sight and be filled with the Holy Spirit [in order to proclaim Christ to both Jews and Gentiles]."

18 Immediately something like scales fell from Saul's eyes, and he regained his sight. Then he got up and was baptized;

19 and he took some food and was strengthened. For several days [afterward] Saul remained with the disciples who were at Damascus.

20 And immediately he began proclaiming Jesus in the synagogues, saying, "This Man is the Son of God [the promised Messiah]!"

447

LIGHT ON THE WORD

Saul/Paul. First known as Saul, his birthplace was Tarsus, the major city in Cilicia. Saul was born a citizen of Rome. Paul was his Roman name and his father was probably a Roman. He also had a Jewish name, "Saul." Saul saw the Christian church in Jerusalem as a threat to the things that were so dear to him. Then Saul had an encounter with God on the road to Damascus. This experience changed his life forever. He became an apostle to the Gentiles.

TEACHING THE BIBLE LESSON

LIFE NEED FOR TODAY'S LESSON

AIM: Students will acknowledge that is it vital to share God's Holy Word.

INTRODUCTION

Saul Encounters Jesus

Saul showed harsh aggression against the disciples. He went to the high priest, Caiaphas, to obtain permission to arrest those of "the Way." Saul was headed to Damascus, because this city had a great number of Jewish people. On his way, he saw a great light from Heaven and fell to the ground. Then God spoke to him. The Lord asked Saul why he was persecuting Him. After his dialogue with Jesus, Saul was both trembling and astonished and he asked Jesus another question: "What shall I do, LORD?" (**Acts 22:10**). Jesus told him to get up and go to the city, where he would be told what to do.

BIBLE LEARNING

AIM: Students will agree that although Ananias was hesitant to visit Saul, he was obedient to God, and Saul's sight was restored.

I. ANANIAS ASSIGNED (Acts 9:10–12)

Although Saul came to arrest Christians, he was stopped on the road to Damascus and told to wait for a man he had never met. **Verse 10** tells about a man named Ananias. The Lord speaks to him and gives him his assignment: rise and go. Ananias would be the one to first show Christian compassion to Saul of Tarsus. God told him what to do—find Saul and lay hands on him—and He told him what would happen—Saul would see again. God will prepare the way for you to minister. In some cases, the Lord will give you assignments and tell you where to go, what to do, and what to expect. Be ready and say, "Hear am I, Lord. Send me. I'll go."

A Reluctant Disciple (vv. 10–12)

10 And there was a certain disciple at Damascus, named Ananias; and to him said the Lord in a vision, Ananias. And he said, Behold, I am here, Lord.

Ananias is identified as a "disciple" (Gk. *mathetes*, **mah-they-TASE**), and Paul later describes him as "a devout man according to the law" (**Acts 22:12**). The pattern of call and response is similar to that of Samuel's (**1 Samuel 3:4, 10**). Ananias' response contradicts the fear he later experiences.

11 And the Lord said unto him, Arise, and go into the street which is called Straight, and enquire in the house of Judas for one called Saul, of Tarsus: for, behold, he prayeth, 12 And hath seen in a vision a man named Ananias coming in, and putting his hand on him, that he might receive his sight.

The vivid details in the message—the name of the street, the owner of the house, and the place of Saul's origin—are compatible with reliable historical traditions and good storytelling. We are never told about Saul's vision of Ananias from his own point of view, but only indirectly through the means of another vision.

II. ANANIAS ANSWERS (vv. 13–15)

Ananias answered his call from the Lord, but when he heard the assignment, he experienced some apprehension. He told the Lord that he has heard about this Saul and what he has done to the saints in Jerusalem. He tells the Lord about the authority that Saul has. The Lord heard what Ananias said, but He did not change His mind about the call He had given to him. God knows sometimes you will be fearful. He assures you He has a plan for you (**Jeremiah 29:11**).

13 Then Ananias answered, Lord, I have heard by many of this man, how much evil he hath done to thy saints at Jerusalem.

Ananias is allowed not only to voice his (understandable) reluctance to encounter such a dangerous person, but to help the reader deal with the obvious objections. Human hesitancy is legitimate, but it can be overturned by the command of the Lord. Ananias's version of the events gives us a slightly different perspective. Luke uses the term "saints" or "holy ones" (Gk. *hagios*, **HAH-gee-ose**) to refer to God's people (**Acts 9:41, 26:10**). Later Paul frequently used this term for the same purpose (**Romans 1:7, 15:25; 2 Corinthians 1:1, 8:4; Philippians 1:1**).

14 And here he hath authority from the chief priests to bind all that call on thy name. 15 But the Lord said unto him, Go thy way: for he is a chosen vessel unto me, to bear my name before the Gentiles, and kings, and the children of Israel:

Saul is explicitly said to have "authority" (Gk. *exousia*, **ek-sue-SEE-ah**) from the chief priests. This word implies having both the political authority and the physical force needed to complete a task. The phrase "all that call on thy name" echoes the statement from **Acts 2:21**: "[W]hosoever shall call on the name of the Lord shall be saved." It also echoes the statement of **Genesis 4:26** as a foundational principle of what it means to trust in the Lord.

Literally, "a vessel" can mean any sort of instrument (**1 Thessalonians 4:4; Hebrews 9:21**), but can be especially used in the context of divine instrumentality (**Romans 9:22–23; 2 Timothy 2:20–21**). Since God speaks of Saul as His "vessel," it is appropriate that Saul will "bear" the Lord's Name, making him a useful instrument for God. The image is remarkably like that used by Paul himself speaking of carrying the glory of God "in earthen vessels" (**2 Corinthians 4:7**). The designation of him as "chosen," in turn, associates him with the description of Jesus as the "chosen of God" (**Luke 23:35**). This terminology has collectively been applied to all believers, although in this sense it speaks of Saul being chosen for his unique and particular task.

III. ANANIAS ACTS (vv. 16–20)

Ananias went to find Saul, to lay hands on him in order for him to receive his sight. The Lord is looking for people who will act on what He has called them to do. Ananias did not do what he wanted, but instead what God had asked him to do. Ananias had to change his attitude about Saul and not see him for what he was, but what he would become.

The Opening of Saul's Eyes (vv. 16–20)

16 For I will shew him how great things he must suffer for my name's sake. 17 And Ananias went his way, and entered into the house; and putting his hands on him said, Brother Saul, the Lord, even Jesus, that appeared unto thee in the way as thou camest, hath sent me, that thou mightest receive thy sight, and be filled with the Holy Ghost.

The use of the phrase "must suffer" places Saul directly and deliberately in the line of suffering prophets like Moses and Jesus (**Luke 9:22, 24:26, Hebrews 11:24–26**). To suffer for Jesus'

Name, in turn, means that he does so as Jesus' representative (**Luke 6:22, 21:12, 17; Acts 5:41**).

The gesture of laying on of hands symbolizes the transfer of power. It appears in sacrificial rites (**Exodus 29:10, 19; Leviticus 1:4; 4:15, 16:21**), and as part of the ordination of priests (**Numbers 8:10**). Even more impressive is the formal transfer of authority from Moses to Joshua through this gesture (**Numbers 27:18–23**). This passage makes clear that the gesture signified that the people should now obey Joshua just as they had Moses. In Luke, the laying on of hands appears as part of Jesus' healings, which Luke clearly understands as a communication of power (**Luke 4:40, 13:13**). In Acts, the gesture accompanies the bestowal of the Spirit in baptism (**8:17, 19, 19:6**), healing (**28:8**), and commissioning for ministry (**13:3**).

In the present case, the laying on of hands works both as a healing and a bestowal of the Holy Spirit. The use of Saul's name with the title "brother" and the physical gesture of touching register as recognitions of his acceptance as a member of God's covenant people.

18 And immediately there fell from his eyes as it had been scales: and he received sight forthwith, and arose, and was baptized. 19 And when he had received meat, he was strengthened. Then was Saul certain days with the disciples which were at Damascus. 20 And straightway he preached Christ in the synagogues, that he is the Son of God.

The composition of what covered Saul's eyes is not clear. The text describes it as something like "scales" that fell from his eyes. This image of scales falling from one's eyes is so iconic that it has become a saying to figuratively describe enlightened understanding or illumination. In the words of the hymn "Amazing Grace," Saul "was blind but now can see." The light that blinded him paradoxically relieved him of his spiritual blindness. In Saul's case, his sight was associated with revelation.

After gaining his sight, Paul takes his first step of obedience in undergoing baptism. He now identifies with the Jesus who is worshiped by the believers he once persecuted. There would be no turning back now. He was part of the Body of Christ.

Once baptized, Saul, who now had his sight, ate and gained strength. Then he connected with the disciples in Damascus. Saul had the opportunity to experience the fellowship of other believers. The same believers whom he had authority to persecute were now welcoming him into their homes. Saul was a different man and preached that Jesus was the Son of God.

SEARCH THE SCRIPTURES
QUESTION 1
Ananias was skeptical to visit Saul because of Saul's reputation. Have you ever hesitated to speak or work with someone because you did not believe they had changed for the better?

Answers will vary.

QUESTION 2
Verse 20 states that Saul immediately began preaching in the synagogues about who Jesus is. What was the first thing you did or said after your conversion to share with someone about who Christ is?

Answers will vary.

LIGHT ON THE WORD
God's Choice
Can God choose anyone He wants to work for Him? God has the plan and He knows the outcome. Are you ready to submit to God's authority? Will you allow Him to depend on you to work His plan? Why or why not?

BIBLE APPLICATION

AIM: Students will affirm that developing a relationship with Christ is important for believers to mature in their calling by God.

Ask God to articulate His calling for you. Be prepared to go beyond your comfort zone to reach those whom God sends to you. Sometimes people have been portrayed as being mean and nasty, but it is up to you to see what God sees in them. Be the Christian that God can count on to do the hard things.

STUDENTS' RESPONSES

AIM: Students will affirm that believers are called by God to serve in obedience.

Many people are ready to do whatever it takes to get money and become famous. Some people would kill, steal, lie, or cheat. But where are the Christians today that will do anything to make sure the Gospel is preached? The things that are important to God should also be important to you. Christians need to be ready to give their lives so others can have eternal life.

PRAYER

Dear Heavenly Father, thank You for counting us worthy to share Your Word. Thank You for giving us moments to seek, share, and live Your Word so that others are drawn to You. May we be faithful and obedient, and have courage to speak as You guide us. In the Blessed Name of Jesus, we pray. Amen.

HOW TO SAY IT

Ananias.   a-nuh-**NIE**-us.

Tarsus.   tar-**SUS**.

DIG A LITTLE DEEPER

This section provides an additional research article to further your study of the lesson:

One of the most remarkable events to read about in the Bible is the conversion of unbelievers. In the book of Acts, the witness of Christ transforms the life of Saul to Paul. The outworking of faith was the preaching of the Gospel. God was able to do what seemed impossible even to Paul. This devotional is a reminder that God is still able to do what seems impossible.

http://odb.org/2010/05/29/never-say-never-2/

PREPARE FOR NEXT SUNDAY

Read **Acts 10:19–33** and "Called to Be Inclusive."

DAILY HOME BIBLE READINGS

MONDAY
Saul's Mandate to Capture Believers
(Acts 22:1–5)

TUESDAY
A Trustworthy Preacher/Teacher
(Titus 1:5–9)

WEDNESDAY
Saul Proclaims Jesus in Damascus
(Acts 9:21–25)

THURSDAY
Saul in Tarsus; Jerusalem at Peace
(Acts 9:26–31)

FRIDAY
Paralytic Aeneas Healed in Lydda
(Acts 9:32–35)

SATURDAY
Jesus Calls Saul on Damascus Road
(Acts 9:1–9)

SUNDAY
Called to Preach
(Acts 9:10–20)

CALLED TO BE INCLUSIVE

BIBLE BASIS: Acts 10:19–33

BIBLE TRUTH: In a vision, God showed Peter that all people can hear and receive God's Word.

MEMORY VERSE: "And he said unto them, Ye know how that it is an unlawful thing for a man that is a Jew to keep company, or come unto one of another nation; but God hath shewed me that I should not call any man common or unclean" (Acts 10:28).

LESSON AIM: By the end of this lesson, we will: EVALUATE the account of Cornelius's meeting with Peter; APPRECIATE that the Gospel is for everyone and desire to reach others with the Gospel; and COMMIT to enhancing the church's cross-cultural mission outreach.

TEACHER PREPARATION

MATERIALS NEEDED: Quarterly Commentary/Teacher Manual, Adult Quarterly, Adult resources—charts, worksheets, and other teaching tools, paper, pens, pencils, Bibles (several different versions)

OTHER MATERIALS NEEDED / TEACHER'S NOTES:

_____

_____

LESSON OVERVIEW

LIFE NEED FOR TODAY'S LESSON
Traditions and cultural understandings often shape our view of the world and our interactions with people.

BIBLE LEARNING
Through a vision from God, Peter was taught how and why to witness to Cornelius and his household.

BIBLE APPLICATION
As witnesses of Christ, we must open our mouths and respond to those who need to know Jesus as Lord and Savior.

STUDENTS' RESPONSES
Christians accept that Jesus is the Savior of the world and that everyone should have the opportunity to know Him.

LESSON SCRIPTURE

ACTS 10:19–33, KJV

19 While Peter thought on the vision, the Spirit said unto him, Behold, three men seek thee.

ACTS 10:19–33, AMP

19 While Peter was thoughtfully considering the vision, the Spirit said to him, "Now listen, three men are looking for you.

20 Arise therefore, and get thee down, and go with them, doubting nothing: for I have sent them.

21 Then Peter went down to the men which were sent unto him from Cornelius; and said, Behold, I am he whom ye seek: what is the cause wherefore ye are come?

22 And they said, Cornelius the centurion, a just man, and one that feareth God, and of good report among all the nation of the Jews, was warned from God by an holy angel to send for thee into his house, and to hear words of thee.

23 Then called he them in, and lodged them. And on the morrow Peter went away with them, and certain brethren from Joppa accompanied him.

24 And the morrow after they entered into Caesarea. And Cornelius waited for them, and he had called together his kinsmen and near friends.

25 And as Peter was coming in, Cornelius met him, and fell down at his feet, and worshipped him.

26 But Peter took him up, saying, Stand up; I myself also am a man.

27 And as he talked with him, he went in, and found many that were come together.

28 And he said unto them, Ye know how that it is an unlawful thing for a man that is a Jew to keep company, or come unto one of another nation; but God hath shewed me that I should not call any man common or unclean.

29 Therefore came I unto you without gainsaying, as soon as I was sent for: I ask therefore for what intent ye have sent for me?

20 Get up, go downstairs and go with them without hesitating or doubting, because I have sent them Myself."

21 Peter went down to the men and said, "I am the one you are looking for. For what reason have you come?"

22 They said, "Cornelius, a centurion, an upright and God-fearing man well spoken of by all the Jewish people, was divinely instructed by a holy angel to send for you to come to his house and hear what you have to say."

23 So Peter invited them in and gave them lodging [for the night]. The next day Peter got up and left with them, and some of the brothers from Joppa went with him.

24 On the following day he [and the others] entered Caesarea. Cornelius was waiting for them, and had called together his relatives and close friends.

25 When Peter arrived, Cornelius met him, and fell down at his feet and worshiped him.

26 But Peter raised him up, saying, "Stand up; I too am only a man."

27 As Peter talked with him, he entered [the house] and found a large group of people assembled.

28 He said to them, "You know that it is unlawful for a Jewish man to associate with or befriend a Gentile, or to visit him; and yet God has shown me that I am not to call anyone common or [ceremonially] unclean.

29 Therefore when I was sent for, I came without raising an objection. So I ask for what reason have you sent for me?"

30 Cornelius said, "Four days ago to this hour, I was praying in my house during the ninth hour (3:00-4:00 p.m.); and a man

30 And Cornelius said, Four days ago I was fasting until this hour; and at the ninth hour I prayed in my house, and, behold, a man stood before me in bright clothing,

31 And said, Cornelius, thy prayer is heard, and thine alms are had in remembrance in the sight of God.

32 Send therefore to Joppa, and call hither Simon, whose surname is Peter; he is lodged in the house of one Simon a tanner by the sea side: who, when he cometh, shall speak unto thee.

33 Immediately therefore I sent to thee; and thou hast well done that thou art come. Now therefore are we all here present before God, to hear all things that are commanded thee of God.

[dressed] in bright, dazzling clothing suddenly stood before me,

31 and he said, 'Cornelius, your prayer has been heard, and your acts of charity have been remembered before God [so that He is about to help you].

32 Therefore send word to Joppa and invite Simon, who is also called Peter, to come to you. He is staying at the house of Simon the tanner by the sea.'

33 So I sent for you at once, and you have been kind enough to come. Now then, we are all here present before God to listen to everything that you have been instructed by the Lord [to say]."

LIGHT ON THE WORD

Tanner. A tanner's job was to clean and prepare animal hides to be used as leather. They employed a process that stripped the remaining hair, fat, and flesh from the animal skins. As one might imagine, it was considered an undesirable job due to the sights and smells it entailed. Furthermore, tanners were considered ceremonially unclean by Jews, because they were in constant contact with dead animals. Tanneries were often required to operate outside of city walls or along the seashore.

TEACHING THE BIBLE LESSON

LIFE NEED FOR TODAY'S LESSON

AIM: Students will evaluate how traditions and cultural understandings have shaped their beliefs and interactions with people.

INTRODUCTION

Dietary Laws Cause Tension

Jewish law was very specific about what Jews were to eat and how they were to conduct themselves. The dietary laws that Peter references are found in **Leviticus 11**. In their original form, these rules were meant to protect the people of Israel and set them apart as God's people. These laws and covenant agreements made it possible for sinful humanity to commune with God. However, through Christ's sacrifice, God had removed the barrier of sin between Himself and His people. Humanity could now commune with God through the acceptance of His Son Jesus Christ (**Romans 3:21–26**). This transition from law to grace through Christ created friction between Jewish Christians who still held to their Jewish culture and the new Gentile believers who hadn't converted to Judaism. Some Jewish believers expected that non-Jewish believers should fully convert to Judaism, taking on all Jewish customs and practices, including circumcision. This tension not only threatened the spread of the Gospel to Gentiles, but also the unity and potency of the Christian church.

BIBLE LEARNING

AIM: Students will analyze Peter's decision to witness to Cornelius and his household.

I. SEEKING (Acts 10:19–23)

The Holy Spirit assures Peter that He sent the men for him. Peter goes with the men and lets them know that he is the person they are seeking. Peter also asks why these men are seeking him. They describe the type of man that Cornelius the centurion is. Peter and Cornelius were both seekers; while Cornelius sought God, Peter sought a confirmation from God.

A Divine Command (Acts 10:19–23)

19 While Peter thought on the vision, the Spirit said unto him, Behold, three men seek thee. 20 Arise therefore, and get thee down, and go with them, doubting nothing: for I have sent them.

The vision was followed by a clear, divine command. Peter was not only addressed by the Spirit, but was told that God was at work in these events. The reader understands with Peter that it was not only the human Cornelius who sent the messengers, but also God.

Peter was commanded to go with the three men, who would take him to the home of Cornelius. "Doubting" (Gk. *diakrino*, **dee-ah-KREE-no**) has a double nuance important for the story. The Greek verb can mean to doubt or hesitate (**James 1:6**), but also to discriminate or choose between (**James 2:4**).

Peter, in effect, is told not to have doubts about the events that will eventually lead him to understand how he should not discriminate between people (see **Acts 15:9**).

21 Then Peter went down to the men which were sent unto him from Cornelius; and said, Behold, I am he whom ye seek: what is the cause wherefore ye are come? 22 And they said, Cornelius the centurion, a just man, and one that feareth God, and of good report among all the nation of the Jews, was warned from God by an holy angel to send for thee into his house, and to hear words of thee. 23 Then called he them in, and lodged them. And on the morrow Peter went away with them, and certain brethren from Joppa accompanied him.

Peter is expecting the men and ready to go with them. He wants to know why they have come. Peter seeks to understand what God is doing, while at the same time showing faith by informing them that he is the one they are looking for. Their description of Cornelius is juxtaposed against his Gentile name. He is described as "one that feareth God," and a "just man." He was "just" (Gk. *dikaios*, **DI-kigh-os**), which means "to be righteous or observing of human and divine laws." He is also of "good report" or reputation among the Jewish people. The messengers here are establishing Cornelius' credibility as a God-fearer. On top of that, they also relay to Peter that God sent an angel to Cornelius to invite Peter to his house.

Peter did not go with the men right away. Because it was too late to take a journey, he invited them to stay at his house. Peter, the men, and others from Joppa travel to Caesarea, where Cornelius was expecting Peter.

II. EXPECTING (vv. 24–29)

Breaking Jewish custom, Peter went inside the Gentile Cornelius' house. Peter first gives a brief history of the Law and a confession that he believed in the Law. But God showed him that he should not call anything "common" or unclean. Peter did not deny what God had revealed to him. The reason he came to Cornelius was the truth God gave to him in a vision. And he would soon find out the full purpose of his visit.

Peter Now Understands (vv. 24–29)

24 And the morrow after they entered into Caesarea. And Cornelius waited for them, and he had called together his kinsmen and near friends.

Peter enters into Caesarea after Cornelius dispatches a group to request his presence in their home. Peter was accompanied by some disciples from Joppa on this journey. This would prove valuable as they would witness what happened during his preaching. Cornelius, seeing the gravity and importance of the occasion, invites his kinsmen and close friends into his house.

25 And as Peter was coming in, Cornelius met him, and fell down at his feet, and worshipped him. 26 But Peter took him up, saying, Stand up; I myself also am a man.

Cornelius is struck with awe at Peter's visit. From this, we can infer that Cornelius believed Peter to be a servant of Jesus, thinking that Peter could impart salvation. As a Gentile steeped in paganism, the centurion offers him the required obeisance as a semi-divine son of God with supernatural powers. Cornelius' reaction is ingrained and reflexive. Peter refuses this worship and tells him to stand up because he was not a god, but a man.

27 And as he talked with him, he went in, and found many that were come together. 28 And he said unto them, Ye know how that it is an unlawful thing for a man that is a Jew to keep company, or come unto one of another nation; but God hath shewed me that I should not call any man common or unclean. 29 Therefore came I unto you without gainsaying, as soon as I was sent for: I ask therefore for what intent ye have sent for me?

Peter talks to Cornelius as they walk into the home. When he sees all the people gathered together, he sees an opportunity to express what God has revealed to him. He reminds them of how his presence there is unlawful (Gk. *athemitos*, **ah-THEH-mee-tose**), or contrary to accepted morality or social convention. This is in contrast to unrighteous (*adikaios*, **ah-dee-KIGH-ose**) which referred to something illegal and wrong.

Peter states that it is contrary to Jewish Law for him to "keep company" with (Gk. *kollao*, **kol-LAH-oh**) or join together with a Gentile or enter a Gentile's home. Such practices were not prohibited by Jewish Law, but Peter is echoing a common Gentile perception at the time which developed out of table fellowship issues. Some Jews avoided eating with Gentiles because certain foods were prohibited in the Mosaic Laws. Of particular issue was food or drink that had been offered as sacrifices and libations to Roman or other foreign gods. So, since it was culturally taboo to inquire about these matters, some Jews avoided eating and drinking with Gentiles all together.

Peter says God has "shewed" (Gk. *deiknumi*, **DAKE-new-mi**) him that he should not call any man common or unclean. The word for "shewed" means to establish the validity of something with an explanation or example. Here the explanation is the vision Peter received on the rooftop of Simon the tanner (**Acts 10:9–16**), which is the basis for Peter's going to Cornelius' house without gainsaying (Gk. *anantirretos*, **ah-nahn-tee-RAY-tose**), or objection.

III. DOING (vv. 30–33)

Cornelius begins to describe what took place four days before as he was fasting. He then says that at the ninth hour he began to pray, and describes his vision. What he describes would be the common description of angels, in the form of man. Luke, the writer of Acts, does not retell Cornelius' vision because it had already been told.

Cornelius' Vision (vv. 30–33)

30 And Cornelius said, Four days ago I was fasting until this hour; and at the ninth hour I prayed in my house, and, behold, a man stood before me in bright clothing,

Cornelius was a Roman centurion, or a captain in the army. Although the term *centurion* means "commander of a hundred," this was just a round estimate. Centurions actually commanded only eighty men. The Bible says he was a "devout man," which means he tried to be godly in his ways and gave God due reverence. His godliness was evident by his positive influence on all those in his house, and his giving money to the poor while praying to God "alway" (**Acts 10:1–2**).

Cornelius recounted to Peter how God had given him a vision to send for Peter. Around the "ninth hour," which was 3 p.m., Cornelius had a supernatural encounter. This mention of the ninth hour indicates Cornelius' adherence to the Jewish times of prayer, which corresponded with the morning and evening offerings in the Temple. As a result of this Gentile man's efforts to know God, he was blessed with the vision, which would start a series of events leading to his salvation. The man who wore "bright clothing" was identified as an angel in the actual vision (**v. 3**).

31 And said, Cornelius, thy prayer is heard, and thine alms are had in remembrance in the sight of God.

The angel in the vision let Cornelius know that God had heard his prayer and his alms were remembered (Gk. *mnaomai*, **MNA-oh-my**) or God was mindful of them. The word for "alms" (Gk. *eleemosune*, **eh-leh-ay-mo-SUE-nay**) is literally "compassion or pity." In Judaism in the Roman period, almsgiving was considered comparable to righteousness. Luke intends to show that Cornelius was a righteous, God-fearing man and that God was answering his prayer. These God-fearers were Gentiles who were sympathetic to the Jewish religion, but not full, circumcised converts. They were not fully initiated as Jews but contributed to the synagogue and demonstrated piety.

32 Send therefore to Joppa, and call hither Simon, whose surname is Peter; he is lodged in the house of one Simon a tanner by the sea side: who, when he cometh, shall speak unto thee.

Peter was lodging with Simon the tanner (Gk. *burseus*, **bur-seh-US**), a leatherworker who created leather from hides and skins by treating them with lime and juices and leaves from various plants. This leather was often used for making tents. The Tabernacle coverings were made from the skins of rams or goats and were more than likely created by tanners (**Exodus 25:5, 26:14, 35:7, 23, 36:19**). Due to the nature of their work, tanners were not regarded highly among Greeks, Romans, or Jews. In Judaism, they were not allowed to go to the Temple during pilgrimage season and also had their own synagogues, due to the bad odor created by the process of curing the animal hides. The Jewish rabbinical tradition (collected in the Mishnah) even allows that in the case of Levirate marriage, the wife of the deceased brother of a tanner was allowed to remain a widow by saying, "I could endure your brother, but I cannot endure you." Due to the odors, tanners were required to do their work outside the gates of the city or by the sea side.

33 Immediately therefore I sent to thee; and thou hast well done that thou art come. Now therefore are we all here present before God, to hear all things that are commanded thee of God.

Cornelius told Peter, "Immediately therefore I sent to thee." Now, Cornelius thanked Peter for coming. But what he did not know was that God gave Peter a vision just before his messengers arrived. And, in Peter's vision, God dealt with Peter's feelings of prejudice toward Gentiles, while telling him to go with Cornelius's messengers (**Acts 10:9–20**). The mighty providence of God works everything out. God can weave a tapestry of people and events in our lives which appear to be unrelated or totally unknown to us. Then, when the time is right, God will pull all the pieces together so that we are blessed with something He has been preparing for us for some time.

Cornelius showed his love for his household by having everyone gathered to hear Peter's words. His example shows that we should not be selfish with God's Word of salvation. We should see to it that all of our relatives and friends get to hear it, whether it comes from us or someone else. We owe it to the ones we love to see that they get a chance to hear the Gospel and receive the gift of salvation through Jesus Christ our Lord.

SEARCH THE SCRIPTURES

QUESTION 1

Verses 25–26 show what interaction between Peter and Cornelius? Why do you think Cornelius responded to Peter this way?

After Peter entered into Caesarea, Cornelius met him, fell at his feet, and worshiped him. Cornelius might have felt honored and relieved that Peter came to share the Gospel with them. Answers will vary.

QUESTION 2

Why are some believers open to sharing the Gospel of Christ with people who are not similar in their way of thinking while others are not? Identify your comfort zone in sharing the Gospel.

Answers will vary.

LIGHT ON THE WORD

Peter Receives God's Assurance

Peter had to be assured of the voice of God in order to embrace the Gentiles. How can we be assured when God wants us to do something beyond our comfort zone?

BIBLE APPLICATION

AIM: Students will decide that believers should actively share the Gospel.

You are often accepted when you buy the name brand clothes, the latest phone, and the coolest glasses. If you speak broken English or a language other than English, you may be talked about and feel like an outcast. It is so easy to make people feel that they are outcast or different. What can you do in your community to help those who are outcasts?

STUDENTS' RESPONSES

AIM: Students will agree that Jesus is the Savior of the world and that everyone should have the opportunity to know Jesus.

How many people do you know who are not native English speakers and could have a speech barrier in communicating? Do you know people who have come to your church who are from a different background or culture? Do you see people who struggle to understand why they are not accepted? Remind yourself about when you felt isolated, and make it your goal to help the people you see in these areas.

PRAYER

Dear Heavenly Father, You are inclusive in sharing Your love, Your mercy, and justice with all. Help us remove the false feelings and thoughts that keep us from witnessing to those who are different from us. Guide us by the Holy Spirit to speak about Jesus and His love. Thank You for the opportunity that You will give us this week to be obedient to the lesson we studied today. In the Name of our Savior, Jesus Christ, we pray. Amen.

HOW TO SAY IT

Caesarea.   seh-**SA**-ree-ah.

Joppa.   **JAH**-puh.

DIG A LITTLE DEEPER

This section provides an additional research article to further your study of the lesson:

How to care for those whom God has entrusted to each believer is often a forgotten principle. This poignant article emphasizes a skill that directly pertains to every person who believes in Jesus Christ. Practical questions are answered with insight into the spiritual formation of disciples. This paradigm shift is both provocative in its approach and sincere in its desire to not only win the lost, but also to participate with God in the transformation of His people.

http://www.dts.edu/read/the-lost-art-of-lingering/

PREPARE FOR NEXT SUNDAY

Read **Isaiah 11:1–9** and "The Peaceful Kingdom."

DAILY HOME BIBLE READINGS

MONDAY
The Servant's Mission to All Nations
(Isaiah 49:1–7)

TUESDAY
Jesus Heals Centurion's Slave
(Luke 7:1–10)

WEDNESDAY
The Lord Meets Cornelius in a Vision
(Acts 10:1–8)

THURSDAY
People Are Neither Unclean Nor Profane
(Acts 10:9–18)

FRIDAY
Gentiles Hear and Accept the Gospel
(Acts 10:34–43)

SATURDAY
Gentiles Included by the Spirit and Water
(Acts 10:44–48)

SUNDAY
Called to Be Inclusive
(Acts 10:19–33)

COMMENTS / NOTES:

_____

_____

_____

_____

_____

_____

_____

_____

_____

_____

_____

_____

ANSWERS TO QUARTERLY QUIZZES

SEPTEMBER • OCTOBER • NOVEMBER 2016

LESSON 1
1. We can judge others unfairly based on appearance, status, job, our own biases, and more. God judges us by justice and righteousness. Answers will vary; 2. We can judge others unfairly based on appearance, status, job, our own biases, and more. God judges us by justice and righteousness. Answers will vary.

LESSON 2
1. God's compassion will be felt and seen by those invited as they feast on the excellent food and drink, His gentle hands of care. They will witness the destruction of those who rejected God and treated His people poorly. Answers will vary; 2. Christians experience health and hope as we witness God's presence and movement at work in the trials, victories, and judgment of believers. Answers will vary.

LESSON 3
1. The eagles' wings can refer to seeking to counsel if needed, helping someone who needs financial assistance, or directing people to resources that will provide relief and/or encouragement. Answers will vary; 2. True. Yes, sometimes we believe God will not intervene or stop us or that we have more power than God. Answers will vary.

LESSON 4
1. God will give His people garments of salvation and the robe of righteousness. God's people will be the bride for Christ, the Messiah, as we develop our relationship and faith in Christ. Answers will vary; 2. The wind brings fresh air to dry places and God will breathe the breath of life into barren places for righteousness and praise to prevail. Answers will vary.

LESSON 5
1. The wind brings fresh air to dry places and God will breathe the breath of life into barren places for righteousness and praise to prevail. Answers will vary; 2. Jesus is the One who gives me directions and who I depend on for understanding, a shoulder to cry on, and my bridge over troubled waters. Answers will vary.

LESSON 6
1. I trust what I see at times and know more than having faith and trusting God. Answers will vary; 2. When I have felt unsure about an important decision for my family, I remember that Jesus says that He "is the way…." (John 14:6) and "take up your bed and follow me" (Matthew 16:24). Both of these Scriptures give me the strength and determination that others see for me to move forward and not become stagnant in my decision-making. Answers will vary.

LESSON 7
1. Believers should approach Jesus with boldness to receive mercy and find grace. We say this because Jesus in our Savior and He wants us to know and feel that we can come to Him and not be afraid. Answers will vary; 2. Believers accept

God's love but do not fully embrace the depth of God's love by choosing to follow things or people (i.e., overindulging in food, drinks, or being apathetic) that take us away from Christ. Answers will vary.

LESSON 8 1. Abraham honored Melchizedek and respected him because he was the king of Salem and a high priest. We should honor Jesus through giving our best financially to the church, our actions of justice, righteousness, and compassion for others. Answers will vary; 2. Jesus gives me more peace that I can find opportunities that are pleasing to God and give me freedom to be myself in Christ. The other things were exciting, but not as fulfilling. Answers will vary.

LESSON 9 1. Answers will vary; 2. God's chastisement reminds me to trust Him more and accept that His ways involve justice for all. I can share with others that Christ has a way of directing that we may not like, but we need to learn how to receive. When we receive His direction, we have more freedom not to worry. Answers will vary.

LESSON 10 1. People would respect God more and honor Him through their actions and hearts that demonstrate their love and loyalty to Him. Answers will vary; 2. The fearful, unbelievers, abominable, murderers, whoremongers, sorcerers, idolaters, and liars. Counseling opportunities, provide for jobs, social activities, address physical or mental health needs, and challenge people to find out if they want to change. Answers will vary.

LESSON 11 1. Answers will vary; 2. Both highlight that Jesus is the only light that we need and will shine through our dark times and gives us joy on earth. Answers will vary.

LESSON 12 1. At first, I was scared, but the more I think about it, I want to be permanently identified as God's in heaven. Answers will vary; 2. Jesus' return means that we are to tell as many people as we can about Jesus, make disciples, and show that we believe in Christ by how we live our lives. Answers will vary.

LESSON 13 1. Jesus is the bright and morning star that outshines everything and everyone. Jesus will return and those who do not believe in Him, will not enter into the New Jerusalem. Answers will vary; 2. For some, I will talk directly to them about who is Christ, and with others, I will invite them to various events to meet people who they can better connect with about Christ. Answers will vary.

DECEMBER 2016 • JANUARY • FEBRUARY 2017

LESSON 1 1. God's favor is always a part of His plan for all of creation and favor that people is based on finite visions and sometimes selfish motives. Answers will vary; 2. This emphasizes that God is sovereign and that I can depend on the Lord. Answers will vary.

LESSON 2   1. I shout with joy or cry or thank the Lord. Answers will vary; 2. Have a special event or program that brings various people together and reintroduce Christ in very practical ways that they identify with in the lives. Answers will vary.

LESSON 3   1. Answers will vary; 2. Have a special event or program that brings various people together and reintroduce Christ in very practical ways that they identify with in the lives. Answers will vary.

LESSON 4   1. The angel said reassuring words to each of them, "Don't be afraid." The angels helped to comfort each so they could hear and listen to the important message about Jesus. Answers will vary; 2. I pray and ask for clarity or reflect upon the times when God has answered or shown me something similar. Answers will vary.

LESSON 5   1. I would write Psalm 33 as a responsive reading and have an instrumental piece with percussion sounds playing in the background. Answers will vary; 2. My worship is strengthened because these verses reflect God's might, care, and attention to detail for nature and humanity. Answers will vary.

LESSON 6   1. I would be more mindful of God's presence and care for me. Answers will vary; 2. I compare how God has responded to the actions and thoughts of the people in the Bible and to our truths today and decide how to proceed. Answers will vary.

LESSON 7   1. Family issues, financial struggles, or making poor choices. Answers will vary; 2. The theme is the abundance of God as shown in nature and in the spiritual lives of His people. God forgives our many sins, shoulders the burden of our sin, and provides more than enough for nature and humanity to co-exist. Answers will vary.

LESSON 8   1. Jesus is my strong foundation, but sometimes there are temptations that shake my relationship with Christ. Answers will vary; 2. Nature is not ashamed of who God is and is reflective of God's beauty. Answers may vary.

LESSON 9   1. I agree that nature worships God more than humanity. I think nature does not hesitate because it knows that God is the Creator and has all power over creation. Answers will vary; 2. Each of these is created by God and are expected to praise Him. Humanity may find this odd because humanity appears to have the only real approaches to praising God. Answers will vary.

LESSON 10   1. I think Paul's statement is not limited to before Christ. Many believers act like children and are unwilling to mature in Christ. Answers will vary; 2. I feel uncomfortable when I read the word slaves. Therefore, I reread the passage, I keep in mind how God loves me in love, and not the historical reality of slavery in my family. Answers will vary.

LESSON 11 1. Yes, if we are not rooted in Christ or value our status, work, family, and more, or worshiping and developing a deeper experience in Christ. Answers will vary; 2. I felt afraid to speak up about Jesus and praise Him, because others might have thought that I was odd. Answers will vary.

LESSON 12 1. Giving extra money through our offerings and tithes, work, doing good deeds, or overvolunteering or becoming involved in the church. Believers do not understand that salvation is not something that we can earn. Answers will vary; 2. False teaching is like yeast because it only takes a small amount of it to spread through the entire batch of dough and cause an effect that you may not want or can control.

LESSON 13 1. In the Chicago area, the problems with laws and traditions have been exposed regarding the police shootings and police behavior. Answers will vary; 2. The fruit of patience and kindness are blooming well and my areas to nurture are joy and peace. I will find Scriptures that speak to joy and peace and practice these as much as possible even when I do not want to. Answers will vary.

MARCH • APRIL • MAY 2017

LESSON 1 1. Giving our best and accepting God's love through Christ, allows us to learn and implement how not to lean to our own ways of loving ourselves and others. Answers will vary; 2. People will get along better, social issues will be eradicated (i.e., poverty, racism, educational inequity), and spiritual obedience would be the norm. Answers will vary.

LESSON 2 1. Our transgressions and sins of the past have been forgiven and reconciled to Christ. We are not bound by our sin to live life in Christ. Answers will vary; 2. The devil is able to move creatively in and out of peoples' lives because they are not as grounded to Jesus or know their power in Christ. Answers will vary.

LESSON 3 1. Cutting away those things or people that have become too much of a burden. Answers will vary; 2. Answers will vary.

LESSON 4 1. God's wrath will come and His love and justice will prevail. Answers will vary; 2. Everyone has the opportunity to come to the Lord and God's Spirit is available to all who want to receive Him. Answers will vary..

LESSON 5 1. I am more confident in God through Christ and how He guides me, comforts me, and provides me joy. Answers will vary; 2. Jesus gives me water in my dry places, He helps me to stand up for myself when I need to, and retreat when to retreat. Answers will vary.

LESSON 6 1. I have felt uncomfortable asking questions about Jesus in front of educated people or my peers, so I seek videos, media preachers, and books to answer my questions. Answers will vary; 2. Depending on where a person's circumstances (i.e., hospital stay, living on the street), baptism may not be an option. Therefore, I believe that our Creator will allow the person to enter into the kingdom of God. Answers will vary.

LESSON 7   1. An empty tomb; "they" may refer to the guards, and "we" may represent the other women, Joanna, Mary (Jesus' mother), and Salome (Mark 6:1). Having other people with you can provide support to what I have seen and heard and challenge what I have not seen or heard. Answers will vary; 2.The linen clothes, the cloth head napkin was folded up, and separated from the linen clothes remind those who would come to the tomb that Jesus has risen because He left the clothes as someone who undressed and left.

LESSON 8   1. It should be enough, but believers sometimes want more tangible expressions of God's love.; 2. When I think of the free love that You give, my heart is joyful. I rejoice that You have given us Christ. I am thankful in so many ways that forgive us and our sins. Thank You Lord! Answers will vary.

LESSON 9   1. Shepherd—courageous, strong, compassionate, loving, and a great leader. Sheep—easily led, nice wool, will listen to its leader, strays from the flock, and needs guidance. Answers will vary; 2. Distinguish the reason(s) Jesus' statement, "I lay down my life for the sheep," is important for believers to embrace (v. 15). Jesus voluntarily sacrificed His life for all humanity, and we have the freedom to live in the love and grace of Christ. Answers will vary.

LESSON 10   1. Believers do not want to trust God, be responsible, or want more control. When believers choose to ignore God, they never fully embrace what He had for their lives. ; 2. Dove—peace, different colors. Jonah spoke God's Word and justice and peace was restored. Jonah had different colors, which can represent his different moods—anger, thankfulness, and obedience.

LESSON 11   1. Answers will vary; 2. Answers will vary.

LESSON 12   1. God's Word was received because they decided that His wrath and power were greater and they could not fight and win. They were afraid of God and wanted to live in peace; 2. Ignored—I was feeling disconnected from God. Answers will vary

LESSON 13   1. God's compassion, love, and His plan for all of creation involves God protecting Jonah and us. He wants the best for us, from us, and gives us an opportunity to show our obedience to Him.; 2. Jonah was upset that God would show love to people who were not Jewish, so he treated the Assyrians with disrespect and disdain. There are times when I think that my way is what I should do and God has agreed with me, but I am wrong. Answers will vary.

LESSON 1   1. Answers will vary; 2. Answers will vary.

LESSON 2   1. Answers will vary; 2. Their relationship is one that requires God to encourage Gideon to believe in himself and trust God. Answers will vary.

LESSON 3   1. Power and authority. Answers will vary; 2. Answers will vary.

LESSON 4   1. Answers will vary; 2. Answers will vary.

LESSON 5   1. Answers will vary; 2. God is pure, and we must respect and honor His holiness.

LESSON 6   1. Answers will vary; 2. Examples: heart, empathize with others. Answers will vary.

LESSON 7   1. Answers will vary; 2. Answers will vary.

LESSON 8   1. Answers will vary; 2. Answers will vary.

LESSON 9   1. Answers will vary; 2. Answers will vary.

LESSON 10   1. Answers will vary; 2. Answers will vary.

LESSON 11   1. Answers will vary; 2. Answers will vary.

LESSON 12   1. Answers will vary; 2. Answers will vary.

LESSON 13   1. Answers will vary; 2. Answers will vary.

SOURCES

SEPTEMBER 2016 QUARTER

Aune, David E. W*ord Biblical Commentary: Revelation 17-22. Vol 52C*. Nashville, TN: Thomas Nelson Publishers, 1982.

Archaeological Study Bible, New International Version: Imperial Cult. Grand Rapids, MI: Zondervan House Publishers, Inc., 2005. 1651

Archaeological Study Bible, New International Version: Josephus and the Fall of Jerusalem Temple Grand Rapids, MI: Zondervan House Publishers, Inc., 2005. 1606

Archaeological Study Bible, New International Version: Major Events in New Testament History in the First Century A.D. Grand Rapids, MI: Zondervan House Publishers, Inc., 2005. 2068

Archaeological Study Bible, New International Version: Patmos Rapids, MI: Zondervan House Publishers, Inc., 2005. 2046

Aune, David E. *Word Biblical Commentary: Revelation 17-22. Vol 52C*. Nashville, TN: Thomas Nelson Publishers, 1982.

Bromiley, Geoffrey W. *The International Standard Bible Encyclopedia*. Grand Rapids, Michigan: W.B. Eerdmans, 1979.

Hebrew-Greek Key Word Study Bible, King James Version. Chattanooga, TN: AMG Publishers, Inc., 1991.

Holy Bible: Holman Christian Standard Version. Nashville, TN: Holman Bible Publishers, 2010. 1625, 2117.

Holy Bible: Holman Christian Standard Version. Nashville, TN: Holman Bible Publishers, 2010. 2112-2115.

Holy Bible New Living Translation: Carol Streams, IL Tyndale House Foundation Pub. (1996, 2004, 2007)

Keck, Leander E. et al. *The New Interpreters Bible Commentary in Twelve Volumes, Hebrews- Revelation Vol. 12* Nashville, TN: Abingdon Press,1998.

Keener, Craig S., T*he IVP Bible Background Commentary: New Testament*. Downers Grove, IL: Intervarsity Press, 1993.

Keener, Craig S., *The IVP Bible Background Commentary: New Testament*. Downers Grove, IL: Intervarsity Press, 1993. 757-763, 815-816.

Keener, Craig S., *The IVP Bible Background Commentary: New Testament*. Downers Grove, IL: Intervarsity Press, 1993.647-650, 678-679.

La Sor, Willian S.; Hubbard, David A; Bush, Frederic Wm. Old Testament Survey: The Message, Form, and Background of the Old Testament, Grand Rapids MI Eerdmans Publishing Co.1982 (Pg 277-312)

Radmacher, Earl D., ed. *Nelson Study Bible, New King James Version*. Nashville, TN: Thomas Nelson Publishers, 1997. 2094-2098.

Radmacher, Earl D., ed. *Nelson Study Bible, New King James Version*. Nashville, TN: Thomas Nelson Publishers, 1997. 2198-2199.

Rendtorff. Rolf, *The Old Testament, An Introduction*. Philadelphia, Fortress Press, 1991, pp. 190-192.

Ryrie, Charles C., *Ryrie Study Bible, New International Version*. Chicago, IL: Moody Press. 1986. 1681-1682.

Ryrie, Charles C., *Ryrie Study Bible, New International Version*. Chicago, IL: Moody Press. 1986. 1744-1745.

Soggin, J. Alberto, *Introduction to the Old Testament From Its Origins to the closing of the Alexandrian Canon*. Louisville, KY, Westminster/John Knox Press, 1987, p. 395.

Unger, Merrill F., *The New Unger's Bible Dictionary*. Chicago, IL: Moody Press, 1988.

Unger, Merrill F., *The New Unger's Bible Dictionary*. Chicago, IL: Moody Press, 1988. 547-548.

Walton, John H. General Ed. *Zondervan Illustrated Bible Background Commentary Vol 4 (Isaiah, Jeremiah, Lamentations, Ezekiel, David)* Grand Rapids, Zondervan Pub 2009 Pg. 56-57

Walvoord, John F., and Roy B. Zuck, eds. The Bible Knowledge Commentary: New Testament. USA: Victor Books, SP Publications, Inc., 1983. 777, 809-810.

Walvoord, John F., and Roy B. Zuck, eds. The Bible Knowledge Commentary: New Testament. USA: Victor Books, SP Publications, Inc., 1983. 925-927, 983-985.

Watson, John H; Matthews, Victor H; Chavalas, Mark W.: *The IVP Bible Background Commentary: Old Testament*. Downers Grove IL (2013)

Young, Edward, J., *The Book of Isaiah: The English Text, with Introduction, Exposition, and Notes (Volume 1 Chapters 1-18)*. Grand Rapids, Eerdmans Publishing Company, (1983) pgs. 378-387)

Youngblood, Ronald F., ed. *Nelson's New Illustrated Bible Dictionary*. Nashville, TN: Thomas Nelson Publishers, 1995. 55, 1035-1039, 551-553.

Youngblood, Ronald F., ed. *Nelson's New Illustrated Bible Dictionary*. Nashville, TN: Thomas Nelson Publishers, 1995.

Zodhiates, Spiros, Warren, Baker. *Hebrew-Greek Key Word Study Bible (KJV)* Chattanooga, TN AMG International, Inc Second Revised Edition 1984, 1990, 2008

Zodhiates, Spiros, *Hebrew-Greek Key Word Study Bible (Key Insights into God's Word)*. King James Version Second

Revised Version. Chattanooga, AMG Publishers, 1984, 1990, 2008

Zondervan Study Bible, New International Version. Grand Rapids, MI: Zondervan Publishers, 2002. 1913-1914.

Zondervan Study Bible, New International Version. Grand Rapids, MI: Zondervan Publishers, 2002. 1988-1989.

DECEMBER 2016 QUARTER

"Lead, Led." *Vines Complete Expository Dictionary of Old and New Testament Words.* Merrill F. Unger and William White, editors. Nashville, TN: Thomas Nelson Publishers, 1996.

Alter, Robert. *The Book of Psalms: A Translation with Commentary.* New York, NY : W.W. Norton & Company., 2007.

Arrington, French L., and Roger Stronstad, eds. *Life in the Spirit New Testament Commentary.* Grand Rapids, MI: Zondervan, 1999. 398-399.

Barclay, William. *The Daily Study Bible Series: The Gospel of Luke.* Philadelphia, PA: The Westminster Press, 1975. 14-16

Brueggemann, Walter. *Psalms.* New York, NY: Cambridge University Press, 2013

Carson, D. A., R. T. France, J. A. Motyer, G. J. Wenham, Eds. *New Bible Commentary* Downer's Grove, IL: Intervarsity Press, 1994.

Craddock, Fred B. *Luke: Interpretation, A Bible Commentary for Preaching and Teaching.* Edited by James Luther Mays, et al. Louisville, KY: John Knox Press, 1990.

Dahood, S. J. *The Anchor Bible: Psalms11.* Garden City, NY : Doubleday & Company., 1968.

Elwell, Walter A. and Comfort, Philip W., *Tyndale Bible Dictionary: Tyndale House Publishers,* Wheaton, IL: 2001, 828

Ferguson, Everett et al. ed. *Encyclopedia of Early Christianity* 2nd ed. New York, NY: Garland Publishing Inc, 1998.

Gaebelein, Frank E., ed. *The Expositor's Bible Commentary Vol. 8.* Grand Rapids, MI: Zondervan, 1984. 835-836

Goldingay, John. Baker *Commentary on the Old Testament. Vol. 3, Psalms 90-150.* Grand Rapids, MI: Baker Academic, 2006.

Guthrie, Donald. *Tyndale New Testament Commentaries: Letter to the Hebrews.* Grand Rapids, MI: Eerdmans, 1983. 216.

Hay, Lewis S. "*Galatians 5: 13 – 26.*" *Interpretation.* 33 no. 1 Jan. 1979, p. 67 – 72.

Hays, Richard B. "*Letter of Paul to the Galatians.*" *The Harper Collins Study Bible,* New Revised Standard Version. Harold W. Attridge, ed. New York, NY.: Harper Collins Publishers, 2006.

Henry, Matthew. "*Galatians 5.*" Complete Bible Commentary Online. http://www.biblestudytools.com/commentaries/matthew-henry-complete/galatians/5.html, accessed on 19 June 2015.

Henry, Matthew. "*Galatians 6.*" Complete Bible Commentary Online. http://www.biblestudytools.com/commentaries/matthew-henry-complete/galatians/6.html, accessed on 29 June 2015.

Holman Pocket Bible Dictionary. Nashville, TN: Holman Bible Publishers, 2004. 762-764, 773.

Johnson, Luke Timothy. *Hebrews: A Commentary.* The New Testament Library. Louisville, KY: Westminster John Knox Press, 2006. 259.

Keener, Craig S. *The IVP Bible Background Commentary: New Testament.* Downers Grove, IL: InterVarsity Press, 1993.

Keener, Craig S. *The IVP Bible Background Commentary: New Testament.* Downers Grove, IL: InterVarsity Press, 1993. 647-650, 670-671.

Lane, William L. *Hebrews 9-13. Word Biblical Commentary,* Vol. 47B. Dallas, TX: Word Inc., 1991.

Life Application Study Bible, New International Version. Wheaton, IL: Tyndale House Publishers, Inc., 1997. 2154-2155, 2170-2172.

NIV Study Bible, 10th Anniversary Edition, Grand Rapids, Mich.: Zondervan, 1995. 1529-1530.

Padgett, Alan G. "'*Walk in the Spirit*': Preaching for Spiritual Growth (Gal. 5: 13 – 6:2.*" World & World.* Vol. 27, Number 3 Summer 2007, p. 342 – 345.

Painter, John. "*The Fruit of the Spirit is Love: Galatians 5: 22 – 23, an Exegetical Note.*" Journal of Theology for Southern Africa. 5 Dec. 1973, p. 57 – 59.

Radmacher, Earl D., ed. *Nelson's New Illustrated Bible Commentary: Spreading the Light of God's Word into Your Life.* Nashville, TN: Thomas Nelson Publishers, 1999. 1648-1653.

Ross, Allen P. *A Commentary on The Psalms. Vol 2* (42-89). Grand Rapids, MI: Kregel Publications, 2013.

Ryken, Leland, ed. "*Farming.*" *Dictionary of Biblical Imagery.* Downers Grove, IL: InterVarsity Press, 2010.

Sakenfield, Katharine Dobb, ed. *New Interpreter's Dictionary of the Bible Me-R Vol. IV.* : Nashville, TN: Abingdon Press, 2009.

Spence, H. D. M., and Joseph S. Exell, eds. *The Pulpit Commentary Vol. 16.* Grand Rapids, MI: Eerdmans Publishing Company, 1980. 22-23

Testament. Grand Rapids, MI: Eerdmans. Reprint, 1988.

The New Interpreter's Bible, General Articles & Introduction, Commentary, & Reflections for each Book of the Bible Including the Apocryphal/Deuterocanonical Books, Volume IV. Nashville, TN: Abingdon Press, 1996, 809-811

Vine, W.E. *"Burden." Vines Complete Expository Dictionary of Old and New Testament Words.* Merrill F. Unger and William White, editors. Nashville, TN: Thomas Nelson Publishers, 1996.

Vine, W.E. *Expository Dictionary of New Testament Words.* Grand Rapids, MI: Zondervan Publishing House, 1981.

Waltner, James H. *Believers Church Bible Commentary* Nelson's. Scottdale, PA: Herald Press, 2006.

Wilson, Gerald H. *The NIV Application Commentary. Psalms Volume 1.* Grand Rapids, MI: Zondervan, 2002.

MARCH 2017 QUARTER

Allen, Leslie C., *The Books of Joel, Obadiah, Jonah and Micah, NICOT.* Grand Rapids: Wm. B. Eerdmans Publishing Co., 1976.

Henry, Matthew. *Matthew Henry's Commentary on the Whole Bible: Complete and Unabridged in One Volume.* Peabody: Hendrickson, 1994.

Jamieson, Robert, A. R. Fausset, and David Brown. *Commentary Critical and Explanatory on the Whole Bible.* Oak Harbor, WA: Logos Research Systems, Inc., 1997.

Knowles, Andrew. *The Bible Guide. 1st Augsburg books ed.* Minneapolis, MN: Augsburg, 2001.

Richards, Larry, and Lawrence O. Richards. *The Teacher's Commentary.* Wheaton, IL: Victor Books, 1987.

Paschall, Franklin H., and Herschel H. Hobbs, eds. *The Teacher's Bible Commentary.* Nashville: Broadman and Holman Publishers, 1972.

Powell, Mark A., *Introducing the New Testament.* Grand Rapids, MI: Baker Academic, 2009. 494-495.

Richards, Lawrence O. *The Bible Reader's Companion. Electronic ed.* Wheaton: Victor Books, 1991.

Walvoord, John F., and Roy B. Zuck, Dallas Theological Seminary. *The Bible Knowledge Commentary: An Exposition of the Scriptures.* Wheaton, IL: Victor Books, 1985.

Wiersbe, Warren W. *The Bible Exposition Commentary.* Wheaton, IL: Victor Books, 1996.

JUNE 2017 QUARTER

Block, Daniel I. *The New American Commentary: Judges, Ruth.* Nashville, TN: B&H Publishing Group, 1999. 391-406, 421-424.

Briggs, Philip. *Ethiopia, Fourth Edition.* Guilford, CT: The Globe Pequot Press, 2005, pp. 26-27.

Bruce, F. F. *The Book of Acts, Revised Edition.* Grand Rapids, MI: Eerdmans. Reprint, 1988, pp. 119-125.

Boling, Robert G. *"The Book of Judges."* In Anchor Bible Dictionary, vol. 3. David Noel Freedman, ed. New York, NY: Doubleday, 1992. 1107-1116.

Cate, Robert L. *Layman's Bible Commentary: Exodus.* Nashville, TN: Broadman Press, 1979. 29-30.

Covey, Stephen R. *Seven Habits of Highly Effective People.* New York, Simon and Schuster. 1989.

Crenshaw, James L. *"Samson." In Anchor Bible Dictionary, Vol. 5.* David Noel Freedman, ed. New York, NY: Doubleday, 1992. 950-954.

Davis, John J. *Moses and the God's of Egypt: Studies in Exodus.* Grand Rapids, MI: Baker Book House, 1986. 67-73.

Drane, John. *Nelson's Illustrated Encyclopedia of the Bible.* Thomas Nelson, Inc. Nashville, TN, 1998. 249

Fensham, F. C. *"In the Old Testament" In the New Bible Dictionary. 3rd Edition.* Leicester, England; Downers Grove, IL: InterVarsity Press, 1996. 1109.

Jamieson, R., A. R. Fausset, and D. Brown. *Commentary Critical and Explanatory on the Whole Bible.* Oak Harbor, WA: Logos Research Systems, Inc, 1997. 167.

Janzen, J. Gerald. *Exodus.* Louisville, KY: Westminster John Knox, 1997.

Kent, Dan G. *Layman's Bible Book Commentary: Joshua, Judges, Ruth, Vol 4.* Nashville, TN: Broadman Press, 1980.

Lockyer, Herbert. *All the Women of the Bible,* Zondervan Publishing, Grand Rapids, MI, 1988

Montonini, M. D. *"Theophany" In The Lexham Bible Dictionary.* John D. Barry, ed. Bellingham, WA: Lexham Press, 2015.

Niditch, Susan. *Judges: A Commentary.* Louisville, KY: Westminster John Knox Press, 2008.

Radmacher, Earl D., ed. *Nelson's New Illustrated Bible Commentary: Spreading the Light of God's Word into Your Life.* Nashville, TN: Thomas Nelson Publishers, 1999. 1648-1653.

Stuart, Douglas K. *The New American Commentary: Exodus.* Nashville, TN: B&H Publishing, 2006. 108-119.

Wells, Bruce. *"Exodus" In Zondervan Illustrated Bible Background Commentary: Genesis, Exodus, Leviticus, Numbers, Deuteronomy.* John H. Walton, ed. Grand Rapids, MI: Zondervan, 2009. 172-175.

Wright, G. E. *"Book of Exodus" In The Interpreters Dictionary of the Bible: An Illustrated Encyclopedia.* George Arthur Buttrick, ed. New York, NY: Abingdon Press, 1962.

Younger, Lawson K. *The NIV Application Commentary: Judges/Ruth.* Grand Rapids, MI: Zondervan, 2002. 285-289, 293-295.

GLOSSARY

A

Abomination: A foul and detestable thing

Affliction: Anguish, burden, persecution, tribulation, or trouble

Angel: A messenger of God, not eternal or all-knowing; specific types include cherubim and seraphim

Ascension: Raising up in authority or physical place. Can especially refer to the event forty days after Jesus' death, burial, and Resurrection, when He went returned to heaven to sit at the right hand of the Father (Acts 1:9–11)

Atone: To propitiate, satisfy the demands of an offended holy God; or reconcile to a holy God after sin

B

Baptize: To dip, immerse, or submerge

Blameless: Irreproachable, faultless, flawless

Blessedness: Happiness, joy, or prosperity, to be well spoken of by God or others

Bless the Lord: To bend the knee in praise to God

Blood of the Lamb: The blood that Jesus shed on the Cross that redeems humanity

Bowels: To ancient Middle Easterners, the place of emotion, distress, or love

C

Called by God: Appointed or commissioned to fulfill a task

Charge: Admonish, order, command

Chosen: To be approved and selected by God

Christ: The Anointed One, the expected Messiah the Jews hoped for and whom Christians believe came as Jesus of Nazareth

Commandments: God's mandates; the entire body of Laws issued by God through Moses for Israel

Conduct: Manner of living

Confess: To acknowledge or fully agree

Consider: To determine or make out

Covenant: An agreement or promise between God and humanity based on God's character, strength, and grace

Crucifixion: A method of Roman execution in which a criminal was hung on a cross

D

Decalogue: From "ten words" in Greek; the Ten Commandments

Desolation: The state of being deserted or uninhabited

Disciples: Learners, students, followers

Dominion: Rule or reign

Dwelling place: A person's refuge or home

E

El: The Hebrew word for "god" or "mighty one"

Evil: Bad, unpleasant, or displeasing things

Evil doer: A malefactor, wrongdoer, criminal, troublemaker

Evil spirits: Messengers and ministers of the devil

Exalt: To raise up to the highest degree possible

Exhortation: Giving someone motivation to change his or her behavior either by rebuke or encouragement

F

Faithfulness: Steadfastness, steadiness

Fear of the Lord: Reverence or awe of who God is resulting in obedience to Him and abstaining from evil

G

Glory: Splendor, unparalleled honor, dignity, or distinction; praise, and worship

God's Bride: The church

God's own hand: God's strength, power

Gospel: The Good News of Jesus the Messiah's arrival and founding of His kingdom

Graven image: An idol cut (often from stone, wood, or metal) and worshiped as a god

Great Tribulation: A time of great suffering that has not been experienced since the world began (Matthew 24:21, Revelation 7:14)

H

Hallowed: Consecrated, dedicated, or set apart

Hear: Listen to, yield to, or obey

Hearken: Pay attention to, give attention to

Heart: The figurative place of emotion and passion

Heathens: The Gentiles, all those who are not a part of the people of God

Holy: Anything consecrated and set aside for sacred use; set apart from sin

Honor: To revere or value

Host: An army or vast number

I

Idolatry: The worship of anything other than God

Infidel: One who is unfaithful, unbelieving, and not to be trusted

Iniquity: Perversity, depravity, guilt, sin

J

Just: Righteous, that which is right and fair

Justice: Righteousness in government

K

Kingdom of Christ: The rule and reign of Christ as king both now and in the age to come

L

Law: Either the Mosiac Law or any human law; synonyms include commandments, ordinances, statutes, legal regulations, authoritative instructions, and teachings

Logos (LOW-gos): (Gk.) Word; the Word of God, either the Bible or Jesus

M

Manna: Food from heaven baked into a kind of bread, which God miraculously gave to the Israelites in the wilderness

Messiah: The Anointed One

Minister: A servant, an attendant, one who executes the commands of another

Mosiac Law: The law passed down by Moses from God to the Hebrew people at Mt. Sinai

O

Omnipotent: All powerful

Omnipresent: All present, being everywhere

Omniscient: All knowing

Ordained: Established and founded by God; founded, fixed, or appointed

P

Parousia (par-oo-SEE-ah): (Gk.) presence; Christ's Second Coming

Peace: Wholeness, quietness, contentment, health, prosperity; more than an absence of conflict or problems, but every part of life being blessed.

Pentateuch: The first five books of the Old Testament

Power: Boldness, might, or strength, especially God's

Prophets: People filled with the Spirit of God and under the authority and command of God, who pleaded His cause and urged humanity to be saved

Profit: To gain or benefit

Prosper: To succeed, especially in spiritual things; to move forward or succeed in one's efforts

Proved: Examined, tested, tried

Psalm: A piece of music or a melody, especially one dedicated to God or a god

Purity: Sinlessness, without blemish spiritually

R

Ransom: To buy back or pay a price for a person, buying their freedom

Redeem: To ransom or purchase

Refuge: A shelter from rain, storm, or danger; stronghold or fortress; a place to run to and be secure when the enemy threatens

Repent: To turn back from sin and turn to God in faith

Righteous: To be declared not guilty

Righteousness: Justness, rightness, especially God's, which He works as a gift in His people; the right way to live as opposed to a lifestyle that treats others unfairly or unjustly

S

Sabbath: From "ceasing (from work)" in Hebrew; the day set aside to worship God

Sanctuary: The holy place, either in the tabernacle or the temple

Salvation: Rescue, safety, or deliverance, especially from eternal punishment

Satan: A fallen angel who is opposed to God and His people

Savior: A defender, rescuer, or deliverer, A term applied to Christ as the rescuer of those who are in bondage to sin and death

Scribes: Secretaries, recorders, men skilled in the Law during Jesus' day

Selah (SEE-lah): (Heb.) A pause in singing to allow for an instrumental musical interlude or silent meditation.

Septuagint: "Seventy" in Latin; the Greek translation of the Hebrew Old Testament made by 70 Jewish scholars beginning in the third century BC.

Servant: A slave, subject, or worshiper

Shalom (sha-LOME): (Heb.) Peace, prosperity, blessing

Shekinah Glory: The awesome presence of the Lord; His honor, fame, and reputation

Shofar (sho-FAR): (Heb.) A ram's horn; commonly used in celebration, as well as in signaling armies or large groups of people in civil assembly

Soul: The immaterial part of a person (what leaves the body after death), or to the whole being, the self, one's life

Stiffnecked: Obstinate and difficult

Strengthen: To secure, make firm

Strive: To struggle, to exert oneself

Supplication: Seeking, asking, entreating, pleading, imploring, or petitioning

T

Tabernacle: A tent; the name of the portable temple constructed by Moses and the people of Israel

Tetragrammaton: YHWH; the four consonants of God's name, as the Jews would often write it

Torah: (Heb.) Law, instrument, or direction; the first five books of the Old Testament

Transfiguration: A change or transformation. Often refers to Jesus' transformation while on the Mount of Olives with His disciples Peter, James, and John, when His face shone like the sun and His clothing was white as snow (Matthew 17:2; Mark 9:2; Luke 9:29).

Transgression: Sin, rebellion, breaking God's Law

Try: In the sense of a test: refined or purified

Trumpet: A ram's horn or simple metal tube used in celebration as well as in signaling armies or large groups of people in civil assembly

V

Vanity (vain): A waste, a worthless thing, or simply emptiness

W

Wisdom: Prudence, an understanding of ethics

Woe: Grief or sorrow

Worship: Bow down deeply, show obedience and reverence

Wrath: Burning anger, rage

Y

Yahweh: God's name, often spelled with consonants only (see Tetragrammaton)

OUR AFFIRMATION OF FAITH

is a reminder of the basic beliefs of the Church Of God In Christ. It witnesses to the reality that God has been active in creation, history, and our lives. Being Trinitarian, our affirmation focuses on the work of the Father, Son, and Holy Spirit, while proclaiming the Gospel holistically. God tells us through Scripture that salvation is available to all through Jesus Christ.

Our Affirmation of Faith is woven throughout the testifying, singing, praying, preaching, and teaching of the Church. Hence, one can hear the cardinal beliefs through these events.

The affirmation makes no pretense of being exhaustive, or being a complete statement of all our beliefs. It presents a set of key beliefs that are grounded in Scripture.

The affirmation echoes the classic testimony: "Giving honor to God in the highest and to the Lord Jesus Christ, I thank God that I'm saved, sanctified, and filled with the Holy Ghost." Our theology begins with God; the doctrine of God shapes all other doctrines for the Church Of God In Christ.

The Church Of God In Christ — Affirmation of Faith

We Believe the Bible to be the inspired and only infallible written Word of God,

We Believe that there is One God, eternally existent in three Persons; God the Father, God the Son, and God the Holy Spirit.

We Believe in the Blessed Hope, which is the rapture of the Church of God, which is in Christ at His return.

We Believe that the only means of being cleansed from sin, is through repentance and faith in the precious Blood of Jesus Christ.

We Believe that regeneration by the Holy Ghost is absolutely essential for personal salvation.

We Believe that the redemptive work of Christ on the Cross provides healing for the human body in answer to believing prayer.

We Believe that the Baptism in the Holy Ghost, according to Acts 2:4, is given to believers who ask for it.

We Believe in the sanctifying power of the Holy Spirit, by whose indwelling, the Christian is enabled to live a Holy and separated life in this present world.

Amen.

THE SYMBOL OF THE CHURCH OF GOD IN CHRIST

The Symbol of the Church Of God In Christ is an outgrowth of the Presiding Bishop's Coat of Arms, which has become quite familiar to the Church. The design of the Official Seal of the Church was created in 1973 and adopted in the General Assembly in 1981 (July Session).

The obvious GARNERED WHEAT in the center of the seal represents all of the people of the Church Of God In Christ, Inc. The ROPE of wheat that holds the shaft together represents the Founding Father of the Church, Bishop Charles Harrison Mason, who, at the call of the Lord, banded us together as a Brotherhood of Churches in the First Pentecostal General Assembly of the Church, in 1907.

The date in the seal has a two-fold purpose: first, to tell us that Bishop Mason received the baptism of the Holy Ghost in March 1907 and, second, to tell us that it was because of this outpouring that Bishop Mason was compelled to call us together in February of 1907 to organize the Church Of God In Christ.

The RAIN in the background represents the Latter Rain, or the End-time Revivals, which brought about the emergence of our Church along with other Pentecostal Holiness Bodies in the same era. The rain also serves as a challenge to the Church to keep Christ in the center of our worship and service, so that He may continue to use the Church Of God In Christ as one of the vehicles of Pentecostal Revival before the return of the Lord.

This information was reprinted from the book *So You Want to KNOW YOUR CHURCH* by Alferd Z. Hall, Jr.

COGIC AFFIRMATION OF FAITH

We believe the Bible to be the inspired and only infallible written Word of God.

We believe that there is One God, eternally existent in three Persons: God the Father, God the Son, and God the Holy Spirit.

We believe in the Blessed Hope, which is the rapture of the Church of God, which is in Christ at His return.

We believe that the only means of being cleansed from sin is through repentance and faith in the precious Blood of Jesus Christ.

We believe that regeneration by the Holy Ghost is absolutely essential for personal salvation.

We believe that the redemptive work of Christ on the Cross provides healing for the human body in answer to believing in prayer.

We believe that the baptism in the Holy Ghost, according to Acts 2:4, is given to believers who ask for it.

We believe in the sanctifying power of the Holy Spirit, by whose indwelling the Christian is enabled to live a Holy and separated life in this present world. Amen.

The Doctrines of the Church Of God In Christ

THE BIBLE

We believe that the Bible is the Word of God and contains one harmonious and sufficiently complete system of doctrine. We believe in the full inspiration of the Word of God. We hold the Word of God to be the only authority in all matters and assert that no doctrine can be true or essential if it does not find a place in this Word.

THE FATHER

We believe in God, the Father Almighty, the Author and Creator of all things. The Old Testament reveals God in diverse manners, by manifesting His nature, character, and dominions. The Gospels in the New Testament give us knowledge of God the "Father" or "My Father," showing the relationship of God to Jesus as Father, or representing Him as the Father in the Godhead, and Jesus himself that Son (St. John 15:8, 14:20). Jesus also gives God the distinction of "Fatherhood" to all believers when He explains God in the light of "Your Father in Heaven" (St. Matthew 6:8).

THE SON

We believe that Jesus Christ is the Son of God, the second person in the Godhead of the Trinity or Triune Godhead. We believe that Jesus was and is eternal in His person and nature as the Son of God who was with God in the beginning of creation (St. John 1:1). We believe that Jesus Christ was born of a virgin called Mary according to the Scripture (St. Matthew 1:18), thus giving rise to our fundamental belief in the Virgin Birth and to all of the miraculous events surrounding the phenomenon (St. Matthew 1:18–25). We believe that Jesus Christ became the "suffering servant" to man; this suffering servant came seeking to redeem man from sin and to reconcile him to God, His Father (Romans 5:10). We believe that Jesus Christ is standing now as mediator between God and man (I Timothy 2:5).

THE HOLY GHOST

We believe the Holy Ghost or Holy Spirit is the third person of the Trinity; proceeds from the Father and the Son; is of the same substance, equal to power and glory; and is together with the Father and the Son, to be believed in, obeyed, and worshiped. The Holy Ghost is a gift bestowed upon the believer for the purpose of equipping and empowering the believer, making him or her a more effective witness for service in the world. He teaches and guides one into all truth (John 16:13; Acts 1:8, 8:39).

THE BAPTISM OF THE HOLY GHOST

We believe that the Baptism of the Holy Ghost is an experience subsequent to conversion and sanctification and that tongue-speaking is the consequence of the baptism in the Holy Ghost with the manifestations of the fruit of the Spirit (Galatians 5:22–23; Acts 10:46, 19:1–6). We believe that we are not baptized with the Holy Ghost in order to be saved (Acts 19:1–6; John 3:5). When one receives a baptismal Holy Ghost experience, we believe one will speak with a tongue unknown to oneself according to the sovereign will of Christ. To be filled with the Spirit means to be Spirit controlled as expressed by Paul in Ephesians 5:18,19. Since the charismatic demonstrations were necessary to help the early church to be successful in implementing the command of Christ, we, therefore, believe that a Holy Ghost experience is mandatory for all believers today.

MAN

We believe that humankind was created holy by God, composed of body, soul, and spirit. We believe that humankind, by nature, is sinful and unholy. Being born in sin, a person needs to be born again, sanctified and cleansed from all sins by the blood of Jesus. We believe that one is saved by confessing and forsaking one's sins, and believing on the Lord Jesus Christ, and that having become a child of God, by being born again and adopted into the family of God, one may, and should, claim the inheritance of the sons of God, namely the baptism of the Holy Ghost.

SIN

Sin, the Bible teaches, began in the angelic world (Ezekiel 28:11–19; Isaiah 14:12–20) and is transmitted into the blood of the human race through disobedience and deception motivated by unbelief (I Timothy 2:14). Adam's sin, committed by eating of the forbidden fruit from the tree of knowledge of good and evil, carried with it permanent pollution or depraved human nature to all his descendants. This is called "original sin." Sin can now be defined as a volitional transgression against God and a lack of conformity to the will of God. We, therefore, conclude that humankind by nature is sinful and has fallen from a glorious and righteous state from which we were created, and has become unrighteous and unholy. We therefore, must be restored to the state of holiness from which we have fallen by being born again (St. John 3:7).

SALVATION

Salvation deals with the application of the work of redemption to the sinner with restoration to divine favor and communion with God. This redemptive operation of the Holy Ghost upon sinners is brought about by repentance toward God and faith toward our Lord Jesus Christ which brings conversion, faith, justification, regeneration, sanctification, and the baptism of the Holy Ghost. Repentance is the work of God, which results in a change of mind in respect to a person's relationship to God

(St. Matthew 3:1–2, 4:17; Acts 20:21). Faith is a certain conviction wrought in the heart by the Holy Spirit, as to the truth of the Gospel and a heart trust in the promises of God in Christ (Romans 1:17, 3:28; St. Matthew 9:22; Acts 26:18). Conversion is that act of God whereby He causes the regenerated sinner, in one's conscious life, to turn to Him in repentance and faith (II Kings 5:15; II Chronicles 33:12,13; St. Luke 19:8,9; Acts 8:30). Regeneration is the act of God by which the principle of the new life is implanted in humankind, the governing disposition of soul is made holy, and the first holy exercise of this new disposition is secured. Sanctification is that gracious and continuous operation of the Holy Ghost, by which He delivers the justified sinner from the pollution of sin, renews a person's whole nature in the image of God, and enables one to perform good works (Romans 6:4, 5:6; Colossians 2:12, 3:1).

ANGELS

The Bible uses the term "angel" (a heavenly body) clearly and primarily to denote messengers or ambassadors of God with such Scripture references as Revelations 4:5, which indicates their duty in Heaven to praise God (Psalm 103:20), to do God's will (St. Matthew 18:10), and to behold His face. But since Heaven must come down to earth, they also have a mission to earth. The Bible indicates that they accompanied God in the Creation, and also that they will accompany Christ in His return in Glory.

DEMONS

Demons denote unclean or evil spirits; they are sometimes called devils or demonic beings. They are evil spirits, belonging to the unseen or spiritual realm, embodied in human beings. The Old Testament refers to the prince of demons, sometimes called Satan (adversary) or Devil, as having power and wisdom, taking the habitation of other forms such as the serpent (Genesis 3:1). The New Testament speaks of the Devil as Tempter (St. Matthew 4:3), and it goes on to tell the works of Satan, the Devil, and demons as combating righteousness and good in any form, proving to be an adversary to the saints. Their chief power is exercised to destroy the mission of Jesus Christ. It can well be said that the Christian Church believes in demons, Satan, and devils. We believe in their power and purpose. We believe they can be subdued and conquered as in the commandment to the believer by Jesus. "In my name they shall cast out Satan and the work of the Devil and to resist him and then he will flee (WITHDRAW) from you" (St. Mark 16:17).

THE CHURCH

The Church forms a spiritual unity of which Christ is the divine head. It is animated by one Spirit, the Spirit of Christ. It professes one faith, shares one hope, and serves one King. It is the citadel of the truth and God's agency for communicating to believers all spiritual blessings. The Church then is the object of our faith rather than of knowledge. The name of our Church, "CHURCH OF GOD IN CHRIST," is supported by I Thessalonians 2:14 and other passages in the Pauline Epistles. The word "CHURCH" or "EKKLESIA" was first applied to the Christian society by Jesus Christ in St. Matthew 16:18, the occasion being that of His benediction of Peter at Caesarea Philippi.

THE SECOND COMING OF CHRIST

We believe in the second coming of Christ; that He shall come from Heaven to earth, personally, bodily, visibly (Acts 1:11; Titus 2:11–13; St. Matthew 16:27, 24:30, 25:30; Luke 21:27; John 1:14, 17; Titus 2:11); and that the Church, the bride, will be caught up to meet Him in the air (I Thessalonians 4:16–17). We admonish all who have this hope to purify themselves as He is pure.

DIVINE HEALING

The Church Of God In Christ believes in and practices Divine Healing. It is a commandment of Jesus to the Apostles (St. Mark 16:18). Jesus affirms His teachings on healing by explaining to His disciples, who were to be Apostles, that healing the afflicted is by faith (St. Luke 9:40–41). Therefore, we believe that healing by faith in God has scriptural support and ordained authority. St. James's writings in his epistle encourage Elders to pray for the sick, lay hands upon them and to anoint them with oil, and state that prayers with faith shall heal the sick and the Lord shall raise them up. Healing is still practiced widely and frequently in the Church Of God In Christ, and testimonies of healing in our Church testify to this fact.

MIRACLES

The Church Of God In Christ believes that miracles occur to convince people that the Bible is God's Word. A miracle can be defined as an extraordinary visible act of divine power, wrought by the efficient agency of the will of God, which has as its final cause the vindication of the righteousness of God's Word. We believe that the works of God, which were performed during the beginnings of Christianity, do and will occur even today where God is preached, faith in Christ is exercised, the Holy Ghost is active, and the Gospel is promulgated in the truth (Acts 5:15, 6:8, 9:40; Luke 4:36, 7:14, 15, 5:5, 6; St. Mark 14:15).

THE ORDINANCES OF THE CHURCH

It is generally admitted that for an ordinance to be valid, it must have been instituted by Christ. When we speak of ordinances of the church, we are speaking of those instituted by Christ, in which by sensible signs the grace of God in Christ and the benefits of the covenant of grace are represented, sealed, and applied to believers, and these in turn give expression to their faith and allegiance to God. The Church Of God In Christ recognizes three ordinances as having been instituted by Christ himself and, therefore, are binding upon the church practice.

THE LORD'S SUPPER (HOLY COMMUNION)

The Lord's Supper symbolizes the Lord's death and suffering for the benefit and in the place of His people. It also symbolizes the believer's participation in the crucified Christ. It represents not only the death of Christ as the object of faith, which unites the believers to Christ, but also the effect of this act as the giving of life, strength, and joy to the soul. The communicant by faith enters into a special spiritual union of one's soul with the glorified Christ.

FOOT WASHING

Foot washing is practiced and recognized as an ordinance in our Church because Christ, by His example, showed that humility characterized greatness in the Kingdom of God, and that service rendered to others gave evidence that humility, motivated by love, exists. These services are held subsequent to the Lord's Supper; however, its regularity is left to the discretion of the pastor in charge.

WATER BAPTISM

We believe that Water Baptism is necessary as instructed by Christ in St. John 3:5, "UNLESS MAN BE BORN AGAIN OF WATER AND OF THE SPIRIT..."

However, we do not believe that water baptism alone is a means of salvation, but is an outward demonstration that one has already had a conversion experience and has accepted Christ as his personal Savior. As Pentecostals, we practice immersion in preference to sprinkling because immersion corresponds more closely to the death, burial, and Resurrection of our Lord (Colossians 2:12). It also symbolizes regeneration and purification more than any other mode. Therefore, we practice immersion as our mode of baptism. We believe that we should use the Baptismal Formula given to us by Christ for all "...IN THE NAME OF THE FATHER, AND OF THE SON, AND OF THE HOLY GHOST..." (Matthew 28:19).

Suggested Order of Service

1. Call to order.

2. Singing.

3. Prayer.

4. Responsive reading:

Supt.: Behold, how good and how pleasant it is for brethren to dwell together in unity!
Psalm 133:1

School: And let the peace of God rule in your hearts, to the which also ye are called in one body; and be ye thankful.
Colossians 3:15

Supt.: Blessed are they that dwell in thy house: they will be still praising thee.
Psalm 84:4

School: Praise ye the LORD. I will praise the LORD with my whole heart, in the assembly of the upright, and in the congregation.
Psalm 111:1

Supt.: And the LORD said unto him, I have heard thy prayer and thy supplication, that thou hast made before me: I have hallowed this house, which thou hast built, to put my name there for ever; and mine eyes and mine heart shall be there perpetually.
1 Kings 9:3

School: Ye shall keep my sabbaths, and reverence my sanctuary: I am the LORD.
Leviticus 19:30

Supt.: And I say also unto thee, That thou art Peter, and upon this rock I will build my church; and the gates of hell shall not prevail against it.
Matthew 16:18

School: My soul longeth, yea, even fainteth for the courts of the LORD: my heart and my flesh crieth out for the living God.
Psalm 84:2

Supt.: And other sheep I have, which are not of this fold: them also I must bring, and they shall hear my voice; and there shall be one fold, and one shepherd.
John 10:16

School: But if I tarry long, that thou mayest know how thou oughtest to behave thyself in the house of God, which is the church of the living God, the pillar and ground of the truth.
1 Timothy 3:15

All: Lift up your hands in the sanctuary, and bless the LORD.
Psalm 134:2

5. Singing.

6. Reading lesson by school and superintendent.

7. Classes assemble for lesson study.

8. Sunday School offering.

9. Five-minute warning bell.

10. Closing bell.

11. Brief lesson review by pastor or superintendent.

12. Secretary's report.

13. Announcements.

14. Dismissal.

History

The Church Of God In Christ Publishing House is one of the oldest businesses in our religious organization. Through the God-given vision of our founder, Bishop Charles Harrison Mason, the Publishing House vitally impacted the ministry of Christian education. Under the leadership of historic individuals such as Bishop J. O. Patterson Sr. and the first chairman of the Publishing Board, Bishop F.D. Washington, the Publishing House's foundational structure began. From 1968 forward, chairmen Bishop Roy L. H. Winbush and Bishop Norman Quick took the ministry to a greater productive level.

Brother Huegha Terry, the first president of the Publishing House, began working there in 1965 and worked diligently until his retirement in 1995. Bishop David A. Hall Sr., former editor of *The Whole Truth* magazine, received the reins from Brother Terry and propelled the Publishing House into the 21st century as CEO.

The goal of producing curriculum that represents the doctrine and traditions of Pentecostalism is more vital today! As the Publishing House serves the Church worldwide, its members can be confident they are using ministry tools that will help win and mature souls for Christ. An extended part of our ministry is the growing number of ministries that are independent charismatic organizations that need materials. Our lessons are derived from the International Sunday School Literature and share the very same subject matter of other groups. There is uniformity in the ranks of Christian churches. However, when a more Pentecostal or doctrinal emphasis is needed, our materials are true to our biblical holiness interpretation.

In 2009, Presiding Bishop Charles E. Blake Sr. appointed Attorney John W. Daniels Jr. the Chairman of the Publishing Board, and under his administration, the Publishing House moved into the digital age. The ministry accelerated, and the vast improvements in productivity are a witness to God's blessing upon our business. Major enhancements in productivity, product design, product content, customer service, website and Internet service, and business in general have been implemented for our customers.

Our motto, "The Lord gave the word: great was the company of those that published it" (Psalm 68:11), has been the Church Of God In Christ Publishing House inspiration. Our staff is called to "Get the Word Out" and commits to provide exemplary customer service.

The current Chairman of the Publishing Board, Superintendent Mark A. Ellis, is

Biblical Statement of Purpose

"The Lord gave the word: great was the company of those that published it" (Psalm 68:11).

Mission Statement

The Church Of God In Christ Publishing House exists to fulfill Psalm 68:11 by creating, publishing, and distributing the highest-quality Christian educational resources that educate, inspire, and equip God's people with Power For Living, thus enabling them to become committed disciples who are dedicated to evangelizing the world for Jesus Christ.

a revolutionary leader and is committed to the success of this great company. The Publishing Board members, along with the staff of the Publishing House and Book Store, are continuing the legacy laid by their predecessors.